GENEALOG
929.3
Notes

R02000 03296

NOTES AND QUERIES

HISTORICAL,
BIOGRAPHICAL AND GENEALOGICAL

RELATING CHIEFLY TO

INTERIOR PENNSYLVANIA.

EDITED BY

WILLIAM HENRY EGLE, M.D., M.A.

ANNUAL VOLUME, 1899.

Baltimore
GENEALOGICAL PUBLISHING COMPANY
1970

Originally Published
Harrisburg, 1900

Reprinted with the cooperation of the
Pennsylvania State Library
Genealogical Publishing Company
Baltimore, 1970

Standard Book Number 0-8063-0413-8
Library of Congress Catalog Card Number 70-114834

Made in the United States of America

INDEX.

Antes, Henry, sketch of, ... 76
Antes, Philip, of the West Branch, 1
Associators, The Forerunners of
  the Pensylvania Line, ...97, 102
Atkinson Family data, ...54, 73
Ayres, George Bucher, contribution by, ... 51
Bedford, Pa., burial records at, 113, 118
Biographical Sketches:
  Campbell, Lawrence, of Northumberland, ... 113
  Darby, William, the American Geographer, ... 234
  McArthur, Duncan, ... 237
  Yoder, Moses, of Oley, ... 121
Bird, Ulysses, contribution by,... 163
Bruner, Daniel Pastorius, contribution by, ...144, 157
Butler wills at Carlisle, ... 230
Campbellstown Evangelical Lutheran Church, ... 227
Carlisle, tombstone records of persons born prior to 1800, ...64, 69, 74, 80
Chapman, Thomas J., contribution by, ... 224
Church Yard Records:
  Ephrata Community, ... 173
  Family, some old, ... 231
  Jordan Lutheran Church, Lehigh county, ... 45
  Lutheran Church, at York Springs, ... 211
  Middle Spring Church, ... 169
  Mennonite, at Hanover, ... 204
  Pennepeck Baptist Church, ... 147
  Penn'a-German in the South,... 128
  Presbyterian Church, Bedford, 113
  Reformed Church, Bedford,..... 118
  St. John's Church at Compass, ...15, 22, 25

Sunnyside Cemetery, York Springs, ... 210
Warrington Friend's Meeting, 220
Craig of the "Irish Settlement," 239
Craig, Samuel, contribution by,... 190
Compass, Pa., records of St. John's Cemetery at, ...15, 22, 25
Cumberland County Marriages, 58, 87
Dawson, John L., ancestry of,.... 216
Deaths of prominent persons,..... 224
Dewey and Schley, ancestry of,... 76
Dewitt, Rev. William R., reminiscences of, ... 109
Early or Oehrle family, ...21, 95
Early, Rev. John W., contributions by, 21, 95, 185, 190, 205, 212, 216, 227
Fortune-hunters, about, ... 167
Garber family, ... 44
Genealogical Data:
  Adams, ... 209
  Agnew, ... 61
  Aigler, ... 185
  Albert, ... 185
  Alexander, ... 225
  Antes, ... 1
  Arnold, ... 185
  Atkinson, ...54, 73
  Attleman, ... 225
  Aulenbach, ... 186
  Baecker, ... 186
  Bargman, ... 129
  Bard, ... 159
  Barnett, ... 144
  Barron, ... 189
  Bauer, ... 186
  Bauman, ... 173
  Bechtel, ... 186
  Bender, ... 159
  Berryhill, ... 231
  Beyer, ... 186
  Bickel, ... 186

Binckley,	173	Dyre,	148
Black,	32	Early,	21, 95
Bogenreiff,	186	Eaton,	148
Bollenbacher,	187	Ebelhare,	160
Bortner,	187	Edwards,	148
Bower,	139	Elder,	67, 167, 209
Bowersox,	166	Emert,	187
Brackenridge,	169	Eppicher,	187
Brown,	201	Ernest,	187
Bruner,	113, 126, 156, 161, 162	Euler,	187
Bucher,	173	Evans,	113, 126, 144, 157
Burriett,	225	Ewig,	187
Butler,	230	Ewing,	86
Campbell,	138	Fahnestock,	174
Canan,	14	Fauss,	187
Carl,	187	Fehler,	187
Carpenter,	160	Fengel,	187
Carson,	160	Fiedler,	187
Cessna,	204	Fiery,	129
Chapman,	209	Findley,	68
Charlton,	188	Fischer,	187
Christie,	188	Fox,	187
Clark,	138, 162	Frazer,	170
Colwell,	169	Frembling,	214
Cookman,	161	Freymeyer,	187
Craig,	238	Fries,	187
Curry,	224	Fuess,	187
Davidson,	107	Fulton,	170
Davies,	144	Galbreath,	177
Davis,	148	Garber,	44
Dawson,	216	Garrigues,	159
Denter,	187	Gebhart,	188
Derr,	61	Geddes,	151
Deveny,	209	Gehr,	188
Devor,	152, 225	Gehrhart,	188
Dewey,	76	Geiger,	159
Diebo,	187	Geiss,	188
Dieter,	187	Gelliger,	188
Dill,	139	Gensemer,	188
Dilley,	225	George,	148
Dornbach,	187	Gilbert,	188
Dunbar,	32	Gitter,	132
Duncan,	148, 170, 225	Given,	162
Duffield,	148	Gorgas,	174
Dunham,	225	Graham,	21

Greber,	191	Keiser,	43
Grever,	174	Keller,	191
Grier,	61	Kelso,	86
Griffiths,	148	Kendell,	209
Gross,	188	Kennedy,	160
Gruber,	188, 190	Kercher,	191
Gueseman,	191	Kern,	191
Gutlender,	191	Kettner,	191
Gutman,	191	Kichel,	191
Haack,	191	Kiester,	225
Haas,	191	Kilgore,	109
Haeny,	152	Kinkead,	160
Halferty,	152	Kinnersley,	153
Halstead,	225	Kirkpatrick,	32
Hamborger,	191	Klee,	192
Hamill,	209	Klinger,	53
Hanna,	155	Knoll,	192
Harlow,	188	Knopff,	192
Hartzler,	103	Kochendoerffer,	192
Hays,	116, 189	Koehl,	192
Hedderich,	191	Konigmacher,	175
Heiliger,	191	Krafft,	192
Heinrich,	191	Kuehler,	192
Hemphill,	170	Landis,	144, 175
Hendricks,	177	Lang,	192
Herron,	170, 171	Leavitt,	109
Himmelberger,	191	Lefler,	44
Hinckel,	191	Leonard,	193
Hoge,	215	Lerch,	192
Holme,	148	Lewis,	153
Hottenstein,	219	Lieb,	214
Houston,	38	Lingle,	192, 193, 214
Hunter,	14	Linn,	68
Irwin,	117	Livingstouse,	61
Jackson,	149	Lloyd,	158
Jenkins,	215	Lochry,	62
Jennings,	91	Logan,	139
Johnson,	170	Lutz,	193
Johnston,	171	McAllister,	5
Jones,	149, 158	McBryar,	63
Kaltglesser,	103	McCallen,	181
Keblinger,	191	McCauley,	154
Keck,	224	McClay,	170
Keen,	152	McClure,	72, 139

McCune,	170	Perschinger,	205
McCurdy,	232	Petry,	205
McDonal,	14	Pfatticher,	205
McDowell,	107, 189	Philbert,	205
McKnight,	171	Phillips,	206
McLene,	112	Phipps,	151, 189
McNair,	101	Placing,	210
McVaugh,	153	Plattner,	206
Maghee,	153	Polk,	194
Mahon,	170	Porter,	176
Marple,	153	Powell,	229
Maris,	153	Power,	152, 176
Marshall,	53, 151	Preston,	160
Martin,	175	Pumroy,	68
Matthews,	108	Radebach,	206
Means,	209	Rankin,	32
Meeth,	193	Rea,	112
Meharg,	68	Renick,	83
Mentzer,	32	Rennie,	226
Mercer,	201	Renno,	206
Messerschmidt,	193	Reynolds,	58, 171
Metz,	233	Richey,	210
Meyer,	193	Riegel,	206
Michael,	193	Riehl,	206
Miles,	153	Rigg,	157, 159
Miller,	20, 193	Ripley,	189
Misner,	226	Ritschart,	214
Mitchell,	49, 139	Rodgers,	171
Montgomery,	215	Roeger,	206
Moore,	153	Rohn,	206, 214
Morris,	201	Rost,	206
Motz,	166	Ryan,	171
Mueller,	193, 194, 205	Salter,	214
Muench,	205	Sawyer,	181
Nevin,	171	Schade,	207
Nicholas,	158	Schaeffer,	207
Nixon,	209	Scharff,	207
Northrop,	153	Schauer,	207
Oehrlin, or Oehrle,	21, 95	Schell,	207
Ogden,	152	Schirmann,	207
O'Hale,	139	Schley,	77
Pastorius,	156	Schmidt,	207
Patterson,	20, 95, 170	Schneider,	208
Pennock,	53	Schroff,	208
		Schropp,	208

Schuler,	212	Wenderich,	213
Seaman,	207	Wenrich,	213
Senseman,	176	Wertz,	213
Shearer,	153	Widener,	132
Shepherd,	153	Wier,	226
Shields,	68	Wiley,	138
Singer,	112	Wilhelm,	213
Sloan,	14, 68, 210, 226	Williams,	201
Smith,	62, 139, 171	Wilson,	139
Somer,	208	Wingert,	213
Sox,	139	Wishart,	151
St. Clair,	68	Witmayer,	213
Sterrett,	162	Witmer,	165
Stewart,	38, 229	Woods,	160
Strauss,	212	Wright,	154, 170
Stroh-Schneider,	212	Young,	219
Sturgeon,	171	Zechman,	213
Summerville,	170	Zerfass,	176
Swift,	153	Zerwe,	213, 214
Swinehart,	161	Zweysich,	214
Tappen,	109	Gnadenhutten Massacre, The,	232
Taylor,	154	Graham of Bedford County,	21
Thomas,	153, 212	Hanover Church and Donegal Presbytery,	77
Thompson,	63, 101		
Thomson,	112	Harrisburg:	
Thortheuer,	212	Memories of Market Square,	28, 33
Torrence,	138	The First Graveyards at,	51
Troester,	212	The Old Bridge,	39
Updegraff,	152	Hart, Gustavus N., contributions by,	55, 147, 152
Urich,	176, 212		
Urie,	226	Hays of Northampton County,	189
Unruh,	212	Historical Works, recent:	
VanBuren,	154	American Genealogist—Thomas Allen Glenn,	25
Vandike,	154		
Vaughn,	266	Brule's Discoveries and Explorations,	1
Vollmar,	212		
Waddell,	161	Fries Rebellion—Gen. W. H. H. Davis,	67
Wade,	226		
Wagner,	212, 213	Keagy Family History,	194
Walker,	160	Penn'a Railroad—Wm. Bender Wilson,	156
Ward,	85		
Watts,	154	The Perkiomen Region—Henry S. Dotterer,	155
Weaver,	15		
Weber,	213	Thirty Thousand Names—I. D. Rupp,	194
Webster,	154		

Wyoming Historical Society Publications, ... 116
Holme, Thomas, Penn's first Surveyor General, ... 83
Houston family data, ... 38
"Indiana," The latest history of, 224
Indians at Wekquitank in 1760,... 125
Irwin of Cumberland Valley, ... 117
Jordan Church, Lehigh county, graveyard records of, ... 45
Jordan, John Wolfe, contributions by, ...123, 129, 134, 140, 142
Kelker, Rudolph F., contribution by, ... 197
Kelker, William A., contribution by, ... 39
Klein, Theodore B., contributions by, ...28, 33, 109, 182
Klinger family data, ... 53
Lancaster County Divorces, 1788-1800, ... 101
Interments, 1841-1856, ... 178
Landis and Smolnicker, ... 122
Letter, A, of the Old Tune, ... 117
Lewis County, ... 163
Lochry, Col. Archibald, ... 62
Lutz, William Filler, contributions by, ...113, 118
Marriages, Cumberland County, 58, 87
Masonic Funeral in 1779, ... 162
Matthews, James P., contribution by, ... 7
Meginness, John Franklin, the Historian of the West Branch Valley, ...180, 195
Contributions by, 1, 76, 121, 132, 226
Mentzer family data, ... 33
Mifflinburg, the early dead at,.... 89
Mitchell of Cumberland Valley, .. 49
Morton, John, "the Signer,"...... 91
Morus Multicaulis Craze, 1830-1841, ... 197
Myers, Albert Cook, contributions by, ...210, 211, 220
McDowell family data, ... 108
McNair family data, ... 101

Nead, Benjamin M., contribution by, ... 201
Necrological Notices:
Bailey, Charles Lukens, ... 149
Butterfield, Consul Willshire, .. 177
Kell, James, of York, ... 86
McIlhenny, Samuel, ... 228
Meginness, John Franklin, ..180, 195
Metz, Sarah Fisher, ... 233
Swope, Gilbert E., of Newville, 95
Northumberland, first burgess of, 113
County, prothonotaries of, 1772-1899, ... 226
Old-Time Reminiscences, ... 182
Opequon, The, ... 129
Owen, B. F., contributions by, 15, 22, 25
Parthemore, E. W. S., contributions by, ...173, 233
Pennock and Marshall families, .. 53
Penn's first Surveyor General,.... 83
Pennsylvania, an official map of, 201
Pennsylvania-German Emigration North and West, ... 93
Prehistoric Earthworks in Central Pennsylvania, ... 168
Railroad Reminiscences of Half a Century Ago, ... 18
The "Tape Worm," 3, 6, 11
Revolution, Heroes of the:
Alison, Dr. Benjamin, ... 91
Brisbin, Captain John, ... 93
Leddick, Philip, ... 5
Lochry, Col. Archibald, ... 62
Scott, Capt. Matthew, ... 3
Revolution, Matrons of the:
Irish, Elizabeth Thomas, ... 72
Kirkpatrick, Ann, ... 60
Parke, Margaret, ... 9
Stewart, Deborah McClenahan,.. 2
Revolution, application for pension by a soldier of the, ... 238
Revolutionary Officers from Pennsylvania who died in service, 127
Revolutionary Relic, how it was lost, ... 49
Reynolds family data, ... 58

Robinson, Rev. Thomas H., contribution by, ... 76
Runkle family graveyard, ... 51
Rutherford, W. Franklin, contributions by, ...9, 60
Sener, Samuel S., contributions by, 15, 33, 38, 54, 58, 73, 113, 122, 178
Stapleton, Rev. A., contributions by, 89, 128, 138, 154, 165, 168, 204
Stevens, Thaddeus, and his "Tape Worm" railroad, ...3, 6, 11
Stewart, of Cumberland Valley, .. 229
Sturgeon Family Reunion, ... 171
Sullivan Expedition of 1779, ... 239
Susquehanna, an Early Settler on the, ... 83
Time-piece, an old, ... 92
Tulpehocken Church, The Little, ...185, 190, 205, 212, 216

Vandegrift Burial Records, ... 55
Venerable Couples, Three, ... 172
Wagoning in ye Olden Time,.... 229
Watts, Anna H., contribution by, 169
Weaver family data, ... 15
Weiser, Conrad, and the Indians, 57
Wekquitank, Annals of, ...
.............123, 129, 134, 140, 142
Welsh Settlers in Earl and Caernarvon, ... 147
Westmoreland County Families, 67, 176
White Deer township, Lycoming county, ... 132
Wilson, William Bender, contributions by, ...3, 12
Woods, M. M., and Parkinson, S. W., contributions by, 64, 69, 74, 80

NOTES AND QUERIES.

HISTORICAL AND GENEALOGICAL.

NOTES AND QUERIES.

Historical, Biographical, and Genealogical.

I.

"Brule's Discoveries and Explorations," by Consul Willshire Butterfield, is the latest publication having special reference to the earliest explorations—the first made by civilized man—of the Susquehanna river throughout its entire course. Etienne Brule, "the pioneer of pioneers," as Parkman denominates him, was one of those indomitable French explorers to whom the world owes much for his hardihood and valor. In the year 1615, with a handful of Hurons, he ventured upon the perilous journey of exploring the Susquehanna from its headwaters in the Iroquois country—State of New York—to where it empties into the Chesapeake Bay, or as Brule thought, the Atlantic. Mr. Butterfield, who is one of the most conscientious of our historians, has gathered up most interesting details of the discoveries and wanderings of Brule, who lost his life at the hands of the savages, being not only killed, but eaten by them. The work is such a valuable contribution to the early discovery of Pennsylvania, that it ought to find a place in the library of every Pennsylvanian who wants to acquaint himself with every portion of its history. The volume is published at Cleveland, but copies may be secured through any live bookseller.

Philip Antes of the West Branch.

Philip Antes was a son of Col. John Henry Antes, who took such an active part in the West Branch Valley during the Indian troubles, and was born at Falkner Swamp, Montgomery county, August 26, 1759. After reaching early manhood he settled in what is now Dauphin county, and there married Susannah Williams, February 21, 1780. Through the influence of his father he was induced to remove to the mouth of Antes creek and settle at the mill which had been built by the former, and stood near Antes Fort. Not liking the location, he purchased a tract of land from Samuel Wallis, in Bald Eagle Valley (now Curtin's abandoned iron works) for which he was to pay "thirty shillings per acre, in four equal payments." This transaction took place May 3, 1787. He at once built a log house and removed there in July of the same year.

Philip Antes was an early convert to the doctrines of the Methodist Episcopal Church, and at his humble log house, at Curtins, the first society was formed in 1787. The names of the first members that have come down to us are Philip Antes, Christopher Helford, Philip Barnhart, Jacob Lee and Lawrence Bathurst, and their respective families. This antedates the first society formed at the house of Arad Sutton, on Lycoming creek, in 1791, by four years.

In the course of time Philip Antes sold his improvement to Roland Curtin and locatel in Lawrence township, Clearfield county, where his wife died May 2, 1826. He survived her till August 14, 1831, when he passed away in his 73d year. They had children as follows:

i. Frederick, b. Jan. 18, 1781; lived and died on the farm at Curtins.

ii. John, b. Oct. 4, 1782; d. at his son's, in Moshannon, in 1852.

iii. Henry, b. Dec. 4, 1784; lived and died in Harrisburg.

iv. Philip, Jr., b. —, 1785; lived near

Clearfield, and died at his daughter's, in the town of Clearfield.

v. Polly, b. June 3, 1788; married Hiram J. Miller, and afterwards Isaiah oGodfellow.

vi. Susannah, b. May 10, 1791; married John Patton, father of Gen. John Patton, of Curwinsville, and died at the great age of 92 or 93 years.

viii. Elizabeth, b. July 31, 1794; married Moses Boggs, associate judge of Clearfield county for seventeen years.

J. F. M.

MATRONS OF THE REVOLUTION.

Deborah McClenachan Stewart.

Deborah McClenachan, eldest daughter of Blair McClenachan and his wife Ann Derragh, was born June 4, 1763, in the city of Philadelphia. Deborah's early training was chiefly confined to her mother's care, who was an exemplar in all that pertained to household life. She had only been placed a few months at school, when the revolutionary struggle began, and her native city was aroused from its long slumber of peace to an eventful era of the scenes of war. Philadelphia, true to her name, has always been a quiet, conservative city, but slow as she is so frequently termed by those who know her incorrectly, she has been determined and firm in every crisis of America's affairs, holding aloft the honor of her country as if it were solely hers. Blair McClenachan was an earnest advocate for independence, and co-operated with every patriotic movement. He was a member of the City Troop, and his statue representing that of a private soldier is at the foot of the pedestal commemorating the battle on the field of Trenton. In 1780 he subscribed ten thousand pounds sterling to supply the starving army. His patriotism and self-sacrifice ought not to be forgotten by Americans. This was the father of our Deborah, and she inherited much of his Irish warmth of temperament—was extremely ladylike in demeanor, and owing to the fact that her mother was somewhat of an invalid, was early installed as the entertainer of her honored father's guests. It was at her own home she met Col. Walter Stewart. He had a'ways been considered the handsomest man in the Continental army, while Miss Deborah's winning manners, grace, and sweet features were remarked by all. Youthful, only seventeen, she won the heart of that son of Mars, and on the 11th of April, 1781, they were married by the Rev. Dr. White in old Christ Church. The war soon thereafter ended, and the family settled down to domestic peace in the metropolis. Until her life's close, as the wife and widow of that gallant officer of the Revolution, Mrs. Stewart was highly honored and revered; philanthropic, her mission of life was one continuous service in doing good to those around her, and when at last the stillness of death came, on the 20th of March, 1823, the surviving soldiers of the Cincinnati and other comrades-in-arms of her husband's, gathered around her bier to show their sympathy and love for a Matron of the Revolution. She was buried by the side of the General in St. Paul's churchyard.

Walter Stewart, son of William Stewart, was born near Londonderry, Ireland, January 16, 1752. At the age of eighteen he came to America, and engaged in mercantile pursuits in Philadelphia. Having received a good education with some military training, at the time when resistance to British tyranny was dtermined upon, he raised a company for the Third Pennsylvania battalion, of which he was commissioned captain, January 6, 1776. On the 26th of May, he was appointed aide-de-camp to Major-General Gates. June 17, 1777, he was appointed colonel of the State Regiment of Foot. He took command of the regiment July 6 following, and was in command at Brandywine and Germantown, where his regimental loss was heavy. On Nov. 12, 1777, by resolution of Congress, Colonel Stewart's regiment was annexed to the Pennsylvania Line, and formed the Thirteenth Pennsylvania. On the 1st of July, 1778, when the Thirteenth was incorporated with the Second Pennsylvania, Col. Stewart took command. He served until the end of the war, winning a high reputation for gallantry, and retired January 1, 1783, with the title of Brevet-Brigadier-General. He was an intimate friend of Washington, who was god-father to his eldest son. After the war General Stewart engaged in business in Philadelphia and was quite successful, although he lost heavily in the Morris failure. He took a great interest in military matters and was Major-General of the First division, Pennsylvania militia, in 1794. He died in Philadelphia, June 14, 1796, and was buried on the 16th with the honors of war, the Society of the Cincinnati, and the officers of the First division following the corpse as mourners. Custis in his "Recollections" states that "Colonel Stewart had a fair, florid complexion, was vivacious, intelligent, and well educated, and it was said was the handsomest man in the American army." His portrait is full length in Trumbull's picture of the surrender of Cornwallis, to the left of the last of the American officers.

NOTES AND QUERIES.

Historical, Biographical, and Genealogical.

II.

CAPTAIN MATTHEW SCOTT.

The "Carlisle Gazette" makes this comment on this brave officer of the Revolution, who died May 20, 1798, "at his seat in Shippensburgh:" "A worthy citizen, indulgent parent, a loving husband and a kind friend. He has long been a resident of this little town, where he is universally lamented. He was an early patriot in the Revolution, of this county, and was taken prisoner in the battle of Long island—where he endured unparalleled hardships, but when exchanged he continued a considerable time in the service, until sickness and other hardships obliged him to resign and retire from a public life to the more pleasing cares of a family—in which he behaved wisely."

THE "TAPE WORM" RAILROAD.

From William Bender Wilson's Forthcoming History of the Pennsylvania Railroad Company.

From the incipiency of the Cumberland Valley Railroad its importance as a part of a great railway line to be constructed between Philadelphia and Pittsburgh was constantly kept in public view. It had, however, a rival which greatly disturbed its friends.

Thaddeus Stevens, who was a power in the State, and one of the closest advisers of Governor Ritner, was in possession of very valuable iron lands in Franklin and Adams counties, the latter of which he represented in the lower house of the Legislature. He conceived the idea of extending the public works from Columbia and Wrightsville to York and Gettysburg, and thence through his lands to the Maryland line to connect with the Baltimore and Ohio Railroad. This road was known as "Stevens' Tape Worm," and its construction and completion threatened the prospective business of the Cumberland Valley project. In consequence of that Charles B. Penrose, who, in all else, was a close political co-laborer with Stevens, deeply interested in the Cumberland Valley route, used his influence to such an extent that he had referred to the Committee on Roads, Bridges, etc., in the Senate, for investigation and report, the subject of the relative merits of the two routes. That committee reported through Senator John Strohm, January 29, 1838, partly, as follows:

"Where a single improvement, whether canal, railroad or turnpike, opens a communication between two given points, the amount of business on that improvement can only be limited by the whole amount of transportation offered between these points, or the capacity of the improvement itself in affording facilities for transportation. But where different improvements converge to the same or similar points, that which affords the easiest, quickest, safest and cheapest conveyance will certainly engross the greatest amount of business; and such, your committee conceives, is the relation which the connection about to be formed between the Baltimore and Ohio Railroad and the Columbia and Philadelphia Railroad, by means of the Harrisburg and Mount Joy Railroad, the Cumberland Valley Railroad, and the Franklin Railroad. The difference in the distance between these routes may readily be seen by comparing the following statements, which, from the best information the committee could obtain, will, it is believed, not vary much from the actual survey:

From Hagerstown to Gettysburg, by the Waynesboro route	47¼ miles
From Gettysburg to Wrightsville	41¼ "
From Wrightsville to Philadelphia	82½ "
From Hagerstown to the point of intersection with the Franklin road (supposed near Williamsport)	4¼ "
	175 miles
From the point of intersection about two miles from Williamsport to Chambersburg	23 miles
From Chambersburg to Harrisburg	51 "
From Harrisburg to Lancaster	37 "
From Lancaster to Philadelphia	70 "
	181 miles

"From this statement it will be perceived the distance from the point where it is supposed the Franklin Railroad will intersect the Baltimore and Ohio Railroad to Philadelphia, the distance by the Chambersburg route is but six miles longer than the other. But, in computing the advantages of railroads, distance is not the only consideration. The number and radius of the curves, and the degree of grade frequently present greater obstacles than even a considerable difference of distance, and in this respect, the Chambersburg route has a decided advantage over that which runs through Gettysburg. The former extends in an almost direct line, through the fertile and highly cultivated valley of Cumberland, over ground nearly level, with scarcely any deep excavations and very few heavy embankments. The traveler always finds himself near the surface of the ground, and is, at all times, gratified with the view of neat and thriving villages, or of comfortable and elegant dwellings, and well improved plantations, indicative at once of the industry and enterprise as well as of the independence and prosperity of the envied proprietors of the soil. He feels secure that if accident should arrest the progress of the train with which he is moving, he could immediately find shelter in a neighboring farmhouse, or be furnished with the means of conveyance to the next town. But, on the latter, for about twenty-five miles, he is either ascending or descending at a grade of fifty feet to the mile a rugged, solitary, and barren mountain, uninhabited, and almost uninhabitable. On the one hand he sees perpendicular cliffs, rising like towering steeples above his head, covered with projecting rocks, which seem threatening him with instant death for his temerity; on the other, he perceives a frightful precipice, over which he is in imminent danger of being hurled to the abyss below, with the certain prospect of being dashed to pieces by the fall. Now he is whirled over a ravine, on an embankment of some fifty or sixty feet in height, and now engulfed in an excavation from whence he can scarce see the sun; or immured in a tunnel where daylight may enter, but cannot penetrate. The slightest accident must expose him to danger of life, limb and property, from which nothing short of a miracle can save him.

"This is no fancied sketch or overwrought picture. He who will traverse these routes and examine them carefully, in a spirit of candor, and with an eye of impartiality—without suffering himself to be misled by the delusive mists of prejudice, or the dazzling rays of interest, will have no hesitation in subscribing to the truth of what is here asserted.

"Another circumstance in favor of the Cumberland Valley Railroad arises from the cheapness of its construction, owing to the favorableness of the ground on which it is located. This connected with the fact that a locomotive will take a greater number of cars on that road than on the other will enable that company to transport passengers and produce at a cheaper rate than can be done on the Gettysburg road, unless the interest of the State is sacrificed to the detriment of an enterprising company. From these views of the two contemplated routes, your committee have no hesitation in declaring their belief that the Chambersburg, or

Cumberland Valley route, will be the easiest, cheapest, safest, pleasantest and shortest route to Philadelphia; and in consequence of those pre-eminent advantages, this road, which is being constructed and is now nearly completed, without any expense to the Commonwealth, will engross by far the greater portion of the trade which can be diverted from the Baltimore & Ohio Railroad in the direction of Philadelphia. In calling it the shortest, your committee would beg leave that they refer to time and not to distance. For although the Chambersburg route is a few miles the longest they are fully persuaded that in consequence of the numerous advantages which this route possesses, it can and will be traveled over in less time than the other; and that either passengers or produce will reach Lancaster or Philadelphia sooner by this route than the other.

"For the reasons above stated your committee believe that but a small portion of the trade destined for Philadelphia can be expected to take the Gettysburg route. Yet there are others, which, though less cogent, are not undeserving of notice nor unworthy of consideration in the decision of this question."

This report gave encouragement to the friends of the Cumberland Valley Railroad Company. Thaddeus Stevens' road, however, proceeded under his direction, he having been appointed Canal Commissioner and made President of the Board, May 17, 1838, for the purpose of not only controlling that road, but using the tremendous political leverage of the Public Works of Pennsylvania in the direction of the re-election of Governor Ritner. The Gettysburg Railroad became one of the leading issues during the campaign, and when that was ended by the election of Governor Porter, work on it was abandoned by the new administration, after Stevens had expended $766,127.39½ of State funds in its promotion and construction, and after a committee of the House of Representatives upon an exhaustive examination had reported that:

"Of all the works of doubtful expediency constructed by the State, in the opinion of your committee there is none so useless, so expensive or of as little value as the Gettysburg Railroad. It was commenced by fraud and intrigue, and will end in disgrace and loss to the Commonwealth. The means of the Commonwealth are inadequate to its completion, and if completed, it would never be productive of general benefit."

The amount in cash expended by Thaddeus Stevens on the Gettysburg Railway up to time of its suspension was $620,-819.61, and that left unpaid by the Commonwealth $145,307.78½, made the total of $766,127.39½ as above of Commonwealth's money squandered on this work.

The Board of Canal Commissioners, in their report for 1839, regarded the amount expended on the road as literally thrown away and expressed the opinion that it should never have been commenced, and that the work upon it should never be resumed. They declared the practicability of the undertaking at best as doubtful, and if completed, by being a source of continued expense, worse than worthless to the Commonwealth.

The work was suspended in pursuance of an act of Assembly, approved February 19, 1839.

NOTES AND QUERIES.

Historical, Biographical, and Genealogical.

III.

PHILIP LEDDICK.

A Revolutionary soldier died at Fayette, N. Y., in 1839, in his 79th year. His son Samuel, who is still living at the age of 90 years, says that his father was born in Germany in 1760 and came to this country with his parents when about three years old. Samuel also says that his father enlisted in the Revolutionary service in 1776, and took the oath of allegiance at Lancaster, Pennsylvania, at the time. What is known of this record of Revolutionary service?   D. W.

McALLISTER.

I have recently been looking up some facts as to Hugh McAllister, who settled in Fayette (New York) in 1804, and was a magistrate and prominent man of Scotch ancestry. A grandson says his ancestors came over in 1732, and that Hugh McAllister, who died in 1850, aged 84 years, was born in Shearman's Valley about 1765. When a young man he removed to Philadelphia, and from that city to Fayette. He was a thrifty old Scotch-Irish Presbyterian deacon. Can you furnish any information of this family?

D. W.

AN OLD STORY REVIVED.

Thaddeus Stevens and the State Railroad—Why it Stopped Short at Columbia—The Abandoned "Western Division."

To the Editor:

After reading the advance chapter of Mr. William Bender Wilson's history of the Pennsylvania Railroad, published in the "Telegraph" of January 21st, it seems to me that there is at least one passage which needs revision before this sketch of the beginning of a great enterprise takes its place in accepted history. I quote the second paragraph:

"Thaddeus Stevens, who was a power in the State, and one of the closest advisers of Governor Ritner, was in possession of very valuable iron lands in Franklin and Adams counties, the latter of which he represented in the lower house of the Legislature. He conceived the idea of extending the public works from Columbia and Wrightsville to York and Gettysburg, and thence through his lands to the Maryland line to connect with the Baltimore and Ohio Railroad. This road was known as "Stevens' Tape Worm," and its construction and completion threatened the prospective business of the Cumberland Valley project. In consequence of that Charles B. Penrose, who, in all else, was a close political co-laborer with Stevens, deeply interested in the Cumberland Valley route, used his influence to such an extent that he had referred to the Committee on Roads, Bridges, etc., in the Senate, for investigation and report, the subject of the relative merits of the two routes."

By some accident, this decayed relic of a political campaign, conspicuous for its shameless falsehoods, has survived the period and purpose which gave it birth, and it is now paraded as a fact worthy of permanent record. Before Mr. Wilson gets through with his railroad studies he probably will have discovered that the project of connecting Philadelphia with the great West by constructing a branch to meet the Baltimore & Ohio at Hagerstown, did not originate with Mr. Stevens, nor with Governor Ritner's administration. The Baltimore & Ohio Company was chartered both in Maryland and Pennsylvania in 1827-1828. The acts of incorporation were substantially the same, except in the Pennsylvania act there was a limitation requiring the road to be completed to Pittsburg within fifteen years, under penalty of forfeiture of the charter.

The route as then projected, was by the most practicable line from Baltimore to Hagerstown; thence by the Potomac Valley to Cumberland, Md.; thence through Wills Gap into Pennsylvania, and up the eastern slope of the main range of the Alleghenies to the headwaters of the Youghiogheny, and with the line of that stream to its junction with the Monongahela; thence to Pittsburg. Nearly one-half of the contemplated road was in Pennsylvania.

Perhaps in succeeding chapters of his history, Mr. Wilson has detailed the successive steps taken by the State of Pennsylvania to construct the Philadelphia branch of the Baltimore & Ohio, for it is part of the story which he has essayed to tell. The work was done under the direction of the Canal Commissioners, and at the period referred to, in the paragraph quoted above, the road had been completed as far as Columbia.

Thaddeus Stevens was one of the colossal men of his generation. He saw the railroad age coming in, and his brain was big enough to comprehend its possibilities. In practical statesmanship he was as far ahead of most of his cotemporaries, as he was in his conception of popular education, human liberty, and the rights of man. He saw that Pennsylvania must have a railroad to the West, and he believed that the best way to get it was to co-operate with the Maryland enterprise. In this opinion he was in accord with the most enlightened and sagacious men in both States.

To tell how the contemplated junction of the Pennsylvania State Railroad with the Baltimore & Ohio, at Hagerstown, came to naught, would far transcend the limits of a newspaper article. The trouble began in Maryland, and had its origin in a most unfortunate selection of a route from Baltimore to Hagerstown. The first survey was substantially by the route now occupied by the Western Maryland Railroad, and if this line had been adopted, the junction with the Pennsylvania State road would have been made at Monterey, fifteen miles east of Hagerstown, and Philadelphia and Pittsburg would have had a connecting railroad (shorter than the great Pennsylvania route) as early as 1840, instead of waiting till 1852.

There were influential local interests in the Valley of the Patapsco which finally determined the choice of that route. When the engineer corps struck the Potomac river at Point of Rocks, some sixty-five miles west of Baltimore, an injunction was sued out by the Chesapeake & Ohio Canal Company, which stopped further operations. The Canal Company chartered in 1824, was the successor of the Potomac Navigation Company, chartered in 1784, of which George Washington was the chief promoter. By virtue of the franchises inherited from the original corporation, the Canal Company laid claim to all the passes of the Potomac, and after long litigation, it was decided by the courts that the Canal Company had the "paramount right" to the passes, and that no other corporation could intrude until the canal had been located, and the company had taken possession of whatever ground was needed. Under pressure from the Legislature, the Canal Company finally consented to allow the railroad track to be laid between the Point of Rocks and the bank of the river, upon payment of $226,000 for the privilege.

The same opposition was encountered when the railroad entered the next narrow pass, near Harper's Ferry, and after much vexatious litigation and delay, the Baltimore & Ohio Company determined to cross over into Virginia, and leave the Canal to the full enjoyment of its "paramount right" to the passes on the Maryland side. There was a tremendous protest against this move in Maryland, but the Virginia Legislature encouraged it with large promises of aid. In 1836 the Maryland Legislature came to the aid of the railroad company by making the State the guarantor of a new issue of its bonds, and a clause was inserted in the bill, providing that the company must locate its road through Hagerstown, or forfeit to Washington county one million dollars. After the company had decided to go into Virginia, Washington county brought suit for the one million dollars. An extra session of the Legislature was called, and this clause of the act of 1836 was repealed. The suit went on, it being contended on the part of the county that the Legislature had no power to impair the obligation of a contract. The Court of Appeals finally decided that while the Legislature could not rescind a contract, it could remit a penalty, and that this provision of the act of 1836 was not a contract, but was in the nature of a penalty. Thus Hagerstown lost the railroad, and the people of the county lost the million dollars.

Up to this time the connection of the Pennsylvania State Railroad with the Baltimore & Ohio, at Hagerstown, was contemplated in both States, and was provided for by legislation in both States. In 1835 the Pennsylvania Legislature in giving the Susquehanna Canal the right to connevt with the Pennsylvania Canal at Columbia, made it a condition that the State of Maryland should permit a road from the Cumberland Valley to connect with the Baltimore & Ohio, at Hagerstown, or in that vicinity. By this time, however, the westward extension of the Baltimore and Ohio had been suspended. From 1835 to 1838 nothing was done, the western terminus remaining at Harper's Ferry. The Virginians, however, were tightening their grip, and when construction was resumed, it was a condition that the track should be laid in Virginia as far west as Cumberland. Of course, Pennsylvania gave up all hope of a connection at Hagerstown.

After the failure of the scheme from the causes already related, Mr. Stevens was roundly abused for the part he had taken in promoting it, and in the gubernatorial campaign which ensued, he was charged by the Democratic stump-speakers with using the State's money in building a railroad for the benefit of a little charcoal furnace at the foot of the South mountain, of which he was the owner, and some facetious fellow designated the uncompleted road the "Thaddeus Stevens Tape-worm."

There was no truth in the charge, or appropriateness in the name, but it caught the popular ear, and Mr. Wilson's history will probably give it new currency. The line from Philadelphia to Monterey or Hagerstown by way of Lancaster, Columbia, York and Gettysburg, as contemplated by the leading men of Pennsylvania sixty-five years ago, was exceedingly direct, and even when projected to Pittsburg by way of Cumberland and Wills' Gap, was shorter than any existing route between the Delaware and the Ohio. If it were not for the chronic impecuniosity of the Reading Company, it would have long since bridged the Susquehanna at Chickies, and would now be running its passenger and freight trains to the West by this very route, which is now occupied by the Western Maryland and the Pittsburg Division of the Baltimore & Ohio.

In those days it was supposed that a grade of fifty feet to the mile was the utmost that the locomotive could climb, consequently when the State Road entered the foot-hills of the South Mountain, it made some turns and curves which may have suggested the ribald epithet, but under the conditions which then obtained, the mountain grades were overcome with remarkable skill. When the Western Maryland Company took possession of the abandoned road-bed fifty years later, it straightened out some of the original curves, but the great "Horse Shoe Bend," which takes in Maria Furnace in its mighty sweep, remains as located by the first engineers, because it would be impossible to bridge the deep ravine which the curve outflanks. This big bend furnished material for many jokes at the expense of Mr. Stevens and "Maria Furnace," but the political orators and wits of 1837 were not practical civil engineers.

When the last appropriation ($500,000) was made by the Pennsylvania Legislature for the State Railroad, it was provided that the money should be expended on the "Western Division," which comprised the twenty-three miles between Gettysburg and a point on Mason and Dixon's Line near Monterey. It is reasonable to suppose that Mr. Stevens exerted his influence with the Legislature to secure this appropriation with the mandate directing where the money should be expended, but that he was influenced by any corrupt motive, or was contemplating his own advantage rather than the public good, is a slander too absurd to be repeated at this day. It is true that the last appropriation was included in an omnibus bill, the title to which did not fully disclose its purpose, but that was a common mode of legislation in those days.

The failure to complete the projected railroad connecting Baltimore and Philadelphia with Pittsburg by 1842, as was provided in the charter granted by the Pennsylvania Legislature, was a great disappointment to many people besides Mr. Stevens; but the Baltimore & Ohio stockholders suffered most of all. The road lay inert and helpless with its western terminus at Harper's Ferry from 1835 to 1838. During the next four years it reached Cumberland by the Virginia route. By this time both its Pennsylvania and its Virginia charters had expired. Virginia influences were still dominant, and after a rest of five or six years, a capable and energetic Virginian residing in Maryland (the late Governor Swann), was put at the head of the company. The Virginia charter was renewed on condition that the road should go from Cumberland to Wheeling. It reached that city in 1852 through a territory which to this day yields an utterly inadequate local revenue.

Twenty years later the company tried to retrieve the colossal blunder by building the Pittsburg Division (Cumberland to Pittsburg) over the route originally projected as the main line, and up to the death of President Garrett, in 1884, this branch line supported the whole structure, and kept its stock above par. The accumulated burden of debt, however, finally broke the camel's back, and the foreclosure and sale now in progress is the melancholy culmination of a series of mistakes, beginning with the choice of the Southern route, which took the road out of the reach of the Pennsylvania connection which Mr. Stevens and the ablest of his cotemporaries were most anxious to make.

JAMES P. MATTHEWS.
Baltimore, Jan. 30, 1899.

NOTES AND QUERIES.

Historical, Biographical, and Genealogical.

IV.

[The "Women of the Revolution" deserve, at the hands of the various hereditary societies, far more consideration than they receive. There is not one of whom something delightful cannot be said, and family tradition has preserved many incidents. Would it not be good policy, if naught else, for the "Daughters" to gather up some of these precious morsels of Revolutionary biography, that they be not lost. We commend to them the perusal of the sketch in this number of "Notes and Queries." They can do likewise.]

Margaret Parke—1737-1810.

Among the women of the Revolutionary period, in Pennsylvania, no one is more deserving of honorable mention than Margaret Parke, wife of Captain John Rutherford. Born in 1737 and married in 1762, she was the mother of six children when the thunders of the Revolution burst upon the colonies. Her husband had joined the Liberty Association of Lancaster county, and held himself in readiness to answer the call of his country at any moment. This call was repeatedly given and as readily answered, thereby leaving Margaret as practical manager of the farm and sole guardian of his children during much of the period covered by the seven years of war. The mannr in which she fulfilled these trusts has been the subject of traditionary eulogy ever since. Of her history previous to her marriage, little has come down to us, and of that little scarcely anything rests upon documentary evidence, so fully occupied were the settlers of that day with the overwhelming problems of the hour that neither time nor energy were available for the noting of personal affairs. We are able, however, to state, with a reasonable degree of certainty, that Margaret Parke was the granddaughter of Arthur and Mary Parke, of Ballybagly, County Donegal, Ireland, who came to America with their family, consisting of three sons and one daughter about the beginning of the eighteenth century and took up a large body of land in Chester county, now divided into seven farms, lying along the Limestone road, near the present town of Parkesburg, and that her father, who was a miller by trade, came to Paxtang in Lancaster county at a very early day and operated a mill which stood on or near the site of the present Dauphin county mill in Swatara township. His wife died in 1737, leaving him with four daughters, the youngest of whom, Margaret, was an infant but a few weeks old and the eldest, Martha, a maiden of sixteen. Mr. Parke never married again, and the care of his household thenceforth devolved upon Martha, who proved to be a superior girl and in many respects a remarkable woman. It is said of her that in her youth she had many offers of marriage, but rejected them all, being convinced that her first duty lay at home. Under her guidance the sisters were taught industry, economy, a knowledge of the Scriptures, and so thoroughly drilled in the Shorter Catechism as to be able to recite that excellent summary of Christian faith and doctrine, from end to end, without the book, a foundation than which no better can be laid, either for this life or that which is to come. Martha remained steadfast in her determination never to marry, until she reached the age of twenty-five, when she surrendered to Francis McKnight. Twice afterwards in the course of her long life, she was called to a similar experience, and at the age of one hundred and four, Mattie Moore, as her name then was, in taking a retrospect of her life, remarked upon the inscrutable ways of Providence, as illustrated in her own career. She, who, in early life, had determined never to marry, had been preceded to the grave by no less than three husbands. A letter written by her to her nephew, William Rutherford, in her one hundred and third year, has been preserved, and exhibits a spirit of piety and trust in God which is refreshing, as well as a concentration of thought not often surpassed by persons in the prime of life. She died at the home of her daughter in Bart township, Lancaster county, in 1830. Mr. Parke and his remaining daughters continued to run the mill until William Thome, of Hanover, and Andrew Huston, of Paxtang, took away two of them, when advancing years and diminished help warned him to retire from active life and in 1758 we find him with his youngest daughter, Margaret, living on a property near the present village of Oberlin, now owned by James Boyd.

Among the reminiscences of this place which Margaret often recalled was the march, past their house, of the British army under General Forbes on its way to Fort Duquesne. She was scutching flax in the yard when the head of the column appeared. Here Mr. Parke died about the year 1760 and was buried in Paxtang churchyard beside his wife. The spot lies about fifty feet southeast of the entrance gate and was originally marked by two red sandstones, both of which were in place within the memory of one or two persons still living.

On the 4th of February, 1762, Margaret became the wife of John Rutherford. In person she is represented as having been above the average height, of pleasing countenance, dark hair, and more than ordinary physical strength. She is said to have been able to meet, with ease, that well known test of muscular development, in vogue a century ago, of shouldering three bushels of wheat, standing with the feet upon the bottom of an inverted half bushel measure. This statement will probably seem incredible to the colonial dames and daughters of to-day, but it must be remembered that the frontier women of the Revolutionary period were obliged to keep their muscles in constant use, and as a consequence were strangers to many of the weaknesses which accompany a more advanced state of society. Moreover, the feat in question is one in which skill plays almost as gerat a part as bodily strength, and doubtless Margaret's early training in the mill had much to do with her ability to handle heavy bags of grain. The spirit of invention by which mankind has been relieved of much of the drudgery of life had not yet been awakened.

But it was to the qualities of her mind and heart, that Margaret Parke owed the position which she held among the women of her day and neighborhood. Whilst she never aspired to leadership, her advice was constantly sought and followed. She was known as a peacemaker, and to be a successful peacemaker among the turbulant Scotch-Irish of that day, or indeed of any other period, requires a degree of judgment and insight into human nature not very common. As an instance of the confidence reposed in her integrity and discretion, it may be stated that in the wills of several contemporary men and women, the division of wearing apparel and other personal effects among the heirs is left to her sole judgment, and in the performance of these delicate tasks all parties interested seem to have been entirely satisfied. She and her husband began housekeeping on the farm at Rutherford Station (then containing about four hundred acres), in 1762. Within a year or two thereafter they erected and occupied the house which is still in use and in which she died, January 18, 1810, outliving her husband by six years.

There is yet preserved in the family the cane with which she supported the steps of her declining years. It had lain in the garret for seventy-eight years, when in 1888, in one of the upheavals of removal, is was brought forth, and upon being shown to one of her grandsons, then in his eighty-seventh year, he immediately recognized it as "Granny's Cane." "Why," said he, "I have used it as a horse many and many a time," and as the recollection of her (to him) beautiful face and her kindly sympathy in the joys and sorrows of childhood rolled back upon his memory, he seemed to throw off the weight of years and live over again the days of his childhood, and to see again her slightly bent form as she came along the path leading to his father's house, leaning upon that very cane, and to anticipate once more the pleasures which her visit, coupled with a search in her wonderful pocket would produce.

No one, now living, remembers her, but her name still continues to be a synonym for patriotism, virtue and Christian motherhood among her descendants.

W. F. R.

THE "STEVENS" RAILROAD.

Another Opinion as to the Wisdom of Its Location.

To the Editor: The admirable contribution of Mr. James P. Matthews to the railroad history of Pennsylvania, appearing in the "Telegraph" of February 4th, contains an inaccuracy, or what might perhaps be termed an error of opinion.

The assertion that "If it were not for the chronic impecuniousity of the Reading company, it would have long since bridged the Susquehanna at Chickies, and would now be running its passenger and freight trains to the West via this very route (the Gettysburg Railroad), etc.," would indicate that the writer thereof is not well acquainted with certain existing railroad connections, while in answering Mr. Wilson as to the practicability of the Gettysburg route as a legitimate connection of the old Columbia road, he is led into making the assertion that such a line crossing the river at Chickies would be a proper highway to the West for the Reading system.

The fact that the direct route talked of more than fifty years ago, connecting the West and the East by linking the Baltimore & Ohio Railroad with the railroads of Pennsylvania via a line through the Cumberland Valley, intersecting the Baltimore & Ohio at Cherry Run, W. Va. (seven miles east of Hancck, Md.) is today in full operation, may be unknown to Mr. Matthews but the fine steel bridge which spans the Susquehanna at Harrisburg over which pass many hundreds of cars daily laden with the products of the great West or returning with the valuable output of Eastern and European mills is substantial proof that what was dreamed of two generations ago has come to pass, and the great natural route for a Southerly crossing of the Alleghenies into the Ohio basin is open to the commerce of the State of Pennsylvania and its sisters.

The route via the Gettysburg Railroad to and from the West, could not be a feasible connection for the Reading, whatever may be said as to the possible advantages to be gained in crossing the river at Chickies, in relation to traffic destined to or originating at Baltimore or in the section east of the South Mountain. Any project for a western connection for the Reading which would contemplate the moving of heavy low-paying tonnage (such as coal and lumber) over the crest of the South Mountain and thence over the rising and falling grades of the Reading and Columbia Railroad to the city of Reading etc., could not be seriously urged against the direct route through the Lebanon and Cumberland valleys, saving many miles in distance and avoiding entirely all mountain grades.

Indeed, the assertion might well be ventured that not only was a line via the Getttysburg Railroad and the Reading infeasible, but that the route via the Gettysburg road and the Columbia Railroad was likewise quite unfitted for sustaining itself, and same be based not upon the deficiencies of the Gettysburg end, but upon the fact that the Columbia Railroad as constructed by the State was inherently wrong in construction for economical work. From the day the State works passed into the hands of the Pennsylvania Railroad Company, down to the present time, the task of reducing the grades, taking out curves and relocating the line between Columbia and Philadelphia has been pursued unremittingly and untold money spent in endeavoring to correct the primal mistake—that is in locating the line at all over the rough country traversed.

The Lebanon Valley Railroad, an independent corporation, was completed in 1856, between Harrisburg and Reading, 54 miles, an almost ideal line, with a maximum gradient of 26 feet to the mile and that for a short distance only. It connected at Reading with the Reading Railroad, a line with an utter absence of visible grades, but with a slight descent toward tide water, "the direction of the traffic." Against such a combination the Columbia Railroad if left to depend upon its own earning capacities would have utterly failed, a condition which would have been in no way improved by the completion of the Gettysburg road as a connecting link with the Baltimore & Ohio Railroad.

Traffic like water will seek of its own accord that channel which affords the most direct route with the least resistance, and the stern logic of cost always determines which competitor will endure.

That it was a mistake to locate the joint canal and railroad terminus of the State works at Columbia is probably generally now agreed. The reports of the Canal Commissioners are full of the troubles direct and indirect experienced by reason of the selection of Columbia for that purpose.

Had the canal terminated at Harrisburg, and the State had built its railroad through the Lebanon and Schuylkill valleys, or indeed only as far as Reading, connecting there first with the private canal of the Schuylkill Navigation Company and later with the Reading Railroad, not only would the line thus formed have been greatly superior to the Columbia route as regards engineering work and economical operating, but the advantages gained by traversing a densely populated manufacturing district wuld have inured to the benefit of the State, and assisted in supporting the line, a condition clearly out of the question along the route of the Columbia Railroad.

When the Lebanon Valley route fell into control of a private corporation which built its own line therein, the fate of the Columbia Railroad was sealed; its only chance for successful continued existence was that which came to pass, the Pennsylvania Railroad Company purchased it, and made it a link of their through line. That done, work was begun at once to make the most of the bargain and to convert it into the best shape possible under the disadvantageous natural conditions surrounding it.

But in the gradual evolution of the two great railroad systems of Pennsylvania, the Gettysburg Railroad had no part, and whether considered upon the grounds of physical possibilities of engineering and economy or upon the equally important basis of railroad policy it seems indeed doubtful if under any circumstances that line could have achieved the purposes for which it was inaugurated. B.
February 6th, 1899.

Mr. Wilson's Answer to Mr. Mathews Criticism.

Waldon, Holmesburg, Philadelphia, Pa., Feb. 7, 1899.—Editor "The Evening Telegraph."—My Dear Mr. McAlarney: Mr. James P. Matthews, of Baltimore, Md., after reading an excerpt from the article on the Cumberland Valley Railroad in my History of the Pennsylvania Railroad Company, which appeared in your columns, takes occasion, in the very interesting letter he contributes to the issue of February 4th, 1899, to take advantage of a word to eulogize Thaddeus Stevens, and outline the early attempts of the Baltimore & Ohio Railroad to pass through Pennsylvania.

I have no desire to dispute the estimate placed on Mr. Stevens, whose fame has passed into history, and which no words of Mr. Matthews or mine can add to or detract from. That Mr. Stevens ended his life as a national colossus is no reason to assert that he never was wrong. As a matter of fact, his strong partisan character had an element of ferocity in it which led him at times to oppose what he believed to be right. An instance of that was found in his well-known opposition to the renomination of Abraham Lincoln. Another was in the heated question of the introduction of steam power on the public works. Mr. Stevens led the opposition in the Legislature, contending that to authorize the purchase of locomotives would place the motive power in the hands of the State, and increase the patronage of the Board of Canal Commissioners. He was perfectly willing to sink his progressive spirit sooner than allow his political opponents to obtain an advantage. Eventually, under the pressure of prominent men of his own party in the State, and in accordance with his own progressive ideas, he dropped his active opposition and permitted the passage of an act of Assembly, approved April 15th, 1834, which authorized the purchase by the Board of Canal Commissioners. These illustrations are simply given to show the extent to which he would sometimes go in his ultra partisanism.

The relation of the incorporation of the

Baltimore & Ohio Railroad, of its struggle with the Chesapeake & Ohio Canal Company, and their diverse interests, being subjects without any particular relation to the history of the Pennsylvania Railroad Company, and as the facts had already been made a matter of historic record by the gifted William Prescott Smith, of Baltimore, in his well-told "Railroad Celebrations of 1857,' there was no occasion for me to incorporate them into my work.

Whilst Thaddeus Stevens was not the father of the suggestion for the extension of the Baltimore & Ohio Railroad through Pennsylvania, to connect with the Public Works at Columbia, he had "conceived" the idea of the practical construction of the so-called "Tape-Worm" Railroad, and as president of the Board of Canal Commissioners, vigorously pushed forward the work.

The attempt of Baltimore corporations to lay Philadelphia under contribution to them had its origin in commercial rivalry, and was resisted by the people of Pennsylvania, whose civic pride would not permit the accomplishment of the various schemes which had been formulated to attain that object. The Baltimore & Susquehanna Company was organized under its Maryland charter, May 5th, 1828, with George Winchester, a public-spirited citizen of that city, and one of its bright legal lights as president. In the winter of 1828-29, several influential gentlemen from Baltimore, under the leadership of Mr. Winchester, appeared at Harrisburg in advocacy of the construction of a railroad from Baltimore to the Susquehanna River; thence to the borough of Carlisle. The measure was presented to the House of Representatives, and referred to the Committee on Inland Navigation and Internal Improvements, which reported against it, February 3d, 1829. The report, which outlines the policy of Pennsylvania at that date, exhibiting the sensitiveness of trade centers, and giving an insight into the jealous care taken of the Commonwealth's interests by the promoters of public improvements, is well worthy of a liberal quotation from its text: It says: "That the time has arrived when Pennsylvania has the means, without the aid of other States, of making such improvements as will accommodate all parts of the Commonwealth; and that the Committee believe that, as a sovereign State of the American Confederacy, it is her policy and her right, as far as possible to adopt the principle that her highways are to be kept under her own control. The expediency of placing the leading roads of a State in the hands of corporations has in all ages been questioned, and some of the wisest statesmen inculcate the maxim that roads and canals are to be made by the State and kept in the hands of the State. Whatever may be thought of the wisdom of this maxim, so far as respects the incorporation of our own citizens, it is believed that the incorporation of persons who are not citizens of Pennsylvania, for the objects of the petition, with power to raise a revenue from the people, and who may contrive to conduct their business beyond the vigilance and reach of our laws, ought not to engage the serious attention of the Legislature.

"The petitioners ask for a charter to citizens of Maryland to make a railroad, which is to begin in Baltimore, and to pass in front of the Pennsylvania Capitol, under the eye of the Pennsylvania Legislature, and penetrate through the heart of Pennsylvania, for the purpose of securing the profits of Pennsylvania trade to a city which pays no revenue to the State and is beyond her jurisdiction.

"The petitioners further ask that the corporation be allowed to act as a transportation company, and that their property be exempted from taxation, and that they make the road, not as a public highway, but as a monopoly, to be exclusively used by the company, or at the pleasure of the company. It is believed that the grant of such privileges is not due to any principle of comity or justice, and is repugnant to every principle of State pride and State policy. It would have a tendency to deprive the State of the trade which will be one of the elements of her future greatness; and with whatever care the charter might be guarded, the humiliating spectacle would soon be exhibited of the country of Penn and Franklin pleading for her rights at Washington, in the courts of the United States, against a corporate power located in one of the streets of Baltimore. An absolute and exclusive control over the highways, excepting only what is conceded to the paternal government of the United States, is the constitutional right, and is a part of the sovereign power of the State, and ought only to be given up when absolutely necessary for the construction of works bearing a national impress. The work in contemplation is urged upon the ground of mere local accommodation, so far as respects our own citizens,, and when it becomes expedient to construct it a due regard for the character and interest of the State will require its construction, either by the Government or by our own citizens."

As a matter of fact the so-called Pennsylvania branch of the Baltimore & Ohio Railroad and the extension of the Baltimore & Susquehanna Railroad fell through because the people of Pennsylvania were not willing that its territory should be invaded to build up the commercial supremacy of Baltimore at the expense of the city of Philadelphia.

Mr. Matthews' study of the public improvements of Pennsylvania must have been cursory, or he has overlooked the permanent records of the Commonwealth which have stood for sixty years, lest he would not have made the assertion that "by some accident this decayed relic of a political campaign conspicuous for its shameless falsehoods has survived the period and purpose which gave it birth, and it is now paraded as a fact worthy of permanent record." The "permanent records" show that Mr. Stevens was president of the Board of Canal Commissioners and dominated its councils when the Gettysburg Railroad was under construction. They further contain a report of a committee of the House of Representatives in which appear these strong words: "Of all the works of doubtful expediency constructed by the State, in the opinion of your committee, there is none so useless, so expensive or of as little value, as the Gettysburg Railroad. It was commenced by fraud and intrigue; and will end in disgrace and loss to the Commonwealth.—"

After the retirement of Mr. Stevens from the Board of Canal Commissioners, that body, in its report for 1839, regarded the amount expended on the road as literally thrown away, and expressed the opinion that it should never have been commenced, and that the work upon it should not be resumed. They declared the practicability of the undertaking at best as doubtful, and if completed, as being a source of expense, "worse than worthless to the Commonwealth. "And the records also show that there was squandered on the work over three-quarters of a million dollars; that work was suspended on it in pursuance of an act of Assembly approved February 19th, 1839; nd that it has never been resumed to this day.

Surely these "permanent records" of the Commonwealth cannot be flauntingly thrown aside by any conscientious student of the truths of history as "decayed relics of political campaigns."

WILLIAM BENDER WILSON.

NOTES AND QUERIES.

Historical, Biographical, and Genealogical.

V.

HUNTER, CANON, McDONALD, SLOAN.

My great-great grandfather, Thomas Hunter, lived in Newberry township, York county, Pa., and his will was probated November 19, 1777. His wife's name was Mary Canon. Their children were James, Ephraim, Jane, Mary, Margaret, Alice, Joseph, William; grandchildren: Thomas Aston, William Aston and Allen Hay. James was my great grandfather. His wife was Elizabeth McDonald. They were living in Westmoreland county, Pa., Feb. 14, 1777, as on that date my grandfather, James (2d) was born. The latter married Nancy Sloan. My father claimed during his lifetime relationship to Thomas A. Hendricks. I observe the name Hendricks associated with that of Colonel Samuel Hunter. Can any one give me information as to any of the persons mentioned above?

W. H. Hunter,
Editor Gazette.
Steubenville, O.

Some Weaver Data.

About 1715 or 1717 Jacob Weber, John Weber, George Weber and Henry Weber settled in what is known as "Weber Thal," in Earl township, Lancaster county, Pa. Very little is known about Jacob or John. The wife of George was named Barbara ———, and his children were:

i. Magdalene, b. Jan. 13, 1727.
ii. John, b. Feb. 10, 1728.
iii. Anna, b. April 30, 1729.
iv. Maria, b. Dec. 30, 1730.
v. Samuel, b. Aug. 8, 1732.
vi. Barbara, b. May 11, 1734.
vii. Henry, b. Oct. 20, 1738.

The children of Henry Weaver were:
i. Mary.
ii. Magdalene.
iii. Ann.
iv. Elizabeth.
v. Christian, b. Dec. 25, 1731.
vi. Henry.

Later in the last century a George Weber married a Frances Brechbiel and they had issue:
i. Samuel.
ii. John.
iii. George.
iv. Henry.
v. Ann.
vi. Frances.
vii. Elizabeth.

Whose son was George Weber, who married Frances Brechbiel? The supposition is that he was either a son or grandson of John (Hans) Weber, one of the four original settlers. This can't be substantiated, however, as the will of Hans Weber, dated Jan. 8, 1755, mentions as legatees a wife Barbara and one son, Jacob. The name of Jacob (original settler) Weber's wife is supposed to have been Mary Elizabeth ——— or Ann Elizabeth ———. Can some reader of "Notes and Queries" enlighten us on the subject?
S. M. S.

OLD CHURCHYARD RECORDS

In St. John's Cemetery at Compass, Pa.

[The readers of Notes and Queries are indebted to the courtesy of B. F. Owen, Esq., of Reading, for the valuable contribution herewith given. The old graveyard at Compass is one of the most interesting "God's Acre" in Pennsylvania, and the records will furnish the antiquary with priceless data.]

Nathan Wilson, d. Oct. 2, 1835.
Margaret Wilson, b. Oct. 19, 1777; d. May 16, 1852.
Thomas Skiles, d. March 20, 1811, aged 52y 3m 5d.
Elizabeth Skiles, wf. of Thomas Skiles, d. July 3, 1839, aged 80y 8m.
Jane Skiles, b. Oct. 26, 1802; d. Sept. 1, 1889.
Andrew Lytle Skiles, b. Dec. 11, 1809; d. Oct. 26, 1875.
Henry Skiles, d. Jan. 7, 1866, in his 88th year.
Rebecca Skiles, wf. of Henry Skiles, d. Sept. 18, 1858, aged 79y.
James G. Skiles, b. Sept. 15, 1822; d. July 16, 1853.
Anna Rachel Skiles, dau. of Amos and Elizabeth Skiles, d. May 14, 1861, aged 1m 22d.
Isaac S. Skiles, s. of Amos and Elizabeth Skiles, d. April 27, 1866, aged 3y 10m.
Adam Rutter, d. Nov. 25, 1810, aged 37y.
John Skiles, d. April 3, 1855, in his 79th year.
Elizabeth Skiles, wf. of John Skiles, d. Feb. 23, 1854, in her 62d year.
Elizabeth Griffith, d. Jan. 8, 1850, aged 56y 4m 10d.
Thomas Griffith, d. Sept. 28, 1840, aged 72y 6m 17d.
Elizabeth Griffith, d. Jan. 15, 1850, aged 76y 10m 22d.
David Christy, d. Feb. 9, 1817, aged 18y 5m.
John Walker, d. Jan. 6, 1807, in his 76th year.
Mary Walker, wf. of John Walker, d. Feb. 28, 1802, in her 86th year.
Mary E. Hollis, d. Nov. 19, 1856, aged 2y 7m 23d.
Jacob Ecker Hollis, d. Aug. 19, 1851, aged 3y 4m.
Hyrem Meginnis, d. Dec. 26, 1867, in his 64th year.
John Walker, d. Oct. 19, 1831, aged 46y.
Anna Jones, wf. of John Walker, d. Aug. 4, 1856, aged 65y.
Elizabeth, wf. of David Davis, d. May 4th, 1756, aged 23y 2m.
William and Mary Cowan. (No age on Record.)

Susan Cowan, d. March 16, 1829, in her 85th year.
George Cowan, d. Feb. 21, 1799, in his 36th year.
Olivia C. Fleming, wf. of James Fleming, b. Sept. 21, 1807; d. March 19, 1895.
James P., s. of Wm. H. and Sarah B. Brown, b. Jan. 5, 1854; d. Feb. 6, 1857.
John Anderson, d. Oct. 24, 1818, aged 90y 3m.
Susanna Anderson, d. Nov. 14, 1815, aged 79y 11m.
William Leech, b. Dec. 24, 1777; d. Dec. 1831.
Ann Leech, b. Aug. 17, 1784; d. Sept. 27, 1873.
Elizabeth Leech, b. Feb. 22, 1787; d. April 10, 1877.
George Leech, d. 1798, aged 45y.
Elizabeth Leech, d. 1838, in her 77th year.
Thomas H. Leech, b. Oct. 31, 1794; d. Feb. 24, 1875.
Catharine, wf. of Thomas H. Leech, d. July 20, 1867, aged 70y 7m 28d.
Jacob R. Leech, s. of Thomas H. and Catharine Leech, d. Nov. 16, 1847, aged 20y 6m 13d.
George Leech, s. of Thomas H. and Catharine Leech, d. Sept. 3, 1849, aged 21y 7m 26d.
Andrew Lytle, d. April 2, 1849, in his 77th year.
Catharine, wf. of Andrew Lytle, d. Nov. 24, 1849, in her 79th year.
Susanna E., dau. of Thomas and Susanna Lytle, d. Dec. 9, 1845, in her 14th year.
Susanna Lytle, wf. of Thomas Lytle, d. Feb. 1, 1832, in her 32d year.
Mary Lytle, d. Oct. 30, 1823, in her 73d year.
Mary Adams, d. June 16, 1875, in her 84th year.
James Lytle, d. Dec. 7, 1820, in his 93d year.
Anna Mary, dau. of John H. and Sophia Skiles, b. Aug. 31, 1854; d. Dec. 21, 1857.
Archibald Lytle, d. Feb. 26, 1749, aged 46y.
Andrew Lytle, d. Aug. 15, 1785, aged 54y.
Archibald Lytle, d. Sept. 15, 1762, aged 26y.
Andrew Lytle, Jr., d. July 11, 1808, in his 24th year.
Margaret C. Dunlap, d. Feb. 22, 1868, in her 67th year.

John London (colored), d. May 26, 1856, aged 48y.
Ellen, wf. of John London (colored), d. Feb. 13, 1892, aged 71y 4d.
Hettee M., dau. of H. and M. Meginnis, d. Jan. 30, 1874, in her 19th year.
Robert Baldwin, d. Aug. 8, 1773, aged 36y.
John McNeil Skiles, b. March 15, 1825; d. Sept. 2, 1875.
Grace Clarkson, dau. of John M. and Elvina Skiles, b. Sept. 22, 1873; d. Feb. 21, 1876.
Mary Darlington, consort of Joseph Darlington, d. Aug. 7, 1813, aged 76y 3m.
Joseph Darlington, d. Feb. 22, 1805, aged 76y.
William Darlington, d. Sept. 10, 1757, in his 67th year.
Jane Dunlap, wf. of Andrew Little and James Dunlap, d. Nov. 30, 1841, aged 90y 5m 8d.
Jane Little, d. Feb. 13, 1868, in her 87th year.
Esquire George, only s. of Andrew W. and Jane Douglass, b. March 25, 1726; d. March 10, 1799; buried in Morlatton graveyard, St. Gabriel's Church, Amity township, Berks Co., Pa.
Richard, oldest s. of George and Mary Piersol Douglass, b. Nov. 25, 1748.
Esquire Andrew Douglass, d. Jan. 20, 1742, aged 40y.
Jane, w. of Andrew Douglass, d. Jan. 24, 1742, aged 35y.
Mary, only dau. of Andrew and Jane Douglass, wf. of John Elliott, d. Feb. 14, 1807, aged 73y.
—— wf. of James Douglass, d. Nov. 8, 1757, aged 60 y. (Stone broken, name gone.)
Archibald Douglass, d. Nov. 25, 1756, aged 61y.
Thomas Douglass, d. May 27, 1794, aged 72y.
Patrick Carrigan, d. June 5, 1779, aged 24y.
Margaret Wilson, wf. of John Wilson, d. April 6, 1786, aged 56y.
John Wilson, d. Oct. 9, 1799, aged 75y.
Francis M. Wilson, d. July 7, 1863, aged 33y.
Charlot Wilson, d. May 3, 1809, aged 9y 3m.
Thomas Wilson, d. Oct. 10, 1793, aged 1y 7m.

Mary Henriett, dau. of Francis N. and L. Louisa Wilson, d. Jan. 6, 1863, aged 3y and 6m.
Grace, wf. of Frederick London (colored), d. July 11, 1843, aged 68y.
Isaac J. Henderson, s. of Dr. Matthew Henderson, d. Sept. 14, 1823, in his 8th year.
Margaret Henderson, wf. of Dr. Matthew Henderson, d. Sept. 3, 1825, in her 34th year.
Dr. Matthew Henderson, d. April 27, 1855, in his 67th year.
Thomas Gilfillan, s. of Thomas G. and Mary Ann Henderson, b. July 16, 1839; d. Aug. 16, 1859.
Mary Skidmore Henderson, d. Sept. 24, 1841, in her 12th year.
Eliza Jacobs Henderson, d. Sept. 23, 1841, aged 10m 1d. Children of Thomas C. and Mary Ann Henderson.
Thomas C. Henderson, b. April 4, 1789; d. Aug. 4, 1870.
Mary Ann, wf. of Thomas C. Henderson, dau. of Samuel and Sarah Jacobs, b. July 20, 1796; d. June 13, 1863.
Barton Henderson, d. Oct. 1, 1823, in his 49th year.
Elizabeth, wf. of Barton Henderson, d. Aug. 13, 1851, aged 65y.
Eliza Henderson, dau. of Jarvis and Isabella Mott, d. Feb. 6, 1833, aged 11m 10d.
Rachel Eliza, dau. of Barton and Elizabeth Henderson, d. Feb. 19, 1823, aged 5y 4m 10d.
James Barton Henderson, s. of Barton and Elizabeth Henderson, d. Oct. 29, 1818, aged 3y 9m 24d.
Jarvis B. Mott, b. March 26, 1806; d, Jan. 26, 1863.
Oscar, s. of J. B. and I. I. Mott, b. Feb. 20, 1850; d. June 30, 1856.
John Boyd, d. June 15, 1811, aged 72y.
George Boyd, d. April 23, 1799, aged 45y.
Thomas Boyd, d. May 15, 1789, in his 27th year; b. in Philadelphia.
George Boyd, Sen., George Boyd, Jun., and George Boyd, 3d. The first d. about the year 1731, aged near 40y; the second June 12, aged about 48y, and the third about the year 1753, aged 3y.
Mathtew Henderson, d. May 7, in his 73d year.
Rachel Henderson, wf. of Matthew, d. Aug. 27 in her 66th year; b. 1806.

James Henderson, d. Nov. 14, 1821, in his 66th year.
Mary, wf. of James Henderson, d. Jan. 27, 1793, in her 24 year.
Archibald Henderson, d. Aug. 23, 1799, in his 35th year.
Catharine Clarkson, aged 91 (no dates given).
Margaret Henderson, wf. of David Henderson, d. Jan. 14, 1818, aged 24y 11m 20d.
David Henderson, d. Aug 24, 1839, aged 66y 7m 12 d.
Rachel, dau. of Matthew and Catherine E. Henderson, d. April 12, 1857, aged 7m 19d.
A son of Matthew and Catherine Henderson, d. May 16, 1858.
Catherine E, wf. of Matthew Henderson, d. May 16, 1858, aged 41y 2m 9d.
Matthew Henderson, b. May 17, 1814; d. May 6, 1861.
Catherine Elizabeth, dau. of Archibald and Barbara Henderson, d. April 9, 1850, aged 25y.
Anna R. Haines, dau. of Matthew and Catherine E. Henderson, d. June 24, 1872, aged 30y 1m 9d.
Mary Gardner, dau. of Francis and Mary Gardner, d. March 31, 1831, aged 25y 7m.
Dr. Francis Gardner, d. Jan. 21, 1816, aged 41y 11m 2d.
Mary Gardner, wf. of Francis Gardner, M. D., d. Sept. 2, 1833, in her 60th year.
John Etton, d, March 5, 1778, aged 52y.
Thomas Hartt, d. May 18, 1774, in his 84th year.
John Coombe, d. Sept. 10, 1736, aged 78y.
Peter Bezellon, d. July 18, 1742, aged 80y.
Martha Bezellon, relict of Peter Bezellon, d. June 18, 1764, aged 78y. [Peter Bezellon was the noted Italian trader. Mrs. Bezellon was identified with the first St. John's church.]
John Hetherenton, d. June 6, 1749, aged 61y.
Jane Davidson, d. Jan. 7, 1846, aged 79y 6m 7d.
Jerman Davis, d. Sept. 15, 1795, aged 58y.
Jerman Davis, d. Dec. 20, 1821, aged 84y.
Amenta Moore, wife of William Moore, d. Oct. 3, 1805, aged 29y 5d.
Jerman Davis, s. of Jerman Davis, d. March 20, 1825, aged 45y.

Mary Davis, dau. of Jerman Davis, d. Aug. 3, 1827, aged 57y.
Jane Bowen Jacobs, wf. of W. C. Henderson, d. Oct. 23, 1866, in her 38th year.
Grant, s. of W. C. and J. B. J. Henderson, d. Aug. 11, 1866, aged 10m.
John Hyman Henderson, s. of W. C. and J. B. J. Henderson, b. Oct. 16, 1862; d. Jan. 29, 1863.
Harriet Amelia, wf. of James S. Twells, dau. of Barton and Elizabeth Henderson, d. Dec. 21, 1849, aged 30y.
Malvina, wf. of Amos S. Henderson, b. Sept. 15, 1815; d. Nov. 19, 1859.
Alfred C. Henderson, b. Nov. 9, 1843; d. Sept. 18, 1867.
Rebecca Hopkins, b. Jan. 19, 1849; d. Nov. 3, 1844. William Patterson, b. Feb. 27, 1852; d. July 31, 1856. Children of Amos S. and Malvina Henderson.
Thomas Henderson, b. Feb. 8, 1773; d. Oct. 17, 1857.
Julia, wf. of Captain Thomas Henderson, b. June 29, 1782; d. Jan. 25, 1847.
Mary, dau. of Thomas W. and Mary C. Henderson, d. May 6, 1868, aged 4y 2m 16d.
William Archibald, s. of Thomas and Juliana Henderson, d. Nov. 9, 182—.
A. Lightner Henderson, b. May 19, 1803; d. Dec. 5, 1869.
Lorenzo Henderson, M. D., b. Sept. 14, 1805; d. Feb. 4, 1844.
Kate Lorenzo Roland, dau. of Lorenzo N. and Susan C. Henderson, b. Feb. 4, 1844; d. June 1, 1859.
Lorenzo Nelson, s. of Dr. Lorenzo N. and Susan C. Henderson, d. Oct. 19, 1810, aged 4m 13d.
Susan Helen, dau. of Dr. Lorenzo and Susan C. Henderson, b. Sept. 17, 1841; d. Jan. 11, 1846.
John Roland, s. of Dr. Lorenzo and Susan C. Henderson, d. July 30, 1834, aged 4m 26d.
William L. s. of Dr. Lorenzo and Susan C. Henderson, d. May 1, 1833, aged 6m 7d.

RAILROAD REMINISCENCES

Or the Projects of Half a Century Ago.

The decade beginning about the year 1850 was prolific with railroad plans and schemes in which the interests of Harrisburg and Dauphin county were largely involved. Some of the plans were realized, others came to naught and are well nigh forgotten. One of them at least seriously threatened the supremacy of Harrisburg as a railroad center.

In order to properly undestand the causes of this activity, let us glance at the actual conditions prevailing.

The line of the new Pennsylvania railroad extending from Harrisburg to Pittsburg was nearing completion, excepting the mountain section, where the Alleghny Portage, owned and operated by the State, formed the connecting link. The new company had leased the Harrisburg and Lancaster railroad on April 21, 1849, for twenty years under a contract whereby the lessee became the owner of the rolling stock and machinery of the H. and L. R. R., and had the exclusive right to run engines over the road, but its authority over traffic was limited to "through" business, the local trade between Harrisburg via the Mount Joy line, also between Columbia and Middletown via the line following the river remaining under the control of the Harrisburg and Lancaster company.

From Columbia and Lancaster eastwardly the traffic of the Pennsylvania railroad passed over the State or Columbia railroad. The management of the Columbia road was not particularly friendly to the new private corporation, and while the old troubles are now seldom recalled, the mention made in one of the annual reports of that period of the Pennsylvania Railroad company that the State authorities had arbitrarily ruled off the Columbia road the cars of the Pennsylvania causing that company to turn over its traffic to one of the numerous private car lines then existing, gives an inkling to some of the differences which prevailed.

But there were other obstacles as well in the way which prevented through train service between the State road and the new line leading west from Harrisburg. The two tracks of the Columbia railroad were laid but four feet six inches apart, much too close together for the new equipment then coming into use. The best that could be done so far as passenger traffic was concerned was to employ one set of coaches east of Harrisburg and the larger and wider cars west, which plan was followed for many years. It was not until 1858 that passenger cars actually ran through from west of Harrisburg to the Philadelphia terminus.

Maentime, the possibilities of opening new routes to Philadelphia and New York to carry the prospectively valuable trade of the Pennsylvania Railroad were fully appreciated by far-sighted capitalists. The bituminous coal of the Broad Top region began moving long before the completion of the road west of Johnstown, and with lumber traffic the tonnage quickly became heavy. This, apart from the large volume of high class goods destined to Pittsburg and beyond, or moving in the reverse direction. The anthracite from the Lykens Valley and the Treverton railroads was also a tonnage eagerly sought.

A charter had been taken out as early as 1836 for a railroad through the Lebanon Valley between Harrisburg and Reading, but the prospect lay dormant until the capabilities of the line as a connecting link between the Pennsylvania Railroad and the Philadelphia and Reading railroad at Reading were seen. Then the Lebanon Valley railroad was pushed to completion, this being in 1855 and succeeding years.

But the builders of the Lebanon Valley railroad were not alone in their efforts to catch and divert this profitable interior trade from the State works. Another body of men figured out a plan to take away this traffic fro mboth the Columbia railroad and the Lebanon Valley railroad, bringing into play a propesed route which now seems odd enough.

By act of Legislature approved April 5th, 1826, a corporation termed the Dauphin and Susquehanna Coal Company was incorporated "To prosecute the coal trade on Short Mountain and Stony Creek." The next year authority was given to make a canal from the mouth of Stony creek to the coal mines. In 1838 the charter was renewed with permission to make either a railroad or a canal along Stony creek. By act of March 18, 1848, the corporation was allowed to provide locomotives and cars.

About this time the value of this line as a connecting link for the eastern traffic of the Pennsylvania railroad became apparent, and new life was injected into the company. By act of February 26, 1852, authority was given to extend the railroad to connect with the public improvements in Schuylkill county. Ostensibly this meant the Reading railroad and Schuylkill canal, but there was a deeper purpose not revealed until the following year, when a charter was taken out for a railroad extending from Port Clinton to Allentown (one of the incorporators being Mr. Simon Cameron) followed by another in 1854 for a line from Auburn to Port Clinton. This then provided through connections from Dauphin to Allentown, there joining the Lehigh Valley railroad already existing to Easton and connecting at Easton with the Central Railroad of New Jersey for New York.

It is not to be inferred that the line from Auburn to Allentown was projected for the sole purpose of handling the traffic of the Pennsylvania railroad. On the contrary that was probably but a minor matter, the main object having been to provide a line competitive to the Reading as an outlet for anthracite coal seeking the eastern markets. The Dauphin and Susquehanna road was duly built from Dauphin to Auburn, and much work was done on the line from Auburn to Allentown, the construction being in charge of Mr. George B. Roberts, the late president of the Pennsylvania Railroad company, at that time an independent engineer.

Meantime the Lebanon Valley Railroad interests were not idle. On March 9, 1856, the Reading and Lehigh railroad was incorporated and power to construct a railroad from Reading to a junction with the Lehigh Valley railroad. The next year its title was changed to the East Pennsylvania Railroad, and it was built. The preliminary report of the engineer, bearing date of May 21, 1856, is a highly interesting document, not only as relating to the comparison drawn between the line from Harrisburg to Allentown via Reading and the line from Dauphin to Allentown via Auburn, but as concerning the development of through western connections up the Cumberland Valley with the Baltimore and Ohio railroad, competitive with the Pennsylvania railroad, a development which came about but not until almost forty years later, showing the far-sightedness of the individual.

The route to and from New York via Allentown and Harrisburg was a very popular one for passengers, and was kept in operation for many years. Indeed, up to the time that the Pennsylvania secured a direct track connection at Philadelphia with what is now its New York line, the sleeping car service was operated via Allentown, a circumstance probably yet well remembered by many of the readers of the "Telegraph."

But meantime, while the promoters of the Lebanon Valley and the Auburn routes were endeavoring to further the interests of their respective companies, changes occurred in the situation which cut off the hopes of both lines so far as the Pennsylvania connection was concerned. The State calculated to sell the public works for good reasons unnecessary to name here, except the suggestion that the various schemes above mentioned had no doubt a certain degree of weight in the premises, and on August 1st, 1857, the Governor by proclamation transferred the main lines to the new owners, the Pennsylvania Railroad company. Forthwith that company set to work to so rebuild the Columbia Railroad as to adopt it to modern conditions, and in the course of time a new agreement was made with the Harrisburg and Lancaster railroad under which the latter line passed into the full control of the great corporation wherein it has now so fully lost its identity.

The Allentown Railroad was never completed. Its embankments may yet be traced near Port Clinton, but its future lost all significance for Harrisburg at the time when the Columbia railroad passed into the hands of the Pennsylvania. The line from Dauphin to Auburn fell into the possession of the Reading. Thus ended plans which, had they culminated, would have materially affected our railroad systems of the present day, and so perished Dauphin's brief dream of outdoing Harrisburg as a railroad centre. B.

NOTES AND QUERIES.

Historical, Biographical and Genealogical.

VI.

MILLER.

The children of John and Elizabeth Miller, of Lebanon county were:

i. John-Peter, b. Feb. 15, 1759; d. March 30, 1838. Reared in the Reformed faith, he became an early Methodist. His wife was Philopena Steinman, b. in 1773; d. Jan. 15, 1831.

ii. Margaret, b. May 28, 1760; d. May 3, 1850; m. Adam Mark, b. March 20, 1757; d. Oct. 20, 1814.

iii. John-Adam, b. May 26, 1777; d. Dec. 3, 1845. Was for many years a class leader in the M. E. Church. He m. Catharine Kramer, b. October 26, 1775; d. August 27, 1814; daughter of Jacob Kramer.

iv. Elizabeth, b. November 18, 1780; d. January 24, 1859; m. John Runkle, b. April 5, 1779; d. May 31, 1845; son of Henry Runkle and —— Ziegler. P.

ROBERT PATTERSON.

Robert Patterson's will is dated Sept. 26th, 1792, and shows he was of East Pennsboro township, Cumberland county, Pa. In this document are named sons William, Samuel, Robert, Timothy, John, Millard, and daughters Hannah, Jane, wife of Henry Furry or Forrer, and Martha. His wife survived him. Her maiden name is not given and she is mentioned as "my beloved wife." I have a portion of the old record, and in it I find one "John P. Patterson, son of Robert and Mary Patterson, was born Feb. 26th, 1787." I judge this was the John named in Robert Patterson's will, and that Mary was the name of Patterson's wife. The will shows the name is spelled Paterson, but in his signature he spells it Patterson. The will was witnesses by Jonathan Hoge and William Diven, and was admitted to probate October 9, 1792. In your Notes and Queries, Third Series, vol. i, p. 392, you speak of Robert Patterson's tomb, etc. I have heard and I believe that Robert Pat-

terson was a Revolutionary soldier, but I have no authentic proof of his service.
KATE DUNCAN SMITH.
Birmingham, Ala.

Graham of Bedford County.

I. John Graham was an early settler in the Cumberland Valley, removing to Bedford township, Bedford county, in 1775, where he took up a tract of land. On subsequent assessment lists he appears to own grist and saw mills and owned land on "Shawanese Cabbin Creek." He died in October, 1804, his will being probated the 13th day of that month. He left a wife Agnes, and children:
i. John.
2. ii. George.
iii. Esther; m. James Burns.
iv. Eleanor; m. John Wilster.
v. Agnes; m. John Parker.
vi. Martha.
vii. Catharine.

II. George Graham, son of John Graham, d. in June, 1839, leaving a wife Elizabeth, and children:
i. George; settled in Cincinnati, O.
ii. John; removed to Michigan.
iii. Mary; m. Dr. Charms.
iv. Jean; m. Alexander Thomson; they were the parents of Mr. Frank Thomson, president Pennsylvania R. R.
v. Julia; d. inf.
vi. Elizabeth; m. and removed to State of Indiana.
vii. [A dau.]; m. Abraham Schell, of Schellsburg. S.

Oehrlin--Oehrle--Early.

On February 25, 1710, Thomas Oehrlin, sometimes also written Oehrle, son of Thomas Oehrlin, deceased, formerly the school teacher and town clerk of Jesingen, Wuertemberg, married Margaret Fensterle, daughter of Jacob Fensterle, judge and treasurer of the same town. They had ten children. She died February 8, 1735. The third son, John Jacob, was born 1714. The fifth, or possibly the seventh son, John, was born Jan. 9, 1724. He was the ninth child. It is not stated whether twins born 1722 were both boys, or both girls, or a boy and a girl.

Thomas Oehrlin (Early) evidently married a second time, as the names of five other children of his born between 1737 and 1746 are given in the church record at Jesingen. Aug. 24, 1750, John arrived at Philadelphia in the ship Brothers. Jan. 6, 1752, he had taken up his residence at or near Reading, Pa., being appointed a member of the building committee of Trinity church on that day. Where he spent the intervening fifteen or sixteen months is not certainly known. April 10, 1753, he married Susanna Brumbach. Christian, their first and only child, was born Jan. 13, 1754. The mother died between September 22 and Oct 12 of the same year. Soon thereafter he removed to the vicinity of the Bindnagle's church, and Mch. 11, 1755, married Regina (full name Mary Regina), daughter of John Albrecht Sichele, by whom he had nine children. Five of them, John, John William, Thomas, Anna Catharine and Anna Margaret, after their marriage, with the exception of John, went to Centre county, Pa., and remained there until about 1806 or 1808. John Early, Sen., died Oct 19, 1796, aged 72 y. 8 m. 10 d. Jacob Early (vid. Notes and Queries, vol. ii, Third Series, p. 258), who died in Donegal township, Lancaster county, Apr., 1777, and who, according to the statements of some of his descendants, was also a German, was a member of the Swamp or New Hanover Church in 1752. His oldest son, John, was born Sept. 17, 1752, and baptized by Rev. H. M. Muhlenberg, December, of the same year. His place of residence this time is not positively known, but 1758-60 he was an inhabitant of Amity township, Berks county, 10 or 15 miles south of east from Reading and from 6 to 9 from New Hanover. His name appears on at least four lists of taxables in that township. He may have resided there during the entire period of 1752-60. His widow, Christina, died Apr. 16, 1782, and was buried by Rev. J. D. Schroeder, pastor of the Ev. Luth. church near Elizabethtown. Her age was sixty-six years, making the year of her birth 1716, and so the husband was probably born about 1710-15, possibly 1714. Can any one tell whether he was that older brother of John, John Jacob, born 1714? It would certainly have been natural that if they were brothers, John should have spent those 15-16 months with Jacob, especially in view of the fact that Peter Schneider, the other member of the building committee of Trinity also resided in Amity. In addition to this it is but 6 to 9 miles on the usual route to Reading from Jacob's residence to Black Bear and St. Lawrence, where the Brumbach's have resided for a century or more. They probably had their home there when John Early married into the family.

J. W. EARLY.

OLD CHURCHYARD RECORDS

In St. John's Cemetery at Compass Pa.

Hannah, wife of Archibald Henderson, d. August 13, 1809, aged 57y.
Archibald Henderson, b. June 7, 1763; d. Nov. 8, 1847.
William Henderson, b. June 8, 1775; d. April 11, 1853.
Rachel Malinda, only dau. of John B. and Mary Henderson, d. Aug. 26, 1808, aged 1y 11m and 8d.
Thomas Barton Henderson, d. Oct. 29, 1819, aged 11m.
Maria Louisa Henderson, d. Oct. 16, 1831, aged 3y 10m 10d.
John Deboise Henderson, d. March 12, 1833, aged 21y 2 m 25d.
John Withers, d. Oct. 17, in his 86th year.
Mary Hannah, wf. of John Withers, d. Dec. 26, 1860, in her 86th year.
Dianah Smith (colored), d. Nov. 4, 1875, in her 84th year.
Ida F. Coleman (colored), b. Feb. 27, 1862; d. April 29, 1879.
Samuel Nocho (colored), b. Dec. 18, 1855, d. Oct. 26, 1859.
Harriet Nocho (colored), d. Dec. 12, 1856.
Mary Nocho (colored), d. Dec. 29, 1856.
George W. Wilson, b. Nov. 12, 1838; d. May 24, 1867.
John D. Wilson, Sr., d. July 10, 1864, aged 74y 3m 5d.
Rachel, wife of John D. Wilson, Sr., b. Jan. 15, 1801; d. Oct. 7, 1870.
William Mulberry, b. July 18, 1781; d. June 30, 1862.
Sarah, wf. of William Mulberry, b. July 10, 1787; d. Oct. 1, 1854.
Adam D. Leaman, husband of Esther Leaman, d. March 5, 1864, aged 29y 26d.
William, s. of William and Sarah Mulberry, d. May 30, 1849, aged 19y 10d.
Elias Eaby, b. April 18, 1813; d. May 24, 1874.
Emma Eaby, b. Feb. 24, 1839; d. Jan. 2, 1879.
Elizabeth Eaby, wf. of Jacob Stott, b. Oct. 23, 1840; d. Jan. 24, 1873.
Jacob Stott, b. Nov. 23, 1835; d. Nov. 19, 1879.
Adalaide ———, b. Jan. 31, 1835; d. May 31, 1856. [This lady married contrary to the wishes of her mother. Her husband erected the monument—shortly after; all but first name was stricken from the stone.]
Cyrus M. Davis, Co. C, 97th Regt., P. V., b. March 25, 1836; d. May 6, 1894.
James Ubil, d. April 15, 1850, aged 64y 6m 18d.
Abner Ubil, d. Dec. 30, 1850, aged 78y 4m 13d.
Elizabeth, wf. of Abner Ubil, d. Oct. 5, 1838, aged 61y.
Peter Ubil, s. of Abner and Elizabeth Ubil, d. June 16, 1834, aged 31y 5m 8d.
Isaac Ubil, s. of Abner and Elizabeth Ubil, d. March 31, 1827, aged 29y 4m 1d.
Peter Ubil, d. Jan. 6, 1825, in his 84th year.
Ruth Ubil, wf. of Peter Ubil, d. March 19, 1830, in her 75th year.
William Ubil, b. June 8, 1777; d. Sept. 9, 1856.
Rachel Ubil, b. March 20, 1779; d. May 1, 1868.
George Ubil, b. Sept. 24, 1791; d. Oct. 12, 1874.
Hannah Ubil, b. April 2, 1789; d. July 22, 1880.
Peter Ubil, b. Aug. 29, 1812; d. Oct. 7, 1854.
Margaret Ubil, wf. of Peter Ubil, dau. of J. M. Fiester, d. May 16, 1850, aged 35y 11m 6d
John Henck, Sr., d. Feb. 20, 1802, aged 84y.
Anna Mary Hencks, d. Jan: 16, 1805, in her 79th year.
Jacob Hencks, d. Feb. 20, 1822, aged 57y.

Margaret Hencks, d. April 8, 1832, aged 59y.
Susanna, wf. of William Russell, b. Sept. 6, 1800; d. June 3, 1849.
John Addleman, d. June 27, 1841, in his 48th year.
Mary, wf. of John Addleman, d. Dec. 14, 1856, in her 56th year.
John M., s. of John and Mary Addleman, d. Feb. 13, 1842, aged 4y 4m 14d.
Jacob Greenleaf, b. Dec. 2, 1800; d. Feb. 25, 1885.
Anna, wf. of Jacob Greenleaf, b. Feb. 28, 1803; d. June 19, 1871.
Bruner Greenleaf, Co. K., 124th Regt., P. V. Inf.
Elizabeth Nelson, d. March 23, 1876, aged 88y 11m and 11d.
Margaret Nelson, d. Nov. 22, 1857, in her 74th year.
Rachel, wf. of James Stewart, d. April 7, 1854, in her 73d year.
Andrew Dague, d. Sept. 12, 1866, in his 66th year.
Mary, w. of Andrew Dague, d. May 21, 1866, aged 66y.
William Wagner, b. Feb. 25, 1812; d. April 1, 1893.
Barbara Wagner, b. Oct. 15, 1796; d. Dec. 14, 1879.
Jane Wagner, wf. of John W. Wagner, b. Jan. 29, 1807; d. Feb. 24, 1877.
Mary S. Wagner, dau. of John W. and Jane Wagner, b. June 20, 1846; d. March 17, 1861.
John Wagner, d. Aug. 30, 1856, aged 21y 7m 22d.
Anna Elizabeth, dau. of James and Margaret Wagner, d. Jan. 28, 1846, aged 6m.
Margaret Wagner, wf. of George Wagner, d. Dec. 19, 1819, in her 37th year.
John Wagner, d. Sept. 20, 1774, aged 41y.
George, s. of John Wagner, d. Jan. 25, 1809, aged 42y.
Barbara Wagner, wf. of John Wagner, d. March 17, 1777, aged 47y.
William Wagner, d. Sept. 18, 1793, aged 32y.
Elizabeth, wf. of William Wagner, d. June 18, 1790, aged 18y.
Peter Wagner, d. April 1, 1832, in his 67th year.
Mary, wf. of Peter Wagner, d. June 7, 1847, aged 76y 6m 12d.
Peter Wagner, d. Dec. 30, 1848, aged 47y.
Maria Wagner, d. June 16, 1854, aged 55y 5m 4d.
Mary Louisa, consort of Rev. J. A. Kirkpatrick, of the Baptist Church, d. Nov. 19, 1864, aged 26y 10m 14d.
Eugene Kincaid, s. of Rev. J. A. Kirkpatrick, b. Aug. 27, 1864; d. March 30, 1865, aged 7m 3d.
William A. Gibbs, d. July 22, 1849, aged 55y.
Mary Gibbs, wf. of William A. Gibbs, d. June 18, 1838, in her 40th year.
James Gibbs, b. Aug. 11, 1792; d. Nov. 16, 1877.
Sarah Gibb, wf. of Michael R. Johnston, d. April 15, 1861, aged 75y 5m 28d.
Susanna Gibb, wf. of Gilbert Gibb, d. Aug. 24, 1822, aged 69y 4m 28d.
Jane Gibb, d. April 10, 1868, aged 77y 11m 26d.
Susan A. Gibb, d. March 7, 1863, aged 76y 6m.
John Armstrong, d. Sept. 18, 1875, aged 86y 11m 5d.
Margaret Armstrong, wf. of John Armstrong, b. Dec. 18, 1798; d. July 21, 1893.
John Williams, b. Sept. 8, 1802; d. Oct. 27, 1867.
Ruth Ann Williams, b. Oct. 16, 1840; d. May 20, 1864.
Rebecca Williams, b. April 7, 1809; d. Nov. 8, 1883.
Abner Ubil, s. of John and Susanna Ubil, b. May 6, 1819; d. July 5, 1862.
Sarah, wf. of Abner Ubil, d. Aug. 27, 1896, aged 77y 1m 27d.
John, s. of Abner and Sarah Ubil, b. Aug. 22, 1842; d. March 23, 1862.
Abner R. Ubil, son of Abner and Sarah Ubil, d. Aug. 9, 1859, aged 1y 3m 20d
Mary Ubil, d. June 11, 1855, aged 5y 5m 4d.
Hugh Tearney, b. Oct. 2, 1855; d. Dec. 7, 1857.
Mary Purell, d. 1835, in her 65th year.
Daniel Ubil, b. Jan. 20, 1817; d. Aug. 18, 1854.
Hannah Ubil, b. Feb. 12, 1815; d. Dec. 31, 1896.
Susanna Ubil, b. Jan. 27, 1792; d. Nov. 9, 1863.
John Ubil, b. Jan. 23, 1783; d. Dec. 9, 1862.

John, s. of John and Susanna Ubil, d. Feb. 27, 1852, aged 27y 10m 6d.
James Ubil, s. of John and Susanna Ubil, d. Feb. 25, 1852, aged 25y 5m 11d.
Ruth Ann, dau. of John and Susanna Ubil, d. Aug. 25, 1851, aged 22y 11m 23d.
Samuel Ubil, s. of John and Susanna Ubil, d. April 18, 1851, aged 13 y 11m 13d.
Frederick D. Baker, d. May 12, 1845, in his 60th year.
Alice Abigale, wf. of Frederick D. Baker, d. Dec. 15, 1848, aged 63y 8m 7d.
Frederick Baker, d. May 24, 1815, in his 67th year.
Margaret Baker, d. Nov. 29, 1831, in her 76th year.
Eliza N. Baker, dau. of F. M. Baker, b. Dec. 4, 1842; d. Dec. 14, 1842.
Juliana Teresa, wf. of Thomas Mee, d. May 24, 1820, aged 45y.
Thomas Mee, d. Nov. 26, 1820, aged 57y.
Margaret Virginia, dau. of Samuel M. and Margaret Armstrong, b. Sept. 1, 1854; d. Dec. 19, 1863.
John Read, s. of Samuel M. and Margaret Armstrong, b. Oct. 8, 1860; d. Dec. 23, 1863.
John McNeil, d. Aug. 9, 1812, in his 73d year.
Mary, wf. of John McNeil, d. Aug. 5, 1819, in her 65th year.
Matilda Ann, dau. of John and Mary McNeil, d. May 1, 1884.
Thomas A., only s. of John and Mary McNeil, b. May 4, 1817; d. Sept. 6, 1896.
Mary, dau. of John and Mary McNeil, d. March 10, 1851, in her 36th year.
Robert McNeil, d. April 6, 1833, aged 49y 3m 13d.
Ann Thomas, consort of Owen Thomas, d. June 12, 1802, aged 50y 25d.
John M. Thomas, b. Oct. 3, 1819; d. Sept. 26, 1882.
Sarah A., wf. of John M. Thomas, d. April 22, 1884, in her 56th year.
Edith, dau. of J. and S. A. Thomas, b. Oct. 15, 1861; d. Feb. 19, 1876.
S. Ida, dau. of John M. and Sarah A. Thomas, aged 15m.
Archibald Thomas, d. May 15, 1859, aged 66y 8m 7d.
Hannah D. Thomas, b. March 16, 1831; d. Dec. 22, 1831.

Charlotte T. Thomas, b. Oct. 10, 1837; d. Sept. 21, 1841.
Sarah, wf. of John Stanton, d. Jan. 26, 1866, in her 66th year.
John Hull, d. May 7, 1861, in his 82d year.
Mary Hull, wf. of John Hull, d. Nov. 20, 1859, in her 76th year.
William Tullidge, M. D., b. in Rorchester, England, d. March 6, 1852, aged 75 years.
Hannah, wf. of William Tullidge, M. D., b. in Dorchester, England, d. June 14, 1851.
Robert Bower, s. of Rev. Henry and Mary Ann Tullidge, b. Jan. 3, 1853; d. Sept. 19, 1853.
Charles Foote, s. of Rev. Henry and Mary Ann Tullidge, b. March 19, 1848; d. July 29, 1850.
Louisa Bower, dau. Rev. Henry and Mary Ann Tullidge, b. Aug. 6, 1850; d. Oct. 21, 1853.
Ann Warren, wf. of James Warren, d. Nov. 12, 1802, in her 43d year.
Amanda, wf. of William Martin, d. July 12, 1857, aged 40 years.
William Ely, M. D.. b. March 28, 1833; d. Dec. 27, 1878.
Hugh T. Skiles, b. Jan. 27, 1812; d. Jan. 27, 1889.
Grace A. Mayberry, d. Sept. 11, 1868, in her 69th year.
Mary Ann, dau. of William and Christiana Murray, d. April 15, 1858, aged 1y 6m 22d.
Elizabeth, wf. of Henry Platt, d. March 15, 1849, in her 58th year.
George W., s. of Henry and Elizabeth Platt, b. Dec. 27, 1827; d. March, 1837.
John Davis, s. of Gabriel and Jane Davis, b. Aug. 9, 1760; d. Jan. 13, 1811.
Gabriel Davis, s. of Reese Davis, of Wales, b. in 1728; d. Feb. 1, 1813, in his 86th year.
Jane Davis, wf. of Gabriel Davis, and dau. of Archibald Douglass, d. March 3, 1777, in her 49th year. Buried in the grave of her uncle, James Douglass, in this yard.
Archibald Douglass Davis, s. of Gabriel and Jane Davis, b. Aug. 21, 1776; d. Dec. 4, 1803.
Gabriel Davis, s. of Gabriel and Jane Davis, b. April 26, 1771; d. April 16, 1801.

Historical and Genealogical.

Mary Davis, dau. of Gabriel and Jane Davis, b. March 18, 1758; d. Nov. 7, 1798.
Jane Davis, dau. of Gabriel and Jane Davis, b. March 13, 1768; d. April 24, 1846.
Julianna Barton Davis, wf. of Archibald Douglass Davis, and dau. of John and Susanna Anderson, b. Sept. 12, 1779; d. May 11, 1837.
Zaccheus Piersol, d. Nov. 18, 1804, in his 40th year.
Margaret Piersol, wf. of Zaccheus Piersol, and dau. of Gabriel and Jane Davis, b. Sept. 15, 1756; d. Feb. 10, 1839.
George Davis, s. of Gabriel and Jane Davis, b. Sept. 7, 1765; d. April 23, 1829.
John Piersol, d. Sept. 14, 1816, in his 34th year.
Catharine, wf. of John Piersol, d. Sept. 23, 1825, in her 37th year.
Jacob Keiser, d. May 14, 1874, in his 88th year.
Mary, wf. of Jacob Keiser, d. April 19, 1838, in her 57th year.
Elizabeth, wf. of Jacob Keiser, d. Sept. 27, 1873, in her 86th year.
Amos Clemson, b. June 9, 1783; d. Sept. 3, 1857.
Maria A. Clemson, d. Feb. 13, 1873, in her 71st year.
Caroline, wf. of Jacob Evans, d. March 17th, 1882, aged 52y 3m 20d.
Elizabeth Kyle, d. Nov. 27, 1881, in her 83d year.
Rudolph Fiester, d. Sept. 14, 1859, in his 75th year.
Mary, wf. of Rudolph Fiester, d. Dec. 10, 1874, in her 85th year.
James Ernst, s. of Rudolph and Mary Fiester, d. Oct. 26, 1866, in his 54th year.

NOTES AND QUERIES.

Historical, Biographical, and Genealogical.

VII.

"The American Genealogist," edited by Captain Thomas Allen Glenn has just appeared. The initial number is a valuable contribution to Pennsylvania genealogy, although the editor proposes to make his magazine cosmopolitan in its scope. What will interest Pennsylvanians the most, however, is a list of the Scotch planters of Ulster, Ireland. This is to be continued. John W. Jordan, who is an undoubted authority on the subject, contributes an instructive article on the "Moravian Immigration into Pennsylvania." The Genealogist is published monthly at one dollar per annum, at Ardmore, Pa., and ought, at that price, on account of its sterling character, have a wide circulation.

OLD CHURCHYARD RECORDS.

St. John's Cemetery at Compass, Pa.

Davis Clemson, d. Nov. 29, 1871, aged 84y 1m 14d.
Rebecca, wf. of Davis Clemson, d. Feb. 14, 1890, aged 93 y 4m 15d.
James Clemson, Esq., d. April 4, 1820, aged 65y 14d.
Mary Clemson, wf. of James Clemson, d. April 21, 1819, aged 66 y 4m 11d.
James Clemson, Esq., d. Sept. 20, 1833, aged 41y 4m 24d.
James Clemson, Esq., d. July 13, 1792, in his 63d year.
Leonard Ellmaker, d. Jan. 14, 1829, in his 88th year.
Elizabeth, wf. of Leonard Ellmaker, d. Dec. 26, 1825, in her 83d year.
Peter Ellmaker, Esq., d. Aug 20, 1798, aged 32y 4m 2d.
Susan, widow of Peter Ellmaker, Esq., d. Dec. 27, 1831.
Jacob C. Ellmaker, d. May 28, 1816, aged 28y 2m 18d.
Frederick C. Ellmaker, d. May 10, 1812, aged 3y 6m.
David Ferree, d. July 17, 1832, aged 60y 2m.
Mary, wf. of David Ferree, d. Jan. 20, 1858, in her 83d year.
Diller B. Ferree, d. Dec. 10, 1865, aged 69y 5m 14d.
Christianna Ferree, d. Aug. 6, 1816, aged 1y 11m.
Elizabeth S. Ferree, consort of Diller B. Ferree, d. Dec. 12, 1844, aged 44y 11m 11d.
Allen W. Ferree, d. Dec. 8, 1852, aged 23y 4m 6d.
Adam Ferree, b. Sept. 2, 1805; d. March 27, 1868.
Elizabeth Ferree, consort of Adam Ferree, d. Sept. 4, 1847, aged 41y 3d.

Clemson M. Ferree, d. Oct. 14, 1852, aged 5y 1m 23d.
D. Dewees Ferree, b. Sept. 9, 1826; d. May 20, 1869.
William Richardson, d. April, 1749, aged 52 years.
Catharine Hopkins, wf. of John R. Hopkins, d. Dec. 2, 1817, aged 27y 6m 26d.
John Hopkins, d. Nov. 29, 1820, in his 70th year.
John R. Hopkins, s. of John and Mary Hopkins, d. Aug. 24, 1817, aged 27y 4m 25d.
John Hopkins, s. of John and Mary Hopkins, d. May 28,1787, aged 11y 6m 28d.
Isaac, s. of John and Mary Hopkins, d. Nov. 4, 1780, aged 11m 26d.
Mary Hopkins, wf. of John Hopkins, d. April 25, 1818, aged 66y.
Anna Catharine, dau. of John R. and Catharine Hopkins, d. March 13, 1817, aged 9m 26d.

In the New Cemetery,

John Reeser, b. Nov. 15, 1830; d. May 26, 1896.
Catharine, wf. of John Reeser, b. Sept. 4, 1833; d. Jan. 13, 1892.
Maggie, dau. of William and Rhoda Skiles, b. Sept. 12, 1847; d. May 11, 1878.
Willie, s. of J. L. and S. J. Schrack, d. Sept. 20, 1865, aged 5m 8d.
Harvie, s. of J. L. and S. J. Schrack, d. June 8, 1867, aged 5m 28d.
William, s. of J. L. and S. J. Schrack, d. July 22, 1871, aged 5m 26d.
Alfred G., s. of J. L. and S. J. Schrack, d. Aug. 27, 1873, aged 8m 9d.
Clara M., dau. of J. L. and S. J. Schrack, d. May 29, 1875, aged 10m 11d.
John R. Englerth, d. Oct. 23, 1893, aged 75y.
Mary C. Englerth, b. Oct. 15, 1856; d. June 16, 1880.
Linton P. Rissel, d. March 30, 1894, aged 43y 2m 19d.
William Rissel, d. Aug. 17, 1889, aged 61y 11m 17d.
Helen Matilda, dau. of A. G. and A. M. Good, d. Dec. 26, 1895, aged 1y 2m 20d.
Nellie Jane, dau. of A. G. and A. M. Good, d. March 7, 1893, aged 1y 4m 4d.
Mary Olive, dau. of A. G. and A. M. Good, d. Sept. 3, 1884, aged 7m 14d.
Sarah Jane, dau. of John and Sarah Martin, d. Nov. 29, 1885, aged 25y 10m 22d.
Cora, dau. of Isaac H. and Annie Mason, d. July 24, 1888, aged 6y 9m.
Harry, s. of B. and M. Evanson, b. Feb. 1, 1859; d. May 28, 1883.
Mary E., dau. of B. and M. Evanson, b. Aug. 8, 1861; d. Sept. 1, 1863.
Clara, dau. of B. and M. Evanson, b. May 15, 1865; d. Dec. 11, 1876.
George Weaver, s. of John and Justina Mason, d. June 28, 1881, aged 25y 9m 13d.
John Mason, b. Dec. 21, 1817; d. Jan. 5, 1884.
Justina Mason, wf. of John Mason, b. April 21, 1820; d. Nov. 26, 1884.
Ida Virginia, dau. of John and Justina Mason, d. Aug. 13, 1849, aged —y 11m 21d.
William Forrest, s. of John and Justina Mason, d. March 16, 1854, aged 3y 2m 1d.
Charles E. Mason, b. Jun 11, 1853; d. July 17, 1887.
John A. P. Mason, b. Nov. 30, 1859; d. Feb. 12, 1885.
John David Evans, b. Jan. 1, 1814; d. Oct. 12, 1881.
Richard Montgomery Wilson, b. May 6, 1833; d. at Tucson, Arizona, Jan. 27, 1882.
John W. Eby, b. Nov. 27, 1836; d. May 29, 1880.
Lafayette Kennedy, b. July 22, 1847; d. Aug. 18, 1866.
Grace Ella, dau. of D. and J. Rockafellow, d. Nov. 14, 1881, aged 1y 7m 24d.
Samuel Martin, b. Feb. 12, 1822; d. Oct. 23, 1880.
Jane, wf. of Samuel Martin, b. Feb. 17, 1826; d. Feb. 17, 1896.
Peter Worrest, b. March 26, 1790; d. April 22, 1838.
Margaret Ferree, wf. of Peter Worrest, b. Dec. 14, 1797; d. June 25, 1879.
David, s. of Peter and Margaret Worrest, b. Aug. 30, 1822; d. April 19, 1824.
Grace E., d. of A. H. and K. Worrest, d. August 11, 1882, aged 9m 26d.
Frederick Worrest, M. D., s. of Peter and Margaret Worrest, d. Oct. 4, 1853, aged 22y 3m 26d.
Henry W. Worrest, b. August 30, 1822; d. May 1, 1884.

Henry W., s. of Henry W and Hannah Worrest, d. April 5, 1861, aged 2y 7m 17d.

Margaret, wf. of H. B. Skiles, b. Dec. 17, 1831: d. Dec. 31, 1880.

Harriet R., dau. of J. and D. Skiles, b. April 9, 1889; d. Aug. 18, 1889.

Capt. George Oldmixon, R. N., d. April 8, 1880. He was a retired English officer about 75 years old at death.

George W. Wagner, b. June 10, 1829; d. Jan. 30, 1893.

Robert Baldwin, b. July 12, 1805; d. Jan. 30, 1888.

Phoebe Baldwin, dau. of Levi and Edith Baldwin, d. Sept. 20, 1841.

Alfred N. Baldwin, s. of Robert and Harriet A. Baldwin, b. Oct. 20, 1845; d. March 27, 1846.

Theodore F., s. of Robert and Harriet N. Baldwin, b. Feb. 5, 1847; d. June 17, 1848.

George Rutter, b. Oct. 14, 1831; d. July 16, 1869.

Adam Rutter, b. Nov. 28, 1808; d. April 21, 1885.

Margaret, wf. of Adam Rutter, b. Aug. 3, 1807; d. Oct. 5, 1893.

Thomas W. Henderson, b. June 30, 1821; d. Jan. 2, 1897.

David Ferree, b. Nov. 24, 1815; d. March 24, 1893.

Elizabeth Ferree, b. Oct. 28, 1801; d. March 6, 1889.

Jos. W. Stott, b. March 6, 1839; d. at Asheville, N. C., Feb. 8, 1883.

David H., s. of Joseph W. and Rachel Stott, b. March 30, 1882; d. Sept. 6, 1882.

Elizabeth, dau. of Thos. W. and S. W. Brownell, b. March 24, 1872; d. July 31, 1872.

Rev. A. Louderback (no dates.)

Harriet Jane Pearl, wf. of James B. McCowan, b. March 19, 1836; d. July 18, 1883.

Michael Cafrode, d. March 26, 1881, aged 73y 7m 23d.

Susanna Cafrode, wf. of Perry Thompson, b. July 13, 1855; d. July 23, 1881.

George Ubil, b. Dec. 8, 1821 (Co. I, 91st Regt. P. V.) ; d. July 6, 1885.

Sarah Ann, wf. of Reuben Trego, b. July 11, 1857; d. July 22, 1892.

Jos. Mash, Co. F., 2d Pa. Artillery, d. in 1891.

J. Hayes Plank, d. Aug. 13, 1886, aged 41y 3m and 3d. Served in Co. H, 20th Penn. Cavalry.

Isabella Glendenning, d. March 22, 1888, in her 66th year.

Christian Eaby, b. Aug. 16, 1812; d. Dec. 7, 1857.

Margaret Eaby, wf. of Christian Eaby, d. Feb. 1, 1849, in her 38th year.

Capt. George W. Seaman, d. April 25, 1891, aged 91y 7m 8d.

Matilda, wf. of George W. Seaman, d. July 10, 1893, aged 72y 1m 8d.

Mary Matilda, dau. of George W. and Matilda Seaman, d. March 8, 1887, aged 42y and 7d.

Newton Kelso, s. of I. D. and Esther Worst, d. May 7, 1887, aged 14y 5m 24d.

George G. Worst, b. July 21, 1826; d. June 4, 1892.

Jacob Kramer, d. Feb. 1, 1892, aged 77y 16d.

Bell Mina, wf. of Charles T. Gabel, b. June 21, 1859; d. May 27, 1889.

Cora R., dau. Charles T. and B. M. Gabel, b. June 4, 1888; d. Feb. 18, 1889.

Martha A., dau. of R. and S. A. Bilger, b. July 4, 1885; d. June 26, 1886.

John Pearl, d. Jan. 23, 1867, in his 78th year.

Rachel Pearl, d. May 28, 1875, in her 87th year.

Samuel C. Pearl, d. June 1, 1897, in his 73d year.

J. Harrison Pearl, d. May 31, 1893, aged 66y 1mo 25d.

Jennie Jackson, dau. of George and Rachel Jackson, b. May 27, 1862; d. Oct. 9, 1876.

Mary, wf. of Archibald Thomas, b. Aug. 29, 1794; d. Oct. 30, 1883. (In old cemetery).

Sophia Elinor, wf. of John H. Skiles, b. Aug. 7, 1821; d. Aug. 9, 1883.

Wilkes B. Booth, b. Oct. 31, 1868; d. Dec. 23, 1896.

Harry E. Skiles, b. Feb. 7, 1869; d. Dec. 8, 1897.

James Clemson, d. April 12, 1891, aged 68y 9mos.

Amos B. Echoff, d. April 20, 1891, aged

55y. Served in Co. L., 17th Penna. Cav.
John Waddell, d. Oct. 30, 1880, aged 70y.
Margaret Elizabeth, dau. of James and Catharine Waddell, b. May 31, 1878; d. Aug. 14, 1879.
Emma, wf. of George Clevenstine, d. Mch. 4, in her 30th year.
John Clevenstine, b. Jan. 13, 1798; d. Jan. 6, 1883.
Leah R. Dague, wf. of Hanford Greenleaf, d. Dec. 13, 1888, aged 60y 1m 17d.
Jacob Thompson (colored), d. Sept. 23, 1891, in his 91st year.
Prudence Ann Thompson (colored), wf. of Jacob Thompson, d. Oct. 11, 1888, aged 101 years.
Lloyd Parker (colored), d. May 16, 1880, aged 88 years.
Nehemiah Coleman Brown (colored), b. June 20, 1881; d. Sept. 17, 1887.
Ida K. Thompson (colored), dau. of Matthew H. and Martha Thompson, d. Dec. 16, 1886, aged 6m 3d.
Samuel Coleman (colored), b. Jan. 27, 1842; d. Feb. 15, 1887.
John Coleman (colored), b. Dec. 7, 1858; d. Oct. 20, 1884.
Martha, wf. of Nehemiah Coleman (colored), b. April 12, 1820; d. Sept. 5,
Nehemiah Coleman (colored), b. April 4, 1811; d. April 5, 1887.
Jacob Nocho (colored), b. Nov. 1, 1812; d. April 22, 1885.
Letitia, dau. of Jacob and Rachel Nocho (colored), d. Feb. 10, 1896, in her 19th year.
William Parker (colored), d. Feb. 22, 1887, aged 73y 12d 4m.
Samuel Nocho (colored), d. Aug. 5, 1883, aged 72y 6m 15d.
Harriet N. Nocho (colored), wf. of Samuel Nocho, d. Dec. 31, 1894, in her 77th year.
Martha A., wf. of George London (colored), b. May 5, 1863; d. May 27, 1890.
Anna Bertha (colored), dau. of John and Margaret London, b. June 21, 1885; d. Dec. 3, 1890.
Reece M. Dixon (colored), d. March 12, 1893, aged 56y.
James Jones (colored), d. July 4; 1897, aged 47y.
William Skiles, b. Dec. 7, 1805; d. Oct. 9, 1864.
Rhoda Skiles, wf. of William Skiles, b. Feb. 9, 1814; d. June 13, 1896.

B. F. O.
Reading, Pa.

MEMORIES OF MARKET SQUARE

And Its Inhabitants in the Decade From 1840 to 1850, With Incidentals.

[Paper read before the Dauphin County Historical Society, by Theodore B. Klein.]

The central rallying point of the ancient Harrisburger on all extraordinary occasions in general, and on Wednesday and Saturday mornings between the hours of 4 and 9 in particular, was the rectangular plot assigned by John Harris at the intersections of the great thoroughfares known as Market and Second streets; and that plot covering an area of less than 100,000 square feet with its adjoining domiciles of the date I write, has more local history to the square inch than any other portion of this domain that we know of.

Some of the glories that crowned the space have departed, but the memories (of the old market houses) remain. We all remember the substantial unpretentious buildings, well ventilated and airy, through which the blasts of winter swept without hindrance, and where the snows piled up in pretty hillocks. The borough authorities had the fire ladders hung aloft against the supporting columns of the roof, and the small boy and at times the romping girl practiced the first principles of gymnastics from the suspended rongs thereof.

When we recall the tons and tons of all manner of produce and luxuries to tickle the palates of hungry men, women and children, and the barrels and barrels of "Smear Kase" and apple butter that were distributed from the venerable structures, and the ship loads of eels and "catties" and shad, and the ark loads of juicy beef and mutton and pork, and the miles of sausages and puddings, and the ten thousand bushels of apples and peaches and pears and plums, and the pyramids of golden butter and millions of fresh laid eggs that were carried away from the old market, we stand aghast and wonder where it all came from, and ask where are all the consumers thereof? And then, the monies given in exchange, what a compound of gold and silver, and copper and greenbacks and shinplasters and battered fips and rags and Spanish pistareens would fill the bags of the butchers and bakers and fishermen and hucksters and farmers of the period.

Oh, the grand parade of the housekeeper semi-weekly in order to keep the larder in good supply. And oh, the financiering to make the dollar buy the butter and the eggs, the meat, and the vegetables.

In the interim, between Wednesday and Saturday the boys and girls made use of the sheltering structures, and the meat market was a royal place for games of high-spy, which games were rudely broken up by Conrad Knepley, the then high constable of the town, who would attack on a double quick, shouting: "Now boys, I got you all like a bundle of straw," but his voice gave ample warning, and a safe retreat was generally accomplished. Here, too, in the odoriferous shade the weary Willies and tired colored boys came to sleep, and many a glorious snooze was disturbed by the ever-present small boy, who was inclined to rival the frisky fly, who longed to tickle the nose and lip or ear of the weary one snoring under the protecting roof of the market house. But they are gone, and the old cake women who were stationed at either end with their little stock of small beer, and mead, and sugar biscuits, and ginger bread, and mint sticks, and sour drops, who gathered in the coppers of the youth of the period, have also departed, and the humming trolley cars now speed over the site they once occupied.

The rattling sabres of the dragoons, the martial tread of the light infantry, and the rumbling of the artillery that was heard on Independence Day in 1796, have been followed annually by the patriots of the town and country, and a panoramic view of the hosts that have marched and countermarched over and around our memorable square would more than equal the standing armies of the Czar of all the Russias, and the old Guard of Napoleon—made up of the militia and the political paraders, and the inauguration regiments, and the circus processions, and the Sunday school celebrators, and the secret societies, and the cold water armies and the firemen, all have from time to time, to the present day, tread in the footsteps of the old forefathers. But, in 1840, the Tippecanoe boys rolled the great canvas globes and sang:

"Oh, what has caused this great commotion, motion, motion,
The whole land through?
It is the ball a rolling on for Tippecanoe
and Tyler too,
For Tippecanoe and Tyler, too.
And with them we will beat little Van,
Van, Van.
Van is a used up man.
And with them we will beat little Van.

On review of some of these gatherings we glean from history that the immortal Washington, on the 3d of October, 1794, and his compatriot, Lafayette, on January 30th, 1825, honored the town and delighted the assembled multitude gathered to honor the distinguished guests. Since those days many celebrated men have passed over the same ground, including General Zachary Taylor, Daniel Webster, Louis Kossuth, the Prince of Wales, Abraham Lincoln and General Grant.

Between the market houses the old-time method of jubilees were exemplified by bonfires on election nights (of which in some years there were three). A week before the time many empty barrels and boxes disappeared mysteriously from their accustomed places in front of stores and were stored in a back lot not far from where the great fire was to be lighted. After the ordinary bedtime (which was then earlier than at present) the fire was silently started, the great blaze startling the slumber of the citizens in the neighborhood and the sparks alarmingly distributed upon the adjoining roofs, caused no little annoyance. After the conflagration was well under way a general collection of anything and everything combustible left outside, in the way of empty boxes was made, and very often the good cases of the dry goods merchants furnished fuel for the lively fire—leaving only a blackened mass of ashes for the hoodlums to scatter in the morning in search of tempered nails.

But let us retrace our steps from the central square, and going through the old meat market pass the well-filled stalls of Anthony Nininger, Nicholas Reamshart, William Metzgar, John Young, George Neuer, Louis Metzgar, Charles Pray, George Sawyer, Michael Reaver, William Bostwick, all substantial citizens and active in their business.

We reach the northwest corner of the square and begin our call upon the old residents. We first meet the familiar form of Adam K. Fahnestock, who has a large establishment, and furnished hats and caps and furs and a variety of articles in housefurnishing and for travelers. Mr. Fahnestock seemed to us boys a stern parent, but he was systematic and not given to follies, and his children, Harris and Louis and Wallace and James and Morris and Sybel and Charles, are remembered with pleasure. Across the avenue we meet Mr. William Calder, one of the pioneers of the transportation of passengers by stage and canal packet lines in the early days before railroads were built. He delighted in his pet herd of cattle and was often seen to walk leisurely after the sleek Durhams as they wended their way to the green pastures beyond the canal after the morning gathering of the creamy milk. The early morning stages to Reading, to York, to Gettysburg and to Jonestown, left the day quite free and the afternoon packet in summer or the night stages departing for the west and north in the winter gave time for scientific farming, in which Mr. Calder delighted; and then the boys, William and John and James, were efficient assistants to their father, while the girls, Mary and Matilda, were the hand maidens of the household and that part of the domicile was well kept, notwithstanding the care of the employes was part of the domestic economy. We see James B. Thompson and Jonas Gish and Simon Duey under the paternal roof, and they were as part of the family.

Next door we tarry a moment at the dwelling of Jacob M. Awl, a manufacturer of standard boots and shoes—a devout and zealous disciple of John Wesley and Methodism, and withal active in municipal affairs and in business with his neghbors. His boys, John Wesley and F. Asbury, and his daughter, Fannie, all worthy children of a worthy sire.

In the adjoining residence we meet Christopher C. Hynicka in his large and roomy store, ever busy handling the pliant leather to be made for the protection of the feet of his many customers. His colony was large and it has spread abroad from the old homestead, some to fulfill their mission and depart and the rest to tarry and to work on to the end. I call the roll but some will not respond. When all at home it was a jolly good family and an extra boy or two or three never raised a murmur from the motherly wife because of a crowded house. Catharine and Luther and Adelaide and George and Rebecca and John and Mary and Christopher and Fannie formed the family circle around the parents in Market Square.

The neighbors, "Mother Wiestling" and her sons, Joseph and Samuel, with a daughter, occupied the next house, and we will go into Joseph's shop and lean or sit upon his stool or shop board, as he industriously sews at a suit of clothes, meanwhile discussing politics or religion or the local gossip of the town.

We go on to the windows of Confectioner Henry Felix and gaze upon the toothsome sweetmeats displayed. What a Mecca it was for the boys and girls all the year round, and at Christmas times what a crowd assembled and took possession of the whole house in the race for articles to distribute thro' St. Nicholas. Here too was a little family, and Samuel and Kate and Sarah and Agnes and Addie and Mary will join our company in the footing up at the end of our stroll.

At the adjoining curb stands the saddle horse of Joshua M. Wiestling in waiting for the morning calls of the Doctor, who will soon be ready to mount. He is a very busy man, and he may be taking the surplus blood from a calling patient in his office before he begins his morning visits. We will not peer into the mysterious-looking case in the corner, for we know there is a great skeleton in it. His good wife and children represent the domestic circle and have important places in the church and in society. Mary Ellen and Catherine and Jacob and Annie and Joshua and Julia fill up the family board and will long be remembered with pleasure by their acquaintances.

Grandmother Ingram lives quietly next door with her daughter and young grand daughters, respected by all. Their neighbors were the family of George Mish, an old-time gentleman, prominent in his day in our local government. His boys, Harry and Cameron and Jacob and George formed a quartette in the square contingent, and Dr. George F, now of Middletown, alone represents the family.

Mr. Whitman occupied the adjoining house and was engaged as a jeweler. Three or four children formed his household circle, several of whom survive the departed parents.

We have now reached the corner, the old, familiar corner occupied by the bachelor merchant, John Rhoads. His stock was staple and fashionable and good. His boys were not his own (but they were yet his own). J. Monroe Kreiter, afterwards cashier of the Dauphin Deposit Bank, and Samuel Reinhart, were his faithful employes, and they were popular with the lady customers who purchased at the old store. Mr. Rhoads kept a burly bull dog as a watch, and the boys who took pleasure in capsizing the empty store boxes from the pavement at night had a wholesome dread of the animal. Mr. Rhoads continued in business until the time of his decease, leaving a comfortable estate for his heirs.

And now we are ready to cross the main street of our borough, the great thoroughfare to the west, by the way of the Cumberland Valley. A great herd of cattle may be plodding by, following the leader, who has the extra wardrobe of the herdsman looped at the base of the horns of the king of the herd. The man marches slowly in front and as he yodels "Hookie, hookie," the sturdy beeves follow and follow in steady march until they reach the shambles in the Eastern cities.

In the opposite direction we may see approaching one or more great canvasscovered Conestoga wagons, drawn by four or six stalwart horses, with an arch of sweet-toned bells suspended above their collars. The wagons creak with the loads of merchandise being transported to Western points from the Eastern markets, and the lively crack of the waggoner's whip and the music of the bells, cheer up the noble animals of the team to a rapid step toward the old bridge and on to their destination.

The southwest corner was an ancient building occupied by Philip Wolfersberger, who had a variety store and had everything for sale, from a nail to an anchor in iron, and all manner of wooden and textile fabrics, from a goose yoke to a rag carpet, as well as birds and beasts, alligators and parrots, and a mammoth pig, a regular curiosity shop and museum worthy of the late Barnum. It was not a financial success. Perhaps it was in advance of the times, when department stores are the popular attraction.

Mr. William Root adjoined the museum on the south and served the public with all manner of tin utensils and stopped the leaks in the coffee pots and drinking cups of the day when they could not be purchased at a penny apiece.

The next house was occupied by the sisters Eliza and Sarah Hoyer. What kind and gentle aunties they were to all the children of the neighborhood, and their nephews, Frank and George and Jacob and Joseph knew where aunties lived and knew of the favors awaiting them when they called. Miss Kate, the sister of the aforenamed boys, was at home with Aunts Eliza and Sarah during their sojourn in the square.

The adjoining premises belonged to the Hoyer estate until 1846, when it was sold, and in 1847 in the march of improvement, the late Dr. William C. McPherson had a substantial brick house erected upon the lot, taking the place of an ancient domicile grown old and dilapidated. Our worthy member, the Hon. John B., and his sister were the children of the parents residing here.

A "ten foot" alley separated these premises from the property of George and Bernard Geiger, who were prominent merchants and prosperous. The three daughters of Bernard became Mrs. Daniel

Eppley, Mrs. David J. Unger and Mrs. Alexander Roberts.

Adjoining the Geigers is the residence of George Washington Harris, a lineal descendant of the founder of the town, and an attorney-at-law practicing at the Bar. You may remember his stately bearing, with all the attributes of an old-time gentleman. His sons, Robert and William, and his daughters, Elizabeth and Catharine and Julia, are remembered in our midst, but they have all, save Mrs. Morris, gone to the great majority on the other side.

We have now reached the next corner and stop to take a sip of cool water at the pump where many a weary pilgrim has quenched his thirst in front of the old and staunch financial institution of the Capital town, the Harrisburg Bank. Thomas Elder is the president, and Henry Walters is the cashier, who, with the tellers, James W. Wier and George H. Small, manage the institution. The storms of panics and grips of hard times have dashed against the bulwarks of the old vaults and safes, but they are still intact, and the stockholders view the accumulated surplus with complacency, as they have just drawn their 172d semi-annual dividend with a dozen or more of busy tellers serving the patrons of the now "National Institution," doing business at the old stand.

Across the classical avenue called Blackberry alley, we come to the old colonial mansion occupied by the Lesleys at the time of which we speak. The Pennsylvania Branch Bank had been there, but had gone under on the downfall of Nicholas Biddle and his associates. The garden on the south side was a picture of beauty. Edward and James Lesley, Jr., were the young men up in society. The old mansion served a good purpose for a long time as post office and residences of Dr. Whitehead, Dr. Hammond and James R. Jones, and at last gave place to the present temple of the Presbyterian congregation, starting under the pastorate of the Rev. Dr. William R. DeWitt.

Another twenty paces to the East, and we reach the welcome hostelrie of the town, celebrated in its day as a first class refuge for travelers and sojourners, known as George Nagle's "Union Hotel." It is a comfortable and inviting looking place to rest, and in the shade of the linden trees on the Second street front, we will tarry for a time and then resume our journey up the east side of the Square, and call upon the residents thereof, finding quite a number of old schoolmates and familiar faces which will be a pleasure to recall to our memories.

NOTES AND QUERIES.

Historical, Biographical, and Genealogical.

VIII.

DUNBAR.

William Dunbar, of Cumberland county, d. prior to August, 1769, leaving a wife and children:
i. John.
ii. Jane.
ii. Francis.
iv. Thomas, b. 1752.
v. Elizabeth, b. 1754.
vi. Mary, b. 1756.
vii. Sarah, b. 1758.
viii. Martha, b. 1760.
ix. William, b. 1762.
x. Samuel, b. 1764.

KIRKPATRICK.

John Kirkpatrick, of Lack township, Cumberland county, d. prior to August, 1762, leaving a wife, Jane, and children:
i. James.
ii. William.
iii. Joseph.
iv. Benjamin.
v. Mary, dec'd.; m. —— Miller, and had a son John.
vi. Elizabeth.
vii. Jane.

BLACK.

Robert Black, of Peters township, Cumberland county, d. prior to June, 1751, and left children, among others:
i. James.
ii. [A dau.] m. John Thomas.
iii. Thomas.
iv. Elizabeth, m. Robert Beck.
v. Robert.
vi. Ann.
vii. John.

Some Mentzer Data.

The writer recently saw several manuscript records in German which were dated 1751, and which are transcripts of records in Germany. He has had them translated and forwards them to "Notes and Queries" for preservation. The papers referred to the Mentzer family, which located in Lancaster county in 1751. The first is an emigration certificate granted on April 13, 1751, to Johan Maintzern, of Jagsfeld, Baden, Oberomt Jorlagh, which allows said John Mentzer, his wife and four lhildren to emigrate to Pennsylvania.

The second paper is a marriage record and birth record, given by the "Stadt Pforamt" in Jagsfeld, on May 11, 1751, and states that:

Johan Maintzer, burgher of Jagsfeld, was a son of Johan George Mentzer, and was born March 2, 1701.

He was married the first time on March 3, 1722, to Anna Maria Meyer, of Barechig, and had issue:

i. Johan, b. Jan. 20, 1723 (married in 1751, and remarried in Germany).
ii. George, b. July 21, 1727.
iii. Anna-Maria, b. April 1, 1729.

He was married the second time to Catharine Spirgi, daughter of Johan Spirgi, on Aug. 11, 1733, and had issue:

i. Conradt, b. May 21, 1734.
ii. Johan-Michael, b. April 20, 1741.

By reference to "Rupp's Collection of 30,000 Names of Emigrants," it is seen that Johan Maintzern, his wife and four children arrived in Philadelphia, Pa., and qualified on September 16, 1751, on the ship "Brothers," Capt. William Muir.

S. M. S.
Lancaster, Pa.

MEMORIES OF MARKET SQUARE

And Its Inhabitants in the Decade From 1840 to 1850, With Incidentals.

IV.

Paper reatd before the Dauphin County Historical Society by Theodore B. Klein.

At our last meeting, the Society journeyed with me over the historic ground of the old market house square, and along its western side, looking in upon the old residents thereof and recalling incidents by the way, tarrying in the stroll at Nagle's "Union Hotel," where under the lindens we stopped for a breathing spell before resuming our march to the point of our destination, which is now in sight, toward the setting sun.

We will pay our respects to Mr. George Nagle, the jolly host of the hotel, and be introduced to his son-in-law, Frederick Showers, who drives an elegant team of fine horses and takes delight in his high steppers of blue-blooded stock. We will also meet Robert Gilmor (a retired gentleman), Daniel Sturgeon, the State Treasurer, and James Snyder, all guests of the house, who are there for the present and well cared for by mine host Nagle. James B. Rupley, George S. Wharton, Edward Smith, James G. Sturgeon and Alexander P. Miller, all employed in the departments on Capitol Hill, are also here.

We will not tarry long, but recross Blackberry alley and stop at the quaint old mansion of George Ziegler—the maternal great grandfather of our own Edward Ziegler Gross. The house was once a hotel, but now an old-time grocery store; a large part of the stock being in liquid form on tap, considered indispensible (in the days before harvesting machines were invented) for the reapers, and also for the sons of the Emerald Isle, who had to dig the canals and build the railways that were in course of construction at that time. In those days many of our good people were patrons of the old-time grocery, and kept a little good old rye, with a bottle of some old vintage of Port or Madeira wine, which was used strictly in accordance to the directions of Saint Paul to Timothy and only for the "stomach's sake." Some of us boys remember the round-bellied decanter, draped in a red silk handkerchief in one hand, and a dollar in the other, passing to and fro between home and the grocery about once a month.

Another step, and the domicile of Elias Zollinger, one of the original hatters of the borough, is reached. The house was a roomy mansion b,ut none too large for the growing boys and girls in the home nest. Mary Ann, and Elias, and George, and John, and Ellen, and Almeda and Warren, and Clara, were there until the separations came, sometimes in joy and sometimes in sorrow, but the old homestead is still revered and occupied by the junior son, who is the worthy successor of his worthy father and the only surviving descendant to perpetuate the name of his branch of the ancient family, and even now a junior member of this ancient and honorable society.

Neighbors for years were found in the family of Daniel Shellenberger, who left the rural home of his forefathers in the Hanovers to try his fortune in the Capital town of the State. After a little while, he bravely settled in its busy center, in the place vacated by the publisher, Barnes, and entered the lists in business, doing what he could to keep the community tidy and well clothed. His efforts were successful, and he took his place among the financiers of his day, and was classed with the prudent investors and conservative advisors in the management of our monied institutions. His family almost equaled in number that of his neighbor, and Henry and Augustus, and Mary, and Esther, and Ellen, and Edwin survived the parents, and in various directions filled, or are filling, the mission assigned by the Director of Humanity in the paths of life.

Mr. William Catrell and his goodly dame occupied the adjoining house and lived a quiet life, beloved by all, and their memories are cherished as worthy people and devout Christians. The death of the head of the family was a sad break in the household, and the homestead was soon after occupied by E. M. Pollock. The head of this house was a worthy son of Erin, dealing in literature and supplies for the diffusion of knowledge. His was a standard establishment and furnished the departments of the Commonwealth on the Capitol Hill many of the materials required in the conducting of the affairs of the Executive Departments; and the legal profession with the standard publications in law and equity. Edward and his five sisters formed the family circle with the mother during their sojourn in the old homestead.

Their neighbors were Charles C. Rawn, a barrister and member of the Dauphin County Bar since 1831. He was a vigorous pleader and an advocate for, and defender of the fugitive slave when captured in his flight from the South. His children joined the circle of youth in our review, and Charles and John Calvin and Fannie were a trio to be enumerated in our summing up.

Miss Mary Clendenin was a sister of Mrs. Rawn's, quite a prominent lady in society, and afterwards became the wife of William P. Beatty, an officer of the Harrisburg & Lancaster railroad company.

A representative of an ancient and honorable family of the county occupied the adjoining house in the person of David Hummel. His family was large and have taken prominent places in the hearts of many who were their associates and friends. His sons, David and George and Albert, and his daughters, Mrs. Gorgas, Mrs. Seibert, Mrs. Alex. Watson, Mrs. James Reily, Mrs. Dr. Eli H. Coover and Miss Emma, will be enumerated among the goodly company of our ancient Square. The family mansion, with its neighbor, is now absorbed in the new Commonwealth Hotel. Mr. Hummel delighted in caring for a sleek herd of good cows, and many a quart of delicious milk submerged the hot porridge, and apple-dumplings of the neighborhood, and the boys and girls thereof delighted to revel in the toothsome pottage that was made up from the product of the dairy.

And now we step upon real historic ground and stand in the shadow of the Washington Hotel. We see a stout mast planted in the ground at the corner of the pavement, and in mid-air, twenty feet above, from the heavy yard arm of the mast swings a full-length portrait of the "Father of His Country" in the position we would imagine him to be when delivering his farewell address. Many a day the heavy sign swung to and fro, wafted by every little breeze, and we remember well the creaking of the iron bolt in the rings late at night, when the wintry winds played with the huge picture of the immortal Washington. The building, built of brick, solid and strong, was well up from the sidewalk. Entrance was had into the hall from the Square and to the bar from Market street and Square also.

The windows of 7x9 glass, were close together and old-fashioned in the extreme. The stone steps leading up into the house served as the platform from which to address the multitudes on political occasions. Alexander Ramsey in his youth began his stump speeches from this point, and his arguments gathered the yeomanry to his standard, and, whether in the English language or German, he was at home with the voters. His success as a public man was insured and he filled many places of honor: Congressman, United States Senator, Secretary of War and Governor of Minnesota.

The mere mention of the many guests quartered at the old Washington Hotel would fill a book. The host of the house in my time was John Smull, who was a popular landlord, the picture of good living, and his table gave evidence of the fact that his guests were well provided for. His boys, Levan, and John, and William, and his daughter Annie, were the pets of the household, and Mother Smull will be remembered long by all who knew her as a good mother to her little ones, and ever anxious for their welfare. In later years William E. Camp was keeper of the Washington. He lost his life by the burning of the steamer Lexington, whilst journeying across Lake Erie.

Passing on a Tuesday or Friday evening we see the wagon of "Pap" Hetrick, at the curb, who came from over the river with quite a load of poultry and country produce, to be sold on Market day. The pretty face and form of his daughter, who always came with him, was a winning card for the old man, and helped very largely to sell the contents of the wagon in good time and at tiptop prices.

We now recross Market street and reach the substantial corner of John Wyeth, who has had built (after a disastrous fire in 1828) the brick buildings, still standing at that place. John Wyeth, Jr., has the corner room for a drug store and our friend, the late Dr. George Ross, of Lebanon, was the compounding clerk of the establishment,—the dispenser of calomel and jalap, paregoric and quinine, and was succeeded by Major Harry J. Shaffer. Mr. Wyeth's family, in the mansion attached to the store, was interesting, and included quite a little colony, beginning with a comely daughter, Gertrude, who had the company of brothers John and Lewis, and sisters Mary and Lucy, to complete the family circle.

The adjoining domicile was occupied by the popular hatter, John L. Speel, always called "Jack," a jovial, good fellow, and a brother-in-law of Alexander Ramsey. His hat store was a rallying place where in the evening jokes and stories went round and round. If we drop in we will find here and there on the boxes around the store Clinton Brooks, Justus Ramsey, Jimmy Allison, Frederick Trace, Oliver Bellman, I. S. Waterbury, George Fager, Lewey De Carlton, Davy Krause, John Edwards, Alfred Adams, John Calder, Wash. Simmons, John Cruikshank, and others, who were always ready with some jollity as they sat around until bedtime.

The children of the household were Mary and Lily, and John and Alexander, all of whom, I believe, survive the parents,

Their neighbors were the family of George Beatty, the silversmith, who furnished the pure metal to his patrons, and kept the chronometers in pace with the sun, and true time in the tall old clocks of our grandfathers His daughters Mary and Sarah and Eliza, graced the household, with the boys Harry and Irwin, and as a fatherly guardian he had the family of the Lairds, including Beatty Laird and his sisters, and also a grandson, who was George Beatty to us boys, and a boy with the other boys of the neighborhood. He is now a prosperous farmer in a western State.

On the Square, next door to the post office, there was an office kept by one John Snevily, who styled himself "Stock and Exchange Broker," who professed to pay the highest price for foreign coin and uncurrent bank notes. He was rather an eccentric gentleman, with a lofty bearing and ruffled shirt, and would at this time be classed a promoter, and perhaps a dude. He was quite active in the "morus multicaulus" scheme of the day, and "cocoons" and silk worms could be explained to the unwary investor quite plausibly, much to the loss and regret of many of the old citizens, who placed their savings in the speculative enterprise. With the silk scheme and the exchange of wild cat bank notes, Mr. Snevily did a profitable trade;

and a pair of handsome black horses often pranced by in front of the gentleman, who was quite a good judge of horseflesh.

Now we reach the post office, in charge of James Peacock. It was a modest, and except on extraordinary occasions, a very quiet place. Correspondence was then quite expensive, for the postage on a letter from our relatives beyond the mountains was twenty-five cents, and from the eastern foot of the mountain at Hollidaysburg, and from Philadelphia, required a payment of twelve and a-half cents, which the old Mexican or Spanish levy represented. The postage on a letter from Lancaster was 10c. When we called tri-weekly for the "United States Gazette," published in Philadelphia, two pennies were paid on delivery of the paper for postage. In Mr. Peacock's time Daniel D. Boas and John Carson had charge of the office as clerks, and David Smith and Jonas Rudy, with great diligence and regularity, knew where to deliver the letters not called for, and they knew where to take them without any special address, for they knew everybody in town who received letters. B. Gibson Peacock, a son, a young attorney in 1844, and four daughters, were the children of the postmaster. Gibson became a noted editor in Philadelphia and proprietor of the "Evening Bulletin." He was a fine singer.

Next door the respected families of the brothers Samuel and William Hays resided. The children of William, viz: William and Margaret, were orphaned in early life, but kind relatives took the place of parents and reared them well. William was mayor of the new city for a term and Margaret was a respected teacher in the public schools. The only daughter of Samuel Hays is the surviving widow of our late president, A. Boyd Hamilton.

Another step or two westwardly and we come to the shoe store of Oliver Bellman. His junior brothers, Washington and Jackson, who were practical shoemakers, and his sisters, afterward Mrs. Yoder and Mrs. Benjamin, formed the household until the bachelor Oliver joined the benedicts and took up his abode a few doors to the east in the mansion occupied by the post office in former times.

And now we have reached the abode of Catharine or Miss Kitty Kapp, a maiden sister of the celebrated Amos Kapp (a partner with our old friend William Calder in the transportation business), who resided in Northumberland county and gave his attention to the lines at Sunbury and Northumberland. Miss Kitty cared nothing for the fashions, and did not adopt the full bloomer costume, but was very shy of anything looking like a train. She knew the pedigree of the whole town, and was considered somewhat eccentric, but she was kind and was a mother to several orphan girls who had their homes with her.

The large yard attached to the premises was filled with fine fruit trees and the boy poachers often annoyed her in their efforts to reach a luscious plum from the top of a high fence enclosing the garden. The stage office, in the height of the staging time, occupied a one-story building on the lot, and it was also a resort for the old gentlemen of the neighborhood where the current gossip of the town was discussed. The first news was generally received there from the stage drivers on their arrival in election times, long before telegraphy and electricity annihilated the distances to the outlying counties.

Across the alley we recall the barber shop of the Dorseys. They were a respectable family of high-toned colored people, polite and accommodating and had many patrons and friends. Henry and Felix were fine fellows, but a shade removed in color from the full-blooded Caucasian.

And now we have almost reached the end of our journey and our history, and we will assemble under the wings of the Golden Spread Eagle which spans the sidewalk in front of the hotel then of Henry Buehler, the headquarters of the ruling Democracy of the State and the place of sojourn of many of the statesmen of the period who remained in the capital more than three days in the week during the entire session of the Legislature. In the spring of 1842 we will find Mr. Charles Dickens, the famous English novelist, now in the house as a guest, but will not disturb him in his reveries after his reception. The Buehlers were of the good, old-time stock, and established the well-known hostelrie at the corner of the square and sustained its good reputation for many years. George and Mary were the children of Henry Buehler and the grandchildren of George Wolf, who was elected Governor of Pennsylvania in 1829.

In the old days of staging this was the starting place of the regular lines to the north and west, connecting with the lines from Philadelphia by way of Reading and from Washington and Baltimore by way of York. The comfortable Concord coach having taken the manifest on at the stage office nearby and the mails at the post office, stands at the curb and takes the dozen or more waiting travelers from the home-like hotel. The luggage is now securely strapped in the great leather boot on the rear end of the vehicle. The passengers are snugly packed three and sometimes four abreast in the capacious coach. The driver, seated high in front with the precious mail bags in the receptacle under the seat with his right foot upon the brake and the lines of his team securely in hand, waits patiently for the last passenger and the signal, "All aboard. The anxious horses are pawing restlessly and impatiently for the expected tension upon their bridle bits, and now the sharp but innocent crack of the whip and the well-known voice of the driver gives notice that all is ready; the horses start away at a brisk trot and out into the darkness and the night the rumbling coach rolls up the street and out into the road that winds up the broad Susquehanna to its junction with the Juniata and through the mountain gap and onward and upward and northward and westward, bearing weary pilgrims to their homes and from their homes far away. It was an interesting sight and there was always a curious group at hand to see the departure of the stages from the old corner at the sign of the Golden Spread Eagle.

And now as we turn our faces in retrospect we see the open, broad square traversed by the steel rails of the traction company. We see but few of the old-time marks of 1840, but we note the march of improvement. To the right we see the stately Calder building and the enlarged Felix and Kelker buildings. We see the Hummel corner rebuilt and the old curiosity shop removed. New structures have taken the place of the modest sized buildings all along, and the massive brownstone bank building adorns the corner. The handsome church of the Presbyterians, with its lofty spire, takes the place of the old colonial mansion of the Lesleys, while upon the opposite side the Dauphin building, with others enlarged, improves the eastern side, whilst the great Commonwealth Hotel is a fitting finish to the block. To our left we note the extensive structure of the Russ building, which completes the recent changes in the way of improvement.

But in ou retrospect "The gate of memory swings back upon its golden hinge," and we see in fancy the more than two hundred members of the households we have visited, the large circle indicating a prolific, prosperous and healthy community in this the capital town of the Keystone State. But the number to-day is sadly reduced and so many, oh, so many of our friends and acquaintances have laid their armor down and are now resting from their labors, whilst we are left to recall their memories and these little incidents by the wayside in the times of our boyhood. With the poet, we know that

"They loved, but the story we cannot unfold;
They scorned, but the heart of the haughty is cold;
They grieved, but no wail from their slumbers will come;
They joyed, but the tongue of their gladness is dumb."

And we that are left may remember that
"We are the same as our fathers have been,
We see the same sights our fathers have seen,
We drink the same stream, we view the same sun,
And shall run the same course our fathers have run,"
leaving others perchance to note the incidents in our lives and record the work of our hands.

NOTES AND QUERIES.

Historical, Biographical and Genealogical.

IX.

STEWART.

In a deed dated Oct. 10, 1801, recorded in Westmoreland county, Robert Stewart is designated as Robert Stewart of the "Stage Inn, Gentleman." The Stage Inn is still standing in Stewartville and is used as a farm house. It was a tavern where stages stopped in the days before the Pennsylvania railroad, when the old turnpike was a great artery of trade and travel. It was kept by Robert Stewart, and after his death, by Colonel Daily. It is eighteen miles east of Pittsburgh, and in its day was one of the best of the old-fashioned taverns. This Robert Stewart was one of sixteen brothers, none of whom I have been able to trace, which is singular, among so many representatives of the name. Can any one furnish information relating to Robert Stewart, his brothers and their parents? H.

The Houston Family.

Having had occasion recently to make some researches in reference to this family, the writer came across considerable data which should be preserved in "Notes and Queries." There seems to be considerable confusion among the different branches as to the progenitor of the family in America.

I. John Houston settled in Lancaster county, Pa, in 1735 and had issue:
 i. Robert.
 ii. Isabella.
 iii. Esther.
 iv. John.
 v. Samuel.
 vi. Matthew.

An elder son, James, had been left in Ireland. The above family remained some time in Lancaster county and then removed to Virginia. His will is of record in Augusta county, Va., in Will Book No. 2, p. 40, and was admitted to probate May 15, 1755.

II. Robert Houston, son of John, married Margaret Davidson and had issue:
 i. John, m. ——Logan.
 ii. Samuel, m. Elizabeth Paxton.
 iii. Bettie.
 iv. Margaret.
 v. Esther.
 vi. Mary.

III. Samuel Houston, who married Elizabeth Paxton, had nine children, among whom were General Samuel Houston, of Texan fame, born March 2, 1793.

Another John Houston came from Ireland about 1750, and with his family of five children located in South Carolina. His wife was a Row. Three children were born after the family came to this country.

A William Houston and family, his wife having been a Margaret Hinman, born in Scotland, settled in Connecticut early in the last century, and had nine children, among them being a Robert Houston.

William Houston, either brother or son of John, son of John of Lancaster county, married Polly Montgomery and settled in Kentucky and some of the children located in Kansas. Among his children was also a Robert.

A branch of the family located in Tennessee. It is stated that their progenitor was a John Houston who located in Lancaster county, where he married a Martha Walker, about 1735, and had issue:
 i. Robert, b. about 1736.
 ii. Samuel.
 iii. James.
 iv. John.
 v. Christopher.
 vi. Prudence.
 vii. Rebecca.
 vii. Mary.

Of these children Samuel settled in Tennessee; James was killed in a fight with the Tories at Ransom's Mills, June 20, 1780; John located in Kentucky; Christopher in Tennessee, and of Robert nothing is known. Who can give information concerning this Robert Houston?

A Robert Houston was married at the "Big Spring" Presbyterian Church, in Pennsylvania, September 2, 1793, to Agnes Bell, and there are records extant showing that a Robert Houston married an Ann Owens in the latter part of the last century. Can any of the readers of "Notes and Queries" give information concerning?

The Lancaster Houstons state that their ancestor was John Houston, who located

near the Gap, about 1720 or 1725, and had issue:
  i. David.
  ii. John.
  iii. William.
  iv. James.
  v. Thomas.
  vi. Samuel, m. Miss Hopkins.

There were also two daughters, whose names are not given. Thomas went to Virginia and John became a physician.

John Houston's will, Lancaster county records, dated Aug. 10, 1769, probated Dec. 4, 1769, (Record Book of Wills B, vol. i, p. 527,) shows that he resided in Paxtang township, and left a widow, Martha, and issue:
  i. William.
  ii. Ann.
  iii. Thomas.
  iv. Samuel.
  v. Daniel.
  vi. James.

There are also of record and which have been printed in former issues of "Notes and Queries," the wills of Andrew Houston, of Paxtang, and James Houston, of Salisbury.

A grant of land in Londonderry was given by Malcolm IV to Hugo de Padvinaw and this was called "Hugostown," afterward "Hughtown" and finally corrupted into "Houston," whence the origin of the name. The arms given to Hugo were:

"Or—a chevron, chequey, sable and argent between three mantles of the second crest. A sandglass winged, P. Pr. supporters. On either side a greyhound, P. Pr. chained and collared. Or—motto over the crest, 'In Tempore.'"

This and the line of descent since that period is given in Crawford's "History of Renfrewshire" as follows.
1. Hugo de Padvinaw.
2. Reginal.
3. Hugh.
4. Findlay de Huston, 1298.
5. Patrick, 1450.
6. John, 1458.
7. Peter, 1513. (Flodden Field fame.)
8. Patrick, 1526.
9. John, 1542.
10. Patrick, 1605.
11. Ludovic, 1620.
12. Patrick, 1696. This Patrick came to America and is interred in a graveyard in Savannah, Georgia; his tombstone inscribed among other data: "Sir Patrick Houston, Bart."
13. John Ludovic.
14. George Ludovic, 1757.
15. John.
16. George, 1815.
17. Ludovic.
18. George Ludovic.
19. John.
20. Patrick, present incumbent, 1897.

Lancaster, Pa.   S. M. S.

THE OLD HARRISBURG BRIDGE

Paper read before the Historical Society of Dauphin County March 9th, 1899, by William A. Kelker.

Prior to the building of the Harrisburg bridge, the people of this vicinity and the traveling public who wished to cross the Susquehanna river at this point, resorted to the private boats and the public ferries, of which the town had two, the one at the foot of Paxton street known as Harris' ferry, crossing the river to the Kelso ferry house, and the other from the foot of North street, landing its passengers and freight at the Wormley ferry house on the Cumberland county shore. Both of these buildings are still standing, the former having been built in 1734 and is the oldest building west of the Susquehanna. The latter was erected in 1810.

The building of a bridge at Harrisburg was contemplated as early as 1809, probably prior, but it was some time before the work was commenced. Many persons did not think a bridge could be constructed that would withstand the great ice floods which visited the Susquehanna valley annually, and which were not impeded at that early day by the dams crossing the river at Clark's Ferry and Sunbury, both tending to lessen the damage done by large floes of ice. After some talk at the several meetings held in Dauphin, Cumberland and York counties, shares were sold and the bridge building commenced in 1813. During the second year of the work the Harrisburg contingent of the soldiers of the War of 1812 returned and were greeted by the home folk with fire-works, bonfires and good things in the way of edibles. Their return was on the 8th of December, 1814, and part of the demonstration was a display of fire-works upon the partly finished first pier of the new bridge. It so happened that our aged townsman, Mr. George C. Fager, was born upon this day, and he avers that, owing to this great display of fire-works, he became the fireman that he has been; and is now, we believe, the oldest volunteer fireman in the State of Pennsylvania. Whatever effect this display of fire-works may have had upon the baby boy of eighty-four odd years ago, we all know that he has been a noted fireman during his lifetime, and has also served the town in many ways of usefulness.

The bridge was finished in 1817 by Theodore Burr, the contractor, and cost $192,138. The United States mail stage, however, crossed it for the first time April 1st, 1816. Early in the progress of the work many persons took advantage of the one and two-plank wide walk made especially for the convenience of the workmen engaged upon the structcure and used it frequently to cross the river.

The first toll was collected October 23d, 1816, and at this point we will name the collectors in the order in which they served in that capacity, beginning with those collecting at the eastern or Dauphin county end of the bridge, following with those in the same work at the western or Cumberland county end. The yearly meetings of the bridge company were held from the opening of the bridge until 1844 in the log house of Mr. John Shoch, which was built in 1791 and removed in 1896 to make room for the present house belonging to the Harrisburg Club, situated on the north corner of Front and Market streets. Since 1844 the annual meetings have been held in the eastern toll-house. The bridge company directors met September 14th, 1816, at which time George Pearson was the first collector elected. He was to begin work on the 23d of October, 1816, at the eastern end of the bridge. He was succeeded by William Dock, on the 1st of October, 1819, who continued in office unil the election of John Fager, on the 29th of January, 1825. The company continued to re-elect Mr. Fager annually until the 31st of March, 1846, the eastern portion of the bridge having been carried away by the freshet on the 15th of March, 1846. Mr. Fager was the last survivor of that band of men who founded the Evangelical Lutheran Church in Harrisburg.

Then followed the election of Jeremiah Rees on the 17th of September, 1847, who was to serve from the 20th of September, 1847, to the 19th of September, 1848. He was, however, re-elected and continued in service until the election of George Steiner, the 29th of March, 1856, who served in this capacity until the 27th of October, 1867, when the board elected Samuel Denning, who, according to the minutes, was the first collector elected for an indefinite period. All the former ones had been chosen annually and, according to the record, after Mr. Denning's election, the collectors were to serve "during the pleasure of the said company." Thomas Reckord succeeded Mr. Denning on the 25th of March, 1874, and he in turn by David Stephenson, the 24th of January, 1878, who was followed on the 18th of July, 1879, by David Zarker, when on the 7th of December, 1893, he was relieved on account of ill health by the present incumbent, Solomon Rhoads, who assumed the duties the 28th of December, 1893.

The following named persons have acted as collectors at the Cumberland county or western end óf the bridge: The first person elected to serve there was William Dock, who took ehage on the 23d of October, 1816. He was succeeded on the 25th of September, 1819, by Jeremiah Rees, who was annually re-elected for twenty years and was succeeded on the 3d of March, 1839, by Jacob Kuhn, who continued in office unil the 17th of September, 1847, when William Lamb was elected, who served the company until the 6th of November, 1852. He was succeeded the same year by William Quigg, who collected tolls for seven years, when, in 1859, 3d of January, his son, John F. Quigg, became the collector. At this date the company dispensed with the rule or custom of electing the collectors for the western end of the bridge "annually" and concluded to have them serve "during the pleasure of the said company" instead. David Stephenson became the first collector under the new rule. He took the office the 21st of October, 1867. His successor was David Zarker, on the 7th of July, 1873, who was followed on the 1st of March, 1879, by William D. Banks, a storekeeper of West Fairview. Owing to the death of Mr. Banks, which occurred in December, 1883, the present incumbent, Lewis C. Danner, was elected and took charge of affairs the 3d day of the same month.

The early toll collectors were required to receive for toll only specie and such notes as were taken on deposit by the banks of Harrisburg. It was also part of their business to look after the replacing of planks in the floors and broken glass in the windows of the bridge. Comparatively few people know that the present old bridge, as well as the eastern section, had window sashes and that in bad weather these slides were closed, much to the comfort of the public and to secure the preservation of the timbers.

The troubles of the gate-keeper were many—subjected to all sorts of annoyances by men and boys. It was no wonder that they sometimes felt like retaliating upon their tormentors. To cheat a corporation is not thought to be a sin by many individuals and to pass "bad money" upon the collector was considered legitimate and smart, especially if not detected. As an instance in point, you all likely remember seeing the old penalty signs on and inside the bridge prohibiting the carrying of fire, fast driving, &c., $5 to $30 the fine. One day during Mr. Fager's administration two men were arrested for fast driving over the bridge and had the exteme penalty of $30 charged up to their account, which was paid, and they were allowed to proceed on their way, but on examination of the notes Mr. Fager found that the three $10-bills were counterfeits. You can imagine his frame of mind on making this discovery. Sometimes he got the better of his tormentors, as the following conversation will prove. About 2 o'clock one August morning in 1840 two men from the Cumberland county side awakened Mr. Fager by their loud cries of "Open the gates, we want out," adding a great deal of profanity to their request. They continued in their rough language while he pretended to open the padlock on the gate. He then asked them in his usual quiet manner "if they were done." They replied, "We are." He in turn replied "So am I, gentlemen." With this remark he relocked the gates and went into the toll-house and would not let them through. They had nothing else to do but to return to the Cumberland county shore and, of course, had to awaken the collector at that end of the bridge to relieve them of their dilemma.

We have several reminiscenees which occurred during the administration of George Steiner, nick-named by the boys of that period "Pete Steiner." He was a terror to all evil-doers and persons who tried to evade the paying of toll. The writer remembers the long "black-snake" whip which he had hanging inside the toll office near the door, and many a boy who attempted to "run the gates" felt the keen, thin lash about the calves of his legs. Another mode adopted by Mr. Steiner to stop the gate runners was to stone them, and for this purpose he kept a stock of stones on the frame work just inside the bridge, and woe betide the boy who made the dash through the gates in the presence of Mr. Steiner, for the volley of stones that was sure to follow him would do credit to a gattling gun of the present date. Mr. Steiner was fond of frogs and enjoyed the sport of hunting them, and it was the greatest pleasure imaginable for the boys of that period to worry him by lying flat on their stomachs back of the fence in the park opposite the toll house and croak like frogs. This performance would certainly bring him out with his "black-snake" whip.

The boys of that date seemed to have more business over the river than those of the present day. Swimming at the island was a great enjoyment. There was a certain lot of youths who could be now named to the lad, who frequently took Fager & Maeyer's old red push-cart along with them on these evening excursions and for no other purpose than to make trouble for Mr. Steiner. They can be heard yet in imagination coming through the carriage way of the bridge, say 9:30 or 10

P. M., and trotting out to the closed gates with a loud "whoa," as if it was a team of horses. Of course the gate-keeper had to get up and open the large gates to leave them out, for the foot gate was too narrow to allow its passage.

In the bridge destroyed by fire at midnight, 25th of May, 1866, the base of the arches were not covered with planking at the abutments, as is the case with the present structure. This opening enabled the boys who had climbed the abutments from the river shore to enter the bridge. Many a boy performed this rather perilous feat and made his way to the island, and just as many were surprised to find Mr. Steiner waiting on them to come through the opening and nearly have the life shaken out of them while being escorted by him out of the gateway. It is said that in early times, the company had tarred the timbers at these openings, but this did not prevent the boys from climbing through. Another trick was to place one of the two benches (which you have often seen at the toll house) across the doorway while the gate-keeper was taking his afternoon nap, and then call out as if a team had come, which would awaken the sleeper and in his half-wakened condition would stumble over the bench. In his confusion the culprits would hurry over without paying their toll. Another scheme was for half a dozen boys to walk through the gateway, each one saying "the last man pays the toll," and then the last one would make a break and follow his companions, who by that time were midway to the first pier. One more of the many pranks and I will stop on this subject. Towards 9 or 10 o'clock P. M. a party of boys would come through the bridge bleating as sheep do after a long drive. The gate-keeper, thinking that it was a belated drover with his flock, would hurry to open the gates, only to be met by a troop of noisy boys, who would dash by him, the last one of the crowd generally receiving a few spanks if he was so unfortunate as to fall into the hands of Mr. Steiner.

Previous to the period of transporting cattle of all kinds by rail, it was the custom to drive them to the great cities over the country roads, and owing to heavy toll rates they were often compelled to ford the Susquehanna at this point on their way to the eastern markets. Sheep and hogs were ferried over and in later years brought through the bridge in great droves, while cattle were sometimes driven through at the ford, which, after leaving the Cumberland county shore, crossed the lower end of Maclay's, now Watts' Island, and came out at the foot of Paxton street. Some little distance from the west end of the bridge on the south side there was (and it still remains) a gate used by the collector by which to confine the droves that they might be counted, for they passed through it at so much a score. This counting was done by driving them through one at a time, thus insuring a fair count. How the boys enjoyed the fun of assisting the drovers in bringing the cattle through the bridge, and going down to the "Black Horse" tavern at the head of Race street. Here the droves were taken into the tavern yard to rest and feed, while the drovers ate their noon meal. Few were the boys who did not own a whip of plaited leather, nicely rounded, with an A No. 1 cracker at the end of the lash. Many a waxed end was begged from Mr. John Edwards or Mr. Myers or Mr. X. Miller, out of which to make crackers for our whips. The sheep always followed their leader, and it was no unusual sight to see the leader (instead of going through the gateway on coming out of the bridge) suddenly turn to his right and leap the low wall, thus gaining the green grass of the park sooner than going by the roadway—followed by the whole drove before the drovers could stop the panic among them.

Mules also were brought over in great numbers and in nearly every case the person leading the drove rode a sorrel horse This leader greatly amused the youngsters by continually calling out "Come boys, come boys!" to the mules following him The drove was usually rounded up by a couple of mounted drivers who knew how to use the long-lashed whips they carried with them The writer remembers crossing the bridge with his father on an errand into Cumberland county during the Civil War. On the way over a small drove of seventeen mules were being brought to Harrisburg. By the time we reached the center of the old "camel-back" bridge, we heard great cries of "Drive on; drive on!" from a couple of teamsters back of our carriage. The old bridge was doing its best to jump off the piers, so greatly was it swaying, and it was all caused by these seventeen contrary mules, who had turned on their drivers and recrossed the bridge at a break-neck speed, terrifying everyone who they overtook during their mad charge. Not being able to quiet our team, we jumped out of the vehicle and got into the footway and took the horse by the head, but he soon got the better of us and went along with the runaway mules, who passed out the gateway with a grand rush, leaving our team to be captured by a soldier who was doing guard duty at the western end of the bridge.

The stone tablet now to be seen in the wall at the eastern toll-gate was ordered by the board of directors, 30th October, 1819. The work was done by George O'Donnel, and the inscription which he cut upon the stone reads:

This Bridge
Built by
Theodore Burr, 1813-1817.
Cost 192,138 Dollars.

On the 27th of November, 1819 the well which has been doing duty fo the past eighty years at the western toll-house was dug, and many a person has quenched his thirst by its cool water. It was on the 27th of January, 1820, that William Ross asked permission to place a floating mill in the eddy of one of the piers. The kind of a mill he proposed to erect and whether his request was granted, is not known.

The old-time market on Tuesday and Friday mornings of each week originated and were continued during the incumbency of John Fager. The benches in front of the toll-house were occupied by the baskets of the nearby farmers of Cumberland and York counties, who brought for sale their butter, eggs and poultry—all of the best quality. These markets were a great convenience to the townfolk. Mr. Fager was so obliging that citizens often left their baskets and money with him with orders to purchase supplies for them. Wagons were stationed on either side of the toll-house in the berry season, and when peaches, apples and cider were brought to town.

It should be stated that after the destruction of the eastern section of the bridge by the ice flood in March, 1846, a ferry was established from the eastern shore to the island. A new superstructure was erected upon the old piers in 1847. This structure was in turn destroyed by fire on the night of the 25th of May, 1866, when the ferry to the island was re-established, and was conducted until the present structure was erected in 1867. These ferries were immediately above the bridge.

During the summer months in years gone by, the eastern toll-house was a favorite resort of the older citizens, especially those residing in the immediate neighborhood. They would usually assemble there between the hours of three and four o'clock in the afternoon. The current news of the time, politics and the gossip of the town were the themes of conversation. It was not an uncommon sight for the passers-by on the other side of the street to observe the worthy old gentlemen sitting on the benches and chairs provided by the genial gate-keeper, fast asleep. In those happy days of old the village was small and there was a degree of warm-heartedness which does not now seem to exist for all is hurry and unrest, and every family is fed by the daily newspaper with news good and bad, especially the latter, gathered up from all ends of the earth. The generation of that day has been gathered to their fathers, and rest from their labors in the quiet cemetery. Industry, honesty and frugality were the notable characteristics of their lives, in marked contrast with the indolence, fraud and wasteful extravagance which prevail to such a great extent at the present time.

NOTES AND QUERIES.

Historical Biographical and Genealogical.

X.

KEISER.
Wanted to know the ancestry of John Keiser and his wife, Catharine ———,

who lived in Bedford county, Penn'a., in 1794. They had children:
i. Philip, b. 1794, in Bedford county, Pa.
ii. Elizabeth.
iii. Mary.
iv. Conrad.
v. John.
vi. Margaret.
Catharine Keiser died in Pennsylvania. John was married three times. I do not know whether Catharine was first or second wife. E. L. H.
Cncinnati.

LEFLER.
John Christopher Lefler, or Lafler, who was ensign in the New York Continental Line, Revolutionary War, married about 1792, Jemima Kendle, or Kendell (second wife), who it is thought belonged to Pennsylvania. Their children were:
i. Sarah.
ii. Henry.
iii. Jacob.
iv. Elizabeth.
v. William.
vi. Peter.
vii. David.
viii. George.
ix. Joseph.
x. James.
xi. Eli.
xii. Rachel.
xiii. Ann.
Wanted to know the ancestry of John Christopher Lefler and Jemima Kendell and place of marriage. The first ten children were born in Pennsylvania, it is thought.
Wanted to know the ancestry of George Lewis Lefler, first town clerk of York town, York county, Pa., in 1780; also justice of the Peace, York borough in 1795. Was he a brother of John Christopher Lefler? E. L. H.
Cincinnati.

The Garber Family.

I. Benedict Garber, b. Oct. 18, 1732; d. June 12, 1817. He came to America from Alsace, Germany, in 1741, when a lad, with his parents, who died on shipboard. He settled in Upper Providence, now Montgomery county, Pa., two and a half miles south of the Trappe. He became an extensive land proprietor. The homestead, beautifully located, was named "Garwood." He served in the war of the Revolution as a private in Captain Jacob Peterman's (Fourth) company, Sixth battalion, Philadelphia county militia, in 1780. He m. Nov. 12, 1758, Dorothea Loreht (Loreth), b. 1733; d. 1807. They had issue:
i. John-Henry, b. Feb. 3, 1759; d. Nov. 24, 1786; m. and had issue:
1. Deborah.
2. Anna.
3. Lydia, m. ——Kelly.
2. ii. Jacob-A., b. July 3, 1761; m. Elizabeth Reiner.
3. iii. John-Charles, b. July 12, 1762; m. and left issue.
iv. Catharine, b. July 4, 1765; m. —— Essig, and had issue (surname Essig):
1. Hannah.
2. Mary, m. —— Turner.
3. Elizabeth, m. —— Grisbock.
v. John, b. July 4, 1767; m. and had issue:
1. Nultame, b. July 8, 1789; d. Aug. 22, 1792.
4. vi Benjamin, b. Feb. 19, 1769; m. Hannah Reiner.
vii. Joseph, b. Feb. 27, 1772; d. Feb. 20, 1773.
II. Jacob A. Garber (Benedict), b. July 3, 1761; d. ——. He was choir master of the old Augustus church at the Trappe, and noted for his powerful bass voice. He m. in 1791, Elizabeth Reiner, and they had issue:
i. Adam, b. April 13, 1792; d. Sept. 10, 1799.
ii. John.
iii. Benedict.
iv. Jacob.
v. Susanna, m. —— Peterman.
vi. Sarah, m. —— Miller.
vii. Hannah, m. —— Croll.
viii. Elizabeth, m. —— Pennypacker.
III. John Charles Garber (Benedict), b. July 12, 1762; d. July 14, 1819; m. in 1785, and had issue:
i. Joseph, b. Feb. 17, 1786.
ii. Hannah, b. Oct. 4, 1787; d. Feb. 3, 1835.
iii. Isaac, b. Oct. 16, 1792.
5. iv. Samuel, b. Feb. 3, 1798; m. Susan Hiltebeidel.

6. v. Charles, b. March 22, 1806; m. Harriet ——.

IV. Benjamin Garber (Benedict), b. February 19, 1769; d. August 6, 1818. He resided on the old homestead, "Garwood." He m. Hannah Reiner, b. May 5, 1774; d. April 27, 1861. They had issue.
   7. i. Charles, b. 1790; m. Sarah Paul.
   8. ii. Henry, b. March 23, 1792; m. Susanna Paul.
   iii. Angelina, b. 1806; m. Rev. Frederick William Waage; served the Lutheran St. Paul's congregation of East Greenville, Pa., for half a century, and was succeeded by his son; they had issue (surname Waage):
      1. Rev. Oswin F.
   iv. Rebecca; m. —— Harper.
   v. Rachel; m. —— Harpel.
   vi. Maria; m. Feb. 25, 1836, Rev. Samuel A. Bumstead.

V. Samuel Garber (John-Charles, Benedict) b. Feb. 3, 1798; d. May 30, 1877. He m. in 1833 Susan Hiltebeidel, b. 1809; d. Feb. 7, 1895. They had issue:
   i. Hannah, b. Sept. 26, 1835; d. Dec. 2, 1873; m. ——Roger.
   ii. Mary-Ann, b. Aug. 1, 1837; d. March 19, 1884; m. —— Priest.
   iii. Davis, b. Feb. 10, 1839; d. Sept. 27, 1896; was Professor of mathematics at Muhlenberg College; m. Dec. 26, 1878, Kate Grim, of Allentown.
   iv. Benjamin, b. July 8, 1840; m. and had issue:
      1. Samuel.
      2. Daniel.
      3. Davis.
      4. Susan.
   v. Rebecca, b. 1844; d. Feb. 11, 1895; unm.
   vi. John-H., b. Jan. 13, 1844; resides at Salina, Cal.

VI. Charles Garber (John-Charles, Benedict) b. March 22, 1806; d. Oct. 11 1882; m. Harriet ——, b. Dec. 14, 1814; d. April 19, 1886. They had issue:
   i. Frank.
   ii. Eve-Anna; m. —— Vanderslice; and had issue (surname Vanderslice).
      1. Charles.
      2. Harriet.
   iii. Elizabeth, m. —— Fetterolf; and had issue (surname Fetterolf):
      1. Adela.
      2. Harriet.
      3. Ross.

VII. Charles Garber (Benjamin, Benedict) b. 1790; m. Sarah Paul: They had issue:
   i. William-F.; m. Jane Rowe; and they had issue:
      1. Henry, b. Nov. 30, 1849.
      2. William.
      3. Sarah-Andora, b. une 2, 1856; m. March 20, 1876, John Lofland, b. Nov. 12, 1850; and had issue (surname Lofland): Jane, Florence-Henri, Lucille, and Paul.

VIII. Henry Garber (Benjamin, Benedict), b. March 23, 1792; d. Nov. 1, 1848; m. Dec. 9, 1814, Susanna Paul, b. Sept. 2, 1789; d. June 4, 1832. They had issue:
   i. Andora, b. May 21, 1815; d. May 26, 1892; m. May 21, 1835, Rev. John William Richards, D. D., b. April 18, 1803; d. Jan. 24, 1854. He was pastor of the Augusta Church, at the Trappe. They left descendants.
   ii. Theodore, b. Dec. 9, 1816; d. Jan. 6, 1884; m. Feb. 5, 1850, his first cousin, Emma Paul, b. Sept. 30, 1825; d. Jan. 31, 1872; and they had issue:
      1. Ada-Virginia, b. Nov. 30, 1850.
      2. Katharine-Paul, b. June 7, 1855.
   iii. Benjamin-Franklin, b. Jan. 5, 1819; d. Oct. 13, 1863; m. Mary Weaver, b. 1820; d. Jan. 29, 1863; no issue.
   iv. Paul-Reiner, d. young.
   v. Sarah-Elvina, d. young.
   vi. Charles-Henry, b. July 3, 1823; m. Feb. 23, 1847, Annie Boileau, b. June 25, 1826; and they had issue:
      1. Henry-Boilean, m. Oct. 1, 1890, Emily May Boyer, and they had Mariam-Boyer.

GRAVEYARD INSCRIPTIONS

In Jordan Lutheran Church, Lehigh County, Penna.

Beidel, Magdalena, b. Steininger, b. Sept. 27, 1793; d. Aug. 23, 1817.
Botz, Mary, wf. of Johan, b. April 11, 1829; d. Nov. 18, 1854.
Bortz, John, b. Dec. 20, 1772; d. Feb. 17, 1852.
Bortz, Jacob, b. Dec. 11, 1777; d. Sept. 22, 1847.
Bortz, Mary, b. Oct. 28, 1782; d. Oct. 24, 1851.

Cope, Anna aMry, wf. of Michael, b. Mar. 31, 1770; d. Jan. 28, 1848.
Derr, Hannah, b. Guth, wf. of Christian, b. Aug. 10, 1873; d. Jan. 15, 1853.
Derr, Moses, s. of James and Catherine, b. Jan. 12, 1831; d. Apr. 6, 1854.
Dormeijein, Martin, b. Jan. 1, 1744; d. Dec. 11, 1802.
Eckel, Catherine, b. Reifschneider, wf. of Sebastian, b. Sept. 6, 1776; d. Apr. 19, 1844.
Eisenhart, Elizabeth, wf. of Andreas, b. May 5, 1793; d. Feb. 4, 1824. "She was a born Kitt." H. S. F., 1710.
Gangwer, Catharine; a tribute by her son, Louis L. Pauly; b. Dec. 19, 1781; d. Oct. 4, 1852.
Gold, Catherine, b. Seigfried, b. July 2, 1750; d. Oct. 2, 1820.
Hamon, Lydia, wf. of Jacob, b. Mar. 18, 1800; d. Apr. 9, 1824.
Hamon, Jacob, b. Jan. 16, 1752; d. Oct. 9, 1804.
Hamon, Matilda, b. July 25, 1822; d. Nov. 27, 1822.
Hamman, Hiram, s. of Jonathan and Maria, b. Sept. 12, 1827; d. Jan. 29, 1834.
Hamman, Cornelius, s. of Jonathan and Maria, b. Nov. 4, 1835; d. Dec. 23, 1835.
Hammon, Willoughby, Geo. Jonas, s. of George and Lydia, b. Jan. 20, 1835; d. May 4, 1835.
Heilman, Elizabeth, wf. of Jacob, b. June 15, 1749; d. Apr. 3, 1822.
Heilman, Jacob, m. Elizabeth Stechlinger, b. Oct. 1, 1740; d. Aug. 25, 1806; 11 children, 7 s. 4 dau.
Heilman, Jacob, s. of Jacob and Magdalena, b. Feb. 9, 1806; d. Aug. 3, 1836.
Heilman, Maria T., dau. Charles and Maria, b. July 26, 1851; d. Mar. 6, 1852.
Heilman, Franklin P., s. of Charles and Maria, b. Jan. 1, 1853; d. Dec. 13, 1853.
Heiberger, Germania, b. Kunz, wf. of Thomas, b. Sept. 23, 1823; d. Jan. 29, 1849.
Heilman, Mary M., "A born Ban," wf. of John Jacob, b. Sept. 17, 1777; ,d. Mar. 22, 1850.
Henninger, Anna Elizabeth, b. Aug. 25, 1742; d. Sept. 26, 1784.
Heller, Elmina, wf. of Jonas, b. Kuhns, b. July 8, 1826; d. Oct. 7, 1859.

Henninger, Christian, b. Oct. 29, 1784; d. Dec. 9, 1826.
Henninger, Elizabeth, dau. of Daniel and Elizabeth, b. Mar. 8, 1824; d. June 5, 1827.
Henninger, Jacob, b. Feb. 12, 1739; d. Sept. 22, 1823.
Henninger, Catherine, b. Kemmerer, wf. of Jacob, b. Aug. 15, 1757; d. June 16, 1837.
Herbele, Crisse Carolina, dau. of Moses and Sarah, b. Oct. 9, 1849; d. Sept. 7, 1853.
Hertzel, Eva, wf. of Johannes B., b. Strauss, b. Feb. 3, 1787; d. Dec. 28, 1851.
Hoffman, Anna Maria, wf, of Jerry, b. Jan. 1, 1735; d. Jan. 19, 1822.
Hoffman, George, b. Sept. 13, 1798; d. Jan. 25, 1821. His sponsor was his grandmother, Anna Maria Hoffman.
Hoffman, Jacob, b. Jan. 8, 1766; d. Oct. 25, 1834.
Hoffman, Maria Elizabeth, wf. of Jacob, b. Nov. 27, 1772; d. Feb. 5, 1844.
Hoffman, George, m. Ann Maria Hornberger, b. Feb. 26, 1733; d. Sept. 24, 1789.
Houser, Salome, b. Hommel, wf. of David, b. July 18, 1796; d. June 19, 1860.
Houser, Edward, s. of David and Salome, b. Sept. 6, 1821; d. Feb. 11, 1851.
Houser, James, b. Sept. 28; d. Dec. 26, 1867.
Houser, Elizabeth, dau. of James and Sarah, b. Aug. 7, 1838; d. Apr. 16, 1852.
Houser, A. J.
Houser, Sarah Susanna, dau. of Jos. and Salome, b. Aug. 9, 1852; d. Aug. 24, 1852.
Houser, David, m. Salome Hommel, b. Nov. 20, 1792; d. Nov. 30, 1846; 9 children.
Kammerer, Jacob, s. of John and Magdalena, b. Jan. 5, 1808; d. Jan. 18, 1838.
Kemsehr, Joseph, b. Oct. 14, 1809; d. Aug. 30, 1834.
Kline, John Peter (War of 1812), b. Mar. 6, 1794; d. July 15, 1872.
Kline, Susanna, wf. of John Peter, b. 1810; d. Oct. 8, 1855.
Klotz, Johanes, b. 1746; d. [oblit.]
Knappenberger, Eliza Emelia, dau. of Har-

rison and Cora, b. Feb. 6, 1854; d. Mar. 14, 1854.
Kock, Reuben, s. of Johann and Susanna, b. Jan. 12, 1813; d. Aug. 17, 1833.
Koch, Susanna, b. Rabenold, wf. of Johan, b. Oct. 28, 1782; d. Jan. 20, 1853.
Koch, Johannes (War 1812), b. Nov. 7, 1782; d. Nov. 29, 1862.
Koch, Samuel, b. Feb. 13, 1812; d. Jan. 8, 1813.
Koch, Heinrich, b. Mar. 2, 1744; d. Jan. 18, 1835.
Kochen, Anna Maria, b. ——; d. 1776 [oblit.]
Kraus, Andrew, b. Feb. 3, 1777; d. Sept. 10, 1847.
Kraus, Maria Barbara, b. ——, 177--; d. Sept., 1802 [oblit.]
Kremer, Sarah Anna, dau. of George and Elizabeth, b. Sept. 12, 1829; d. Aug. 12, 1830.
Kuhns, Henry, s. of Jonathan and Judith, b. Nov. 3, 1826; d. Aug. 3, 1851.
Kuhns, Lowina, dau. of Dewald and Lydia, b. Apr. 30, 1834; d. Aug. 7, 1849.
Kuhns, Emenda Eliza, dau. of Samuel and Rebecca, b. Apr. 25, 1847; d. Sept., 1847.
Kuhns, Lidia, b. Schmitin, wf. of Dewald, b. Aug. 8, 1789; d. Apr. 7, 1844; 15 children.
Kuhns, Dewald, b. Sept. 30, 1777; d. Oct. 16, 1857.
Kuhns, Lidia, dau. of Dewald and Lydia, b. June 16, 1815; d. July 7, 1850.
Kuhns, Amanda Elizabeth, dau. David and Maria, b. Nov. 22, 1842; d. Aug. 16, 1845.
Kuhns, Sarah Elizabeth, dau. of Reuben and Sarah, b. Nov. 25, 1840; d. June 1, 1841.
Kuhns, Eva, wf. of Philip, b. Mar. 15, 1788; d. May 9, 1854.
Kuntz, Carolina, dau. of Lydia and George, b. Steininger, b. Jan. 15, 1828; d. Aug. 28, 1838.
Kuntz, Johan Philip, b. June 3, 1762; d. Jan. 3, 1832.
Kuntz, Jacob, b. Dec. 6, 1753; d. Dec. 27, 1831.
Kuntz, Elemenda, dau. of Johannes and Maria, b. Mar. 14, 1851; d. Mar. 17, 1853.
Kuntz, Heinrich, b. Feby. 17, 1806; d. 1812.
Litzenberger, Alfred James, s. of Jacob L. and Catherine, b. June 21, 1839; d. Oct. 23, 1843.
Landes, George (War of 1812), b. Sept. 13, 1779; d. June 9, 1845.
Landes, Maria Magdalena, b. Schrieber, wf. of J. George, b. Nov. 5, 1779; d. Oct. 21, 1863.
Lichtenwalner, Johnnes, 12 children, b. June 29, 1738; d. Oct. 30, 1794; m. 1763; m. Catherine Stettler.
Lichten, Walner Catherine, b. Stauffer, b. Oct. 17, 1744; d. 1802; 6 sons, 6 daughters.
Lichtenwalner, Johan, b. 1794; d. Aug., 22, 1816.
Lindes, Jacob, b. 1801; d. Aug. 27, 1815.
Litzenberger, Benjamin Franklin, s. of Jacob and Catherine, b. Apr. 17, 1841; d. Sept. 1, 1842.
Maria, Catherine, [oblit] b. 1727; d. Dec. 28, 1802.
Miller, Benjamin, s. of Daniel and Maria, b. Jan. 7, 1833; d. Sept. 11, 1833.
Miller, Josia, s. of Johan and Anna, b. Sept. 26, 1831; d. Dec. 6, 1846.
Miller, Ellen T. M., dau. of Jesse and Marietta, b. Nov. 13, 1853; d. May 13, 1853.
Minet, Johan Heinreich, b. Sept. 1779; d. July 16, 1832; m. Nov. 27, 1802 Catherine Stremy.
Mosser, Johannes, b. April 16, 1741; d. Oct. 11, 1810; m. 1702 Elizabeth Ster; 8 children, Mosser Elizabeth, 3 sons, 5 daughters, b. 7th, 1743; d. Feb. 15, 1808; m. Johannes Mosser, b. April 16, 1762; Mosser Tobias, 2 sons 7 daughters, b. May 24, 1743; d. July 22, 1800; m. Christina Maurin.
Mosser, Hannes, b. Oct. 3, 1776; d. April 1814; m. Feb. 5, 1793.
Mosser, Maria Barbara, b. Moyer, wf. Johannes; b. Jan. 10, 1772; d. April 7, 1838.
Moyer, Barbara, w. John, b. Oct. 15, 1794; d. Jan. 26, 1821.
Noll, Philip, s. of George and Catherine, b. March 28, 1828; d. Aug. 8, 1850.
Rabenold, Albin Daniel, s. of Benjamin and Hanna, b. April 12, 1853; d. Aug. 26, 1853.
Rabenold, Elizabeth, b. Riter; w. of Daniel, b. March 22, 1784; d. April 28, 1835.

Rabenold, Daniel, b. May 4, 1774; d. Dec. 1883,
Rabenold, Cassie Jane Elizabeth, dau. Solomon and Sarah Jane, b. Oct. 28, 1856; d. Feb. 27, 1856.
Reinert, Catherine, wf. of Nathan, Moyer; b. Dec. 28, 1815; d. June 3, 1842.
Ruch, Georg, b. 1664 in Elsas, in Zuzendorfund; d. 1768; very old, his entire age is 104 yrs, 11 mos.
Sager, Aaron, s. of George and Elizabeth, b. April 11, 1822; d. Feb. 24, 1832.
Schantz, Elizabeth, wf. of Philip, b. Sept. 28, 1768; d.—— 31, 1833.
Schantz, Maria, wf. of Jacob, b. Aug. 28, 1760; d. Oct. 16, 1848; m. 1778.
Schantz, Jacob, m. 1778, b. April 26, 1761; d. 1816.
Schantz, John Philip, b. Sept. 2, 1763; d. Aug. 3, 1834; m. Elizabeth Neff, 1790; 7 children.
Schantz, Johan G., b. May 7, 1765; d. Sept. 10, 1851.
Schantz, Jacob, b. Nov. 28, 1791; d. June 2, 1843.
Schiffert, John Henry, s. of Johann and Elizabeth, b. Sept. 12, 1829; d. May 27, 1852.
Schneider, Eva, wf. of Abraham, b. May 15, 1785; d. March 28, 1854.
Schindel, Horace, s. of Henry and Lavina Litzenberger, b. Feb. 4, 1852; d. May 12, 1854.
Schindel, Martin Luther, s. of Rev. Jeremiah and Elizabeth, b. Dec. 4, 1863; d. April 14, 1838.
Schloszer, Bernhardt, b. in Bohemia, 1735; d. June 20, 1814; m. Barbara Crist.
Semel, H. T.
Schwayer, Elizabeth, dau. of Johan and Elizabeth, b. March 10, 1844; d. July 15, 1845.
Sieger, Elizabeth, wf. of Samuel, b. March 1, 1757; d. —— 18, 1826; m. 1771, 6 sons and 6 daughters.
Sieger, George, b. April 12, 1800; d. April 17, 1852.
Sieger, Elizabeth, wf. of George, d. of Jacob and Chris Stopp, b. Sept. 23, 1794; d. Dec. 25, 1876.
Sieger, Elias, b. Nov. 24, 1807; d. June 2, 1848.
Sieger, Mary Matilda, dau. of Elias and
Salanda, b. Aug. 29, 1855; d. March 15, 1855.
Sieger, Samuel, (War 1812), b. July 2, 1760; d. Nov. 28, 1835.
Sherer, Soloman, m. Esther Wieand, b. March 2, 1802; d. Oct. 8, 1853; 8 ch.
Sherer, Lavinus, s. of Solomon and Esther, b. Aug. 12, 1851; d. Aug. 28, 1855.
Sherer, Levi, s. of Johannes and Margaret, b. Nov. 7, 1809; d. Dec. 28, 1836.
Sherer, Johan, b. May 14, 1773; d. Oct. 10, 1855.
Sherer, Margaret, wf. of Johan, b. March 11, 1776; d. —— 14, 1797.
Sieger, Michael, s. of Samuel and Elizabeth Snider, m. Juliana Kern, 1804; 6 children, b. Sept. 25, 1781; d. Jan. 12, 1829.
Steinninger, Maria Margaret, w. of Philip, b. Aug. 30, 1781; d. Oct. 16, 1803.
Steininger, Barbara, b. Stauffer, wf. of George, b. June 18, 1743; d. April, 1817.
Steahapp, Barbara, b. Sept. 12, 1714; d. April 5, 1774.
Steininger, Johannes Philip, b. June 16, 1775; d. April 15, 1870.
Steininger, Maria Magdalena, wf. of Philip, b. —— 26, 1782; d. April 23, 1858.
Steininger, Solomon, s. of Philip and Margaret, b. Jan. 29, 1814; d. March 16, 1843.
Steininger, John Leon, b. Nov. 20, 1762; d. March 4, 1849.
Steininger, Catherine Margaretta, wf. of John Leonard, b. Aug. 5, 1769; d. July 11, 1857.
Steininger, Jonas, s. of John Leon and Margaret, b. April 25, 1808; d. June 13, 1850.
Steininger, Anna Maria, b. May 27, 1811; d. June 16, 1845.
Steininger, Anna, dau. Philip and Maria, b. June 18, 1816; d. Aug. 26, 1817.
Strauss, Maria Magdalena, b. Gluck, wf. of Heinerich, b. June 26, 1775; d. —— 31, 1849.
Strauss, Polloy Ann, dau. of William and Henrietta, b. July 8, 1844; d. June 2, 1845.
Strauss, Leandi, b. Dec. 21, 1844; d. Sept. 10, 1820.
Unger, Nathan, s. of Christian and Susanna, b. Oct. 18, 1808; d. Aug. 31, 1833.

Wartman, Ephraim, s. of George and Hanna, b. Aug. 23, 1828; d. April 19, 1838.
Wartman, George Israel, s. of Rev. George and Hannah, b. Feb. 27, 1823; d. May 2, 1853.
Wartman, George, Rev., b. Nov. 29, 1793; d. Jan. 27, 1837; m. 1823; 4 sons, 2 daughters.
Xander, Johanes, b. July 15, 1803; d. Feb. 21, 1855; m. Anna Maria Hoffman.

NOTES AND QUERIES.

Historical, Biographical, and Genealogical.

XI.

Mitchell of Cumberland Valley.

I. Gorge Mitchell, of Letterkenny township, Cumberland county, d. prior to February, 1763, leaving a wife and three children—that of Joseph only being named.

II. John Mitchell, of Antrim township, Cumberland county, made his will January 9, 1756, which was probated on the 17th of the same month. He left a wife Elizabeth, who d. in April, 1765; and children:
  i. Jane, m. and had a son George.
  ii. Elizabeth.
  iii. Margaret.
  iv. Martha.
  v. Mary.
  vi. Ann-Mary.
  vii. John.
  viii. Robert.
  ix. Rachel.
Granddaughter, Elizabeth Gable.
Executors were wife and son Robert.

III. John Mitchell, of Rye township (now Perry county), Cumberland county, d. in May, 1774, leaving a wife Agnes, and children:
  i. David; was a brigadier-general at the close of the Revolution.
  ii. James.
  iii. Jane, m. ——Parkeson.
  iv. Sarah, m. —— Hart.
  v. Mary.
  vi. Joseph.

IV. Gawin Mitchell, of Newton township, Cumberland county, d. in September, 1782, leaving a wife Isabella, and children:
  i. Alexander.
  ii. Ezekiel.
  iii. Susanna.
  iv. Margaret.
  v. Agnes.
  vi. Jean.
  vii. Ruth.
  viii. James.
  ix. Robert.
Executors, wife and son-in-law, Josiah Brown.

V. Samuel Mitchell, of Fermanagh township, Cumberland county, d. in May, 1783, leaving a wife Ann, and children:
  i. William.
  ii. Robert.
  iii. Jennett.
  iv. Mary.
  v. [Posthumous.]
Executors, Hugh McAlister and Samuel Sharon.

How a Revolutionary Relic Was Lost

When Uncle Robin Gray had served his fourth "tour" of duty to the State of Pennsylvania, the mustering out officer informed him and his fellow-soldiers that he had no money to pay them for their services; that continental paper was worthless, and the State was "flat broke." Continuing, he said: "I can give you a certificate only; take your arms home with you; they will be a souvenir at least, and if you are ever called back to service you will have them ready for duty. Perhaps the State may some day be able to redeem these certificates and arms which you have so honorably earned."

Uncle was no grumbler; he was a young man and felt able to spare that much for his country. He took his "musquet" home, stored it away, and there it remained for fifty years.

One bright summer morning, away back towards the beginning of the "twenties," in my own early "kid" days, I made my way over to Uncle Gray's to have a play-day with his younger children. We romped through the house, even to the garret, taking with us to the latter place the big black dog, Rover, hoping to victimize a rat. A garret, in the old time farm-house, especially in the summer season, was a general lumber room, where winter clothing, bedding, spinning wheels, reels and all sorts of family jim-cracks were stored for the time being. Among these stow-aways was a strange-looking gun, which Cousin Ellen said was her father's cld "musquet." I had heard the name before and knew it was a weapon of war, but had never seen one. I looked it over with a child's curiosity, noted the massive lock with a large fire stone in place, the suspension rings, and above all the iron ram-rod, not forgetting the bayonet and cartridge box. The stock was in excellent preservation and not a speck of rust was on the barrel. It was of the old French pattern, and might have been one of the twelve thousand brought over by General Lafayette with which he bought his commission. Its regulation weight was nine pounds, whilst the British arm of the same period weighed eleven. It was two or three inches longer than the regulation gun of to-day.

Somewhere about 1830 or '31 Congress passed a pension act, covering all who had done service in the war for independence. Uncle had in one of his six-months' "tours" borne a lieutenant's commission, and was entitled to considerable pay. He was a scrupulous, conscientious man, had given his services ungrudgingly, and in accordance with the sentiment of his day regarded a pension application as the nearest of kin to the "beggar's petition." This point of honor to-day looks odd, but seventy years ago was a ruling force. Uncle was not a rich man by any means; his life had been a life of saving economy, necessary to make the "two ends of the year meet." The temptation was great, but for the time being he decided to hold back. It was at this point that Chief Justice Marshall and General Sumpter, both men of ample estate, came forward and received pensions. Uncle reconsidered his position. "If," said he, "as great a man as John Marshall can honorably take a pension, I think I may." That pension gave him more ready money than he had ever had. He treated himself to a new suit, a new hat, and the first overcoat I had ever seen him wear.

The pension bureau had required his certificates and discharges from service and they had been duly submitted, but it took no account of the old musket. Expecting nothing, he felt that he had been paid and overpaid beyond his wildest dreams; everything had been redeemed by the United States, including the musket. It was his no longer, it belonged to the States, and, taking it on his shoulder he trudged into Harrisburg and there deposited it in the State arsenal, where it was piled up with a great lot of other old guns of like character and its identity lost forever.

On the day of that delivery my mother happened to be on a social visit to Aunt Polly and on her return home related the incident. "Out of sight, out of mind," the old musket was soon forgotten, and did not come back to memory for more than fifty years, only to regret that as a first-class relic and heirloom it was lost forever.

In the summer of 1837 the writer was mustered into Captain John Wise's company, Harrisburg battalion, Pennsylvania militia. Captain Wise was a hatter and had his store on Front street, between Market and Blackberry alley. The battalion lined up on Walnut street for inspection. About one man in twenty had a gun; sticks, big and little, were the main armament. He who had an old blunderbuss or horse-pistol was in good form. Inspector Reily took a look or two at us and then marched us to the arsenal. Here, in one of the rooms, were wagon-loads of old rusty muskets, nearly all without bayonets. Arming us with these terrible weapons we went forth to drill and manouvre in a style that would have brought tears to the eyes of a West Point military artist. Having exhausted Steuben and Scott, we returned to the arsenal to deposit our arms, and so ended an old-time muster-day in Harrisburg.

Query—What became of those old and time-honored muskets? If the editor of Notes and Queries doesn't know, who does? H. RUTHERFORD.
Oakland, Ill.

[In reply to our esteemed octogenarian friend, we can only say that we saw this pile of rubbish, so called, auctioneered and bought by Mr. Washington Barr, in the "forties." Had we known then what we subsequently realized, how many relics of the days of the Revolution might have

Historical and Genealogical.

been preserved. Those of to-day are being educated to a higher standard, and the past is more dearly prized. Would that our fathers had one-half the appreciation; and yet perchance it may be well, as they who come after will have the greater responsibility. "Remember the days of old," is a precious saying, but the preservation of the records of the past is grander and nobler.]

Runkel Family Graveyard.

[In West Hanover township, Dauphin county, on the farm owned so many years by the Runkel family, is the private burial ground from which the following transcripts were taken.—E. W. S. P.]:

Miller, George, b. Oct. 5, 1769; d. Jan. 17, 1829.
Miller, Margaret E., wf. of George, b. Oct. 10, 1773; d. Aug. 8, 1847.
Miller, Elizabeth, wf. of John Runkel, b. Nov. 18, 1780; d. Jan. 24, 1859.
Miller, John, b. Sept. 18, 1801; d. June 6, 1858.
Miller, Sarah, b. Sept. 29, 1809; d. Aug. 8, 1847.
Miller, Mary, dau. of George and Margaret E., b. Nov. 11, 1812; d. Sept. 28, 1818.
Runkel, John, b. April 5, 1799; d. May 30, 1845.
Runkel, Elizabeth, b. Sept. 10, 1802; d. June 20, 1851.
Runkel, Catharine, b. Oct. 2, 1803; d. Aug. 25, 1868.
Runkel, Mary, wf. of Henry Bomgardner, b. May 2, 1806; d. April 28, 1889.
Runkel, George, b. Oct. 3, 1810; d. June 28, 1889.
Runkel, Sarah, b. Oct. 23, 1812; d. Oct. 5, 1865.
Runkel, Lydia, b. May 15, 1814; d. Feb. 14, 1874.
Runkel, Catharine Mark, wf. of George Runkel, b. Dec. 13, 1818; d. Sept. 21, 1860.
Runkel, Nellie, b. Aug. 6, 1818; d. Dec. 20, 1897.
Runkel, Levi, b. May 18, 1822; d. June 10, 1873.
Runkel, Willie, b. July 12, 1842; d. Aug. 30, 1842.
Runkel, Eliza, b. June 16, 1849; d. March 31, 1865.
Runkel, John, s. of Levi and Harriet, b. June 3, 1853; d. Sept. 22, 1877.
Runkel, Mary Jane, b. Oct. 1, 1856; d. Nov. 1, 1856.
Runkel, Alfred, s. of Aaron and Mazie Runkel, b. Feb. 27, 1896; d. Sept. 3, 1896.
Radabaugh, Mary E., b. Feb. 19, 1851; d. March 28, 1863.
Gerberich, Catharine, wf. of Leonard, b. Aug. 23, 1793; d. Aug. 30, 1826.

The First Graveyards of Harrisburg

[Paper read before the Dauphin County Historical Society, 13th April, 1899.]

It is not a sprightly topic. But in the interest of local history I will take up this grave subject, which, so far as I remember, has not been written upon—the old-time graveyards of Harrisburg.

These were within the limits of the old town and subsequently incorporated borough. The largest piece of ground appropriated to burial purposes, was the angular space lying partially behind and east of the Lutheran church; bounded by Fourth street, Chestnut street, and Meadow Lane as its longest side.

This tract was owned and used by four churches or congregations, thus: Immediately in the rear of the Lutheran church, extending to Meadow Lane, and its western line, being the rear boundary of the properties on Market street, was the section occupied by the Presbyterians. Entrance was had from Fourth street, by a way along the eastern side of the Lutheran church; and this also extended at a right angle to Market street.

Right in the corner of Chestnut street and Meadow Lane was a small portion for use of the colored people in general.

The remainder, being also the largest part of the tract, belonged to the German Reformed and Lutheran denominations together; a circumstance which no doubt resulted from the fact that those two congregations had worshipped together, in the first church building erected in the town (1787), and so continued until 1814, when the Lutherans built their own separate church on Fourth street.

The union of these graveyards at this location was quite convenient, as things were then; because they were merely on the edge of the town—and a "ragged edge" it was, too—and no residences were beyond them; only the warehouses along the old canal, meadows bordering Paxtang creek, and the rugged hills beyond.

More than that, the old-time funerals were always afoot, and the body was borne by carriers upon a bier. The custom of using a hearse was yet to come, within the town, and was only in vogue for long distances in the country. To have hauled a body, and not carried it, would then have been considered most disrespectful, and hence it was not practiced.

That portion of these burial grounds lying close along the fence on Meadow Lane, contained the graves of the very poor people, unable to purchase their own lots. It was also a sort of "Potter's Field" for unknown strangers dying in the town, friendless persons killed by accident, and a few criminals who died in the county jail.

I do not recall any monuments (upright structures) in any of the graveyards; but there were many large flat slabs at various heights. There was one vault, in the Presbyterian ground, belonging to the Wyeth family; in which also Samuel Douglas, a distinguished lawyer of his time, was deposited. Occasionally some venerable member of the Presbyterian church was taken out to the historic graveyard of old Paxtang church, mother of the congregation in town.

The Methodist graveyard was located on the west side of North street, above Third, opposite the Capitol grounds. But when the original waterworks were constructed, in 1839, the laying out of the reservoir required this ground for public use, and it was vacated accordingly. The bodies were removed to a new location on Ridge Road, a short distance west of the reservoir. The delicate work of removal was undertaken by Conrad Kneepley, a famous old-time High Constable. But he shocked the Methodists and the whole community by reinterring a number of the coffins in a north and south direction, instead of the traditional east and west—"without malice aforethought," no doubt. However, it was deemed unpardonable, the contractor was instantly deprived of his job, and it was bestowed on Mr. Ross Meredith, who conformed to the sensibilities of the congregation and the prejudice of the times, by completing the work decently and in order.

The Episcopalians had their graveyard in the rear of the church at Front and Pine streets, and it was amply sufficient for their small congregation at that time. It was neatly kept, and was noted for containing the remains of Joseph Jefferson—grandfather of our Joe Jefferson—who had died while acting in Harrisburg.

The Roman Catholic graveyard occupied ground along the north side and rear of their church building, on State street, above Second. The lot was bordered with stately shade-trees; between this and Third street the open square was low and swampy.

There were two other very small churches, Baptist and Winebrennarian, which I presume buried their dead with the other denominations.

The establishment of a public cemetery, however, changed the whole course of things in this regard. Its need was greatly felt, as the old burial grounds had become very much crowded, and when it was dedicated to its sacred purposes, September 30, 1845, a new era dawned upon the matter of burial in Harrisburg. There was now a feeling of permanancy harmonizing all interests in the new "God's-acre," and the business of removal from the old yards in town began in due time.

The ground selected for the new cemetery had always been regarded as one of the loveliest and most inviting spots adjoining the town. "Mount Kalmia" was suggested as a handy name for it, but not altogether appropriate; for the laurel (kalmia) was of small account here in the shady wood, as compared with its luxuriant growth on the neighboring bluffs.

The hillside, with its jutting knoll, was known as "Hare's (Herr's) Hill," and the ravine within was called "Fairy Valley." This was our most charming resort for May parties and picnics in general, when life was young. A beautiful rivulet gurgled down the shady dell, the grassy sod was velvety and cool, and here in summer-time gathered many bright eyes and happy hearts—"in the days when we went gipsying, a long time ago"—who now 'sleep in Jesus' under the grand old oaks above.

If I remember correctly, the first person buried in the new cemetery was Gen. James Steele, whose family resided on Front street. The second an infant child of William Kepner's. The third was one of my own lovely companions, Miss Anna Doll—the extremes of life with youth and beauty.

At the opening ceremonies, the dedicatory address was delivered by Rev. Dr. William R. DeWitt, the senior pastor of the borough. The day was pleasant and a large gathering of people heard it. The impressive personality of Dr. DeWitt, and the special adaption of his refined poetic style to the expression of his thoughts on such an occasion, can be easily imagined by all who remember him. The address was afterwards published.

GEORGE BUCHER AYRES.

NOTES AND QUERIES.

Historical, Biographical, and Genealogical.

XII.

KLINGER.

John Philip Klinger was born July 11, 1723, in Poffenbeerfurt, Odenwald, Germany. He came to America and settled near Reading, Penna. Later on, he removed to Lykens township, Dauphin county, near Klinger's Church, where he died September 30, 1811, leaving four sons and one daughter:
i. John-Philip; m. and had sons:
 1. John-Philip, Jr.
 2. Peter.
 3. Daniel.
 4. John.
ii. George; m. and had sons:
 1. Alexander.
 2. George.
 3. Philip.
 4. Peter.
 5. John.
iii. Alexander; m. and had sons:
 1. George.
 2. Alexander.
iv. Peter; m. and had sons:
 1. Philip.
 2. Peter.
 3. George.
 4. John-Alexander.

 5. Jacob.
 6. John-Adam.
 7. David.
v. [a dau.]; m. —— Weiser.

None of the foregoing are living. A grandson, Jacob Klinger, a nephew of Daniel, who was a son of Peter Klinger, resides with his family at Loyalton.

Pennock—Marshall Families.

[From a letter written to Dr. Vincent C. Marshall, of Cincinnati, O., by his father, dated "East Marlborough," 11th mo., 22 d., 1826, we glean the following genealogical facts relating to the Pennock and Marshall families of Chester county]:

Christopher Pennock, a native of Germany, went to England, thence to Ireland, where he married Mary Collett, daughter of George Collett, of Clonmell, County of Tipperary, Ireland. He is said to have been an officer under William of Orange, subsequently emigrating to Pennsylvania. He died in 1701 in Philadelphia. Of his children, only one reached maturity—Joseph Pennock, who in 1702 became a merchant in Philadelphia. In 1714 he settled on a tract of land in West Marlborough township, Chester county, granted by the Founder to his grandfather, George Collett. Here he erected a large mansion, "Primitive Hall." He was, in his younger day, "a dashing young Irishman," and very hospitable. He married Mary Levis, daughter of Samuel Levis. Their children were:
i. Elizabeth.
ii. Samuel; m. Mary Hadley.
iii. William; m. Alice Mendenhall.
iv. Mary.
v. Joseph; d. inf.
vi. Nathaniel.
vii. Joseph (second).
viii. Ann.
ix. Sarah; m. Humphrey Marshall.
x. Hannah; m. Jacob Marshall.
xi. Lewis; m. Ruth Marshall.
xii. Susanna.

Abraham Marshall, born in Derbyshire, England, joined the Society of Friends and about the year 1700 came to America, and was a highly esteemed minister. He married Mary Hunt, daughter of John Hunt, of Kingsessing, a native of Kent, England.

He died in 1767, his wife surviving two years. Their children were:
i. Samuel.
ii. Elizabeth.
iii. John; m. Hannah Caldwell.
iv. Abraham; m. Rachel Carter.
v. Hannah.
vi. Isaac; m. first Ann Vernon; m. secondly Mary (Evans) Clayton.
vii. Jacob; m. Hanah Pennock.
viii. Humphrey; b. 1722; d. 1801; m. first Sarah Pennock; m. secondly Margaret Minshall. He was the earliest of our native botanists, and wrote the first work on that subject.
ix. James; m. Sarah Waite.

John Marshall, who married Hannah Caldwell, daughter of Vincent Caldwell and his wife Betty Peirce, left children:
i. Joseph; d. young.
ii. Ruth; m. Lewis Pennock.
iii. Betty; d. young.
iv. Ann; m. first Amos Hope; m. secondly Joseph Peirce.
v. Mary; m. Solomon Harlan.
vi. John; m. Sarah Miller; s. p.
vii. Abraham; m. Alice Pennock; from whose letter to his son these notes are gleaned. Their children were Hannah, John, Joseph, George, Levis, Vincent C., Israel, Eliza, Abraham, Milton, Mora and Pennock. Vincent Caldwell Marshall became a prominent physician of Cincinnati and died in 1844. He m. first a Miss Pugh; secondly Ann Cassilly. By first wife he had a son David P. Marshall, who m. and went to California in the "gold fever days." There was a daughter by the second wife, who m. Henry Miller and d. s. p. Abraham Marshall, a brother of Dr. Vincent C., in 1832 was living at Rushville, Ill.
viii. Hannah.

Atkinson Family Data.

In volume ii, third series of Notes and Queries, page 166, appear some notes concerning the family of Atkinson, and in reference thereto the following data may be of value:

Stephen Atkinson had a fulling mill on the Conestoga creek from 1720 to 1730. He married Ann Wilton, and his will, which is of record in Lancaster county, dated Sept. 14, 1739, mentions children:
i. Matthew.
ii. Elizabeth, m. Thomas Doyle.
iii. Jane, m. Joshua Minshall.
iv. [A dau.] —— m. Samuel Reed.

Matthew Atkinson, was twice married, his first wife, name unknown; his second wife was Margaret Thornbrough, daughter of Thomas Thornbrough, of Lancaster. Matthew died in 1756, and his will mentions the following issue:
i. Stephen.
ii. Wilton.
iii. Ann, m. ——Davis, of Lancaster.
iv. Margaret.
v. Matthew.
vi. Hannah, m. James Brown.

The will of Thomas Thornbrough is of record in Lancaster county, he having died July 20, 1758.

Margaret, the widow of Matthew Atkinson, died in 1798; her will being dated Sept. 7, 1798. In it she mentions her daughter Ann Davis; Matthew; Hannah Brown.

Stephen Atkinson (son of Stephen) m. Jane Holliday, daughter of Thomas Holliday, and died in 1765, leaving a widow and a posthumous child. His will is of record at Lancaster and is dated Sept. 5, 1765. Thomas Holliday was a brother of Adam Holliday, who laid out Hollidaysburg in 1768. (See Notes and Queries, 1897 series.)

Wilton Atkinson married Ann Maria Leroy, at St. James' Episcopal Church, Lancaster, Pa., on April 24, 1762, and left issue, two daughters and three sons. The sons names were Thomas-Wilton, Matthew-Abraham and William-Benjamin. The birth record of only one can be found and that is:

Thomas Wilton Atkinson, son of Wilton and Ann Maria Atkinson, was baptized at the Reformed Church, Lancaster, Pa., on Oct. 5, 1766, having been born June 8, 1766. Ann Maria LeRoy was a daughter of —— LeRoy and Maria ——. The will of the widow Maria LeRoy, of Heidelberg township, died about 1801, showing that she left surviving:
i. Ann-Maria, m. Thomas W. Atkinson.
ii. Maria-Salome, m. Chas. Hall.

iii. Elizabeth, m. Rev. Dr. W. Hendel. (See Notes and Queries, vol. iii, 3d series, p. 507.)

On the records of the Moravian church, Lancaster, are baptisms of Thomas Atkinson, born Oct. 1, 1815, bap. Oct. 6, 1815, sick; Matthew, bap. April 2, 1819, dying; both were children of Matthew Atkinson, printer, and his wife, who was Caroline Rabenthal.

Hannah Atkinson m. James Brown and had issue (surname Brown):
 i. Juliana.
 ii. David, m. Mary Beck, of Philadelphia, and moved west.
 iii. Harriet, m. Thomas Williams, at St. George's church, Philadelphia, Pa., in 1817, and had Harriet, who married Joseph Severns, of Philadelphia; and had Clara, who married Walter Raleigh, of Philadelphia.

The "Lancaster Journal" during September, 1796, contains an advertisement announcing the opening of a school for young ladies by Hannah Brown. Information is desired as to date of marriage of Hannah Atkinson and James Brown.

The following abstracts are from "Friend's Records in Ireland:"

"Sarah Atkinson, daughter of Stephen and Isabel, of Ballinacor, County Armagh, b. 18, 12 mo., 1656, m. John Robson, of Sligo, County Armagh, son of Francis and Isabel, on the 29, 1 mo., 1676."

"Abigail Atkinson, daughter of Stephen and Isabel, married George Bell, of Ballinderry, on the 11, 8 mo., 1692".

"Lydia Atkinson (whose parents' names are not mentioned), of Sligo, County Armagh, married Henry Hollingsworth, of Pennsylvania, America, on the 22, 6 mo., 1688."

"Edward Atkinson, died 22, 11 mo., 1865."

S. M. S.
Lancaster, Pa.

Vandegrift Burial Records.

Located on the Bristol turnpike, near Cornwall, Bucks county, Pa., is the private burial ground of the Vandegrift family. This tract was set apart by the emigrant Folkart Vandegrift from a grant of land secured by him about 1720, the exact date being effaced from the records. (See Pennsylvania Archives, 3d ser. vol. iii.)

The lot contains about an half acre of land and is used exclusively by his descendants and those marrying into the Vandegrift family. It is nearly filled with graves and kept in an excellent condition. Joseph Vandegrift, a great-grandson of the donor, takes care of the ground, digs the graves and keeps the records, but in his head only. He remembers all who have been interred in this cemetery for the past fifty years, but neither before his time nor since has any written record of an official character been kept.

It is for this reason I give below the inscriptions on the older stones as far as they are decipherable. It will preserve the names of some of the earliest settlers in this section of Bensalem township, Bucks county. I find that the church records in this neighborhood are next to worthless, being inaccurate, registries having been made without dates and often without full names, thereby making it impossible to discover the sex of persons where simply the family name is shown.

Vandegrift, Folkart, b. 1695; d. Oct. 24, 1775.
Vandegrift, John, b. 1723; d. Mar. 25, 1805.
Vandegrift, Catherine, wf. of John, b. Oct. 11, 1735; d. Jany. 16; 1794.
Vandegrift, Mary, wf. of John, b. 1726; d. Aug. 3, 1784.
Vandegrift, Jacob, b. 1696; d. Mar. 26, 1771.
Vandegrift, Jane, wf. of Jacob, b. 1697; d. April 15, 1766.
Vandegrift, Jacob, b. 1731; d. Oct. 7, 1769.
 Farewell friends and wife so dear,
 I'm not dead but sleeping here;
 My debts are paid, my grave you see,
 Prepare for death and follow me.
Vandegrift, John, husband of Ann, b. 1687; d. Aug. 27, 1765.
Vandegrift, Elizabeth, wf. of Joseph, b. 1736; d. Sep. 21, 1772.
Vandegrift, Catherine, wf. of Joseph, b. 1743; d. Mar. 8, 1781.
Vandegrift, Abraham, b. 1698; d. Feb. 20, 1781.
Vandegrift, Charity, wf. of Abraham Van-

degrift, sen., b. July, 1700; d. Jan. 6, 1786.
Vandegrift, Folkart, b. 1734; d. Oct. 10, 1795.
Vaudegrift, Elizabeth, wf. of Folkart, b. 1735; d. Apr. 5, 1813.
Vandegrift, Catherine, b. 1731; d. Dec. 31, 1772.
Vandegrift, Jacob, b. March 3, 1729; d. Apr. 28, 1800.
Vandegrift, Sarah, 2d wf. of Jacob, b. 1742; d. Oct. 14, 1822.
Vandegrift, Jacob, b. 1763; d. Aug. 10, 1808.
Vandegrift, Benjamin, b. 1761; d. Jan. 29, 1811.
Vandegrift, Elizabeth, wf. of Benj., b. 1769; d. Apr. 11, 1844.
Vandegrift, Amos, b. Oct. 28, 1768; d. Sep. 2, 1817.
Vandegrift, Hannah, wf, of Amos, b. Jan. 14, 1769; d. Mar. 9, 1854.
Spunway, Catherine, dau. of Francis Le Jau, b. 1700; d. July 10, 1750.
Daniel, Margeret, b. 1727; d. Aug. 1, 1745.
Van Kirk, Barnet, b. 1747; d. Sept. 17, 1817.
Van Kirk, William, b. 1764; d. Mar. 14, 1817.
Van Sant, Abraham, b. April, 1779; d. June 30, 1821.
Van Sant, Mary, wf. of Abraham, b. Feb. 6, 1755; d. Oct. 1, 1810.
Vanhorn, John, b. 1698; d. Feb. 15, 1758.
Aublag, Edmund, b. Jan. 18, 1767; d. May 30, 1796.
Jackson, Jacob, b. 1740; d. Jan. 31, 1814.
Jackson, Martha, wf. of Jacob, b. Aug. 20, 1740; d. Nov. 20, 1809.
Jackson, John, b. 1739; d. Jan. 26, 1766.
McMullen, Alexander, b. Aug. 25, 1750; d. Jan. 28, 1787.
McMullen, Abigail, wf. of Alex, b. 1753; d. April 29, 1783.
McMullen, Elizabeth, wf. of Alex, b. 1757; d. Aug. 19, 1786.
McMullen, Isaac, b. 1784; d. May 26, 1823.
McMullen, Rebecca, wf. of Alex, b. 1766; d. July 13, 1825.
McMullen, John, b. 1759; d. April 30, 1824.
McMullen, Mary, wf. of John, b. 1765; d. Oct. 3, 1823.
States, Elizabeth, dau. of Alex and Rebecca McMullen, b. 1791; d. July 24, 1823.
Oliver, Rees, b. 1769; d. Aug. 13, 1798.

G. U. HART.

Philadelphia.

Will of Col. William Crawford.

The will of Colonel William Crawford, dated 16th May, 1792; proved September 10, 1782, and recorded 29th Dec. 1819, in Will Book No. 1, page 9, in the Register's office in and for Westmoreland county, Penna. It reads as follows:

"In the name of God. Amen. I, William Crawford, of the county of Westmoreland, and State of Pennsylvania, being in perfect health of body and sound memory, do make, ordain and constitute this my last will and testament in manner and form following, that is to say:

"I give and bequeath unto my much beloved wife, Hannah Crawford all that tract of land wherein I now live, situate lying and being on the River Youghioghania, in the county and State aforesaid, during her natural life. I do also give and bequeath unto my said wife one negro man named Dick and one mulatto man Daniel, also all my household furniture and stock of every kind and nature whatsoever for and during her natural life and after the decease of my said wife the above mentioned negroes, Dick and Daniel, to descend to my loving son, John Crawford, and after his decease to the heirs of his body and lawfully begotten.

"I give and bequeath unto my loving son, John Crawford, and his heirs lawfully begotten, five hundred acres of land to be laid off out of lands located down the River Ohio by me, to be laid off by my executors, reserving to my son the choice of said lands and also the tract of land wherein I now live at Stewart's Crossings, at the decease of my said wife, Hannah; and at the decease of said son, John Crawford, to descend to his son, William Crawford, and his heirs forever, but if he die without heirs then and in that case to descend to his next eldest brother.

"And I do give and bequeath unto Moses Crawford, son of the above said John Crawford and to his heirs forever, four hundred acres of land to be laid off out of my lands located down the River Ohio as before mentioned.

"I do give and bequeath unto Richard Crawford, son of the above said John Crawford, and to his heirs forever, four hundred acres of land out of and to be laid off as above mentioned. I do give and bequeath unto Anne McCormick, daughter of William and Effe McCormick, four hundred acres of land to be laid off as above mentioned. Also I do give and bequeath unto Anne Connell all that tract of land whereon she now lives, lying and being on the north side of Youghioghania River, about two miles from said river, and on Braddock's old road, together with all the stock of every kind whatsoever and all the household furniture and farming utentials now in her possession for and during her natural life, and after the said Anne Connell's decease my will is and I do hereby ordain that the said land, goods and chattels of every kind whatsoever be sold by my executors and the money arising therefrom be equally divided amongst her four children, to wit: William, James, Nancy and Polly, but nevertheless in case the said Anne Connell should think it more proper that the two boys or either of them, the said William or James, should keep the said land, &c., that then and in that case the said lands, goods and chattels of every kind be appraised and an equal fourth of the said appraisement be paid to the other children as they may arrive at the age by law affixed, or the survivors of them. Also do I give and bequeath unto William Connell son of the said Anne Connell, and his heirs forever, five hundred acres of land located by me down the Ohio River, there being a warrant for that quantity in his name from the land office, Virginia.

"Also I give and bequeath unto James Connell, son of the said Anne Connell, and his heirs forever, five hundred acres of land down the River Ohio, there being a warrant for that quantity in his name, which was also located by me as above mentioned, as soon as they arrive at full age.

Also do I give and bequeath unto Nancy and Polly, daughters of said Anne Connell, six hundred acres of land located by me down the River Ohio to be equally divided between them by my executors. And my will is that after my accounts are adjusted and settled and all my just debts and legacies and bequeaths paid, that all and singular my estate, real and personal of every kind and whatsoever, except a mulatto boy named Martin, which I give to my son John Crawford, and a mulatto girl named Hannah, be equally divided between my three beloved children, viz: John Crawford, Effe McCormick and Sarah Harrison, and their heirs forever.

And I do will, constitute and appoint my much beloved wife, Hanna Crawford, my loving brother, John Stephenson, and William Harrison, executrix and executors of this my last will and testament, ratifying and confirming this to be my last will and testament.

"In witness whereof I have hereunto set my hand and affixed my seal this sixteenth day of May, in the year of our Lord one thousand seven hundred and eighty-two.

W. CRAWFORD.

"Signed, sealed, published, pronounced and declared by the said William Crawford as his last will and testament in the presence of us,

Thos. Gist,
John Ecales,
Mary Wright,
Nancy McKee.

NOTES AND QUERIES.

Historical, Biographical, and Genealogical.

XIII.

CONRAD WEISER.

A correspondent sends Notes and Queries the following, taken from the Universal Magazine of Knowledge and Pleasure," London, November, 1749: "They write from Philadelphia that on the 13th of August last, arrived there Conrad Weiser, Esq., and with him the deputies of eleven different nations of Indians, in order to transact some affairs with that government, viz., the Deputies of the Onondagas, Senecas, Mohawks, Cayugas, Oneidas, Tuscaroras, Shawanese, Nanticokes, Delawares, Mohigans and Tutelos; the whole number amounting to 260 persons."

Reynolds Family Data.

John Reynolds was born near Lancaster in 17—. He was the son of William Reynolds, a Protestant Irishman, who came to America in 1762 and who was in the "Flying Camp" in 1776. In 1778 he married Catharine Ferree Le Fevre, great granddaughter of Mary Ferree, a French Huguenot, who had come from the Rhine Provinces and whose ancestors settled in Lancaster county in 1711.

John Reynolds, son of the foregoing, married a ——— Moore and had William and John Fulton Reynolds, the latter being born in 1787. John Fulton Reynolds also married a Moore, Lydia by name, and had among other children the late Admiral Reynolds and General John F. Reynolds.

William Reynolds, of Strasburg township, left widow Catherine and heirs, Samuel, William, John and Lydia. His will was probated Sept. 28, 1801.

William Reynolds was the eldest son of John and Mary Magaw Reynolds and was born in Hopewell township, Cumberland, then Lancaster county, in 1730. He was commissioned a lieutenant on Dec. 19, 1757, in Colonel James Burd's battalion; was wounded at Fort Duquesne Sept. 17, 1758, and resigned March 17, 1760. He died in February, 1769. Married to Margaret Williamson and had issue: Mary, Agnes, Margaret and one dead (name unknown). "Notes and Queries," Third Series, vol. iii, p. 233.

David Reynolds, 1734-1816. Private in Third company, Capt. John Dixon, Third battalion, Col. Comfort Sage, General James Wadsworth's brigade, Connecticut militia, 1776. Private in Captain Paul Brigham's company, Fifth brigade, Conn. Line, Jan 1, 1787. Jan. 1, 1783, at Long Island and White Plains.

Thomas Reynolds, lieutenant-colonel Second regiment, Burlington county, New Jersey militia. Promoted colonel June 6, 1777. Resigned Dec. 18, 1782. Prisoner of war and paroled; exchanged for Colonel Simcoe, British Foot.

William Reynolds, ———, 1792. Private 24th Regt., Conecticut militia, Colonel Nathan Denison, in a detachment commanded by Colonel Zebulon Butler, June 24-Oct. 1, 1778.   S. M. SENER.
Lancaster, Pa.

Cumberland County Marriages.

Loudon, Archibald, m. Nov. 17, 1796, Mrs. Hannah Holcham.

Ligget, James, of Newberry township, York county, m. Isabella Hannah, Oct. 31, 1797, of Lisburn, Allen township.

Lyne, John, m. Dec. 13, 1798, Miss Barbara Lefevre.

Latshaw, Joseph, m. Nov. 21, 1799, Miss Polly Riddle, both of Carlisle.

Linn, William, of Franklin county, m. Jane, dau. of Abraham Smith, of Cumberland county, Dec. 18, 1800, by Rev. Francis Herron.

Longenecker, Martin, m. June 14, 1801, Mrs. Weiser, of Carlisle.

Line, Henry, m. Jan. 12, 1802, Letitia Coleman, both of East Pennsboro'.

Logue, Joseph, m. Feb. 11, 1802, Nancy Jumper, dau. of Conrad Jumper.

Laird, James, Esq., of Frankfort township, m. May 27, 1802, Mrs. Allen, of Baltimore.

Loudon, Archibald, Peggy, dau. of, m. Jan. 12, 1804, David Woods, of Dickinson township.

Lyon, John, m. April 29, 1808, by Rev. Mr. Sharon, Jane, dau. of late William Maclay.

Leyburn, James, m. April 13, 1804, Miss Anne McGabey, both of Carlisle.

Leckey, George, m. Nov. 22, 1808, Miss Crowell, dau. of Capt. Crowell, of Newville.

Longenecker, Isaac, m. Feb. 8, 1810, Veronico Eshleman, both of Cumberland county.

Leib, Gen. Michael, m. at Philadelphia, Nov. 9, 1808, by Rev. White, Miss Susan Kennedy, of that place.

Lacock, Gen. Abner, of Beaver, Bethsheba, dau. of, m. Aug. 31, 1809, Ephraim Pentland, Esq., editor of "The Commonwealth," of Beaver.

Lyon, Alice, dau. of William Lyon, dec'd., m., March 6, 1810, George Chambers, Esq., of Chambersburg.

Lamberton, Jane, dau. o James Lamberton, Esq., of Carlisle, m. April 12, 1810, John Noble, of Carlisle, by Rev. Mr. Wilson.

Loudon, Archibald, Miss Rebecca Hocham, step-daughter of, m. Alexander I. W. Jackson, printer, May 8, 1810, by Rev. Mr. Campbell.

Lowrey, James, Esq., Senator for Cumberland county, m. Mrs. Peebles, widow of Col. Robert Peebles, late of Franklin county, May 24, 1810, at Shippensburg.

Lyon, Rebecca, formerly of Carlisle, m. at Washington, Pa., by Rev. Matthew Brown, Feb. 6, 1812, James M. Russell, Esq., of Bedford.

Lenich, David, m. Nov. 5, 1816, Elizabeth Butler, both of Carlisle, by Rev. Richard Tydings.

Ludlam, Smith, m. Dec. 26, 1816, Polly, dau. of John Reed, innkeeper, of Carlisle, by Rev. Mr. Tydings.

Lechler, Henry, m. Dec. 26, 1816, Catharine Copp, of Harrisburg, bq Rev. Mr. Keller.

Murray, George, m. June 21, 1804, by Rev. Dr. Davidson, Polly Denny, all of Carlisle.

McKnight, Elizabeth, m. Nov. 8, 1803, Hugh Moffet, both of West Pennsboro'.

McClellan, Joseph, m. June 26, 1788, Polly Irwin.

McKibben, twin brothers of, m. June 22, 1790, twin sisers of Beard, of Clark's Gap, Franklin county.

Magaw, Dr. William, of Mercersburg, m. Oct. 20, 1790, Miss McDowell, dau. of William McDowell, Esq.

Morrison, James, Esq., of Pittsburgh, m. Sept. 28, 1791, Esther Montgomery, dau. of John Montgomery, Esq.

McDannell, Daniel, Jr., m. Jan. 17, 1793, Elizabeth Jumper, dau. of Conrad Jumper, of Cumberland county.

Michael, Wendle, merchant, of Carlisle, m. July 30, 1795, Miss Margaret Clouser, of Cumberland county, by Rev. Mr. Dubendorf.

Montgomery, John, Jr., Esq., Attorney-at-Law, of the State of Maryland, m. June 2, 1796, at York, Miss Polly Harris, dau. of William Harris, Esq., of York.

McClure, Charles, m. March 9, 1797, Mrs. Rebecca Parker, dau. of William Blair.

McKeehan, Capt. George, of West Pennsboro', m. Jan. 12, 1801, Jane Johnston, dau. of James Johnston, of Frankford township.

McIntyre, Thomas, m. Jan. 7, 1801, Polly McAlister, both of this county.

Martin, Samuel, of Cumberland county, m. Feb. 5, 1801, Mrs. Polly Taylor, of Monaghan township, York county.

McClintock, John, of Middleton township, Patsy, dau. of, m. April 23, 1801, Richard Gilson, of East Pennsboro'.

McKinstry, James, of Dickinson township, m. June, 1801, Jane, dau. of John McCullough, of West Pennsboro'.

McCullough, William, m. June 23, 1801, Sarah, dau. of Alexander McBride, Jr., of Dickinson township.

Morel, David Louis, aged 66 years, m., Jan. 14, 1802, at Petersburgh, Rye township, "The agreeable Miss Nancy Huston, aged 19 years."

McCullough, Matthew, m. Feb. 1, 1803, Miss Jane Hunter, both of Mifflin township.

McClean, Robert, of Georgetown, D. C., m., June 20, 1811, Mrs. Eliza Cart, of Carlisle.

Mayer, Benjamin, editor of the German Aurora, Harrisburg, m. Aug. 1, 1809, Miss Elizabeth, dau. of Michael Wetzel, of Paxtang.

McLaughlin, Neal, of Carlisle, m. Oct. 30, 1810, by Rev. Dr. Campbell, Esther Lewis, of Dauphin county.

Moore, Howard, m. Feb. 27, 1810, Miss Waugh, both of Cumberland county.

McLean, William, m. June 21, 1810, by Rev. James Walker, of Shippensburgh, Nancy McCoobsey, both of Southampton township.

McCord, Alexander, of Shearman's Valley, m. April 9, 1812, Eliza Shrom, of Carlisle.

McClure, Polly dau. of Charles McClure, dec'd., m. Aug. 20, 1812, Joseph Knox, merchant, of Carlisle.

McCool, David, m. April 1, 1813, at the home of David Moreland, Esq., in Shearman's Valley, Mary Morrison, both of Toboyne.

Miller, John, saddler, of Newville, m. April 15, 1813, Catharine Butt, step-daughter of Jacob Keigley, stocking weaver, of Carlisle.

McCoy, Robert, Esq., m. June 29, 1813, Elizabeth Dunn, dau. of Andrew Dunn, both of Carlisle.

Martin, Benjamin, m. Oct. 28, 1813, Sally Long, both of Toboyne township.

McCord, Andrew, Esq., P. M. at Newville, m. Feb. 13, 1814, Miss Davidson, dau. of John Davidson, of West Pennsboro', by Rev. Williams.

Ann Kirkpatrick 1750-1842.

The subject of this sketch was born on the banks of the Swatara, on the farm adjoining the present borough of Middletown, January 11, 1750. Her father, William Kirkpatrick, son of Samuel, of Armagh, Ireland, emigrated to America in 1738, became possessed of a large body of land at Middletown, much of which is now owned by the Frey estate, married Margaret Waugh, and died there in 1760, at the early age of 41, leaving a wife, two sons, John and and William, and two daughters, Ann and Sarah. He was buried in a picturesque spot on the brow of the hill above his house, overlooking the winding course of the Swatara as it emerges from the bluffs beyond and mingles its waters with those of the broad Susquehanna. His grave was afterwards surrounded by a wall of red sandstone from the neighboring quarries, which incloses a space about sixteen feet square, and it is probable that his son John rests within the same enclosure as no mention of him is made in the settlement of the estate, and tradition has it that one of the children was buried there. At the present moment this spot presents the aspect of a small clump of trees, surrounded by a dilapidated wall, in the center of a cultivated field, and in times gone by, was given a wide berth by the superstitious dwellers in the region around about.

Mr. Kirkpatrick was a man of means and intelligence, and was doubtless somewhat in advance of his age, as he made special provision in his will for the education of his daughters, directing that they be "brought up and trained in a manner suitable to their station," leaving his wife as principal executrix and sole manager of his estate until the youngest child should reach the age of twenty-one, a period, in this case, of about two decades.

Ann was ten years old when her father died, and nine years later she married Josiah Espy, of Hanover township, near Indiantown Gap, where they began housekeeping, but soon afterwards purchased and took possession of the estate in Paxtang, now Susquehanna township, Dauphin county, at present owned in part by the heirs of William Trullinger; here they spent the remainder of their lives, Mr. Espy passing away on the 23d day of July, 1813, and she remaining until May 30th, 1842.

During the Revolutionary War, Mr. Espy, in common with every other ablebodied Scotch-Irishman in Paxtang, devoted much of his time to public affairs, and the fact that he and others who had wives and children were able to do this and at the same time contribute of their substance to the cause, speaks volumes for the energy, ability and patriotism of the women, upon whom rested, very largely, the domestic interests of the community during the struggle for independence. In this respect Ann Kirkpatrick proved herself equal to the situation. The multitudinous affairs of the old time farm establishment were almost as well conducted as when the master himself was at the helm, nor was the education of the children for a moment neglected, especially the shorter catechism side of it, of which it has been said that even the youngest, "tho' scarcely longer than my leg, could screed you off effectual calling as fast as any in the dwalling."

In person Ann Kirkpatrick was of medium height, blue eyes, fair complexion, symetrical figure and a countenance which betokened intelligence and geniality. Intellectually she was endowed with a memory so astonishing that her husband found it unnecessary to trouble himself with account books, as to minor affairs, relying solely upon her unerring recollection of details. This faculty, coupled with her habit of reading almost every book that came her way, rendered her one of the best conversationalists of her time. During her long widowhood, after her children were settled in life, she spent considerable time travelling, chiefly on horseback, visiting friends in Wilkes-Barre, Bedford, Gettysburg, Lewisburg, Lancaster, etc., excursions which required as much time and energy as a trip around the globe in these days of her great-grandchildren, the relation of the "uncos" of which afforded vastly more entertainment to the home people than the stories of the "globe trotters" of to-day. In her later years it was a great treat to make one of a company around the evening fire and listen to her graphic accounts of bygone events. Unfortunately she committed nothing to paper and there was no Boswell among her hearers.

The estimation in which she was held by her contemporaries can be gathered from an obituary notice written doubtless by Rev. James Sharon, from which we quote a few paragraphs:

"Died.—At the residence of her son, in Susquehanna township, Dauphin county, on Monday, the 30th day of May, 1842. Mrs. Ann Kirkpatrick Espy, in the 93d year of her age. Her remains were interred in the Paxton burying ground on Wednesday last. 'And she died in a good old age, full of years, and was gathered to her people.' The brief but appropriate and impressive language of the Bible, used to note the death of an aged patriarch, who lived out his years and God took to himself, is almost all that is necessary to add to the record of this good and venerable lady's decease. Of no disease; of no blast, she died." * * * * * "Her character as a member of society needs no panegyric; it was formed by all those qualities * * * which make up the characters of the truly good. To the largest extent of her means, she was charitable and beneficent; the highest pleasure of her life was in contributing to the comfort and happiness of those who surrounded her. * * * * * And with so little display was her charity administered that * * * the recipients of her bounty knew not, frequently the hand and the heart from whence the kindness came. * * * Mrs. Espy was the oldest person residing in Dauphin county at her decease, and never resided out of its present limits." * * *
W. F. R.

NOTES AND QUERIES.

Historical, Biographical, and Genealogical.

XIV.

LIVINGHOUSE.

Frederick Livinghouse, or Leveringhouse, was born in Morrison's Cove, Bedford county, Pa., about 1790. He married in 1814, Elizabeth Jacobs, daughter of Daniel Jacobs, of that locality. Two sons, Daniel and William, were born in Pennsylvania. He subsequently removed to Montgomery county, O., and later to Indiana. What information can be gained of the ancestors of this family? F. A. L.
Lincoln, Neb.

AGNEW.

James Agnew, with other Scotch-Irish emigrants, settled on Marsh creek, York now Adams county, Pa. David Agnew, his son, settled in Franklin county, and married, in 1777, Mary Erwin [Irwin]. It is recorded of David Agnew that he was quite as ready to resist oppression as his ancestors had been, and at the outset of the Revolution, espoused the patriot cause. I am desirous of ascertaining the services of James Agnew in the early days of Penn's Province. M. V. A.
Alexandria, Va.

DERR—SWINEHART.

Prior to 1734 Christopher Wagenseil settled in Hanover township, Philadelphia, now Montgomery county, Pa., near Pennsburg. He had two daughters, Mary Ann, who married John Derr, and Elizabeth Catharine married David Haag. The Derr and Haag ancestors and descendants are desired.

John Wagenseil, a son of Christopher Wagenseil, had daughters: Susanna, m. Conrad Swinehart; Anna-Maria, m. Benjamin Royer, and Maria-Margaret, m. Matthias Walter. The descendants of these families are desired.
G. W. WAGENSELLER.
Middleburgh, Pa.

A LOST MANUSCRIPT.

A correspondent of "Notes and Queries" writes to this effect: "Would like to purchase the manuscript of 'The Return of the Spinsters from Oklohoma.' If any of our readers can furnish a reply, address 'M. S. P., P. O. Box 24, Henderson, Ky.'"

SMITH—GRIER.

John Jacob Smith, of Lancaster, Pa., m. Catharine Greer and had issue:
  i. John-Jacob, m. —— Reigart.
  ii. Nancy, m. March 22, 1810, Joseph Severus and had issue: Joseph Severus, m. Harriet Wiliams, and they had Clara, m. Walter Raleigh.
  iii. Sarah, m. —— McKenny.
  iv. Susan, m. —— Duncan.
  v. Catharine, m. —— Reigart.
  vi. Mary, m. —— Frey.
  vii. Betsy, m. Jabez Carter.
  viii. Martin, m. Jan. 14, 1803; m. Lucy Yates in 1828.
  ix. James-Grier, b. 1805.

Information is desired concerning ancestry of Catharine Greer or Grier.

S. M. S.
Lancaster, Pa.

Colonel Archibald Lochry.

Next to the sad story of the commander of the expedition to the Sandusky Indian towns, Colonel William Crawford, in 1782, is the brief recital of the mournful tragedy near the mouth of the Miami on the 24th of August, 1781, when the gallant Col. Lochry fell a victim to Indian hate. It is not the purpose of the writer at this time to give an account of the ill-fated expedition which had been sent to the relief of Gen. Clark, who had been directed to capture Vincennes from the British. Archibald Lochry, son of Jeremiah Lochry, was born April 15, 1733, in the North of Ireland. His father emigrated with his family to Pennsylvania prior to the year 1740, locating on the extreme confines of Cumberland county in what was subsequently Lurgan township. Here the father died prior to 1750, and his children were brought up as youthful pioneers. During the French and Indian war Archibald Lochry was commissioned July 10, 1763, an ensign in the Second battalion of the provincial forces, his elder brother, Jeremiah, also being an officer in the service. After Bouquet had compelled the Northwest Indians to sue for peace, he took up large tracts of land, in what was subsequently Westmoreland county. Here he and some members of his family located. The principal tract lies in what is now Unity township. The land is quite valuable, being underlaid with the thick vein of Connellsville coal. He dated his official correspondence at the "Twelve-Mile Run," which was the name of the small stream which flows into the Fourteen-Mile Run before it empties into the Loyalhanna. When the War of the Revolution opened he was one of the active spirits of that patriotic section of the State, and his services throughout the struggle were gallant and heroic. In the summer of 1781, in command of several companies, he was ordered to the support of General Clark's forces in the western country. Embarking in frail boats, Col. Lochry's command reached Fort Henry, where they were to join those of General Clark. They pushed on down the river, but their provisions and forage having been nearly exhausted, the army halted at a spot which appeared to have attracted them by its inviting beauty. They had not been many hours in the locality when they were attacked by Indians awaiting them in ambush. Few escaped save those who escaped after being taken prisoners. Col. Lochry was among the first who were killed. The entire story is a sad one, and yet it remains to be written in full. Will not some of those interested in the early history of Western Pennsylvania take up the subject, and do justice to the exploits and memory of as brave a pioneer as ever lived—the gallant Colonel Archibald Lochry? A correspondent has sent us a copy of Colonel Lochry's will, which is on record at Greensburgh:

The will is dated Nov. 20, 1778, and probated before James Kinkaid, Esq., by Jeremiah Lochry and George Henry, on July 11, 1782. Recorded in Will Book No. 1, page 31, in the office of the Register of Wills in and for Westmoreland county, Pa.

"In the name of God, amen! I, Archibald Lochry, of Hannastown, in Westmoreland county, etc., being through the goodness of God in sound judgment and memory, therefore calling to mind the mortality of my body and that it is appointed for all men once to die, do make this my last will and testament that is to say:

"Principally and first of all, I give and bequeath my soul to God, who gave it, beseeching his most gracious acceptance of it in and through the merits and mediation of my most compassionate Saviour and Redeemer Jesus Christ. My body I give to the earth, nothing doubting but I shall receive the same again at the general resurrection, and as touching such worldly estate as I am blessed with in this world, it is my will and order that all my just debts be fully paid and that my public accounts may be settled with all convenient speed; and it is my will that all and singular my estate, real and personal, shall be equally divided between my well beloved wife and my only daughter Elizabeth. My land adjoining Col. John Proctor to be rented until my said daughter arrives at the age of twenty-one years, and one-half the rents thereof applied for her boarding and schooling, the other half for the use of my wife, and in case one or either of them should die before my daughter comes to age or is married, the whole to devolve to the survivor and all my claims or rights to my lands, only the lands above mentioned, I desire may be sold.

"And I hereby constitute and appoint John Proctor whole and sole executor of this, my last will and testament, to see it duly executed according to my true interest and meaning, revoking and disannuling all former wills, ratifying and confirming this and no other to be my last will and testament.

"Witness my hand and seal this 20th November, 1778.
"A LOCHRY.
"Signed, sealed pronounced and declared and confirmed in presence of
JEREMIAH LOCHRY,
DAVID PHILSON,
JAMES KINKAID.
"Thanks to God I am now in my right senses, and do allow this to be my last will and testament, except that my daughter Betsey to receive her equal lots of my estate. A. LOCHRY.
Attest:
JEREMIAH LOCHRY,
GEORGE HENRY.

"I, John Proctor, the executor within named, do by these presents absolutely, freely and voluntarily resign my right of executorship to the within will, but will for the sake of the deceased and his relict, join in administration with the widow. Witness my hand, the 11th day of July, 1782.
Attest: JOHN PROCTOR.
WM. JACK,
JOHN PUMROY.
Proved by Jeremiah Lochry and George Henry, the 11th July, 1782, before James Kinkaid.

Col. Lochry had two children, viz: Elizabeth and Jane [or Jean], born April 15th, 1776, and August 3d, 1780, respectively. One of the children was born after the Colonel had written his will. Colonel Lochry was killed by the Indians August 24, 1781.

Mrs. Lochry afterwards became the wife of Captain John Guthrie and they had issue. Mrs. Lochry was a daughter of Capt. Joseph Erwin, of the Ninth Pennsylvania Regiment, who died in Armstrong county, Pa., in 1825, leaving to survive him a widow, Elizabeth Erwin.

i. Elizabeth Lochry, b. April 15, 1776; d. 1860; m. David McBryar, son of Nathaniel McBryar; he died in 1843. They had issue (surname MrBryar):
 1. James.
 2. Mary, m. John Duff.
 3. David.
 4. Nathaniel-Watson.
 5. John.

ii. Jane (Jean) Lochry, b. Aug. 3, 1780; m. Samuel Thompson and had issue (surname Thompson):
 1. Alexander.
 2. Mary, m. Andrew Garley.
 3. Nancy
 4. William.
 5. Elizabeth, d. 25th Feb. 1852; m.

31st May, 1832, Joseph McQuilkin.
6. Sarah, b. 1804; d. Jan. 1890; m. Nov. 24, 1824, John Paul.
7. David.
8. Jane, m. Thomas Adair.
9. Lydia.
10. Lucy.
11. Watson.
12. Samuel.

TOMBSTONE RECORD

From Town Graveyard, Carlisle, of Persons Born Prior to 1800.

[Notes and Queries are indebted to two indefatigable correspondents at Carlisle, Pa., for the "Record" given in this and several succeeding numbers. Many of the heroes of the Revolution rest in the old graveyard at Carlisle, but unfortunately most of the graves of these patriots are unmarked. This "Record" is, however, valuable, and will preserve the names of numbers, whose names are becoming obliterated from the weather-beaten and perishable character of the stones. To the descendants far away from the old ancestral town, these will be dearly cherished.]

I.

Agnew, John, b. 1778; d. Sept. 28, 1850.
Agnew, Margaretta, wf. of John, b. 1792; d. April 11, 1852.
Agnew, Samuel, s. of John and Margaret, b. Jan. 19, 1978; d. April 13, 1838.
Alexander, Sam, b. 1788; d. 1841.
Alexander, Ann, d. June 26, 1877.
Allen, David, b. 1732; d. Nov. 10, 1790.
Allen, Sarah, b. 1738; d. Feb. 28, 1794.
Anderson, Jane, wf. of William, b. 1796; d. June 18, 1847.
Andrews, Rev. Abraham, d. Nov. 1800.
Armor, Edward P., b. 1789; d. Feb. 28, 1862.
Armor, Rebecca, wf. of E. P.
Armor, Willam, b. 1758; d. Sept. 18, 1820.
Armor, Rachel Pontone, wf. of William, b. 1762; d. June 2, 1833.
Armor, Sarah, dau. of William and R. P., b. 1798; d. Feb. 27, 1878.
Armstrong, General John, s. of James, of Brookboro, County Fermanagh, Ireland, b. 1717; d. March 9, 1795. Commander Kittaning expedition, 1756; brigadier general Continental Army, 1776; major-general Pennsylvania militia, 1777; member Continental Congress, 1778-88.
Armstrong, Rebecca Lyon, wf. of General John, b. at Enniskillen, Ireland, May 2, 1719; d. at Carlisle, Pa., Nov. 16, 1797.
Armstrong, Mary, wf. of Dr. James, dau. of George Stevenson, Esq., b. 1766; d. May 27, 1813.
Armstrong, Dr. James, b. 1746; d. May, 1828.
Armstrong, John Wilkins, M. D., s. of James, M. D., b. at Carlisle, Jan. 17, 1798; d. at Princeton, N. J., Feb. 19, 1870.
Armstrong, Mary Shell, wf. of John Wilkins, M. D., b. 1813; d. 1855.
Armstrong, James, b. 1746; d. Sept. 21, 1821.
Armstrong, wf. of Daniel, dau. of John Noble, sr., b. 1797; d. Oct. 9, 1833.
Armstrong, Mary Ann, b. 1798; d. Aug. 15, 1874.
Armstrong, James, b. 1785; d. Aug. 1,1855.
Armstrong, Robert, b. 1785; d. Oct. 8, 1839.
Auckinbaugh, Mary, b. 1780; d. May 1, 1861.
Alspaugh, Elizabeth, b. Jan. 16, 1785; d. Sept. 16, 1887.
Battersby, Haynes Wade, b. 1765; d. Oct. 14, 1840.
Bautz, Susannah, b. June 14, 1796; d. Jan. 31, 1873.
Baggs, Anna, b. Feb. 27, 1771; d. Feb. 10, 1849.
Baker, Rachel, widow of William, dau. of William Spotswood, b. April, 1789; d. Oct. 16, 1847.
Baker, Phillip, b. 1780; d. Aug. 20, 1834.
Baker, Mary M., wf. J. H. William, b. 1783; d. Jan. 12, 1855.
Baker, J. H. William, b. 1778; d. Feb. 28, 1851.
Barnet, Abram, b. May 4, 1788; d. May 7, 1881.
Barnet, Elizabeth, b. Aug. 25, 1793; d. March 1, 1878.
Baughman, Mrs. Nancy, b. Sept. 1774; d. Oct. 22, 1852.
Baughman, Christian, b. 1763; d. Sept. 8, 1812.

Bawler, Capt. Samuel, b. 1771; d. Sept, 29, 1840.
Barkley, Robert, b. 1750; d. Feb. 20, 1839.
Barkley, Isabella, wf. of Robert, d. Sept. 29, 1826.
Beers, William, b. 1793; d. Nov. 13, 1860.
Bell, Charles, b. 1749; d. Sept. 27, 1785.
Bell, Charles, b. 1786; d. July 12, 1859.
Bell, Mary Ann, wf. of Charles, b. 1789; d. July 18, 1853.
Bell, Henrietta P., dau. of Charles and Mary Ann, b. 1829; d. April 1, 1836.
Bell, Sarah, b. Oct. 3, 1775; d. Dec. 18, 1841.
Bell, John, b. April 9, ——; d. —— ——, 1859. (stone broken).
Beales, Elizabeh, b. 1773; d. Sept. 1, 1856.
Bell, James, b. 1768; d. 1842.
Bell, Hannah, b. 1771; d. 1834.
Bellman, Mary J. Bennett, wf. of Henry W., b. 1829; d. Sept. 5, 1857.
Bennett, Elizabeth, wf. of Rev. Joseph, b. March 18, 1786; d. Sept. 25, 1868.
Bentz, Weirich, b. March 15, 1789; d. Nov. 19, 1850.
Bentz, Elizabeth Follinger, wf. of Weirich, b. March 10, 1788; d. July 23, 1860.
Berry, Sarah, wf. of Jeremiah, dau. of Walter Glagett (or Clacett), b. Nov. 5, 1786; d. Dec. 28, 1857.
Boyd, Priscilla, wf. of Simon, dau. of Wm. Denny, b. 1763; d. Feb. 22, 1849.
Boyd, Simon, b. 1752; d. Oct. 6, 1816.
Burkholder, Elizabeth, b. Feb. 11, 1777; d. Dec. 29, 1836.
Biddle, Julia Montgomery, wf. of Wm. M., b. 1797; d. Feb. 23, 1883.
Biearbower, Henry, b. 1778; d. 1825.
Black, John, sr., b. Feb. 22, 1780; d. March 30, 1863.
Black, Barbara, wf. of John, sr., b. 1785; d. —— 24, 1857.
Blaine, Robert, b. 1766; d. Jan. 8, 1826.
Blaine, Susan, wf. of Robert, b. 1771; d. Aug. 19, 1853.
Blaine, Jane, wf. of James, b. 1769; d. April 15, 1793.
Blair, Wm., jr., b. 1760; d. March 21, 1792.
Blair, Susan, wf. of Wm., jr., b. 1763; d. June 9, 1827.
Blair, Susannah; Blair, Elizabeth; Blair, ——, stones partly under ground.
Blair, Henry C., b. 1792; d. June 19, 1814.

Blair, Andrew, b. 1744; d. July 21, 1816.
Blair, Elizabeth Hays, wf. of Andrew, dau. of Hays, b. 1791; d. Jan. 2, 1842.
Blair, Wm., s. of Wm. and S. [Stone pierced by a shell during shelling of Carlisle, 1863.]
Boden, Mary, wf. of A., dau. of D. and J. King, b. 1777; d. June 17, 1812.
Boden, Rebekah, wf. of Andrew, b. April 15, 1781; d. Dec. 18, 1833.
Bolander, Sarah, wf. of Conrad, b. 1780; d. Feb. 9, 1842.
Brackenridge, Hugh Henry, Judge of Supreme Court of Penn., b. 1749; d. June 25, 1816.
Bradley, Mary, wf. of Geo., b. Nov. 12, 1796; d. Sept. 5, 1849.
Bredin, James, b. 1789; d. July 2, 1838.
Brannon, Mary, wf. of John, b. 1796; d. June 24, 1880.
Bullock, Eliza, wf. of Ezekiel, b. 1797; d. Jan. 10, 1833.
Butler, John M., b. Jan. 10, 1790; d. March 4, 1874.
Butler, Martha, b. 1798; d. July 22, 1849.
Butler, Margaret, wf. of Rev. W., b. Sept., 1783; d. at Gettysburg, Aug., 1831.
Butler, Anna, wf.. of Rev. W., b. Feb. 18, 1793; d. Dec. 6, 1847.
Butler, Rev. W., b. Sept. 15, 1783; d. Jan. 11, 1852.
Call, Ann, b. 1750; d. Nov. 1, 1820.
Callender, Capt. Robert, b. 1726; d. July 29, 1776.
Callender, Mary, wf. of Capt. Robert, b. 1731; d. Sept. 21, 1765.
Callisshaw, Henrietta, b. 1794; d. April 17, 1861.
Cameron, Robert, s. of James and Margaret, b. June 14, 1799; d. Jan. 27, 1843.
Cameron, Catherine, wf. of Wm., sr., b. May 16, 1799; d. Aug. 15, 1862.
Cameron, Wm., husband of Catherine, b. 1791; d. Aug. 20, 1869.
Campbell, Rev. John, b. 1752; d. May 16, 1819.
Carothers, Isabella, wf. of Andrew, b. Sept. 2, 1786; d. June 4, 1881.
Carter, John, b. Dec. 25, 1800; d. Oct. 19, 1872.
Carter, William Farley, b. Jan. 16, 1796; d. June 29, 1813.
Chambers, Margaret, consort of Robert, b. 1755; d. May 2, 1790.

Chambers, Robert, b. 1740; d. Sept., 1802.
Chambers, Jane, dau. of Robert, b. 1776; d. Feb., 1797.
Chambers, Ruhamah, dau. of Robert, b. 1788; d. May 10, 1800.
Chambers, Wm., b. 1744; d. Dec. 6, 1809.
Chambers, Arthur, b. Nov. 22, 1792; d. March 16, 1814.
Clark, Ann, b. Sept. 6, 1779; d. Aug. 3, 1865.
Clark, Joseph, b. 1771; d. May 18, 1845.
Clark, Wm., b. 1740; d. March 28, 1804.
Clark, Margaret, wf. of William, b. 1740; d. Sept. 9, 1821.
Clark, Mary, dau. of Wm., b. 1779; d. Oct. 31, 1829.
Clark, Nancy, wf. of Robert, b. 1772; d. March 17, 1823.
Clark, Robert, b. July 2, 1774; d. Jan. 7, 1850.
Clark, Margaret, wf. of Robert, b. 1785; d. Nov. 30, 1865.
Clark, Sarah, b. 1790; d. Dec. 6, 1859.
Cook, Capt. David, b. 1767; d. July 11, 1842.
Cook, Hannah, consort of Capt. David, b. 1782; d. Jan. 5, 1837.
Cornman, Anna M., b. 1800; d. Oct. 9, 1882.
Cornman, John, b. 1787; d. April 17, 1862.
Crabb, Plunkett A., b. 1788; d. 1850.
Craighead, Thomas, b. March, 1738; d. Nov. 13, 1808.
Craighead, Margaret, wf. of Thomas, b. 1740; d. Dec. 17, 1815.
Craighead, Richard, b. 1765; d. July 3, 1848.
Craighead, Wm., b. April 23, 1779; d. Dec. 15, 1843.
Craighead, Hetty Weakley, b. July 10, 1789; d. March 24, 1875.
Craighead, Mary, wf. of George, b. 1780; d. June 15, 1839.
Craighead, Geo., b. 1773, d. Aug. 30, 1848.
Craighead, Jane, b. May 7, 1765; d. Feb. 23, 1809.
Graighead, John, b. Jan., 1764; d. Feb. 19, 1814.
Craighead, Rebecca, wf. of Thos., b. July 27, 1773; d. Aug. 21, 1858.
Craighead, Wm., s. of Thos. and Rebecca, b. Feb. 5, 1798; d. Nov. 5, 1844.
Cregg, Phebe M., wf. of James, b. 1782; d. Sept. 5, 1862.

Cregg, James, b. April 16, 1776; d. June 10, 1848.
Crider, Mary, b. 1790; d. June 18, 1874.
Cullin, David, b. 1790; d. Aug. 28, 1827.
Crawford, Eunice, b. 1774; d. Aug. 20, 1802.
Collier, Lieut. Joseph, b. 1755; d. 1799. Served in American army from commencement of the war to the end of it in 1785.
Creigh, Jane, wf. of John, Esq., b. 1749; d. Oct. 31, 1808.
Creigh, Jane, mother of John, Esq., b. 1716; d. Jan. 9, 1797.
Creigh, John, Esq., b. 1741; d. Feb. 13, 1813.
Creigh, Thomas, Esq., b. 1768; d. Oct. 29, 1809.
Creigh, Ann Hunter, wf. of Rev. Thomas Creigh, dau. of James O. and Margaret Jacobs, of Lancaster Co., Pa., b. July 3, 1809; d. Oct. 16, 1836.
Creigh, Dr. John, b. 1772; d. Nov. 7, 1848.
Creigh, Eleanor, wf. of Dr. John, b. 1774; d. Aug. 11, 1861.
Davis, Mary, wf. of Joshua, b. 1764; d. Sept. 1848.
Denny, Nancy, dau. of Wm., b. 1768; d. Jan. 11, 1845.
Denny, Wm., b. 1781; d. March 27, 1848.
Davidson, Agnes, mother of R. D. D. D.
Davidson, Abigail, wf. of R. D., D. D., d. 1806.
Davidson, Margaret, wf. of R. D., D. D., b. 1781; d. March 27, 1809.
Davidson, Robert, D. D., b. 1750; d. Dec. 13, 1812.
Day, Elizabeth, b. 1782; d. May 16, 1817.
Dinkle, Rebecca, b. Oct. 10, 1785; d. June 26, 1845.
Dinkle, Rebecca R., b. 1827; d. Sept. 19, 1840.
Dinkle, Daniel, b. Jan. 4, 1779; d. July 18, 1854.
Dixon, Catherine, b. Aug. 22, 1768; d. May 28, 1842.
Donavan, Mary, b. Jan. 28, 1799; d. April 11, 1865.
Donnelly, John, b. Feb. 10, 1776; d. Oct. 10, 1834.
Donnelly, Dorothy, wf. of John, b. Nov., 1778; d. May 5, 1842.

Dorward, Sabina Sener, b. Feb. 22, 1766; d. March 10, 1846.
Douglass, John, b. 1738; d. April 30, 1803.
Douglass, Margaret, widow of John, b. in Dublin, Ireland, 1749; d. Sept. 5, 1804.
Dowling, Catherine, wf. of Daniel, b. March 16, 1784; d. Dec. 25, 1856.
Duey, Jacob, b. 1787; d. Aug, 15, 1862.
Duey, Sarah, b. 1794; d. June 14, 1874.
Duey, Hester, wf. of Jacob, b. June 22, 1793; d. Sept. 28, 1867.
Douglas, Agnes, b. 1778; d. April 14, 1848.
Douglas, Wm., b. 1741; d. Dec. 10, 1833.
Duncan, Margaret Loue, wf. of Stephen D., b. at the Island of Bermuda, June 20, 1793; d. Dec. 20, 1813.
Duncan, Robert Callender, s. of Thos. and Martha D., b. 1786; d. Sept. 1, 1817.
Duncan, Thos., Esq., L. L. D., b. Nov. 20, 1760; d. Nov. 16, 1827; Judge of Supreme Court of Penn.
Duncan, Martha, wf. of Thomas, b. June, 1768; d. Feb., 1852.

S. W. PARKINSON,
M. M. WOODS.
Carlisle.

NOTES AND QUERIES.

Historical, Biographical, and Genealogical.

XV.

WESTERN PENNSYLVANIA,
During the struggle for independence, forms a series of valuable historical articles from the pen of Edgar W. Hassler of the "Dispatch," Pittsburgh, published in that newspaper. The initial number appeared in December last, and some five or six more numbers will complete them. Mr. Hassler has done good service in this work, his object being to create general public interest in the early history of Western Pennsylvania. As it is impossible to secure the issues of the "Dispatch" containing these interesting sketches, it is hoped that they be promptly put into permanent form—so that the lover of Pennsylvania history, aye of American history, may secure the collection. Mr. Hassler, no doubt, can quickly dispose of a limited edition—they deserve reproduction.

"THE FRIES REBELLION,"
By Gen. W. W. H. Davis, of Doylestown, is the latest contribution to Pennsylvania history. So little is known of this, the so-called "Window Tax War," sometimes the "Hot Water War," that the warrior-author has placed the reading public under many obligations for this interesting monograph on an episode of our State history one hundred years ago. Of the causes which led to this incipient rebellion against a revenue measure of the Federal Government the author enters into detail, and gives many new facts concerning the attempt made by John Fries and others to resist the law. There is no doubt that Fries was fanatical in his zeal to oppose the government, and little account would have been paid to the Falstaff martial array gathered under his banner, had it not followed close upon that other rebellious transaction in Western Pennsylvania, the so-called Whiskey Insurrection. Fries was a deluded, ignorant fellow, but unfortunately others gave heed to him and the Federal authorities sent troops to check the outrages committed and arrest the conspirators. Fries and fourteen others were charged with treason. He was tried and with two confederates found guilty. A second trial was had with the same result, and they were duly sentenced. A violent political discussion ensued, inflaming the minds of the people, and efforts were made to obtain a reprieve. After some dissention in his Cabinet, President Adams granted a pardon. The volume is replete with interesting data, and is worth preserving. In reading the book one wonders, as in the case of prior and subsequent rebellions in the United States, if "treason" can ever be made odious.

Westmoreland County Families.

ELDER.
John Elder, of Armstrong township, made his will October 14, 1800, which was probated November 14th following. He left a wife Mary, and children:
i. Robert.
ii. Thomas.
iii. James.
iv. Joseph.
v. lizabeth.
vi. Isabella, m. Alexander Thompson.

Executors, wife, son Thomas and son-in-law Alex Thompson.

ST. CLAIR.
Andrew St. Clair, of Ligonier township, died in February, 1835, leaving his estate to his "present wife, for the maintenance and support of my children and herself."

FINDLEY.
William Findley, of Unity township, "died at 10 o'clock, Wednesday, April 4, 1821, eighty years old, and buried at Unity meeting house, April 6th, at 11 A. M." He left a wife, Mary, who died November 12, 1825, at an advanced age," and children:
i. John.
ii. Elizabeth, m. —— Patterson.
iii. Mary, m. John Black.
iv. Eleanor, m. Richard E. Carothers.
v. David; d. prior to his father and left children:
  1. Mary.
  2. Nancy.
  3. John.
  4. David.
  5. William.

Mrs. Mary Findlay Black, b. 1789; d. 1835; was editor of the "Westmoreland Intelligencer," from January, 1832, to August, 1835. William Findley Black, son of John and Mary Findley Black, b. 1807; d. 1834; was co-editor of the "Intelligencer" from January, 1834, to July 4, 1834.

Richard E. Carothers and Eleanor Findley, his wife, had issue (surname Carothers):
i. Rev. John, b. May 5, 1807; d. Nov. 27, 1880; was twice married; m. first, March 24, 1840, Sophia Huston, and secondly, January 1, 1867, Mary Kirkpatrick, dau. of Rev. David Kirkpatrick.
ii. Rev. R. Alexander.
iii. Rev. James E., b. May 6, 1821; d. March 7, 1875, leaving a widow, one daughter and one son, Rev. J. B. Carothers.
iv. Thomas.
v. Nancy.
vi. Eleanor, m. William Findley.

There were six other children.

Richard E. Carothers wih his wife and children removed from Westmoreland county, in 1830, to Rural Valley, Armstrong county, about eight miles east of Kittanning.

PUMROY.
John Pumroy, of Derry township, made his will December 10, 1808; probated March 9, 1809. He left a wife Hannah, and children:
i. Margaret, m. —— Boyd.
ii. Francis.
iii. George.
iv. John.
v. Mary, m. —— Gibson.
vi. Thomas.

LINN.
Andrew Linn, of Donegal township, made her will April 12, 1811; probated April 24, 1811. He left a wife Margaret, and a sister, Sarah Labba, of Philadelphia.

SLOAN.
Robert Sloan (township not given) made his will April 20, 1812; probated May 17, 1816. He left children:
i. Susannah.
ii. John.
iii. Ann.
iv. Elizabeth.
v. Mary.

SHIELDS.
David Shields, late of the township of Letterkenny, Cumberland county, made his will May 27, 1766; probated may 8, 1773, before Arthur St. Clair, register of wills in and for Westmoreland county. He left a wife Mary, and children:
i. Matthew.
ii. Thomas.
iii. Robert, m. and had issue:
  1. George.
  2. David.
  3. John.
  4. Matthew.
  5. Robert.
  6. James.
  7. Hannah.
iv. Isabel.
v. Rebecca.
vi. Janet.

MEHARG.
Peter MeHarg, of Fairfield township, made his will September 6, 1803. In it he

mentions his wife Ann, and children:
i. Ann, m. Samuel Knox; d. 1817; son of Robert Knox and wife nee Herron.
ii. Jean.
iii. John, m. Mary Hendricks, dau. of Abraham and Ann Hendricks.

TOMBSTONE RECORDS

From Town Graveyard, Carlisle, of Persons Born Prior to 1800.

II.

Ecker, Anna M., d. Aug. 16, 1867, aged 83y.
Ecker, John, d. April 17, 1867, aged 42y.
Eckels, Robert D., b. June 21, 1798; d. Nov. 5, 1857.
Eckels, Sarah, wf. of Robert D., d. Nov. 14, 1873, aged 87y.
Eckels, Francis, d. Aug. 25, 1814, aged 63y.
Eckels, Mabel, wf. of Francis, d. May 31, 1816, aged 86y.
Ege, Elizabeth, consort of Capt. George, b. March 1, 1788; d. Dec. 6, 1848.
Egolff, Elizabeth, wf. of Michael, d. Sept. 8, 1795, aged 66y.
Egolff, Michael, d. April 8, 1817, aged 91y, 6m, 6d.
Egolff, Valentine, d. Dec. 1832, aged 42y.
Elliot, Sarah, b. Aug. 22, 1793; d. June 13, 1875.
Elliot, Mary, wf. of J., d. Sept. 29, 1863, aged 78y, 8m, 11d.
Ensminger, Elizabeth, consort of Michael, d. Oct. 10, 1849, aged 73y, 10m, 10d.
Etter, Catharine, d. July 6, 1813, aged 42y, 2m, 16d.
Edwards, Joseph, b. May 9, 1789; d. Dec. 26, 1822.
Edwards, Margaret, b. Sept. 22, 1791; d. May 16, 1879.
Elliott, Samuel, d. Aug. 1863, aged 68y.
Filey, Christiana, wf. of John, d. Nov. 11, 1864, aged 71y.
Fisher, Samuel, b. Oct. 17, 1798; d. April 30, 1830.
Fisher, Daniel, b. Feb. 11, 1797; d. Feb. 28, 1828.
Fisher, Susan A., wf. of Daniel, b. July 15, 1800; d. Jan. 5, 1872.
Fleming, James, d. Feb. 12, 1823, aged 63y.
Fleming, Margaret, wf. of James, dau. of William Clark, b. Oct. 23, 1772; d. Sept. 3, 1856.
Foster, Alex., d. June 20, 1812, aged 22y.
Foster, Alfred, M. D., b. 1790; d. 1847.
Foster, Thomas, d. Jan. 29, 1829, aged 76y.
Foster, Rebecca, wf of Thomas, d. Feb. 23, 1812, aged 56y.
Foulke, Dr. Geo. D., b. Nov. 12, 1780; d. Aug. 14, 1849.
Foulke, Mrs. Mary, relict of Dr. George D., d. May 16, 1861, aged 80y.
Galbraith, Eleanor M., d. April 26, 1858, aged 58y.
Galbraith, Samuel, d. Feb. 10, 1851, aged 87y.
Garney, Brien, d. April 13, 1859, aged 75y.
Garney, Catharine, wf. of Brien, d. Aug. 24, 1867, aged 72y.
Gibson, Robert, d. April 30, 1798, aged 87y.
Gibson, Margaretta, wf. of Robert.
Gibson, John Bannister, b. Nov. 8, 1780; d. May 22, 1853. For many years Chief Justice of Pennsylvania.
Gibson, Sarah W., wf. of John Bannister, b. Jan. 25, 1791; d. Jan. 25, 1861.
Gill, Robert, d. May 12, 1872, aged 76y, 6m, 4d.
Gill, Nancy, wf. of Robert, d. Oct. 13, 1870, aged 72y, 5m, 19d.
Gilmore, John, d. April 7, 1871, aged 85y.
Given, Joseph, d. Oct. 26, 1791, aged 26y.
Glauser, Elizabeth, b. April 20, 1800; d. May 12, 1838.
Glenn, David, d. April 11, 1857, aged 74y.
Glenn, Jane, wf. of David, d. June 21, 1868, aged 81y.
Glass Abraham, d. Dec. 24, 1853, aged 75y.
Gordon, Alexander, d. Dec. 30, 1794, aged 73y.
Gordon, ——, footstone beside above grave marked G.
Gould, Samuel, b. Sept. 10, 1794; d. Aug. 25, 1863.
Gould, Frederick, d. Jan. 19, 1857, aged 66y.
Gould, Margaret, wf. of Frederick d. in Philadelphia, July 10, 1864, aged 72y, 2m, 12d.
Gould, Elizabeth, d. Sept. 2, 1865, aged 85y, 5d.
Grove, Catharine, d. Oct. 25, 1877, aged 90y, 9m, 29d.

Notes and Queries.

Gustine, D. Lewis, d. Oct. 17, 1805, aged 56y.
Gustine, Rebekah, consort of D. Lewis, d. Oct. 6, 1826, aged 65y.
Harkniss, Isabella Park, wf. of Wm. Sr., d. March 10, 1859, aged 76y.
Halbert, Joseph, d. Oct. 14, 1825, aged 49y.
Halbert, Elizabeth, wf. of Joseph, d. Oct. 2, 1848, aged 70y.
Halbert, Charles L., d. Sept. 28, 1872, aged 84y.
Hall, Letitia, d. Nov. 5, 1852, aged 60y.
Hamilton, Adelina, dau. of James and Sarah, d. March 14, 1800, aged 1y, 2m.
Hamilton, James, d. Feb. 13, 1819, aged 67y. President of the Ninth Judicial District of Pennsylvania.
Hamilton, Mary, b. Aug. 2, 1796; d. Dec. 17, 1851.
Hamilton, Sarah, relict of Judge J., d. Dec. 28, 1843, aged 73y.
Handschuh, George, d. Jan. 15, 1852, aged 65y, 14d.
Handschuh, Dorothea, wf. of Geor., d. Oct. 15, 1869, aged 83y.
Harmon, ———, wf. of John, b. Sept. 17, 1785.
Harlan, Lewis, b. Feb. 19, 1787, d. Oct. 3, 1843.
Harlan, Rebecca, b. April 26, 1784; d. Feb. 23, 1859.
Hays, Joseph, Sr., d. July 24, 1841, aged 77y.
Hays, Nancy, wf. of Joseph, Sr., d. Sept. 8, 1827, aged 54y.
Hays, Nancy, dau. of Joseph and Nancy Hays, d. June 13, 1816, aged 18y.
Haxtum, Cornet Milton, d. Dec. 29, 1809, aged 20y.
Heagel, Wm., b. July 16, 1769; d. Oct. 4, 1802.
Heckman, Catharine, wf. of James, d. Oct. 19, 1861, aged 66y, 8m, 9d.
Hendel, Bernard, d. Jan. 7, 1849, aged 62y.
Hendel, Rebecca, wf. of Bernard, dau. of George Kline, d. May 25, 1837, aged 45y.
Hendel, Jacob, d. Nov. 2, 1835, aged 65y.
Hendel, Mary G., wf. of Jacob, d. Oct. 6, 1833, aged 61y.
Heavaner, John, d. May 30, —, aged 80y.
Hevner, Elizabeth, wf. of John b. Sept. 14, 1796; d. Jan. 26, 1844.
Hendel, Capt. Geo., d. April 1, 1812, aged 61y.
Hendel, Rosanna, wf. of Capt. Geo., b. July 16, 1787; d. May 6, 1846.
Hettrick, Catherine A., d. July 1, 1861, Aged 85y.
Helfenstein, Anna Mary, consort of Albert; d. Nov. 24, 1859, aged 70y.
Hoffer, Melchor, d. Jan. 1, 1849, aged 52y.
Hoffer, Catherine, d. Jan. 17, 1884, aged 86y, 6m.
Hoffer, James, d. Oct. 13, 1851, aged 51y.
Hoffer, Melchor, d. March 31, 1843, aged 81y.
Hoffer, Martha, wf. of Melchor, d. July 8, 1847, aged 81y.
Hogue, Nancy, d. June 13, 1841, aged 74y.
Hogue, John W. L., d. April 15, 1828, aged 65y.
Holcomb, Hannah, wf. of M. Esq., b. Feb. 15, 1800; d. May 7, 1867.
Holmes, Eliza, wf. of Jonathan, dau. of Com. O'Brien, U. S. N., b. in Algiers, March 22, 1800; d. Jan. 3, 1870.
Holmes, Daniel, d. March 27, 1832, aged 33y.
Holmes, Margaret, wf. of Daniel, d. March 25, 1832, aged 61y.
Holmes, Daniel, d. March 15, 1810, aged 49y.
Holmes, Mary, d. July 9, 1816, aged 39y.
Holmes Jane, wf. of Andrew, d. July 4, 1815, aged 74y.
Holmes, Andrew, d. Feb. 20, 1810, aged 39y.
Holmes, Andrew, b. May 24, 1770; d. Nov. 27, 1855.
Holmes, Ann, wf. of Andrew, d. June 16, 1850, aged 79y.
Hood, Andrew, d. Dec. 3, 1843, aged 55y.
Hood, Mary, d. June 29, 1869, aged 79y.
Howard, Peres, b. in Mass., Dec. 11, 1795; d. April 23, 1867.
Huston, Sarah, d. March 12, 1851, aged 73y.
Irvine, Capt. Andrew, b. in Ireland, 1749; d. 1789. Served as an officer in American Army from the commencement of the war until it was ended in 1785.
Irvine, James, b. Oct. 28, 1796; d. May 21, 1848.
Irvine, Mary, d. Nov. 8, 1781, aged 1y.
Irvine, William, d. Aug. 21, 1852 aged 80y.
Irvine Jane, d. June 10, 1857, aged 78y.
Irvine, Robert, b. Sep. 21, 1781; d. Aug. 22, 1864.

Irvine, Eleanor, wf. of Robert, b. June 26, 1781; d. Aug. 29, 1854.
Johnson, Anastasia, d. Nov. 5, 1835, aged 70y.
Jones, David, d. March 28, 1861, aged 64y.
Jones, Thomas, jr., b. Birmingham, Eng., May 4, 1785; d. in Carlisle, April 18, 1829.
Kane, Robert Van Rensselaer, d. March 8, 1815, aged 15y., 9m., 19d.
Kauffman, Jane A., d. Aug. 11, 1859, aged 69y.
Keeny, Mrs. Eliza, d. Oct. 31, 1882, aged 85y.
Kelso, Elizabeth, d. May 30, 1808, aged 36y.
Keller, Leonard, d. May 24, 1843, aged 81y.
Keller, Ann Catherine, wf. of Leonard, d. Oct. 22, 1820, aged 71y.
Keller, John, d. Aug. 28, 1878 aged 82y.
Keller Susan, wf. of John, d. Aug. 16, 1891, aged 75y.
Kerr, Andrew, d. Jan. 7, 1849, aged 83y.
Kerr, Elizabeth, d. Aug. 5, 1842, aged 70y.
King, David d. July 11 1823, aged 84y.
King, Jane, d. May 17, 1820, aged 76y.
King, James, son of D. and J., d. Aug. 10, 1810, aged 24y.
Kinter, Susan A., dau. of Jacob and Mary, d. Jan. 3, 1833, aged 61y.
Kline, Lawrence, d. Aug. 5, 1858, aged 78y., 3m., 21d.
Kleffman, John Henry, d. Sep. 1, 1847, aged 62y.
Knox, Joseph, d. Sep. 10, 1827, aged 51y.
Kraft, Mrs. Ann Maria, dau. of Berstecher, b. Feb. 4, 1780, d. July 4, 1860.
Kurn, Christian, b. in Germany, Nov. 20, 1799; d. in Carlisle, Nov. 21 1863.
Laley, John, sr., d. July 16, 1853, aged 84y.
Laley, Catherine, wf. of John, d. Jan. 23, 1858, aged 71y.
Lamberton, James, d. Sep. 10, 1822, aged 72y. 1 m.
Lamberton, Robert, d. Aug. 9, 1852, aged 67y.
Lamberton, Mary Harkness, wf. of Robert, d. Dec. 28, 1880, aged 90y.
Lamberton, James, d. July 28, 1846, aged 95y.
Lamberton, Jane, wf. of James, d. Sep. 1, 1812, aged 56y.

Lamberton, James, b. June 15, 1793; d. Dec. 3, 1871.
Lamberton, Alexander, b. 1790; d. Oct., 1868.
Lamberton, Esther, b. April, 1800; d. March 27, 1880,
Lee, Mary, wf. of Thomas, Sr., d. Aug. 27, 1862, aged 68y., 5 m.
Lee, Thomas, Sr., d. May 21, 1871, aged 85y., 10m., 29d.
Lee, Mary, wf. of Thoms., d. Sep. 21, 1811, aged 67y.
Lee, Elizabeth dau. of T. and M., d. —12, 1852, aged 71y.
Lee, Mrs. Mary, d. March 30, 1862, aged 79y., 10m., 8d.
Lee, Miss Margaret, d. Dec. 22, 1862, aged 87y.
Leeds, Mrs. Rachel, d. April 24, 1860, aged 85y.
Leiby, John, b. June 20, 1791; d. July 30, 1863.
Leiby, Barbara, wf. of John, d. Jan. 10, 1869, aged 81y., 10m., 28d.
Leonard, Margaret, d. Feb. 10, 1841, aged 56y.
Leonard, Sarah, d. March 11, 1850, aged 57y.
Leonard, Wm. H., d. Jan. 8, 1860, aged 68y.
Logan, Margaret, wf. of John, d. July 29, 1799, aged 24y.
Logan, Alexander, d. Nov. 29, 1819, aged 60y.
Logue, Geo., Esq., d. March 8, 1814, aged 51y., 7d.
Logue, Jane, relict of Geo., Esq., b. Dec. 25., 1758; d. Dec. 6, 1839.
Long, James, d. Dec. 25, 1805, aged 58y.
Love, James, d. March, 1817, aged 61y.
Lynch, Sarah, wf. of Matthew, d. Oct. 31, 1779, aged 71y., 5m.
Lyon, George A., b. 1784; d. 1855.
Lyon, Anna, wf. of George A., dau. of Thomas Lyttleton Savage, of Virginia, b. Feb. 10, 1797; d. Aug. 25, 1876.
Lyon, Wm., Esq., b. March 7, 1729; d. June 12, 1808, aged 52y.
Macdonald, Mrs. Sarah, wf. of Duncan, d. 1795, aged 51y.
Macdonald, Margaret, dau. of Duncan and Sarah, b. June 22, 1760; d. May 27, 1844.
Magauran, Margaretta, wf. of Edward, d. June 7, 1850, aged 83y.

Magaran, Mary, wf. of Edward, d. Nov. 19, 1803, aged 45y.
Magauran, Jane, dau. of Mary and Edward, d. Nov. 7, 1792, aged 10m.
Magauran, Edward, d. Nov. 10, 1825, aged 75y.
Martin, James, native of Barnymahayr, County Down, Ireland, d. April 18, 1869, aged 86y.

NOTES AND QUERIES.

Historical, Biographical, and Genealogical.

XVI.

McCLURE.
Nathan McClure, b. Sept. 11, 1789; d. August 8, 1855; was an elder in Falling Spring Church. He m. February 22, 1821, Jane McChesney, b. Nov. 15, 1793; d. Feb. 16, 1845; daughter of Robert McChesney. Information is desired relating to the ancestry of this McClure family as well of the McChesneys.

A MATRON OF THE REVOLUTION.

Elizabeth Thomas Irish.

Elizabeth Thomas, daughter of John Thomas, iron master, was born August 14, 1735, in Merion, Philadelphia county, Penna. Her parents were early Welsh settlers in that locality, persons of prominence among their Quaker neighbors. Elizabeth was educated in Philadelphia in one of the Friends' schools, was well read in the sparse literature of that day, the paucity of which was felt in many families in the early days of settlement. In 1758 she married Nathaniel Irish, manager of Union Furnace, Hunterdon county, New Jersey, evidently becoming acquainted with him through his business relations with her father. They took up their residence in New Jersey for awhile, but at the opening of the Revolution we find them located in their native State. During that severe struggle for independence, Mrs. Irish resided in a neighborhood where there were numerous loyalists, who commonly went by the name of tories. Unmindful of these she was truly patriotic and the cause found in her a noble handmaid. Apart from the care of a large family, which included for a long period several members of her father's household, her industry manifested itself in sending to the gallant men connected with her husband's valiant command many of life's necessities, and especially was this the case when Washington's army lay at Valley Forge. Writers of the Revolutionary period indulge in laudation of the doings of mythic personages, but here we have the story of a veritable heroine—one who liberally ministered to the wants of the soldiers of the Declaration. Without depreciating the good work of other Pennsylvania women in that contest, the services and good deeds of the wife of Nathaniel Irish shall be told of her in connection with the heroism of woman in every age. The "Daughters" have no nobler example, molded as she was in the heroic life of a glorious matron of the Revolution. When the struggle ended —and peace dawned over the hills and valleys of Pennsylvania, the family removed to a tract of land on Plum Creek, in Pitt township, Allegheny county, Pa., where Mrs. Irish spent her few remaining years. She died there on the 11th of July, 1789, and was buried in a private graveyard nearby.

Nathaniel Irish, son of Nathaniel Irish, was born in Saucon township, now Northampton county, Pa., May 8, 1737. Nathaniel Irish, Sen., was a native of the Island of Montserrat, in the West Indies, removed to the American colonies about the year 1730. He died at Union Furnace, Hunterdon county, New Jersey, in 1748. The only son, Nathaniel, was partly educated in Philadelphia, and under private instructors, his parents being persons of means. He was only eleven years of age when his father died, and early manifesting an interest in the iron business established by his father, he became the manager of Union Furnace. It is here that we find him at the beginning of the Revolution, in which he took the deepest welfare. He commenced the manufacture of cannon from wrought iron, but the British obtaining knowledge of this sent out a secret expedition and destroyed the furnace. Nowise undaunted, he raised a company of artillery artificers and was commissioned captain February 7, 1777. He continued in active service until January 1, 1783. He was one of the original members of the Society of the Cincinnati. After the war Captain Irish settled on a tract of land he had taken up on Plum Creek, Westmoreland, now Allegheny county. The State of Pennsylvania gave him a warrant for five hundred acres of Donation land, which was located in the first district in what was subsequently Lawrence county. A portion of this tract remains in the possession of the family. Early in the "nineties" Captain Irish located in the town of Pittsburgh, of which borough he was chosen the first assistant burgess. His later years he spent quite retired, and died there September 11, 1816, aged seventy-nine years. Capt. Irish m. secondly Mary Irwin. She and her husband lie buried in the First Presbyterian churchyard, Pittsburgh. By the second marriage there was no issue. The descendants by the first are quite numerous, a grandson, D. Cadwallader Irish, Esq., representing him in the hereditary societies of the Revolution.

THE ATKINSON FAMILY.

The following data in addition to that published in "Notes and Queries," (No. xii) in regard to the Atkinson family has come to hand:

The will of Thomas Adkinson (Atkinson), of Bucks county, yeoman, dated 10th of 8 mo., 1687, is of record. He left a wife, Jane, executrix, to sell 100 acres which he bought of Joseph English. To his brother John he gave 100 acres of land, on which he dwelt, on condition that if John die without issue the land was to revert to testator's children, Isaac, William and Samuel. To his wife the remainder of estate during her lifetime and then to children above mentioned. The witnesses were Joseph Kirkbride, Richard Londy. Letters were granted to Jane on the 21st of 3 mo., 1688. The inventory was made 31st of 8 mo., 1687, appraised 11th of 12 mo., 1687 by William Biles and Joseph Krikbride, amounting to £85, 16s. It was recorded 5th of 5 mo., 1688, in Bucks county, where the will is also of record.

James Atkinson was one of the executors of Ralph Smith, of Bucks county, whose will was probated the 27th of 3 mo. 1685.

William Atkinson owned 50 acres of land in Upper Dublin, Philadelphia county n 1734, as shown by the list of landholders of that county.

The minutes of the Friends' monthly meeting of Philadelphia, dated the 6th of 1 mo., 1682, set forth that a certificate dated at Clonbragill, County Armagh, Ireland, touching the coming into Pennsylvania of one James Atkinson, who then resided with Griffith Jones, contrary to the wishes of Friends in place from whence he came, was presented, and it was agreed that James Atkinson should come before the meeting and give satisfaction touching his arrival.

At the meeting held 3d of 5 mo., 1683, Thomas Holme, Thomas Wynne and Griffith Jones, were directed to ratify, by writing a few lines, the Friends in Clonbragill.

At the quarterly meeting of the same held 2d of 7 mo,, 1684, James Atkinson announced his intentions of marrying Hannah Newby, and three Friends were appointed to enquire into the clearness of said intention.

At the meeting held 7th of 8 mo., 1684, James Atkinson's clearness being shown he was allowed to marry said Hannah Newby, of Jersey, and a certificate was drawn up.

Amos Atkinson, of Mass., was a second lieutenant of Little's Massachusetts regiment, 19th of May to Dec. —, 1775; first lieutenant of Twelfth Continental infantry, 1st January to 31st December, 1776.

Milton Atkinson, of Pennsylvania, was quartermaster of Twelfth Pennsylvania, 11th of January, 1777.

Moses Atkinson, R. I., was an ensign of Ninth Continental infantry, 1st of Jan., 1776.

Samuel Atkinson, N. H., was first lieutenant of the First New Hampshire, on the 23d May, 1775.

The following are from "Pennsylvania Marriages," vol. ii, 2d series Archives:

Oct. 2, 1775, Isaac Atkinson and Elizabeth Toy.

Nov. 18, 1769, John Atkinson and Margaret Whitehead.
Jan. 22, 1766, Joseph Atkinson and Elizabeth Croxford.
Feb. 10, 1777, Samuel Atkinson and Elizabeth Conaroe.
May 11, 1774, William Atkinson and Ann Lawrence.
Nov. 20, 1759, William Atkinson and Cath. Kreemer.
March 28, 1771, William Atkinson and Charity Hoyer.
July 9, 1745, Mary Atkinson and Daniel Bankson.

The following appears in the New York State Marriages, History Bulletin of N. Y., No. 1, p. 8:

Feb. 10, 1753, William Atkinson and Leonah Claus.

S. M. SENER.
Lancaster, Pa.

TOMBSTONE RECORDS.

From Town Graveyard, Carlisle, of Persons Prior to 1800.

III.

Matson, Peter, d. March 27, 1846, aged 49y.
Mayberry, Jane, wf. of William, d. March 28, 1878, aged 85y.
Mayberry—(Stone broken).
Mayberry, Rev. Sylvanus, d. Sept. 19, 1816, aged 62y.
McCarter, John, b. June 24, 1765; d. Aug. 22, 1854.
McCarter, Jane, wf. of John, d. June 25, 1843, aged 83y.
McCauley, Mollie, renowned in history as Mollie Pitcher, the heroine of Monmouth, d. Jan. 1833, aged 79y. Erected by the citizens of Cumberland co., July 4, 1876. [b. Oct. 13, 1744; d. Jan. 22, 1832.]
McCommon, Sarah, d. July 3, 1844, aged 68y.
McCoskey, Hon. Samuel A., d. Sept. 4, 1818, aged 67y.
McCoskey, William, d. Dec. 2, 1771, aged 43y.
McCoskey, Ann Susannah, wf. of Dr. Samuel Allen, d. Nov. 12, 1792, aged 38y.
McCord, Catharine, wf. of Alexander, d. Nov. 20, 1832, aged 49y.
McCord, Robert, d. March 9, 1826, aged 59y.
McCord, Lacy, d. Sept. 5, 1824, aged 57y.
McClure, Emilia, wf. of Charles, d. Feb. 1, 1793, aged 28y.
McClure, Charles, d. Feb. 8, 1811, aged 72y.
McClure, Rebecca, relict of Charles, d. April 23, 1826, aged 63y.
McClure, John, d. March 20, 1841, aged 57y.
McClure, Jane, wf. of John, d. Aug. 13, 1864, aged 79y.
McFate, John, d. March 30, 1866, aged 73y.
McGonegal, William, b. July 29, 1791; d. Aug. 21, 1860.
McGinnis, John, b. March 25, 1793, d. Jan. 13, 1870.
McGinnis, Charlotte R., dau. of Richard and Elizabeth O'Brian, consort of John McGinnis, Jr., b. in Algiers, April 10, 1801; d. in Carlisle, Aug. 27, 1827.
McGinnis, John, Sr., d. Jan. 6, 1847.
McGinnis, Martha, consort of John, Sr., d. Sept. 13, 1836.
McKim, James, d. Nov. 13, 1831, aged 53y.
McKim, Catharine, wf. of James, d. March 1, 1831, aged 47y.
McKinley, Esther, wf. of Daniel, d. March 27, 1846, aged 76y.
McKinley, Rev. Daniel, D. D., aged 55y.
McKinley, Mary W., wf. of Daniel, b. Sept. 25, 1800; d. Jan. 15, 1892.
McNaughton, Anna, d. Jan. 1, 1861, aged 71y.
McMath, James, d. Nov. 6, 1873, aged 77y, 5m, 29d.
Mell, John, d. Jan. 23, 1877, aged 83y.
Metzger, George, Esq., b. Nov. 19, 1782; d. June 10, 1879.
Miller, Dr. Matthew, b. Feb. 13, 1800; d. Nov. 4, 1877.
Miller, Robert, d. Nov. 10, 1795, aged 73y.
Miller, Capt. William, d. Jan. 22, 1781, aged 25y.
Miller, Elizabeth, wf. of Robert, d. Sept. 12, 1799, aged 70y.
Miller, Gen. Henry, d. April 5, 1824, aged 73y.
Miller, Sarah Ursula, wf. og Gen. Henry, d. July 16, 1829, aged 79y.
Miller, E., d. April 23, 1832, aged 72y.
Miller, S., d. Feb. 2, 1842, aged 62y.
Miller, William, b. Oct. 27, 1768; d. Oct. 15, 1815.
Miller, Mary, wf. of William, b. Dec. 30, 1768; d. Feb. 12, 1851.

Miller, Elizabeth, dau. of William and Mary, b. Feb. 8, 1800; d. Jan. 5, 1837.
Mitchel, Elizabeth B., d. July 8, 1826, aged 41y, 8m, 2d.
Montgomery, Mrs. Mary, widow of Dr. Thomas, of New York city, d. at Carlisle, Oct. 25, 1850, aged 85y.
Moore, Robert, b. in Ireland; d. at Carlisle, June 16, 1848, aged 87y.
Moore, Mary, consort of Robert, d. 1812, aged 47y.
Moore, Jane, d. Sept. 23, 1785.
Moore, Robert, s. of Jane, killed by the fall of a scaffold, Nov. 30, 1805, aged 25y.
Moore, Mrs. Margaret, d. March 17, 1854, aged 66y, 1m, 9d.
Moore, Mr. James, d. Jan. 24, 1854, aged 54y, 8m, 14d.
Moore, William, Esq., d. Aug. 31, 1804, aged 75y.
Moore, James, d. June 18, 1767, aged 72y.
Moore, James, Esq., d. 1813, aged 48y.
Moore, Nancy, d. 1828, aged 54y.
Moore, John, d. 1822, aged 82y.
Moore, Eleanor Thompson, wf. of John, d. 1817, aged 71y.
Moore, Robert, d. 1795.
Moore William, b. Jan. 22, 1795; d. Oct. 16, 1866.
Moore, Catharine, wf. of William, d. July 6, 1864, aged 68y.
Moore, William, his wf. Elizabeth, also their dau. Mary, who d. Feb. 7, 1857, aged 77y.
Moore, William, merchant of Carlisle, by birth a Virginian, d. June 29, 1812, aged 36y.
Morrow, John, native of Raffrey, County Down, Ireland, d. Oct. 11, 1824, aged 64y.
Morrow, Jane Hamilton, wf. of John, d. Oct. 1, 1859, aged 84y.
Mullin, Mrs. Nancy, d. Feb. 5, 1863, aged 45y.
Munro, William, d. Oct. 10, 1823, aged 45y.
Munro, Hetty, wf. of William, d. March 18, 1831, aged 42y.
Murray, Geo., d. May 6, 1855, aged 94y.
Murray, Mary, dau. of Wm. Denny, and wife of Geo., d. April 10, 1845, aged 68y.
Myers, Theodore, d. Feb. 19, 1839, aged 36y.
Myers, Sarah, wf. of Theodore, d. Dec. 17, 1875, aged 76y.
Myers, Sarah, wf. of Jacob, of Baltimore, d. Oct. 10, 1826, aged 54y.
Nesbit, Charles, S. T. D., b. 1785; d. Feb. 14, 1804.
Nesbit, Mrs. Anne Tweedie, wf. of Charles, d. Aug. 12, 1794, aged 20y.
Neil, Elizabeth, dau. of William and Isabella, d. Aug. 12, 1794, aged 20y.
Nevel, Magdalene, b. Jan. 8, 1797; d. June 8, 1880.
Nevel, Catharine, b. Oct. 14, 1824; d.
Noble, John, d. April 10, 1804, aged 54y.
Noble, Margaret, widow of John. d. March 8, 1830, aged 74y.
Noble, Elizabeth, dau. of John, b. May 17, 1787; d. Aug. 12, 1864.
Noble, Margaret, dau. of John, b. Nov. 28, 1784; d. Dec. 2, 1866.
Noble, Mary, b. June 21, 1778; d. July 21, 1853.
Noble, James, b. Sep. 16, 1775; entered Sep. 16, 1836.
Officer, Alex., d. Oct. 3, 1805, aged 77y.
Officer (stone broken), James, aged 83y.
Officer, John, b. April, 1757; d. March 14, 1831.
Officer, Margaret, wf. of John, d. Aug. 27, 1829, aged 63y.
Officer, John, Jr., b. Nov. 22, 1800; d. Feb. 12, 1851.
Officer, Nancy, wf. of John, d. April 30, 1794, aged 32y.
Officer, Thomas, d. March 5, 1815, aged 90y.
Oliver, Sarah, b. June 22, 1800; d. Sep. 24, 1874.
Paine, Seth, Esq., only s. of Dr. James and S., of Portland, Maine, d. at Carlisle, May 14, 1866.
Paine, Sarah, d. Dec. 20, 1880.
Paine, ——— d. Jan. 26., 1872.
Park, John, d. March 1, 1850, aged 95y.
Park, Isabella, wf. of John, d. Aug. 17, 1848, aged 70y.
Parker, Ann Alexander, d. April, 1809, aged 18y.
Parker, Isaac Brown, b. Nov. 8, 1783; d. Sep. 19, 1865.
Parker, Maria Veasey, b. July 6, 1788; d. Oct. 10, 1865.
Parker, Elizabeth, d. Sep. 6, 1871, aged 84y, 5m, 9d.

Patterson, Wm., d. Sep. 4, 1804, aged 50y.
Paul, John, d. March 28, 1834, aged 60y.
Peffer, Elizabeth, consort of John, d. March 22, 1812, aged 22y.
Peffer, Adam, b. Dec. 14, 1797; d. Jan. 16, 1872.
Pollock, Jane S., d. 1800, aged 72y.
Pool, John, d. June 17, 1857, aged 67y.
Pool, Mary D., mother of John.
Porter, Wm., d. Dec. 1, 1819, aged 37y.
Porter, Sarah M., wife of Wm.
Postlethwaite, James, d. Aug. 7, 1866, aged 72y.
Postlethwaite, Catharine, wf. of James, d. Nov. 13, 1862, aged 63y.
Procter, John, b. Aug. 10, 1784; d. Jan. 10, 1847.
Procter, Mary Officer, wf. of John, b. March 18, 1797; d. April 6, 1882.
Quigley, Andrew, d. April 26, 1853, aged 69y.
Quigley, Nancy, wf. of Andrew, d. March 3, 1835, aged 50y.
Quigley, Christopher, b. March 23, 1797; d. June 24, 1867.
Ramsey, Elizabeth, d. Nov. 2, 1855, aged 59y.
Ramsey, James, d. July 11, 1797, aged 72y.
Ramsey, aJnet Woods, wf. of James, stone damaged).
Reed, Hon. Hugh, d. April 7, 1845, aged 68y.
Reed, Sarah Ann, wf. of Hon. Hugh.
Reighter, John, d. March 26, 1839, aged 76y.
Reighter, Mary, consort of John, d. Sep. 21, 1830, aged 70y.
Reighter, b. July 4, 1793; d. Dec. 5, 1881.
Reighter ——, b. July 4, 1793; d. Dec. 5, 1831.
Rinehart, ——, b. Dec. 1779; d. Oct. 16, 1843.
Rhoads, Mary, wf. of Philip—(stone damaged.)
Rhoads, John, d. Aug., 1854, aged 72y.
Rhoads, Henry, b. Feb. 28, 1784; d. Feb. 7, 1864.
Rhoads, Margaret, wf. of Henry, d. Dec. 28, 1850, aged 67y.
Ringwalt, Jacob, d. Dec. 24, 1824, aged 63y.
Ringwalt, Our Mother, d. March 27, 1858, aged 83y.

NOTES AND QUERIES.

Historical, Biographical, and Genealogical.

XVII.

HENRY ANTES.

He was a son of Joseph Antes and a great-grandson of Col. John Henry Antes, who built the fort at the mouth of what is known as Antes creek, and was born in Nippenose township, Lycoming county, April 20, 1818. After living for sixty-eight years in the place of his birth, he left there in 1886 and settled at Bloomsburg, Columbia county, where he died, March 18, 1895. Mr. Antes was the last of the numerous posterity of the revolutionary hero to leave the township of Nippenose, though the family name still clings to the stream and the post office at Jersey Shore station, on the Philadelphia and Erie railroad. The christian virtues so noted in his ancestors were prominent throughout his entire life, and he left to his family the comfort and consolation of a memory of seventy-seven years, filled with the fruits of a peaceful disposition, sterling integrity, untiring energy and a calm submission to the final summons to his future reward. The surviving members of his family consist of his son James, a veteran of the Thirteenth Pennsylvania cavalry, and a resident of Elmira; Mrs. Mary F. Caswell and Miss Kate, who with their widowed mother, still reside in Bloomsburg.

J. F. MEGINNESS.

Williamsport, Pa.

DEWEY AND SCHLEY.

[In these days when the names of two of the greatest naval heroes the century has produced are upon every one's lips, it may be interesting to the readers of "Notes and Queries" to give the following genealogical records of George Dewey and Winfield Scott Schley.]

Rear Admiral Dewey's Ancestry.

1. Thomas Dewey came from Sandwich, Kent, England, in the year 1633, to Dorchester, Mass. He removed about 1638 to Windsor, Conn., where, on March 22, 1638, he married the Widow Frances Clarke. He died at Windsor, April 27, 1648.

2. Josiah Dewey, born 1641. Settled first at Westfield, but subsequently removed to Lebanon, Conn. He married in 1662, Hepzibah Lyman.
3. Josiah Dewey, of Lebanon, Conn., born, 1666.
4. William Dewey, of Lebanon, Conn., born, 1692; died, 1759.
5. Simeon Dewey, of Lebanon, Conn., born, 1718; died, 1751.
6. William Dewey, settled at Hanover, N. H.; born, 1746; died, 1813.
7. Capt. Simeon Dewey, of Berlin, Vt., born, 1770; died 1863.
7. Dr. Julius Y. Dewey, of Montpelier, Vt., born, 1801; died, 1877.
9. Admiral George Dewey, born, 1837.

Admiral Schley's Ancestry.

1. John Schley, b. Jan. 2, 1767; d. Oct. 31, 1835. His grandfather, John Thomas Schley, laid out the town of Frederick, Md., and was one of the most distinguished jurists of Maryland. His wife was Mary Shriver, dau. of David Shriver and his wife Rebecca Ferree. The latter was a granddaughter of Philip Ferree and his wife Elizabeth Dubois, of Pennsylvania Huguenot ancestry.
2. John Thomas Schley was one of the sons of the former. He was b. Nov. 4, 1806; d. Oct. 1876. His wife was Georgiana McClure, of Baltimore. They were the parents of:
3. Winfield Scott Schley, b. Oct. 9, 1839, at Richfields, near Frederick, Md.

OLD HANOVER CHURCH.

Notes From the Minutes of Donegal Presbytery.

[Our readers are indebted to the Rev. Thomas H. Robinson, D. D., for the following notes concerning the church at Manada and the ordination of the Rev. Richard Sankey.]

Sept. 3, 1735.—Meeting at Notingham.
A supplication from a people on the borders of Suitara congregation desire the countenance of the Presbytery in building a new meeting house in order to have supplies—being read.
Mr. Bertram reports that his people desire him to signify to the Presbytery that they desire us to defer granting said supplication till they be heard. Judgment deferred till next meeting.
Oct. 3, 1735.—Meeting at Notingham. The affair of the people of Manada Creek deferred.
Oct. 10, 1735.—Meeting at Notingham.
Mr. Sankey, a student from Ireland, having produced his certificate last meeting before the members of the Presbytery, the Presbytery order that he endeavor to acquaint himself with the brethren before our next and endeavor to prepare for some preliminary emtemporary trial against our next meeting.
Nov. 20, 1735.—Middle Octorara.
Lazarus Stewart appeared to prosecute a supplication for a new erection of Manada Creek. Mr. Creaghead and Mr. Anderson had made a report to Presbytery concerning Mr. Bertram's congregation that the people of Derry desired to be organized into a separate congregation and have their bounds defined.
The Presbytery considered it not convenient to come to a determination on these matters until better informed about distance and situation of these people, and therefore appoint Mr. Anderson and any other brother whom the Standing Committee may appoint to serve with him, to perambulate the bounds and borders of the congregation of Derry and people of Manada some time next spring—said brethren to take particular notice of the meeting house of Manada, and its distance from the meeting house of Derry. They are also empowered to fix the bounds of said people and to determine concerning the situation of the meeting house of Manada. [Note—Paxtang, Derry and Manada were under Mr Bertram's charge at this time. Meeting houses at Paxtang and Derry.]
Nov. 20, 1735.—
Mr. Sankey questioned in divinity and philosophy. Presbytery satisfied with his answers and appoint him a sermon on Prov. iii, 6, "In All Thy Ways," to be delivered before the Standing Committee at their first meeting, who, if they see cause, shall appoint him another subject to prepare a discourse upon, to be delivered before Presbytery at their next meeting, to be received at peice of trial.

Dec. 10, 1735.—Octorara.

Mr. Sankey delivered a discourse on Prov. iii, 6, as a specimen to further trial, which was approved as such. Appointed to prepare a discourse on Psalm xliii, 3, "O, Lord, Send Forth Thy Light and Thy Truth," &c., to be delivered at next meeting of Presbytery.

May 25, 1736.—Notingham.

Mr. Anderson, Andrew Galbraith and one of the elders from Paxtang (Wm. Maxwell by name), are ordered to meet on the Tuesday before the next meeting of Presbytery at Derry the first Monday of September, in order to perambulate the bounds between the people of Derry and of Manada.

May 26, 1736.—

Mr. Sankey delivered a lecture on Psalm xxiii, which was approved, and he was ordered to prepare an exegesis on "Au Christus qui sit orderanda" against next meeting and a Presbyterial exercise on Rom. ii, 13, "For not the hearers of the law," &c.

Sept. 1, 1736.—Derry.

Mr. Anderson reported that the perambulation between Derry and Manada had been fulfilled and gave in the statements of their committee in writing. Debate and pleadings between parties followed.

Lazarus Stewart engages to the Presbytery that all persons who belong or shall join themselves to the new erection, who are in arrears to Mr. Bertram shall pay up.

Sept. 2, 1736.—

The Presbytery inquired into the affair of Mr. Bertram's release from a part of his charge. The people of Paxtang asked what they could afford yearly for support of their minister. Their answer was that they were willing to engage for 60 pounds, one-half in money and one-half in hay, flax, linen or linen cloth at market price. The people of Derry in like manner promise £55, to be paid in like manner, both declaring, however, that they would allow their minister the benefit of overplus subscriptions, yet they will expect a congregational discharge yearly on the payment of said expected quota. Both parties engaged to choose collectors for their respective quotas. It is further agreed by the people of Manada and Derry, and ordered by Presbytery, upon the borders of these two congregations that is between the meeting houses and beyond the creek of Swatara shall on or before the first of November next declare in an orderly way, i. e., before some elder or principal man of the congregation which they make choice of, whether they will join the congregation of Derry or Manada, and after said 1st day of November none who dwell in bounds shall be at liberty to alter their choice but by concurrence of both congregations, or order of the Presbytery.

Both congregations of Derry and Paxtang want Mr. Bertram.

Mr. Bertram not ready to decide to which he will go.

Mr. Sankey delivers his discourse on Rom. ii, 3, and his exegesis on "Au Christus," &c., both approved. Ordered to prepare a sermon on Rom. iii, 31, "Do we make void the law?" &c., and also be prepared to defend his thesis against next meeting.

Oct. 26, 1736.—Dunagal.

Lazarus Stewart reports nothing done in paying arrears due to Mr. Bertram because no list of arrears rendered, but they are ready to act when an account is rendered.

Oct. 27, 1736.—

Mr. Sankey gives popular sermon and is further examined in languages and philosophy, acknowledges the Westminster Confession and Catechism, promises to conform to the Directory, and to give subjection to the Presbytery, and is then licensed to preach the Gospel as a probationer.

Nov. 10, 1736.—Forks of Brandywine.

Messrs. Gerston and Sankey ordered to supply Pequea and Manada by monthly turns alternately till next meeting of Presbytery.

April 6, 1737.—Chestnut Level.

In pursuance of a supplication from the people of Manada, Mr. Bertram ordered to supply that people on the last Sabbth of April and on some following day of the week convene the people in order to moderate a call to Mr. Sankey. Mr. Sankey to preach at Conedoguinet, Paxtang and Manada until next meeting.

June 22, 1737.—Notingham.

Upon a supplication and a call to Mr. Sankey, presented by John Cunningham and Robert Grier, commissioners from the congregation of Hanover, by which said commissioners are empowered to promise toward Mr. Sankey's outward support among that people as their orderly pastor the annual payment of 60 pounds—that is, one-half in money and the other in particular commodities, as flax, hemp, linen, yarn and cloth, together with several gratuities mentioned in said supplication. Said call was recommended to Mr. Richard Sankey's consideration till next meeting of Presbytery.

June 23.—

Mr. Sankey to supply Paxtang and Hanover alternately, to open next Presbytery with a sermon from Rom. vi, 21, "What fruit have ye then?" &c.

August 31.—Octorara.

Mr. Sankey preached by mistake from Rom. vi, 22, but discourse approved as part of trial. Ordered to prepare an exegetical discourse on the Resurrection of Christ as a common head.

He accepts the call from Hanover, and is appointed to supply the people for ordinary till next meeting of Presbytery.

Oct. 5, 1737.—Pequa.

Mr. Sankey opens Presbytery with a discourse from Mark xvi, 9, according to appointment. It is accepted as part of trial.

Oct. 6.—

Supplication from Hanover that Mr. Sankey's ordination be hastened before next winter. Presbytery not opposed to it. Ordered to supply Hanover till next meeting.

Nov. 17, 1737.—Derry.

It having been reported at our last Presbytery that there was great offence taken at a certain piece of conduct by Mr. Sankey, both by ministers and people, especially in the bounds of New Castle Presbytery, viz., his sending a copy of a sermon to Mr. Hunter containing very considerable error in point of very momentous doctrines of religion by which Mr. Hunter was laid aside in one of his trial discourses before said Presbytery, the Presbytery then agreed that Mr. Sankey should be appointed correspondent to attend said Presbytery in order to the clearing up of the matter, which he did, and it being joined, found upon inquiry that Mr. Sankey had sent said notes as above, and that said notes did contain such errors as were reported, but that Mr. Sankey had not only condemned and accordingly laid aside said erroneous notes from all use, but had sent a letter of caution with said notes to Mr. Hunter, which did not come to Mr. Hunter's hand. The Presbytery, after much serious consideration, came to the conclusion, viz., that, although upon a serious review of Mr. Sankey's conduct both before and since his being a preacher, yet cannot see any ground to suspect him of unsoundness of the faith, yet we condemn it as a great and gross imprudence in Mr. Sankey's conduct, his writing and sending forth such erroneous notes and thereby giving such occasion of stumbling, both to ministers and people, and therefore judge that he deserves to be severely rebuked by the Moderator for the same, and strictly cautioned to act with more circumspection for the future and guard against all offensive conduct in this or any other kind. Mr. Sankey being called in, was accordingly rebuked, which he cheerfully submitted unto. A copy of above minute sent to New Castle Presbytery.. Mr. Sankey ordered to deliver an exposition of xv Psalm and a Presbyterial exercise from Rom. viii, 4, at next meeting.

April 17, 1738.—Dunagal.

Mr. Sankey opens Presbytery with an exposition of xv Psalm. Presbyterial exercise deferred till next meeting; appointed a popular sermon, John i, 29.

Jlne 28, 1738—Forks of Brandywine.

Mr. Sankey delivers his Presbyterial exercise, also his popular sermon; both approved. Next meeting of Presbytery at Hanover last Wednesday of August and then Mr. Sankey have his extempore trial and if approved he to be ordained next day—last Thursday of August—Mr. Bertram to preside.

Aug. 30, 1738.—Hanover.

First meeting of Presbytery in Hanover. Present, Thomas Craighead, Alex. Craighead, Bertram, Thomson, Boyd, Paul, Black and Anderson, (Elders) Matthew Atchison, Daniel Henderson, James Carothers, John Christy, Hugh Scott. Mr.

Alexander opened with a Presbyterial exercise.

Mr. Elder delivered a common head.

Mr. Sankey's extempore trial approved and all other parts of trial, and it was ordered he be ordained to-morrow. Aug. 31, 1738.—

Mr. Sankey ordained and received as a member of Presbytery.

TOMBSTONE RECORDS

From Town Graveyard, Carlisle, of Persons Born Prior to 1800.

IV.

Robb, Charles, b. Feb. 4, 1734, d. May 2, 1757. Oldest date in graveyard.
Rodgers, Margaret, formerly relict of Capt. John Scott, b. Nov. 16, 1763; d. Feb. 11, 1852.
Rouey, Charles, Sr., d. Dec. 27, 1843, aged 46y.
Ross, James, L.L. D., d. July 6, 1827, aged 84y.
Ross, Catharine Irvine, relict of James, L.L. D.; d. Dec. 1, 1846, aged 82y.
Ross, Rasanna, wf. of James, d. April 13, 1738, aged 42y.
Rowan, Charles, d. Oct. 24, 1844, aged 65y.
Rowan, David, d. Oct. 7, 1830, aged 86y.
Rowan, Jane, d. Dec. 12, 1827, aged 80y.
Rowney, William, d. April 3, 1851, aged 61y.
Rowney, Mary, sister of William, d. April 28, 1875, aged 82y.
Rowney, Mary, consort of James, d. Feb. 9, 1831, aged 84y.
Rowney, James, d. Feb. 1, 1816, aged 77y.
Rustan, Mary, d. March 18, 1832, aged 63y.
Sanderson, John, b. Feb. 27, 1798; d. April 11, 1862.
Schpitzner, Y. Christianna, wf. of Frederick, d. Aug. 31, 1868, aged 84y.
Schpitzer, Frederick, d. Dec., 1865, aged 79y.
Schmohl, S. Jacob, d. Sept. 15, 1868, aged 73y, 9m, 10d.
Schmohl, Mary Dorothe, wf. of Jacob, d. Feb. 28, 1859, aged 58y, 3m.
Scott, Capt. William, d. March 26, 1806, aged 51y, 7m.
Scott, Jane, wf. of Capt. William, dau. of John McCausland, of Lancaster county, d. Sept. 26, 1785, aged 23y.

Scott, Mrs. Mary, b. in Freemont, N. J., November 2, 1772, d. April 11, 1847.
Scobey, David, b. Dec. 13, 1791; d. May 27, 1874.
Scobey, Catharine Myers, wf. of David, b. June 9, 1794; d. June 2, 18 .
Sener, Jacob, Sr., b. July 16, 1792; d. Aug. 3, 1887.
Sener, Barbara Ann, wf. of Jacob, Sr., b. July 5, 1796; d. April 11, 1873.
Seymour, Anne Upshur, wf. of William D., b. Dec. 7, 1779; d. Nov. 10, 1873.
Shapley, Rufus E., b. Dec. 22, 1786; d. May 21, 1864.
Shapley, Lydia, b. July 16, 1788; d. March 1, 1876.
Shelly, Percy B., d. April 15, 1855, aged 55y.
Shrom, Joseph, b. June 8, 1792; d. March 2, 1865.
Shrom, Ann, wf. of Joseph, d. Dec. 28, 1828, aged 32y.
Simison, Parker, d. Oct. 3, 1867, aged 74y.
Simison, Margaret, dau. of William Denny and wf. of Samuel. d. Dec. 8, 1847, aged 76y.
Skiles, John, Sr., d. July 27, 1841, aged 81y. He served his country in the Revolution of 1776.
Smiley, Margaret, consort of George, d. Feb. 24, 1824, aged 33y.
Smith, John. Esq., b. at Middlesex, Cumberland county, 1757; d. at Carlisle, October 6, 1839. He was a soldier in the Revolution.
Smith, Jane, wf. of Thomas, d. March 27, 1822, aged 42y, 2m, 10d.
Smith, Lieut. Nathaniel, of the Third regiment of the Pennsylvania line in the army of the United States, b. Jan. 19, 1765; d. Nov. 9, 1790.
Smith, James, d. Sept. 14, 1791, aged 52y.
Smith, Simon, d. Jan. 6, 1851, aged 73y, 4m, 6d.
Spahr, John, d. Nov. 19, 1844, aged 62y, 8m, 2d.
Spahr, Elizabeth, wf. of John, b. Oct. 12, 1783; d. Jan. 19, 1858.
Speck, Mary Ann, wf. of Dr. Joseph, dau. of Jacob and Elizabeth Matter, d. Feb. 20, 1830, aged 40y.
Sponsler, Mrs. Susan, d. Feb. 22, 1863, aged 39y.
Steele, Ephraim, d. April 12, 1868, aged 76y.

Steele, Capt. John, Third United States regulars, b. Aug. 22, 1764; d. Nov. 6, 1800.
Steel, Margaret, wf. of Jno., d. Nov. 19, 17-1, aged 41y.
Steel, Margaret ——, dau. of John.
Steel, in memory of John or Josiah.
Steel, Rev. John, d. Aug. 1779, aged 64y.
Steel, Margaret, wf. of Rev. John, d. Feb., 1779, aged 58y.
Steel, Capt. John, s. of Rev. John and Margaret, d. Dec., 1819, aged 98y.
Sterrett, Mrs. Catherine, dau. of Duncan and Sarah Macdonald, d. 1825, aged 59y.
Stephens, Thomas, d. June 2, 1795, aged 66y.
Stephens, John, Sr., d. at Middlesex, Cumberland county, April 2, 1813, aged about 51y.
Stephens, Hannah, wf. of John, Sr., d. Oct. 14, 1818, aged about 56y.
Stephens, John, Jr., b. Jan. 2, 1790; d. Feb. 9, 1808.
Stevenson, Hon. George, LL. D., d. July 13, 1783, aged 65y.
Stevenson, Mary, d. Oct. 15, 1791, aged 65y.
Stevenson, Dr. Geo., s. of Hon. George and Mary, d. May 8, 1829, aged 70y. Buried in graveyard of Old Swedes church in Wilmington, Del. Served in Continental Army and one of the "Original Members and Founders of Society of the Cincinnati."
Strum, George, d. Nov. 27, 1804, aged 46y.
Sturgeon, Robert, b. March 7, 1795; d. Feb. 10, 1845.
Sturgeon, Eliza A., wf. of Robert, b. Aug. 25, 1798; d. Aug. 26, 1852.
Searight, Francis, d. Jan. 22, 1824, aged 42y.
Searight, Jane, wf. of Francis, d. March 4, 1860, aged 69y.
Searight, Gilbert, d. Sept. 30, 1815, aged 75y.
Searight, Esther, wf. of Gilbert, d. 1792, aged 35y.
Searight, Gilbert, Sr., d. Dec. 1, 1856, aged 69y.
Searight, Sarah, wf. of Gilbert, d. Jan. 21, 1853, aged 53y.
Stuart, Miss Margaret, d. July 23, 1833, aged 44y.
Stuart, Ann, b. June 17, 1789; d. Aug. 10, 1865.
Stuart, James, Esq., d. Oct. 8, 1830, aged 53y.
Stuart, Samuel, d. Sept. 11, 1828, aged 83y.
Stuart, Margaret, wf. of Samuel, d. Feb. 20, 1844, aged 92y.
Stuart, Hon. John, b. Oct. 26, 1794; d. March 28, 1870. Associate Judge of Cumberland co., 1835-1851.
Stuart, Barbara, wf. of Hon. John, b. Aug. 15, 1798; d. Aug. 28, 1873.
Stuart, Miss Sarah, d. Feb. 18, 1870, aged 71y.
Swartz, John, d. Oct. 8, 1845, aged 52y, 4m.
Thompson, Samuel, d. Aug. 12, 1850, aged 75y.
Thompson, Mrs. Letitia, d. Oct. 8, 1863, aged 71y, 4m.
Thompson, Gen. William, d. Sept. 3, 1781, aged 45y.
Todd, Isaac, b. June 30, 1783; d. Feb. 1, 1851.
Todd, Elizabeth, b. May 5, 1787; d. Sept. 25, 1858.
Trimble, Sarah, wf. of Thomas, dau. of Thomas Urie, d. July 26, 1844, aged 48y.
Trimble, Thomas, Esq., d. Aug. 17, 1844, aged 62y.
Trimble, Mary, wf. of Thomas, dau. of Samuel and Frances Woods, d. Sept. 24, 1821, aged 27y.
Thornborough, Rebecca, wf. of Joseph, d. Jan. 9, 1792, aged 32y.
Underwood, Joseph, d. Feb. 10, 1823. aged 24y.
Underwood, John, d. Sept. 1, 1827, aged 78y.
Underwood, Sarah, wf. of John, d. June 24, 1827, aged 78y.
Underwood, James, b. Oct. 14, 1789; d. Nov. 8, 1834.
Underwood, Catherine Todd, wf. of James, b. Feb. 1, 1796; d. April 8, 1879.
Underwood, James, d. March 25, 1811, aged 53y.
Underwood, Sarah, wf. of James, d. March 8, 1832, aged 85y.
Ulrich, Mary, d. June 30, 1863, aged 80y.
Vance, Ann, d. May 29, 1878, aged 90y.
Vaughn, Catherine, d. March 26, 1843, aged 44y.
Vaughn, John, d. Sept. 10, 1760, aged 74y.

Notes and Queries.

Veazey, Mary, relict of Thomas B., M. D., of Cecil co., Maryland, b. Jan. 9, 1765; d. Feb. 5, 1826.
Vickers, Daniel, b. March 12, 1865, aged 65y.
Walker, James, d. April 25, 1816, aged 54y.
Wallace, Patrick, d. March 15, 1813, aged 75y.
Watts, David, b. Oct. 29, 1794; d. Sept. 15, 1819.
Watts, Juliana, wf. of David, d. Feb. 20, 1869.
Watts, Matilda B., b. Oct. 25, 1797; d. Sept. 29, 1885.
Wareham, Philip, b. Dec. 25, 1770; d. Oct. 16, 1831.
Wareham, Mary, wf. of Philip, d. Aug. 20, 1848, aged 65y, 8d.
Weakley, Mrs. M., d. 1800.
Weakley, James, d. Dec. 8, 1831, aged 51y.
Weakley, Daniel, d. Feb. 28, 1829, aged 37y.
Weakley, Edward, d. May 29, 1817, aged 74y.
Weakley, Margaret, wf. of Edward, d. April 12, 1834, aged 79y.
Weakley, Nathaniel, d. Oct. 6, 1858, aged 70y, 7m.
Weakley, Sarah, wf. of Nathaniel, d. Sept. 15, 1869, aged 78y, 16d.
Weakley, James, d. Jan. 20, 1820, aged 80y.
Weakley, Rebecca, wf. of James, d. Dec. 12, 1817, aged 64y.
Weakley, Isaac, d. Dec. 7, 1848, aged 71y.
Weakley, Isabella, d. July 20, 1839, aged 24y.
Weakley, Rebecca, wf. of Nathaniel, d. Dec. 10, 1818, aged 26y.
Weaver, Philip, d. May 24, 1861, aged 77y, 4m.
Weaver, Laura, wf. of Philip, b. May 2, 1788; d. March 10 1817.
Whiteman, Caroline B., wf. of Jacob, b. Aug. 4, 1798; d. Aug. 26, 1885.
Weidman, Jacob, b. Nov. 16, 1796; d. Sept. 28, 1870.
Wetzel, Jacob, d. Oct. 15, 1828; aged 57y, 7m, 4d.
Wetzel, Phebe, wf. of Jacob, d. Oct. 14, 1825, aged 53y, 8m.
Wheaton, Levi, b. at Richmond, Va., Sept. 6, 1796; d. Sept. 24, 1822.

Wise, Frederick, b. Oct. 14, 1772; d. Nov. 13, 1846.
Wise, Elizabeth, •wf. of Fred., b. Sept. 9, 1781; d. March 1, 1843.
Williamson, Capt. Thomas, d. Sept. 17, 1832, aged 73y.
Williamson, Rebecca, d. April 21, 1853, aged 82y.
Williamson, Col. James, d. Feb. 4, 1881, aged 86y.
Winard, Lewis, b. Oct. 27, 1798; d. April, 1867.
Winard, Maria, b. March 29, 1791; d. Jan. 13, 1878.
Wynkoop, John, b. March 20, 1784; d. Jan. 23, 1860.
Wynkoop, Ann, wf. of John, b. April 18, 1792; d. March 18, 1850.
Wilson, John, d. July 29, 1828, aged 46y.
Wilson, Mary Davis, d. June 4, 1838, aged 58y.
Woods, Richard, d. Jan. 28, 1788, aged 31y, 3d.
Woods, Samuel, s. of Samuel and Frances, d. Aug. 27, 1817, aged 21y, 8m, 22d.
Woods, Samuel, s. of William, d. Dec. 5, 1836, aged 79y.
Woods, Frances, wf. of Samuel, dau. of James and Sarah Sterrett, of Rapho township, Lancaster county, d. Oct. 15, 1824, aged 64y, 12d.
Woods, Samuel, b. April 5, 1787; d. Nov. 11, 1862.
Woods, Lillias, wf. of Samuel, b. Oct. 23, 1793; d. Oct. 23, 1827.
Woods, Rebecca, b. March 23, 1797; d. March 7, 1844.
Woods, Nathan, b. Sept. 27, 1770; d. Aug. 29, 1853.
Woods, Jane M., b. March 31, 1783; d. May 2, 1857.
Woods, James, d. April 19, 1856, aged 75y.
Woods, Jane, d. Dec. 12, 1865, aged 81y.
Woods, Nathan, d. Aug. 17, 1812, aged 50y.
Woods, Jane, wf. of Nathan, d. Sept. 3, 1847, aged 73y.
Woods, Alexander, d. Sept. 15, 1868, aged 81y.
Woods, Mary, wf. of Alex., d. Jan. 21, 1837, aged 60y.
Woodruff, Rev. George Houston, d. March 28, 1822, aged 25y.
Woodburn, Hon. Samuel, b. March 27, 1791; d. Oct. 7, 1860.

Young, Hannah, wf. of Samuel, b. Jan. 27, 1799; d. April 2, 1821.
Zarmen, Martin, d. March 16, 1840, aged 60y.
Zarmen, E., d. March 2, 1781, aged 79y.
Ziegler, Geo., d. Jan. 17, 1889, aged 93y.
Ziegler, J—, b. March 11, 1785; d. July 2, 1864.
Zollinger, Jacob, d. April 6, 1820, aged 66y, 20d.
Zollinger, Dr. John, d. Oct. 10, 1868, aged 74y.

(MRS. C. A.) S. W. PARKINSON,
M. M. WOODS.

NOTES AND QUERIES.

Historical, Biographical, and Genealogical.

XVIII.

An Early Settler on the Susquehanna

Whereas George Renick, late of Iniskillen, having about eleven years since arrived in this province with the first settlers of Donegal, yet has never obtained leave to settle on any of the proprietor's lands, without which leave he never would presume to attempt it, and being now desirous that himself and three sons, William, Thomas and Robert and his son-in-law, Robert Polke, might be allowed to settle down on some tract together in one neighbourhood, I therefore think it advisable that pursuant to his request he and his said sons and son-in-law be suffered to enter on the quantity of one thousand acres, near Susquehanna, between Sohataroe and Pextan, and that the same may be marked out to him and his said sons in a regular tract by the surveyor of Lancaster county or his order at the said George's charge, upon this express condition, that he and his said sons and son-in-law shall comply with such terms as shall be proposed by the proprietors or their agents, when lands in those parts shall be granted, or other wise shall quietly quitt the same. Dated at Stenton, the 25th day of January, 1730-1. JAMES LOGAN.

Lett him begin on Susquehanna at least two miles above Sohataroe, running a proper distance back, and he may take in any settlement that is only begun and not actually inhabited. J. L.

Pennsylvania's First Surveyor-General.

Located near Roland Station, about a mile northwest of Holmesburg, Philadelphia, in a secluded spot surrounded by woodland, with no other means of approach than a foot-path, apparently seldom used, is an old, deserted burial lot, perhaps less than 300 feet square. It is here that the remains of Thomas Holme, surveyor-general under William Penn, are deposited. It is one of the oldest burial grounds in the State. There is a small monument erected to the memory of Holme, the inscriptions on which are given below, together with several other tombstone records of less importance. Many stones are fallen and scattered about the ground. Quite a number of graves are marked with large pieces of building stone, without inscriptions.
[North side.]
In Memory of
THOMAS HOLME,
Died 1695—Aged 71.
Surveyor-General of William Penn. He Drafted the Plan and Laid Out the City of Philadelphia.

[West side.]
This stone was erected in 1863 by the following-named trustees of Lower Dublin Academy, a mark of respect to the memory of the originator of the school.
Benjamin Crispin,
Jonathan Enoch,
George W. Holme,
Isaac Pearson,
George Fox,
Henry Dewees,
Samuel C. Willits,
Charles W. Harrison,
George Wagner,
Alfred Enoch,
Thomas Shallcross,
Firman D. Holme.

[East side.]
In lieu of a donation in his will for school purposes his heirs gave the land on which the Lower Dublin Academy is erected.

[South side.]
He became the proprietor of 1646 acres

of land in one tract by grant of Penn in 1684, named this Well Spring Plantation, of which this is part.

James Creighton, s. of John and Margaret Creighton, b. Mar. 3, 1731; d. Nov. 27, 1818.
Rebecca Creighton, his wf., and dau. of Wm. and Elizabeth Ingles, b. Nov. 19, 1752; d. Apl. 13, 1825.
Engles, Elizabeth, d. Dec. 9, 1773, aged 8 mo. 21 d.
Engles, Sarah, d. 1768, aged 10 mo.
Engles, Joseph, d. 1766, aged 5 yrs.
Engles, Jane, d. 1757, aged 3 yrs.
Bowers, Margerth, b. 1762; d. Oct. 21, 1766.

GUSTAVUS N. HART.

Cumberland County Marriages.

Mateer, Major Andrew, m. Marh 31, 1814, Ann, dau. of John Huston, of Dickinson township.
Moore, John, of South Middleton township, m. Oct. 22, 1816, Ann, dau. of Robert Grayson, Esq., dec'd., of Carlisle.
McClure, Charlotte, dau. of Charles McClure, dec'd., m. Dr. Adam Hays, June 19, 1817, by Dr. Duffield.
Musselman, Christian, m. June 14, 1804, by Rev. Mr. Sano, Miss Betsy Sano, both of Cumberland.
Noland, William, of Virginia, m. April 12, 1796, Catherine Callender, of Carlisle.
Neely, James, of York county, m. April 3, 1798, Miss Peggy McBeth, of Cumberland county.
Noble, James, m. Feb. 19, 1801, Miss Polly Cooper, both of Carlisle.
Nevin, Mr. ——, merchant, of Springfield township, m. Feb. 1, 1810, by Rev. Williams, Mary, dau. of Joseph Pierce, dec'd.
Noble,Francis, of E.Pennsboro', m. March 15, 1810, Margaret, dau. of Samuel Martin, of Allen township.
Nesbit, Alex, Esq., of Wiliamsburg, Huntingdon county, m. Nov. 5, 1816,Mrs.Martha Brooks, dau. of Mrs. Mary Ramsey, of Carlisle, by Rev. Mr. Pringle.
Noble, Francis, of Carlisle, m. at Baltimore, June 3, 1817, Miss Mary Brown, of Ohio.
Officer, John, of Carlisle, m. May 31, 1796, Mrs. Officer, of Cumberland county.
Offley, Lieut., quartermaster Tenth regiment, m. March 31, 1800, Miss Polly Greer, of Carlisle.
Oliver, John, merchant, of Carlisle, m. Aug. 17, 1800, at the residence of Wiliam Godfrey, in York county, Miss Hannah God frey, dau. of William Godfrey.
Oliver, Jane, of Carlisle, m. April 25, 1811, William Laughlin, of Newton township.
Oliver, Miss Margaret, m. June 24, 1817, Benjamin Fernald, both of Carlisle.
Parker, Andrew, of Cumberland county,m. June 25, 1793, Margaret Williams, dau. of John Williams, of Cumberland county.
Peebles, Miss Elizabeth, m. June 19, 1794, Dr. John Geddis, of Newville.
Pollock, Miss Margaret, dau. of John, of Carlisle, m. Nov. 12, 1795, Hance Morrison, of Pittsburgh.
Postlethwaite, Dr. James, m. April 11, 1799, Betsy, dau. of the late Major James Smith, of this county.
Pollock, Miss Polly, eldest dau. of Oliver Pollock, Esq., of Silvers Spring, m. Dr. Samuel Robinson, July 9, 1799, by Rev. Snowden.
Pollock, Jerrat, m.Feb. 13,1800, Miss Polly Briggs, both of Cumberland county.
Pattison, Charles, of Carlisle, m. Sept. 16, 1800, Miss Polly Mateer, of Allen township.
Postlethwaite, Miss Amelia, dau. of Col. Samuel, m. Jan., 1801, Henry Coulton, of Greensburg.
Pollock, Oliver, of Carlisle, m. last week in October, 1805, Mrs. Dady, of Baltimore.
Pendergrass, Edward, of Carlisle, m. May 20, 1810, Jane Pence, of West Pennsboro', by Rev. Campbell.
Purcell, Edward, of Millerstown, m. June 6, 1810, Miss Grizel Wood, of Thompsontown, by Rev. John Thomas.
Parker, Miss Mary E., dau.of the late Capt. Alexander Parker, of this county, m. at Pittsburgh, July 3d, 1810, William Robinson, Esq., of Pittsburgh, by Rev. Mr. Taylor.
Peacock, James, editor Pennsylvania Reporter, m. September 25, 1813, by Rev. Buchanan, Frances C. Slough, at Harrisburg.
Province, Robert, Esq., of Huntingdon, m. Jan. 20, 1814, Mary Ramsey, of Carlisle, by Rev. Dr. Atwater.

Patton, Robert, formerly of Cumberland county, m. April 25, 1814, in Mifflintown, Mrs. Mary Cottle.
Pratt, Robert, m. Oct. 29, 1816, by Rev. Mr. Keller, Sarah Lamberton, all of Cumberland county.
Quigley, Christopher, Esq., of Allen twp., m. March 25, 1806, Mrs. Katharine Longenecker, of Carlisle.
Quigley, Wm., of Cumberland county, m. March 5, 1807, Elizabeth Adams, by Rev. Snowden.
Quigley, Christopher, m. March 7, 1809, Mary Hunter, both of Allen twp.
Quigley, Miss Sarah, m. March 3, 1813, by Rev. Dr. Campbell, David Reisinger, all of Carlisle.
Ross, James, Esq., of Washington county, Pa., m. Jan. 13, 1791, Nancy Woods, dau. of George Woods, Esq., of Bedford.
Rippey, Ruth, dau. of Capt. William, of Shippensburg, m. Dec. 12, 1791, Joseph Duncan.
Rippey, Isabel, dau. of Capt. William, of Shippensburg, m. Aug. 8, 1793, Joseph Kerr, merchant, of Strasburg.
Ramsey, Peggy, dau. of James, of Carlisle, m. May 8, 1794, Major Samuel Jackson, of Mifflintown.
Ream, Henry, of Baltimore, m. Feb. 9, 1797, Polly Crever, dau. of John Crever, of Carlisle.
Ramsey, James, merchant, of Carlisle, m. Sept. 25, 1800, Elizabeth Smith, dau. of Capt. John Smith, of Adams county.
Ramsey, Wm., Esq., Dep. Surveyor of this county, m. June 15, 1804, at Clark's Ferry, by Rev. John Linn, Miss Nancy Clark.
Reehm, Englehardt, cabinet maker, of Carlisle, m. June 28, 1804, Miss Betsy Black, dau. of Peter Black, of East Pennsboro', by Rev. Mr. Sano.
Reynolds, Benjamin, m. June 26, 1806, Mary, dau. of Patrick Cochran, all of Shippensburg, by Rev. Moody.
Radatt, Samuel, m. June 14, 1810, by Rev. John F. Moeller, Sarah Bell, all of Shippensburg.
Riley, James, m. April 23, 1812, by Rev. Dr. Davidson, Sarah Frank, both of Carlisle.
Reed, Hugh, m. Jan. 14, 1813, Nancy Kennedy, both of Carlisle, by Rev. Mr. Houston.

Rowan, David, Peggy, dau. of, m. April 15, 1813, Joseph Edwards, cabinet maker, all of Carlisle.
Roland, Philip, of Cocalico twp., Lancaster county, m. Oct. 3, 1816, Elizabeth Markle, of Allen twp., Cumberland county.
Remp, Samuel, m. Oct. 3, 1816, Elizabeth Worst, both of Mifflin twp.
Scott, Capt. Wm., Margaret, widow of, m. at Carlisle, April 17, 1809, William Rodgers.
Smith, William, m. Oct. 5, 1809, Martha Carr, both of Carlisle.
Seely, Lieut., U. S., A., m. Jan. 30, 1810, Miss Gray, dau. of Capt. William Gray, of Sunbury.
Sheldon, Richard, of Cumberland county, ironmaster, m. April 3, 1792, by Rev. John Campbell, Susanna Foulk, dau. of Stephen Foulk, Sr., at his seat near Carlisle.
Sterrett, Nancy, dau. of Ralph Sterrett, m. June 28, 1792, Adam Logue, of Carlisle, by Rev. Dr. Davidson.
Sanderson, Patty, dau. of Robert, m. Nov. 20, 1792, James McClean, of Leesburg, Va.
Semple, Steele, attorney-at-law, at Pittsburgh, m. Dec. 17, 1793, Kitty Fowler, dau. of Capt. George Fowler, of Wingfield, Allegheny county, Pa.
Steel, John, Esq., Amelia, dau. of, m. Feb. 4, 1794, James Given, merchant, of Carlisle.
Semple, Jean, dau. of Robert, m. April 15, 1794, John Miller, of Mount Rock.
Smith, James, m. Oct. 26, 1795, Miss Betsey Dunlap, both of Cumberland county.
Steele, Joseph, clockmaker, m. Sept, 8, 1796, Miss Johnston.
Sanderson, Robert, of Middleton twp., Jean, dau. of, m. June 5, 1800, Wm. Holling, of Virginia.

NOTES AND QUERIES.

Historical, Biographical and Genealogical.

XIX.

WARD.

My great-grandfather, George Ward, father of my grandmother Jordan, who was Letitia Ward, was born in now Dauphin county, Pa., the first in 1755, the other about 1780. My object is to ascertain if there are any Wards of this same family residing in that county. My grandfather Ward removed to Warren county, Ohio, during the 'nineties.

JOHN WARD JORDAN.
Louisville, Ky.

EWING.

I wish to find out the maiden name of the wife of Thomas Ewing, who lived in Manor township, Lancaster county, Pa. They had a son who became General James Ewing and lived in York county, Pa. His father having died, his mother married a man by the name of Connolly and they had a son, who was known in Western Pennsylvania as Dr. John Connolly. Lord Dunmore appointed Connolly a justice of the peace in what he was pleased to style West Augusta, being all of Pennsylvania west of the mountains. He gave much trouble to Western Pennsylvania and was arrested near Hagerstown, Md. His half brother, General James Ewing, of York, joined him on his way to Philadelphia, where he was to be imprisoned and tried to reason with him and induce him to be loyal to the country, but without avail. It is said this Dr. John Connolly was a nephew of Col. George Croghan, who was Sir William Johnson's agent in Western Pennsylvania. Can you give me the maiden name of General James Ewing's and Dr. John Connolly's mother?

N. B. H.
Pittsburgh, Pa.

KELSO.

John Kelso came to Erie county from near Harrisburg, I think from Cumberland county, with Col. Thomas Forster, Jacob Weis and others in 1797, and located in Fairview, twelve miles west of Erie. In 1800 he removed near Erie and purchased lands still in his family. In 1803 he located in Erie; was appointed Associate Judge for Erie county July 4th, 1800, but refused the commission; was appointed Prothonotary for Erie county December 1st, 1804; served a year, resigned and was appointed commissioner of land sales and lots in Erie; on January 18, 1809, reappointed Prothonotary for Erie county, which he held until his death in 1819. He was also brigadier-general at Erie during the War of 1812. He had five sons and two daughters.

Edwin G. Kelso, born in 1800, was appointed Prothonotary of Erie county Oct. 21, 1824, and held the office until Jan. 8, 1836. He was appointed Collector of the Port of Erie July 1, 1836, and held it ten years. He died in Erie twenty years ago and left children.

Henry B. Kelso died at Mackinaw prior to the Civil War.

Albert G. Kelso resided three miles west of Erie on his father's early purchase, and William C. Kelso, an attorney, in Erie.

Melvin M. Kelso was a successful farmer.

Caroline Kelso married Hon. Elijah Babbitt in 1828, and they both lived in Erie.

Adaline Kelso married Rev. James M. Whallan in 1829. She and her husband both died prior to 1880.

This is the history of John Kelso and his children in Erie county. Mrs. Kelso died at the old Kelso homestead, in Erie, about 1870.

Mr. Kelso brought a female slave when he came to Erie county who was too old to be emancipated and was a slave for life, the only one that ever lived and died in Erie county and has descendants there.

N. W. R.
Erie, Pa.

James Kell, Esq. of York, Pa.

James Kell, a prominent citizen and leading lawyer, of York, Pa., died in that city June 4th, 1899, after an illness of tbout six months. He was born in Youngstown, Westmoreland county, Pa., December 14, 1828, of Scotch-Irish parentage, his father being Samuel Kell (son of James), who was born in Hummelstown, Dauphin county, Pa., his mother Margaret Mears (daughter of John and Anne Baldridge), who was born in Path Valley, Franklin county, Pa. Mr. Kell's early life was spent in the latter county, and in 1856 he removed to York, where for several years he taught in the public schools, subsequently studied law with Henry L.

Fisher, Esq., and was admitted to the bar in 1862, from which time until within a few months of his death he was in continuous practice. He was long prominent in the leadership of the Republican party of York county, holding the chairmanship of the county organization for a number of terms. He was the Register of Wills in 1877 by appointment of Governor Hartranft, and postmaster of the city of York from 1884 to 1888. At the first election (in 1875) for additional law judge of the courts of York, he was the Republican candidate against Hon. Pere L. Wicks, who was elected. Mr. Kell occupied a number of positions of trust, among which may be mentioned those of director of the old North ward school district of the then borough of York, president of the Union Fire Engine Company during the latter sixties, trustee of the York Collegiate Institute from its incorporation in 1873, and of the Children's Home from its foundation shortly after the close of the war between the States. He was a past master of York Lodge, No. 266, F. & A. M., and secretary and charter member of Willis Council, No. 508, Royal Arcanum. James Kell was married in 1862 to Miss Jane Elizabeth Fischer, daughter of Dr. John Frey Fischer, one of the leading physicians in his day in York county. To this union were born eight children, all of whom, with his widow, survive, viz: John F., a lawyer of York, James A. and William S., of Philadelphia, where both are connected with the Bradstreet Mercantile Agency, Helen M., Mary C., Alfred M., Jane F. and Eliza K. Kell.

Mr. Kell was a painstaking lawyer, faithful to his clients' interests and careful in the preparation of legal papers, many of which were frequently taken as models of their kind. He was a member of the First Presbyterian Church of York for many years.

Cumberland County Marriages.

Sterrett, John, of Allen township, m. Oct. 27, 1801, Nancy, dau. of Robert Chambers, residence "on his farm on the K¾ banks of the Conedoguinet creek."
Stewart, Dr. Alexander, m. Nov. 17, 1801, Jane, dau. of Capt. William Rippey, all of Shippensburg.
Snowden, John M., one of the editors of the "Farmer's Register," Greensburg, m. Nov. 24, 1801, Elizabeth, dau. of John Moore, Esq., all of Westmoreland county.
Schouller, John, of Mifflin township, m. Dec. 30, 1802, Mary, dau. of Joseph McKee, of Springfield.
Stevenson, Dr. George, m. at Pittsburgh, Jan. 27, 1803, Maria Barker, youngest dau. of Joseph Barker, merchant of that place.
Skiles, John, m. Nov. 1, 1803, Betsy, dau. of Percival Kean, all of West Pennsboro'.
Searight, Lieut. Alexander, of Middleton township, m. [1804] Elizabeth, dau. of Andrew Lobaugh, of Adams county.
Stear, Jacob, m. Sept. 4, 1806, Magdalena Bacher, both of East Pennsboro'.
Scott, Jane, dau. of John Scott, Esq., of Shippensburg, m. Dec. 1, 1808, by Rev. Mr. Burge, John Bowman, all of Shippensburg.
Semple, Joseph, m. June 5, 1810, Ann Noble, both of East Pennsboro'.
Sturges, James, hatter, of Shippensburg, m. Sept. 29, 1810, by Rev. Job Guest, Miss Polly Bradenbury.
Smith, Mary, dau. of John Smith, shoemaker, of Carlisle, m. Jan. 21, 1811, Edward McGunagle, shoemaker, of Shippensburg.
Sturm, George, merchant, m. March 19, 1811, Miss Elizabeth Fisher, all of Carlisle.
Shryock, John, Esq., m. Sept. 12, 1811, the amiable Martha Cochran, dau. of Patrick Cochran, of Shippensburg.
Sharp, Capt. Alexander, of Newton township, m. Jan. 14, 1812, Miss Isabella Oliver, of East Pennsboro', by Rev. John Hayes.
Scroggs, John A., Esq., of Beaver county, m. March 1, 1814, Anna White, dau. of John White, of Mercer county.
Steel, Mary, m. May 12, 1814, Jacob Bishop, all of Carlisle.
Shannon, James, m. Nov. 7, 1816, by Rev. Mr. Moody, Jane, dau. of John Wilson, all of Newton township.

Stewart, Samuel, m. May 22, 1817, Ann Donnalson, both of Dickinson township.
Thompson, Gen. William, Elizabeth, dau. of m. April 24, 1800, at New Castle, Del., by Rev. Robert Clay, Mr. Jh. L. D'Happart.
Todd, Isaac, m. June 16, 1807, Elizabeth Keller, dau, of Leonard Keller, all of Carl sle.
Thompson, Samuel, m. Oct. 10, 1808, Miss Leticia Brown, all of Carlisle.
Trindle, Mrs. Sarah, widow of Capt. Alexander Trindle, m. Jan. 24, 1792, William Gibson, of East Pennsboro'.
Trindle, William, s. of Capt. Alexander Trindle, m. Jan. 31, 1792, Betsy Gibson, dau. of William Gibson.
Urie, Thomas, m. Feb. 7, 1793, Margaret, dau. of John Dunbar, of Cumberland county.
Urie, Thomas, Esq., of Middleton township, m. Oct. 30, 1809, Mrs. Margaret Parker, of East Pennsboro'.
Ulrich, Mary, dau. of Nicholas, of Carlisle, m. Sept. 12, 1816, George Knitzman, of Carlisle.
Villard, A. J., of Washington city, Sophie, dau. of, m. Feb. 26, 1814, Jacint Laval, colonel of First Light Dragoons.
Walters, Jacob, merchant, of Chambersburg, m. Nov. 8, 1791, Miss Patty Stuart, of Carlisle.
Wallace, William, of Carlisle, m. Miss Jean Gray, of Northumberland county, Nov. 9, 1791.
Woods, Nathan, m. May 31, 1796, Jean Weakley, dau. of James, both of this county.
Watts, David, Esq., m. Sept. 14, 1796, by Rev. Mr. Campbell, Miss Juliana Miller, dau. of Gen. Henry Miller, of York.
Weakley, Miss Rebecca, m. Nov. 17, 1796, Thomas Craighead.
Wise, George, saddler, m. March 2, 1797, Mrs. Fisher, both of Carlisle.
Wilson, George, of Mifflin county, member of the Senate of Pennsylvania, m. March 15, 1798, by Rev. Dr. Rogers, Miss Isabella White, of Philadelphia.
Wright, Robert, of Carlisle, m. Nov. 20, 1798, Nancy Holmes, dau. of Thomas Holmes, of York county.
Watson, Dr. William, of Mifflintown, m. December 10, 1801, Miss Polly Davis, dau. of the late Col. John Davis, of Middlesex.
Wilson, Samuel, of Fairfield, Ohio, m. Oct. 13, 1803, Miss Sarah Martin, eldest dau. of Samuel Martin, of Allen township.
Williams, Abraham, of Allen township, m. March 29, 1804, Miss McElhaney, of York county.
Williams, David, of Monaghan township, York county, m. April 5, 1804, Miss Jane Neel, of same place.
Wallace, Miss Elizabeth, of Cumberland county, m. April 21, 1804, at Harrisburg, Gilbert Burnett, of Baltimore.
Wise, Frederick, m. Sept. 4, 1806, Mrs. Elizabeth Solander, both of Middleton township.
Wise, Jacob, m. Sept. 4, 1806, Miss Elizabeth Weaver, both of Middleton township.
Wheeler, William, Esq., Deputy Surveyor for this county, m. Feb. 22, 1807, Miss Polly Fisher, of Carlisle.
Williams, David, saddler, from Baltimore county, Md., m. Sept. 10, 1807, Sarah, dau. of John Smith, blacksmith, of Carlisle.
Waggoner, Abraham, m. Nov. 12, 1807, Mary Thuma, both of Cumberland county.
Wonderlich, Susan, dau. of David, of Middleton township, m. Nov. 15, 1807, Abraham Herr, of Carlisle.
Waugh, Samuel, of East Pennsboro', m. Nov. 3, 1806, Elizabeth Seidel, of Rye township.
Weakley, Thomas, of Dickinson township, m. March 30, 1809, Nancy Alexander, of Carlisle.
Wilson, Robert, of State of Ohio, m. Junt 1, 1809, Jane, dau. of Robert Donavan, of Lurgan township, Franklin county.
Wood, George, of Mifflin county, m. Aug. 24, 1809, Margaret Purcell, of Millerstown, Cumberland county.
Wright, Rev. John, pastor of the church in New Lancaster, Ohio, m. Oct. 16, 1809, Jane, dau. of Edward Weakley, of Cumberland county.
Weaver, Adam, Esq., of Jefferson county, Va., m. Nov., 1806, Mrs. Lydia McCalla at the residence of Derrick Peterson, Esq., Lower Dublin, by Rev. Dr. Rogers.

Waugh, Miss ——, m. Feb. 27, 1810, Howard Moore, both of this county.
Weakley, James, s. of Edward, m. March 24, 1811, Miss Priscilla Foulke, both of Middleton township.
Wright, James, of Chambersburg, m. March 14, 1811, Jane Kennedy, dau. of Hugh Kennedy, shoemaker, of Carlisle.
Wiestling, John S., printer, m. Dec. 24, 1811, at Harrisburg, by Rev. Gloninger, Sarah Youse, of Harrisburg.
Wingart, Valentine, hatter, of Huntingdon, m. Feb. 4, 1812, by Rev. Mr. Reed, Miss Rebecca Todd, of Carlisle.
Wright, Ensign William, m. April 14, 1812, Miss Peggy Shields, both of Carlisle.
Wilkins, William, Esq., attorey-at-aw, of Pittsburgh, m. Oct. 13, 1812, Catharine Holmes, dau. of John Holmes, of Baltimore.
Wolf, John, of North Middleton, m. Dec. 22, 1812, Mary Hock, of East Pennsboro'.
Weakley, William, of Dickinson township, m. Nov. 25, 1813, by Rev. Dr. Atwater, Isabella, dau. of Thomas Alexander, dec'd.
Woodney, John, of Path Valley, m. April 7, 1814, by Rev. Mr. Linn, Ann Patterson, of Shearman's Valley.
Walters, Henry, Esq., of Liverpool, Cumberland county, m. Jane M. Thompson, of Thompsontown, May 6, 1817, by Rev. Thomas Smith.
Wilson, James, merchant, of Chambersburg, m. July 22, 1817, Eliza Ege, dau. of Michael Ege, dec'd., of Cumberland county.

The Early Dead at Mifflinburg.

Mifflinburg is a beautiful and thriving town in the heart of Buffalo Valley in Union county, Pa., and was founded over a century ago by Elias Youngman, and for that reason was called Youngmanstown. Immediately south of the town is the cemetery, the outgrowth of the churchyard connected with the Union church, built about 1806, and still standing, but used as a warehouse. In the old part of the cemetery, in front of the old church, are buried many of the German settlers of the valley, but most of their graves are unmarked. In the following list will be found a few whose names prominently occur in the early history of this region. Perhaps half of the inscriptions herewith given are in the German language. The tombstone of the proprietor and his wife are inscribed in German and fairly legible, as follows, in literal English:

"Here rests—Elias Youngman—Born the 15th August, 1738—Married the 15th of January with Catharine Nagel—Lived 54 years, 3 months and 6 days in—Matrimony—Begat 2 sons and 1—Daughter—Died the 17th April, 1817, as—Proprietor of Youngmanstown, Union county—Was aged 78 years, 8mo. and 2d.—Text, Psa. 92, Vers. 13-15."

"To the memory dedicated—Catharine Youngman—A Born Nagle's Daughter—Was the 4th April, 1743—In Kafferoth in Germany born—Came with her father to America—Married to Elias Youngman—Had three children—George, Catharine and Thomas—And died the 23 January, 1822—In Mifflinburg, Union county—Her age was 78 years, 9 mo. and 19 days—Text, John xvii, 14."

Two of Mr. Youngman's children lie close to him, viz., Thomas, who died in 1812, aged 40 years, and Catharine, wife of John Dreisbach, born 1766, and died 1852. The tombstone of Dreisbach is a model one, as it has on it valuable family history, including a list of all his children. He was the son of the Emigrant Dreisbach, who came to Pennsylvania from Wettgenstein, Westphalia, Ger., in 1751. (See N. & Q., No. vii—1898). He was born in Berks county, Pa., 1762; m. to Cath. Youngman 1788, and d. 1823. Children were Samuel, John, Thomas, Elias, Cath., Joseph, George and Maria. By the side of Thomas Youngman lies his "former wife," Amelia Foster, who died 1842, aged 69 y.

Aumiller, John, b. 1799; d. 1883.
Aumiller, Eve, wf., b. 1803; d. 1892.
Aurand, Henry, b. 1782; d. 1844.
Aurand, Eve, wf., b. 1783; d. 1842.
Aurand, Sarah, b. 1815; d. 1856.
Bartges, Fred, b. 1779; d. 1853.
Bartges, Elisabeth, wf., and dau. of Peter Zeller, d. 1811.
Bartges, Henry, b. 1808; d. 1842.

Beachler, John, b. 1797; d. 1855.
Beachler, Elis, wf., b. 1797; d. 1884.
Bishop, John, b. 1789; d. 1848.
Bogenreif, David, b. 1796; d. 1881.
Bogenreif, Cath., wf., b. 1798; d. 1852.
Boyer, Jacob, b. 1793; d. 1863.
Boyer, Sarah, wf., b. 1797; d. 1869.
Boope, John, b. 1776; d. 1851.
Boope, Mary, wf., b. 1783; d. 1862.
Clark, Mary, wf. of Aaron, b. 1755; d. 1841.
Cronemiller, Martin, b. 1761; d. 1838 (Rev. soldier).
Cronemiller, Jacob, b. 1787; d. 1840.
Cronemiller, Susan, wf., b. 1788; d. 1839.
Cummings, Cath., wf. of John, b. 1779; d. 1837.
Dreisbach, John (see above).
Dreisbach, Thomas, b. 1797; d. 1872. (In War of 1812).
Dreisbach, Mary, wf., b. 1798; d. 1862.
Fox, Peter, b. 1773; d. 1856.
Fox, Henry, b. 1786; d. 1856.
Gillfillin, Dr. E, b. 1769; d. 1833.
Gillfillin, Eliz., wf., b. 1794; d. 1832.
Gilard, Christopher, b. 1760; d. 1824.
Gilard, Magdalena, wf., b. 1758; d. 1829.
Gutilius, Fred, Esq., b. 1767; d. 1839.
Gutilius, Anna Cath., wf., b. 1773; d. 1838.
Hassenpflug, John Henry, b. at Harrisburg (?) Aug. 20, 1750; m. to Maria Seebolt, 1790; begat 9 sons and 5 daughters, and d. 1829.
Hassenpflug, Maria, wf., b. 1769; d. 1852.
Hassenpflug, Samuel, b. 1794; d. 1871.
Hassenpflug, Rachel, wf., b. 1797; d. 1863.
Hassenpflug, Solomon, d. 1812.
Hixon, G. W. b. 1804; d. 1853.
Hoy, John, b. 1767; d. 1849.
Hoy, Mary, b. 1781; d. 1848.
Hoy, Lydia, b. 1816; d. 1897.
Hoy, John, b. 1768; d. 1854.
Hoy, Mary, wf., b. 1774; d. 1833.
Hoy, Elisabeth, b. 1785; d. 1822.
Houtz, Henry, b. 1802; d. 1867.
Hoffman, Jos., b. 1800; d. 1878.
Hoffman, Lydia, wf., b. 1802; d. 1872.
Imschaffstall, Eve, b. 1773; d. 1851.
[Note—This is a most peculiar German name, and in literal English is "Insheepstable."—In the sheep stable.]
Kaupp, J. Charles, b. 1775; d. 1851.
Kaupp, Ann Maria, wf., b. 1783; d. 1872.
Kauffman, Peter, b. 1762; d. 1845.
Kauffman, Ann Maria, b. 1769; d. 1857.
Kauffman, David, b. 1775; d. 1853.
Kauffman, Elis, wf., b. 1784; d. 1862.
Klein, Jacob, b. 1765; d. 1849.
Katherman, Fred., b. 1790; d. 1850.
Katherman, Christina, wf., b. 1799; d. 1867.
Kleckner, Abr., b. 1750; d. 1839.
Kleckner, Anna Barb., wf., b. 1760; d. 1849.
Kleckner, Daniel, b. 1780; d. 1833.
Latshaw, Jacob, b. 1780; d. 1870.
Latshaw, Marg., wf., b. 1800; d. 1876.
Lenhart, Jacob, b. 1783; d. 1845.
Lenhart, Christianna, wf., b. 1783; d. 1837.
Maize, Jacob, b. 1777; d. 1836.
Maize, Elis, wf., b. 1767; d. 1842.
Maderia, Abr., b. 1779; d. 1852.
Maderia, Maria, wf., b. 1794; d. 1847.
Meyer, George, b. 1771; d. 1850.
Meyer, Eve, wf., b. 1774; d. 1848.
Meyer, Marg., dau., b. 1814; d. 1885.
Millhouse, John Nich., b. in Germany, 1753; m. to Juliana Welker, 1783; begat 4 sons and 7 dau. and d. 1835.
Millhouse, Julianna, wf. (Welcher), b. in Oley, Berks county, 1761; d. 1845.
Moss, Patrick, b. 1762; d. 1834.
Moss, Elenore, wf., b. 1765; d. 1839.
Moll, Conrad, b. 1779; d. 1848.
Moll, Susan, wf., b. 1787; d. 1863.
Musser, Deborah, wf. of John, b. 1792; d. 1873.
Orwig, George, b. 1759; d. 1841.
Orwig, wf., b. 1760; d. 1842.
Orwig, Elis, wf. of Abr., b. 1792; d. 1828.
[Note—George Orwig was the son of Gottfried Orbig, who came from Germany in 1741, b. 1719, and his wife Gloria, b. 1713, and who settled near the present site of Orwigsburg, Pa.]
Pellman, Mary, relict of Dr. Conrad Pellman, b. 1764; d. 1850.
Pontius, Peter, b. 1783; d. 1862.
Pontius, Barb., wf., b. 1791; d. 1877.
Rinkard, John, b. 1808; d. 1888.
Rinkard, Barb., b. 1813; d. 1889.
Rinkard, Jos., b. 1809; d. 1887.
Ruhl, George Philip, b. 1760; d. 1843.
Ruhl, Elis, wf., b. 1768; d. 1841.
Rezner, John, b. 1774; d. 1836.
Rezner, Anna Mary, wf., b. 1773; d. 1826.
Rockey, William, b. 1759, and m. 1782, to Margaret Leader; begat 9 children; d. 1816.

Rockey, Margaret, wf., b. 1759; d. 1837.
Rockey, William, b. 1793; d. 1849.
Rockey, George, b. 1786; d. 1855.
Rockey, Mary, b. 1790; d. 1848.
Silverwood, Thomas, b. in England, 1790; d. 1834.
Silverwood, Mary, wf., b. 1800; d. 1857.
Spieglemyer, Elis, b. 1785; d. 1822.
Shoch, Mich., b. 1763; d. 1864.
Shoch, Anna, wf., b. 1769; d. 1823.
Shoch, Maria, wf. 2nd, b. 1782; d. 1856.
Stitzer, John, b. 1778; d. 1846.
Stitzer, Christena, wf., b. 1783; d. 1853.
Stitzer, John, b. 1808; d. 1859.
Shoemaker, Christina, wf. of John, b. 1781; d. 1842.
Sechler, Samuel, b. 1787; d. 1867.
Sechler, Elis, wf., b. 1787; d. 1840.
Walter, Abr., b. 1812; d. 1869.
Walter, Christina, b. 1817; d. 1867.
Walter, Jacob, b. 1798; d. 1873.
Wingert, Elis, wf. of John, b. 1787; d. 1852.
Welcher, Fred., b. in Oley, Berks county, 1774; d. 1846.
Welcher, George, b. in Oley, 1791; d. 1835.
Witmer, Sebastian, b. 1776; d. 1846.
Witmer, Mary, wf., b. 1776; d. 1824.
Witmer, Anna, wf. 2nd, b. 1775; d. 1845.
Wehr, Simon, b. 1769; d. 1840.
Wehr, Anna Cath., b. 1774; d. 1854.
Yearick, Simon, b. 1755; d. 1831 (Revolutionary soldier).
Yearick, Samuel, b. 1786; d. 1854.
Yearick, Christian, b. 1814; d. 1856.
Yearick, Henry, Esq., b. 1780; d. 1856.
Yearick, Maria Cath., wf., b. 1787; d. 1837.
Zellers, Peter, b. 1745, in Tulpehocken twp., Berks county; d. 1817.
Zellers Catharine, wf. and dau. of Jacob Willhelm, b. 1742; d. 1808.
Zellers, Henry, b. 1778; d. 1846.
Zellers, Mary, wf., b. 1782; d. 1858.
Zellers, George, b. 1806; d. 1892.
Zellers, Marg., wf., b. 1809; d. 1863.
Zerby, George, b. 1774; d. 1853.
Zerby, Susanna Cath., b. 1775; d. 1847.

A. STAPLETON.
Lewisburg, Pa.

A Patriot of the Revolution.

Dr. Benjamin Alison, son of Rev. Francis Alison, vice provost, University of Pennsylvania, and Hannah Armitage, was b. 1745, in New London township, Chester county, Pa., and d. in Philadelphia in the autumn of 1872. He entered the University of Pennsylvania in May of 1761 and graduated in the class of 1765; N. M., 1767; B. M., 1771. Commissioned surgeon First Pennsylvania Battalion, Col. John Philip deHaas, June 3, 1776; served in the Canada campaign and resigned January 1, 1777. It is inferred from his will that he was unmarried, as he left his estate to nephews and nieces and Col. Hunter, commandant of Fort Augusta.

NOTES AND QUERIES.

Historical, Biographical, and Genealogical.

XX.

JENNINGS.
I. Zebulon Jennings, b. 1709; d. 1777, in New Jersey. By first wife Sarah ——, they had issue:
II. Zebulon, b. 1735; d. 1776; m. in 1762, Joanna Little. Among other children they had issue:
III. Jonathan, b. May 14, 1769, in New Jersey; d. Nov. 2, 1808, in Ohio. He m. in arch, 1791, Elizabeth Stephenson, b. June 27, 1775; d. August 22, 1825. They had, among others:
IV. Junia, b. Sept. 10, 1800, in Fayette county, Pa.; d. Feb. 19, 1871, in Marietta, O. He m. in 1820, Hannah McCabe, b. in 1794; d. Dec. 19, 1831. She was the daughter of Robert McCabe (1770-1823) and Polly McCracken (1774-1823) his wife, who was a daughter of Rev. Alexander McCracken.
Information concerning other branches of this family is desired.

John Morton the "Signer."

I am somewhat surprised at the meagre information you have of the services of my ancestor, John Morton, a signer of the Declaration of Independence. The data I have show the following, which ought to be recorded and hence my reason for supplying it for future inquirers, should there be any, for his descendants are numerous. He was as follows:

Member of the Provincial Assembly 1756-1767.
Justice of County Court, 1757.
Member of Stamp Act Congress in 1765.
Sheriff of his county 1766-1769.
Member of Pennsylvania Assembly 1772-1775, being its Speaker in 1775.
Associate Judge Supreme Court of Pennsylvania 1774.
Delegate to the Continental Congress 1774 and 1776.

A signer of the Declaration of Independence of July 4th, 1776, when, by giving the deciding vote of the Pennsylvania delegation in favor of that Magna Charta of our liberty, he, in the language of John Adams on that occasion, "crowned Pennsylvania the 'Keystone of the Arch of Liberty," thus giving origin to the appellation "Keystone State" applied to Pennsylvania. He died April, 1777, the first signer to die. It is said that his decease was largely due to grief at the ill success then attending our arms. On his death-bed he used these words, referring to those who censured him for his boldness in giving the deciding vote of his delegation, in favor of independence: "Tell them they will live to see the hour when they shall acknowledge it to have been the most glorious service that I ever rendered my country."

CHAS. L. DAVIS, U. S. A.

An Old Timepiece.

The Misses Kurtz, of North George street, York, Pa., have an old "Grandfather's Clock" that was made by their great grandfather, John Fisher, of "Yorktown," Pa. Upon the inside of the door is the following newspaper clipping which was taken from a local paper, evidently published in the latter part of the eighteenth century:

"York, Pa., July 28, 1790.—Messrs. Edie & Wilcoks, by giving the following a place in your useful and impartial paper you will oblige a constant reader: A description of a curious timepiece completed by Mr. John Fisher, Sr., Yorktown, Pa., May 23d, 1790, the astronomical part of which does the greatest honor to the inventor. The timepiece performs the office of a common eight-day clock, but runs thirty-five days. It exhibits the time of the sun's rising and setting, its declination, the longest and shortest days in the year and the hours of the day in the most distant parts of the world, all of which is clearly elucidated by the globe affixed about three inches from the center. It has the moon circulating around the verge of the globe, which makes all the different vicissitudes that the real moon seems to make to us in the heavens. The dial plate is circular and of fourteen inches in diameter, in the center are disposed the date, minute and second hands, and to the north of them the hour hand operates. The plate is elegantly engraved, and is by no means void of taste. Round the verge it is ornamented with the twelve signs of the zodiac, the seven planets and twelve months, with the exact number of days in each month in a year.

"The operation of winding this machine is performed on an entire new plan and constructed in such a manner as not to affect its going. The whole is executed with fourteen wheels and a suitable number of pinions, and contained between two brass plates six inches long and three wide. It is kept in motion by two common weights, and that motion kept regulated by a second pendulum.

"This is not the only performance of Mr. John Fisher's that deserves notice, for besides this he has constructed and finished several other pieces of clock work, equally curious, by which he has gained very distinguished professional celebrity. I cannot omit mentioning that Mr. Fisher possesses fine natural talents in drawing, painting, engraving, etc., to enter into detail of which would appear to be too prolix, suffice it to say that they have already rendered him eminently conspicuous among such of the admirers of the fine arts as have had the pleasure of his acquaintance."

John Fisher resided in York at the time of the American Revolution and was intimate with the national celebrities of the times who visited York, especially during the sitting there of the Continental Congress in 1777. His son was Dr. John Fisher and the latter's son was Dr. John Frey Fisher, whose daughters, Mrs. Dr.

Luther M. Lochman and Mrs. James Kell (both widows), still survive and live in York.
J. A. K.

Early Pennsylvania--German Emigration North and West.

About the beginning of the present century there was a very considerable emigration of Mennonites from Lancaster county, Pa., to Upper Canada. Among the names I now recall are such familiar ones as Groff (Grove), Eby, Webber (Weaver), Eyer, &c. A large number of Pennsylvania Germans settled along the Niagara river, some on the American side. Several Lancaster county families settled at the falls, where a Mr. Witmer built the first grist mill, about 1811-12.

Another line of German emigration was deflected to Erie county, Pa. Scores of families settled in the vicinity of North East several miles distant from Erie. Among them were the Hersheys and Wilhelms (Williams) from Lancaster county, and the Heiss' from Berks county.

Fairfield county, Ohio, was almost wholly settled by Pennsylvania Germans. The pioneer was named Seitz, from York county, in 1801. He was followed in a few years by a very large number of friends and relatives.

Pickaway and Stark counties also had originally a preponderating Pennsylvania German population. The Sandusky region, Sandusky and Seneca counties, recived from 1820 to 1835 great colonies of Germans from Pennsylvania. In one instance almost an entire congregation from Mifflin county, Pa., emigrated thither.

The Pennsylvania Germans originally settled a number of counties in Indiana and Illinois. Probably two-thirds of the original settlers of Stephenson county, Ill., were Pennsylvania Germans. In 1839 an entire class or congregation emigrated thither from Centre county, Pa. Before going they elected a full complement of church officials.

Some years later a very large colony emigrated from Cedar Creek Valley, Lehigh county, to Page county, Ill. The emigrants traveled in caravans. Their wagons were great, wide-tired canvas-covered prairie schooners. The cattle were driven along. Small pigs, chickens, etc., were taken along. The trip required many weeks to accomplish. In the case of the emigration of religious societies, family worship and the bi-weekly prayer meetings were regularly maintained.

The Mr. Seitz who has figured prominently in Ohio politics, is a descendant of the York county Seitz mentioned. The "Buckwalters," also prominent in Ohio, are descendants of the Buckwalters who removed to Ross county, O., from Colebrookdale, Berks county, Pa. They were originally Mennonites.

A. STAPLETON.

Captain John Brisbin of the Revolution

[The following communication came into our hands a number of years ago. The writer was George Mytinger Brisbin, Esq., of Osceola Mills, Pa. Accompanying was the roll of Capt. Brisbin's company, but as this is published in the History of the Pensylvania Line in the Revolution, does not occasion its reproduction here. There are some points, however, in the letter which are interesting, and hence given.]

In compliance with the promise I made you I have carefully copied the names from my grandfather's roll book, and forward them to you. There is some explanation which I deem necessary and will endeavor to make. Many of the names are spelled in different ways, where they occur in different places in the book. Grandfather spells his sometimes Brisben, and again Brisbin. I think he was unsettled about that time, as to the spelling of Brisbin. He was from Scotland, and the name in Scotland is spelled "Brisbane," where the title is still in existence. Dr. William Brisbane, of Philadelphia, is my authority for the Scotch way of spelling the name. While in Europe he visited Scotland, and had a copy of the "Brisbane" coat of arms taken, and brought it home. Dr. Brisbane, I believe, is the son of William Brisbin, who was the son of grandfather. I have frequently heard my father say, many years ago, that his father and a brother came to this country together; another brother held a commission in the English army; that the two brothers at once espoused the Revolutionary cause and entered the army; the third brother was with Gen. Howe, at New York, and whenever the opportunity offered showed his tyranny over those he termed "rebbles." This fact becoming known to the "rebble" brothers, they determined to alter the manner of spelling the name, that their descendants might never have the sins of the tyrannical brother to answer for—hence "Brisbin." Grandfather had been in the English army before the Revolution, but what service he rendered I never knew, but he had a large land grant from George the III. which was located on Green river, Kentucky, but during the war his papers became scattered, the land was monopolized by strangers and lost to him.

The baptismal name of Lieut. Sitz, as it is sometimes spelled, and that of Lieut. Gross, does not occur anywhere in the book—they are always styled "Lieut." Gross, or Sitz, as the case may be.

The baptismal name of McGraw, soldier, is omitted.

The name of "Oogon" is spelled in some places with one "o" in the commencement of the name, thus, "Ogon."

General St. Clair's name is frequently made mention of in the accounts of the soldiers, from which I infer the regiment was in his immediate command, although my father at one time had a letter from Maj. Gen. Anthony Wayne, highly extoling Captain John Brisbin's services, but that letter was taken to Washington for some purpose and never returned to him again.

Grandfather raised his company in Lancaster county—disposing of his farm for the purpose—which, I believe, at that time included the territory now covered by Dauphin and Lebanon counties. His headquarters while enlisting the company was at Harrisburg, although his home was afterwards at Bird-in-Hand, where my father was born in 1784, after the war was over, of course, and where grandfather married again, for the third time. He was a widower during the war. His third wife was a widow named Wood, who was my father's mother—whether she was the widow of the Col. Wood, who commanded the regiment, I have forgotten if I ever was informed, but somehow it occurs to me she was.

I have copied a receipt which is in the book of one of the soldiers, a copy, I suppose, of the many given. It is as follows:

April 10th, 1777.

"This is to certify that I have received from Capt. John Brisbin, of Col. Wood's regiment, in full of all demands, as wages for my services in said regiment, as witness my hand. Hugh Reed.

"Attest—A. Steel."

Grandfather had gone into the continental service in easy circumstances and came out of it poor, and long after the war was over he was harrassed by creditors, from whom he had gotten supplies for his company, but before he died he had paid everything. A copy of a letter which is preserved in this book will serve to illustrate what I have asserted. It is as follows, to wit:

"Mill Creek, Jan'y 12th, 1783.

"Sir: I just now received your letter concerning the two steers I bought from John Logan. I bought them for nine pound, Congress money, in the year 1777, the 12th day of July. You wrote to me I bought them in the year 1776. Sir, I was in Canada that year. I have sent the depreciation of nine pound by John Craige, Esq., which was three for one. If you find any error in it, send me word by John Craige, and your receipt for the money. I am, with respect, your humble servant, John Brisbin."

"Mr. Daniel Climer."

This book, made up of the stamp paper, is in a dilapidated and torn condition, as it naturally should be, after having been carried and used nightly, from camp to camp all through the eight years' war of the Revolution, and handled since then for a hundred years, but there is still enough of it left, strange to say, to make it a very desirable relic for those interested.

John Brisbin, a son of Capt. John's, was also a soldier of the Revolution. He settled in Centre county and some of his descendants are residing there now.

Captain John Brisbin is buried in old Paxtang churchyard. The inscription on the stone is as follows:

CAPT. JOHN BRISBAN,
Soldier of the Revolution,
Who Departed This Life
March 13, 1822,
Aged 91 years.
G. M. B.

NOTES AND QUERIES.

Historical, Biographical, and Genealogical.

XXI.

PATTERSON.

Robert Patterson, who died in East Pennsboro' township, Cumberland county, Pa., three miles west of Harrisburg, in 1792, was an officer in the Revolution. After the war he removed to Cumberland county and kept the Black Horse Tavern at the large spring in the location referred to. His wife was Mary Millard. Descendants residing in Virginia desire information concerning his ancestry. K. D. S.

Gilbert E. Swope, of Newville.

It is with very deep regret that we chronicle the death of a faithful correspondent of "Notes and Queries," Mr. Gilbert Ernest Swope, of Newville, Pa., which occurred on Saturday, June 17, 1899. Gilbert E. Swope was born January 24, 1860, at Dansville, N. Y. His father was the Rev. David Swope, a native of Gettysburg, Pennsylvania, who was for many years an eminent clergyman of the Lutheran Church. His mother was a daughter of Dr. Jesse Gilbert. The father died at Newville in 1881, the widowed mother surviving. Gilbert E. Swope received a good education, studied pharmacy and established himself in business at Newville, Pa., in which he was eminently successful. In his moments of leisure Mr. Swope began the preparation of the genealogy of the Swope family and allied branches, and which with all the love and fascination for family history he completed. The work is certainly an enduring monument of his untiring devotion to genealogical pursuits. His adaptability as well as fondness for historical research has given to Pennsylvania local lore, the history of the Big Spring Presbyterian church, while he almost completed a similar record of the Middle Spring Presbyterian church. Other historic labors demanded his attention and it is to be regretted that life was not spared him a few years longer to enable further research and the completion of contemplated contributions to the history of his locality. He was an indefatigable worker in this peculiar field and in the thirty years of his noble young life he certainly accomplished much. He was earnest and conscientious in his researches and his faithfulness cannot be questioned. Pity it is that there are so few to take his place. He was a frequent contributor to Notes and Queries, and no one regrets more sincerely the death of that noble genealogist than the Editor. Mr. Swope was exceedingly anxious to complete his history of Middle Spring church referred to, but finding this impossible, he committed it to his devoted wife, who rendered him such valuable assistance in his disinterested labors, to issue to the world. It is fondly hoped that she may have the strength, for she has the ability, to do this. Looking over his work for the past ten years and what he accomplished, it behooves those who take interest in the lore of the Cumberland Valley to be up and doing. It is to be wished that the mantle of this faithful friend of historical research will fall upon the shoulders of as able and devoted a chronicler. In the waning twilight of the 19th of June, loving and sympathetic hearts followed his remains to the church he revered, and in the God's acre within its shadows committed them to the earth, "Dust to dust, ashes to ashes." Mr. Swope labored for the good of others and his life destiny is hallowed by the thought that without selfish motives he accomplished much and left a name to be long remembered in the annals of Pennsylvania local history.

OEHRLE (EARLY) GENEALOGY.

I. The first Thomas Oehrle (Early) of whom we know, and who was a school teacher and court clerk at Jesingen, Wuertemberg, together with his wife, died prior to 1710. We know of but two of their children.

i. Jacob, b. Sept. 1679; on Feby. 5, 1704, married Anna Regina Kihlkopf. He was a weaver and day laborer. He died Sept. 26, 1744, aged 65 years.

ii. Thomas, b. May, 1687, a carpenter and afterwards a magistrate or judge in the congregation, or township. Died Nov. 25, 1746, aged 59½ years.

II. Thomas Oehrle (Early), b. May, 1687; died Nov. 25, 1746. Married Margaret, dau. of Jacob Fensterlin (Fensterle), judge and treasurer at Jesingen. The wife died Feby 8, 1735. They had children:

i. Thomas, b. 1710; died in infancy.
ii. Christian, b. 1712.
iii. John Jacob, b. 1714. Was this Jacob Early, of Amity township, Berks and Donegal, Lanc. co.?
iv. John Martin, b. 1716; died in infancy.
v. Anna Catharine, b. 1718.
vi. Anna Margaret, b. 1721; died in infancy.
vii. Twin, b. 1722; d. inf.
viii. Twin, b. 1722; d. inf.
ix. John, b. Jan. 9, 1724. Sp. at bapt., George Spitz and Anna Catharine, wf., of George Conrad Algayer, a subaltern or non-commissioned officer. John Early came to America Aug., 1750.
x. Thomas, no date of birth given; died 1745, aged 9y and 8m.

Thomas Early m. a second time but no details given.

xi. John George, b. 1737.
xii. Agnes, b .1740; d. inf.
xiii. Anna Barbara, b. 1741; d. 1798.
xiv. Christine, b. 1743.
xv. Conrad, b. 1746.

III. John Early (Thomas, Thomas), b. Jan. 9, 1724, at Jesingen, Wuertemburg. Arrived at Philadelphia August 24, 1750, in ship Brothers. Married, first, Susanna Brumbach, Apr. 10, 1753, at Reading, Pa. She died between Sept. 22 and Oct. 12, 1754. They had:

i. Christian, b. Jan. 13, 1754. Sp. Eberhart Mathieu and wf., Jacobina.

He m. second, Mary Regina, d. of John Albrecht Sichele, Mch. 11, 1755. Stoever's Record says, Mch. 10. By this marriage:

ii. John, b. July 31, 1757. Sp. John Albrecht Sichele and wf., Eva Elizabeth.

iii. John William, b. Aug. 10, 1763. Sp. Michael Zimmerman and wf., Eve Koenig.
iv. Thomas, b. Nov. 4, 1767. Sp. Michael Riecks and wf., Elizabeth.
v. (Anna) Catharine, b. July 7, 1772. Sp. George Peder (Peter) and wf. Catharine (Sichele). Bindnagel record gives only Catharine, but in other instances her name is given as Anna Catharine, and as that was the name of Mrs. Peters, her aunt, for whom she was evidently named, the full name is given here.
vi. Anna Margaret, b. Feb. 29, 1779. Sp. Christopher Ernst and wf. Anna Margaret (Sichele). The date of birth here is evidently a mistake, as there could be no Feb. 29, 1779, but it is so given in Bindnagel's church record. Aug. 24, 1795, Anna Margaret was married to Peter Eisenhauer, of Bethel township, and Sept. 5, 1803, (Anna) Catharine was married to Michael Breitenbach, of Potter township, Centre county.

There were four other children, who evidently died in early infancy, as their names are nowhere recorded.

IV. Christian Early, (John, Thomas, Thomas,) b. Jan. 13, 1754; m. Elizabeth Killinger, May 24, 1779. (The dates are from family Bible).

i. Christian, b. Aug. 25, 1780; bapt. Sept. 3, 1780. Sp. John Early and wf. Regina. Died Sept. 4, 1781, aged 1y and 11d.
ii. John, b. Feb. 18, 1783.
iii. (Anna) Catharine, b. May 13, 1784.
iv. William, b. Aug. 20, 1785.
v. John George, b. March 29, 1787.
vi. Susanna, b. Dec. 7, 1788.
vii. Elizabeth, b. March 15, 1790.
viii. Name illegible; b. —, 1793.
ix. Christian, b. Jan. 1, 1795. This is the Christian who attained man's estate and whose descendants are in Hanover.
x. Jacob, b. April 5, 1797.
xi. Regina (not Rachel), b. Feb. 25, 1799.
xii. Thomas, b. March 29, 1801.
xiii. Margaret, b. June 12, 1803.

The name of the other child, there were 14, is not given. It should probably be placed between the first Christian and John.

V. John Early,(John,Thomas, Thomas,) b. July 31, 1757; married Margaret, dau. of John Adam Deininger, Sr., Sept. 4, 1777.

He died March 1, 1810. She died August 8, 1810. (From family Bible).
  i. Magdalena, b. Feb. 24, 1778; bapt. March 6, 1778. Sp. George Peter and wf.; was married to David Ernst, Oct. 17, 1798. (From family Bible—Ernst's).
  ii. John-Jacob, b. Dec. 12, 1779; bapt. Jan. 20, 1780. Sp. John Oehrle and wf. Regina.
  iii. John-William, b. March 5, 1782; bapt. March 17, 1782. Sp. Michael Feininger (Deininger) and Barbara Bindnagel. N. B.—"Both single," is the record.
  iv. Daniel, b. Feb. 9, 1784; bapt. March 7, 1784. Sp. Daniel Wunderly and Regina Feininger.

These last two from Bindnagel church record. Daniel Early died March 4, 1813, aged 25y and 25d, single person. (Campbellstown church record).

THE ASSOCIATORS.

The Fore-Runners of the Pennsylvania Line.

[A paper read before the Wyoming Historical Society, May 22d, 1891.]

I.

The story of the Revolution is one of fascination, and we cannot hear it too often—it should be ever new. The accounts we read in our childhood of the battles of Brandywine and Germantown, of the Paoli, and of Wyoming, have to-day the same charm, with thrill of patriotic ardor, as in the olden time. We never tire of it —and facts and incidents glow with the warmth of love for our land of liberty. Patriotism is not a rank and pestiferous weed which will grow upon any soil. It requires nurturing care and protection. The hereditary societies of the Revolution, filled with ancestral pride, honoring the memories of the fathers of the Republic —they who fought in defense of independence—seek by their example to instill into the minds and hearts of those who follow after, that the fires of patriotism are just as necessary for the safety of a country, as are the armaments of war. The descendants of a loyal ancestry, of which they are justly proud, have thus graceful recognition. Honor be to them and theirs, as the years roll on. And so with this, by way of prelude, permit me to turn to my paper for the evening—promising you only a brief outline of the part taken by the early Associators in the War for Independence. And here it may be proper to remark that the Associators of the dawn of the Revolution should no more be confounded with the militia of a later period, than the National Guard of Pennsylvania, with the ununiformed militia enrolled as such. Their services to the State and to the colonies were of incalculable importance, and their history, if ever written, would be that of as brave a body of men as ever stood up "in defense of their country, their lives, and their sacred honor."

The primary organization and regulation of the military forces of one war have generally been confided to the heroes of a prior conflict of arms. When the mutterings of discontent with the Government of England presaged disruption, the stern old heroes of the French and Indian War —they who had fought under Braddock, Forbes and Bouquet—forged to the front, and to them are we indebted for the disciplining and the establishing of the Associators—the forerunners, nay, the vanguard, of the Pennsylvania Line of the Revolution. Of the field officers serving in that contest, scarcely any save the gallant Mercer, who fell at Princeton at the outset of the struggle for independence, and General John Armstrong, are known in connection with the glory of the Revolution; and yet, to them—strict disciplinarians and good soldiers, was chiefly due the effectiveness of that band of heroes, immortal, who fought and fell all the way from the assault upon Quebec to the Siege of Yorktown. As in the late War for the Union, although the names of Scott and his illustrious compeers, the general officers of the former contest, are scarcely remembered in connection with the history of that terrific civil strife, yet their duties well performed, were of the utmost effect. It is, moreover, true that the central figures of that struggle saw service in the former war, yet they were not the full-fledged warriors of the campaign against Mexico. Grant, McClellan, and Meade, and other generals, around whom cluster the exploits of victory, were scarcely recognized in the achievements which so richly emblazoned the second conquest of the Land of the Aztecs. And thus it was that the successful leaders in the contest of 1776 were either those hardly known as subordinates fifteen years before, or those who had "smelled the battle from afar"— their good training, however, due to the veterans who instructed them in military discipline and the art of war.

Such men as Burd, of Lancaster, Montgomery, Maclay and Postlethwaite, of the Cumberland Valley; Plunkett, of Northumberland, Proctor of Westmoreland, and others who held prominent commands in the Provincial forces during the French and Indian War, although not so thoroughly identified with the struggle for independence as men like Thompson, DeHaas, Miles, Potter, Piper, Bull, Irvine, and Johnston, who filled subaltern positions in the former war, yet in their immediate localities became the leaders of mighty thought and patriotic action. Not only was their influence manifested in the "Resolves" which showed their hostility to the tyranny of the English Government, but all their energies were earnestly and actively exerted in the formation of the Committees of Observation in every county of the Province. And it is also a significant fact that most of the men who were chosen upon these first committees, like Wayne, and Mifflin, and Reed, either served throughout the war in the Army of the Declaration or were among the more prominent in the councils of the Confederation and of the State. They, however, saw the ensigns of that service promoted to the first positions—and yet they patriotically gave their time and their substance to the common cause—that cause, the independence of the colonies.

From the year 1774, when the exactions of the British Government grew unbearable and intolerable, the people of the Province of Pennsylvania, in the interior counties especially, were carefully led to ponder the steps they were not slow in taking, to repel tyranny in whatever form it might manifest itself—act upon the defensive, and stand up for their rights boldly. The love of liberty was a leading trait of the vast majority of the people who settled the State of Pennsylvania. The tyranny and oppression of Europe drove them to seek an asylum among the primeval forests. Persecution for conscience sake compelled alike the Scotch-Irish, the German of the Palatinate, the Swiss and the Huguenot to come hither and rear their altars dedicated to God and freedom to man. With them, independence was as much their dream as the realization. And such was the feeling in the Province that years before the commencement of the War for Independence, Governor John Penn in writing to his brother in England, expressed himself in these almost prophetic words: "Their next move will be to subvert the Government and establish one of their own."

At times, the Associators were slow in coming out, and great stress has been laid upon this fact, charging them with unwillingness to perform military duty in the field. It was just the reverse. Too frequently an unnecessary alarm was created in Philadelphia—that the British army was threatening, and the call was at once made to the Associators of the frontier counties. The Associators of the city and county stated they had enough to do to guard their homes. Withal, there were several matters of moment which at times interfered with their ordinary promptness —"seed-time and harvest." In the second place the passiveness, aye, the disloyalty, of the non-Associators in their midst. Gen. Roberdeau's plan was that the latter "should get in the harvest for those who are—that all must bear their part in some line or other, and those who make a conscience of using the sword, can offer none against using the sickle." Unfortunately this class banded together and defeated the object proposed. The non-Associators were composed chiefly of Mennonites and Quakers, with a few other religious sects —people who were perfectly satisfied to live under any form of government which did not interfere with their rights of conscience. In a great measure was this spirit of indifference manifested by the major part of the inhabitants of the eastern counties. And this has been so largely dwelt upon by those who have never understood the history of our State, that it becomes a duty to refer to it just now. Although for several decades disagreements existed between the Proprietary Governors, and the Assembly of the Province (which was controlled by the dominant religious body, the Quakers), yet the latter opposed everything which would interfere with their feudal rights. And when the era of Liberty dawned upon them, they attempted to skulk behind the Penn Provincial Charter. This particular party never gracefully submitted to the inevitable—the ridding of the charter at the suggestion of the Congress by revolutionary methods being absolutely necessary—and although some of their young men (who were disowned for it) became identified with the events which resulted in independency, not only in civil but military life, the older portion never became truly loyal—it was the end of Quaker supremacy in Pennsylvania.

Only in the frontier counties of the Province were military organizations kept up. There it was necessary, especially from the period of Braddock's defeat down to the Revolution. As early as 1774, however, when the struggle became imminent, the people generally banded themselves together into what were called Associations, formed for their mutual defense and protection.

In their original Articles of Association it was usually set forth that it was only "to make the subscribers perfect in the art of the Military," that they had "associated, agreed, promised and resolved" concerning certain rules for their government. The "Resolves" specified the commanding officers of the companies to whom all promised obedience, penalties for the violation of the rules being fixed; each member of the company to provide himself with a good gun or musket, and ordered to supply himself with a cartouch box or shot bag, a powder horn, with a certain quantity of powder and lead. Certain days, especially Saturdays of each week, were fixed for the mustering of arms and the exercising of commands. Penalties for nonattendance were provided for, as well for members of it appearing drunk or conducting themselves in any such manner as to be considered unworthy of being members, when the majority of the officers and compañy either fined them heavily or promptly expelled them. The companies did not exceed one hundred men, the average number being, however, about eighty, rank and file. It required a majority of the officers with the consent of a majority of the soldiers to march out of the Province with the command. The Association was to be continued for a limited period, but this could be enlarged at any time, and by a majority of the subscribers of the Association be dissolved by a vote of two-thirds. The officers appointed the sergeants, corporals, and company drummer, and as a general thing all officers were fined for offenses equally with the privates. As heretofore stated, the preamble and articles of association simply recited the object to be "the perfecting of the subscribers, in the military art," without any reference to the political affairs which then agitated the minds of all classes of people. It may not be relevant to our subject but perfectly proper to state, that of the men whose signatures are attached to the various articles of association there were only a few who made their mark, whether they were Scotch-Irish or German, disproving any charge of illiteracy. One-half of the early Associators (of 1774-1775) were either of American birth or of Scotch-Irish extraction, the Germanic-Swiss settler vying with them in patriotic valor, the drawback at first, being mainly the language of the latter.

In the year 1775, there were no less than fifty-three battalions of Associators, regularly formed and well disciplined in the Province of Pennsylvania, comprising a body of over twenty-five thousand men, and it is safe to infer that during the entire period of the Revolution this Province could have been depended upon at any time for that number of men at arms. Pennsylvania has never had proper credit given for her forces in the war of the Revolution, and we presume never will. Many of the battalions which were not incorporated by degrees into the ranks of the Pennsylvania Line were almost constantly in active service during every year, and at one time or another, upon the frontiers of the State.

These voluntary articles of association preceded any adopted in any other province or colony, and formed the basis of the articles of association of Pennsylvania adopted by the Council of Safety on the twelfth of August, 1775. The preamble of these later articles reads as follows:

"We, the officers and soldiers, engaged in the present association for the defence of American liberty, being fully sensible that the strength and security of any body of men, acting together, consists in just regularity, due subordination and exact obedience to command, without which no individual can have that confidence in the support of those about him, that is so necessary to give firmness and resolution to the whole, do voluntarily and freely, after consideration of the following articles, adopt the same as the rules by which we agree and resolve to be governed in all our military concerns and operations until the same, or any of them shall be changed or dissolved by the Assembly, or Provincial Convention, or in their recess by the Committee of Safety, or a happy reconciliation shall take place between Great Britain and the colonies."

These articles, thirty-two in number, provided for almost every contingency that might arise to the troops in active service. It provided for the punishment of officers and soldiers, for various offences; their conduct towards each other as well as upon the failure of either of them in the non-performing such duties as might be required of them upon duty. Each battalion of associators selected, for a general court-martial to all cases, six men, drawn by lot. The same authority was given to commissioned officers below the rank of field officers, and these entire twelve men were to select a field officer who should act as president and have the casting vote. These articles were subscribed to by each and every associator to whom they were deliberately read or each having been allowed carefully to peruse the same.

Of the colonels in command of the battalions of associators in the early part of the year 1775, we have the honored names of Thomas McKean, George Ross, James Smith, James Wilson and George Taylor, signers of the immortal Declaration of Independence. Of the other men who became more or less prominent in political or public affairs of the State during the Revolutionary era were John Dickinson, author of the Farmer's Letters, Tench Francis, Timothy Matlack, William Hamilton, and James Moore. When the receipt of the news of the battle of Lexington reached the valleys and hills of Pennsylvania it found the entire region organized for the defence of their liberties. The performance of military duty was no new thing to men who had been cradled amidst the clash of arms in the protection of the frontiers made desolate so many years by the ruthless savages, the merciless Delawares and the perfidious Shawanese. When the exciting story of Lexington became generally known the sensation was intense, and in every portion of the Province local committees of saety and Associators met in conference, and with great unanimity and with one voice resolved that they would defend with their arms their property, liberty and lives, all attempts to deprive them of either. They were only reiterating what they had resolved upon as early as June, 1774, "That in the event of Great Britain attempting to force unjust laws upon us by strength of arms, our cause we leave to heaven—and our rifles." Nerved with patriotic zeal, and the fire of liberty burning in their breasts, the Associators in all sections of Pennsylvania were aroused to the dangers which threatened the country and were ready for the common defence.

The efficiency of the workings of the organization of the Associators was, at this crisis fully exemplified. When the Congress, by its resolution of June 14th, 1775, directed the raising of a battalion of expert riflemen in Pennsylvania, within twenty-four hours after their resolve was made known in the different localities, where Associators had previously been organized, companies of volunteers were formed, and although the final resolution of the Congress was passed on the 22d of June, three days after, on the 25th, the entire battalion of riflemen was ready for the field. Expert riflemen having been called for, the Associators upon the frontiers were promptly selected. These were the sharpshooters of their day, and their effectiveness in the use of their favorite arms was fully appreciated by the British when these provincials reached Boston, as none of the officers or soldiers of the former dared expose themselves to view, even at more than double the distance of the common musket shot. They were remarkable for the accuracy of their aim.

Now, who were the men composing this battalion? First, we have Colonel William Thompson, of Carlisle, who not only served in the French and Indian war with distinction, but was efficient upon the first Comimttee of Observation, and in the organization of the Associated Battalions of Cumberland county. Under him were Chambers, and Grier, and Doudel, and Cluggage, and Hendricks, west of the Susquehanna, with Miller and Nagle, and Ross, and Lowdon, and Smith, east of that river—men who had all seen valiant service upon the frontiers of the Province. And these were the first of the Continental Line, and this battalion was formed from the Associators, organized by the men who eventually became their leaders, so they in turn became the officers of the First Pennsylvania regiment upon the continental establishment.

Following the battalion of riflemen, during the year 1775, were formed the battalions of DeHaas, of St. Clair, of Shee, of Wayne, of Magaw, and of Irvine. Notwithstanding the depletion by the formation of these battalions, the Associators outside of the three original counties kept up their organization ready for the emergency, at every call of their country, and especially to defend the frontiers from the wily savage and tory outlaws upon the borders of the Great Lakes;—being in constant deadly peril.

Lancaster County Divorces 1788-1800

The following divorces were granted to Lancaster county parties by the Supreme Court between 1788 and 1800:

Joseph Wright, from Catharine Wright, nee Leek, married Sept. 8, 1784; divorced Sept. 24, 1788.

Catharine Leamon, from Samuel Leamon, married in 1792; divorced April 6, 1795.

Agnes Henry from John Henry, married Nov. 18, 1792; divorced Dec. 14, 1795.

George Waggoner, from Dorothea Waggoner, nee Foulke, married Feb. 25, 1775; divorced Sept. 7, 1795.

Cornelius Moyer, from Catharine Moyer, nee Kendrick, of Conestoga township, married Nov. 1, 1791; divorced Sept. 7, 1795.

John Steinman, from Maria Christina Steinman, married Mar. 5, 1794; divorced Dec. 10, 1797.   S. M. S.

NOTES AND QUERIES.

Historical, Biographical, and Genealogical,

XXII.

THOMPSON.

In volume two of the second series of "Notes and Queries" reference is made to Captain William Thompson. He went to Mason county, Kentucky, in 1773, and laid out large tracts of land which were divided by lot at Pittsburg. He resided some years in the Cumberland Valley, when he removed to Westmoreland county, being among the early Scotch-Irish settlers in that region. He was among the first to join in the struggle for independence. His wife was a daughter of John Jack, who participated in the Hannastown "Declaration," and a cousin of that Patrick Jack who carried the "Mecklenberg Declaration" to Philadelphia. Hugh Thompson was a son of William Thompson and his wife, Mary Jack. He was their fifth child and born near Mount Pleasant about 1788. A daughter was Mary Jane Logan, born Nov. 13, 1811. She died about two years ago. Hugh Thompson had brothers Andrew F. Thompson and Joseph Thompson. What is known of them or their descendants?

HUGH T. LOGAN.

Danville, Ill.

McNair Genealogical Data.

[The following record is taken from the McNair family Bible at "Oak Grove," North Sparta, Livingston county, N. Y., in the possession of Judge Hugh McNair.]

Hugh McNair, b. in Northampton county, Penna., January 1, 1765; d. Dec. 27, 1844. He m., first, Phoebe Torbert, b. Dec. 20, 1777; d. May 1, 1817. He m., secondly, Nov. 12, 1818, at Canandaigua, N. Y., Elizabeth Tate Boyd, widow of Dr. Samuel Dungan, b. at Newtown, Pa., July 30, 1783; d. in Kalamazoo, Mich., March, 1853. The children of Hugh McNair and Elizabeth Tate Boyd Dungan were:

2. i. David-Anthony, m. Juliana Trumbull Wilcox.

ii. Clement-Dungan, b. Apl. 9, 1823; d. unm. in Cal., 1864.

II. David Anthony McNair, born in Canandaigua, N. Y., Aug. 19, 1819; d. in Minneapolis, Minn., June 15, 1895; m. in Detroit, May 7, 1844; Juliana Trumbull Wilcox, b. in Detroit May 7, 1825; d. Aug. 15, 1878. Their children, all born in Kalamazoo, Mich., were:

3. i. Julia-Wilcox, b. Jan. 11, 1845.

ii. Myra-Elizabeth, d. in infnacy.

iii. Eben-Orlando, b. Jan. 1, 1850.

iv. Orlando-Clement, b. Feb. 21, 1852.

v. David-William, b. Jan. 25, 1855.

vi. Marie-Louise, b. Oct. 21, 1862.

III. Julia Willcox McNair, b. in Kalamazoo, Mich., Jany. 11, 1845; m. in Washington, D. C., Oct. 30, 1866, William Mitchell Tenney (son of William H. Tenney and Eliza Bird Cropley, of Boston, England), b. Jan. 12, 1843, in Georgetown, now Washington, D. C. Their children (surname Tenney) were:

i. Julia-McNair, b. Oct. 21, 1870; d. Sept. 12, 1871.

ii. William-Mitchell, b. Jan. 15, 1875; d. Aug. 4, 1875.

iii. William-Darrow, b. Aug. 15, 1877.

iv. Frank-Chester, b. Nov. 15, 1883.

Kaltglesser—Hartzler.

On September 15, 1729, Jacob Kalckglaesser emigrated to this country from the Palitinate in Germany, in the ship Allen, James Craigie, master, from Rotterdam. He settled in Pennsylvania in the region in which later was erected York county. The name has since undergone several changes, two spellings prevailing, Kaltglesser and Colclesser. About the year 1740 his son Johan Kaltglesser was born. The date of the father's death is not definitely known. Johan Kaltglesser died in the year 1804.

John Kaltglesser, the son of Johan, was born in the year 1779, married Elizabeth Newcomer, in the year 1807; he was killed by the explosion of a boiler in the year 1816, and was buried in Hellam township, York county.

In the year 1817, his wife, Elizabeth Kaltglesser, married John Huston, of Irish descent, from whom are descended the Huston family now living on the old homestead in Hellam township.

The children of John and Elizabeth Kaltglesser, born in the township of Hellam, York county, were:

Solomon; he changed the spelling of his name to Colclesser; b. 1809; d. 1891; for many years burgess of Hagerstown, Maryland, whose only daughter, Mrs. Mary Lang, is still living in Hagerstown.

Magdalena, b. October 12, 1810; d. April 18, 1887; m. May 14, 1830, Jacob Hartzler.

John, b. 1812; went to sea and was never heard of afterward.

The children of Jacob and Magdalena Hartzler, who are still living, are the Rev. Jacob Hartzler, of Alberton, Maryland; Mrs. Susan E. Burns, of Selin's Grove, Pa.; Mrs. Emma Mundis, of Shrewsbury township, York co., Pa.; Rev. H. B. Hartzler, D. D., of Harrisburg, Pa., and M. E. Hartzler, of York, Pa. This branch of the family tree then, is, in brief, as follows: The Hartzler family, descended from Jacob and Magdalena Hartzler; Magdalena Hartzler's maiden name was Magdalena Kaltglesser; she was the daughter of John Kaltglesser, who was the son of Johan Kaltglesser, who in turn, was the son of Jacob Kalckglaesser, who was a Palatinate German and emigrated to this country in the year 1729, from Germany.

R. Z. HARTZLER.

THE ASSOCIATORS.

The Forerunners of the Pennsylvania Line.

II.

At the suggestion of the Committee of Safety, in the month of February, 1776, the Assembly took into their consideration measures necessary for the home-defense of the Province of Pennsylvania. A few days thereafter, they directed the raising of not more than two thousand men in the pay of the State, to serve until the first of January, 1777, subject to discharge at any time, upon the advance of a month's pay to each man. This body of men was to be recruited from the Associators, only for State service and solely for its defense. The command of the two battalions, composing what was the Rifle Regiment, was confided to Colonel Samuel Miles, while the Musketry Battalion was given to Samuel John Atlee. Both of these men were distinguished for their intrepidity and bravery in the French and Indian War. Of the two battalions of the Rifle Regiment John Cadwalader, of Philadelphia, was appointed second in command, but this honor was refused by him, as he did not desire to be subordinate to Colonel Miles. Within a space of six weeks this entire body of men, fifteen hundred in number, was organized from the various Associated Battalions in the Province. But scarcely had they been constituted, when the necessities of the Continental service caused the Council of Safety to place these troops at the disposal of the Congress. In this instance, we find a notable example how the Associators became incorporated as a portion of the Pennsylvania Line, if not entirely absorbed therein. Although these commands suffered dissolution in the defeat of the American forces upon the evacuation of Long Island on the 27th of November, 1776, yet their services were just as honorable as those of any other regiments in the Line. History has, in this fact, repeated itself. During the War of the Rebellion, when the famous Pennsylvania Reserve Corps was organized and mustered into the State service for its sole protection and the defense of its borders, upon the pressing call of the Federal authorities the Commonwealth of Pennsylvania yielded to the greater emergency and hastened the troops to the relief of the National Capital, menaced by the Confederate forces, and henceforward the Reserves became incorporated into the great Union Army, while the State for whose protection and by whose authority they were raised had its borders left open to the invasion of the Army of Virginia, bringing destruction and desolation in its path; and its loyal citizens have to this day never been reimbursed for their losses.

On the 18th of June, 1776, the Committees of the different counties met in conference at the Carpenters' Hall, in the city of Philadelphia. The exigency of affairs, and the demands made by the Continental Congress, with the determination to wrest from the old Proprietaries their powers and establish the government of a sovereign State, demanded prompt and energetic action. Already had Pennsylvania, as previously stated, in its pay the battalions of Miles and Atlee, formed from the Associated battalions, as well as the State regiment of foot under command of Col. John Bull, also formed from associated companies; but the exactions of the Congress of 3d June, 1776, were further increased, requesting the raising by the State of six thousand militia towards the establishment of the Flying Camp. The failure of the Assembly, owing to a hasty adjournment, in making provision for the organizing this additional force, left the entire subject in the hands of the Provincial Conference. That body promptly recommended to the Committees and Associators of the Province to embody forty-five hundred of the latter, which, with the battalions heretofore referred to (Miles and Atlee's) consisting of fifteen hundred men then in the pay of Pennsylvania, although in the Continental service, would have been the full quota required by Congress. An address to the Associators was issued, from which we quote the following patriotic passages:

"We need not remind you that you are now furnished with new motives to animate and support your courage. You are now about to contend against the power of Great Britain in order to displace one set of villains, to make room for another. Your arms will not be enervated in the day of battle, with the reflection that you are to risk your lives, or shed your blood for a British tyrant, or that your posterity will have your work to do over again.—You are about to contend for permanent freedom, to be supported by a government which will be derived from yourselves, and which will have for its object not the emolument of one man, or class of men only, but the safety, liberty, and happiness of every individual in the community.

"We call upon you, therefore, by the respect and obedience which are due to the authority of the United Colonies, to concur in this important feature. The present campaign will probably decide the fate of America. It is now in your power to immortalize your names by mingling your achievements with the events of the year 1776, a year which we hope will be famed in the annals of history to the end of time, for establishing upon a lasting foundation the liberties of one-quarter of the globe.

"Remember the honor of our colony is at stake. Should you desert the common cause at the present juncture, the glory you have acquired in your former exertions of strength and virtue will be tarnished, and our friends and brethren who are now acquiring laurels in the most remote parts of America will reproach us, and blush to own themselves natives or inhabitants of Pennsylvania.

"But there are other motives before you —your houses, your fields, the legacies of your ancestors, or the dear-bought fruits of your own industry and your liberty, now urge you to the field. These cannot plead with you in vain, or we might point out to you further—your wives, your children, your aged fathers and mothers, who now look up to you for aid, and hope for salvation in this day of calamity, only from the instrumentality of your swords.

"Remember the name of Pennsylvania. Think of your ancestors, and of your posterity."

A meeting of delegates from the officers and privates of the several Battalions of Associators was called for the fourth of July, in the town of Lancaster. Fifty-three battalions were represented—of which eleven were from the county of Lancaster, the hot-bed of rebellion. Notwithstanding there were objections made by the five battalions of the City and Liberties of Philadelphia, who entered a protest against the assembling of the convention and against the action to be had therein, the prominent men who composed the majority of this body, however, did not hesitate to undertake the work assigned to them. Upon the election of two brigadier generals, Daniel Roberdeau and James Ewing, power was given them to call out any number of the Associators of the Province whenever it was deemed important so to do. At once measures were taken, and the Flying Camp was formed of volunteer details from the different Associated battalions. It will be seen, therefore, that about one-third of the entire body of Associators was brought into the field during the year 1776. How effective these men were, and how helpful in their duties to the Continental Army, are beyond all praise—we refer to their heroic services on Long Island, at Fort Washington, on the retreat through the Jerseys—at Trenton and Princeton.

With the evacuation of Long Island, and the surrender of Fort Washington, the retreat of the little army of Washington through the Jerseys brought, as was naturally expected, alarm to the city of Philadelphia, for the British army followed the retreating Continentals. Again at this crisis in the war, the Associators were called upon by President Wharton in his manly and patriotic address of December 23d, which appealed to every friend of his country:

"Friends and Countrymen," thus he invoked, "The pressing exigencies of the times induce us once more to address you, while we can deplore the calamities of our country without restraint, and before the voice of truth and execrations of tyranny are forced back into the bosom of the wretched sufferer. On your vigorous exertions alone, at this time, will depend the privilege of ever addressing you by the title of freemen. Should the enemy be encouraged by further success, devastation and ruin must mark their footsteps.

"We call upon you, we entreat and beseech you, to come forth to the assistance of our worthy General Washington, and our invaded brethren in the Jerseys. If you wish to secure your property from being plundered, and to protect the innocence of your wives and children—and if you wish to live in freedom and are determined to maintain that best boon of heaven, you have no time to deliberate. A manly resistance will secure every blessing; inactivity and sloth will bring horror and destruction. Step forth like men—feed not yourselves with the vain expectation of peace and security, should the enemy succeed in reducing this country. Such hopes will vanish like the dreams of the night and plunge you into an irretrievable abyss of unspeakable misery.

"Shall we, with heaven and justice on our side (unless we could impiously suppose that the Almighty has devoted mankind to slavery), shall we hesitate to meet our enemies in the hostile field? The sons of America have not drawn their swords to invade the rights of others, nor to reduce populous countries to a state of desolation. It was not to plunder the wealthy, nor to wrest from the laborious farmer or industrious mechanic his hard-earned blessings, that America had recourse to arms. No! Whilst our most humble petitions and pathetic expostulations yet rung in the ears of our enemies, they wantonly attacked us on our own peaceful shores.

"May Heaven, who bestowed the blessing of liberty upon you, awaken you to a proper sense of your danger, and rouse that manly spirit of virtuous resolution which has ever bid defiance to the efforts of tyranny. May you ever have the glorious prize of liberty in view, and bear with becoming fortitude the fatigues and severities of a winter campaign. That, and that only, will entitle you to the superlative distinction of being deemed, under God, the deliverers of your country."

This spirited and soul-stirring address had its effect upon the Associators. General Mifflin, one of the most fascinating orators of the day, was also sent through the State by the order of the Assembly to stir up the people, and the committees of the different counties were called upon to assist him. The enthusiasm was so great in "the back counties" that the quota was easily raised. It was very different in the threatened city of Philadelphia, and yet if we are to believe a recent writer, the Associators and militia of the metropolis "saved the country" on numerous occasions without any assistance from the counties. Although the military ardor of its patriotic and loyal citizens was thoroughly aroused and they were prepared for the crisis, yet the claims of their families weighed heavily upon them, causing great anxiety. It became necessary, therefore, to offer bounties to the volunteers, and this, with enlistment of substitutes, had its effect in filling the quota. As stated, it was entirely different distant from the city of Philadelphia. There most of the Associators had little needs pressing them—at this time of year most of the farm work had been accomplished—the abundant harvests had been gathered and secured—their families well supplied—while from the scenes of the threatened clash of arms they were far removed.

Although, what has been stated was true as to the patriotic aspirations of the Associators, Congress itself exhibited that alarm and indecision which was exceedingly injurious to the cause of independency. Naturally, General Washington was extremely solicitous for the safety of Philadelphia. His army had been reduced to four thousand men, regular troops, and this was daily wasting away by desertion and by the expiration of the terms of service of the soldiers. Once again, the Associators hastened to the relief of the beleagured army in the Jerseys, and in a few days three thousand men from the interior counties arrived in the city of Philadelphia ready for prompt movement across the Delaware, to the succor of the commander-in-chief. Subsequently came the victories of Trenton and Princeton, and largely instrumental in securing them were the Associators of Pennsylvania. To their support, under the able command of Cadwalader, Ewing and others, there is a credit due which has never been accorded. No one but the commander-in-chief of the American forces appreciated so fully the invaluable aid thus tendered him in gaining these victories, which buoyed up the hearts of the Americans and checked that spirit of revolt and insubordination among the New England and New York officers who clamored for Washington's removal. We know that it has been charged that some of the companies of Associators outside of Philadelphia, after the battle of Princeton deserted in full bodies, leaving only their officers. This has never been authenticated, and we know of no record among the archives of the State which verify such statements in the case of the troops actually mustered into the State or Continental service.

Moreover, it is true, the law governing the Associators was in itself weak; and in some instances the disciplining of the undisciplined officers was bad. Having been found, therefore, that the system of the association had become too uncertain to depend upon in case of an emergency, the Assembly, at its next meeting, devoted itself to the preparation of a bill relating to the militia, and it was passed. This militia bill provided that the various counties throughout the State, including the city of Philadelphia, should be divided into six districts, each of which was to have within it not less than six hundred and forty, nor more than six hundred and eighty men fit for military duty. Over these divisions were placed lieutenants for each county and for the city of Philadelphia, and sub-lieutenants for each district. Each district was subdivided into eight parts or companies, and each district was to elect its own lieutenant-colonel, major, captain and other officers. The lieutenants and sub-lieutenants of the counties took lists of the inhabitants of their respective districts, collected fines and superintended the general details of the law. The companies were divided by lots into classes and provision was made for the calling out of these classes as they were wanted. Persons enrolled, on refusing to parade, were ordered to be fined seven shillings six pence, per day; officers absent, ten shillings per day; non-commissioned officers, five shillings per day, and field officers not attending were fined five pounds and non-commissioned officers and privates, fifteen shillings. The companies were required to be exercised at least two days in April, three days in May, two days in August and two days in September and October of each year. Battalions were to parade once in May and once in October. To the command of these militia forces, John Armstrong, John Cadwalader, James Porter, and Samuel Meredith were appointed brigadier generals.

Under this law most of the men who were efficient in organizing the associated battalions at the outset of the Revolution on account of their military training, were appointed the lieutenants and sub-lieutenants of their respective counties and districts. In connection with the important provisions of the law, a test and oath of allegiance were established. This was deemed eminently necessary as a war measure, the reasons therefor being given in the preamble which recited: "That from sordid and mercenary motives, or other causes inconsistent with the happiness of a free and independent people, sundry persons had been induced to withhold their service and allegiance from the Commonwealth of Pennsylvania as a free and independent State, as declared by Congress; and that sundry other persons, in their several capacities had, at the risk of their lives and fortunes, rendered great and eminent service in defence and support of Independence, and that they remained in some measure undistinguished from the disaffected who were deriving undeserved service from the faithful and well affected, and as allegiance and protection were reciprocal, those who would not bear the former, should not be entitled to the benefits of the latter."

Once more do we hear of the Associators —when again fearing an attack by the British army upon Philadelphia, the Supreme Executive Council in a proclamation of the 9th of April, 1777, after stating the causes of alarm and calling upon the people to prepare for defence, used this language:

"This city has once been saved by the vigorous, manly efforts of a few brave Associators, who generously stepped forth in defence of their country; and it has been repeatedly and justly observed, and ought to be acknowledged as a signal evidence of the favor of Divine Providence that the lives of the associated militia in every battle during this just war have been remarkably spared. Confiding, therefore, in the continuance of His blessing, by Him, who is indeed the God of Armies, let every man among us hold himself ready to march into the field whenever he shall be called upon to do so."

With the passage and promulgation of the new militia law, the Associated Battalions as such, ceased to exist. The days of the Associators had passed away, and the Pennsylvania militia came upon the stage of action. It was naturally anticipated that greater thoroughness in discipline would be the result, yet this was never realized. Although these served well in the campaign around Philadelphia, in September, 1777, yet their duties were afterwards chiefly confined either in the protecting the frontiers, standing sentinel while the back-woodsman sowed his grain and reaped his harvest, or yet in guarding prisoners of war. The influence of the Association was nevertheless felt throughout the contest for Independence.

In conclusion, those who had associated themselves three years before had either gone into the Continental Line where they remained, or had fallen in the disastrous battles and skirmishes which so fearfully decimated our little army, or yet, sick and wounded dragged their emaciated bodies and torn limbs to die in their native valleys. As honored descendants of noble sires, let us cherish holy memories of our suffering ancestry—let us as descendants of those patriots drink renewed inspiration, that as our fathers fought to establish a nation, so may we ever hallow their memories, not only by recording their chivalrous deeds—but to assist in promoting the cause of liberty and humanity in every country on the habitable face of the globe. Over a century ago our ancestors promulgated the immortal Declaration, and we who remain must by right and duty aid in perpetuating the principles guaranteed by that magna charta of our civil and religious liberty.

NOTES AND QUERIES.

Historical, Biographical, and Genealogical.

XXIII.

DAVIDSON.

James Davidson married Esther Findley. They resided in the Cumberland Valley until 1798, when they removed to the Ohio. They had the following children:

i. William; m. Mary Aiken Ramsey, it is said, in Ireland.
ii. Esther; d. May 18, 1848, at an advanced age; unm.
iii. Sally; m. Nathan Blaine.
iv. James; lived and died in Coitsville, Ohio.
v. Lydia; m. ——— Alexander.
vi. Peggy; m. Robert Stewart.
vii. Mary; m. ——— Junkin, of near Carlisle.
viii. Robert; resided in Hopedale, near Cadiz, Ohio; d. about 1860.

What is known of James Davidson's ancestors, and of his services in the Revolution. MRS. ROSA H. SEXTON. Seward, Neb.

The McDowell Family.

McDowell is a Lowland corruption of the Highland McDougall, the name of an old famous clan. Our ancestors were once powerful in old Scotland, even making kings. A John McDowell, a Romish priest converted to Protestantism, and a refugee with Calvin in Geneva, is not improbably our remote ancestor. In this country our records begin with Ephraim McDowell.

Ephraim McDowell sailed from Londonderry, Ireland, on May 9, 1729, in the "George and Ann," landed at Philadelphia; settled first in Hunterdon county, New Jersey, then moved to Somerset county, on the Raritan. He is buried in the Leamington churchyard. He had two sons Ephraim and John, who in 1736, in the "John and Margaret," brought settlers to the Borden Tract, Berkeley county, Virginia.

Capt. John McDowell was of Scotch descent and born in the Province of Ulster, Ireland. In early manhood he came to America, settling first in Pennsylvania, and then in Virginia. He became one of the surveyors of Benjamin Borden and was killed by the Indians, December 14, 1742, in the first battle between the whites and Indians in the Virginia valley. He left a family of three children. In 1744 Benjamin Borden married his widow. In Lexington, Va., a monument is erected to the memory of the McDowells.

Collin's History of Kentucky says:

When John McDowell, of Rockbridge county, Virginia, was killed, he left three children. Of these Samuel, the elder, with his wife, Mary McClurg, emigrated to Danville, Ky.. in 1784. Abram, the son of Samuel, was the father of Gen. Irvine McDowell.

John had a son Alexander, who became an eminent Presbyterian clergyman. He was educated in Glasgow, Scotland, and prepared for the ministry at the University of Edinburg, Scotland. He was pastor of Rock congregation in Cecil county, Maryland; principal of the classical academy, afterwards Delaware College, Newark, Delaware. He died January 13, 1782, and is buried in the Stone graveyard, Lewisville, Chester county, Penna., with his wife, Alice Craighead, and his infant son, Thomas.

His son John was born in Cecil county, Maryland, in 1750; was educated as a physician at the medical school of the University of Pennsylvania. He married Martha Johnston, at New London X-Roads, Chester county. About the year 1804 he removed to Steubenville, Ohio, and died there January 1, 1825. He was an officer and surgeon in the Continental and United States army. In the Revolutionary War he served with distinction and honor; was engaged in the "Crossing of the Delaware," the battle of Princeton, Trenton and others. Congress presented him with a sword. He was a close personal friend of Gen. George Washington, and one of the original members of the Society of the Cincinnati. His military record is as follows: First lieutenant and surgeon's mate, Sixth Pennsylvania Battalion, Jan. 9, 1776; first lieutenant, no date, and captain Seventh Pennsylvania, March 20th, 1777; transferred to First Pennsylvania, Jan. 1, 1783, and served to Nov. 3, 1783; surgeon United States infantry regiment, Aug. 12, 1784; resigned, July 24, 1788.

He served his State as a member of the Executive Council for three years and was also a member of the Legislature.

Martha Johnston, the wife of John McDowell, was the third child of Alexander and Martha Johnston. She was born at New London X-Roads. In a lot about fifty feet west of the New London Presbyterian Church is a tombstone with the following inscription:

In memory of Alexander Johnston, Esq., who departed this life August 8th, A. D. 1790, aged 84 years.

Martha Johnston, wife of Alexander Johnston, who departed this life February 8th, A. D. 1784, aged 66 years.

John McDowell and Martha Johnston had five children:
i. John.
ii. Alexander-Johnston.
iii. Anna.
iv. Eliza.
v. Marie-Antoinette.

John McDowell, Jr., m. Catherine Wells, who died in Steubenville, O. They had children:
i. George-Wood; d. young.
ii. Bazaleel-Wells; d. young.
iii. Martha; m. Dr. John L. Matthews, and they had children (surname Matthews):
1. Kate.
2. Mary-A.
3. Alice.
4. Belle.
5. George-McDowell.
6. Alexander.

Alexander Johnston McDowell (son of Dr. John), b. at New London X-Roads, Chester county, Pa., in 1788; d. at Steubenville, December 6, 1871. He m. Mary Sheldon, of Steubenville. They had children:
i. Marie-Anna.
ii. Sheldon-Woodbridge.
iii. John; d. inf.
iv. Martha-Johnston.
v. Lydia-L.
vi. Alexander-Johnston, Jr.

Marie Anna McDowell, b. at Steubenville, O.; m. Dr. Joseph Mitchell; no children; d. at Steubenville, O.

Sheldon Woodbridge McDowell, b. at Steubenville; d. at Lexington, Va., in 1856; buried at Steubenville; unm.

Martha Johnston McDowell, b. at Steubenville, May 20, 1823; m. Abner Lord Frazer, August 20, 1844; d. at Youngstown, O.; buried in Cincinnati. Their children were (surname Frazer):
i. Sheldon-Lord.
ii. Mary-McDowell.
iii. James-Alexander; d. young.

iv. Abner-Lord, Jr.
v. Alexander-McDowell; d young.
vi. Betsy-Lord.
Sheldon Lord Frazer, b. at Steubenville, Oct. 8, 1845; m. Elise McDowell Backus, at Toledo, O., Oct. 29, 1874; had one child, Elizabeth, b. Oct. 2, 1878, at Cincinnati, O.
Mary McDowell Frazer, b. at Steubenville, Aug. 1, 1847; m. Joseph Sill, Dec. 1, 1880, and had one child, Katharine, b. Oct. 1, 1881, at Chilicothe, O.
Abner Lord Frazer, Jr., b. at Cincinnati, O., July 20, 1858; m. Carrie Hume, of Lima, March 1, 1892, and had one child, Hume McDowell, b. at Youngstown, June 8, 1894.
Betsy Lord Frazer, b. at Cincinnati, Nov. 9, 1862; m. Thomas Stokely Wood at Milford, O., Nov. 24, 1892; have one child, Elizabeth McDowell, b. at Duluth, Minn., April 18, 1895.
Lydia L. McDowell, b. at Steubenville, O.; m. Eli T. Tappan, at Steubenville. They had (surname Tappen):
i. Mary T., b at Steubenville; m. Prof. John H. Wright, of Columbus, O., and have:
1. Bessie, d. young.
2. Austin.
3. John.
ii. Charles.
Alexander Johnston McDowell, Jr., b. at Steubenville, O.; m. Ella Kilgore. He died at Albuquerque, New Mexico, April 8, 1889. They had two children:
i. Mary-Eleanor.
ii. Lucy-Alice, b. at Steubenville; m. Lee Douglass Meader, April 18, 1896, at Cincinnati, O.

Anna McDowell, dau. of Dr. John McDowell, d. at Steubenville; m. George Wood and had children (surname Wood):
i. Anna; m. Nathaniel Dike, and they had Virginia and William, who died unm. Virginia m. Thomas S. Blair and left three children.
ii. Margaretta; m. John Dike; no children.
iii. Mary; d. young.
Eliza McDowell, dau. of Dr. John McDowell, m. William R. Dickinson; no children.
Marie Antoinette McDowell, dau. of Dr. John McDowell, b. at New London X-Roads, Chester county, Pa., April 10, 1797; d. at Cincinnati in January, 1868; m. Humphrey H. Leavitt, at Steubenville, O. They had three children (surname Leavitt):
i. John-McDowell, b. at Steubenville; m. Bithia Brooks, of Cincinnati, O., and had issue (surname Leavitte:
1. John-Brook; m. Mary Weith.
2. Bithia; m. W. M. Mersereau.
3. Frank.
4. Edwin.
5. Humphrey-H.; d. young.
6 Anna; m. Lieut. Cresup, U. S. N., and had Logan and John.
ii. Edwin; b. at Steubenville; m. Emily Sherman and had Edwin.
iii. Frank; d. unm.

REV. WILLIAM R. DEWITT.

A Venerable Pastor and Some of His People.

[Paper read before the Historical Society of Dauphin County, June 8, 1899, by Theodore B. Klein.]

In the bosom of mother earth, on the western bluff in the city of the dead, now in the deep shadow of this summer day twilight, surrounded by the perfume of countless June roses, sleeps one who was a father in Israel, and in his day a vigorous leader and a patriarch of the children of 'John Calvin," whose tabernacles now occupy many favored spots in our city and county, and whose disciples are numbered by the thousands in our midst—active and aggressive in every good work. Let us, for a little while, recall the memories of the Reverend Doctor William R. Dewitt and some of his people who are gathered with him in the sacred precincts of our "Mount Kalmia," and almost as we read can hear in the evening carol of the robins a sweet dirge as the names of the departed are remembered.

Upon the tablet of the massive monument erected to his memory we read the simple inscription:

REV. WILLIAM R. DEWITT,
Born in Dutchess County, New York,
February 25, 1792.
Died December 23, 1867.

From published annals, we learn that in February, 1809, a brick church was built by the Presbyterians on Second street and Blackberry alley, in which, on the second Sabbath of September, 1818, Rev. William R. Dewitt, of the Presbytery of New York, delivered his first sermon to the congregation worshiping in that church. It was a living branch of the mother church at Paxtang, and has proved a sprightly child of the famous stock, whose fathers, in the Rutherfords and Elders, and Grays and Wilsons, and others, will long be remembered in the beautiful Lebanon Valley.

The pastor was then 26 years of age, and shortly afterwards received a call from the congregation, which he accepted, and he was regularly installed on the 12th of November, 1819.

He continued to go in and out among his people and to break unto them the bread of life in the old church until 1841, a period of twenty-two years, when a new church was erected upon the same site, and from the beautiful Italian marble pulpit thereof he continued his ministrations alone until 1854, another period of thirteen years, when the Rev. Thomas H. Robinson was called as his associate, and in companionship the service of the Master was continued (until the destruction of the church by fire and until the new temple was constructed at Market Square and Second street), up to within a short period of the demise of the senior pastor in 1867—thus completing a pastorate of forty-nine years, a marvelous time for a man to serve continuously in one parish in this country.

In the early evening hours of the night of March 30th, 1858, he witnessed the cruel flames of a supposed incendiary fire envelop and consume his house of worship, and in a few short hours there was nothing left but a mass of blackened, smouldering ruins to mark the spot of his Sabbath home, where he and his people delighted to assemble in public service on the "Day of Rest."

The sermons of the Doctor, carefully prepared, were fine models of pulpit oratory and delivered with force and power. His reading was excellent, and many of his perorations were eloquent and impressive. His prayers were earnest, and his ascriptions of praise to the Deity were often favorite quotations from the Psalms, frequently beginning: "Of old hast thou laid the foundation of the earth, and the heavens are the work of thy hands." * * * "They shall perish but thou shalt endure; yea all of them shall wax old like a garment; as a vesture shalt thou change them and they shall be changed." * * * "But thou art the same, and thy years shall have no end." "The children of thy servants shall continue, and their seed shall be established before thee." A fitting tribute indeed as a prelude to the petitions presented to the "Giver of every good and perfect gift."

A review of his work in our midst would be very interesting history and the records of his church would recall a long line of familiar names and faces. The names of all the precious infants baptized in the name of the Trinity; the names of the youths and adults confirmed as members of the congregation before the altar; the names of the many couples united in the bonds of holy wedlock; the names of many who were consigned to the dust and ashes of their mother earth, and the host of names of his people to whom he ministered in life, in sickness and in health, in joy and in sorrow, would fill a large, a very large, volume indeed.

His experience as a pastor was large and varied, a veritable Moses as it were, leading his children through the troubles and trials incident in the progress of the church through the intervening years. The building up of his congregation and their dependent missions, the destruction of his new church by fire, the division of a strong congregation and the building of the last beautiful temple at Second and Market Square, were trying periods in his ministry, requiring a strong executive ability which he was possessed of to a great degree but withal placed heavy burdens and cares upon the active pastor.

Fortunately there were Aarons and Hurs to hold up his hands and to assist him, and with the Brothers Weir and their faithful associates, men and women, and children, too, success followed their every effort, and the monuments of their work remain upon the favored spots occupied by their temples and in the hearts of the surviving descendants of the Presbyterian brethren who have been taught to revere the name and memory of Doctor Dewitt, who now sleeps with his kindred and friends.

In the family plot the wife of his youth reposes: "Julia Anna, daughter of Rev. Nathan Woodhull, who passed away May 1, 1822, aged 23 years." The dust of children and grandchildren is deposited in close proximity to that of the patriarchal father who with the last partner of his joys and sorrows, Mary Elizabeth Wallace, who died October 16, 1881, form the silent family circle in God's acre, and there too sleep a daughter, Mary Wallace, who was called to the eternal home at the age of 24, and a son Wallace, who was cut off in the full vigor of manhood, aged 53. There, too, is the infant son of Dr. William, Jr., and Susan named John Hamilton, whose father removed from our midst, spending the latter years of his life amid the orange groves in Florida, where his ashes are deposited, and Edward, a son of George E. and Kate Dewitt Sterry, who survived but one short year in this troublous world. The wife of the Doctor's son, the Rev. John (Laura Beaver Dewitt), who lived 46 years and was gathered to her kindred, and it is written of her in the chiseled granite that "she was a woman full of good work and alms deed which she did" like unto her sister of Apostolic times. Her husband survives, and continues in faithful service. He has filled prominent places in the church of his fathers and now occupies a chair in the celebrated Theological Seminary at Princeton. The parishioners of his flock embraced the families of our most prominent and influential citizens and we can in fancy call a congregation as it were within hailing distance from his last resting place and almost in touch with the mouldering dust beneath his tomb.

Hard by, we find the families of the Brothers R. Jackson, David, and James Fleming, all active in the work of the church, when the final summons from the arch angels trump shall call forth the sleepers from their last resting place the reunion of the families of the old pastor's flock, including the Boyds and Sloans, the Ayres and Graydons, and Borders and McKinneys, the Mowreys and Weirs, the Rutherfords, and Hannas, the Haldemans, and Geigers, the Ingrams and Jones, the Roberts and Hays, the Hamiltons and Wallaces, the Wyeths and Pollocks, the Carsons and Wilsons, the Briggs and Pearsons, the Herrs and McCormicks, the Gilberts and Harris, the Porters and Shunks, and a host of their descendants who will follow, will indeed form a grand army of one faith as taught by the pastor who for so many years was the faithful teacher and bishop in their midst.

His success in the church of his fathers have proven worthy of the inheritance improving and enlarging on every hand and the seed sown in his time and that of his successors has increased a hundred fold, and the talents distributed have not been "laid away in a napkin" but have largely developed in the interest of humanity and the Master; and if it were possible for the body of the reverend pastor to return to the scenes of his earthly labor he would gladly say "Well done, good and faithful servants," for they have been good husbandmen and the branches have reached out far and wide; and we may fancy that he would lay his venerable hand upon the head of his successors and their flocks and bid them God speed in their work until called to lay their armor aside and bid adieu to the cares and labors in the Master's field, cheering them on and forward with the exhortation and comforting assurance—

"That hope and despondency, pleasure
 and pain, together
Are mingled, in sunshine and rain,
And the smiles and the tears, the song
 and the dirge,
Still follow each other like surge upon
 surge,"
until the end comes with its eternal rest upon the other shore.

NOTES AND QUERIES.

Historical, Biographical, and Genealogical.

XXIV.

McLENE.

James McLene, of Antrim township, Franklin county, d. in March, 1806, leaving a wife Christine and children:
 i. Daniel
 ii. Thomas-Brown.
 iii. Mary, m. Samuel Smith.
 iv. James.
 v. Lazarus-Brown.
 vi. [A dau.] dec'd; m. Samuel McFerran, and left children Eliza, Christine, Mary-Ann, and Samuel.
Executors were the sons.

REA.

I. John Rea, Sen., of Montgomery township, Franklin county, d. in April, 1807, leaving a wife Jane, and children:
 i. Daniel.
 ii. Isaac.
 iii. Ann, m. —— Powell.
 iv. Elizabeth, m. —— Taylor.
 v. James.
 vi. John.
 vii. Henry
The executors were sons Henry and Daniel.

II. Martha Rea (widow), of Greene township, Franklin county, d. in April, 1824, leaving her estate to daughter Elizabeth, nephew Samuel, son of Gen. John Rea.
The executors were Gen. John Rea and John Grevin. Letters of administration were granted to Andrew Thomson, Esq. The witnesses were John Rea, of James, and William McKean.

III. James Rea, of Metal township, Franklin county, d. in May, 1812, leaving a wife Ann and children:
 i. Willy, m. —— Blaine.
 ii. Nancy, m. —— Madeira and had Stophel.
 iii. Sally, m. —— Veah.
 iv. John.
 v. David.
The executors were wife John Rea and Nancy Madeira.

THOMSON.

I. Alexander Thomson, of Greene township, Franklin county, d. in February, 1800, leaving a wife Elizabeth and children:
 i. John.
 ii. William.
 iii. Alexander.
 iv. Archibald.
 v. Elizabeth, m. —— Purviance.
 vi. Margaret, m. —— Watson.
 vii. Barbara, m. —— Watson.
 viii. Mary, m. —— Cowan.
 ix. Jannett, m. —— Shaw.
 x. Andrew.
 xi. Ann, m. —— Logan.
 xii. James.
 xiii. Jane, m. ——Shields.
The executor was son John.

II. Archibald Thomson, son of the above, of Greene township, Franklin county, d. in December, 1801, leaving a wife Ann, and children:
 i. Alexander.
 ii. James.
 iii. Elizabeth.
 iv. Jane.
 v. Agnes.
 vi. Hannah.
The executor was the wife.

III. Jenny Thomson, daughter of John Thomson, late of Guilford township, Franklin county, d. in July, 1797, making bequests as follows:
Sister Martha McMurran.
Bro. Henry.
Brother Samuel.
Bro. William.
Bro. John.
Bro. Robert.
The executors were Henry Thomson and James Brotherton. The witnesses to the will, William Brotherton and Francis McMurran.

SINGER.

Catharine Singer, bron Sept. 5, 1781, in Carlisle, Pa. Married, 1796, Robert Irwin, born Nov. 15, 1775.
Can any one assist me in finding the parents of both Robert Irwin and Catharine Singer?
Were there any Singers at that time in Carlisle? I. J.

First Burgess of Northumberland.

Lawrence Campbell, born in Ireland in 1765, emigrated to Pennsylvania in 1784, just after the close of the Revolution, and located at Northumberland town in 1792. He was attracted thither by the large number of Scotch-Irish who had settled in and around that place. On the incorporation of Northumberland as a borough, January 16, 1828, Lawrence Campbell was chosen the first burgess at an election held April 6, 1829, and he was re-elected thereafter for five years, making six consecutive years of service. Only a few months after the close of his last term he died, November 8, 1834, at the age of sixty-eight years.   J. F. M.

EVANS-BRUNER.

Nathan Evans, b. 1683, d. December, 1763. He m. Susanna ——, and settled at Radnor, Chester county. In 1730, with a number of others, he moved to Caernarron township, Lancaster county, where he founded Churchtown. His children were:
i. Nathan; m. Mary ——, and had Evan and Nathan.
ii. John.
iii. James; m. Elizabeth ——.
iv. Ann; m. Eleazer Evans, and had John and David.
v. Mary; m. Thomas Nicholas.

James Evans, son of Nathan and Mary, b. circa, 1724; d. 1801; m. Elizabeth ——; and according to his will had:
i. Nathan.
ii. William.
iii. James; m. Ann Cunningham.
iv. John.
v. Caleb; d. May, 1802; m. Sarah Edwards, dau. of David Edwards; and had Caleb.

James Evans (James. Nathan), d. April 2, 1802; m. Jan. 22, 1794, Ann Cunningham, b. Nov. 22, 1764; d. May 14, 1838; and had issue:
i. Hiram.
ii. Rebecca; m. Abraham Bruner.
iii. Davies.

Rebecca Evans (James, James, Nathan), m. Abraham Bruner, lumber merchant at Columbia; their son, Davies Evans Bruner, is an attorney at the Lancaster county bar.

Abraham Bruner, above named, was a son of Ulrick Bruner, b. July 5, 1762; d. Nov. 29, 1843; m. March 20, 1787, Elizabeth Weaver, b. April 12, 1768; d. March 12, 1853; a daughter of John Weaver and his wife, Barbara Buckwalter. Ulrick Bruner was a son of Ulrick Bruner, b. June 4, 1730; d. Feb. 19, 1821; m. in 1755, Fronica Bross, who d. Jan. 27, 1796.

Information is desired of the maiden name of Susanna, wife of Nathan Evans, and Elizabeth, wife of James Evans. Also, concerning Ann Cunningham, whose mother, Rebecca, married John Kirkpatrick (her second husband), dying Feb. 11, 1804.   S. M. SENER.
Lancaster, Pa.

BURIAL RECORDS

From the Old Presbyterian Churchyard, Bedford, Pa.

[Notes and Queries are indebted to William Filler Lutz for this and subsequent tombstone records at Bedford, Pa.]

Anderson, Ann, wf. Thos. Anderson.
Anderson, Thos., b. 1727 in or near the town of McGuire Bridge, County Fermanagh, Ireland; d. about 1799.
Beaty, Rebecca, d. 22 Nov., 1792, aged 36 yrs.
Barclay, Samuel M., Esq., b. 17 Oct., 1802; d. 3 Jan., 1852.
Barclay, Samuel M., b. 11 Mch., 1831; d. 20 Aug., 1880.
Barclay, Josiah E., Esq., b. 13 Nov., 1825; d. 24 Nov., 1852.
Barclay, Francis B., M. D., b. 20 Mch., 1797; d. 12 July, 1851.
Barclay, Camela B., wf. Francis B. Barclay, M. D., b. 14 Oct., 1800; d. 1 Oct., 1872.
Barclay, Hester A., b. 29 Aug., 1827; d. 25 Mch., 1878.
Boyd, John, d. 1 Aug., 1822, aged 44 yrs.
Boyd, Margaret, wf. Rev. Alex. Boyd, d. 20 Feb., 1816, aged 28 yrs.
Brooks, Sarah S., wf. David S. Brooks, d. 4 April, 1850, aged 32-11-12.
Colvin, James, b. 11 June, 1809; d. 19 Sept., 1831.
Creutzborg, Wm., b. 13 Mch., 1826.
Carns, Sam'l, d. 10 Sept., 1835, aged 26-4-0.

Notes and Queries.

Crothers, Samuel, d. 10 Sept., 1835, aged 41-4-0.
Cromwell, Benj., s. of Sam'l V. M. Cromwell, d. 27 Nov., 1847, aged 2-6-24.
Cromwell, Sam'l S., s. of Sam'l V. M. Cromwell, d. 12 Feb., 1844, aged 0-3-9.
Carothers, Mary, d. of Sam'l and Eliza Carothers, b. 18 April, 1831; d. 21 Feb., 1833, aged 1-10-3.
Cromwell, Eliz. Loyer, d. of Sam'l V. M. Cromwell, d. 28 Nov., 1847, aged 6-0-21.
Duncan, Reuben R. McDowell, b. 19 Dec., 1833; d. 9 Sept., 1834.
Duncan, Chas. Edwd., b. 11 Dec., 1829; d. 29 Jan., 1830.
Dean, Mrs. Jane, wf. of Daniel Dean, d. 9 June, 1821, aged 23-8-22.
Davidson, Mary Ann, d. 26 Jan., 1858. aged 70 yrs.
Davidson, Margaret, d. 24 Aug., 1856, aged 66.
Davidson, Matthew, b. 20 Dec., 1780; d. Sept., 1825.
Davidson, Geo., b. 24 Jan., 1784.
Davidson, Margery Reynolds, b. 26 Aug., 1786.
Davidson, Col. Samuel, d. 1803.
Davidson, Margery, relict of Col. Samuel Davidson, d. 23 Dec., 1832.
Davidson, Mary, wf. of Matthew Davidson, b. 3 Feb., 1792; d. 8 Oct., 1876.
Daily, Eleanor, b. 3 Feb., 1771.
Davidson, Jno., b. 10 April, 1773.
Davidson, Wm. T., M. D., b. 5 Oct., 1775.
Davidson, Maj. Sam'l, b. 27 Jan., 1778; d. 20 Feb., 1842.
Davidson, Wm., s. of Jno. and Mary Davidson, d. 26 June, 1849, aged 3-8-22.
Davis, Margaret, wf. of John Davis, and daughter of E. and S. Adams, d. 7 Sept., 1858, aged 35 yrs.
Denison, Hugh, d. 24 Feb., 1819, aged 36-5-13.
Espy, Mrs. Jane, wf. of David Espy, Esq., d. 12 June, 1813, aged 58 yrs.
Fletcher, Juliana, consort of Col. John Piper, d. 6 July, 1837, aged 36-1-0.
Funk, Geo., d. 12 Oct., 1844, aged 69 yrs.
Frazer, James, b. 2 Oct., 1787; d. 10 April, 1811.
Gibson, Mary, d. 6 Dec., 1839, aged 51-11-0.
Gibsond, Bert, d. 7 Oct., 1804.
Gillam, Mary C., wf. of Henry Gillam, d. 19 Aug., 1830, aged 44-5-0.

Henry, Elizabeth, d. 14 Dec., 1818, aged 88.
Hunter, Silas Brow (d. on a visit to the psrings), of Fauquier Co., Va., where he was b., Oct., 1792.
Hoge, James, of Huntsville, Ala., d. 2 July, 1832, aged about 35 yrs.
Henry, George, d. 10 March, 1834, aged 62-2-21.
Henry, Elizabeth, wf. of Geo. Henry, d. 9 Jan., 1820, aged 37 yrs.
Hammer, Eliza Jane, d. of Jos. and Nancy Hammer, d. 6 Aug., 1835, aged 1-3-27.
Hafer, Margaret A., wf. of Johnson Hafer, d. 31 Jan., 1859, aged 32-1-9.
Harmer, Richard, s. of Elwood and Charlotte Harmer, d. 9th mo., 30th, 1853, aged 1-8-22.
James, David, d. 6 Nov., 1852, aged about 65 yrs.
Jones, Abel, d. 9 Oct., 1862, aged 55 yrs.
Kerns, Abraham, d. 16 Sept., 1838, aged 50 yrs.
Kerns, Caroline, d. of Abr. and Naomi Kerns, b. Mch., 1822; d. 19 Dec., 1847.
Kerns, Abraham, s. of Abr. and Naomi Kerns, b. 19 Dec., 1827; d. 9 Oct., 1828.
Kerns, Mary, d. Abr. and Naomi Kerns, b. 12 Aug., 1829; d. 27 Apl., 1833.
Kerns, Watson, s. of Abr. and Naomi Kerns, b. 30 Dec., 1834; d. 20 May, 1836.
Kerns, Macdonald Ridgley, aged 54-7-0. Harvie M., his only child, aged 4-9-17.
Harmer, Elwood, s. of Jos. and Ann Harmer, b. 2nd mo., 17th, 1819; d. 6th mo., 5th, 1856.
Kean, John, d. 28 Jan., 1843, aged 48 yrs.
Kean, Jane, d. 24 Mch., 1868, aged 73.
Lybarger, Jane, wf. of Dan'l Lybarger, d. 27 Mch., 1822, aged 51-2-15.
Lybarger, Rosanna, d. of Dan'l and Jane Lybarger, d. 30 May, aged 72-1-15.
Lybarger, Hester, d. of Dan'l Lybarger.
Loy, Martin, d. 1 Jan., 1847, aged 62-8-4.
Loy, Linnent Wm., s. of Jno. F. and Mary A. Loy, d. 15 Dec., 1844, aged 0-5-9.
Leader, H. J. F., s. of Senary and Maria Leader.
Longstreth, Jane, wf. of Martin Longstreth, d. 4 July, 1860, aged 93 yrs.
Miller, Thos. B., d. 15 Nov., 1854, aged 54-1-15.
Miller, Charlotte H., wf. of Thomas B. Miller, d. 8 July, 1846, aged 39-6-23.
Miller, Chas. Edw., s. of Thos. B. and

Charl. Miller, d. 14 Mch., 1853, aged 12-3-23.
McDowell, Charles, d. 20 Feb., 1843, aged 66-4-24. A native of Ireland; came to U. S. 1795 and settled in Bedford Co.
McDowell, Elizabeth, wf. of Chas. McDowell, d. in Pittsburgh, Pa., 12 Oct., 1859, aged 77.
McGahe, Jane, b. 25 Dec., 1763; d. 4 Feb., 1798.
McGaughey, Jno., d. 20 Mch., 1794, aged 85 yrs.
Morrison, Ann Eliza, d. 20 Apl., 1820, aged 2-0-0.
Morrison, Jos. Todd, d. 8 Oct., 1825, aged 2 yrs.
Morrison, Jno. E., d. 9 Jan., 1835, aged 20-8-0.
Morrison, Henry Clay, d. 3 Sept., 1835, aged 4-6-0.
Morrison, Sophia, b. 14 Mch., 1821; mar. S. M. Barclay 31 Jan., 1839; d. 26 Nov., 1839.
Morrison, Jos. S., d. 25 Sept., 1851, aged 71.
Morrison, Mary, d. 1 May, 1814, aged 78.
Morrison, Joseph, d. 2 May, 1791, aged 65.
M'Grady, Jas., d. 15 Oct., 1822, aged 19-8-5.
Mullin, Eliza, d. of Geo. Mullin, d. 4 Mch., 1833, aged 20-4-9.
Metzger, Markes, consort of Hannah Wertz, d. 10 Jan. 1838, aged 40-2-16.
Metzger, Andrew, b. 29 Apl., 1793; d. 20 Aug., 1830, aged 37-3-21.
McElwee, Thos. B., b. 31 Oct., 1792; d. 23 Aug., 1843.
Moore, Sam'l, b. 11 Jan., 1772; d. 4 Aug., 1812.
Moore, Agnes, b. 28 Oct., 1810.
Moore, Cornelia, d. of Geo. and Mary Moore, d. 9 Dec., 1855, aged 7-2-13.
Moore, Mary, b. 3 Jan., 1808; d. 15 Oct., 1808.
Moore, James, b. 13 May, 1803; d. 3 July, 1805.
Moore, James, d. 29 June, 1853, aged 70-7-29.
Moore, Fanny, wf. of Jas. Moore, d. 24 Aug., 1836, aged 52-9-8.
Myers, Sallie, d. of B. F. and S. C. Myers, d. 8 Mch., 1862, aged 0-1-14.
Murving, Jno. W., s. of Thos. and H. E. Murving, d. 16 Jan., 1862, aged 0-4-15.
Mills, Wm., of Essex Co., N. J., d. 1815.

Metzger, Sol., d. 27 Sept., 1838, aged 35.
Metzger, Jas., s. of Sol. and Ann Jane Metzger, d. 3 Aug., 1830, aged 1-1-29.
Metzger, Matilda, d. of Sol. and Ann Jane Metzger, d. 10 Aug., 1833, aged 1-10-26.
Metzger, Ann Jane, relict of Sol. Metzger, d. 13 May, 1850, aged 45-2-4.
Minnick, Frank, s. of John and Emmarine Minnick, d. 23 Dec., 1838, aged 1-6-4.
McVicker, Jno. A., s. of Jas. and Mary Ann McVicker, d. 5 Sept. 1840, aged 1-1-18.
Patterson, Jos., of Balto., Md., d. 26 Aug., 1829, aged 49 years.
Powell, Col. Levin, of Va., d. in Bedford 23 Aug., 1810, aged 73 yrs.
Patterson, Rebecca, d. of David and Elizabeth Patterson, d. 23 Sept., 1840, aged 5-7-13.
Perry, Mrs. Anna, wf. of Samuel Perry, d. 23 Aug., 1823.
Perry, Wm., d. 11 May, 1834, aged 44-6-0.
Reiley, Hetty, d. 22 Nov., 1807, aged 48 yrs.
Reily, Martin, d. 5 Oct., 1829, aged 70 yrs.
Reynolds, John, b. 2 May, 1769; d. 24 Oct., 1838.
Reynolds, Margery Davidson, b. 26 Aug., 1786; d. 29 Dec., 1838.
Reynolds, Susan Sarah, b. 3 Jan., 1826; d. 2 May, 1833.
Reynolds, Rebecca, wf. of John Reynolds, d. 9 May., 1811, aged 35 years; also, Geo. W. Reynolds, d. 6 Apl., 1813, aged 6 yrs.
Rea, Thomas, b. 22 Mch., 1770; d. 8 Mch., 1843, aged 72-11-14.
Rea, Margaret, b. 8 Sept., 1791; d. 17 Sept., 1826, aged 35 yrs.
Rea, Martha, b. 22 Feb., 1779; d. 23 Nov., 1813, aged 34-8-1.
Rea, Mary, d. 27 Sept., 1845, aged 41 yrs.
Rea, John M., b. 2 July, 1816; d. 8 Sept., 1846, aged 30-12-6.
Stuckey, David C., d. 7 Mch., 1841, aged 10 mo. 3 da.
Stewart, Mary E., d. of Henry and Margaret Stewart, d. 26 Jan., 1850, aged 4-2-27.
Scott, Jane, widow of Robert Scott, d. 7 7Mch., 1819, aged 70 yrs.

Steckman, Susan, d. 7 Dec., 1860, aged 42-3-27.
Steckman, Valentine P., d. 17 Apl., 1878, aged 58-4-23.
Smith, Charles J., d. 24 Apl., 1813, aged 50 yrs.
Shaffer, Jane, wf. of Tobias Shaffer, b. 28 Nov., 1813; d. 22 Feb., 1836, aged 23-3-8.
Sills, Geo., s. of John and Maria E. Sills, d. 6 Dec., 1829, aged 26-10-21.
Sills, John, Sr., d. 2 Mch., 1837, aged 69-1-5.
Snively, Sarah Emily, d. of Andrew J. and Juliana Snively, d. 9 Aug., 1846, aged 1-8-23.
Snively, Jas. Albert, s. of Andrew J. and Juliana Snively, d. 7 May, 1848, aged 1-10-16.
Thompson, Abbey, wf. of the Hon. Alex. Thompson.
Weaver, Sam'l G., d. 13 Mch., 1854.
Weisel, Jane, wf. of Wm. Weisel, d. 11 Oct., 1854, aged 33 yrs.
Weisel, Samuel, infant son of Wm., and Jane Weisel, d. 22 Oct., 1854, aged 28 days.
Williams, Mary Ellen, d. of Philip B. and Ann Williams, d. 14 July, 1851, aged 25-3-23.
Williams, Ann, wid. of Philip Williams, d. 9 June, 1853, aged 71-2-7.
Williams, Philip, d. 2 Nov., 1831, aged 48 yrs.
Williams, Philip P., s. of Philip P. and M. A. Williams, d. 15 May, 1849, aged 18-8-5.
Williams, Martha D., d. 1827.
Williams, Henry C., s. of Philip P. and Ann Willims, d. 1 Oct., 1853, aged 25-3-15.
[In many cases the tombstones have entirely disappeared and in some the inscriptions are worn away and cannot be read.—W. F. L.]

NOTES AND QUERIES.

Historical, Biographical, and Genealogical.

XXV.

HAYS.
John Hays, of Allen township, Northampton county, d. in March, 1790, leaving a wife Jean, who was a daughter of John Walker [d. 1777], of Allen township, and children:
i. William; was the eldest.
ii. John.
iii. Isabel, m. —— Patton.
iv. Mary.
v. Elizabeth, m. —— Wilson.
vi. James, m. and had John.
vii. Robert, m. and had John.
viii. Jean, m. James Brown; d. 1800.
ix. Francis.
x. Mary, m. Neigel Gray .
Bequests were made to the following persons, but relationship not given:
Jane Rosbrugh, wife of Rev. John.
John Dunlys.
Thomas Boyd.
John Hays, Jr.
Robert Hays.
In this connection we find a Jean Ralston, who m. a John Hays. Who were they?

The Wyoming Historical and Geological Society

Have just issued volume four of their Proceedings and Collections, a volume of over two hundred and fifty pages. Apart from the admirable "Memoir of Sheldon Reynolds, Esq.," the most interesting and valuable paper is that by Judge Stanley Woodward, "The Yankee and the Pennamite in the Wyoming Valley." He gives a brief yet succinct account of the struggle for dominion, touching upon later events in that historic region, now as he fitly says, "The synonym for material prosperity and widespread wealth." Other papers especially of local interest, as well the "Record of Marriages and Deaths in the Wyoming Valley, 1826-1836," are included. A list of papers read before the society, many of which have been published in their Collections, shows what excellent work that society has been doing. It is the most prosperous of all the local historical societies in the State, has a large membership of active men and women, and all connected therewith are to be congratulated on the noble results they are now accomplishing. It is certainly the model of all local societies, and Notes and Queries extends its congratulations on the value of the publication under consideration.

Irwin of Cumberland Valley.

[Recently, in making researches among the records at Chambersburg, we came upon the following concerning the Irwin family.]

I. Mary Irwin (widow), of Peters township, Franklin county, d. in December, 1784, leaving children:
i. Samuel.
ii. William.
iii. Martha, m. —— Lapsley.

The witnesses were John Orbison, George Duffield and William Duffield, Jr. The executors were William Duffield and Thomas Orbison.

II. James Irwin, of Peters township, Franklin county, d. in December, 1785, leaving a wife Rebecca, and a son John. Bequests were made as follows:
James Irwin, son of my brother Archibald.
James Irwin, son of my brother Joseph.
Brother John.
Brother Archibald.
Sister Elizabeth, m. —— Torrence.
Sister Martha, m. —— Neely.
Sister Margaret, m. Thomas Patton.
Sister Mary, m. William Nesbit.
Sister Lidia, m. Moses Porter.

The executors were James Irwin, son of his brother Archibald, and John Maxwell.

September 21, 1790, John Irwin and David Somerville administered on the estate of William Irwin, dec'd.

November 12, 1792, William Strain and John Ogleby administered on the estate of John Irwin, dec'd.

III. Martha Irwin (widow), of Southampton township Franklin county, d. in August, 1794, leaving children:
i. Mary, m. John Mitchell.
ii. Jean, m. William Strain.
iii. Martha, m. David Simral (Somerville).
v. Margaret.
vi. Ann, m. John Ogilbe.

The executors were John Ogilbe and David Somerville.

IV. John Irwin, of Antrim township, Franklin county, d. in January, 1796, leaving a wife Mary, and children:
i. John.
ii. Robert.
iii. Mary, m. David Agnew.
iv. (A dau.) m. James Ramsey and had son James.

The executors were son-in-law James Ramsey and James McLene.

October 2, 1798, letters of administration on the estate of William Irwin were granted to Jane Irwin and John Irwin.

V. Archibald Irwin, of Montgomery township, Franklin county, d. in January, 1799, leaving a wife Jane, and children:
i. James.
ii. William.
iii. Archibald.
iv. Agnes, m. William Findlay.
v. Elizabeth, m. Robert Smith.
vi. Jane.
vii. Mary, m. Matthew Van Lear.

The executors were son James and Matthew Van Lear.

An Old-Time Friendly Letter.

[The following copy of a letter written one hundred and twenty years ago is at least entertaining, if not interesting. Our readers will find it both. "Dear Kitty" was Kitty Shepard, who was more properly known as Miss Catharine Schaffer. When the British army approached Philadelphia, in 1777, many families who were able sent their daughters away. Miss Kitty was sent to friends in Newport, R. I. It was only at rare intervals that she heard news from home. The accompanying letter is one that she received from her intimate friend, Miss Magill, by the hand of Mr. Joseph Pfeiffer, a friend of the family. Their families resided in the neighborhood of Third and Branch streets, Philadelphia.

Kitty Shepard afterwards married Ensign Philip Hagner, of the Philadelphia county militia. Their marriage is recorded at St. Michael and Zion Lutheran Church, Philadelphia, as occurring on the 8th of November, 1783. One of their sons was Charles V. Hagner, author of the "History of the Falls of Schuylkill." The Hagner property included the ground now occupied by Dobson's Mills. The homestead is still standing, shut in by the walls of the immense factories. Ensign Philip Hagner's record in the Philadelphia county militia is recorded in Pennsylvania Archives, Second Series, vol. xiii, p. 583, 601, 745, 765, and in vol. xv, p. 677.—M. B. H.]

1778.

Dear Kitty:

I received your Letter and think you have no rite to Scold at all when you hear how it was * * * * * on hand Sleep for my friend I should never think Sacrifised if I had an opportunity. I rote and got all the things that I had. Mr. Twiring told your Mama not to send them by John for he was going in a little wagon himself and would take them. I think you ought to beg pardon. I am not very entertaining at any time, but sutch as I have you are welcome to. I am very happey to be sure. Capten Sandey drank tea hear yesterday, and would have gallanted me but I did not choose to walk. I was afraid I had lost him, but I am happy to find I have not. He said I had everything to make me happy but a smart young man. I suppose he meant himself for the person, but Polley Porchan was there, so there was nothing more said. I think you might have put your name and mine to the Letter. I beg there may be no more scolding, for I think I am very good in righting all the nonsense I can think of. Mr. Aufray has got better and intends the beginning of next week to breakfast or dine with you; he presents his compliments. Mr. Pfeifer's family are all well and send their love. Polly begs Betsey would rite to her mama. The girls are all well; they were here last night, but I was out and did not see them. Poor Polly Cruthers is very bad. I have sent all the things but the rings and Tasels. I will get them as soon as possible. We are all well, thank God, and in high spirits about the arrival of the French fleet. God grant they may take New York, and I think the Toreys situation will be bad enuf. Mr. Haneal's Compliments. Please to give our love to Mrs. Twining and Riah, and be sure to kiss Anna twenty times for me. I shall conclude without scolding. Yours,

LATITIA MAGILL.

Next Friday week Mr. Johnston says he wil take me down. I am very sorry the stages are gone from Third street for it makes it very dull. Mrs. Bougan is come home. Past twelve, and all the family has been a sleep this hour.

To Mr. Joseph Pfeiffer, for Miss Kitty Shepard, Newport, R. I.

BURIAL RECORDS.

From the Reformed Church Graveyard at Bedford, Pa.

Arnold, Mary Ann, b. I April, 1810; d. 8 Feb., 1846.

Arnold, Wm., d. 20 March, 18ɔɔ, aged 2 y., 7 m.

Arnold, Mary E., d. 10 Feb., 1836, aged 2 y., 11 m., 13 d.

Arnold, Henry W., d. 27 March, 1847, aged 3 y., 11 m., 20 d.

Anderson, Henrietta, d. 16 Sept., 1833, aged 4 y., 11 m.

Anderson, Elizabeth., d. 12 Sept., 1836, aged 60 y., 7 m., 14 d.

Beegle, Charles, d. 21 June, 1853, aged 52 y., 1 m., 16 d.

Beegle, Frederick, b. 19 Dec., 1777; d. 11 May, 1844, aged 67 y., 5 m., 2 d.

Beegle, Mary Magdalene, b. 9 June, 1780; d. 14 Feb., 1846, aged 65 y., 8 m., 5 d.

Beegle, Susannah, d. 9 Oct., 1838, aged 32 y.

Beegle, John A. J., d. 4 May, 1839, aged 11 y., 11 m., 2 d.

Beegle, George A., son of C. and S. Beegle, d. 13 April, 1841, aged 2 y., 6 m., 17 d.

Beegle, George W., d. 22 April, 1840, aged 4 m., 13 d.

Bechel, William, d. 19 March, 1840, aged 2 y., 11 m., 2 d.

Beckwith, Virginia M., dau. of James and Ann Beckwith; d. 11 Jan., 1860, aged 7 y., 11 m.

Bechel, Appolonia, dau. of J. M. and Rebecca Bechel; d. 20 Jan., 1847, aged 3 m., 13 d.

Bechel, Eliza Ann, dau. of J. ---. and Re-

Historical and Genealogical. 119

becca Bechel; d. 14 March, 1847, aged 3 y., 3 m., 7 d.
Bechel, Reuben, son of John M. and Rebecca; d. 20 March, 1847, aged 1 y., 7 m., 28 d.
Beegle, Mary M., dau. of William and Eve Beegle, b. 6 Sept., 1849; d. 5 Nov., 1849.
Barkheimer, Susan, d. 11 Aug., 1859, aged 48 y.
Border, John, d. 11 July, 1856, aged 80 y., 7 m., 16 d.
Border, Ellen, son of David and Amelia Border, d. 1 July, 1857, aged 5 y., 9 m., 16 d.
Bollinger, Margaret, b. 13 July, 1804; d. 9 Aug., 1840, aged 36 y., 9 d.
Burkholder, Ruth Ellen, dau. of H. and E. Burkholder, d. 28 Dec., 1852, aged 1 y., 10 m., 28 d.
Bonnett, Jacob, d. 27 Feb., 1837, in his 60th year.
Bonnett, Anna, wf. of Jacob Bonnet, b. 17 March, 1763; d. 7 April, 1835, aged 72 y., 21 d.
Bonnett, Thos. J., b. 22 Jan., 1803; d. 10 Sept., 1835.
Bonnett, George W., b. 22 Jan., 1803; d. 30 March, 1805.
Bonnett, Ann Eliza, dau. of Thos. J. and Ann Bonnett, b. 27 Aug., 1831; d. 25 April, 1832.
Bonnett, Richard E., son of Thos. J. and Ann Bonnett, b. 4 Jan., 1833; d. 19 Oct., 1852.
Bonnett, John J., son of Thos. J. and Ann Bonnett, b. 13 Feb., 1830; d. 18 Jan., 1853.
Beegle, Paul, son of S. and C. B. Beegel, d. 8 Nov., 1851, aged 1 y., 10 m.
Baylor, Adam, d. 1 Aug., 1827, aged 33 y., 1 m., 4 d.
Baylor, William, d. 10 April, 1841, aged 36 y., 6 m., 14 d.
Brown, Walter, d. 3 Feb., 1856, aged 74 y., 1 m., 3 d.
Corl, Sarahan, b. 1 April, 1819; d. 25 Sept., 1841.
Corle, Sara Mc., dau. of Samuel and Sara Corl, d. 15 May, 1817, aged 5 y., 8 m., 24 d.
Claar, Emily, d. 3 Sept., 1833, aged 9 m.
Cromwell, Daniel, b. 4 Nov., 1806; d. 27 Aug., 1813.

Cromwell, Samuel, d. 10 Feb., 1836, aged 1 m., 2 d.
Cromwell, Sarah, d. 3 Sept., 1831, aged 1 y., 11 m., 17 d.
Cromwell, Holland B., b. 30 Jan., 1828; d. 18 Sept., 1842.
Claar, George, b. 1 July, 1793; d. 31 Aug., 1828.
Claar, Simon, d. 19 Sept., 1812, aged 80 y.
Difibaugh, Elizabeth, wf. of Samuel, d. 6 April, 1842, aged 27 y., 9 m., 5 d.
Dibert, Elizabeth, d. 11 Aug., 1828, aged 21 y., 11m., 6 d.
Dibert, Mary J., dau. of Thomas and Elizabeth Dibert, d. 11 Oct., 1811, aged 2 m., 11 d.
Dively, Caroline, dau. of J. A. and J. C. Dively, d. 25 Aug., 1853, aged 29 y., 11 m., 28 d.
Dibert, Mary, relict of Charles Dibert, d. 24 Aug., 1852, aged 85 y., 3 m., 25 d.
Dibert, Charles, d. 13 Jan., 1842, aged 79 y., 4 m., 28 d.
Dibert, Thomas, d. 28 March, 1854, aged 52 y., 26 d.
Dibert, Frances M., w. of Henry Dibert, d. 6 March, 1856, aged 23 y., 6 m., 8 d.
Dull, George, d. 21 June, 1853, aged 42 y., 4 m., 19 d.
Dunkel, George Oliver, son of William and Mary Dunkel, d. 13 May, 1857, aged 1 m., 22 d.
Difibaugh, Alex S., son of A. L. and Elizabeth Difibaugh, d. 24 Aug., 1853, aged 2 m., 14 d.
Essick, Rachel, b. 4 Feb., 1786; d. 11 Feb., 1836.
Filler, Lydia, d. 26 Aug., 1837, aged 26 y., 3 m., 24 d.
Filler, George R., d. 4 May, 1838, aged 21 y., 11 m.
Frazer, Margaret, d. 30 Jan., 1824, aged 25 y.
Fulford, Sarah, wf. Jacob Fulford, d. 5 Sept., 1860, aged 79 y., 8 m., 11 d.
Fulford, Sarah E., d. 25 April, 1835, aged 1 y., 4 m.
Gilson, Hannah Mary, d. 11 Oct., 1838, aged 4 y., 21 d.
Gilson, Frances, wf. Alex. Gilson, d. 6 June, 1859, aged 47 y., 11 m.
Gilson, Alex., d 6 April, 1864, aged 68 y., 2 m., 4 d.

Notes and Queries.

Gilson, Selina Mary., dau. Alex. and F. Gilson, d. 25 Sept., 1859, aged 17 y., 11 m., 11 d.
Herring, Elizabeth, wf. George Herring, d. 15 Jan., 1850, aged 29 y.
Hofius, Dechart, son J. H. and A. M. Hofius, b. 16 May, 1823; d. 25 July, 1859, aged 17 y., 2 m., 7 d.
Hofius, Dr. John H., d. 10 June, 1851, aged 65 y.
Herring, Corp. C. W., Co. K, 55th Pa. Inf.
Holderbaum, John, d. 23 March, 1817, aged 62 y., 8 m., 2 d.
Haultorbaum, Margaret, d. 1 July, 1840, aged 75 y.
Keeffe, Ann Margaret, dau. William Keeffe and Mary Zimmers, d. 6 Sept., 1853, aged 4 m., 13 d.
Koons, David, son Henry and Catharine Koons, b 1 Jan., 1834; d. 6 Jan., 1835.
Koons, Odilla, consort of Henry Koons, d. 16 March, 1844, aged 72 y.
Koons, Henry, d. 1 Feb., 1855, aged 90 y.
Ketterman, Lilly G., dau. Samuel and Jane Ketterman, d. 10 Aug., 1861, aged 7 m., 22 d.
Lowry, Sara Ann., dau. J. and M. A. Lowry, d. 23 Sept., 1836, aged 1 y., 2 m., 10 d.
Lysinger, Eve, relict of Dewalt Lysinger, d. 19 May, 1854, aged 75 y., 4 m., 24 d.
Light, Mary, d. 23 April, 1833, aged 5 y., 10 m.
Light, Julian, d. 12 Dec., 1835, aged 5 y., 9 m.
Lowery, Elenor, b. 12 Dec., 1814; d. 7 Jan., 1816.
Leader, Henry S., son G. W. and Sarah Leader, d. 8 Aug., 1855, aged 23 y., 1 m., 24 d.
Mortimore, Mary Ann, wf. Jacob, d. 14 Aug., 1860., aged 29 y., 6 m., 18 d.
Mortimore, Emily Jane, dau. Jacob and Mary Ann Mortimore, d. 3 Dec., 1856, aged 1 y., 3 m., 14 d.
Miller, John W., d. 21 Aug., 1850, aged 9 y., 8 m., 10.
Miller, Eve, d. 29 March, 1839, aged 56 y., 7 m., 18 d.
May, Julian, d. 8 Dec., 1834, aged 1 y., 6 m., 23 d.
Miller, Henry, b. 7 Dec., 1782; d. 16 July, 1818.
Messersmith, Sharlotte, dau. Henry and Elizabeth Messersmith, b. 16 Jan., 1810; d. 1 March, 1815.
McFadden, Daniel, d. 22 Sept., 1831, aged 40 y.
McFadden, Evy C., d. 18 Sept., 1830, aged 1 y., 10 m.
Moses, Elizabeth, wf. Jacob Moses, d. 16 March, 1-852, aged 41 y., 4 m., 13 d.
Minten, Sarahan, d. 16 Nov., 1838, aged 21 y., 9 m., 7 d.
Mardoff, Mary, wf. William Mardoff, d. 18 Dec., 1872, aged 84 y.
Nycuem, William, consort Mary Nycuem, d. 13 Feb., 1849, aged 38 y., 6 m., 30 d.
Nycuem, Lorenia, dau. William and Mary Nycuem, b. 25 Sept., 1836; d. 20 Aug., 1838.
Naugle, Thomas J., b. 25 Nov., 1831; d. 6 March, 1844.
Oylar, John, b. 18 June, 1787; d. 2 July, 1834.
Over. Mrs. Henrietta Over, dau. Jacob and Margaret Zimmers, d. 9 Sept., 1826, aged 21 y., 8 m., 9 d. Erected by her only son. D. Jacob Over.
Peck, Jacob, d. 13 Nov., 1838, aged 19 y., 10 m., 2 d.
Pheifer, Martin, d. 27 Feb., 1837, in 60th y.
Russell, Thomas E., son George and Susan Russell, d. 17 Dec., 1852, aged 7 y., 7 m., 13 d.
Russell, George, b. 23 Aug., 1831; d. 9 May, 1839.
Reimund, John, b 18 April, 1761; d. 1 Sept., 1845.
Radebaugh, Alverda, son Samuel and Charlotte Radebaugh, d. 7 Aug., 1857, aged 4 y., 16 m., 7 d.
Radebaugh, Jeremiah, son Jacob Radebaugh, b. — July, 1800; d. 12 Feb., 1817.
Radebaugh, Sharlotte, dau. Jacob Radebaugh, b. 14 Feb., 1798; d. 14 Nov., 1845.
Reiley, Martin, d. 22 Oct., 1821, aged 24 y.
Silver, Mary, wf. John Silver, b. 9 Jan., 1801; d. 21 Oct., 1832.
Stahl, Margaret, d. 28 Oct., 1834, aged 34 y., 8 m., 4 d.
Stahl, Susanna, d. 28 April, 1835, aged 13 y., 9 m., 21.
Stahl, John C., d. 13 April, 1843, aged 3 y., 9 m., 18 d.
Stahl, Sarah Ellen, d. 29 Aug., 1845, aged 3 m., 3 d.

Stahl, Mary, d. 26 Sept., 1834, aged 1 y., 2 m., 11 d.
Stahl, Sarah, wf. William, d. 3 Jan., 1853, aged 43 y., 8 m., 25 d.
Stahl, William, b. at Melsingen, Hesse Cassel, 27 Feb., 1788; d. 28 Jan., 1867.
Stahl, Jacob Z., son William and Sarah Stahl, b. 28 June, 1847; d. 11 Aug., 1868.
Surins, Andrew, d. 6 April, 1828, aged 43 y.
Stevens, Henry, b. 11 Feb., 1814; d. 5 Sept., 1849.
Stevens, Rebecca, wf. Henry Stevens, b. 22 Oct., 1819; d. 29 Feb., 1868.
Sands, Simon, d. 23 Oct., 1840, aged 3 y., 1 m., 26 d.
Sands, Mary, consort Dunbar Sands, d. 8 Jan., 1848, aged 32 y., 10 m., 7 d.
Smith, Susan, dau. G. W. and E. Smith, d. 8 April, 1853, aged 14 d.
Smith, David E., d. 3 Dec., 1850, aged 20 y., 7 m., 19 d.
Stouffer, Mary Virginia, dau. Christian and Mary E. Stouffer, b. 16 July, 1852; d. 18 July, 1854.
Shuck, William and James, sons of Daniel and Susan Shuck, b. 17 May; d. 26 June, 1815.
Weisel, Simon Peter, son A. and E. Weisel, d. 25 April, 1851 ,aged 20 y., 5 m., 24 d.
Weisel, Samuel, d. 23 Feb., 1853, aged 27 y., 11 m., 23 d.
Weisel, Mary E., dau. S. W. and B. Weisel, 22 Nov., 1851, aged 3 y., 2 m., 1 d.
Weisel, Anna Barbara, wf. John Weisel, d. 14 Nov., 1857, aged 77 y., 10 m., 11 d.
Weisel, Jos. Frank, son A. and E. Weisel, d. 9 May, 1851, aged 5 y., 7 m., 12 d.
Wortz, Valentine, about 65 y.
Wortz, Rachel, consort of Valentine Wortz, d. 15 March, 1841, aged 69 y., 16 d.
Welch, Susan, wf. William F. Welch, d. 3 April, 1858, aged 22 y., 10 m., 20 d.
Walleck, Sharlotte, d. 24 March, 1841, aged 90 y.
Zimmers, Margaret, d. 8 Oct., 1843, aged 72 y., 9 m., 7 d.
Zimmers, Frederick, d. 23 Dec., 1837, aged 82 y.
Zimmers, Henry, b. 1 May, 1830; d. 25 April, 1847.
Zimmers, Sarah, dau. Philip and Rachel Zimmers, d. 2 May, 1853, aged 28 y., 11 m., 15 d.
Zimmers, Philip, d. 5 Nov., 1862, aged 70 y., 2 m., 24 d.
Zimmers, Rachel, wf. Philip Zimmers, d. 15 Dec., 1855, aged 61 y., 4 m., 4 d.
Zimmers, Samuel, d. 26 Aug., 1857, aged 36 y., 5 m., 28 d.

Bedford, Pa.   W. F. L.

NOTES AND QUERIES.

Historical, Biographical and Genealogical.

XXVI.

MOSES YODER.

Among the early settlers in Oley township, Berks county, was Samuel Yoder. His ancestors came from Germany. Samuel Yoder had issue:
i. Maria, b. 1750; d. 1812.
ii. George, b. 1752.
iii. Peter, b. 1763.
iv. David, b. 1765; d. Jan., 1826.
v. Abraham, b. 1768.

Of the above descendants, David married Catharine High. He died in 1826, and his wife in 1845. They had issue:
i. Joshua; m. Elizabeth Brown.
ii. Samuel; m. Sarah Mackey.
iii. David; d. young.
iv. Moses, b. April 1, 1810; d. ——.
v. Benneville; d. young.
vi. Isaac; m. Deborah Fowler.
vii. Aaron; d. young.
viii. Eliza; d. young.
ix. Phoebe; m. Jeremiah Taylor.
x. Anna; m. Frederick Dersham.

Moses Yoder, fourth son of David, emigrated from Berks county with his parents to Union county in 1815, and settled in White Deer township. He purchased 60 acres of land lying on the river and subsequently laid out the village of New Columbia. He married Elizabeth Ranck in 1834. She died without issue November 23, 1848, and in July, 1854, he married, secondly, Mrs. Ann Van Wagner. She was born February 21, 1818, her parents being James and Ann Craft Fowler. Her father died in 1858.

Moses Yoder was an active and hard-working man in various lines of business.

In 1864 he purchased a store at White Deer Mills and engaged in that business. In 1875 he was appointed postmaster at White Deer Mills and held the office for a number of years. Mr. Yoder joined the Lutheran church in 1845 and remained a consistent member until his death a few years ago. By his last marriage he had one daughter, Kate Datesman Yoder, born May 7, 1855. On the 27th of December, 1876, she married Cyrus Leinbach and they had: Merle Yoder, born January 6, 1878, and Mabel Inez, born July 15, 1881.   J. F. M.

LANDIS AND SMOLNIKAR

Two Eccentric Men of Bygone Days.

In "Notes and Queries," Second Series, pp. 464-5-6 and pp. 469-70, appear notes in regard to John Landis, the eccentric poet, artist and tourist. The data there found does not, however, mention when John Landis was born. The writer recently saw a copy of a 177 page book entitled "Discourses on the Depravity of the Human Family, Particularly Applied to These Times; by John Landis, Poet, and Annointed of God. Printed by R. S. Elliott & Co., Harrisburg, Pa., 1839," in which the author gives an account of himself in the preface. Among other things Landis writes that he was "born October 15, 1805, in Dauphin county, one mile from Hummelstown and ten from Harrisburg, on the Engle farm, where 'Echo Cave' is located." That he was of Lutheran parentage; began printer's trade with Mr. (Francis) Wyeth, of Harrisburg, in 1822; became a partner in the only Jacksonian Democratic paper printed in Reading and was a partner for six months; lived at York, Harrisburg, Reading and Lancaster up to 1833, when he took a trip to foreign lands; began painting in 1830; the picture of "Christ Preaching" was destroyed when the Lutheran church in Harrisburg was burned in October, 1838.

The writer further states that he had the small-pox in 1830, and while lying abed with the disease had a vision of the Lord, who called him "annointed," and told him to preach, which he did after that period. When recovering from that disease, he started from Harrisburg for Lancaster, and between Columbia and Lancaster a break-down of the wagon occurred and Landis suffered a fractured arm. Other data which Landis details is similar to that contained in "Notes and Queries," Second Series, above mentioned.

In this connection it may be stated that another eccentric character, who visited Lancaster forty years ago, and even less than that, was "Smolnikar," his name being Andrew D. Smolnikar. He was a mild crank of the religious type, and usually wore a linen "duster" which extended to his knees and carried a grip in his hand. He was the author of several pamphlets, among them being "Secret Enemies of True Republicanism." On the title of this book, a copy of which the writer owns, he claims to have been "Formerly for eighteen years, priest and Benedictine monk and Imperial Royal Professor of Biblical Literature; Afterwards, since 1838, by signs declared a messenger of the Universal Republic, improperly called the Millenium." This book was printed in 1859. He states that he was born on November 29, 1795, in Kamnik, Lithipolia, or the City of Stein, in Illyria. He was ordained a priest in 1819. He remained such until January 5, 1837, 5 o'clock P. M., when he claims to have had a visit from an angel, who ordered him to go to America where he (Smolnikar) should begin to establish Christ's peaceful reign on earth. He came to America and began to lecture in Boston, Mass., on January 7, 1838, having arrived in this country on November 29, 1837. He had numerous followers, who believed in the coming of the Millenium, and he and his followers made furious attacks upon the Presidents of the United States from 1849 to 1860, claiming that they were particularly in need of understanding the message of peace.

The writer has two other pamphlets written by Smolnikar, anl in one of them he states that he studied for the priesthood with the monks in Laibach, and was ordained a priest of the Diocese of Laibach, Carniola of Illyria, in 1819; afterwards entered the Benedictine order of monks in 1825 in the St. Paul monastery in Carinthia, and in 1827 became Professor of Biblical Literature in that monastery. He came to Philadelphia in 1852 and there met a shoemaker named Peter Bunney who had been a Mormon preacher in England. Peter Bunney joined the Millenium movement with Smalnikar, both of whom went among the Mennonites endeavoring to make converts. Bunney went to Canada, where he died in June, 1863. Smolnikar established his headquarters in Donally's Mills, Tuscarora township, Perry county, Pa., where he had quite a following. He was sued in the courts of Perry county by one Levi Carstetter for debt contracted by furnishing lumber, etc., for erecting a building to be used as a "temple of worship and headquarters of the Peace Union."

The last public appearance in print made by Smolnikar was in June, 1866, when he addressed "An Earnest Appeal" to the President and Senate of the United States for the introduction of Christ's peaceable reign on earth. This was addressed from Baltimore. After this Smolnikar drifted agout for some time and finally all trace of him became lost and no one can state positively where he died or when, or where buried. In this regard he is a similar case to Landis, whose date and place of death or burial are unknown.   S. M. SENER.
Lancaster, Pa.

Annals of Wekquitank.

1760-1763.

[In "Notes and Queries" for 1897, p. 153, reference is made to "Wekquitank," one of the Moravian Indian missions. To John W. Jordan, of the Historical Society of Pennsylvania, are our readers indebted for the following "Extracts from the Diaries" of that mission, covering a period of three years and six months. As a part of the early history of our Commonwealth these records are of inestimable value.]

I.

1760.

April 24.—We set out from Nain and came to Christian's Spring, where Bro. [Joachim] Senseman and [John Joseph] Schebosch received their instructions from Bro. Peter Boehler. Camped that night at "The Rose," kept by Ephraim Colver and wife. (1.)

April 25.—Continued our journey this morning, and towards evening reached Wekquitank. Here the Indians encamped along the fence, near the site of the former house and mill [Hoeth's], while we missionaries went farther on to Boemper's former place, where we found a part of the old stable and crib standing, and fed our horses. Bro. Senseman held a "Quarter Hour" [a short devotional service] for the Indians.

April 26.—The Indians shot two deer. Bro. Senseman pointed out the spot selected for the settlement, near an excellent spring. Bro. Schebosch went in search of the cows that had strayed off in the night. The Indians fired the site for the settlement to burn up the brush, but the wind set an old tree on fire, which fell across the creek and set fire to the fences there.

April 27.—Busy all day building huts.

April 28.—Bro. Schebosch began to plant corn, while the Indians were kept busy peeling bark for the huts. Young Philip went in search of our cows that have not yet returned. The first meeting in the new town was held this evening.

April 29.—Several of the Indians went to Nain, to bring their friends here.

April 30.—Christian and his two brothers went for his mother and their effects; and young Philip went home.

May 2.—After the "Morgen Segen" [morning prayer] Anton (2) and David went to Nain, and the two widows Emma and Sarah with their children came from thence and desire to live here. We occupied Anton's house.

May 3.—Bro. Schebosch rode to Christian's Spring on business. (3)

May 4 (Sunday).—Preached on John iii, 14.

May 5.—Bro. Senseman was busily engaged in burning brush on the village site, while Bro. Schebosch ploughed. David returned from Nain.

May 6.—We occupied our own house, as Anton with his wife and child, Christian Gottlieb, are expected.

May 7.—Anton with his family arrived to-day.

May 8.—Anton brought a large beaver home, and invited us all to dine on it.

May 10.—David went to Nain.

May 11 (Sunday).—Bro. Schebosch held "Morgen Segen," and at noon a discourse on 1 Corinthians. Two white men, who live four miles from here, visited us. Anton held "Abend Segen" [evening prayer], after which Bro. Schebosch rode to Christian's Spring to have a plow-share sharpened.

May 12.—Anton and Zacharias went out to hunt and the former shot a deer. Bro. Schebosch returned. Bro. Senseman began to set the fence, where two years ago it was burnd by the bush fire.

May 13.—Were anxious about Zacharias' absence. The rain prevented our ploughing.

May 15.—Six white men rode thro' to-day, and inquired whether we designed soon to rebuild the mill.

May 17.—Anton went to Nain.

May 18 (Sunday).—Christian went to Nain. The meetings to-day were kept in English, as we had no interpreter; but most of the Indians understand English.

May 19.—Some of the Indians began to plant. Sam Evans (5) and Ruth came to-day, our first visit from Indians.

May 20.—The brethren Schulze and Reichardt arrived with a team from Nain, with the effects of our Indians. Justina, with her children, David and his wife Charity, came here to reside; and Sam Evans departed.

May 21.—Bro. Schebosch held "Morgen Segen." Anton, with his wife Johanna and child, came from Nain.

May 22.—The Indians were busy planting. Zaccheus, and wife, and Beata, came to reside here, so land was allotted them.

May 23.—Finished planting Indian corn. Bro. Schebosch, with his team, went to Bethlehem for his wife.

May 24.—Joel and his wife Regina came here to reside.

May 25 (Sunday).—Discoursed on the Acts of the Apostles. The first Children's "Quarter Hour" held to-day. Anton held "Abend Segen."

May 28.—Bro. Schebosch and wife arrived from Nain, with their child Joseph. Anton, Zaccheus and Christian went to Fort Allen (6) on business.

May 29.—Bro. Schebosch began to plough for oats. Anton and brethren while on their return from the fort shot a deer.

June 1 (Sunday).—At noon preaching; "Abend Segen" kept by Anton.

June 2.—Set the fence. Zacharias went to Fort Allen for provisions for us.

June 3-4.—Busy at the fence. Zacharias returned from the fort, and Peter went to Nain.

June 6.—Rained the whole day. Anton helped Joel to roof his house, which he occupied to-day.

June 8.—Anton preached on Isaiah lv, 6, after which we held a conference.

June 9.—Bro. Schebosch held "Morgen Segen." To-day we finished setting the fence. Sam Evans and Ruth came from Nain, also Isaac Nutimaes. (7) Bro. Senseman cautioned Anton to be watchful that no rum be smuggled into the settlement, whereupon the latter spoke to Nutimaes.

June 10.—Nutimaes left, having told us that everything was quiet on the Susquehanna.

June 11.—To-day we began to haul timber, to repair the spring-house on the Boemper place, which we design for the present to use as a meeting house.

June 13.—Bishop Spangenberg and Bro. [John J.] Schmick (8) arrived from Bethlehem. After extending to them a hearty welcome, and partaken of some refreshments, they viewed the site for the village, the creek, and the spot selected for the clergy house; also the site selected by Bro. Senseman for a burying-ground. Next was visited the spot where the Hoeths had lived, and had been murdered, and where their race, grist and saw mill had stood. The neighbors are clamorous that we should rebuild the mills. Spangenberg kept "Abend Segen:" then he and Schmick retired to their little tent, that had been struck for them on the site of our settlement.

June 14.—Bro. Schmick held "Morgen Segen:" then Spangenberg spoke, Schebosch's and Schmick's wives interpreting.

Next a Children's Love Feast was held, in which Spangenberg related about events in North Carolina, Anton interpreting, and German and Indian hymns were sung. In the afternoon the widow Emma, a sister of Capt. John, who had formerly lived on the Nazareth tract with her brother, was admitted to church fellowship; and then the Lord's Supper was celebrated, three Indians and eight whites partaking.

Catalogue of Indians in Wekquitank
Married.
1. Anton and Johanna (communicants).
2. David and Charity.
3. Zacharias and Elizabeth.
4. Joel and Regina.
5. Zaccheus and Beata.
6. Peter and Lucia.
Widows.
1. Justina, [of Nicodemus,] (communicant).
2. Emma or Naemi, [Capt. Jno. Hains' and Peter's sister].
3. Sarah [Jo Peepe's wife and Hains' and Peter's sister].
Single Brethren.
1. Christian, (candidate for Communion).
3. Nathan [son of Justina].
3. Thomas [son of Justina].
Youths.
1. Doosch [son of Peter].
2. Jonathan [son of Peter].
3. Gaschaschis [son of Justina].
4. John [son of Nathaniel].
Boys.
1. Lewis [son of Joel].
2. Christian Gottlieb [son of Amelia].
Girls.
1. Dorothea [daugh. of Zacharias].
2. Mary [daugh. of Jo. Peepe's].
Infants.
1. John [son of Zaccheus].
2. Joseph [son of Schebosch].
Unbaptized.
1. Zaccheus and Beata's infant son.
Missionaries.
Joachim Senseman.
John Joseph Schebosch and his wife Christiana [Warden].

June 15.—(Sunday.) Bro Schmick kept "Morgen Segen;" then Spangenberg kept a "Gemeinrath" [Church Council] with all the adults, and spoke of the design of the settlement. Next he held a "homily" and then our guests took their leave and set out for Nazareth, Bro. Senseman accompanying them some way thro' the woods. Anton, Peter, Christian and others set out for a four days' hunt.

June 17.—Bro. Senseman and Schebosch began to set up the meeting-house, which had been brought from Boemper's place.

June 18.—The hunters returned with nine deer. Zaccheus went on a wolf hunt.

June 19.—Some of our Indians went into the swamp for bark with which to cover the meeting-house.

June 20.—The meeting-house was covered with bark. Several Indian sisters hoed corn.

June 21.—Bro. Schebosch and Christian rode into the woods to get out boards for the meeting-house.

June 22.—(Sunday.) Bro. Senseman preached on Phil. ii, 13, Anton interpreting; after which we had a "Gemeinrath" on temporal affairs.

June 24.—Nearly all the Indian brethren went out to hunt, twenty miles hence, and the sisters hoed corn.

June 25.—Some of the Indian's female friends came to assist them hoe, as the land is covered with a thick sward, from not having been tilled for five years. Bro. Martin Mack (9) with his wife arrived to-day; the former thought the land looked much better than when he was here last winter.

June 26.—We completed the benches or seats for the meeting-house, and in the evening it was dedicated by Bro. Mack, who made first an address, next Anton prayed, and then Bro. Mack sang some Indian and some German verses.

June 27.—Bro. Mack held "Morgen Segen," and then visited the Indians in their huts; after which he returned to Bethlehem. Bro. Senseman and Bro. Schebosch blocked up the latter's house.

June 29.—Preached on Titus iii : 4, 5, 6.

July 1.—Bro Schebosch returned from Bethlehem with the intelligence that Sister Amelia had died on Friday, June 27. Our Indians busy hoeing corn.

July 2.—Peter, Christian and Zacharias returned from the hunt, with sixteen deer.

July 3.—Peter, Christian and Zacharias

the mishap that had befallen him. While chasing a bear he fired on some black object through the bush, which turned out to be a black horse, which a white hunter had hitched to a limb while in pursuit of game. Much frightened, he resulved to wait for the owner and explain. The owner much regretted the loss of his horse, when Zacharias promised to make good his loss in money, when he came to the settlement. He never appeared. Perhaps the horse was only slightly wounded, or perhaps he felt guilty, as there is a fine of £40 for a white man to shoot a deer at this season of the year.

July 9.—Bro. Schebosch went to Boemper's old place to plow for winter wheat, and Bro. Senseman laid the floor of the meeting-house.

July 11.—Bro. Schebosch moved into his house to-day.

July 14.—Some of our Indians went to Fort Allen for provisions.

July 16.—Bro. Senseman and Bro. Schebosch cut grass for hay.

July 19.—Our Indians worked in the corn-field, after which we had a meeting with those who attended the Lord's Supper. At dusk we had Love feast, followed by the Lord's Supper, with six converts.

July 20.—At 9 A. M. held a Liturgy-meeting with the communicants in the chapel.

July 21.—Bro. Schebosch and Christian rode to Christian's Spring on business. We heard that the Indian pow-wow or Doctor had called on the father of Tobias, a sick lad, and returned his rifle, saying: "Here is your piece; I am able to cure your son; I did not come for that purpose, but to join the Brethren.

August 1.—Some of our Indian brethren went on the hunt, and the sisters picked dried huckleberries.

August 2.—Bro. Schebosch ploughed and sowed turnips, and Bro. Senseman made hay. Tobias shot a fine deer.

August 3.—(Sunday.) Text for sermon to-day 1 John i : 8, 9.

August 4.—Sam Evans and Ruth, his wife, came here to-day.

August 9.—We hauled in the hay and built a hay-cock.

August 11.—Began a school for the children.

August 13.—Bro. Schebosch returned from Gnadenthal. [A settlement west of Nazareth].

August 15.—Wood was cut for a spring-house.

August 16.—Anton expressed a wish to visit on the Susquehanna and call on Papunhan (10) and his clan. The Lord's Supper was celebrated.

August 17.—Bro. [John] Roth (11), who lately came here, kept "Morgen Segen."

August 18.—Bro. [Jacob] Fries (12) kept 'Morgen Segen," after which he and Bro. Roth set out for Christian's Spring.

August 20.—Bro. Scheboch and Bro. Senseman worked at the spring-house.

August 23.—Bro. John Bonn and Bro. Lorenz Bagge visited us; from them we learned of the death of the Disciple [Zinzendorf] and Anna Nitschmann. This intelligence moved us unutterably, and we could not sleep.

August 24.—(Sunday.) Bro. Senseman and Schebosch communicated the sad news to the Indians, and Anton was so affected, he could with difficulty interpret. Bro. Bonn viewed the land and reckoned it to be good.

August 25.—Bro. Bonn kept "Morgen Segen," after which he and Bro. Bagge returned to Christian's Spring. Bro. Senseman is indisposed. Some Indians went on a hunt.

August 27.—Our Indians were busy building Peter's house.

August 28.—Anton and Joel were making canoes in the woods.

August 29.—The oats was hauled in and stacked up; and white pine boards were hauled for clap-boards.

NOTES AND QUERIES,

Historical, Biographical and Genealogical.

XXVII.

EVANS-BRUNER.

Nathan Evans (N. & Q., xxiv) was not the founder of Churchtown, any more than other members of the Bangor church, but he was, however, a very liberal contributor to Bangor, for which he deserves all praise. On May 24, 1738, a warrant was issued and survey made to Gabriel Davies (son of Wm. Davies, of Radnor) for 62 acres and 127 perches, "for a church to be erected." Feb. 20, 1755, the patent was issued to Lynford Lardner and John Davies, (son of Wm. Davies, of Radnor), trustees. The patent states the warrant was for a "church to be erected and since erected and called Bangor." Leases were made for lots on this tract, and houses erected by different parties—it was spoken of as the Church Town, since changed to Churchtown. The settlement in Caernarvon was made by the children of the Welsh who settled at Radnor, and the sons of William Davies, of Radnor (John, William and Gabriel), and his sons-in-law, Nathan Evans, Evan Hughes, Hugh Hughes and David Jones, all having land patented to them immediately around Churchtown. The maiden name of Nathan Evans' wife was Susanna Davies (daughter of Wm. Davies, of Radnor). Elizabeth Thomas was the maiden name of the wife of James Evans. Her parents are not known. James Evans (son of James) married Ann Cunningham. I can give no particulars.   O.

OFFICERS OF THE REVOLUTION

From Pennsylvania Who Were Killed or Died in the Service.

[For some time we have endeavored to make a list of the Officers of the Navy, Battalions and Line who were killed or died while in the Revolutionary service. The following, necessarily incomplete, will be valuable for reference. In addition there were losses among Pennsylvanians in other commands—especially the Continental navy.]

Col. Thompson's Battalion:
  William Hendricks, Capt., k. before Quebec, Dec. 31, 1775.
  John McClellan, 1st Lt., d. on the expedition to Quebec.
Second Battalion:
  Samuel Watson, Capt., d. at Three Rivers.
Third Battalion:
  Daniel Brodhead, Jr., 1st Lt., d. in 1779, shortly after released from captivity.

Fourth Battalion:
  Charles C. Beatty, Lt., accid. k. 1777.
  Samuel Kennedy, surgeon, d. 1778.
Fifth Battalion:
  John Miller, Capt., m. w. 1776.
  John Finley, 2d Lt., d. 1781.
Sixth Battalion:
  Robert Adams, Capt., k. 1776.
  Joseph Culbertson. Ens., k. 1776.
  James Calderwood, Qr. Mr., m. w. at Brandywine.
Penn'a Rifle Regt.:
  James Piper, Lt. Col., d. in cap.
  Joseph Jacquet, 2d Lt., k. August, 1776.
  George West, 1st Lt., d. in cap.
  Charles Taylor, 3d Lt., k. August, 1776.
  William Peebles, Capt., d. in cap.
  David Sloan, 2d Lt., k. August, 1776.
Musketry Battalion:
  Caleb Parry, Lt. Col., k. Aug., 1776.
  Alex. Huston, Jr., Ens., k. at Brandywine.
First Penn'a.:
  Charles Craig, Capt., w. at B.
  Thomas Boyd, 1st Lt., k. 1779.
  Michael Hoffman, 2d Lt., d. 1780.
  William Patton, 3d Lt., k. at B.
  Christian Reinick, Surg. M., k at Paoli.
  James Holliday, Ens., k. at B.
Second Penn'a.:
  Major Walborn, 1st Lt., k. at Paoli.
  John Park, 1st ___., d. 1780 from w.
  Jacob M. DeHart, 1st Lt., d. 1780 from w.
  Peter Dietrick, Ens., k. 1780 at Paramus.
Third Penn'a.:
  Rudolph Brunner, Lt. Col., k. 1778, at Monmouth.
  Thomas L. Byles, Major, k. 1780, at Paramus.
  Brice, Innis, Surg. M., d. 1778 in service.
Fourth Penn'a:
  Marien Lamar, Major, k. at Paoli.
Fifth Penn'a:
  Alex McClintock, 1st Lt., w. at B. and d.
  James McCullough, 1st Lt., d. 1782 in service
  William Magee, Ens., k. at Paoli.
Sixth Penn'a.:
  Ezekiel Downey, Surg., d. at York river, Va.
Eighth Penn'a.:
  Eneas Mackey, Col., d. 1777 in service.

George Wilson, Lt. Col., d. 1777 in service.
Samuel Smith, 2d Lt., k. at Ger.
Ninth Penn'a.:
George Grant, Capt., d. 1779 in service.
Tenth Penn'a.:
George Calhoun, Capt., d. 1779 in service.
Adam Bettin, Capt., Lt., k. at the revolt, 1781.
Peter Shiles, 2d Lt., w. 1777 at B. and d.
Eleventh Penn'a.:
Benjamin Hammond, 2d Lt., k. 1778.
Thomas Lucas, 2d Lt., k. at B.
Peter Martin, 2d. Lt., k. at B.
Alex. Carmichael, 2d Lt., k. at B.
Twelfth Penn'a.:
Peter Withington, Capt., d. 1777 in service.
John Carothers, 2d Lt., k. at Ger.
William Boyd, 2d Lt., k. at B.
Thomas Hanson, Adj., d. 1777 in service.
Hartley's Regt.:
Lewis Bush, Major, m. w. at B.
Robert Hopes, Capt., k. at B.
James Dill, Lt., k. at B.
James Lemon, Lt., k. at B.
New Eleventh Penn'a.:
Morgan Connor, Lt. Col., d. 1780 at sea.
Joseph Davis, Capt., k. 1779, near Wyoming.
Isaac Sweeney, Capt., d. 1780 in service.
German Regt.:
Eberhard Michael, Pay, d. 1778 in service.
Penn'a Artillery:
John Martin Strobagh, Lt. Col., d. 1778 in service.
Samuel Stoy, Capt., Lt., d. 1782 in service.
Hugh Montgomery, 1st Lt., d. 1777 in service.
Samuel Boude, 2d Lt., k. at B.
William Newbound, 3d Lt., d. 1778 in service.
Artillery Artificers:
Benjamin Flower, Col., d. 1781 in service.
James Livingston, Qr. Mr., k at B.
Col. Baldwin's Regt. of Art.:
Henry Matthews, Capt., d. 1781 in service.

Penn'a Navy:
James Johnston, 1st Lt., Chatham, d. 1777 in service.
Benj. Thompson, Capt., Dragon, d. 1777 in service.
John Reynolds, 1st Lt., Franklin, d. 1779 in service.
James Fletcher, 2d Lt., Race Horse, d. 1777 in service.

Pennsylvania-German Graveyards in the South.

Recently I had occasion to travel extensively per carriage in Western Maryland and a part of West Virginia where Pennsylvania-Germans settled extensively prior to 1750. The chief settlement was made on the Conecocheague (pronounced locally Con-o-go-jig), in the vicinity of Clear Spring, Washington county, Md. Rev. Michael Schlatter, the founder of the Reformed Church in Pennsylvania, writes in his journal of having visited this place. By the help of the local Reformed pastors I was able to identify the St. Paul Lutheran-Reformed Church, a few miles southeast of Clear Spring, as the original congregation. Upon arrival there, however, I was deeply disappointed. I found a magnificent edifice (the third church), one of the finest country churches to be seen anywhere, but my exploration in the old graveyard, which has grown into a large cemetery was not very satisfactory. The Colonials have simply limestone headstones and there are very few prior to 1800. Inasmuch as this county (Washington) was formed during the Revolution by separation from Frederick county, the historian is obliged to resort to the old records of Frederick county, at Frederick City, for his earliest dates concerning the settlers. I herewith append some Pennsylvania-German names. Numbers are still extant here, while many of the "plantations" are yet in the possession of the descendants of the original settlers:

Brua (now Brewer), Cushwa, Angney (now Ankony), Fiery, Eby, Reidenour (see Notes and Queries, 1898, p. 173), Seybert, Houer, Newcommer, Leight, Kerchner, Wolf, Funk, Klein, Miller, Gehr, Sprecher, Spickler, Holbruner, Huyett,

Kauffman, Swengel, Grosh, Small, Witmer, Mish, Heller, Scheider, Eby, Tice, Whorley, Spitznagel, Biesbecker, Myers, Bergman.

In the new part of the cemetery is a fine monument in memory of the Fiery family. The inscription on one panel is as follows:

"GREAT-GRAND-PARENTS."
Fiery, Joseph, b. Durlach, Germany; d. 1812, aged 67 years.
Fiery, Mary Domer, his wife, d. 1812, aged 74 years.
GRAND-PARENTS.
Fiery, Henry, Sr., d. 1813, aged 47 years.
Fiery, Elizabeth Peters, his wife, d. 1853 aged 83 years.
PARENTS.
Fiery Henry, Jr., d. 1861, aged 68 years.
Fiery, Martha Miller, his wife, d. 1871, aged 70 years.
Erected by Lewis Fiery."

The following person was doubtless an original settler of Berkeley county, W. Va., about six miles distant across the Potomac:

"Bargman, Michael, b. 1738, in Europe; d. Dec. 17, 1818, aged 80y 1m 19d." "Eve Bergman, wife of Michael, b. in Hannau (Hanover, Germany—A. S.), dau. of Anna Eve Brackonier, b. Nov. 30, 1752; d. May 18, 1827, aged 74y 5m 18d. Lived and died a member of the Lutheran Church." "Cath. Smith," dau. of Michael and Eve Bargman, b. March 26, 1776, in Berkeley county, Va., and d. June 5, 1827, aged 51y 2m 10d."

"THE OPEQUON."

From this old settlement I went to Martinsburg, West Virginia. Near by is the Opequon creek, along which the Pennsylvania-Germans settled very early. The oldest graveyard I could find is that of the old Lutheran and Reformed Church, in Martinsburg, and dates back to Colonial times. Here I found a few German inscriptions, but the coarse sand headstones were so eroded as to be indecipherable. I am of the opinion that very little data concerning the German emigration to the South can be derived from tombstones.

In Rev. John Casper Stoever's baptismal record from 1730 to 1750 may be seen the names of many German settlers in the great valley of Virginia, of which a large number are still extant there.

A. STAPLETON.
Carlisle, Pa.

Annals of Wekquitank.

1760-1763.

II.

August 30.—The children attend school regularly, and are improving. To-night the dogs were restless, and a stone was thrown upon Joel's house.
September 1.—Two white men came to look at a plantation in the neighborhood, but on hearing that we had not yet concluded to build a mill, decided not to buy.
September 2.—Bro. [C. F.] Post visited from Bethlehem.
September 4.—Bro. Schebosch and Bro. Post hauled stones for the bake-oven.
September 8.—Bro. Schebosch ploughed for winter wheat.
September 9.—Bro. Post kept "Morgen Segen." The sisters were busy making "agriatkens" [a preparation of Indian corn]. Zacharias went out to hunt.
September 10.—Bro. Schebosch went to Christian's Spring for provisions.
September 11.—Bro. Spangenberg, Boehler and [B. A.] Grube (13) came from Bethlehem to keep the Lord's Supper, to examine our settlement, decide upon a plan for the "Gemeinhaus," and to assist in fitting out Bro. Post, (who has been assisting since the indisposition of Bro. Senseman) and Anton for their visit to the Susquehanna.
September 12.—Bro. Post held "Morgen Segen." Bro. Peter Boehler and wife arrived and subsequently the Lord's Supper was celebrated.
September 13.—Bro. Grube kept "Morgen Segen."
September 16.—Bro. Post kept "Abend Segen" in the Indian language.
September 17.—Bro. Post returned to Bethlehem.
September 18.—Jonas shot a large buck—David made chestnut shingles.

September 20.—David shot two deer.
September 21 (Sunday).—Bro. Post preached.
September 22.—The bake-oven was roofed; Bro. Post split pine shingles, and Peter finished the chimney to his house. Christian shot a deer; Zacharias was at work on his house, and Zaccheus worked in the swamp making "Liver Holly." Bro. Post kept the evening meeting and Anton interpreted.
September 24.—Early this morning Bro. Schebosch went in search of the horses that have strayed off. Christian and Zacharias went to hunt; the latter's wife went on a two days' journey with them to bring back the meat.
September 25.—Bro. Schebosch rode to a neighboring plantation to obtain supplies. Later in the day he mowed the buckwheat.
September 27.—Bro. Schebosch finished mowing the buckwheat and stacked it, and also cut the Indian corn.
September 28.—Bro. Post was indisposed. We learned that Peter and Zacharias, while on the hunt, had visited Gideon (Teedyuscung), and had been drunk.
September 29.—Bro. Post held "Morgen Segen." Zacharias' wife returned with venison. Anton went to Meniolagomeka to get wooden bowls. We worked at the house.
September 30.—Bro. Post held "Morgen Segen," and afterwards made shingles. Lucia returned and told us that the hunters had gone toward Shamokin or the Swatara, and would be absent three weeks.
October 1.—Bro. Schebosch went to, and the Brethren (Matthew) Schropp and Senseman came up from Bethlehem.
October 2.—Bro. Schropp and Bro. Post returned to Bethlehem.
October 4.—Everybody busy, building and making "agritje." Sarah and Emma washed to go Pennsburg, but we disuaded them.
October 6.—Bro. John Bonn and three brethren from Christian's Spring arrived, who are to build a small house for Bro. Grube and to repair the chapel.
October 9.—Anton and Joel went hunting for beaver.
October 12.—The two hunters returned, with some beavers and raccoons.

October 13.—Bro. A. Reincke and Abraham Steiner returned to Christian's Spring.
October 14.—The Surveyor and three others came and asked for lodgings over night.
October 15.—Bro. Klein came with supplies from Christian's Spring.
October 17.—Bro. Grube's house was finished to-day. The following was promulgated:
"Bro. Grube must see to have the wood cut and Bro. Schebosch is to haul it. Bro. Senseman is to return to Bethlehem on account of ill-health. Bro. Schebosch is to attend to externals, e. g., building, planting, etc. Bro. Grube is 'Ordinarius, Pfleger, Gemein Vorsteher, etc.' The Lord's Supper is not to be postponed on account of the absence of certain persons. Anton is to be interpreter, to keep occasionally 'Morgen und Abend Segen,' and to be useful in the care of souls. Bethlehem will provide for the Love-Feasts, until the members are able to provide for themselves. Bro. Grube is to have a cow and one-half of his hay. Bro. Schebosch is to receive an allowance from the Bethlehem Economy and then keep house himself. The large wagon to remain here. Bro. Schebosch must give us a discharge and an indenture for his son. Church intelligence must be communicated to the congregation. Bro. Senseman will leave his mattress and blanket here."
October 18.—The Christian's Spring brethren returned home. In the evening came Bro. Grube and wife, with the Gnadenthal wagon; they are to take charge of the settlement.
October 19.—At noon Bro. Grube preached for the first time, and in the evening celebrated the Lord's Supper.
October 20.—Bro. Senseman went to Bethlehem.
October 23.—Christian and Zaccheus returned from their hunt; the first had shot twelve and the latter nine deer.
October 29.—David, who went on the hunt on the 25th, returned to-day, having shot but five deer. He sent the women after the meat.
November 4.—Samuel asked to be allowed to go to Pennsburg to fetch his old grandmother; we permitted him.

November 6.—Bro. Schebosch went to David's hunting-hut to get some venison, and Peter and family went on the hunt.

November 7.—Sarah and her daughter Elizabeth went out to search for hemp.

November 9 (Sunday).—At noon Bro. Grube preached.

November 11.—Lucia and Emma were appointed "Saal Dienerinen" [sextons].

November 14.—Samuel returned from Pennsburg without his grandmother, who was too ill to travel.

November 16 (Sunday).—Conference to-day resolved upon the following:
I. Every brother who is successful in the hunt must donate 2℔s. of deer tallow for the manufacture of candles for the chapel.
II. On Sundays no one shall follow the chase.
III. Every one must dress tidily and decently.
IV. The sisters shall make two baskets for Love-feast purposes.
V. Wood is to be cut for the use of the chapel.

November 17.—Peter shot 3 deer.

November 19.—Christian returned from the hunt, and had killed 7 deer.

November 21.—Early this morning Anton shot a fine buck; and in the afternoon finished his new chimney-place.

November 24.—Bro. Schebosch went with a load of cooper's wood to Bethlehem.

November 25.—Jonathan and Zacharias shot two deer near to the settlement. Bro. Grube arranged some hymns in the Delaware to-day.

November 29.—Bro. David Zeisberger visited us to-day and on

November 30 (Sunday).—Preached at noon.

December 1.—Bro. Zeisberger kept "Morgen Segen," and then set out for Bethlehem.

December 3.—Bro. Grube kept "Morgen Segen" in Delaware.

December 7 (Sunday).—Before the sermon the Litany was prayed in the Delaware.

December 18.—On Monday, 15th inst., Bro. Grube went to Bethlehem and returned to-day. During his absence Bro. Schebosch held the meetings in English and Mohican.

December 20.—Candles for the chapel to the number of 150 were made out of the deer fat contributed. The deer-skins were sold in Bethlehem by our Indians.

December 21.—Bro. Grube with Anton began a translation of the "Harmony of the Gospels" into the Delaware.

December 24 (Christmas Eve).—At dusk the children had a Love-feast and Vigils; Indian hymns were sung, and each child received a lighted taper, with which they left the chapel for their homes. At 10 P. M. the Vigils of Christmas for the adults was held.

December 25 (Christmas).—At 10 A. M., preaching.

December 26.—Most of the Indians went to hunt.

December 29.—David returned from the Minisinks, whither he had taken his skins to sell.

1761.

January 1.—Jonathan went to-day as our first express to Bethlehem.

January 5.—Our express returned with letters. Bro. Schebosch set out for Nazareth and Bethlehem.

January 8.—He returned in the sleigh, and later the Lord's Supper was celebrated.

January 11.—Bro. Schebosch kept "Children's Meeting" in Mohican.

January 13.—A Susquehanna Indian, John Martin by name, visited us.

January 16.—Jonathan went with the sleigh to Bethlehem for Indian corn.

January 18.—Bro. Grube and Anton worked at the Delaware translation of the "Acts of the Last Day of the Son of Man."

January 26.—Some of the young people went on the hunt. Several Indians arrived from Nain, to visit friends—usual occurrence.

January 28.—Peter went on the hunt.

February 1 (Sunday).—Peter, Gottlieb and Toosch returned. They had lodged in Augustus' old hunting-hut, and while absent, it with their skins and blankets were burned, as the hut had been fired. Christian and party returned with eight deer.

February 3.—Bro. Schebosch and wife went to Nazareth with the sleigh.

February 8.—Some of our young men went to Nain to cut cord-wood for Bethlehem. Bro. Schebosch went to Friedensthal Mill.

February 11.—Bro. Grube kept "Morgen Segen" in Delaware.

February 13.—The hunters who went out for bears met with no success.

February 17.—Zacharias went out to boil sugar.

February 19.—Justina and Sarah with their children went out into tne Great Swamp (14) to make baskets.

February 23.—Bro. Grube went to Bethlehem on business.

February 27.—Deep snow.

March 2.—Anton went on a beaver hunt. Bro. Schebosch returned from Bethlehem and brought the Results of the Last Conference on Indian Affairs.

March 6.—Anton returned and so did Sarah from the Great Swamp.

March 7.—Bro. Grube's wife was confined, but her infant boy died.

March 8.—Dr. Otto (15) came to visit Bro. Grube's wife, who lies very low. Anton went on the beaver-hunt.

March 12.—Bro. Grube began to work in his garden. Sam Evans desires to settle here.

March 19 (Maundy-Thursday).—Began to read the "Acts of the Days of the Son of Man" in Delaware, and celebrated the Lord's Supper.

NOTES AND QUERIES.

Historical, Biographical, and Genealogical.

XXVIII.

WIDENER-GITTER.

Peter Widener married Susanna Gitter, and they lived in Berks county. In 1759 Peter Widener died, and his widow married James Whitehead, of Philadelphia. I am desirous of securing some information relating to the first named families. B. W. S.
Cincinnati, O.

RANKIN.

I. William Rankin, of Antrim township, Franklin county, d. in November, 1792, leaving a wife Mary, and children:
i. Adam; land on Kiskiminetas.
ii. Archibald.
iii. James; land in Penn's Valley, Mifflin county.
iv. William; land in Penn's Valley.
v. John; land on Spring Creek, Penn's Valley.
vi. Jeremiah; land on Spring Creek.
vii. Betsey.
viii. David.
The executors were sons Archibald, James and William.

II. James Rankin, of Montgomery township, Franklin county, d. in October, 1795, leaving a wife Jean, and children:
i. William.
ii. Jeremiah.
iii. James.
iv. David.
v. Ruth; m. John Tool.
vi. [A dau.] m. Samuel Smith, and left a daughter Mary.
The executors were son Jeremiah and David Houston.

III. William Rankin, of Montgomery township, Franklin county, d. in February, 1802, leaving a wife Ann, and children:
i. James.
ii. Elizabeth; m. —— Ritchey.
iii. Jean.
iv. Ann.
v. Ruth.
vi. Mary-Gillespie.
The executors were James McFarland, Sen., wife Ann and son James.

IV. Jeremiah Rankin, of Montgomery township, Franklin county, d. in July, 1803, leaving a wife Mary, and children:
i. James-Clark.
ii. Nancy.
iii. Maria.
iv. Esther.
The executors were brother James, and brothers-in-law James Clark and David Humphreys.

WHITE DEER TOWNSHIP

When It Was Formed, Where It Is Located, and Why So Named.

At February sessions, 1776, four years after the organization of Northumberland county, the court created a new township and named it White Deer. It was made out of territory taken from Buffalo township, which embraced what is now known as the rich and beautiful Buffalo Valley, in the present county of Union, on the west side of the West Branch of the Susquehanna. Briefly, the boundary line of White Deer township was defined: "Beginning at the upper side of Buffalo creek, the northeast branch to its head; thence up the same to the mouth of Spruce Run; up Spruce Run to its forks; thence up the northeast branch ti its head; thence by a straight line to the four-mile tree on Reuben Haines farm, on the line of Potter township (now in Centre county)— the well known four-mile tree in the Penn's Valley Narrows."

Why was such an odd name given to the new township? Tradition says that it was on account of white deer being found by the early settlers in the beautiful valley which its territory embraced. This valley, now partly in Lycoming county, is one of the most charming spots found in the State. It is partly surrounded by mountains and the scenery is incomparably beautiful, while the soil is rich and the husbandman is well rewarded for his labors. On account of its attractiveness, richness and beauty, settlers early flocked to White Deer, and when the land came into market in 1769 there was a rush to secure locations. The existence of white deer in this favored locality is strange and the cause is unexplained to this day. And within recent years old hunters report having seen one or two stragglers.

The original territory of the township was so large that when population increased there was a clamor for a division. Consequently, at August sessions, 1785, a "petition of divers inhabitants was presented to the court setting forth that they labored under great inconvenience, costs and damages, by reason of the extensiveness of the township," and they prayed for a division. The proposed new boundary line was thus set forth in the petition: "Beginning on the banks of the West Branch, a small distance above the Widow Smith's mill; from thence partly westerly along the south side of White Deer Mountain to where Spruce Run crosses through said mountain; thence down Spruce Run till Buffalo Creek, to where it empties into the West Branch. This boundary to remain White Deer township as formerly, and the upper part, above Widow Smith's mills to be formed into a new township."

The Widow Smith lived at the mouth of White Deer creek and owned a small mill, which was a great convenience to the settlers. She also had erected and carried on a mill for repairing and boring gun barrels during the Revolution. This was the only place in the upper Susquehanna valley where such work was done. She was a very patriotic and plucky woman. Once her mills were destroyed by the Indians, but on her return after the Big Runaway, she had them rebuilt.

After hearing the petition, the court made a decree, "that the said division shall be and remain, and the new township shall be called Washington forever." This decree was entered August 23, 1785, and the name of the township was in honor of General Washington, who, at the head of the American armies, had just achieved liberty and independence. It still exists, and now belongs to Lycoming county, but has been greatly reduced from its original size. It has furnished territory to form the townships, in Lycoming, of Brady, Clinton, Armstrong, Limestone, Susquehanna, Bartress and Nippenose, besides several in other counties.

White Deer still remains as a township in Union county. It has suffered some by the curtailment of its territory for the formation of new townships, but not to the extent of Washington. In Indian times many thrilling incidents occurred within its borders, but it rapidly became populous on account of the fertility of its soil, and contains many fine and highly cultivated farms. By the census of 1890 it had 1,907 inhabitants, and Washington had 937.

JOHN OF LANCASTER.

Annals of Wekquitank.

1760–1763.

III.

March 20.—(Good Friday.) The reading of the "Acts" continued at 9 and 12 and 3 P. M.

March 21.—Love Feast held. Joel quite sick.

March 22.—(Easter.) Before sunrise we met in the chapel, where the history of the Resurrection was read, and then went up on the graveyard, where but one body rests. Bro. Schebosch held a conference with the Brethren about plowing.

March 23.—Heard that Elizabeth, wife of Zacharias, while out boiling sugar, was brought to bed of a daughter.

March 24.—Some of the brethren went on the hunt. Peter and family went to "The Rose" for Indian corn.

March 27.—Zacharias and Elizabeth came home; she carried the child born five days ago. Bro. Schebosch began to set the fences.

March 29.—(Sunday.) Elizabeth's infant daughter was baptized, and named Anna.

April 6.—Gottlieb and Jonathan returned from the beaver-hunt, but were not very fortunate.

April 7.—Anton returned with five beaver. Abel, who during the war had left Gnadenhuetten, requested to be allowed to reside here.

April 8.—Bro. Schebosch began to plow.

April 9.—Teedyuscung's oldest son (16) made us a visit.

April 17.—Abel and family went on a hunt.

April 19.—(Sunday.) Bro. Peter Boehler and Senseman visited us.

April 22.—Bro. Boehler administered the Lord's Supper.

April 23.—Bro. Grube accompanied Bro. Senseman to Bethlehem. It being proposed to widow Emma to marry, she said: "I had one husband, to him I will cling, 'till I see him face to face."

April 28.—Bro. Ruch and Bro. Priesing went with the wagon to Christian's Spring for tar. Some young people from Nain came to hunt bear. Owing to the heavy rain the creek overflowed its banks.

May 1.—Bro. Schebosch with Zaccheus and Beata, went to Nain for seed Indian corn. Justina and Sarah, who have been absent two months, returned, the former bringing her brother named Turck from Cranberry [N. J.]

May 4.—Nathaniel came from Nain, searching for his strayed horse.

May 6.—Samuel and Turck went to the Great Swamp to make bowls.

May 9.—Repaired the fences lately damaged by fire. Launched a new canoe on the Wekquitank. Emma set out for Cranberry to visit.

May 11.—Bro. Grube went to Bethlehem via Meneolagomeka, to fetch his wife who is there to recruit her health.

May 14.—Bro. Grue and wife rode from Bethlehem 'till over the Blue Mountains, where he was met by Bro. Ruch, with a cow, which he drove home for his own use.

May 15.—A horse and cow stable were built for Bro. Grube. The sisters planted corn.

May 18.—Some of our Indians went to Bethlehem to buy supplies at the store. Anton and Gottlieb went per canoe down the Wekquirtank vio the Lehigh to Bethlehem. Bro. Grube planted half an acre of Indian corn.

May 21.—Heavy frost—the corn and pumpkins froze. The sisters planted corn a second time. Bro. Schebosch kept "Abend Segen."

May 23.—The Lords Supper was celebrated.

May 24.—A large bear came near the town—was pursued and killed.

May 28.—Bro. Grube planted corn a second time.

May 30.—Six brethren went on the hunt. I advised them to meet in the morning and evening, and sing verses. Bro. Schebosch finished plowing to-day.

June 1.—After "Morgen Segen," some of our Indians went to the Lehigh to fish; Bro. Schebosch went with them.

June 2.—The hunters returned with five deer. Last night a severe frost somewhat damaged the corn.

June 3.—The fishing party returned with several horses loaded with 328 shad.

June 8.—Several brethren went for bark to cover their new huts; and Zacharias went to Christian's Spring to sell brooms.

June 10.—The hunters started on a ten-days' hunt.

June 18.—Bro. Spangenberg and wife, with Bro. Senseman, came on a visit.

June 19.—Bro. Spangenberg kept the early servce, and next the Lord's Supper "Quarter Hour." In the afternoon he visited the farm, after which a conference was held. In the evening a Love feast was held for all, followed by the Lord's Supper. Two Indians from Wyoming, one of whom was Amos, made us a visit.

June 20.—Bro. Spangenberg and party returned to Bethlehem.

June 22.—All of the Indians here hoed corn to-day.

June 23.—Bro. Grube and the Indians began to cut grass and make hay. We learned from Amos that old Paxinosa had died this spring in the Ohio country. (19.)

June 29.—Bro. Grube's hay-stack was completed, after which he planted cabbage. Two traders passed through the town.

June 30.—Everybody busy hoeing corn.

July 1.—Peter returned home, and complained of ill-usage by a white man at Baumann's. (20.)

July 9.—Some of our Indians went to buy cooper's tools. Levi got drunk.

July 11—Supplies and food scarce.

July 17.—Bro. Boehler and wife came up from Bethlehem and inspected the two farms.

July 18.—This evening the Lord's Supper was celebrated.

July 19.—The Boehlers returned home.

July 21.—Isaac Nutimaes and family came from the Susquehanna. His wife, Anna Mary, was baptized by us. He stated that many Indians will attend the Treaty that is to be held at Easton. Peter is invited by his brother Teedyuscung to atend the Treaty, but is undecided what to do. Bro. Grube told him to follow the leadings of the Lord. Samuel told me that he designed going to Bethlehem to-morrow to see Teedyuscung, whose old counselor he had been, and with whom he still is in connection.

July 27.—Isaac Nutimaes and family set out for Tioga.

July 29.—Bro. Grube went to Bethlehem.

July 30.—While on his return, Bro. Grube met old Samuel, in his "Indian costume of state," on his way to Easton to the Treaty. Bro. Grube accompanied him and also Zacharias, thither. The latter goes after his negro wench who has come down from the Susquehanna. Peter and his family went after huckleberries.

August 4.—Bro. Soelle and Bro. Samuel Isles made us a visit.

August 5.—Bro. Isles kept "Morgen Segen." Zacharias returned from Easton with the negress, who had been raised by his wife Elizabeth. We permitted her to keep her here conditionally.

August 6.—Bro. Soelle and Bro. Isles returned home.

August 8.—This evening Peter returned, and then with Zacharias went to Easton to the Treaty.

August 14.—The Lord's Supper was celebrated.

August 17.—The hunters returned with two deer.

August 20.—Bro. David Zeisberger and Bro. John Bonn from Christian's Spring, came on a visit; and Bro. Schebosch went to Friedensthal Mill.

August 21.—After a long drought, fine rain fell, which will benefit the Indian corn.

August 23.—Two of our neighbors visited here to-day.

August 24.—Gottlieb returned with 3 deer.

August 26.—Three white neighbors came to inquire about the murder committed by Indians in the Minisink; and towards dusk two others came to ask advice what they should do, for the people back of the Blue Mountains are all fleeing. Bro. Senseman came up from Bethlehem to notify us of indications of an Indian War.

September 4.—Sam Evans and wife came on a visit.

September 7.—Very hard frost.

September 14.—Bro. Schebosch took a wagon load of staves to Bethlehem, and Verona, Regina and Sarah took baskets to Nazareth.

September 15.—Peter and his son set out for a month's hunt.

September 18.—The sisters began to make "acritje."

September 23.—Our new bell was hung at the Gemein-haus and rung for the first time.

September 30.—Bro. Grube, who went to Bethlehem on the 24th, returned with Bro. [A. A.] Lawatsch, who examined the farms.

October 4.—(Sunday.) At the Meeting this evening Samuel again attended, and expressed himself "as not being at rest in his heart."

October 5.—Charity and Beata went over the Blue Mountains for chestnuts. Old Samuel left for good, without bidding us good-bye, going to Wyoming. He has long been halting between two opinions. We regret his course.

October 10.—(Sunday.) The Lord's Supper was celebrated. A man and woman came from Meniolagomeka to Bro. Schebosch to be bled.

October 14.—Bro. Grube finished gathering his corn. Widow Emma returned from her sojourn at the sea-side among her friends.

October 19.—All the men went out on the hunt, but met with no success; the women dried Indian corn.

October 20.—Bro. Grube almost lost his life while felling a tree.

October 22.—Peter and his son returned from their hunt of five weeks, and report they have shot 50 deer.

October 28.—Bro. Senseman came up from Bethlehem to relieve Bro. Grube for a few days.

October 30.—Some of our sisters went into the woods to gather wild hemp; and Bro. Senseman and Schebosch set up a tar-kiln. Three deer were shot close by the town.

November 2.—While some of the brethren went out on the hunt, Bro. Schebosch burned tar.

November 3.—Levi shot a large bear. Bro. Schebosch gathered in the turnips and cabbage.

November 4.—Bro. Grube returned from Bethlehem.

November 17.—Several sisters went to their husbands' hunting-huts to bring in the venison.

November 22.—Jonathan and his brother Toosch came in from the woods to get horses to bring in the venison from their hunting-huts.

November 30.—(Sunday.) In the Conference this evening, the members were reminded to contribute deer's fat, for the making of candles for the chapel.

December 1.—The first snow of the winter fell. Two horses laden with venison from the hunting-huts were brought in to-night.

December 3.—The children very diligent in school.

December 5.—The Lord's Supper celebrated.

December 9.—Bro. Sturgeous came up from Bethlehem, to set up a store for us.

December 14.—Zacharias and Jonathan's family went to Bethlehem to sell skins.

December 17.—A number of our Indians go with a sleigh-load of skins and tallow to Bethlehem.

December 20.—(Sunday.) Bro. Grube preached in Delaware.

December 24.—(Christmas-Eve.) At dusk a Lovefeast for the children was held, and at 9 P. M. Vigils for the adults.

December 26.—Snow very deep.

December 28.—To-day the brethren opened a road through the snow to Boemper's old place, so as to be able to put their horses in the barn there, as the snow in the woods is so deep.

1762.

January 2.—Sam Evans is visiting here. The Lord's Supper was celebrated.

January 4.—Peter and Lucia went to Baumann's to buy blankets, as they failed to get any in Bethlehem.

January 19.—Some of the brethren went on the hunt, and Bro. Schebosch to the Minisinks to buy corn, but was unsuccessful. Supplies are very scarce with us.

February 1.—Bro. Grube hauled one cord of wood.

February 7.—Bro. Post, who has returned from the Alleghany, visited us.
February 9.—Justina and family went out to sell baskets.
February 10.—Bro. Schebosch began to make shingles for Bethlehem.
February 14.—Bro. Grube busy with his translation of the "Harmony of the Gospels."
February 24.—Bro. Grube hauled firewood. Anton and family went to Nain, to be present at the wedding of their son Gottlieb.
March 1.—Bro. Grube went to Bethlehem, and Bro. Schebosch set out with baskets and brooms to exchange for supplies.
March 3.—The weather excessively cold.
March 4.—Little Abraham was buried to-day.
March 6.—Beata, the mother of Abraham, died. She was baptized at Bethlehem by Bro. Pyrlaeus in 1746, and lived at Gnadenhuetten. As a widow she was married to Zaccheus, with whom she had eleven children—all but one having died. A few years previous to the Indian War she moved up to Nescopec, and after the peace came into the neighborhood of Bethlehem, when, after a period of probation, she was re-admitted to the Communion.
March 8.—Beata's remains interred.
March 9.—Bro. Schebosch went with the sleigh to Friedensthal.
March 11.—Peter and Lucia went to seek for fodder for their cattle.
March 16.—Several of our white neighbors came after Bro. Schesbosch to bleed them.
March 17.—To-day Bro. Grube sent the first sheets of the "Acts of the Last Days of the Son of Man," in Delaware, to Bro. Brandmuller in Friedensthal to print.
March 22.—Bro. Schebosch made shingles, and David and Charity went ten miles to boil sugar. Sam Evans reports that half way between here and Wyoming the snow lies leg-deep.
March 23.—Zacharias and Elizabeth went to boil sugar.
March 26.—Bro. Grube went to Nazareth for supplies.

March 30.—Our Indians were busy making shingles.
April 4.—Began the Passion Week services.
April 5.—Read the "Acts" in Delaware.
April 8.—(Maundy-Thursday.) The Lord's Supper celebrated.
April 9.—(Good Friday.) Services held.
April 10.—(Great Sabbath.) Lovefeast for the congregation.
April 11.—(Easter). We met in the chapel early, and the congregation was greeted with the words "Jesus Christus k'patamosinna kitschiwi aminwa nanneleuch!" We then proceeded to the graveyard where the Litany was read.
April 13.—Bro. Brandmuller sent Bro. Grube proof to read.
April 14.—Bro. Grube went to Bethlehem.
April 24.—Jonathan and Sarah, who had been at service for some weeks among the whites, returned to-day.
April 26.—Anton and Zaccheus finished 2,000 singles.
May 5.—Bro. Grube went to Nazareth for meal and bread.
May 10.—Some of the brethren went to buy seed-corn, and others to the Lehigh to fish for shad.
May 16.—Bro. Schebosch visited our sick neighbor, four miles distant from here.
May 18.—All hands busy planting corn. Toosch shot a wolf.
May 20.—(Ascension Day.) At the services to-day were two white men.
May 24.—Began to keep school again, and afterwards plowed Indian corn. Peter built a stable for his horse and cow.
May 31.—Some of the brethren went out on the wolf-hunt.
June 4.—Hunters returned with two deer.
June 9.—Bro. Grube returned from Bethlehem with his wife; on the road up, the horse shied and threw her.
June 10.—Bro. Grube began to hoe his corn.
June 11.—A load of shingles was taken to Bethlehem by Bro. Schebosch.
June 24.—Bro. Grube began to mow grass to make hay.
June 26.—Peter went to the Treaty at

Easton, despite Bro. Grube's dissuasion. So it is with the Indians; if they have formed a resolution they never abandon it!

June 30.—Peter returned from Easton.

July 3.—Old Samuel came up from the Treaty at Easton on a visit.

July 6.—He left to-day. The Government has presented him with a good horse.

July 12.—Everybody busy hoeing corn and haying.

July 19.—Bro. Schebosch began to harvest wheat.

August 1.—Bro. Grube translated at the "Harmony."

August 2.—The young folks went out to hunt.

August 6.—Bro. Boehler and wife visited here.

August 9.—The sisters went to the Blue Mountains for huckleberries.

August 17.—Some of the Indians went on the hunt. Jonathan notified us that he was going to Lancaster to get his share of the money given to the Indians at the Easton Treaty.

August 19.—Bro. Schmick and wife visited us. He kept all the services in Mohican.

August 24.—Some sisters went with two horses to gather wood for brooms and baskets.

August 31.—A Delaware from Wyoming came to visit his friends.

September 2.—Jonathan returned from Lancaster ill.

September 5.—The settlers above the Blue Mountains must go 20 to 30 miles to mill!

NOTES AND QUERIES,

Historical, Biographical, and Genealogical.

XXIX.

TORRENCE.

Albert Torrence, of Greene township, Franklin county, died in February, 1804, leaving his estate to the following:

Sister Jane, m. Thomas McKean.

Sister Isabella, m. John Ferguson, and had Elizabeth and Hugh.

Sister Mary, m. Hugh Wiley.

Bro. James.

Bro. William.

The executors were John Ferguson, Sr., Thomas McKean and Hugh Ferguson.

WILEY.

Hugh Wiley, of Letterkenny township, Franklin county, d. in November, 1805, leaving children as follows:

i. John.
ii. Hugh, m. Mary Torrence.
iii. Sally.
iv. Betsey, m. Joseph Culbertson, and had son Hugh.
v. Temperance, m. William Means.
vi. Margaret, m. Henry Davis.

The executors were son John and son-in-law William Means.

Some York County Colonial Burial Places.

I recently made an exploration of a number of early York county burial places, my first point being the site of the old Monaghan Presbyterian church situated in the vicinity of the present town of Dillsburg. I was assured by the Hon. J. Esslinger, of Dillsburg, that the records of the church are still extant, and date back to 1737. During my brief stay, however, I could not learn their whereabouts, and gave my attention to the graveyard which forms part of the Dillsburg cemetery, and then only to such subjects as might be of greater historic value. The following were Scotch-Irish immigrants and founders of eminent families: Dill, Logan, O'Hale, Clark, Wilson and Mitchell.

Sacred to
the memory of
Archibald Campbell,
Lieut. in the 6th regiment
of Pennsylvania in the army of
the United States of
America,
who departed this life
the 4th day of Dec., 1784,
aged 29 years.

Clark, John, b. 1727; d. 1805.
Clark, Sarah, wife, b. 1728; d. 1803.
Clark, William, b. 1768; d. 1846.

Historical and Genealogical.

Clark, Sarah, wife, b. 1779; d. 1824.
Clark, Samuel, b. 1812; d. 1860.
"In memory of
George Matthew Dill, Esq.,
who deceased
October ye 13, 1750,
aged 52 years."
[This was the founder, an eminent citizen and father of Colonel Dill, after whom the town was named. The founder's will is on file at York, Pa.]
Dill, Dr. Armstrong, b. 1761; d. 1788.
Dill, Matthew, b. 1790; d. 1868.
Dill, Hannah (wife), b. 1805; d. 1878.
Dill, Dr. Armstrong, b. 1836; d. 1887.
Dill, William, b. 1740; d. 1872.
Dill, Elenore, b. 1758; d. 1826.
Logan, John, b. 1709; d. 1796.
Logan, Ann, b. 1700; d. 1799.
Logan, Henry, b. 1738; d. 1825.
Logan, Susannah (wfe), b. 1743; d. 1817.
Logan, James, b. 1753; d. 1783.
Mitchell, William, b. 1741; d. 1787.
Mitchell, Mary (wife), b. 1741; d. 1792.
Mitchell, Margaret, b. 1773; d. 1798.
Mitchell, James, b.. 1772; d. 1833.
Mitchell, Jane (wife), b. 1791; d. 1852.
McClure, James, b. 1745; d. 1846.
McClure, —— (wife), b. 1750; d. 1847.
McClure, Daniel, b. 1764; d. 1829.
McClure, Margaret, b. 1770; d. 1812.
McClure, Rachel, b. 1799; d. 1870.
McClure, Samuel, b. 1808; d. 1889.
McClure, Margaret (wife), b. 1817; d. 1890.
McCreary, ——, b. 1759; d. 1828.
McClure, Alice (wife), b. 1779; d. 1855.
O'Hale, Edwin, b. 1746; d. 1816.
O'Hale, Jane, b. 1747; d. 1817.
O'Hale, Samuel, b. 1761; d. 1783.
Wilson, John, b. 1729; d. 1803.
Wilson, Prudence, b. 1768; d. 1848.
Wilson, Martha, b. 1778; d. 1858.
Wilson, Thomas, b. 1765; d. 1827.
Wilson, Jean (wife), b. 1761; d. 1826.
Wilson, George, b. 1756; d. 1851.

Bowers—Smith—Graveyard.

Six or more miles east of Dillsburg, where the Redmont cemetery is located may be found the burial place of the old German settlers of that locality. The descendants of the above two families are exceedingly numerous, and scattered far and wide. The old graveyard was once in an open field, but has now grown into a finely kept cemetery. In my researches I confined myself to the old families.
Bower, R. B., d. 1776.
Bower, John, d. 1793.
Bower, Mary, d. 1802.
Bower, Joshua d. 1810.
Bower, Mary, b. 1748; d. 1840.
Bower, Peter, b. 1738; d. 1819.
Bower, John, b. 1728; d. 1803.
Bower, Andrew, b. 1742; d. 1824.
Bower, Abraham, b. 1765; d. 1835.
Bower, Barbara, d. 1795.
Bower, Elisabeth, d. 1784.
Bower, Moses, d. 1784.
Bower, Michael, son of Andrew, b. 1768; d. 1825.
Bower, Sarah, b. 1784; d. 1853.
Bower, Joseph, b. 1776; d. 1841.
Bower, Amy (wife), b. 1772; d. 1833.
Bower, Mary, d. 1806.
Bower, Abraham, b. 1743; d. 1825.
Bower, Naomi (wife), b. 1741; d. 1818.
Bower, Michael, b. 1730; d. 1807.
Bower, Mary (wife), b. 1729; d. 1806.
Bower, Benjamin, d. 1856.
Bower, Elisabeth (wife), b. 1769; d. 1823.
Bower, Elisabeth, b. 1757; d. 1819.
Bower, Solomon, b. 1790; d. 1853.
Bower, Alexander, b. 1790; d. 1855.
Bower, Elisabeth (wife), b. 1795; d. 1845.
Bower, William, b. 1800; d. 1881.
Bower, Isaac, b. 1776; d. 1853.
Bower, Elisabeth (wife), b. 1778; d. 1859.
Bower, Michael, b. 1788; d. 1856.
Smith, Peter, Sen., b. 1738; d. 1812.
Smith, Mary (wife), b. 1728; d. 1804.
Smith, Peter, Jr., b. 1772; d. 1843.
Smith, John, Sen., b. 1730; d. 1786.
Smith, Emanuel, b. 1764; d. 1821.
Smith, John Carpenter, b. 1789; d. 1862.
Smith, Cath (wife), b. 1799; d. 1870.
Smith, Joel, d. 1862.
Smith, Abraham, b. 1766; d. 1822.
Smith, Rebecca (wife), b. 1772; d. 1824.
Scholl, Peter, b. 1768; d. 1828.
Scholl, Sarah (wife), d. 1837.
Shimp, Leonard, b. 1759; d. 1817.
Shimp, Mary (wife), b. 1770; d. 1822.
Sox, Nicholas, d. 1795.
Sox, Sarah, wife, b. 1759; d. 1825.
Eckert, Barbara, b. 1758; d. 1839.
Asper, J., d. 1782.
Webb, Mary, d. 1795.
Hull, Anna, b. 1773; d. 1848.

Lane, Jane, b. 1740; d. 1827.
Fauss, Geo., b. 1780; d. 1848.
Fauss, Hannah (wife), b. 1782; d. 1854.
Krall, Joseph, b. 1761; d. 1839.
Krall, Anna (wife), b. 1773; d. 1849.
Morrison, Jane, b. 1782; d. 1865.

1768
d 2
May
H. D. Kline.

This last inscription is the oldest I can find, and is on a blue slate.

A. STAPLETON.
Carlisle, Pa.

Annals of Wekquitank.

1760—1763.

IV.

September 8.—Our boys caught 100 trout, and shot several deer. Supplies very scarce, no flour, and the unripe corn suffers from the frost. We wonder our people are not discouraged to plant here!
September 17.—Severe frost.
September 24.—Most of the brethren went to hunt.
October 4.—Several brethren went to Christian's Spring to have their rifles repaired.
October 6.—Bro. John Okely visited, and with him an Englishman who desired to see our Indian settlement.
October 7.—Christian and Martha were married to-day.
October 11.—Many of the sisters went after chestnuts. Bro. Grube went in search of his horse which had strayed into the woods, but found only his bell. Later an Indian brought him home.
October 13.—Bro. Nathaniel Seidel and Bro. [Frederick] von Marschall visited us, and on
October 15—returned to Bethlehem.
November 1.—Most of the brethren went on the hunt.
November 8.—Bro. D. Zeisberger, Bro. Denke and Bro. Ekerspear visited here from Christian's Spring.
November 17.—Peter and his son returned from the hunt; in six weeks shot 50 deer.
November 24.—Commemoration of the Massacre on the Mahoning!
November 25.—Bro. [John] Arbo and Bro. Bonn visited us from Bethlehem.
November 26.—Dorothea (a child) was buried to-day. She was born in 1752; and baptized by Bro. J. M. Mack at Gnadenhuetten.
November 28.—First Sunday in Advent.
December 2.—Some of our Indians went on the hunt. Levi returned and had shot 30 deer. Joel and Regina returned from Dansbury [Stroudsburg], where he had sold baskets and brooms. Corn there sells at 4 shillings per bushel.
During the year 1762 three deaths have occurred—Beata and Abraham, wife and child of Zaccheus, and Dorothea, a young girl; and Christian and Martha have been married.

1763.

January 10.—Bro. Grube and eighteen brethren hauled timber, to build a kitchen.
January 29.—Finished hauling wood and stones.
February 1.—Our young folks made snow-shoes, as the snow is so deep no one can go beyond half a mile of the town.
February 6.—All our brethren set out for Bethlehem to make a path through the snow, but could only proceed three miles, and then returned.
February 13.—Bro. Grube and Anton translated 56 chapters of the "Harmony."
February 25.—Bro. Grube finished for himself a new sleigh.
March 8.—Furious storm of rain and high water. Our entire farm under water and don't know how to help ourselves. The water came up to our houses.
April 1.—(Good Friday.) Bro. Brandmuller forwarded to-day the first proof of my "Delaware hymn-book," which rejoiced Anton.
April 28.—Our Indians hard at work fighting a bush-fire, which almost consumed our fences. As it was we lost 1,000 rails.
May 2.—Some of our brethren went down the creek into the Lehigh, with five new canoes for sale. Two were sold—one for 50 shillings, and one for 40 shillings.

Bro. Schebosch began to clear land, on the 40 acre piece, one and a half miles from here.

May 14.—Bro. Nathaniel Seidel came to look over two tracts of land near here.

May 16.—Bro. David Zeisberger and Anton set out for M'chwihilusing, and on June 1—they returned, and the next day Bro. Zeisberger goes on to Christian's Spring.

June 18.—Learned that the Indians on the west side of the Susquehanna were beginning to murder.

June 24.—Our brethren have decided not to go on the hunt, until the disturbances are past.

June 26.—Two white men from the Susquehanna came to ascertain something of the Indian troubles. They propose to leave their farms, but the settlers hereabouts say they will stay as long as we stay.

July 2.—Very unquiet about here during the night; hence have set a watch.

July 24.—The address of the Indians of Nain and Wekquitank, to the Governor, was read to our brethren, and signed by all the adults. They promised to heed our advice as to the manner of deporting themselves towards the white settlers.

July 26.—Six settlers, about three miles from here, came to see whether we intended abandoning the settlement.

July 27.—Zacharias and Thomas, with Paules, Nutimaes' son, and two boys came from Long Island, 60 miles beyond Shamokin, stating that the Indians there were still quiet. One of the party was a French Indian, who, the first day he attended our meeting, came with a "lit pipe" in his mouth. We were told that he had come to maraud.

August 2.—A company of 20 soldiers reached here to-day. Pursuant to orders the Captain agreed with Bro. Grube on a countersign for our Indians. Four French Indians from the Allegheny came to the evening meeting, and afterwards lodged with Peter. They came straight through the woods, and forded the Lehigh 8 miles above Gnadenhuetten so as not to be seen by the whites. They are a wild-looking set. Most of our men kept watch to-night.

August 10.—A company of soldiers passed through to Fort Allen. Peter confessed that there were twelve French Indians on the war-path, and out for scalps, and of the four who were here, but are now hiding in the woods, one is captain of the band, who did not carry a rifle but a spear.

August 14.—The four French Indians took their departure.

August 15. A company of soldiers passed through, most of them dressed similar to Indians, but without breeches.

August 25.—Our hunters shot some deer.

August 28.—Sunday.) A company of soldiers passed through.

August 31.—Two Indians from M'chwihilusing, en route for Bethlehem, with skins to sell, arrived here, and Bro. Grube advised them not to go through the Irish Settlement, as we had no escort for them.

[During the month of September the brave Grube with his flock continued to reside on the Wekquitank, and so long as they did, many of the white settlers in their immediate neighborhood felt secure. The former were, however, much harrassed by the threatenings of a company of Provincials recruited in the Irish Settlement, until 'Squire Timothy Horsfield notified them that the Indian mission was under the special protection of the Governor, and warned them not to destroy their property or molest them in any manner.

[On the 9th of October, Bro. Grube wrote to the Church authorities at Bethlehem, that the whites accused the converts of participating in the late murders in the neighborhood, and that they had been warned to leave or else they would be murdered. Thereupon it was decided to transport the mission flock to Nazareth, and three brethren were sent to assist in the work. Early on the morning of the 11th they set out for Nazareth, two wagons from Christian's Spring carrying the women and children. It was just time to go, for hardly had the line begun to move, when firing was heard on the neighboring hill, followed by the usual shout of Indian triumph.

[The converts, thinking the savages had attacked a company of Provincials, wished to go to their assistance, but this Bro. Grube would not allow, and ordered them to form around the wagons and assume a defensive position. When the firing ceased the march was again resumed. On the 12th they reached Nazareth, where they were welcomed. It was ascertained subsequently that the firing was done by a party of Provincials, who wished to entice the converts out to a fight.

[From October 12 to November 8 they remained at Nazareth. On the 6th of the last mentioned month an express arrived from the Governor, ordering their removal to Philadelphia for better protection. When informed of this they at once began to prepare to obey the order; and on the 8th left Nazareth in wagons, with the best wishes and prayers of the congregation. At noon of the same day they arrived at Bethlehem and repaired to the chapel, where Bishop Peter Boehler delivered to them a farewell address upon the text for the day: "Make thy way straight before my face" (Psalm v, 8). After the service they were furnished with clothing and provisions, and on the banks of the Lehigh united with the Nain congregation and commenced their journey to Philadelphia. From a catalogue of the members o the Wekquitank congregation prepared by Bro. J. J. Schmick, November 10, we find that it consisted of forty-five souls, viz:

Anton's family. . . . . 3 persons
Peter's family. . . . . 4 persons
John's family. . . . . 6 persons
Joel's family. . . . . 4 persons
Christian's family. . . . . 2 persons
Jonathan's family. . . . . 4 persons
David's family. . . . . 4 persons
Sarah's family. . . . . 4 persons
Widow Justina's family. . . . . 4 persons
Widows Sarah, Emma and 1 child. . . . . 3 persons
Abel. . . . . 1 person
Sam Evans' family. . . . . 3 persons
Schebosch's family. . . . . 3 persons

45 persons

[During their sojourn of sixteen months in Philadelphia, they were at times subjected to insults, and threatened with mob violence. Early in the year 1764 the small-pox and dysentery broke out among them, and many died. When the death of the first was announced, the Brethren's congregation determined that the corpse should be interred in their burying-ground, and had a grave dug for its reception; but during the night it was filled up by persons unknown. This fact, and the known strong prejudices existing against the converts, deterred the members of the congregation from acting further in the matter, and all who died were buried in the Potter's Field (Washington Square), receiving Christian burial at the hands of the faithful missionaries. In March of 1765 the converts returned to Bethlehem, and began preparations to remove to Wyalusing, on the Upper Susquehanna, in accordance with the agreement made with the Provincial Government and the Church. Here we leave them.

[On the 21st of November, 1765, intelligence reached Bethlehem that the improvements made at Wekquitank had been destroyed by fire. Subsequently the land was used as a grazing-ground. From Christian's Spring and Gnadenthal the cattle were driven there in the spring and left until winter. Intercourse was kept up with the settlers in the neighborhood as late as 1799 and ministers from Nazareth frequently visited them. The land was finally divided into farms and sold by the Church.]

Notes to "Annals of Wekquitank."

1. Nain was a Moravian Indian village, two miles from Bethlehem, commenced in 1757, and abandoned in 1763.

2. The Rose Tavern was built by the Moravians in 1752, on the northern line of the "Barony of Nazareth," and stood as late as 1858.

3. Anton, a Delaware convert, was baptized by Bishop Cammerhoff at Bethlehem, February 8, 1750. For twenty-three years he was a consistent member of the church, and acted as assistant to the missionaries in Pennsylvania and Ohio. He died at Gnadenhutten, Ohio, in the summer of 1773, aged about seventy-six years.

4. A Moravian settlement on the "Barony of Nazareth."

5. Sam Evans was a Delaware, and a

half-brother of Teedyuscung. In 1756, his daughter Theodora was an inmate of the Single Sisters' House at Bethlehem.

6. Fort Allen was built in January of 1756 by Benjamin Franklin, and stood on the right bank of the Lehigh, nearly opposite the mouth of Mahoning Creek, where Weissport was commenced in 1785.

7. A son of "Old Nutimaes," a well-known chief of the Fork Delawares, who subsequently moved to the Susquehanna.

8. John Jacob Schmick was a native of Prussia, united with the Moravians in 1748, and entered their Indian Mission service in 1751, and became a proficient of the Mohican dialect. He died in 1778, aged 64 years.

9. John Martin Mack, for many years a missionary among the Indians, was born in 1715, in Wurtemberg. He was one of the founders of Bethlehem. In 1761 he was appointed superintendent of the missions in the Danish West Indies; in 1770, consecrated a bishop, and died in Santa Cruz, Jany. 9, 1784.

10. He lived at M'chwilusing, on the site of what was subsequently Wyalusing. On June 26, 1763, he was baptized by David Ziesberger, receiving the name of "John Papoonhank" or "Minsi John." Died May 15, 1775, aged about seventy years.

11. For some years a missionary among the Indians of Pennsylvania and Ohio.

12. Fries was a graduate of the University of Copenhagen, and labored mainly in the Moravian schools in Germany and America.

13. Bernhard Adam Grube was born 1715 in Germany; educated at Jena; came to Pennsylvania in 1746, and was employed in the schools at Bethlehem. In 1752 he entered the Indian mission service and was stationed at Meniolagomeka, where he studied the Delaware dialect. The following year he was dispatched to North Carolina with the first Moravian colony, where he remained until 1755. Re-entering the Indian mission, he was stationed at Gnadenhuetten; in 1758 at Pachgatgoch, Conn., and in 1760 at Weckquitank. When the Indian converts were removed to Philadelphia he accompanied them. After serving as pastor of several congregations in Pennsylvania, in 1780 he visited the mission villages in Ohio, and the evening of his long life was spent at Bethlehem, where he died March 20, 1808. While in charge of the mission at Weckquitank, he compiled in Delaware a "Harmony of the Gospels" and a "Hymn Book" (references to which appear in the diary), which were used by the missionaries until superceded by the works of David Zeisberger. Grube's works were printed by John Brandmiller at Friedensthal, near Nazareth.

14. Also called the "Pine Swamp," and the "Shades of Death," on early maps of the Province.

15. John Matthew Otto, born 1714, in Meinungen. Studied medicine and surgery at Augsburg. Came to Bethlehem in June of 1750. For thirty years physician and surgeon of the Brethren's settlements. Died at Bethlehem in August of 1786.

16. Tachgokanhelle was baptized at Gnadenhuetten, by Bishop Cammerhoff, December 14, 1750, and was named Amos. He was then twenty-four years of age. His wife, Pingtis, who was the sister of Agnes Post, was baptized the same day, receiving the name of Justina. She was a Jersey Delaware.

17. A well-known chief of Susquehanna Shawanese, for many years the friend of the Brethren. His wife was baptized by Bishop Spangenberg.

18. Baumann's plantation was located about five miles from Gnadenthal, and between that settlement and the Lehigh. He was a Schwenkfelder.

JOHN W. JORDAN.
Philadelphia.

NOTES AND QUERIES,

Historical, Biographical, and Genealogical.

XXX.

JOHN LANDIS.

Inquiries are made whether any of the paintings or portraits executed by John Landis are in existence and where. Also if there is a portrait of the author-poet. Any information directed to Notes and Queries will be thankfully received.

BARNETT.

Information is desired of branch of the Hanover Barnett family. Susan and Maria Barnett became the wives of Mathias Winagle, and their descendants are residing in Dauphin county, but none know of their maternal ancestor, excepting they came out of the Hanovers. Can the two wives of Mathias Winagle be sisters of John Barnett, b. May 2, 1765, his wife a Miss Crain, and had the following children:

i. Joseph, b. April 14, 1789; d. 1792.
ii. Margaret-Roan, b. March 23, 1790.
iii. John-Craig, b. Feb. 17, 1792.
iv. Mary, b. July 16, 1793.
v. Joseph-Crain, b. May 7, 1795; settled in Middletown, O.
vi. Juliet, b. August 23, 1797; m. July 7, 1831, John McEwen Barnett; and had William A. Barnett, b. Nov. 28, 1832; residing in Dayton, Ohio.
vii. Sarah, b. Sept. 26, 1799.

Information that wil lead to the Windnagle-Barnett family and ancestry will be appreciated. Address Editor "Notes and Queries." E. W. S. P.

WELSH SETTLERS

In Earl and Caernarvon Townships, Lancaster County.

Nathan Evans was born in the year 1682, in Treve Eghlis, Montgomeryshire, Wales. He came to this country with the Welsh emigration before the year 1700, and settled with his countrymen in the Welsh tract at Radnor, where in the year 1709 he married Susanna, daughter of William and Ann (Miles) Davies. William Davies was a merchant in Philadelphia. He owned vessels, and likely lived at Radnor, where he had a plantation. The following agreement (the original of which is in the possession of the descendants of Nathan Evans) sets forth their occupations:

"Merandum:

"It is agreed by and Between Nathan Evans, of Edgment, in the County of Chester, in the Province of Pensilvania, Mill-right, of the one part, and William Davies, of the Township of Radnor, in the County and Province affors'd, Merch't, of the other part, as followeth (viz't):

"Imprimis. It is agreed and Covenanted by the s'd parties that the s'd William Davies (for the considerations hereafter mentioned) is to Bring and Transport from Great Britain to Pensilvania so many of the s'd Nathan's Kinsfolks and Relations as shall and will be free and willing to venture to come over on the s'd Nathan Evans's account; and also the s'd William Davies is to find and allow them sufficient mentainance During their voyage after they are Shipped on Board a Shipp and Set Sail, in order for their Transportation to Pensilvania as affors'd; and also the s'd William Davies is to assist and help all the s'd Nathan's Kinsfolks and Relations as are willing to venture as affors'd from the place of their abode until they are Shipped as affors'd (if occation be).

"In Consideration whereof the s'd Nathan Evans is to pay or Cause to be paid unto the s'd William Davies the full and just sum of Tenn pounds of Current Money of Pensilvania for every whole passinger that shall venture as afors'd, and five pounds Like money for every half passinger, which s'd sums are to be paid within the Space of fourteen days after the arrivall of the ship where s'd passingers shall be Transported, at Philadelphia or Chester, the one-half thereof in Current Silver or gold money of Pensilvania, and the other half in Contrey produce (viz't): Wheat, flour, or Biscets, at Current Market price when paid; and if any of the s'd passingers shall happen to Die after they are Shipped as affors'd, it is agreed that the s'd Nathan is to pay the same sum or sums, and in the same maner and times as if they had Lived to arive at Pensilvania as affors'd; And also It is agreed by the parties affors'd that the s'd Nathan Evans is to pay and Discharge the s'd William Davies from all such Charges as he shall be att Concerning ye s'd passingers from the place of their abode untill they are Shipped as affors'd in maner following, that is to say: For every shilling English Money that the s'd Wm. Davies shall pay in Great Britain the s'd Nathan is to pay two shillings Pensilvania money unto the s'd William

Davies, along w'th the passage money affors'd; To all which s'd Coven't and agreem't either of ye parties bindeth themselves their heirs execut's and adm'trs firmly by these presents. In Witness whereof they have thereunto set their hands and seals, Interchangably. Dated the 25th day of October, Anno Dom., 1714.

"NATHAN EVANS.

"Sealed and Delivered in the p'sence of us.

"HUGH HUGHES,
"MIRICK DAVIES."

The agreement would lead us to suppose that Nathan Evans had considerable means, if he was prepared in fourteen days after their arrival in America, to pay for the transportation of his kinsfolk, not limiting the number, and that he was very desirous that they should come to this country. It is not known that any dil come over on his account under the agreement. He had a brother, Roger Evans, in the Province and he mentions in his will two nephews in the Province of Maryland, likely sons of Roger.

The agreement is witnessed by Hugh Hughes, who married Mary Davies, another daughter of William Davies, and Mirick Davies, a son of William, who was coroner of Philadelphia in 1720 and 1728. The said William Davies came to America about 1685, purchased a lot in Philadelphia on Walnut street from John Jones, October 30, 1685, and in same year he purchased a plantation at Radnor. He married Ann Miles, sister of Richard Miles, of Radnor. He was originally a Quaker, and his name frequently appears in the Radnor and Haverford meeting records. Afterward he became an ardent Episcopalian. The first Episcopal services in the vicinity were held in his house, then in a log cabin built upon his plantation, which burned down early in 1700, and which was replaced by the present St. David's church, near St. David's Station, on Pennsylvania railroad. His children were members of the church. Nathan Evans' name appears in the records. William Davies was a vestryman and he was prominent in the church as long as he lived. He was a member of the Pennsylvania Assembly in 1712 and 1714. He died in 1734, leaving among his assets a "pew in St. David's church."

In September, 1712, Nathan Evans bought a plantation in Edgmont township, Chester (now Delaware) county, along Ridley creek, and in 1719 he purchased an adjoining farm from Isaac Norris, of Fairhill, Philadelphia county.

From Pennsylvania, Archives, vol. xix, Second Series, we find. In 1715 William Cloud obtained a warrant for 300 acres of land in Chester county which he assigned to his son, Joseph Cloud, who in 1718 had 300 acres surveyed to him on a branch of the Conestoga creek; and in first month, 1720, paid ten pounds in part and since by deed "ye 1st May, 1725, conveyed all his right and title to Nathan Evans, of said county, millwright." This is the property that he finally settled upon and where he built his house, still standing and occupied and owned by a descendant, in now Caeruarvon township, Lancaster county. Again from same volume, "Said Nathan Evans requests a grant of about 100 acres adjoining the east side of the above to erect a mill on." He also requests a grant of a piece of land for a settlement for his brother Roger, on the south side of his tract, and from Surveyor Taylor's papers in Historical Society, Philadelphia, we find that surveys were made January, 1737, to Roger Evans' for 150 acres on the north and south branches of the Brandywine, in Nautmeal township, and to Nathan Evans 150 acres on the the north branch of the Brandywine in Nantmeal township, Chester county, warrant having been given to him September 20, 1718, for 100 acres "on which he intends to build a mill." James Steel gave orders to Isaac Taylor to lay out the land. The above fixes the fact that Nathan Evans' brother Roger was in this country in 1718, and was living in 1737. He sold his farm in Edgmont township in 1724, and since he bought the Conestoga farm about the same time, he must have moved to the Conestoga Valley in this year. He built the house now owned and occupied by one of his descendants, Isaac Evans, on a part of this plantation, which he called the little meadow. The following is taken from the records of Bangor church, Churchtown, Lancaster county:

"By the Honorable William Penn, Esquire, original proprietor of the Province of Pennsylvania, his charter to all persons themselves from any part of Christendom into said Province. It is granted they shall enjoy the free license of the Christian religion under whatever denomination. Upon this, so engaging a plan of privileges, among others, several families of Welsh known by the name of Ancient Britons, did transplant themselves from Wales, in Old England, unto the Province aforesaid and settled themselves at first in the township of Radnor, in the county of Chester, in the Province aforesaid, where they erected a place of worship, where they had divine service, according to the doctrine and discipline of the Episcopal Church of England, of which church they were zealous members, and had for their minister the Rev. Mr. Robert Weyman, the society's missionary for the Propagating of the Gospel in Foreign Parts.

After some years many of them finding their settlement too confined (from the vast number of incomers) they, Anno Domini 1730, removed some miles to the westward into a new county called Lancaster and settled in a township called Caernarvon from a shire of the same name in Wales in Old England, and fixing here, they (in imitation of all good Christians) found that no place would be agreeable to them without the Public Worship of God, therefore unanimously and cordially consented and agreed according to their wordly circumstances to build a church of square logs, which they furnished and gave the name of Bangor from a diocese of that name in Old England. The principal members who built the church were as follows, viz:

Thomas Williams,	Evan Hughs,
George Huttson,	Zaccheus Davies,
Nathan Evans,	George Huttson,
Edward Davies,	Edward Nicholas,
Thomas Morgan,	Edward Davies,
Rees Davies,	Hugh Davies,
Philip Davies,	David Davies,
Gabriel Davies,	Morgan Evans,
Morgan John,	John Davies,
John Bowen,	Charles Huttson,
John Edwards,	Thomas Nicholas,
Nicholas Huttson,	John Davies.

Note.—These Davies were relatives of Susanna Davies, wife of Nathan Evans. Gabriel and John were her brothers. Congressman Edward Davies was a descendant of Gabriel. Nathan Evans moved to this region ahead of his friends from Radnor.

The first pastor was Rev. Griffith Hughs, 1730-1733. Then in succession Rev. Roger Blackwell, 1733-1739; Richard Lock, 1739-1751; George Craig, 1751-1759; Thomas Barton, 1759-1774. (In the interval during the Revolutionary War they had no minister), and Rev. Frederick Illig, 1782.

On the 17th day of November, A. D. 1751, the first record of the church was recorded; when Nathan Evans was chosen a vestryman and he continued each year at the head of the vestry until his death. At a meeting of the vestry on the 7th day of September, A. D. 1754, a subscription was taken up to raise money to build a new church. The largest subscription was given by Nathan Evans, one hundred pounds.

The warrant for the land upon which the church was built (and still stands) is dated May 24, 1738. Survey was made "to Gabriel Davies for a church thereon then intended to be erected and since erected and called Bangor Church, for the use of a congregation of Protestants of the established Church of England." Patent was issued to "Linford Lardner (who was a cousin of William Penn and Treasurer of the Province) and John Davies (the present church wardens,) and their heirs for the use aforesaid." 62 acres and 167 perches. Consideration. 9 pounds, 14 shillings and 8 pence. Quitrent ½ penny per acre. In 1759 Nathan Evans, Senior, paid "for the Glebe land, which lies around the church and cleared it out of the office by a patent for the use of the minister officiating in the church of Bangor, 29 pounds 2 shillings.

GEORGE CRAIG.

From first page of church record:
"Easter Monday, April 7, 1760. Mr. Nathan Evans, Sen., paid into the hands of William Douglass, Treasurer to the Church of Bangor, the sum of nineteen pounds, two shillings, and three pence, being the last payment of a benefaction of

one hundred pounds which he generously contributed towards building said church, and which the congregation acknowledges to have now received in full."

Nathan Evans died December 23, 1763, leaving a will, mentioning his wife, Susanna, sons, Nathan, John and James, and daughters, Ann, wife of Eleazor Evans, and Mary, wife of Thomas Nicholas, grandsons Nathan, son of Nathan; John and David, sons of Ann; Nathan and William, sons of James, and nephews Richard and Jonathan in the Province of Maryland (these were likely sons of his brother Roger) After devising the farm on which he lived to his son James, he bequeathed "Twenty shillings, which it is my will shall be given to the minister of Bangor Church yearly and every year forever, which twenty shillings I charge to and lay upon the meadow commonly known by the name Little Meadow."

One of his descendants now lives upon this farm and the amount has always been and is regularly paid to the church. He also bequeathed 100 pounds to buy three bells for the church, but money was used for other purposes. He also devised a farm in Tredyffrin township, Chester county, to his grandson, Nathan, son of Nathan, subject to an annual payment of twenty shillings to be used toward the support of a school in said township.

A large slab of marble covers his grave in Bangor, chlrchyard, upon which is inscribed:

"Waiting for the glorious resurrection of the faithful,
Here lies the body of Nathan Evans the elder.
Born in Treve Englis, in the county of Montgomery, in the principality of Wales.
A man, humble in affluence and prosperity.
In the duties of religion devout,
In friendship faithful,
In his dealings just,
To the poor he dispensed with a liberal hand.
To the church he was a generous and bountiful benefactor, and to all mankind a loving friend.
Having attained the age of eighty-one years he calmly resigned his soul unto the hands of the Redeemer on the 23d day of Dcember, A. D. 1763.
The memory of the just shall be held in everlasting remembrance."

His descendants are widely distributed throughout the United Sates.

TOMBSTONE INSCRIPTIONS

From the Pennepeck Baptist Grave yard Near Bustleton.

[The first Baptist church was built in 1707 on a piece of ground given by the Rev. Samuel Jones. He was born in Radnor county, Wales, July 9, 1657, and came to America in 1686. Rev. Elias Keach, Rev. Thos. Dungan, Wm. Kinnersley and Rev. Ebenezer Kinnersley, his son, also Rev. Jenkin Jones, were the noted preachers of this congregation, whose energies made the early history of the Baptist church in America. This church and graveyard is one of the most interesting places historically that I have visited in this State. Its condition is excellent, the grounds being well cared for.]

L. B., 1768.
Butchewho, John, d. June 30th, 1777, aged 46 y.; also ye body of Hannah James, died ye 13th. of May, 1731.
Bartolet, Elizabeth, d. May 23, 1805, aged 50 y.
Cart, Margaret, wf. of John Cart, d. Apl. ye 26, 1749, aged 52 y.
Clift, Jonathan, d. 19 ——, 1805, aged 84 y. 7 m. 11 d. Also,
Clift, Christian, d. May 9, 1788, aged 45 y.
C. C., 1788.
F. C., 1787.
E. C., 1766.
[These are in the Clift plot and are undoubtedly of that name and family.]
Clift, Edward, d. July 17, 1801, aged 34 y.
Dungan, Mercy, wf. of Jonathan Dungan, d. 17 Sept., 1735, aged 21 y. and 10 m.

Few did exceed her sober life,
When as a maid or a wife;
But now her spirit dwells on high
Tho' her body here doth lye.

Dungan, Benjamin, b. Apl. 27, 1743; elected deacon of the Baptist church, Pennypeck, Lower Dublin, Pa., Mar.

30, 1782, which office he sustained upwards of 34 years and died the Lord's day, June 23, 1816, anno aet 73.
Dungan, Jesse, d. July 12, 1823, aged 67 y. 4 m. 19 d.
Duncan, Hannah, dau. of William and Maria Duncan, d. Aug. 10, 1805, aged 1 y. 4 m.
Duffield, Peter, d. Aug. 15, 1752, aged about 37 y.
Duffield, John, d. Sept. 12, 1756, aged 36 y.
Duer, Elizabeth, d. Apl. 10, 1817, aged 83 y. 9 m. 13 d.
M. D., d. May 30, 1812, aged 14 y. 2m. 10 d. [This is perhaps a Duer, initials only shown.]
De Nyce, John, d. May 10, 1775, aged 49 y.
De Nyce, Jane, wf. of John De Nyce, d. Dec. 5, 1805, aged 79 y. 5 m. 1 d.
Dyre, Joseph, d. Aug. 19, 1802, aged 1 y. 5 d.
Dyre, Joseph, d. July 23, 1806, aged 1 y. 5 m. 8 d.
Dyre, Joseph, d. Feby. 26, 1835, aged 81 y. 1 m. 6 d.
Dyre, Christianna, consort of Joseph Dyre, b. July 28, 1737; d. Oct. 17, 1829.
Dyre, Hetty, dau. of Joseph and Christianna Dyre, b. Sept. 7, 1783; d. Oct. 25, 1823.
Davis, David Z., d. Sept. 8, 1827, aged 27 y. 7 m. 8 d.
Davis, Mary Ann, d. Sept. 16, 1826, aged 6 m. 10 d.
Davis, Thomas, d. June 13, 1826, aged 3 y. 8 m. 26 d.
Davis, Charles, d. Sept. 16, 1818, aged 1 y. 5 m. 16 d.
Davis, William, d. Oct. 4, 1821, aged 2 y. 7m. 12 d.
Davis, Lewis, d. Oct. 20, 1821, aged 7 m. 12 d.
Davis, Daniel, a native of Carmarthenshire, South Wales, d. Aug. 3, 1824, aged 64 y. 2 m. 1 d.
Eaton, John, d. 3 m., 1702.
Eaton, Rev. George, d. July 1st, 1764, aged 77 y. 11 m.
Eaton, George, d. 7 m., 1706.
Engle, Caroline, dau. of Richard and Thirza Engle, d. Sept. 10, 1820, aged 10 y. 2 m.
Edwards, George, s. of Benjamin and Hannah, d. Aug. 31, 1820, aged 3 y. 10 m. 14 d.
Edwards, Marshall, d. Feb. 9, 1778, aged 31 y.
Edwards, Martha, wf. of Marshall Edwards, d. Feby. 20, aged 36 y.
Edwards, Dr. Enoch, ob. Apl. 18, 1802, aged 52 y.
Edwards, Ann, wf. of Alexander Edwards, d. Sept. 11, 1771.
Edwards, Alexander, d. May 16, 1777, aged 66 y.
Edwards, George, d. June 16, 1797, aged 56 y.
Edwards, Jemimia, wf. of George Edwards, d. Nov. 13, 1807, aged 62 y.
Foster, Thomas, d. Feb. 23, 1771, aged 77 y.
Glen, John, s. of James and Mary, d. Sept. 20, ——.
Gordon, Elizabeth, wf. of Elisha Gordon, d. Mar. 31, 1817, aged 58 y. 3 m.
George, Ann, d. Aug. 14, 1799, aged 10 y.
George, Wm., d. Sept. 3, 1799, aged 8 y.
George, Catherine, d. Sept. 4, 1799, aged 15 y.
George, Ann, wf. of William George, d. Sept. 9, 1801, aged 33 y.
George, Richard, d. Jany. 6th, 1809, aged 2 y.
Griffiths, Thomas, d. June 16, 1783, aged 78 y.
Griffiths, Joseph, s. of Thomas and Elizabeth Griffiths, d. Nov. 16, 1775, aged 28 y.
Griffiths, Thomas, d. June 16, 1783, aged 78 y.
Gillison, Thomas, a native of South Carolina, d. June 2, 1825, aged 53 y. 3m 5 d.
Holme, John, d. July 12, 1775, aged 69 y.
Holme, Jane, wf. of John Holme, d. May 18, 1795, aged 84 y. 6 m.
Holme, Hetty, dau. of Thomas and Rebecca, aged 2 y. 7 m.
Holme, Susan, wf. of George W., d. June 4, 1828, aged 28 y. 5 m. 18 d; also, Holme, Frances, dau. of Geo. and Susan, d. Mar. 23, 1828, aged 2 y. 7 m. 2 d.
Holme, Wm. H., s. of Geo. W. and Susan, d. Aug. 30, 1821, aged 14 m. 5 d.

Holme, Thomas, d. May 26, 1826, aged 78 y.
Holme, Rebecca, wf. of Thomas Holme, d. Oct. 11, 1805, aged 52 y.
Holme, John, d. Mar. 8, 1810, aged 68 y. 22 d.
Holme, Esther, wf. of John Holme, d. Dec- 20, 1816, aged 68 y. 5 m. 13 d.
Harker, John, d. June 15, 1804, aged 43 y. 2 m.
Hall, Susan, of Boston, d. June 4, 1810, aged 42 y.
Hollinger, Achsha, d. Apl. 16, 1812, aged 23 y. 11 m. 8 d.
Haeftee, Charles, d. Sept. 18, 1742, aged 55 y.
Heritage, William F., s. of John and Ann Heritage, d. Nov. 20, 1803, aged 3 y. 11 m. 18 d.
Heritage, Susannah, dau. of John and Jane De Nyce, d. Aug. 27, 1774, aged 24 y.
Hughes, Elizabeth, wf. of John Hughes, d. Dec. 20, 1815, aged 57 y.
Jackson, Joseph, d. Mar. 24, 1807, aged 33 y. 6 m. 2 d.
Jackson, John, d. Apl. 27, 1770, aged 64 y. 7 m.
James, Hannah, d. May 13, 1731.
Jones, George, d. 1701.
Jones, James, d. 1699.
Jones, Joshua, d. Nov. 1st, 1781, aged 80 y.
Jones, Hannah, wf. of Joshua Jones, d. Oct. 2, 1770; also, an infant, 12 d old.
Jones, Joshua, d. Oct. 5, 1823, aged 63 y. wanting 4 d.; also, his wife
Jones, Eleanor, d. Apl. 14, 1815, aged 53 y. 126 d.; also, their daughters,
Jones, Hannah, d. Feb. 13, 1792, aged 2 y. 13 d.
Jones, Lucretia, d. Feb. 17, 1792, aged 47 d.; also,
Jones, Eleanor, d. May 6, 1807, aged 2 y. 185 d.; also, their son,
Jones, Samuel, M. D., d. in Cincinnati, Mar. 22, 1832.
Jones, Sylvia, d. July 20, 1778, aged 11 m. 20 d.
Jones, an infant of S. and S. Jones, b. Feby. 7, 1773, aged 17 d.
Jones, John, d. 1713; also, his wife,
Jones, Rebecca, d. Nov. 3, 1743; also,
Jones, James, d. Oct. 12, 1770, aged 7 y.

Jones, Samuel Spicer, d. May 11, 1769, aged 18 m. 17 d.
All that live must die,
All that die must live;
Endless joy or woe.
Jones, Samuel, d. Aug. 3, 1778, aged 7 y. 3 m. 3 d.
Jones, Thomas Spicer, d. Aug. 4, 1778, aged 13 y. lacking 9 d.
Jones, Reverend Samuel, b. Jan. 14, 1735; d. Feb. 7, 1814.
Jones, Sylvia, the consort of Samuel Jones, D. D., d. July 23, 1802, aged 66 y. 6 m.
Jones, Elizabeth, b. Caernarvonshire, N. Wales, d. July 23, 1808, aged 35 y.

GUSTAVUS N. HART.
Philadelphia.

OBITUARY.

Charles L. Bailey.

Surrounded by all the members of his family, with the exception of his son-in-law, Mr. Robert E. Speer, and daughter-in-law, Mrs. William E. Bailey, who were unable to arrive here in time, Mr. Charles L. Bailey, one of Harrisburg's oldest, most prominent and most universally respected citizens, passed to his reward at his home, Front and Chestnut streets, Tuesday morning, September 5th, 1899. He had been seriously ill but a few days, and on Sunday Drs. Deaver and DeCosta, eminent Philadelphia specialists, were summoned in consultation with the local attending physicians. They gave the members of the family little encouragement as to his recovery. About midnight Mr. Bailey lost consciousness and slowly sank to rest at the hour above indicated.

Many telegrams of sympathy and condolence were received at the Bailey residence during the day, and many friends called and expressed their deep sorrow over the death of Mr. Bailey. Mrs. William E. Bailey, who is a daughter of former Secretary of War Russell A. Alger, was by the bedside of the aged sufferer Monday, and later left for her home.

For more than a quarter of a century Mr. Bailey had been one of the leading citizens of the Capital City. He was distinguished for his broad-mindedness, generosity, public-spirit, pride in his home city, and thorough independence. His fidelity in all the walks of life was one of his most marked characteristics. On all public questions he was independent in the expression of his opinion, and courageous in maintaining it. Energetic and progressive as a business man, he was also free and liberal in the use of his means to promote the good of his community, and church and charity alike were constantly the recipients of his generosity. In his death this community has lost a citizen whose moral influenc was a blessing and an inspiration.

Charles Lukens Bailey, son of Joseph Bailey and Martha (Lukens) Bailey, was born March 9th, 1821, in Chester county, Pa. His paternal ancestors were of English and his maternal ancestors of Welsh descent. His great-grandfather, Edward Bailey, was a resident of Bucks county and his grandfather, William Bailey, a resident farmer in Philadelphia county, Pa. His father was born in 1796 and settled in Chester county in 1819, where he carried on farming until 1838, when he engaged in the iron business at the old Lukens' mill in Coatesville and there manufactured boiler plate for six years. In 1844 he removed to Berks county, near Pottstown, and erected on the site of the "Old Forge" of the Pine Iron Works, a rolling mill and carried on business alone for a few years and afterwards in connection with his sons under the firm name of Joseph Bailey & Sons, until within a short period when he retired from active life, leaving his manufacturing interests then in the hands of his son, Joseph L. Bailey. The children of Joseph and Martha Bailey were: Charles L., Sarah, Edward, formerly manager of the iron works at Glasgow, Montgomery county, deceased; Dr. George, of Philadelphia; William L., treasurer and manager of Thorndale Iron Works; Joseph L., Hannah, and Anne, deceased.

Charles L. Bailey, eldest son, obtained his early education at the Westtown School, Chester county, and for some time thereafter was a clerk in the drug store of Thomas Evans & Co., of Philadelphia. His career in the iron business began in 1838 as a clerk for his father at Coatesville, where he became thoroughly conversant with the details of the business carried on at that place. He removed with his parents to Berks county, where he continued his clerkship for five years, and from 1849 to 1852 was a partner with his father in the Pine Iron Works. In August of the latter year Mr. Bailey removed to Harrisburg and in connection with Morris Patterson, of Philadelphia, founded the Old Central Iron Works, latterly used as a puddling mill. He continued business until 1859, when he became interested with the late James McCormick in the Nail Works at Fairview, Cumberland county, rebuilt the works and carried them on successfully until 1866, when he retired from the firm, and founded and erected the present Chesapeake Nail Works in Harrisburg. Later he associated with him his brother, Dr. George Bailey, under the firm name of Charles L. Bailey & Bro.

In 1869 Mr. Bailey removed to Pottstown, and until 1875 was the treasurer and general manager of the Pottstown Iron Company, manufacturing nails, boiler plate and pig iron. Closing out his interest there he returned to Harrisburg, and in 1877-78 erected the present Central Iron Works, contiguous to the Chesapeake Nail Works. Mr. Bailey was thoroughly imbued with the spirit of progress and enterprise, as his various industrial undertakings attest, and although his mind was largely absorbed in business pursuits, he did not hold entirely aloof from duties incumbent upon him as a citizen. He was president of the board of trustees of the Market Square Presbyterian Church, and in 1880 was appointed by Governor Hoyt a trustee of the Pennsylvania Insane Hospital. He was elected a member of the Select Council of the city in 1877, was a member of the State Legislature in 1879, and in 1881 he was again elected a member of the Select Council, chosen president, and served as chairman of the Finance Committee.

Mr. Bailey married, in 1856, Emma H. Doll, daughter of William Doll and Sarah M. (Elder), of Harrisburg, whose maternal great-grandfather was Rev. John Elder. Their surviving children are: William Elder, a graduate of Yale in the class of

1882; Edward, a graduate of Yale scientific course in the class of 1881, president of the Harrisburg National Bank; Charles L., attorney-at-law and James B., associated with his father in the iron and steel business, also graduates of Yale, and Emma D., wife of Robert E. Speer, of New York, general secretary of the Presbyterian Board of Foreign Missions.

NOTES AND QUERIES.

Historical, Biographical, and Genealogical.

XXXI.

GENEALOGICAL
And Revolutionary Research.—Recently many complaints have reached us regarding the unreliable information furnished by a coterie in this city. We desire it to be distinctly understood, that the Editor of "Notes and Queries" is not responsible for the data sent out by these ignoramuses in genealogical research. If people want accuracy they should seek information from those they know and on whom they can depend.

WISHART.
John Wishart, of Antrim township, Cumberland county, d. in February, 1778, leaving a wife Agnes, d. March, 1793, and children:
i. Joseph, d. prior to 1792, leaving a daughter Jean.
ii. Nancy (Agnes).
iii. John.
iv. James.
v. Edward.
vi. Mary.
The executors are sons John and James. Neither of them are named in their mother's will, her executors being son Edward and James Crooks. Edward and Mary, provably minors in 1778, are not mentioned in their father's will.

GEDDES.
James Geddes came to Pennsylvania in 1752. His son, William Geddes, m. in 1762, Sarah McCallen. She d. in 1773. Their son Robert Geddes, b. Sept. 30, 1771, in Hanover township, Lancaster county, d. July 14, 1832. He married Jane Sawyer, who d. Nov. 29, 1808, leaving six children, one of whom was my grandfather, John Geddes, b. March 19, 1801, and d. Nov. 4, 1889, at Ann Arbor, Mich. My grandfather had a brother William, b. Dec. 28, 1802, and d. March 21, 1877, at his residence in Pittsfield, near Ann Harbor. In his will he speaks of a sword that belonged to Robert McCallen. John Sawyer, father of Jane Sawyer, who m. Robert Geddes, was b. Aug. 4, 1730 (O. S.), and d. Aug. 12, 1813. He was the oldest son of William Sawyer, who settled in Londonderry township, Lancaster county. What I wish to know is whether either of the Sawyers named or Robert McCallen served in the war of the Revolution.
CHARLOTTE RANDALL.
Beliot, Wis.
[Robert McCallen commanded a company of Lancaster county militia, and went into the Jerseys in August, 1776, and in service until January, 1777.]

Some Westmoreland County Families.

[A New York correspondent who is preparing a record of his own family, sends the following to "Notes and Queries." Prechance some of our Westmoreland county friends can help us.]
PHIPPS.
Samuel Phipps died at his home, near Butler, Richland county, Ohio, January 5, 1841, aged 105 years, 7 months and 5 days. He,·consequently, was born either February 25, or June 1, 1735, as the old or new style of calendar and the old-style year beginning March 25th or new-style year, beginning January 1st, be used. Family tradition informs us that he was born near Philadelphia. Where and when was he born, and where married? What the name of his father and date and place of birth, marriage, death and place of burial? What were the full Christian and surname of his mother, dates of birth, death and place of burial? Was Samuel Phipps descended from Joseph Phipps, who came over with William Penn, or how related?

MARSHAL.
Mary Marshal, who married, about 1765, Samuel Phipps, above mentioned,

was a cousin of General Anthony Wayne. What is the date of her birth, where, when married, full name of her father, and Christian and surname of her mother?

UPDEGRAFF.

What were the Christian and surname of the wife of John Updegraff, parents of Edith Updegraff, of West Fairfield township, Ligonier Valley, Westmoreland county, Pennsylvania, who married Nathan Phipps, son of Samuel and Mary Marshal Phipps?

WISE.

William Wise, of Wesmoreland county, Pennsylvania, married Sarah Phipps, daughter of Samuel and Mary Marshal Phipps. Any information about the family and descendants and whereabouts of the Wise family will be greatly appreciated.

DEVOR.

Rebecca Devor or Devour married Eli Phipps, son of Nathan and Edith Updegraff Phipps. What is the date of the birth of Rebecca Devor Phipps and where, what was the name of her father, the maiden, Christian and surname of her mother, date of her birth and where buried?

POWER.

In what capacity and by what authority was George Power sent by the State of Pennsylvania, first temporarily in 1789, and second permanently in 1795 to Franklin, now Venango county, in regard to the settlement of the territory "north and west of the Allegheny River and Conewingo Creek?" What were the maiden, Christian and surname of Margaret, the mother of George Power and wife of William Power, What is the date and place of birth of Margaret Power, and date of her death, as well as where buried? What was the name of her father? What were the full maiden, Christian and surname of her mother? Where did her parents reside? What is the date of the birth of William Power? Where was he born? What is the date of his death? At what place and in what cemetery was William Power buried? What is the date of the marriage of William and Margaret Power? Did Margaret Power, after the death of her husband, William, marry Colonel Daniel Cresap? Family tradition informs us that she did. Was Margaret, the widow of William Power, the mother of the ten children: Thomas (1st), Daniel, Joseph, Van, Robert, James and Thomas (2d), and Elizabeth, Mary and Sarah, born unto Colonel Daniel Cresap by his second wife?

OGDEN.

Armstrong Ogden was born at Elizabethtown, N. J., May 10, 1795. What were the names of his parents? Was his father Col. Joseph Ogden, his mother's maiden name Susannah Woods?

HAENY.

Catherine Haney or Katrina Haeny, of Westmoreland county, Pa., was born June 3, 1773, and married June 5, 1792, John Phipps. What was the name of her father, and the maiden, Christian and surname of her mother?

HALFERTY.

What is the date of the birth of Margaret (about 1790), daughter of Col. Edward and Margaret Flack Halferty, of West Fairfield, Westmoreland county, Pa., who married John Phipps, on January 9, 1812?

SAMUEL PHIPPS BRIGHAM.

TOMBSTONE INSCRIPTIONS

From the Penepeck Graveyard, Bustleton, Pa.

II.

Jalley, Samuel., d. Sept. 5, 1810, aged 40y. A native of County Down, Ireland.
Keen, Mary, wife of John Keen, d. Feb. 14, 1816, aged 74y.
Keen, John, d. May 17, 1808, aged 70y.
Keen, Sarah, wife of John Keen, b. Nov. 28, 1743; d. Sept. 6, 1782.
Kely, Patrick, d. 1716.
Kitchen, Thomas, d. 1706.
Kinnersley, Rev. Ebenezer, d. July 4, 1778, aged 67y.

Kinnersey, Sarah, wife of Ebenezer, d. Nov. 6, 1802, aged 81y.
Kinarsley, William, d. Feb. 17, 1732, aged 63y, 3m.
Lewis, Samuel Ellis, son of Robert and Frances, d. Aug. 8, 1791, aged 11y.
Lewis, Robert, d. July 14, 1795, aged 55y.
Lewis, Frances, wife of Robert, d. April 3, 1820, aged 64y.
McVaugh, Elizabeth, d. March 2, 1821, aged 70y.
McVaugh, Edmond, d. Feb. 14, 1820, aged 72y, 4m.
MccAvoa (McAvoy), Catherine, d. April 6, 1737, aged 45y.
Marshall, William, d. Feb. 20, 1764.
Maghee, Willam, d. Sept. 29, 1825, aged 67y; also
Maghee, Frances, consort of Wm. Maghee, d. Oct. 26, 1835, aged 62y.
Maris, Nathan, son of William and Mary, d. June 6, 1780, aged 1y, 4m; also
Maris, Mathias, their son, d. June 13, 1784, aged 4m, 12d.
Marple, David, d. Oct. 7, 1739, aged 75y.
Marple, Jesse, d. April 21, 1815, aged 34y, 3d.
Miles, Griffith, and his wife,
Miles, Bridget, born in Wales 1670; d. Penna., Jan., 1719.
Miles, John, d. 1717, aged 37y.
Milès, Jacob, d. Aug. 23, 1822, aged 54y.
Miles, Margaret, d. March 3, 1826, aged 70y.
Miles, Lydia, d. Aug. 28, 1841, aged 89y.
Miles, D. [No date, very old piece of rough stone.]
Miles, Samuel, d. Nov. 25, 1825, aged 31y, 6m, 10d.
Miles, Ann, consort of Joseph Miles, d. Dec. 20, 1821, aged 90y.
Miles, Ann I., aged 3y, 1m, 25d. [No year given.]
Morris, Evan, b. in Radnorshire, Great Britain, d. Jan. 25, 1725, aged 25y.
Moulder, William, d. Sept. 24, 1798, aged 73y.
Moore, Dr. Jonathan, b. July 29, 1775; d. March 17, 1815.
Moore, Hamilton, son of Dr. Jonathan, b. Jan. 4, 1811; d. Nov. 20, 1812.
Northrop, George, 3d m, 1707.
Northrop, Mary, dau. of Enoch and Mary Northrop, d. Nov. 14, 1792, aged 6y, 7m.

Owen, Elizabeth, wife of Owen Owen, d. Jan. 1, 1818, aged 33y, 7m, 9d.
L. O., 1768. [This probably an Owen.]
Purnal, Samuel, d. July 20, 1809, aged 22y, 19d.
Parker, Eliabeth, wife of Thomas Parker, d. Nov. 26, 1702, aged 50y.
Powell, Thomas, d. Sept. 26, 1752, aged 55y; also
Powell, Eleanor, d. Dec. 8, 1772, aged 68y.
Rickard, Mary, 3d m, 1702.
Swift, Anthony, d. March 28, 1815, aged 74y; also
Swift, Martha, wife of Anthony, d. April 14, 1830, aged 87y.
Swift, Dr. Samuel, d. Nov. 28, 1784, aged 73y, 7m.
Swift, Elizabeth, wife of Samuel Swift, d. Oct. 20, 1795, aged 78y.
Swift, Mary, dau. of Samuel and Elizabeth, d. Nov. 19, 1787, aged 37y.
Swift, John, d. Dec. 17, 1732, aged 22½y.
Swift, Phebe, b. Feb. 15, 1737; d. Jan. 1, 1814.
Swift, John, b. Oct. 4, 1736; d. Dec. 29, 1813.
Swift, Edward, b. Dec. 11, 1765; d. Dec. 26, 1813; also
Swift, Elizabeth, his widow, d. March 9, 1850, aged 78y.
Swift, Sarah, dau. of Edward and Elizabeth Swift, b. Jan. 14, 1797; d. Jan. 14, 1813.
Swift, Henry, son of Edward and Elizabeth Swift, d. April 14, 1829, aged 15y, 1m.
Sherwell, Sarah, d. Nov. 2, 1822, aged 56y.
Shepherd, Willimina, b. Aug. 14, 1808; d. March 27, 1815.
Shepherd, John Jr., b. Oct. 25, 1792; d. Feb. 28, 1813.
Shepherd, John, b. Oct. 15, 1759; d. Oct. 23, 1809.
Shepherd, Anna B., wife of John Shepherd, d. Oct. 14, 1828, aged 67y.
Shearer, Sarah, wife of Jacob, d. July 27, 1796, aged 35y, 7m.
Shearer, Rachel, wife of Jacob, d. March 9, 1832, aged 67y.
Shearer, Jacob, d. Feb. 12, 1837, aged 82y.
Thomas, James, a native of Wales, d. May 5, 1806, aged 47y.
Thomas, John, d. May 14, 1761, aged 45y; also

Thomas, Lucretia, wife of John, d. Dec. 15, 1760, aged 40y.
Taylor, Malachi, b. Nov. 22, 1770; d. May 9, 1826.
Taylor, Isaac, d. Aug. 27, 1819, aged 21y, 11m, 18d;
Van Beuren, Abraham, of Philadelphia, d. Aug. 11, 1825, aged 63y; also
Van Bueren, Sarah, wife of Abraham, dau. of John Holme, of Holmesburg, Pa., d. Aug. 20, 1839, aged 56y.
Van Beuren, Henry, son of Abraham, d. Jan. 6, 1818, aged 5y, 6m, 17d.
Van Beuren, Frances, dau. of Abraham and Sarah, d. Nov. 13, 1816, aged 2y.
Vandike, Henry, d. April 11, 1825, aged 79y, 8m, 1w.
Vandike, Lucy, wife of Henry Vandike, d. Feb. 19, 1836, aged 77y.
Watts, Silas, d. Aug. 16, 1737, aged 39y.
Watts, Rachel, wife of John Watts, d. Nov., 1765, aged 29y, 4m.
Watts, Stephen, d. 1788, aged 51y.
Watts, Elizabeth, d. 1793, aged 87y.
Watts, Elizabeth, widow of Arthur Watts, dau. of John and Lucretia Thomas, d. April 25, 1835, aged 78y.
Watts, John, b. Sept. 14, 1733; ; d. July 14, 1813; also
Watts, Margaret, wife of John Watts, b. Aug. 3, 1751; d. Jan. 11, 1844.

J—ntered here I be.
O—that you could now see.
H—ow unto Jesus I op to flee,
N—ot in sinn will Io be.

W—arning in time pray take.
A—nd peace by Jesus make;
T—hen att the last when youl wake.
S—ure [illegible]

he died
August ye
27, 1702.

Wright, Rachel, wife of John Wright, d. Nov. 28, 1801, aged 72y.
Wright, John, d. April 13, 1792, aged 63y.
Wright, Rachel, d. March 21, 1833, aged 75y.
Wright, Rebecca, d. April 9, 1813, aged 41y, 8m, 9d.
Wright, Jane, wife of Samuel, d. April 5, 1826, aged 34y.
Wright, Elizabeth, dau. of Samuel and Jane Wright, d. May 28, 1829, aged 8y, 9m.
Wright, Harriet, dau. of Samuel and Jane, d. Aug. 26, 1819, aged 1y, 8m.
Wright, Harriet, dau. of Jesse and Mary, b. Feb. 5, 1811; d. Apl. 4, 1817.
Wright, Elizabeth, wife of John Wright, d. Feb. 1, 1806, aged 44y.
Wright, John, d. Nov. 15, 1841, aged 86y.
Wright, William, d. Apl. 9, 1813, aged 53y, 9d.
Wright, Eleanor, wife of William, d. June 15, 1818; aged 60y, 1d.
Wright, Joseph, d. Feb. 19, 1832, aged 78y, 3m.
Wright, Martha, wife of Joseph Wright, d. Jan. 10, 1814, aged 64y, 6m, 9d.
Webster, Thomas, d. Aug. 20, 1809, aged 85y.
Webster, Susannah, d. Dec. 11, 1785, aged 58y.

GUSTAVUS N. HART.
Philadelphia.

Old Hanna Burying Ground.

Inscriptions on tombstones in the old Hanna burying ground, three miles from Hagerstown, Md.:

In
memory of
Mary MacDill,
who departed this life
February 25, 1808,
aged 80 years, 1 month
and 12 days.

In memory of
Charles McCauley, senior,
who was born March 15, 1754,
and died April 10, 1817, aged
63 years and 25 days.

In memory of
Charles McCauley, junior,
who was born January 1, 1799;
died February 11, 1830.
aged 30 years, 1 month and 11 days.

In memory of
Hannah McCauley,
wife of
Charles McCauley, senior,
who was born October 6, 1757,

and departed this life July 10, 1835, aged 77 years, 3 months and 4 days.

Sacred to the memory of
Catharine
daughter of Billmyer
and wife of Robert Hanna,
who was born October 30, 1805,
and departed this life May 6, 1836,
aged 30 years, 6 months and 6 days.

In memory of
Jackson Hanna,
who was born January 2, 1784,
and departed this life January 18, 1837,
aged 53 years, 16 days.

In
memory of
John Hanna,
who was born October 26,
A. D. 1748, and died May 4,
A. D. 1838, aged 89 years,
6 months and 9 days.

Kind angels watch his deepening dust,
Till Jesus comes to raise the just.
Then may he wake wiht sweet surprise
And in his Saviour's image rise.

(Note)—John Hanna served in the Second Maryland regiment, Revolutionary war, his name appearing on a return and roll on file at the Record and Pension Office, Washington, D. C., as having enlisted May 3, 1782, for three years. His rank is not stated.

In
memory of
Margaret, daughter of
George and Rebecca Hanna,
who was born November 8,
1835, and died February 11, 1839.

Sacred to the memory
of
Elizabeth,
Consort of David Keedy
who was born January 29, 1792,
and departed this life April 5, 1839,
aged 47 years, 2 months and 7 days.

In memory of
Sarah Ann, daughter of
Isaac and Sarah Ann Hanna,
who was born April 9, 1835,
and who died May 30, 1839,
aged 4 years, 1 month and 11 days.

Mary Ann,
daughter of Jeremiah and Susan Huyett,
died February 12, 1840,
aged 4 years, 4 months and 27 days.

In memory of
Isaac Hanna,
who was born November 13, 1793,
died March 14, 1841,
aged 47 years, 4 months and 1 day.

In memory of
Mary Ann,
daughter
of George and Rebecca Hanna,
born October 2, 1830,
died January 26, 1844,
aged 13 years, 3 months and 25 days.

In
memory of
Mrs. Ann Hanna,
wife of the late
John Hanna,
who departed this life
May 25, 1847, in the
92nd year of her age.

Jacob E.,
son of Jacob E. and Nancy Bell
died July 22, 1847,
aged 1 year, 10 months and 21 days.

One grave marked with a rough stone without inscription.

NOTES AND QUERIES.

Historical, Biographical, and Genealogical.

XXXII.

"THE PERKIOMEN REGION, Past and Present," edited by Henry S. Dotterer, of No. 1605 North Thirteenth street, Philadelphia, is a monthly publication which we trust will be found in the possession of every lover of Pennsylvania history. The Editor spent over a year solely in making researches among the archives of Holland, Germany and Switzerland, and has opened his budget for the benefit of the readers of his periodical. To those who peruse "Notes and Queries" we would advise to secure "The Perkiomen Region" at once. They will then know what a good thing they possess.

BRUNER.

I. Ulrick Brunner came to America in 1744 and settled in Morgantown, Berks county, Pa. He m. in Aprin, 1755, Fronica Gross, dau. of Joseph and Magdalena (Roth) Gross, from the Palatinate, Germany. They had, among others:

II. Ulrick Brunner (Ulrick). He changed his name to Owen Bruner. He m. Elizabeth Weaver, dau. of John and Barbara (Buckwalter) Weaver. Her father was a son of Joseph and Ann Weaver, who came from Switzerland in 1706 and settled near New Holland, in now Lancaster county, where they took up a large tract of land called "Weber Thal." Ulrick Bruner and his wife Elizabeth Weaver had among other children:

III. Abraham; m. Rebecca Evans.

PASTORIUS.

I. Christianus Pastorius, of Warburg, Germany, had among other children:

II. Martinus Pastorius, of Erfort; was a lawyer and Imperial Councillor to King Ferdinand II, 1605 to 1629; was killed during the thirty years' war. He m. Bridget von Flinsberg and they had among other children:

III. Melchior Adam Pastorius, b. Sept. 21, 1624, at Erfort, Germany; d. Feb. 4, 1702, at Nuremberg. He was a lawyer, senator, burgomaster, mayor, Beyruth councillor, and judge of Wersheim, Germany. His wife was Magdalena Dietz, and they had among other children:

IV. Francis Daniel Pastorius, b. at Sommerhausen, in 1650; d. Dec. 26, 1719, at Germantown, Pa. He was a lawyer, professor of law, Frankfort. Came to America in 1683, and founded Germantown in 1684; became a judge of the courts and a member of the Provincial Assembly. He m. Ennecke Klostermann, dau. of Dr. Johann Klosterman, of Mulheim. They had among other children:

V. John Samuel Pastorius; m. Hannah Luken, dau. of Jan Luken, and had:

VI. Daniel Pastorius; m. Sarah Shoemaker, dau. of Abraham and Amelia (Levering) Shoemaker, and they had:

VII. Daniel Pastorius; m. Elizabeth Mecklin, dau. of Jacob and Maria (Zimmerman) Mecklin. The latter was a dau. of Sebastian (son of Abraham Zimmerman, of Oley,) and Ann Elizabeth de Levan. Sebastian Zimmerman was the second judge of Berks county. They had:

VIII. Daniel Pastorius, a merchant of Philadelphia. He m. Tacy Styer and they had among others:

IX. Mary M. Pastorius; m. Davies Evans Bruner.

"History of the Pennsylvania Railroad."

William Bender Wilson, of Holmesburg, Pa., has placed the reading public of Pennsylvania, and especially the admirers of that mighty and successful corporation, in ever-living obligation, in this Narrative History of the Pennsylvania Railroad Company. From the earliest inception of that great project, which connects the West with the East, the author gives facts and figures which only a patient delver could furnish. The two handsome volumes which contain the results of years of careful investigation, are replete with the principal incidents in the career of that gigantic enterprise which is the pride and glory of our good old Commonwealth. No other railway system in the world has been more energetic, more successful or more enterprising. View the corporation from whatever standpoint, its equal has never existed, and the whole story is entertainingly told by one of its veteran employees—one who has seen it rise from its infancy to its acme in railroad industry— and whose very life seems to have been interwoven into that history. No living man save William Bender Wilson has the personal intimate knowledge of facts pertaining to a faithful narration. He has done his work well—and no self-styled "official" historian can give a tithe of the information the untiring author of these volumes has gathered, without using this material. The building of the Pennsylvania Railroad gave a great impetus to the industries of the Commonwealth, and with its many branches, which have grid-ironed the State, Progress has been written at the entrance to every village within its goodly domain. We have only to contrast the canal boat of sixty years ago with the transit of the Pennsylvania Limited from Philadelphia to Pittsburg. To those who can grasp the transformation there is food for thought. Up to the "Jubilee" period Mr. Wilson has given us a pleasing resume of its grand history and in conclusion brief sketches of the many noble brain-workers who assisted in the accomplishment of the most wonderful marvel of railroad enterprise the world has ever realized. Mr. Wilson's work ought to occupy a place in the library of all men of thought and action in the State.

EVANS OF CAERNARVON.

I. Nathan Evans, b. 1683; d. Dec. 20, 1763, in Churchtown, Lancaster county, Pa. (See "Welsh Settlers in Earl and Caernarvon," N. & Q., xxx.) He m. in 1709, Susanna Davies, dau. of William and Ann (Miles) Davies, of Radnor. They had issue:
  i. Nathan, b. 4, 8, 1711; d. 1777; m. Mary Fox, widow; resided at Churchtown, Lancaster county, Pa. They had issue:
    1. Evan, m. Dec. 26, 1761, Jane Carson.
    2. Nathan, m. Aug. 9, 1763, Mary Thomas.
  ii. William, b. 4, 9, 1713; d. 1744, unm.
  2. iii. Evan, b. 1, 1, 1717; m. Mary Morgan.
  3. iv. John, b. 11, 20, 1720; m. Mary Hudson.
  4. v. Anne, b. 11, 4, 1722; m. Eleazor Evans.
  5. vi. James, b. 2, 8, 1724; m. Elizabeth Thomas.
  6. vii. Mary, b. 2, 6, 1726; m. Thomas Nicholas.
II. Evan Evans (Nathan), b. 1, 1, 1717; d. 2, 18, 1765; m. Mary Morgan, dau. of John Morgan. They had issue:
  i. David.
  ii. Elizabeth, m. Aquilla Rogers.
  iii. Griffith.
  iv. John.
  v. Susan, m. John Silas, and had issue (surname Silas):
    1. Mary.
    2. Margaret, m. William Ayres.
    3. Elizabeth.
  vi. Margaret.
  vii. Mary, m. June 20, 1768, Charles Cunningham.
  7. viii. Evan, m. Mary Jones.
  ix. Sarah, m. Lot Evans.
  x. James.
III. John Evans (Nathan), b. 11, 20, 1720; d. 12, 1801; m. Mary Hudson, widow. They had issue:
  i. Nathan, b. 1752; d. 1793.
  8. ii. John, b. 1754; m. Margaret Jones.
  iii. David, b. 1758; d. 1, 18, 1801; m. Sarah Waddell; she m. secondly, Dr. Washington Rigg; and they had issue (surname Rigg):
    1. John D., m. Margaret Wilson, of Parkesburg.
  iv. Mary, m. Nathan Edwards.
  v. Elizabeth, m. ——— Douglass.
IV. Anne Evans (Nathan), b. 11, 4, 1722; m. Eleazor Evans; d. 11, 1, 1763; son of David Evans, of Berks county, Pa. They had issue (surname Evans):
  i. Eleazor.
  ii. John.
  iii. David.
  iv. [a dau.] m. John Hinton.
  v. Amos.
  vi. Nathan.
  vii. Sarah.
  viii. [a dau] m. John Pugh.
  iy. Joseph.
V. James Evans (Nathan), b. 2, 8; 1724; d. 10, —, 1801. He was sergeant Fourth Battalion, Berks county militia, and a man of prominence during the War for Independence. He m., in 1750, Elizabeth Thomas. They had issue:
  9. i. Nathan, b. 11, 27, 1752; m. Elizabeth Jones.
  10. ii. William, b. 3, 3, 1756; m. Ann Shay.
  11. iii. James, b. 1762; m. Ann Cunningham.
  iv. John, d. 4, 19, 1794, unm.
  v. Caleb, m. Sarah Edwards, dau. of Daniel Edwards, and had issue:

1. Caleb, d. unm.
vi. Susanna.
VI. Mary Evans (Nathan), b. 2, 6, 1726; m. first, Thomas Nicholas; d. 1760; son of Mordecai Nicholas. They had issue (surname Nicholas):
  i. Thomas, m. Miss English, dau. of Thomas English, of Berks county, and they had issue (surname Nicholas):
    1. Thomas.
  ii. Susanna.
  iii. Bridget.
  iv. Ann.
Mary Evans Nicholas, m. secondly, Thomas Jones, of Berks county, and they had issue (surname Jones):
  i. Samuel.
  ii. Martha.
  iii. Susanna.
  iv. Sarah.
  v. Mary.
VII. Evan Evans (Evan, Nathan). He m. Feb. 25, 1777, Mary Jones, b. 12, 17, 1756; d. 1, 16, 1791; dau. of David and Elizabeth (Davies) Jones. Elizabeth Davies is supposed to be a sister of Susanna, wife of Nathan Evans. They had issue:
12. i. Eleanor, b. 2, 17, 1778; m. George Rigg.
  ii. Elizabeth m. James Evans, son of Nathan and Elizabeth (Jones) Evans, dau. of David and Elizabeth (Davies) Jones. [See family under James Evans.]
  iii. Samuel.
  iv. Mary.
VIII. John Evans (John, Nathan), b. 1754; d. 8, 11, 1813. He m. 3, 9, 1799, Margaret Jones, dau. of Col. Jonathan Jones and his wife Margaret Davis. Colonel Jonathan Jones was a son of David and Elizabeth (Davies) Jones. They had issue:
  i. Reese, b. 1800.
  ii. David, b. 1802; m. Margaret Evans. [See under family of James Evans.]
  iii. Jonathan-Jones, b. 1804.
13. iv. John-Clarkson, b. 1806; m. Ann Jones.
14. v. Nathan, b. 1808; m. Ann Barde.
  vi. Ann, b. 2, 1, 1810; d. 1825.
  vii. George-Washington, b. 5, 1, 1812; surgeon U. S.. N.; lost on ship Pulaski, 8, 9, 1838.

IX. Nathan Evans (James, Nathan), b. 11, 27, 1752; d. 6, 27, 1802. He m. Elizabeth Jones, b. 8, 19, 1754; d. 5, 12, 1823; dau. of David Jones and sister of Col. Jonathan Jones. They had issue:
15. i. Margaret, m. David Evans.
16. ii. James, m. Elizabeth Evans.
17. iii.Susanna, m. John Carson.
  iv. Mary, b. 10, 19, 1781; d. 10, 17, 1841.
  v. Elizabeth, b. 8, 28, 1786; d. 8, 26, 1833; m. 6, 11, 1821, David Jones.
18. vi. Gabriel-Davies, b. 9, 17, 1788; m. Mary McCadden.
  vii. Sarah, b. 6, 24, 1792; d. 8, 8, 1878; m. James Beck, and had issue (surname Beck):
    1. Richard; resides Fairfield, Iowa.
    2. William.
    3. James.
    4. David.
  viii. David Jones, b. 7, 14, 1797; d. 5, 25, 1859; m. Mary Moore.
X. William Evans (James, Nathan), b. 3, 3, 1756; d. 1, 1, 1808, at Churchtown, Pa. He m. Ann Shay, of Churchtown. They had issue:
  i. Mary.
  ii. Jehu.
  iii. Abner.
  iv. Dr. Thomas-Barton, of Wrightsville.
  v. Elizabeth.
  vi. Margaret.
  vii. William.
  viii. [a dau.] m. —— Lloyd, of Columbia, Pa., and had issue (surname Lloyd):
    1. William.
    2. Mary.
    3. Ann.
    4. Dr. Barton.
  ix. Edmund, m, Miss Sterrett.
XI. James Evans (James, Nathan), b. 1762; d. 4, 12, 1802. He m. 1, 22, 1794, Ann Cunningham, b. 1, 22, 1764; d. 5, 14, 1838; dau. of James and Rebecca Cunningham, of Earl township, James being a son of Joseph Cunningham, of Salisbury and Earl townships, of Lancaster county, Pa. They had issue:
19. ii. Hiram, m. Ann Davies.
20. ii. Rebecca, m. Abraham Bruner.
  iii. Davies.
XII. Eleanor Evans (Evan, Nathan),

b. 2, 17, 1778; d. 5, 23, 1855. She m. 7, 4, 1797, George Rigg. They had issue (surname Rigg):
1. George-Davis.
2. Mary-Ann.
3. Eleanor.
4. Hiram-Evans.
5. Margaret, m. Edward Jacksen.
ii. Hiram, m. Rebecca Tumbleston.
iii. Eliza-Jones.
iv. George-Evans, m. Catherine Ziemer, and had issue (surname Rigg):
1. Rachel.
2. John.
3. Isabella.
4. Mary, m. John Clemenson.
5. Harriet, m. Levi Shirk, and had issue (surname Shirk): Catherine, m. Neal Graham.
6. Emily, m. John Kersey, and had issue (surname Kersey): Esther and Florence.
v. Samuel, m. first, 1, 8, 1829, Ellen Shaner, and had issue (surname Rigg):
1. Eliza J., m. Jacob Geiger and had issue (surname Geiger): Olmer.
2. Rebecca.
3. Phoebe.
4. Mary-Ellen.
Samuel Rigg m. secondly 4, 22, 1847, Catherine Styer, and had issue (surname Rigg):
5. Sarah J., m. Martin H. Rosen, and issue (surname Rosen): Irwin and Milton A.
6. Samuel E., m. Ella Ammon.
7. John-Adams, m. Sarah A. Baum, and had issue (surname Rigg): Dorothea, Walter and Samuel.
vi. Rachel, m. 1833, Edward Jackson.
vii. John-Evans, m. 1838, Mary A. Kellar, and had issue (surname Rigg):
1. Heber.
2. Edward.
3. Eleanor.
4. Elizabeth.
5. Sarah.
6. Caroline.
viii. Robert-Coleman.
ix. Reese-Evans, m. Jane Finger, and had issue (surname Rigg):
1. Robert.
2. John.
3. Edward.
4. George.
5. Annie.
6. Lillie.
7. Rebecca.
x. Mary-Ann.
XIII. John Clarkson Evans (John, John, Nathan), b. 1806, was a member of the Pennsylvania Legislature. He m. Ann Jones, dau. of Caleb and Mary (Whitman) Jones. They had issue:
i. David, m. 1st, Rebecca Johnson; m. 2dly, Fanny Bell.
ii. Clara, m. Adam Bard, of Reading, Pa., and had issue (surname Bard):
1. Anna C.
2. Emily.
3. Adam.
iii. Elizabeth-Douglass.
iv. George-Washington, m. Harriet Buckley, and had issue:
1. John N.
2. David-Jones.
v. Ann-Jones.
vi. Nathan, m. Matilda Cochran, and had issue:
1. Clara-B.
2. Lottie.
3. Nathan.
4. John C.
5. Lulu B.
vii. Sarah, m. Gaston Bender, and had issue (surname Bender):
1. John R.
2. Anthony.
3. Helen.
XIV. Nathan Evans (John, John, Nathan), b. circa, 1810. He m. Ann Barde. They had issue:
i. Louisa.
ii. Charles.
iii. Annie.
iv. George, m. Annie ———, and they had issue:
1. George.
2. Horace.
3. Helen.
4. Louisa.
v. Clement, m. Lizzie Chambers, and they had issue:
1. Frank-Howell.
2. Gertrude.
3. Horace, m. Louise Rosengarden, and had Harry.
vi. Mary, m. Louis Garrigues, and had issue (surname Garrigues):
1. Emily.

2. Edward.
3. Horace.
XV. Margaret Evans (Nathan, James, Nathan). She was twice married; m. first, David Evans, son of John and Margaret (Jones) Evans; no issue. She m. secondly, James Kinkead. They had issue (surname Kinkead):
  i. Eliza, m. William Thompson, of Mt. Vernon, O., and had issue (surname Thompson):
    1. William.
  ii. Margaret, m. William M. Woods, of Allegheny, Pa., and had issue (surname Woods):
    1. Mary.
XVI. James Evans (Nathan, James, Nathan). He m: in 1801, Elizabeth Evans, dau. of Evan and Mary (Jones) Evans (see vii). They had issue:
  i. Elizabeth, b. 7, 6, 1804; living (1899); m. John B. Ebelhare, of Honey Brook, Pa. They had issue (surname Ebelhare):
    1. Samuel.
    2. Ann.
    3. James, m. Hannah Buchanan.
    4. Frederick.
    5. Ellen, m. Thomas Walker, and had issue (surname Walker):
      a. Mary-C., m. George Fabian, and had Martha and Ann.
      b. Samuel-C.
      c. Ann-E., m. Richard Frederick, and had Rachel, Ellen and Laura.
      d. Warren, m. Emma Search, and had Edith and Henry.
      e. Eliza-Ellen.
    6. Julia-Ann, m. Thomas Carpenter, and had issue (surname Carpenter):
      a. Charles, m. Laura Lister, and had Elsie, Minnie and Charles.
      b. Emma.
      c. William.
    7. John-Davies.
    8. Sarah-Ann, m. William Kennedy, and had issue (surname Kennedy):
      a. George.
      b. John.
      c. Minnie.
      d. Flora, m. E. A. White, and had Earl and Harold.
      e. Bena, m. John Kennedy.
      f. Lillie.
      g. Laura.
    9. Robert, m. Susan Ammon and had issue (surname Ebelhare):
      a. John.
      b. Clarence.
      c. Lizzie, m. L. Davidson, and had Hollis, James and Susan.
      d. Ida.
      e. James.
      f. Levi.
      g. Ellen.
      h. Celia.
      i. Dora.
      j. Edward.
      k. Francis.
      l. Viola.
    10. Hiram.
    11. Oliver-Perry.
    12. Mary E., m. John Tresler.
    13. George-Davies.
  ii. Eleanor; m. Cornelius Preston, and had issue (surname Preston):
    1. William.
  iii. Sarah.
  iv. James.
  v. Oliver-Perry.
XVII. Susanna Evans (Nathan, James, Nathan) She m. John Carson, who was a grandson of Thomas and Mary (Evans) Nicholas, the latter a dau. of Nathan Evans (first). They had issue (surname Carson):
  i. Sarah.
  ii. Margaret.
  iii. Mary.
  iv. William.
  v. John; m. Ann Lawrence, and had issue (surname Carson):
    1. John; m. Clara Segner, and had issue:
      a. William-Harrison.
      b. Mary.
      c. Charles.
      d. Davis.
      e. Ann-Elizabeth.
      f. Hannah.
  vi. Davies-Evans; m. Elizabeth Townsley and had issue (surname Townsley):
    1. Horace-C.
    2. Margaret.
  vii. Hiram-Evans.
  viii. Barton-Evans; m. Elizabeth McCormick, and had issue (surname Carson):
    1. Benjamin-Franklin.

2. James-Harrison.
3. Susan-A.
4. Barton-Evans.
5. Jennie.
iv. William-Henry-Harrison; m. Isabella Gillespie, and had issue (surname Carson):
  1. Lily.
  2. Emma.
  3. Edward.
  4. Charles.
  5. Ellsworth.
  6. Howard.
  7. Christie.
x. Mary-Evans.
xi. Uriah-B.-Waddell.
xii. Annette; d. inf.
xiii. Grier; m. Lydia Waddell and had issue (surname Carson):
  1. Walter.
  2. Mary.
  3. Charles.
xiv. Annette (second); m. Uriah Waddell, and had issue (surname Waddell):
  1. John.
  2. George.

XVIII. Gabriel Davies Evans (Nathan, James, Nathan, b. 9, 17, 1788; d. 8, 26, 1833. He m. 1, 4, 1821, Mary McCadden, dau. of John and Elizabeth (Silverthorn) McCadden, of Chester county, Pa. They had issue:
 i. William-Davies; m. Mary A. Evans; reside at Malvern, Iowa.; they had issue:
  1. Ida-L., m. Oscar H. Snyder, Plattsburg, Mo.
  2. Joseph-G., m. Sue L. Deckert, Pasco, Wash.
  3. Mary-Ruth, m. William F. Levan, Biloxi, Miss.
  4. Ann-Florence, m. Charles F. Goodwin.
  5. Elizabeth-Jones, m. Zach. T. Lindsay, Omaha, Neb.
  6. George-Davies, m. Ada M. Garretson.
  7. William-Morris, m. Georgie Moore, Malvern, Iowa.
  8. Paul-Whiting, m. Addie Rightmeyer.
  9. Ethel.
  10. Edith-M., m. Judge Joseph R. Reed, Council Bluffs, Iowa.
 ii. Elizabeth-Silverthorn, m. Isaac H. Tallman, Miles, Indian Territory.
 iii. Margaret-L., m. Darwin C. Smith, Tarkio, Mo.
 iv. Sarah-Beck.
 v. John.
 vi. Samuel-Sparks, m. Endarmile Bayless, Tarkio, Mo.
 viii. David-James, m. Ellen Barwell, Detroit, Mich.
 viii. George-VanHorn.

XIX. Hiram Evans (James, James, Nathan). He m. 1, 14, 1819, Ann Davies. They had issue:
 i. Isaac, m. Susan Groff, and they had issue:
  1. Annie.
  2. Blanche.
  3. Hiram.
 ii. James-C., m. Emma Barber.
 iii. Davies-W.
 iv. Andrew-J.
 v. Lydia-Ann.
 vi. Rebecca-E., m. Henry Evans.
 vii. Hiram.

XX. Rebecca Evans (James, James, Nathan). She m. 12, 14, 1814, Abraham Bruner, of Columbia, Penna. They had issue (surname Bruner):
 i. James-Evans.
 ii. Owen.
 iii. Davies-Evans, a lawyer of Columbia, Pa., m. Mary M. Pastorius, and they had issue (surname Bruner):
  1. Davies-Evans.
  2. Daniel-Pastorius, m. Helen S. Fleming.
  3. Rebecca-Tacy.
  4. Abraham, m. Emma R. Boisseau, dau. of Judge James Boisseau, of Petersburg, Va., and had issue—Francis D. Pastorius.
 iv. John-Fletcher.
 v. Ann-Eliza, m. Rev. Alfred Cookman, son of Rev. George G. Cookman, and had issue (surname Cookman):
  1. Alfred-Bruner.
  2. George-G., m. Margaret E. Clarendon, and had Earl-Clarendon.
  3. Rev. Frank-S., m. Mary Hearst.
  4. Anne-Bruner, m. Schurman Halstead, and had issue:
  5. Rev. William W., m. Carrie Taft and had issue:
   a. Alfred.
   b. Carrie.
   c. Annie.

d. William.
  6. Rebecca-Evans.
  7. Mary, m. Sigourney Fay Clark and had issue (surname Clark):
    a. Elizabeth.
    b. Rebecca.
  8. Helen-Kier.
  9. Dr. Alfred.
vi. Rebecca, m. Rev. Joseph B. Dobbins.
viii. Abraham, m. Sarah J. Breneman, and had issue (surname Bruner):
  1. Mary-E., m. Wiliam B. Given, and had issue (surname Given):
    a. Ezra.
    b. Jennie.
    c. William.
    d. Mary.
  2. Alfred-Cookman, m. Annie M. Bruner, dau. of Henry F. Bruner, and had issue:
    a. Abraham.
    b. Henry.
    c. Alfred.
  3. Henry.
  4. William-E., m. Lillie Clark.
  5. James.
viii. Emma.
ix. Cyrus, m. Rebecca J. Groff, and had issue (surname Bruner):
  1. Helen-Groff.
  2. James-Evans.
  3. Elizabeth-Evans.

*Margaret Jones Evans, widow of John Evans, m. secondly, in 1814, Peter Bechtel, and had issue (surname Bechtel).
  i. Caroline, m. Joseph Levan, of Reading.
  ii. Amelia.

NOTES AND QUERIES.

Historical, Biographical, and Genealogical.

XXXIII.

STERRETT.

To what Sterrett family did John and Benjamin Sterrett belong? They took out patent for land together in Donegal township, Lancaster county, in 1738. In 1742 John alone took out patent in Antrim township, Cumberland county, where he died in 1762. In his will he makes a bequest to "Mary, the daughter of Benjamin Sterrett," who was not yet of age and from terms of will appears to have lived in John's family.   C. V. Carlisle.

A Masonic Funeral in 1779.

[The following we copy from the Wilkes-Barre Record of recent date. During the War of the Revolution warrants were issued for what were termed "Army Lodges," the most notable of which was Lodge 19, connected with Col. Proctor's artillery regiment of the Pennsylvania Line. It was this lodge which performed the Masonic services here narrated. After the war the warrant of No. 19, by special request of several of its survivors, was granted them, and the lodge at Norristown is in reality the successor of the Army Lodge of Proctor's artillery.]

As an advance detachment of General Sullivan's army was approaching the Valley of Wyoming in April, 1779, it was fired on by a small band of Indians lying in ambush at a point near where General Oliver's powder mills now are on Laurel Run, and Captain Joseph Davis and Lieut. William Jones, of a Delaware regiment, were slain. The bodies received a hasty burial near the spot where they fell, for soldiers on the march have little time to waste on sympathy. On the arrival of the invading army en route to accomplish its mission of forever wiping out the power of the once mighty Six Nations in the State of New York, in the month of July following, the remains were exhumed and reburied with imposing Masonic services by brother Masons belonging to the army. So far as is known, by either record or tradition, it was on this occasion that the first lodge of Free Masons ever met on this side of the Blue Mountains, was opened in due and ancient form in Colonel Proctor's marquee, which was probably pitched somewhere on what is now the Common on the river front of our city, the object being to arrange a funeral service for the re-interment of their brethren slain on the mountain the preceding April. We have no means of knowing whether the more solemn portion of the Masonic burial service took place in the secrecy of the lodge room at that time, as it does now, or not, but the following account of the imposing ceremony on depositing the bodies in the grave is copied from the Providence, Rhode Island, "Gazette" of Sept. 18, 1779:

"Wyoming, July 31, 1779.—On Tuesday last, the 28th inst., agreeable to previous determination, the bodies of our brethren, Capt. Joseph Davis and Lieut. William Jones, who were massacred by savages near this post on the 23d of April last, were re-interred. This mark of respect we thought necessary for the following reasons; it being expressive of our esteem and their not being buried in the proper grave-yard. The form of procession being fixed upon at Lodge No. 19, was as follows:

1. Twenty-four Musketeers with reversed arms.
2. Two Tylers bearing their swords.
3. A band of music.
4. Two Deacons with wands.
5. Three brethren bearing the orders.
6. The Holy Bible and Book of Constitutions.
7. Two Reverend brothers.
8. The Worshipful Master, with Hon. Major General Sullivan.
9. Senior and Junior Wardens, bearing their columns.
10. The Treasurer and Secretary.
11. Past Master.
12. The brethren, two and two.
13. Gentlemen of the Army.
14. Two corps of drums muffled and fifes playing a solemn dirge.

The brethren were neatly clothed with jewels, etc., and were in numbers odd of one hundred and fifty. Just as we arrived at the ground an exceeding easy gust of rain coming up prevented the delivery of a discourse which had been prepared for the occasion by Brother William Rogers, a short and suitable prayer being by him offered up. We then committed their bodies in Masonic form to the dust. Afterwards three vollies of small arms were discharged. The Brotherhood were attended by the Pennsylvania Regiment of Infantry, commanded by Col. Hubley, as likewise by a great concourse of people, both inhabitants and soldiery.

The melancholy scene was clothed with the usual decorum amongst the brethren and satisfaction to all the bystanders. A stone being prepared by our brethren Forest and Story with suitable inscription, was fixed at the head of their graves."

The first interment was on the top of the Wilkes-Barre Mountain, near where Charles Parrish's sylvan residence now is. The one here spoken of was within a few feet of Market and Washington streets, on ground now occupied by the skating rink, but they were not permitted to enjoy a final resting place even here. A marble headstone had taken the place of the rude one set by their Masonic brethren at the re-interment, so that the graves were readily recognized in after years, and when the removal of the bones of the forefathers of the hamlet were ruthlessly shoveled up by the unsympathizing stranger workmen not many years ago, and some of them removed to the new cemetery, the remains of these two victims of savage warfare were again dug up and removed to the Hollenback cemetery, and again interred with high Masonic ceremonies conducted by old Lodge 61, with Hendrick B. Wright as worshipful master; where it is hoped they may be permitted to rest in undisturbed repose until the last trumpet shall sound and bid the dead awake and come to judgment. W. J.

Lewis County.

Few persons in Pennsylvania have any recollection of the attempt made in 1820-22 to divide Lycoming county by erecting its then three most eastern townships—Elkland, Shrewsbury and Moreland—into a new county. The territory covered by these townships at that time would have included all of what is now Sullivan county, and perhaps a portion one-half or nearly as large as Sullivan from what is now the eastern part of Lycoming county. It was to be called Lewis county, and Mount Lewis was to be the county seat. Thus it will be seen that the attempt made by Judge Jones was not the first effort to have a town at the beautiful lake on the mountain.

George Lewis, Edward J. Eldred, William King, William Molyneux and several others were very active in this movement. Lewis and Eldred visited Harrisburg and spent considerable time trying to get the measure through. Joseph Priestly was also interested in the matter. Although very near, they were not quite successful. Had this scheme succeeded, George Lewis would no doubt have been in some measure remunerated for the vast amount of money he spent developing and starting the glass works at the lake, and Mr. Eldred would have received an appointment to an office to which he was so well qualified and justly merited.

Following will be seen the petition and a letter from George Lewis to Esq. Eldred which quite fully explains the matter. These documents were found among the papers of W. J. Eldred by his executors:

"To the Honorable, the Senate and House of Representatives of the Commonwealth of Pennsylvania in General Assembly Met:

"The petition of the undersigned inhabitants of Elkland, Shrewsbury and a part of the original township of Moreland, or new township of Penn, in the county of Lycoming, respectfully showeth

"That your petitioners are subject to great disadvantages, arising from the distance to their present county town, and the appropriation of their taxes which are drawn from them and expended far away, while their country being new, is consequently much in want of roads and bridges. The inconvenience of attending their present seat of justice at the distance of thirty or forty miles and upwards is thereby much increased. Your petitioners, therefore, pray that the Legislature will be pleased to direct that a separate county district be laid off, bounded at the following lines: Beginning at a post in the line of Northumberland county, a corner lately made on a division of the original township of Moreland into Penn as the corner of No. 103; from thence in a north and northwesterly direction along the dividing line between No. 103 and No. 102 to the line of Muncy Creek township; thence in a northerly direction along the line of Muncy Creek township to the southwest corner of Shrewsbury township; thence in a direct line to a point two miles below the mouth of Plunkett's Creek on the Loyal Sock Creek; thence continuing the course of the last mentioned line, to the hight of land which divides the waters of the Loyal Sock and Lycoming creeks; thence by several courses corresponding to the general course of the height of ground on the ridge which divides the waters of said creeks and continuing the like on the ridge that divides the waters of the two branches that is the West and North branches of the Susquehanna river to the southeast corner of Bradford county; thence on the line which divides Lycoming and Luzerne counties to the corner of Columbia county; thence along the line that divides Lycoming, Columbia and Northumberland counties to the place of beginning. Your petitioners claim a privilege somewhat peculiar to themselves which your Honorable body will duly appreciate. They do not sue to you for a new county to favor the specuative ideas of a few individuals. This petition breathes the voice of the people.

"It is the prayer of your petitioners that the county may be called Lewis county and that the seat of justice may be established at Mount Lewis on account of the central situation to the lines or boundary enumerated and from the accommodation that it presents, the proprietor having paid out a very large sum of money in erecting a glass house and a number of dwelling houses and having offered to give the use of a commodious house called the boarding house for all county purposes. Your petitioners further beg leave to represent to the Legislature, that in the event of this county being erected that it will promote the object which the Legislature has been solicitous about, namely, the encouragement of manufacturers, as it will prevent the hands being called to a great distance as jurors and other public duties."

In connection with the foregoing petition the letter of George Lewis to 'Squire Eldred, which follows, furnishes data of interest. The letter is dated at "Mount Lewis, Oct. 19, 1820:"

"Dear Sir:—I thank you for the able manner in which you have drawn up the petition and likewise for your letter to Mr. Priestley. Your attendance at Harrisburg does appear to be necessary. On the subject of money (although it is with me a very scarce article indeed), yet, rather than you should not attend, I will do what is needful if you will call at the store at Mount Lewis, and consult with Mr. C. Howlett before you go.

"I expect to meet you at Harrisburg, if you could contrive to be there on the commencement of the session that the petition may be early on the list.

"It appears to me that we must have a county judge and deputy surveyor even if we are promised to get you appointed by the Governor when it is right to apply. I will attend to it and expect likewise to see J. Priestley on the subject. If it was convenient for you to go out on the Berwick turnpike to see what Shiner is after and to represent our interests to the settlers, it might have a good effect. It is said that he is about to have a large town laid out and that he does even talk of its being a county town; if made proper use of in argument it will not injure us.

"If any matter occurs in my absence, be good enough to write to Mr. Howlett, who will forward it to New York.

"Should Mr. King be dilatory on the business of acquiring signatures, I must then leave you to attend to it, to get all we can is desirable. Should you go to the turnpike take it with you probably the less said there the better, least Shiner should be more on the alert.

"I remain respectfully yours,
"Geo. Lewis.
"To Edward J. Eldred, Esq.,
Liberty Hall, Elkland, Pa."

Although Mr. Lewis' new county project failed, and that enterprising gentleman passed from off the stage of action thirty years afterward, the county of Sullivan was formed, yet Lycoming was spared much of the territory to be embraced in the contemplated Lewis county.
ULYSSES BIRD.
Laporte, Pa.

Early Snyder County Families.

WITMER.

Peter Witmer, founder of the Witmer family, seated in the region contiguous to Sunbury, was born in 1737 in Hertzheim, Nassau-Dillenberg, Kingdom of Prussia. He was connected with the older Witmer family of Lancaster county, Pa. Coming to Pennsylvania when young, he married, in 1757, a Miss Marie Solomana, who was born in Upper Alsace, France (now Germany), October 24th, 1740. Rev. Handschue, a noted Lutheran divine, consummated the marriage. The early years of his married life were spent in Lancaster county.

In 1766 he located on a very large tract of land on the west side of the Susquehanna, one mile above the present village of Port Trevorton, in Snyder county. He effected his removal from Columbia to this place by means of a flat-boat. He was one of the first settlers of this region, and a prominent citizen. He died in July, 1793, leaving a wife and family of whom presently. Will filed at Sunbury, probated July 31, 1793. Over 300 acres of the estate is still in the hands of his descendants. The place was an important point in the early days. Witmer carried on a ferry, saw mill and distillery.

The children of Peter and Marie Witmer were the following. The reader's attention is called that five daughters were called Maria.):

i. George, b. April 23, 1758.
ii. Peter, b. Jan. 11, 1760.
iii. Maria-Catharine, b. July —? 1761.
iv. Maria- Solomana, b. Sept. 3, 1762.
v. John-Jacob, b. Feb. —, 1764.
vi. Maria-Magdalena, b. June —, 1766.
vii. Anna-Maria, b. Oct. —, 1767.
viii. Maria-Barbara, b. Jan. —, 1769.
ix. Samuel, b. April 4, 1771.
x. Margaretha, b. Dec. 28, 1772.

Of the above, George died in 1769, and John in 1778. Anna-Maria became the wife of John Motz and removed to Centre county. Maria Magdalena married John Thornton. He died 1816 (?) and the family with the widow, removed to Greensburg, Ohio. Some of the other daughters were also married to men whose names are unknown to the writer.

MOTZ.

I. In 1769, Casper Motz was the grantee of a tract of land near New Berlin, on Penn's Creek, in now Union county. Said Casper Motz was doubtless the John Casper "Mautz," aged 16 years, who, in 1731, arrived in Pennsylvania from Germany with his parents and settled in Oley, Berks county. If Casper Motz ever settled on this land he must have died before the erection of Northumberland county, as we do not find his name among the early taxables. Three brothers, John, Michael and George Motz, presumably sons of Casper Motz, appear in this region in Revolutionary days as taxables. Of these brothers we have the following data:

II. Michael Motz lived in Penn township (now Snyder county). His wife's maiden name was Moyer. He was a soldier of the Revolution. In 1785 he removed to the western extremity of Penn's Valley "Narrows," in Centre county, where Woodward is now situated, and died about 1823, aged about 85 years. He had children:
    i. John; killed accidentally when young.
    ii. Henry; m. Barbara Moyer.
    iii. Eve; m. John Wise.
    iv. Susan; m. George Wise.
    v. Catharine; m. Jacob Wise, who removed to Ohio at an early day.
    vi. Sophia; m. Abraham Hoca; removed to Stephenson county, Ill.
    vii. Rebecca; m. Conrad Wise; removed to Clearfield county, and from thence to "the West." It is a notable circumstance that four sisters married four brothers.

III. John Motz was born in 1758; married Anna Maria Witmer, daughter of Peter Witmer, the pioneer aforenamed. He was associated for some years with his father-in-law in the milling business. In 1785 he purchased a tract of land at the western extremity of Penn's Valley "Narrows," close to that of his brother Michael. Here he erected a large grist and saw mill, and laid the foundation of an extensive business, yet in the hands of his descendants. The thriving town of Woodward was built on the estate. He died here in 1802 and his widow in 1839. He was very sick when he made his will bequeathing his estate to his wife during her natural life and providing for the following children:
    i. John; m. Elisabeth Fisher, of Snyder county, and had children:
      1. Daniel.
      2. John-C.
      3. William.
      4. Lydia.
      5. Sarah.
      6. Catharine.
      7. Mary-Elisabeth.
Of the sons John C. alone reached manhood and inherited his father's business.
    ii. Jacob; m. Elisabeth Hess and had children:
      1. Samuel.
      2. John A.
      3. Emanuel.
      4. Simon.
      5. Mary.
    iii. George.
    iv. Salome.
    v. Susanna.
    vi. "A child expected"—who was named James.

IV. George Motz the third of the presumed sons of Casper Motz, lived near the present town of Middleburg, the county seat of Snyder county. In his will, on file at Sunbury, he says he is sick and anxious about his wife and children. He died in 1806 leaving a wife and children:
    i. John.
    ii. Lorentz.

His descendants still reside about Middleburgh.

BOWERSOX.

Paul Bowersox, founder of the Bowersox family of central Pennsylvania, arrived in Philadelphia in 1771, per brig "Betsy," from the Fatherland. There is an older branch established in Southeastern Pennsylvania, but their connection has not as yet been established. Paul Bowersox settled soon after his arrival in Penn township Northumberland (now Snyder) county where he died in 1806. He had children as follows:
    i. George Bowersox m. Mary Stonebruch. He lived and died near Paxtonville. His children were:
      1. John; m. Magdalena Walter.
      2. George; m. first Kate Clouser; secondly, Anna Berger.

3. Samuel; m. Susan Boyer.
4. Daniel; m. first, Sophia Walter; secondly, —— Kiester.
 ii. Jacob Bowersox, second son of the emigrant Paul, m. Magdalena Bolender, and had children:
1. Frederick; m. —— Long.
2. William; m. first, —— Reitz; secondly, Sarah Rearick.
3. Peter; m. Margaret Decker.
4. Reuben; m. Mary Rich.
5. Isaac; m. Leah Moyer.
6. Leah; m. David Weirick.
7. Amelia; m. Jacob Doebler.
8. Julia; m. John Kline.
9. Matilda; m. first, Henry Walter; secondly, Jonas Renninger.
10. John; m. Sarah Smith.
 iii. Michael Bowersox, third son of the emigrant, m. and had children:
1. David; m.
2. Paul.
3. Catharine; m. Daniel Doebler.
4. Mina.
5. Hannah.
Besides the foregoing the emigrant Bowersox had children of whom we have no data, as follows:
iv. David.
v. Eve; m. Philip Walter.
vi. Benjamin.
vii. John; d.
viii. [a dau.] m. —— Kauffman.
ix. [a dau.] m. —— Bullinger.
Note.—There is a branch of Bowersox established in Centre county who emanate from George and who came from Hanover, where his father, John Michael (who arrived in 1750), settled.
A. STAPLETON.
Carlisle, Pa.

NOTES AND QUERIES.

Historical, Biographical and Genealogical.

XXXIV.

ELDER.
I. Robert Elder, of Fannett township, Franklin county, made his will August 3, 1804 probated August 24, 1804. He left a wife, Susanna, and children:
i. Robert.
ii. William.
There were other children—names not given. The witnesses were Joseph Elder and Matthew Elder. The executors, John Elder and John and James Alexander.
II. Robert Elder, of Fannett township, Franklin county, made his will October 4, 1799, probated April 21, 1807. He left a wife Mary and children:
i. Joseph.
ii. Samuel.
iii. David.
iv. Abraham, of Huntingdon county.
v. Robert.
vi. Matthew.
There may have been other children. The witnesses were Robert Simeson and James Alexander. The executors were sons Joseph and Samuel.

FORTUNE-HUNTERS ABOUT.

Another Snare for the Deluded.

Notwithstanding the repeated admonitions to the "next of kin," every now and then somebody who is anxious to follow the instructions given by an Israelite to his hopeful, "My son make monish, honestly if you can, but anyhow make monish," sends out word to easily gullible people that "millions" are awaiting them. We have had a succession of these, from the Brosius, Baker and other marvelous tales of wealth only awaiting claimants, down to the Sitler family, the latest. It is a positive fact that no "ninety-nine year lease" has matured whereby property now worth "millions" is to be inherited; nor have any of our readers positive knowledge that "millions" of any foreign estate ever came to America. The whole thing is absurd, and any person who takes any stock in these humbugs well merits the contempt of sensible people. In order that our readers may see how gullible seekers after fortune are, we reprint the following from a recent Chambersburg newspaper:

"The Gillespies, Shuman and Cochrane families in Chambersburg are heirs in the Matthias Sitler, jr., estate, which is now receiving the attention of the descendants in Baltimore, Md., Pennsylvania and Central Illinois. The value of the estate is estimated at $75,000,000.

"This claim includes some of the land on which the City Hall and Ford's Opera House is built, and property on Fayette and Baltimore streets in the city of Baltimore. It consisted of about ten acres and was leased for ninety-nine years. The time is now about up. Some time ago a gentleman who is now in the employ of the Pennsylvania Railroad was sent to Baltimore to search the records. He reported that there were more than forty leases in good shape and about to expire. Also that the property was of inestimable value. As he is an expert employed by the above named company as a title searcher, it is presumed he knows what he is talking about."

The following is the brief report of the Sitler estate, as furnished by the Associated Press:

"An estate in Germany worth $63,000,000, and another in Baltimore worth $12,000,000 to $13,000,000 are claimed by the heirs of Matthias Sitler, first, a German baron, who died in 1745, and of his sons, Matthias, second, and Abraham. Mrs. Eliza E. Smith, of Chicago, is entitled to a $500,000 share of the joint property. W. J. Sitler, of Robinson, Ill., is one of the principal prosecutors of the claim.

"There are 200 heirs to the German estate and 150 claimants for a portion of the Baltimore property. The story told by the claimants is as follows:

"Matthias Sitler first lived at Frankfort-on-the-Main in the early part of the eighteenth century. He had vast wealth and was a strict Roman Catholic. His sons, Matthias, second, and Abraham, became adherents of Martin Luther, and the old man cut them adrift, first giving each a considerable sum of money. The old man made a will, leaving his property in charge of the crown to be delivered with its accumulation to the heirs of his sons 100 years after his death.

"The sons went to Baltimore in 1736. Matthias, second, put all his money into real estate. This he leased for ninety-nine year periods. When Matthias died he left between forty and fifty of these leases to his heirs, comprising an area of about ten acres in the city of Baltimore. The property is scattered in different sections."

Prehistoric Earth-Works in Central Pennsylvania.

The general impression prevails that the Aborigines of North America have left but few memorials of their occupancy east of the Mississippi Valley. The great works of Central and South America have been thoroughly explored and well described by competent archaeologists, while Davis, Baldwin, Squier, Lesquereaux, Conant, and others, have ably described the remains of the Mound Builders and Cliff Dwellers of North America. The works of the mound builders were formerly supposed not to extend farther East than Wheeling on the Ohio River, but unmistakable traces on the Monongahela River discovered in recent years extends their settlements into West Virginia and Pennsylvania.

When the whites arrived in Pennsylvania, they found a number of memorials which it is difficult to ascribe to the Delawares and other tribes then occupying the country. Among such works was an immense burial mound on the West Branch of the Susquehanna River. This mound which was situated at Hall's Station, three miles above Muncy, was over fifteen feet high when the first settlers arrived, about 1768. When Conrad Weiser visited it in 1737, he describes it as having the appearance of having been deserted beyond the memory of man. Some claim a recent origin for this mound from the fact that some steel tomahawks and other articles made by Europeans have been discovered among the remains; but this proves nothing, except that interments were made in it after the white man's arrival in America, while its origin may have been centuries before.

The earth work at Bryner's Bridge, near Academia, in Juniata county, was a still far more extensive affair. Besides the tumulus filled with human bones there was an enclosure of about three acres on an elevated plateau. It was semi-circular in form, and the banks were still three feet high within the memory of old residents. There were paved fireplaces and a step-way cut down the rocky embankment to Doyl's Run, which here enters the Tuscarora Creek. It is hardly probable that this was the work of the Tuscarora Indians, who came here from North Carolina to join the Iroquois Confederacy, long after Penn's arrival. Another earth work, and which has never before been described—at least to my knowledge—is situated near Potter's Bank, in Centre county. My first acquaintance with this memorial was in 1872, when I traveled through this region as an "itinerant" preacher. At that time it was a large circle, forty-six paces in diameter. The public road ran through it, one side being in a cultivated field and the ridge barely visible. The other side, however, was a virgin forest, and great trees, pine, hemlock, and oak, growing in the circle and on the embankment, which was about two feet high. The late John Blair Linn, Esq., informed me that he also visited the place to gather information concerning it, but no one could give a clue as to its origin. In company with William Lucas, Esq., who lives near by, I lately visited the place again in order to more fully describe it. The entire circle is now under cultivation, and its outlines can scarcely be made out. Its situation was on a well-rounded hill and commanded a beautiful view of Upper Penn's Valley. At the foot of the hill is Sinking Creek, and also a splendid spring, which supplied the dusky denizens with water. Flint chips and arrow heads are ofund on the hill in abundance. Michael Strohm, merchant and postmaster at Centre Hill, nearby this place, informed me that when he came here in 1835 as a boy from Lebanon county, the "Indian Fort," as they called it, was considered a great curiosity. The entire hill was then thickly wooded. When he came there, some of the first settlers were still living, who told him it had the same appearance as when they came, which was prior to the Revolution. I believe the place to have been of great importance to the Aborigines. It was situated on the great Indian path or trail, which led from the Tuscarora Valley—thence across the Juniata River westward through Big Valley—past Logan's Spring—over the Seven Mountains, thence it debouched into Penn's Valley, at the end of Tussey Mountain, near the circle under consideration—thence northward through the Allegheny Mountain, where it reached the West Branch of the Susquehanna near Karthaus. Considerable portions of this path are still traceable.

A. STAPLETON.
Carlisle, Pa.

TOMBSTONE INSCRIPTIONS

Middle Spring Church, Cumberland County, Pa.

Lower Graveyard.

Barklow, Abraham, b. May 4, 1785; d. May 10, 1842.
Brackenridge, Nancy, wife of John Brackenridge and dau. of James Colwell, b. Dec. 1, 1776; d. Jan. 10, 1803.
Brackenridge, Margaret, wife of John Brackenridge, b. .1782; d. May 20, 1850.
Brackenridge, John, b. 1771; d. July 5, 1851.
Brackenridge, James Colwell and Mary Ann, son and dau. of John and Nancy Brackenridge; also infant son of John and Margaret Brackenridge.
Brackenridge, John, son of John and Margaret Brackenridge, b. 1809; d. March 9, 1833.
Brackenridge, Mrs. Mary Ann, wife of John Brackenridge, b. 1809; d. May 1, 1837.
Brackenridge, William Findley, son of John and Margaret Brackenridge, b. Nov. 1, 1812; d. Nov. 24, 1852.
Colwell, Agnes, wife of late James Colwell, d. August 5, 1804, in the 65th year of his age.
Colwell, Kezia, wife of John Colwell and dau. of Samuel and Mary Cox, b. July 12, 1783; d. May 15, 1804.
Colwell, Martha, relict of John Colwell and dau. of David and Jane King, b. Jan. 1775; d. Dec. 3, 1856.

Cox, Mary, wife of Samuel Cox and dau. of Thomas and Catharine McComb, b. 1760; d. Jan. 18, 1810.
Cummins, Thomas, b. 1760; d. August 8, 1810.
Duncan, Hugh, b. 1823; d. at Ogdensburg, N. Y., Aug. 11, 1865.
Duncan, Isabella, b. April 18, 1797; d. Jan. 25, 1872.
Edgar, Samuel Charles, son of David and Mary Edgar, b. March, 1784; d. Dec. 22, 1811.
Herron, Margaret, consort of James Herron, b. 1766; d. Sept. 16, 1807.
Herron, James, b. 1754; d. Auril 21, 1829.
Johnston, John, b. March 13, 1793; d. June 10, 1846.
Johnston, Elizabeth Brackenridge, wife John Johnston, b. May 28, 1800; d. Sept. 7, 1856.
Johnston, Major Joseph, b. Oct. 11, 1811; d. Feb. 28, 1860.
Johnston, Sarah, b. Jan. 11, 1790; d. May 21, 1828.
Johnston, Jane, consort of Benjamin Johnston, d. Feb. 23d, in 65th year of her age.
Johnston, Benjamin, b. 1760; d. Sept. 11, 1833.
Johnston, Rebecca, b. Sept. 1, 1800; d. Nov. 20, 1881.
Johnston George, b. Sept. 25, 1799; d. May 23, 1884.
Johnston, Sarah, wife of George Johnston, Esq., b. Jan. 6, 1806; d. March 31, 1859.
Johnston, Robert, b. 1804; d. March 25, 1841.
Johnston, Samuel, b. 1727; d. April 4, 1777; also
Johnston, Mary, consort of Samuel Johnston, b. 1728; d. Nov. 5, 1794.
Mahon, David, b. 1744; d. Oct. 5, 1813.
Mahon, Sarah, consort of David Mahon, b. 1752; d. Dec. 23, 1839.
Maclay, David, Esq., b. 1762; d. Feb. 20, 1839; on same stone.
Maclay, Eleanor, dau. Hon. Samuel Maclay, of Northumberland county, Pa., who died 4th day of April, 1802, in the 25th year of her age.
Maclay, Eleanor, wife of David Maclay and dau. of John Herron, Esq., b. 1784; d. Feb. 23, 1825.

"Death gives us more than was in Eden lost."
McCune, Robert, b. 1753; d. Aug. 29, 1816.
McCune, Mary, consort of Robert McCune, b. 1761; d. Feb. 4, 1837.
McCune, Robert, b. 1795; d. Oct. 30, 1857.
McCune, Elizabeth, wife of Robert McCune, b. 1794; d. Dec. 11, 1863.
Patterson, Eleanor Peebles, wife of Francis G. Patterson, b. Aug. 7, 1803; d. March 13, 1843.
Patterson, Francis G., b. Dec. 1, 1789; d. Jan. 21, 1850.
Pomeroy, Mary A., wife of Thomas Pomeroy and dau. of Col. Stephen Wilson, b. May 30, 1811; d. Dec. 8, 1882.
Reynolds, John, Esq., b. 1749; d. Oct. 20, 1789.
Renshaw, Isabella, wife of Simpson Renshaw, b. Dec. 1808; d. July, 1841.
Ritchie, John, b. Jan. 7, 1766; d. Feb. 4, 1814.
Ritchie, Mary, consort of John Ritchie, b. March 1, 1765; d. Oct. 26, 1844.
Sumerville, David, b. 1749; d. Sept., 1749; also
Martha, his wife, b. 1759; d. May 3, 1831.
Sumerville, Margaret, dau. of the above, b 1781; d. Jan. 23, 1847.
Wright, George, Sr., b. 1714; d. March 26, 1779.
Wright, Susanna, wife of George Wright, b. 1726; d. Dec. 11, 1781.

Upper Graveyard.

Frazer, Andrew, b. March 1, 1789; d. March 29, 1829.
Frazer, Annie Wilson, wife of Andrew Frazer, b. Oct. 5, 1799; d. Dec. 8, 1857.
Fulton, William, b. 1738; d. Sept. 3, 1803.
Fulton, Elizabeth, relict of William Fulton, b. 1739; d. July 4, 1828.
Fulton, Margaret, b. 1769; d. Nov. 22, 1816.
Fulton, Jane, b. 1800; d. April 18, 1830.
Fulton, William, Jr., d. July 28, 1837; aged about 66 years.
Fulton, James, b. 1757; d. Nov. 25, 1820.
Hemphill, Cynthia Jack, wife of James

Hemphill and dau. of James and Jane Jack, of Big Spring, b. 1767; d. Feb. 19, 1827.

Hemphill, Martha Strain, wife of James Hemphill and dau. of William and Jane Strain, b. 1773; d. July 30, 1830.

Hemphill, James, b. Jan. 10, 1770; d. July 25, 1852.

Herron, Mary, wife of John Herron and dau. of James and Jane Jack, b. 1753; d. Jan. 28, 1808.

Herron, John, Esq., b. 1750; d. Oct. 2, 1815.

Herron, Jane, wife of John Herron, b. 1761; d. Oct. 3, 1815.

Lindsay, Margaret M., wife of Thomas Lindsay, b. 1812; d. April 19, 1884.

McKnight, John, b. 1769; d. May 6, 1855.

McKnight, Elizabeth, wife of John McKnight, b. Aug. 19, 1790; d. Feb. 3, 1865.

McKnight, Jane, b. Feb., 1823; d. Jan. 28, 1858.

Nevin, Margaret, b. at the residence of her father, John Williamson, on the banks of Octoraro Creek, Lancaster county, Oct. 21, 1741; d. at Shippensburg May 2, 1822.

Nevin, Daniel, b. in city of New York, Aug. 23, 1744; d. at his residence on Herron's Branch, Dec., 1815.

Nevin, John, b. 1777; d. Oct. 19, 1829.

Nevin, Martha M., b. 1779; d. Feb. 12, 1854.

Reynolds, William, b. Aug. 24, 1769; d. Nov. 3, 1824.

Reynolds, Elizabeth, wife of William Reynolds, b. Nov. 21, 1773; d. June 26, 1848.

Reynolds, William, b. May 5, 1798; d. July 4, 1873.

Rodgers, Rachel, wife of Richard Rodgers, b. 1748; d. April, 1812.

Rodgers, Denny, son of Richard and Rachel Rodgers, b. Dec., 1784; d. March, 1831.

Smith, John, b. 1766; d. Nov. 17, 1836.

Smith, Elizabeth, b. 1772; d. Feb. 7, 1854.

A. H. W.
Carlisle, Pa.

NOTES AND QUERIES.

Historical, Biographical and Genealogical.

XXXV.

RYAN.

Isaac Ryan and Hannah Townsend were married October 24, 1774, at old Swede's Church, Wilmington, Delaware, by the Rev. Lawrence Girelius, and had issue:
i. Joseph.
ii. John.
iii. Ann.
iv. Abner.
v. Issac.

Isaac Ryan, son of Isaac, married Sophia Davis, August 16, 1808, at Trinity Lutheran Church, Lancaster, Pa., by Rev. G. H. E. Muhlenberg.

Can any reader of Notes and Queries furnish data showing to what families of Townsend and Davis, Hannah Townsend and Sophia Davis belonged? They were both supposed to belong to Chester county families.

S. M. S.

Sturgeon Family Re-union.

A correspondent has sent us a clipping from a Beaver Falls, Pa., newspaper, giving an account of a reunion of the Sturgeon family at the old homestead at Oakdale, Allegheny county, Pa., on August 24, 1899, at which time there were assembled thirty of the collateral relatives. The place where the reunion was held was purchased by Henry Sturgeon in 1790 and has never passed out the Sturgeon name and is still owned by Samuel H. and Joseph Sturgeon. A more beautiful spot could not have been selected as well as appropriate for the first reunion. It was a beautiful morning and as the trains from the east and west arrived the relatives were taken to the home of Joseph Sturgeon, which is located on a high elevation overlooking the surrounding country and the villages of Noblestown and Ooakdale, the latter being built on what was formerly a part of the original farm.

The history of the different branches of the Sturgeon family was given by Miss Margaret S. Sturgeon, of Candor, Pa., who gave a history of the Adams county branch, which extended back over a period of 200 years, showing that the Sturgeons were originally Hollanders, carrying the linen trade to Ireland; and the first to come to his country was Jeremiah Sturgeon with his two sons in 1720 and located near Harrisburg, Pa. From them have come the descendants who were represented at this reunion. John Calvin Sturgeon, Esq., of Erie, Pa., who also has been quite active in securing a history of the Dauphin county branch and in his recital gave much the same history as the Sturgeon ancestry.

Three Venerable Couples.

[Our "ancient" friend, Gernerd, in a communication to "The Muncy Luminary," furnishes the following facts concerning more "ancient" inhabitants of the West Branch Valley. Along with this comes the information that our "venerable" friend of the Otzinachson will be "at home" on Wednesday, the twenty-fifth of October. Although premature, we extend our warmest congratulations to the distinguished historian of the West Branch, and his amiable wife.]

Mr. John F. Meginness, in his recently published and very interesting Annals of Montoursville, says that place "can probably boast of having the oldest married couple of any town in the county. Mr. Jonathan O. Crawford and Abigail Wilson, his wife, celebrated the fifty-seventh anniversary of their marriage on the 3d of October, 1898."

When the aged historian of the West Branch of the Susquehanna made this statement he was of course not aware that Muncy can boast of having a married couple still older. We would therefore call attention to the fact that our esteemed citizens, J. Roan Barr and Cassandra Smith Miller were married July 7th, 1840, and that they had commenced their matrimonial life one year and nearly three months before Mr. and Mrs. Crawford, of Montoursville, were married.

Muncy's most venerable married pair can next July celebrate their sixtieth wedding anniversary—an event that comparatively few married couples ever live to commemorate. "A golden wedding (50 years) is of rare occurrence," says Meginness, when speaking of Mr. and Mrs. Crawford, "but a fifty-seventh anniversary is rarer." And a sixtieth is still more remarkable.

How many changes in our town and neighborhood this aged couple have lived to witness. Mr. Barr remarked to us a few days ago that he came to Muncy and united with the Presbyterian Church in the spring of 1839, and that of nearly one hundred communicants of that period he is now the only one still remaining with the congregation. He suffers greatly at times from rheumatism—an affliction not often fatal, but one that is very trying, and of which Saint Paul is supposed to have complained when he spoke of "a thorn in the flesh"—but he has a good, strong constitution, otherwise enjoys the best of health, and says he can hardly realize that his eighty-sixth birthday will come on the 17th day of next February.

Mr. John F. Meginness and his esteemed wife, Martha Jane King, are also a truly venerable couple, as they were united in marriage way back in October, 1849, and will therefore in a few more days celebrate their golden wedding.

Mr. Meginness still handles a pen with apparently unabated vigor, but he is not nearly so active on foot as he was in 1847 and 8 when he was one of the few of the Fifth United States infantry who had the distinction of carrying a musket, with forty rounds of ammunition and a lot of accoutrements, from Vera Cruz to the City of Mexico and all the way back again, without once falling out of rank and taking a ride in a wagon. If the Mexican musket ball that grazed his body in a fight with guerillas on the old battle ground of Cerro Gordo had laid him under the dust of Mexico, he would never have written the twenty or more historical and genealogical books and pamphlets of which he is now the distinguished author. If the guerilla did not make a very good shot, he certainly made a very good miss.

May these esteemed couples of Williamsport, Montoursville and Muncy live long into the twentieth century, enjoy life to the last, and have yet many happy wedding anniversaries. J. M. M. G.

THE EPHRATA COMMUNITY,

Its Graveyard and Tombstone Record

[One of the easliest German settlements in the Province of Pennsylvania, was that on the Cocalico, in Lancaster county. The following transcript of the tombstone record in this ancient burial place of that peculiar sect was made several years ago. As many of the descendants of these people are scattered over many States of the Union, no doubt this record will be greatly appreciated.
E. W. S. P.]

Addams, Orion, b. March 22, 1833; d. Dec. 25, 1856.
Bauman, Sarah, b. Oct. 30, 1776; d. July 30, 1792.
Bauman, Joseph, b. Jan. 16, 1808; d. Feb. 24, 1859.
Bauman, Benjamin, b. Jan. 22, 1784; d. Feb. 22, 1828.
Bauman, Elizabeth, b. March 15, 1783; d. May 19, 1850.
Bollinger, Hannah, wf. of David and dau. of John Fahnestock, b. 1780; d. 1867.
Bauman, Joseph, b. July 10, 1796; d. May 11, 1872.
Bauman, Mary, wf. of Daniel, b. June 4, 1803; d. Sept. 22, 1886.
Bauman, Daniel, b. April 1, 1796; d. Sept. 22, 1886.
Bauman, Peter, b. Sept. 14, 1791; d. Feb. 18, 1857.
Bauman, Hannah, wf. of Peter, b. Jan. 18, 1791; d. Oct. 17, 1856.
Bauman, Samuel, b. June 5, 1788; d. April 8, 1820.
Bauman, William, b. Aug. 8, 1791; d. April 9, 1826.
Bauman, Susannah, nee Weaver, b. Oct. 7, 1788; d. Oct. 9, 1875.
Bucher, Polly, b. July 2, 1823; d. April 5, 1825.
Bucher, Catharine, wf. of Benedict, nee Mellinger, b. Dec. 3, 1795; d. Jan. 26, 1849.
Binkley, Elizabeth, wf. of Henry, b. Jan. 4, 1792; d. June 21, 1878.
Binkley, Elizabeth, b. July 14, 1824; d. April 28, 1866.
Bechtle, Lusella, wf. of John, b. Sept. 2, 1830; d. May 29, 1866.
Binkley, Henry L., b. May 6, 1799; d. May 8, 1855.
Brenizer, Harriet, wf. of J. B., nee Gorgas, b. February 24, 1839; d. April 27, 1865.
Bollinger, John b. March 12, 1799; d. Oct. 18, 1850.

Hier ruht eine ungfbint der Liebe Gottes,
FRIEDSAM.
Ein einsamer nachmals
aber geworden an unsirhrer unssehern Lehrer
der Linsamen u. Geineine
Chrissi in u. um Ephrata.
Geborn in Eberbach im
der Pfaltz, genent Conrad
Beissel, entschlief den 6 ten
Julius A. O. 1768, Seiner
Geistlichen Lebens 52 aber
des naturchen 77 jahr, 4
monat.

[The translation read as follows.]

Here rests an outgrowth of the love of God "Friedsam," a solitary brother, afterwards a leader and religious teacher of the solitary and the Congregation of Grace in and around Ephrata. Born in Eberbach, Palatinate, called Conrad Beissel. Fell asleep July 6, 1768, in the 52d year of his spiritual life, but the 72d year and 4th month of his natural life.

Connell, Moore, b. Sept. 26, 1830; d. Aug. 9, 1881.
Carter, Matilda, b. 1802; d. Aug. 20, 1855.
Davis, Johannes, b. May 21, 1780; d. Jan. 24, 1829.
Dewees, Elizabeth, b. May 11, 1779; d. July 13, 1849.
Dishong, Dietrich W., b. Feb. 2, 1767; d. Sept. 27, 1845.
Deshong, Hannah, b. Oct. 29, 1768; d. June 29, 1830.

Fahnestock, Diedrich, b. Feb. 2, 1696; d. Oct. 10, 1775.
Fahnestock, Margaret, b. July 23, 1702; d. December 29, 1785.
[The above have also another marble stone with the following:
"In memory of
Diedrick and Margaret
Father and Mother of the
Tribe of Fahnestock
in the United States, who
Emigrated from Prussia in
1726,
and setttled near Ephrata,
Penna.
We reverence their our most
Worthy Progenitors.
Erected by the Tribe,
1878."
They are the ancestors of the family surname so long known in this city.]
Hier liegt begraben
der Ehr wurdige Bruder
Gideon, sonst D.
Christian Eckstein
micdglied der Bruder Schaff-
in Ephrata. Starb d. 26
Julius ihm jahr 1787,
Seine alters 70 jahr,
1 monat, 7 tag.
Fahnestock, Esther, b. March 27, 1740; d. Dec. 6, 1792.
Fahnestock, Diedrich, b. Dec. 5, 1732; d. Dec. 20, 1818.
Fahnestock, Daniel, b. Dec. 18, 1773; d. July 29, 1829.
Fahnestock, Christian, b. Sept. 8, 1763; d. March 19, 1853.
Fahnestock, Benjamin, b. May 2, 1741; d. July 27, 1820.
Fahnestock, Rebecca, wf. of Johannes, b. 1715; d. Jan. 17, 1775.
Fahnestock, Elizabeth , wf. of Daniel, b. March 24, 1779; d. May 20, 1831.
Fahnestock, Johannes, b. 1735; d. May 22, 1812.
Fahnestock, Catharine, b. 1745; d. May 13, 1822.
Fahnestock, Peter, b. Feb. 3, 1730; d. Sept. 15, 1805.
Funck, Christian, b. Jan. 17, 1796; d. March 10, 1880.
Fausit John, b. 1811; d. November 10, 1882.

Fink, Mary, wf. of Peter, b. May 18, 1815; d. April 9, 1847.
Gorgas, Jacob, b. April 9, 1728; d. Nov. 21, 1798.
Gorrgas, Christina, b. March 29, 1734; d. Oct. 20, 1804.
Gorgas, Margaret, wf. of S., nee Firestone, b. Feb. 5, 1815; d. June 20, 1886.
Gorgas, George, b. Sept. 21, 1832; d. Jan. 21, 1857.
Gorgas, Christina, wf. of B., b. June 10, 1774; d. May 31, 1848.
Gorgas, Benjamin, b. Sept. 16, 1762; d. Oct. 5, 1836.
[The first Jacob was the progenitor of the Gorgas' of Dauphin and Cumberland counties.]
Graver, Mary, b. Aug. 8, 1797; d. March 9, 1873.
Graver, Philip, b. Nov. 1, 1750; d. March 30, 1837.
Grever, Felbina, b. Dec. 18, 1762; d. Feb. 4, 1844.
Graver, Catharine, b. April 18, 1786; d. April 18, 1879.

Rachel Hoeffley,
b. 1743;
d. March, 1825.
Alt zu Gott Hinauf hab-
ich geschrien und geboten,
Am tage meiner threbsahl
fleht ch zu thin; miteilen
Half er mir aus alten
Meinen Nothen.

St.
Albina
Sonst
Margaret Hoecker,
d. April 20, 1767.

Hier Rhuet
Bruder
Obed.
Sonst
Ludwig Hoecker,
Strab den Julius 25 monat
Anne un Jahr 1772, alt 72
Jahr 11 monat.
[He was the founder of the first Sunday school in the world, antedating Robert Raikes' school by 45 years.]
Hay, Seba, wf. of George, dau. of Dietrich

and Esther Fahnestock, b. June 18, 1775; d. October 19, 1800.
Hoffli, Salma, b. February 6, 1727; d. Sept. 26, 1807.
Hahn, Henry K., b. Oct. 20, 1848; d. Oct. 7, 1862.
Hostetter, Henry, b. Aug. 14, 1796; d. June 9, 1833.
"A citizen highly esteemed and much respected and in the years 1828 and 1829 honored by his fellow-citizens with a seat in the House of Representatives of his native State, Pennsylvania."
John, Susannah, w. of J., b. May 8, 1792; d. Aug. 17, 1847.

Br.
Naeman
Sonst,
Adam Koenigmacher,
b. July 30, 1737;
d. January 30, 1793.

Konigmacher, Christian, b. Nov. 11, 1745; d. January 26, 1816.
Koenigmacher, Hannah, dau. of Benj., b. June 18, 1808; d. Dec. 30, 1884.
Konigmacher, Christina, nee Fahnestock, b. 1804; d. March 1, 1871.
Koenigmacher, Sarah, b. May 7, 1803; d. Nov. 28, 1871.
Koenigmacher, Joseph, b. Dec. 12, 1805; d. April 4, 1861.
Konigmacher, Cecelia, wf. of Jos., dau. of Henry F. Slaymaker, b. May 3, 1817; d. Sept. 3, 1859.
Koenigmacher, Abraham, b. Nov. 14, 1769; d. Sept. 17, 1825.
Koenigmacher, Samuel, b. May 16, 1799; d. Nov. 23, 1835, in Philadelphia.
Koenigmacher, Benjamin, b. Sept. 12, 1773; d. March 24, 1850.
Koenigmacher, Margaret, wf. of B., dau. of Peter Fahnestock, b. March 5, 1772; d. June 12, 1847.
Koenigmacher, William, b. Jan. 5, 1797; d. Feb. 10, 1881.
Koenigmacher, Susanna, wf. of William, dau. of Jacob Bauman, b. May 20, 1798; d. June 15, 1833.
Konigmacher, Adam, s. of Jacob, b. March 7, 1799; d. Nov. 7, 1815.
Konigmacher, Elizabeth, dau. of John Royer, b. Nov. 7, 1831; d. Sept. 15, 1857.
Konigmacher, Lydia, dau. of Henry Mohler, b. July 3, 1829; d. April 18, 1866.

Konigmacher, Adam, b. Dec. 24, 1821; d. Nov. 11, 1887.
Konigmacher, Rebecca, dau. of Johannes Fahnestock, b. July 7, 1775; d. Dec. 5, 1832.
Konigmacher, Doctor Jacob, b. June 4, 1771; d. Sept. 18, 1839.
Konigmacher, wf. of Abraham, b. May 15, 1780; d. March 27, 1868.
Kurtz, Catharine, b. Aug. 20, 1809; d. Oct. 9, 1831.
Kimmel, Elizabeth, wf. of Jacob, nee Grever, b. Sept. 11, 1777; d. Feb. 1, 1861.

Hier Lieght Bruder
Frederick Keller,
Starb November 10,
1771, alt 34 jahr
10 monath.

Keiper, Barbara, b. Dec. 20, 1771; d. March 16, 1852.
Landes, Hannah, nee Heffley, b. May 25, 1776; d. Nov. 11, 1849.
Landes, Esther, b. Dec. 20, 1797; d. Dec. 2, 1873.

Heir Ruhen,
die gebenig
des hoen Filosofen,
Jacob Martin,
Er ist in Europe geboren
den 10 ten Juni, 1725, und
ist gestorben als ein guter
Christ den 19 ten Julius, 1790
im 66 Jahr seines alter.

Miller, Heinrich, b. May 12, 1728; d. Jan. 12, 1778.
Martin, Charlotte, wf. of Peter, Jr., dau. of Abraham Koenigmacher.
Martin, Johannes, b. Jan. 12, 1748; d. May 14, 1874.
Martin, Jacob, b. Feb. 11, 1779; d. July 13, 1849.
Martin, George, b. April 31, 1790; d. Jan. 2, 1821.

Peter Miller,
Gebutig in Oberamt
Lautern, im Enur Pfaltz
Kam als Reformerter
Pridiger nach America
In Julius, 1730, wurde
unter die Gemeine im
Jahr 1735, und genant
Bruder Jabez auch warder nachmals hr Lehrer
Bis an sein ende entschlief

den 25 sten September, 1796, Alter 86 Jahr und 9 monath.
Pfautz, Michael, b. Dec. 12, 1802; d. Jan. 13, 1874.
Roland, Rosina, nee Martin, b. Aug. 4, 1762; d. Oct. 4, 1821.
Royer, Samuel, b. Nov. 6, 1797; d. April 23, 1864.
Royer, Catharine, b. Jan. 31, 1804; d. March 7, 1885.
Somony, John Jacob, b. 1715; d. Nov. 2, 1789.
Senseman, Anna, wf. of Jos., dau. of Michael Sherick, b. March 5, 1800; d. April 9, 1856.
Senseman, Joseph, b. Sept. 29, 1785; d. March, 1819.
Senseman, Johannes, b. July 17, 1757; d. March 11, 1819.
Senseman, Michael, b. Aug. 18, 1809; d. Nov. 11, 1819.
Steinmetz, Isaac B., b. Aug. 1, 1838; d. Oct. 29, 1875.
Urich, Elizabeth, wf. of Jos., b. Feb. 10, 1780; d. Sept. 16, 1850.
Urich, Joseph, b. May 15, 1781; d. Nov. 16, 1864.
Urich, Andrew, b. Nov. 11, 1805; d. Dec. 22, 1879.
Urich, Mary, b. March 18, 1799; d. Jan. 5, 1880.

Dr.
Jacobus Sen
SEMANISHIER.
Gesamlet zu
[Following this is illegible.]

St.
Petronella,
Starb July 27, 1791,
Alt 52 Jahr 11 monat.

Bruder
Philemon,
Starb 30 Martz, 1785,
Altes 75 Jahr.

Zerfass, Sarah, b. Dec. 6, 1799; d. June 18, 1852.
Zerfass, Samuel, b. Jan. 7, 1767; d. April 30, 1843.
Zerfass, Magdalena, nee Eckert, b. Aug. 26, 1765; d. July 18, 1853.
Zarfass, Elizabeth, wf. of S., nee Royer, b. Oct. 1, 1799; d. April 12, 1860.
Zerfass, Samuel, b. May 12, 1802; d. April 25, 1872.
Zerfass, Judith, wf. of S., b. May 11, 1809; d. April 24, 1891.
Zirvin, Veronica, b. Nov. 17, 1734; d. Jan. 4, 1815.
Ziegler, Louisa, b. Oct. 30, 1818; d. Sept. 4, 1879.

NOTES AND QUERIES,

Historical, Biographical, and Genealogical.

XXXVI.

IMPORTANT DOCUMENTS relating to the soldiers of the Revolution have recently been transcribed for the Editor of "Notes and Queries," and as occasion may offer will be published in these columns. To prevent pirating these rolls and papers will be copyrighted.

Westmoreland County Families.

Rev. James Power's will is dated January 26, 1828; and probated August 24, 1830. He makes bequests to children and grandchildren as follows:
 i. Elizabeth.
 ii. Jane.
 iii. Rachel.
 iv. Mary.
 v. Rebecca, m. —— Smith.
 vi. Isabella.
 vii. Hannah.
 viii. Margaret.
Grandchildren:
Rachel Findley.
James Smith.
Rev. Joseph Smith.

Rev. Samuel Porter, of Congruity, in Salem township, Westmoreland county, made his will, dated June 1, 1825, which was probated Oct. 3, 1825. He makes bequests to his wife, Jane, and children:
 i. William
 ii. John.
Bro. William Porter.
Grandchildren:
Nancy Porter and Peggy Wright.

Thomas Jamison by will dated July 9, 1774, and probated March 1, 1775; makes bequests to wife Ann and children:
i. William.
ii. Mary.
iii. Ann, m. Abraham Hendricks.

Also makes bequests to Thomas Hendricks, his grandson, Abraham Hendricks, his son-in-law, and Thomas Roberts, a son of his wife by her former husband.
I. Ann Jamison, b. 1752. d. Dec. 23, 1834; m. Abraham Hendricks, b. 1749; d. Jan. 2, 1819. They had issue:
i. Abraham.
ii. Daniel.
iii. William.
iv. Jamison, m. Elizabeth Ogden.
v. Ann, m. William Henderson.
vi. John.
vii. Thomas.
viii. Rachel, m. Thomas Pollock.
ix. Mary, m. John McHarg.
II. Mary Jamison.
III. William Jamison d. May 11, 1800. He married March 11, 1783, Elizabeth Galbreath [daughter of Thomas Galbreath], b. 1765; d. March 11, 1845. They had five children.

Thomas Galbreath, of Scotch-Irish descent, was a merchant in North Carolina, and came to Cumberland county, Pa., in 1764 settling near Carlisle. Soon afterwards he removed into Ligonier Valley, Fairfield township, Westmoreland county, Pa. His children were:
i. Elizabeth m. William Jamison.
ii. Martha, m. John Irwin.
iii. James.
iv. John.

Thomas Galbreath on 29th August, 1774, bought 270 acres of land in Fairfield township, from John Hinkson. The tract was "The Squirrel Hill" tract upon which New Florence is now located. He also obtained on the 13th June, 1777, three tracts of land from General Arthur St. Clair, one of which did embrace "Fort Ligonier." The same tract was sold by the sheriff on 10th June, 1795, to James Ramsey. Col. Ramsey laid out the town on the site of old Fort Ligonier and called it "Wellington." In 1817 he changed the name to Ligonier as appears by a notice in the Greensburg Gazette of February 15, 1817:

"Col. Ramsay has changed the name of his new town at Ligonier Old Fort from Wellington to Ligonier. The sale of lots in the said town is postponed to Monday, the third day of March next."

In the partition among Thomas Galbreath's heirs, in 1800, James Galbreath got "The Squirrel Hill Old Town" plantation, which had been bought from Capt. John Hinkson.

Consul Willshire Butterfield.

Consul Willshire Butterfield, the historian of early Western Pennsylvania, and of the Northwest Territory, died at his residence in South Omaha, September 25th, 1899. Mr. Butterfield was born in Mexico, Oswego county, N. Y., on July 28th, 1824, and spent the early years of his life in that section. Later on he removed to Ohio and at the age of twenty-two published his first book, a history of Seneca county, Ohio, Altogether, Mr. Butterfield has written and published twenty-five books and at the time of his death was engaged in writing a history of the early days of Chicago. No title has been chosen for this book, but it was nearly completed and would have soon been sent to the publishers.

Among Mr. Butterfield's later books was the "History of the Girtys," which is an account of the Girty brothers, Thomas, Simon, James and George, and the part taken by them in Lord Dunmore's war on the western border, War of the Revolution and in the Indian wars of 1790 and 1795. This book was written since Mr. Butterfield removed to South Omaha in 1888. It was published in 1890. One of Mr. Butterfield's books which attracted widespread attention was his account of the "Expedition Against Sandusky," under Colonel William Crawford in 1782.

The latest book given to the public by this author was "Brule's Discoveries and Explorations, 1610-1628," being a narrative of the discovery by Stephen Brule of Lakes Huron, Ontario and Superior and of his exploration of Pennsylvania, Western New York and Ontario, Canada. This book was published last year and received much favorable comment from the critics, especially from those in the Dominion of Canada. Mr. Butterfield gave this book to the Western Reserve Historical Society, of Cleveland, O., and it was published under the direction of that society. The "Washington-Irvine Correspondence," published in 1882, was another book which attracted considerable attention from the reading public and added considerably to the laurels of **the author.** This book deals with the official letters which passed between Washington and Brigadier General William Irvine and between Irvine and others concerning miliary affairs in the West from 1781 to 1783. "The History of the Discovery of the Northwest by John Nicollet in 1634" is another book by Mr. Butterfield which has been widely read.

As Pennsylvanians we are greatly indebted to the indefatigable labors of Mr. Butterfield. He was a hard-working and conscientious historian. He was no writer of fiction under the guise of history, or he might have gained a comprotence, as well as ephemeral or present day fame. But his works will live after him, and are his eternal monument.

Some Lancaster Interments.

[The writer has in his possession sixty-three invitations which were received by his great-grandmother during 1841-1855, and later, to attend the funeral obsequies and interments of a number of old Lancaster residents. The age of the person, however, is not mentioned, but as the invitation gives the date of interment, they will answer as a guide to those who may be searching after such data. The writer has accordingly made a list for publication in "Notes and Queries" and herewith appends the same.
S. M. SENER.]

Washington Newton King, son of David and Margaret King, interred Wednesday, March 14, 1848, from parent's residence on East King street.

Catharine King, from residence of her husband, Jacob King, South Duke street, on Thursday afternoon, October 19, 1848.

Ross Simpson, from George King's residence, East King street, on Wednesday, February 22, 1848.

Samuel Powell, from his residence on Church street, near Vine, on Sunday, September 27, 1851.

Jacob H. Locher, of Harrisburg, formerly of Lancaster, from his brother's residence, East King street, Lancaster, on Thursday, February 22, 1855.

Samuel Herman Riley, son of S. J. J. and Martha Riley, from his parent's residence, East King street, on Monday, December 31, 1849.

Frederick Alphonsus Westhaeffer, son of J. M. and M. C. Westhaeffer, from parents residence, East King street, on Wednesday, July 14, 1847.

Serena Smith, from the residence of her son, George H. Smith, East King street, on Sunday, July 28, 1850.

William Bender White, from residence of his father, Joseph White, East King street, on Saturday, August 14, 1851.

Eliza Musketnuss, daughter of Jacob Musketnuss, from Henry Nauman's residence, East King street, on Thursday, March 5th, 1851.

Samuel Swope, infant son of Maria and Levi Swope, (innkeeper) from father's home, East King street, Thursday, January 27, 1848, to proceed to the country.

Levi Swope, from his late residence, East King street, on Sunday, February 16, 1851, to proceed to the country.

Rosanna Eichenbroad, from residence of Joseph White, East King street, on Friday, June 22, 1855.

Emily Lauretta Kieffer, from residence of her father, Thompson Kieffer, on West Chestnut street, on Friday afternoon, September 24, 1847.

Mrs. Catharine Light, from her late residence, East King street, on Thursday, January 28, 1846.

Mrs. Ann Knight, from her late residence on South Queen street, on Sunday afternoon, January 30, 1847.

William Ball, from the residence of Adam Metzger, East King street, on Monday, March 1, 1847.

Jacob Eicholtz, from his late residence, on Friday, May 13, 1842.

Margaret Ehler, from residence of John Retallick, East King street, on Sunday afternoon. September 21, 1851.

Jacob Ehler, from his residence on

Church street, near Vine, on Friday, March 26, 1852.

William T. Bomberger, infant child of William and Mary Bomberger, from their home on East King street, on Sunday, September 8, 1850.

Elizabeth Pinkerton, widow of late Henry Pinkerton, Esq., from her residence, East King street, on Saturday, November 2, 1844.

Henry A. Pinkerton, from residence of his mother, Mrs. C. E. Pinkerton, corner of East King and Lime, on Tuesday, September 24, 1850.

Mary Catharine Pinkerton, wife of John L. Pinkerton, from her husband's residence on North Lime street, on Friday, August 31, 1850.

Mrs. Hannah Pinkerton, from residence of her husband, Henry Pinkerton, Sr., in Centre Square, on Tuesday, September 26, 1854.

Catharine Sener, from her residence on North Prince street, on Sunday afternoon, November 22, 1851. She was the great-grandmother of the writer. She was born on May 20, 1770 and was a daughter of Heinrich Rung, who came to America from Grimlauf, landing on December 12, 1734, at Philadelphia. She was the wife of Johannes Sener, born October 7, 1765; died July 11, 1814.

Mrs. Christianna Aune, from her residence on Middle street, on Friday, June 2, 1853.

George Leonard, Sr., from the residence of his son Philip Leonard, on East King street, on Tuesday, May 11, 1847. He was the great-great-grandfather of the writer and was born September 13, 1755, and was a Revolutionary soldier, serving nearly three years, and was at Trenton, Princeton and Germantown.

John Leonard, from his residence on East King street, on Tuesday, January 26, 1847.

John Leonard, Sr., from the residence of his son, John Leonard, Jr., corner Vine and Christian streets, on Sunday, January 28, 1849.

John K. Harkins, from residence of his father, Eugene Harkins, East King street, on Wednesday August 24, 1847.

John Charles Harkins, from the residence of his father, Eugene Harkins, corner East King and Church streets, on Friday, September 12, 1851.

Thomas B. Sparks, from residence of Jacob Gumpf, Church street, on Friday, August 18, 1848.

Elizabeth M. Eausman, from home of her mother, East Orange street, on Friday, February 25, 1853.

Mrs. Mary Ann Winouer, from her husband's residence, Church near South Queen street, on Monday, February 19, 1849.

William Wineow (Winouer), from residence of his mother, West Orange street, on Tuesday, March 9, 1852.

Ann Margaret McGonigle, from the residence of her parents, Michael and Mary McGonigle, on East King street, on Monday, August 18, 1851.

Hiram Shofstall, from home of his mother, East King street, on Friday, June 25, 1847.

Magdalena Roeting from residence of her husband, East King street, on Friday, July 23, 1847.

William Roeting, from residence of his son-in-law, Charles Nauman (Graeff's Landing), on Sunday, September 1, 1850.

Mrs. Unity Stroble, from her residence, corner East Orange and Lime streets, on Sunday, February 22, 1852.

Thomas Jefferies, from his residence, East King street, on Wednesday, June 26, 1850.

Patrick Ferry from his residence, East King street, on Thursday, May 23, 1845.

Jerome A. Lechler, from residence of his mother (Mrs. Zimmerer) on High street, on Thursday, December 26, 1849.

Mrs. Jane Lewars, from her residence on East King street, on Wednesday, February 2, 1848.

Peter Reinhart, from residence of his son-in-law, Dennis Coyle, on Church street, on Sunday, March 26, 1854.

Catharine Demuth, from the residence of her son-in-law, Henry Kepple, on East King street, on Wednesday, May 16, 1855.

John Lindman, from residence of his son, East King street, on January 6, 1848.

Elizabeth Hallacher, from residence of her husband, Adam Hallacher, on East King street, on Thursday, November 30,

1848. "The funeral will move to the country."

Mrs. Catharine Gloninger, from her residence on East King street, on Saturday, January 4, 1845.

Mary Ann Beck, from her husband, L. Beck's residence, corner of Lime and Church streets, on Sunday, January 18, 1852.

Joseph Huber, from his father's residence on North Queen street, on Sunday, May 11, 1845.

Peter Huber, Sr., from his residence on North Queen street, on Tuesday, October 29, 1850.

Mrs. Mary Huber, from her residence, North Queen street, on Sunday, July 1, 1855.

Mrs. Ann Gemperling, from residence of her husband, Daniel Gemperling, on Middle street, on Thursday, September 20, 1849.

William Demuth Gemperling, son of Daniel Gemperling, from his father's residence, on Wednesday, August 6, 1851.

Mrs. Elizabeth Gemperling, from residence of her son-in-law, George P. King, corner of East Orange and Plumb (Plum) streets, on Saturday, March 25, 1854.

William Rhoads, infant son of Jacob and Eliza Rhoads, from their residence on East King street, on December 29, 1848.

Mrs. Elizabeth (Eliza) Rhoads, wife of John Rhoads, from her husband's home on East King street, on Wednesday, July 25, 1850.

Mrs. Margaret Gumpf, from the residence of her husband, Michael Gumpf, on Middle street, on Sunday, July 17, 1853.

Mrs. Mary Halbach, from her late residence, East Orange street, on Wednesday, September 24, 1851.

Henry Nauman, from his late residence on Mulberry street, near Chestnut street, on Sunday, April 23, 1854.

Benjamin Franklin White, eldest son of Joseph and Catharine White, from their residence on East King street, on Thursday, September 4, 1851.

JOHN F. MEGINNESS

Death of the Veteran Editor and Historian.

The Williamsport Gazette and Bulletin of November 13th gives the following particulars of the death of John F. Meginness, the veteran journalist and newspaper man, which occurred in that city on Saturday night, November 11th, 1899.

"John F. Meginness, the veteran journalist and historian, died suddenly at his home, 621 Grace street, Saturday night. Death came in an instant and at a moment of complete happiness, for he was exhibiting the last link in the chain which surrounded the celebration of his golden wedding—an event that had been looked forward to by him during the past decade.

"On October 25th last Mr. and Mrs. Meginness celebrated their golden wedding, guests having assembled here from considerable distance. Among the number was Miss Sally H. Bryan, of Philadelphia, and she had been requested to stay until Saturday, Mr. Meginness promising to accompany her as far as Harrisburg. He had sent to Sunbury to be bound by a particular friend what is known as his "Golden Wedding Book," a unique affair containing the original newspaper clippings from various papers throughout this section, relative to the golden wedding, letters from friends, their marriage certificate, etc., so that it could be bound in golden morrocco. Saturday he was to get the book, and he combined the pleasure of traveling with his cousin and getting his book, in which he set great store.

"He returned to this city on the 10.40 Pennsylvania train, which was late. Besides this Golden Wedding Book he had other books to the weight of twenty pounds. He hastened home, walking faster than was his wont, and entered the house glowing with happiness and apparently in the best of health he ever enjoyed. He was short of breath and sat down for a moment. Without waiting to remove either hat or overcoat, so anxious was he to show his Golden Wedding Book, he stood up and unbound the wrapper. At his side were his wife and daughter-in-law, Mrs. Harry M. Meginness. They were standing in the dining-room. Mr. Meginness, with the glow of pride upon his face, opened the book and pointed to it with the words:

"'Look at the title page,' (It contained the marriage certificate).

"As he uttered these words he staggered backwards against the door and his wife and daughter-in-law each caught one of his arms. He sank to the floor, dying instantly and without a struggle. He had no premonition of death—it came to him at a moment of complete happiness.

"Dr. Stickel, the nearest physician, was instantly summoned, and arrived within five minutes. He gave it as his opinion that death was due to heart disease, the fatal attack being brought on by overexertion.

John Franklin Meginness was born in Lancaster county in 1827, and his early boyhood was passed upon the farm. In 1843 he went West to battle his own way through life, but not meeting with much encouragement he returned to Lancaster county in 1847 and enlisted in the regular army for service during the Mexican War, in which he served with much credit, entering the City of Mexico with the victorious American army. He subsequently taught school in Lycoming county where, in October, 1849, he married Martha Jane King. His first experience as an editor was in Jersey Shore in June, 1852, and from that time up until 1857 he remained there as editor of various papers. In 1855 he wrote a history of the West Branch Valley of the Susquehanna, which was the pioneer history of that part of the State. He subsequently edited newspapers in various cities in Illinois and in 1862 returned with his family to Williamsport. During the war he was connected with the quartermaster's department from Washington and subsequently in the treasury department. In 1869 he returned to Williamsport as editor of the Gazette and Bulletin, which position he filled until 1889, when he retired. Soon after this he published an exhaustive biography of Frances Slocum, the lost sister of Wyoming. He subsequently published a history of Lycoming county and wrote a number of histories of like character, being engaged on that work at the time of his death. He was a voluminous contributor to the press over the signature of John of Lancaster.

Mr. and Mrs. Meginness were the parents of ten children, seven of whom survive, as follows: Mary Virginia, who married William C. Arp; Alice, who married Ira B. Waite; William Warren Meginness, editor-in-chief of the Gazette and Bulletin; Henry Harvey Meginness; Ida Jane, wife of H. J. Edwards; Carrie, wife of H. A. Van Gilder, of Morristown, N. J., and Herbert Eugene Meginness.

NOTES AND QUERIES.

Historical, Biographical, and Genealogical.

XXXVII.

McCALLEN—SAWYER.

My great-great-grandfather's name was Willam Geddes. He came to America with his father, James Geddes, in 1752. He married in 1762, Sarah McCallen, who died in 1773, leaving six children, one of whom was Robert Geddes, my great-grandfather, who was born September 30, 1771, in Derry township, then Lancaster county, Pa., now Londonderry township, Lebanon county. He married Jane Sawyer, who died November 29, 1808, leaving six children, one of whom was my grandfather, John Geddes. He was born March 19, 1801, in Derry township, and died November 4, 1889, at Ann Arbor, Michigan. My grandfather had a brother, William Geddes, who was born, December 28, 1802, in Derry, and died March 21, 1877, at his home in Pittsfield, near Ann Arbor. I am anxious to find out if either the father of Jane Sawyer, whose name was John Sawyer, or the father of Sarah McCallen, whose name was Robert McCallen, were either of them a soldier in the War of the Revolution. In my great-grandfather's will he refers to a sword that Robert McCallen once owned. John Sawyer was born August 4, 1730 (old style) and died August 12, 1813. He was the eldest son of William Sawyer, an Englishman from Bristol. C. R. Beloit, Wis.

[In reply to the foregoing inquiry, we may state that Robert McCallen commanded a company of Associators in the Jersey campaign of 1776. John Sawyer also served in the militia as a private on several tours of duty.]

OLD TIME REMINISCENCES.

The Awakening of a Citizen of Harrisburg Who Slumbered Since 1845.

[Paper read before the Historical Society of Dauphin County, by Theodore B. Klein.]

In fancy we arouse a citizen of 1845 from his deep slumber, supposed to have been enjoyed for more than half a century in the recesses of the hill at the gate of the beautiful Cumberland Valley, on the westerly bank of the Susquehanna, within cannon shot of the society's home-nest. During the days, weeks, months and years that have passed since he lay him down to sleep, great events have taken place in the world; great advances have been made in the fields of art and sciences; great inventions developed and utilized, to all of which he has given no heed.

He has not heard the clink of the sledge upon the steel, nor the explosion of the giant powder that crushed the rocks of the hill under which he slept to make way for the track of the railway that joins the Keystone State to its neighbors on the North and South. He heard not of the angry debates in Congress on the slavery question; he heard not of the election of Abraham Lincoln as President of the United States; he heard not the threatenings of secession and a dissolution of the Union; he heard not of the bombardment of Fort Sumpter by the fiery South Carolinians; he heard not of the call of Lincoln for men to preserve the Union of States; he heard not of the grand armies assembling in response to that call; he heard not of the heavy battles from Bull Run and on through the weary, sad years to the surrender at Appomattox; and not even when the hosts gathered in hot haste over his resting place to fortify the hill as a protection to his native town, he slept on and on. The booming artillery at Gettysburg disturbed him not, nor did the shouts of victory from the boys in blue, as Lee's discomfited army retired behind Seminary Ridge seeking refuge beyond the Potomac, arouse him from his slumbers. He heard not of the brilliant campaigns of McClellan, and Grant, and Sherman and Sheridan, and their comrades in arms and witnessed not the return of the victorious hosts who had defended the nation's flag to the bitter end and sustained its every star inviolate.

He heard not the wail of the Cuban insurgents, nor the cry of the helpless victims of Spain's tyranny in the Philippines and the West Indies. He heard not of the explosion of the ill-fated ship of his country in Havanna harbor. He heard not of the exploit of Dewey in the far-away waters of the Eastern Hemisphere. He heard not of the naval victory on the Cuban coast where Spanish pride was humbled and her navy destroyed.

The click of the magnetic spark that recorded the current events of the day even to the uttermost parts of the earth, that comes and goes under the fathomless depths of the vast oceans was unheard. The cheery "Hello! Hello!" through the transmitter of the telephone that carries the human voice as it were for hundreds of miles in familiar tones, he heard not.

On this bright September day the hypnotic influence is dispelled and he stands upon the summit of the lofty hill overlooking the Susquehanna and his native Harrisburg, and in amazement his vision takes in the great clouds of smoke and exhausted steam rising from the easterly bank of the river for miles along its shore. He is told that steel rails and steel bridges and all manner of iron and steel products are being turned out by day and by night as rapidly as mighty engines and ten thousand men can manipulate the ore and raw materials into the finished metals.

He notices the airy superstructure of the new bridges across the river and learns the purposes of their erection. He sees at his feet the mysterious moving of the trolley car, and learns a part of the practical uses to which the harnessed lightning is applied. He remembers the familiar old "Camel-back" bridge in his immediate front, yet looks in vain for the dome of the State Capitol; but sees the mass of brick upon the site thereof and learns the fate of the time-honored structure with regret. His vision extended, he sees the growth of the new city up and down the river and out beyond Paxton creek, covering the plateau toward Prospect Hill, and the old flag from Reservoir Park greets his dimmed vision, and the enclosed lake of Susquehanna water upon the hill side is pointed out to him as a transformation scene, for he remembers the old terraced spot on North street in his early days as the place from whence flowed the liquid stream into the domicile of his father.

He is anxious to descend the slope and visit the scenes of his boyhood, and we clamber down the steep and into the old bridge, as full of kinks as the limbs of the awakened sleeper, but it is the same dear old bridge, and even the dust and cobwebs of '45 clusters in its nooks and corners. The island is still there but looks changed, and he inquires for Wesley Van-Horn and his melon patches, where often he regaled himself in days of yore. He sees the new bridge which will carry him to the new city, and he wonders where the twin sister of the "Camel-back" has gone; but looks in vain for the wreck in the waves of the placid stream that was wild and dangerous when the destructive flood of ice cut the bridge away. He looks over the side at the entrance to the bridge, but does not see Jacob Stees or Charlie Wingert busy unloading their sand flats.

The denizens of the old gate house on the Dauphin shore are strange to him— and greet him not, but he sees wonderful things upon every hand. Upon the smooth asphalt of Market street there is a group of merry wheelers to welcome him, and as he casts his eyes upon a pair of almond-eyed children of China in flowing robes scorching upon their noiseless steeds his mother tongue breaks out in the exclamation: "Pots tousand was is das?" He is delighted with the graceful movements of the expert cyclers, and from them gazes in admiration upon the stately structure of the Harrisburg Club, that has superseded the old building which he remembered so well. He looks for his old acquaintance, Judge Bucher, on his right, but he cannot be seen. He catches a glimpse of his old companion, George Fager, whom he hails, but the mutual greetings are short and tinged with sadness because his old friend cannot distinguish the joy of his countenance at his return to his native heath.

How the scene in view seems to draw the now stranger as he hastens along the once familiar street. Upon his right he expects to see old General Forster, or some of the Geigers, or Mr. Ingram, and upon his left some of the Stehleys, the proprietors of the Dock and Gilliard grocery, or Mr. Lyman Gilbert or his son Henry, but the stately building that occupies the old corner upon which is carved in letters of granite: "Board of Trade Building," looks strange to him, and he is told that the people whom he expected to see are gone.

He looks again to his right and misses the modest old homestead of the Kunkel's, but he sees the familiar name of Gross, who was a neighbor, and well he remembers the genial Daniel W. His son Edward Z. represents the old firm and tells of the departure of his good father. He asks for the Emersons upon his left, but no one responds to his inquiry. Where is Gustavus S. Peters, who printed the colored picture books, and Martin Lutz and his son Henry (of the old Dauphin Guards), and Mr. Rhoads and Philip Wolfersberger, who all lived in this block? The same answer applied to his every question—all gone since you have been absent from the town.

With wonder and surprise he looks for the market houses in which he had often romped in his boyhood days, and from which he had carried the basket for his mother, but they have been removed and he now sees the swift trolley cars speed along, driven by an invisible power, and hears the gong of the motorman warning him of danger.

He anxiously looks for the picture of George Washington swinging at the opposite corner where the old hotel stood in his day, and he can hardly realize the transformation that has taken place. The old John Wyeth corner looks familiar, but he sees not the colored globes in the windows of the store where he often bought quinine. The book store of Francis Wyeth is not there either. The merchants of his day have been supplanted by others. Davy Krause is not there with his jolly patrons enjoying their evening smoke, nor is Johnnie Orth and his little colony who were in the days of his youth nestled in an old-time frame house on the ground floor at the corner of what was known as Court House alley. The big store of A. J. & S. T. Jones, across the way, is absorbed by the new hotel. The familiar sign representing the "Death of Gessler" as he receives the arrow from the bow of Tell, is not where it was when he left nor is the old hostelrie that was kept by Christian Haehnlen and his "good frau." He knew the whole family—Lewis and Jacob and John—and Julia and Sophia and Rosie and Kitty. Few remain of those who joined in the merry meetings of that household in the old billiard rooms of the hotel, where bushels of chestnuts were piled in the corner for the youngsters and mice to nibble.

He looks across the street for the old court house, where he had often sat admiring the dignity of the Presiding Judge and enjoyed the pleadings of prominent members of the Bar in behalf of their numerous clients. The old steps from the pavement to the terrace leading into the building are gone. It was a favorite lounging place for the boys in the evening.

He looks in vain for the long frame building which flanked the county property on the east where Printer and Publisher Bergner worked industriously on the upper floor, reached by wooden steps outside from the Court House terrace, and where several attorneys-at-law occupied rooms on the first floor;—and as a tinge of hunger and of past memories comes over him he hurries around the corner to search for the famous oyster cellar of George Chester and his good wife, Eliza, who prepared the toothsome bivalves to the king's taste, and as he remembers the boys Moses and Thomas and Dave, who were the helpers of the parents, exclaims (I would give much to hear Pap Chester say): "Mo-mo-mo-Mose, do-do-do-don't gi-gi-gi-give dem boys mo-mo-mo-more dan to-to-to-two crackers apiece." The enterprise of the late John H. Brant improved the premises, and the Trust Company building, more fully enlarged with its busy places, now occupies the site which was occupied by those mentioned and the drug store of J. G. Schoch and later by John Kepple, Joseph Cook and John Oenslager.

Our friend turns a backward glance to view the south side of the street again, but he does not recognize the homes of Judge Dock, where George and William were of the family. The Graydon and Forster and McCormick homes, too, are deserted and filled with to him strange tenants. Dan Robinson's store, where he received the Philadelphia daily papers at tea time, is not there—when told he can now have them before breakfast he looks doubtingly.

The Matthew Wilson Hotel looks familiar but its improvement and new name is admired, and seated in the spacious reception room of the now handsome Lochiel he takes a survey of the surroundings and notices the changes since his day. Immediately opposite, the place of X. Miller who made the fancy shoes of the day, and Bro. William Duncan, who supplied the Havana sixers for the boys, and Frederick Boas and Judge Krause, who gave their clients their advice in the law, are all gone; while the "Telegraph" building stands in their places.

Across Third street the Ayres building, where George Wolfersberger sold dry goods, is gone to give place to the building of banks, &c. Immediately opposite he looks in vain for Jacob Shell's store and speaks kindly of Cornelius and Rebecca, the children of the family, and taking in the street as far as he can see to the east he notes the procession from the suburban wards that has taken the place of the quiet citizens who came in limited numbers from the canal which bounded the old town in his day on the east.

In his reverie he wonders and exclaims

how can these things be? and on a partial explanation he is convinced that nothing short of a miracle has produced the wonderful results he has witnessed, and admitting the enterprise and industry of his townsmen and their successors, who have toiled and planned and builded during the years of his absence, he rejoices with exceeding great joy and full of gladness and a loud huzza bids us a cheery "Good Night."

BAPTISMAL AND OTHER RECORDS

Of the "Little Tulpehocken Church":

The Little Tulpehocken Church, also known as Christ Church, is located one and one half miles south of Bernville, in Jefferson township, Berks Berriville, in Jefferson township, Berks county. It would be very desirable indeed to have a succinct, yet full history of the this church, especially during its earlier period; but it is not possible to gather such a history from the meagre information contained in the "Church Record and Protocoll." The greater part of the records of baptisms, fully four-fifths and possibly even nine-tenths, as well as the marriages, are unquestionably in Rev. John Casper Stoever's handwriting. These cover the period from 1730 to 1750, or thereabouts, possibly till 1752 or 1753. During this period Rev. Stoever was undoubtedly the pastor. The communicants from 1761 to 1763 are recorded in a different hand, apparently that of Rev. J. N. Kurtz. A large part of the names of those who communed represent families not among the baptisms. All this would seem to indicate that Rev. Stoever was the pastor of the "Little Tulpehocken Church," so called to distinguish it from the larger church or congregation near Stouchsburg, during the first twenty or twenty-five years of its existence. Also that when Rev. Kurtz took charge of the field, Rev. Stoever having retired from it, he, that is Kurtz, served Northkill (Bernville) but one or two miles distant, and succeeded in drawing the larger part of this congregation to that one. Besides this, it would seem to show that when Rev. Schultze came, for some reason or other, after serving the Lutherans of this vicinity a few years, he failed to satisfy them, and that Rev. Stoever was recalled, with the view of reuniting the people and drawing them back to the church at this point, where the Northkill empties into the Tulpehocken. However, if "Records" count for anything, this Little Tulpehocken Church is apparently older than the one called "Northkill Church," at Bernville. Whether the two congregations were the result of a split in this one, or whether this one was organized by Rev. Stoever, and the other soon after by Rev. Wagner in opposition, it is not possible to decide now. But the indications are that in this case, possibly the same influences were at work which produced the two greater Tulpehocken churches, Zion (Reed's) and Christ, near Stouchsburg. Later and fuller investigations may throw more light on the subject.   J. W. EARLY.

"Church Book (record) and Protocoll of (for) the Evangelical Lutheran congregation down at the Tulpehocken near the Northkill. In it are noted and recorded the children baptized in this church and congregation, as well as those regularly joined in matrimony from 1730 on. Derived in part from other church records and in part taken from my (own) manuscripts and collected in this (book)—and to be continued in future, by me, John Caspar Stoever, regularly called and ordained an Evangelical Lutheran minister and pastor in charge of this and other congregations in Lancaster county in the Province of Pennsylvania. Done and executed in the year of our Lord 1742."

JOH. JACOB AIGLER AND WF. CHRISTINA.
Aigler, Simon, b. May 24, 1783; bap. ——
—, ——; spon., Simon Aigler and wf. Anna Catharine (grandparents).

WM. ALBERT.
Albert, John Adam, b. Feb. 27, 1741; bap. April 12, 1741; spon., John Adam Bollman and wf. Hen. Elizabeth (Kraft).

JOHN GEORGE ARNOLD.
Arnold, Anna Catharine, b. May 9, 1743; bap. June 19, 1743; spon., Sophia Catharine Knauss.

Notes and Queries.

ANDREW AULENBACH, Sr.
Aulenbach, Mary Catharine, b. June 9, 1741; bap. July 5, 1741; spon., Andrew Kraft and wf.
Aulenbach, John Nicholas, b. June 15, 1742; bap. Aug. 8, 1742; spon., Joh. Nicholas Weyrich and Mary Barbara Weigel.
Aulenbach, Mary Magdalene, b. Feb. 14, 1744; bap. Jan. 23, 1745; spon., Matthias Wagner and wife.
Aulenbach, Elizabeth, b. Feb. 10, 1751; bap. Dec. 15, 1751; spon., Nicholas Kuntz and his wife.

ANDREW AULENBACH Jr., and Wf.
Aulenbach, a son, b. Feb. 29, 1744; bap. Nov. 17, 1744; spon., John Aulenbach, single.

DANIEL AULENBACH.
Aulenbach, John, b. Feb. 25, 1763; bap. Dec. 9, 1763; spon., Joh. Christian and Elizabeth Aulenbach.
Aulenbach, Conrad, b. Sept. 18, 1764; bap. Sept. 29, 1765; spon., Conrad Christ.
Aulenbach, Mary Elizabeth, b. March 1, 1767; bap. March 11, 1767; spon., Mary Elizabeth Christ.
Aulenbach, Susanna Catharine, b. Jan. 31, 1771; bap. July 7, 1771; spon., Matthew Mueller and wf. Susan Catharine.
Aulenbach, Andrew, b. Feb. 2, 1775; bap. Feb. 19, 1775; spon., John Mueller and wf. Justina.
Aulenbach, John, b. Feb. 17, 1773; bap. Feb. 24, 1773; spon., John Schoch and his wf.

PETER AUMAN AND WF. ELIZABETH
Auman, Sybilla, b. Feb. 12, 1791; bap. March 20, 1791; spon., Sybilla Himmelberger, single.
Auman, George, b. May 4, 1792; bap. June 10, 1792; spon., George Belleman and wf. Sophia.

JOHN MICHAEL BAUER.
Bauer, Mary Magdalene, b. Aug. 15, 1751; bap. Sept. 2, 1751; spon., Nicholas Mardin (Martin) and his wf. Eva Barbara.
Bauer, Mary Margaret, b. Nov. 24, 1754; bap. March 30, 1755; spon., Sigmund Hanle and wf.
Bauer, John, b. Oct. 27, 1765; bap. Dec. 4, 1765; spon., Michael Koehl.
Bauer, Adam, b. Jan. 13, 1767; bap. Feb. 15, 1767; spon., Michael Kettner and wf.

NICHOLAS BECHTEL.
Bechtel, Mary Elizabeth, b. April 6, 1756; bap. April 9, 1756; spon., Anna Mary Pechtler and Valentine Eckert.

TOBIAS BECHTEL.
Bechtel, Joanna Mary, b. May 24, 1740; bap. Aug. 10, 1740; spon., John Meeth and Anna Mary Holder.

JOHN BAECKER AND WF.
Baecker, Amand Hedeyne (?) b. May 11, 1733; bap. Aug. 18, 1733..

ANDREW BEYER.
Beyer, John Jacob, b. March 2, 1731; bap. June 3, 1731; spon., John Jacob Schaeffer and Sybilla Kobel.
Beyer, Elizabeth, b. March 28, 1733; bap. April 2, 1733; spon., John von Hasch and his wf.
Beyer, Samuel, b. April 27, 1737; bap. July 25, 1737; spon., John Hasch and his wf.
Beyer, John, b. Feb. 2, 1740; bap. March 23, 1740; spon., John Hasch and his wf.
Beyer, John Peter, b. Oct. 27, 1742; bap. May 22, 1743; spon., John von Hasch and his wf.
Beyer, Susanna Mary, b. March 2, 1745; bap. Oct. 14, 1750; spon., Adam Fischbach.
Beyer, Abraham, b. May 2, 1747; bap. Oct. 14, 1750; spon., Adam Fishbach.
Beyer, Martin, b. Sep. 21, 1750; bap. Oct. 14, 1750; spon., Martin Schell.

JOHN BEYER.
Beyer, John Henry, b. Dec. 28, 1729; bap. May 18, 1730; spon., Henry Beyer.
Beyer, Catharine Margaret, b. May 16, 1742; bap. July 11, 1742; spon., John Adam Schroff.

FREDERIC BICKEL.
Bickel, John Caspar, b. April 1, 1742; bap. April 18, 1742; spon., Caspar Meeth and his wf.

TOBIAS BICKEL.
Bickel, John Nicholas, b. Oct. 20, 1741; bap. Nov. 8, 1741; spon., John Nicholas Holder and his wf.

SIMON BOGENRAEFF.
Bogenraeff, George Adam, b. April 17, 1756; bap. May 9, 1756; spon., George Adam Bartdorff and his wf.

SIMON BOGENREIFF (apparently same as above.)
Bogenreiff, Joh. Valentine, b. Oct. 17, 1741;

bap. Dec. 7,1741; spon., Valentine Unruh and his wf.

ABRAHAM BOLLENBACHER.
Bollenbacher, Abraham, b. May 16, 1746; bap. Sep. 28, 1746; spon., Abraham Haass and his wf.

GEORGE BOERSTLER.
Boerstler, Catharine, b. Jan. 11, 1779; bap. Apr. 21, 1779; spon., Barbara Geiss.

BALTHASER BORTNER.
Bortner, Mary Elizabeth, b. Mch. 8, 1738; bap. Apr. 30, 1738; spon., John William Leitner and his wf.

JOHN CARL.
Carl, Christian, b. Jan. 24, 1737; bap. Apr. 17, 1737; spon., Lazarus Winger and his sister, Anna.
Carl, Catharine, b. July 2, 1741; bap.Aug. 2, 1741; spon., Lazarus Winger and his wife, Catharine.

JOHN DENTER.
Denter, John David, b. Dec. 1, 1755; bap. Dec. 19, 1755; spon., Jacob Denter and wf., Margaret.

PHILIP DIEBO.
Diebo, Joh. Conrad, b. June 25, 1738; bap Aug. 23, 1738; spon.. Conrad Scharff and wf.

JOHN DIETER.
Dieter, Magdalene, b. Aug. 29, 1743; bap. Sept. 11, 1743; spon., Henry Fiedler and Magdalene Schoener.

ANDREW DORNBACH.
Dornbach, Anna Margaret, b. Dec. 22, 1747; bap. Mch. 6, 1748; spon., Herman Weber and Margaret Schneider.

DAVID EMERT.
Emert, Mary Margaret, b. Oct. 21. ——; bap. Oct. 25, ——; spon., Conrad Scharff and wf. (grandparents).

GEORGE PETER EPPICHER.
Eppicher, Lewis, b. Dec. 10, 1741: bap. July 11, 1742; spon., Joh. Nicholas Klein and wf.

CONRAD ERNST.
Ernst, Susanna Catharine, b. Apr. 27, 1742; bap. May 16, 1742; spon., Wendel Ernst and Barbara Pfatteicher.

ADAM EULER.
Euler, Susanna, b. Mch. 10, 1743; bap. Mch. 20, 1743; spon., Philip Petry and wf.

CHRISTIAN EWIG.
Ewig, Anna Barbara, b. Jan. 26, 1741; bap. July 5, 1741; spon., Conrad Lang and wf.

GEORGE FAUSS.
Fauss, Magdalen, b. Apr. 12, 1747; bap. May 10, 1747; spon., Philip Fauss and wf.

PETER JACOB FEHLER.
Fehler, John, b. Oct. 10, 1742; bap. Mch. 20, 1743; spon., John Schneider and wf.

ADAM FENGEL AND WF., JUSTINA.
Fengel, Christina, b. Apr. 3, 1788; bap. June 16, 1788; spon., John Mueller and wf., Justina.

GOTTFRIED FIEDLER.
Fiedler, Catharine, b. Dec. 18, 1740; bap. July 5, 1741; spon., Michael Schauer and his wf.
Fiedler, Andrew, b. Nov. 6, 1742; bap. Nov. 28, 1742; spon., Andrew Kraft and wf.
Fiedler, Mary, b. Aug. 5, 1745; bap. Sept. 1, 1745; spon., Henry Frey and wf., Catharine.
Fiedler, Mary Margaret, b. Dec. 10, 1747; bap. Dec. 20, 1747; spon., Albrecht Strauss and wf.

JOHN FISCHER.
Fischer, Joh. Henry, b. Oct. 5, 1734; bap. Jan. 8, 1735; spon., Joh. Henry Adam.
Fischer, Catharine Barbara, b. Sept. 8, 1740; bap. Sept. 14, 1740; spon., John Kuerschner and wf.

JOHN FUESS (Fiss in index).
Fuess, a son, b. Sept. 18, 1764; bap. Jan. 13, 1765; spon., Thomas Lang and Susanna Hass.

MICHAEL FRIESS.
Friess, Martin, b. Feb. 16, 1753; bap. Feb. 18, 1753; spon., Martin Schell and wf., Margaret Elizabeth.
Friess, David, b. Aug. 10, 1754; bap. Sept. 1, 1754; spon., Martin Schell and wf., Margaret Elizabeth.
Friess, Joh. Jacob, b. Feby. 9, 1756; bap. Jan. 18, 1757; spon., Jacob Duenter and Catharine Schellenberg.
Friess, Catharine, b. Oct. 30, 1758; bap. —. —, ——; spon., David Meuerle and wf., Catharine.

DANIEL FREYMAEYER AND WF., ELIZABETH.
Freymaeyer, Daniel, b. July 9, 1742; bap. Sept. 11, 1742; spon., John Henny.

JACOB FUCHS.
Fuchs, Emma Elizabeth, b. Nov. 19, 1741;

bap. Dec. 7, 1741; spon., Joh. Rehm and Anna Elizabeth Ermentraut.
Fuchs, Anna Mary, b. Jan. 1, 1743; bap. Jan. 13, 1743; spon., Nicholas Holder and wf.
Fuchs, Anna Margaret, b. Oct. 8, 1747; bap. Oct. 25, 1747; spon., John Eilrat and wf., Engel.

HENRY GEBBERT.
Gebbert, Joh. Adam, b. Mch. 9, 1755; bap. Feb. 6, 1763; spon., Joh. Adam Schmidt and wf., Anna Mary.
Gebbert, Anna Mary, b. Mch. 1, 1760; bap. Feb. 6, 1763; spon., Joh. Adam Schmidt and wf., Anna Mary.
Gebbert, Mary Christina, b. Jan. 25, 1763; bap. Feby. 6, 1763; spon., Joh. Adam Schmidt and wf., Anna Mary.

FREDERICK GEHR.
Gehr, John, b. Jan. 3, 1772; bap. Jan. 5, 1772; spon., John Zanter.

WILLIAM GELLIGER.
Gelliger, Joh. Jac. William, b. Nov. 6, 1741; bap. Dec. 7, 1741; spon., Joh. Jacob Vollmar and wf.

GEORGE DANIEL GENSEMER.
Gensemer, Mary Appolonia, b. Mch. 21, 1740; bap. Mch. 30, 1740; spon., Jacob Vollmar and wf.

JACOB GEHRHART.
Gehrhart, Frederic, b. Apr. 13, 1781; bap. Apr. 22, 1781; spon., Joh. Adam Gruber and wf., Elizabeth.
Gehrhart, John, b. Apr. 11, 1789; bap. May 16, 1789; spon., John Scharff and wf., Eva Rosina.

CONRAD GILBERT (The schoolmaster) AND WF., ELIZABETH.
Gilbert (twin), Susanna Rosina, b. June 22, 1783; bap. June 22, 1783; spon., Henry Graff and wf., Susanna.
Gilbert (twin), Margaret, b. June 22, 1783; bap. June 22, 1783; spon., John Miller and wf., Justina.

GEORGE ADAM GEISS.
Geiss, Henry Adam, b. June 21, 1764 (?); bapt. Sept. 10, 1764 (?); spon., George Henry Kettner and wf., Catharine.

JOHN DANIEL GROSS AND WF., SOPHIA DOROTHEA.
Gross, Anna Mary, b. Feby. 19, 1778; bap. Mch. 12, 1778; spon., Jacob Eichler and Anna Mary Romich.
Gross, Joh. Henry, b. Mch. 17, 1779; bap. Mch. 30, 1779; spon., Andrew Gross and Elizabeth Schmidt.
Gross, Mary Catharine, b. Feby. 15, 1784; bap. Apr. 18, 1784; spon., Simon Eichler and wf., Anna Catharine.

HENRY GRUBER.
Gruber, Joh. Adam, b. Oct. 19, 1735; bap. Jan. 11, 1736; spon., Joh. Adam Schroff and wf., Catharine Elizabeth.
Gruber, Catharine Elizabeth, b. Feby. 6, 1737; bap, Feby. 20, 1737; spon., Joh. Adam Schroff and wf.
Gruber, Mary Eva Rosina, b. Dec. 3, 1738; bap. Dec. 13, 1738; spon., Joh. Adam Schroff and wf.
Gruber, Christian, b. Feby. 18, 1740; bap. Mch. 11, 1740; spon., Christian Gruber and wf.
Gruber, Christopher, b. Dec. 11, 1741; bap. Dec. 27, 1741; spon., Christian Gruber and wf.
Gruber, Henry, b. Aug. 19, 1747.
Gruber, Elizabeth, b. Oct. 10, 1749; bap. Oct. 19, 1749; sp., Conrad Fink and wf., Catharine, and Elizabeth Beyer, dau. of Andrew Beyer.

NOTES AND QUERIES.

Historical, Biographical, and Genealogical.

XXXVIII.

Genealogical Queries.

CHARLTON.
Jeptha Charlton, born in England, and resided in Westmoreland county, Pa., from or before 1800 till 1817, and in 1800, married Rachel, daughter of Samuel and Mary (Marshal) Phipps. Where and when was he born, the full Christian names of his father and mother, and the date of marriage with Rachel Phipps?

CHRISTIE.
What is the date of the birth of Thomas Tilly Christie, son of Marvin and Hannah (Tilly) Christie, of Butler county, Pa.? Mr. Christie was born about 1817. What year, month and day?

HARLOW.
Narcissus D. Harlow, daughter of Mordecai and ——— (———) Harlow,

of Fauquier county, Va., and widow of —— Stiger. She was born about 1814. What did the initial letter "D" stand for, the date of her birth and where, the full maiden, Christian and surname of her mother; the Christian names, date and place of birth, date of death and place of burial of Mr. Stiger and date of marriage?

BARRON.

Elizabeth Barron married George McKinley in Westmoreland county, March 7, 1816, and had two sons: John, born March 23, 1817, and William, born March 15, 1819. What is the date and place of birth of Elizabeth Barron, date of her death and place of burial, what the full Christian name of her father and what were the full maiden, Christian and surname of her mother; also, the names and addresses of the descendants of her sons, John McKinley and William McKinley?

RIPLEY.

Frank L. Ripley married Alice Phipps in Butler, Pa., March 31, 1874. What is the full name of Mr. Ripley, date and place of birth, names of his father, maiden, Christian and surname of his mother and residence of his parents?

PHIPPS.

David Phipps was a resident of North Huntingdon township, Westmoreland county, Pa., in 1805. He gave a bill of sale, recorded in a deed, dated December 30, 1805, to John Sowash to secure him in the sum of $3,100, for signing an administrator's bond. Who was this David Phipps, the date and place of his birth, name of father, maiden name of his mother, residence of his parents, date of death and place of burial; if he married, then also the maiden name of his wife, date and place of her birth, date of her death and place of burial, date of their marriage, addresses of their descendants?

Was the Samuel Phipps, born in 1735, of whom mention was made in "Notes and Queries," September 16, 1899, a son of Nathan Phipps, born 1702, and Sarah Davies or Davis, and the great-grandson of Joseph Phipps, "The Friend?" Where did Joseph (Joseph, 2d) ,son of Joseph Phipps, "The Friend," live? Where did Nathan Phipps, son of Joseph and grandson of Joseph, "The Friend," reside? Did they or either of them first remove from the immediate neighborhood of Chester county, near Easttown, and subsequently, about 1773-5, remove to York county? When and where did the following Revolutionary War event take place, given me by one of the very old members of the family, as he recollects reading it in a family history, lost when fire consumed his parents' home? He writes: "I remember reading in that lost record, an incident of the Revolutionary period, written by an Updegraff, as follows: 'During an engagement or skirmish between Washington's troops and a British column, near Phipp's house, that Washington and his staff passed through the hall passage between the two compartments of the house.'" What were the names and place of residence of the Phipps referred to in this quotation?

McDOWELL.

What are the names of the marines, soldiers or sailors who went with Commodore Perry from the sinking Lawrence to the Niagara in the battle of "We have met the enemy and they are ours," on Lake Erie in 1814? Family tradition informs us that Allen McDowell was one of the volunteers, and before leaving the flagship that he distributed his money and all personal trinkets among his remaining comrades.

[Information in reply to the foregoing questions will be greatly appreciated by one preparing a genealogical table of the Phipps family, descendants of Joseph Phipps, "The Friend," the immigrant with and friend of William Penn, who arrived in 1681.

SAMUEL PHIPPS BRIGHAM.
Mineola (L. I.) N. Y.

Hays of Northampton County.

I. John Hays was one of the early settlers in the "Craig Settlement," Allen township, Northumberland county, Pa. He was an influential man in the "Settlement," and served as an officer on the frontiers during the French and Indian war. An interesting journal by him is printed in the seventh volume of first series, Pennsylvania Archives. Lieut. Hays m. in Ireland Jane Love, b. in 1712, and d. in 1806, in Northumberland county. He was b. in 1704, and d. Nov. 16, 1789. Their children were:

i. William.
2. ii. John, b. circa, 1730; m. first, Barbara King; m. secondly, Jane Walker.
iii. Isabel, m. Thomas Patton.
iv. Mary, d. young.
v. Elizabeth, d. 1818, in Beaver county, Pa.; m. Thomas Wilson, son of Judge Hugh and Sarah Wilson; he d. February 23, 1799.
3. vi. James, b. February 29, 1740; m. Sarah Brown.
vii. Robert, b. 1742; d. 1819; m. Mary Allison, and had issue:
  1. John.
  2. Jane.
  3. William, b. 1776.
  4. James.
  5. Joseph.
  6. Mary, m. —— Walker.
  7. Sarah, m. —— Shipman.
  8. Elizabeth.
viii. Jean, m. James Brown, son of Samuel and Jane (Boyd) Brown.
ix. Francis; removed to Tennessee.
x. Mary (second), m. James Gray; m. secondly —— Steele.

II. John Hays (John), b. about 1730, in Ireland; d. Nov. 3, 1796, at Meadville, Pa., whilst on a journey to Fort Pitt (Pittsburgh). He was an officer during the Revolutionary struggle. He was twice married. Married first, Oct. 16, 1760, Barbara King, b. about 1740; d. August 11, 1770; daughter of James King and his wife, Mary Boyd. They had issue:
i. Mary, b. 1761; d. Sept. 9, 1776.
ii. John, b. 1763; d. Oct. 9, 1821; m. May 21, 1795, Jane Horner, b. Oct. 20, 1765; d. Dec. 15, 1825; daughter of James Horner.
iii. James, b. 1765; d. March 1, 1829; m. Hannah Palmer, dau. of George Palmer.
iv. Jane, b. 1767; m. John Grier.

v. Elizabeth, b. 1769; d. Jan. 27, 1844; m. Dr. Edward Humphrey.

John Hays m., secondly, Jane Walker, d. Dec. 15, 1824, and they had issue:
vi. Ann, b. 1772; m. John Wilson.
vii. William, b. 1774; d. 1848; m. Lydia Temple.
viii. Isabella, b. 1776; m. John Ralston.
ix. Robert, b. 1778; d. Feb. 15, 1843; m. Eliza Hamilton.
x. Thomas, b. 1782; d. Dec. 9, 1847; m. Rachael Hamilton.
xi. Richard, b. 1784; d. Oct. 8, 1856; m. Christian Ralston.
xii. Samuel, d. near Erie, Pa., May 27, 1850.
xiii. Mary, b. 1787; d. Jan. 11, 1851, unm.
xiv. Joseph, b. 1789; d. March 30, 1895; m. Mary Allison.
xv. Rebecca, b. 1791; d. April 10, 1840; unm.

III. James Hays (John), b. Feb. 29, 1740; d. Feb. 14, 1817. He was a lieutenant during the French and Indian war, serving under Colonel Bouquet. He settled on Beach creek and died there. He m. Sarah Brown, b. Feb. 15, 1745; d. May 5, 1823; dau. of Samuel Brown and his wife, Jane Boyd. She was sister to Lieut. Robert Brown, of Colonel Baxter's Flying Camp, captured at Fort Washington, Nov. 16, 1776; and was afterwards major-general of the Pennsylvania militia, and a member of Congress eighteen years.

SAMUEL CRAIG.

Wapakoneta, O.

BAPTISMAL AND OTHER RECORDS

Of "The Little Tulpehocken Church."

II.

CHRISTIAN GRUBER.

Gruber, Joh. George, b. Feb. 16, 1743; bap. Feb. 20, 1743; spon., Henry Gruber and wf.
Gruber, Susanna, b. Aug. 12, 1746; bap. Aug. 31, 1746; spon., Martin Stup and wf. Susanna.

Historical and Genealogical.

JACOB GRETER.
Greter, Joh. George, b. Sep. 7, 1739; bap. Oct. 23, 1739; spon., Joh. George Hess and Mary Barbara Stoer.
Greter, Joh. Henry, b. Feb. 7, 1742; bap. Feb. 21, 1742; spon., Joh. Henry Gruber and wf. Mary Rosina.

GEORGE WILLIAM GUESEMAN.
Gueseman, Ann Margaret, b. Dec. 9, 1749; bap. Jan. 21, 1750; spon., Anna Margaret Heck.
Gueseman, Joh. George, b. ———, ———; bap. March 3, 1754; spon., Joh. George Gueseman.

CHRISTIAN GUTLENDER and wf. Elizabeth.
Gutlender, John Paul, b. June 23, 1788; bap. Aug. 10, 1788; spon., John Paul Wenrich and Mary Barbara Gilbert (both single).
Gutlender, Mary Catharine, b. Oct. 20, 1789; bap. July 18, 1790; spon., George Gutlender and wf. Mary Catharine.
JACOB GUTLENDER and wf. Justina.
Gutlender, George William, b. March 11, 1789; bap. April 14, 1789; spon., George Wm. Berger and wf. Anna Mary.

GEORGE GUTMAN.
Gutman, Joh. Henry, b. May 30, 1742; bap. July 11, 1742; spon., Henry Berger and Rosina Fertig.

JOH. GEORGE HAACK.
Haack, Mary Susanna, b. Nov. 14, 1734; bap. Jan. 8, 1735; spon., Mary Susanna Dieter.

ABRAHAM HAASS.
Haass, John Nicholas, b. June 6, 1742; bap. July 1, 1742; spon., Joh. Nicholas Fuester and wf. Elizabeth.
Haass, Mary Susanna, b. Sept. 28, 1744; bap. Nov. 19, 1744; spon., Samuel Philbert and wf.

MCHAEL HAMBORGER.
Hamborger, Catharine Margaret, b. Nov. 10, 1751; bap. Nov. 17, 1751; spon., Joh. George Muench and Mr. Gutmann.

JOHN HEDDERICH.
Hedderich, John Wirner, b. July 7, 1744; bap. ———, ———; spon., Wirner Weitzel.

JOST HEDDERICH.
Hedderich, Anna Margaret, b. July 26, 1745; bap. Sept. 26, 1745; spon., Anna Margaret, for Magdalena Heddrich, a minor.

PHILIP HEILIGER.
Heiliger, Christina Barbara, b. Feb. 8, 1748; bap. March 6, 1748; spon., Peter Muench and wf., Christina Barbara.

JOHN ADOLPH HEINRICH.
Heinrich, Anna Mary, b. Aug. 21, 1740; bap. Sept. 14, 1740; spon., Joh. Nicholas Holder and wf.
Heinrich, Mary Elizabeth, b.July 24, 1744; bap. Aug. 19, 1744; spon., Tobias Bickel and wf.

VALENTINE HIMMELBERGER.
Himmelberger, Mary Elizabeth, b. July 1, 1741; bap. Oct. 11, 1741; spon., Mary Elizabeth Lehm or Lehmi.

JOHN HIMMELBERGER.
Himmelberger, Catharine, b. April 9, 1797.

CASPAR HINCKEL.
Hinckel, Mary Margaret, b. Oct. 14, 1771; bap. Oct. 27, 1771; spon., Michael Follmer and wf.

JOH. GEORGE KEBLINGER.
Keblinger, Catharine Elizabeth, b. Dec. 2, 1741; bap. Dec. 7, 1741; spon., Paul Keblinger and Catharine Umbehagen.
Keblinger, Joh. Samuel, b. Sept. 14, 1743; bap. Oct. 9, 1743; spon., Joh. Samuel Philbert and wf. Susanna.

JOHN KELLER and wf. Christina.
Keller, Philip Tobias, b. May 1, 1742; bap. May 16, 1742; spon., Tobias Bickel and wf.
Keller, John, b. Sept. 22, 1743; bap. Oct. 9, 1743; spon., Jacob Vollmar, snr., and wf.

FREDERICK KERCHER.
Kercher, Jacob, b. ——— ———, 1754; bap. June 9, 1754; spon., Jacob Beck and wf. Catharine.
Kercher, Jacob Frederic, b. Oct. 10, 1757; bap. Nov. 10, 1757; spon., Jacob Beck and wf. Catharine.

THOMAS KERN.
Kern, Simon, b. Feb. 24, 1742; bap. April 18, 1742; spon., Simon Bogenreif and wf.

GEORGE MICHAEL KITTNER (Kettner in index.)
Kittner, Mary Eve, b. April 7, 1741; bap. May ———, 1741; spon., Mary Eve Friederich.

HENRY KICHEL.
Kichel, Christian, b. March 9, 1743; bap.

March 20, 1743; spon., Christian Meyer and wf.

WILLIAM KLEE.
Klee, Emilia, b. July 4, 1834; bap. Sept. 7, 1834; spon., Catharine Heider.
Klee, Mary Amanda, b. Apr. 4, 1836; bap. July 7, 1836; spon., John Schaefer and wf., Susanna.

JOHN KNOLL.
Knoll, Mary Catharine, b. July 21, 1741; bap. Sept. 4, 1741; spon., George Daniel Gensemer and wf.

PETER KNOPFF.
Knopff, Eva Catharine, b. Feby. 11, 1741; bap. April 22, 1741; spon., Michael Busch and wf.
Knopff, a daughter, b. June 13, 1749; bap. July 2, 1749; spon., John Eckert and wf.

ANDREW KOCHENDOERFFER.
Kochendoerffer, Andrew, b. June 23, 1742; bap. July 11, 1742; spon., Andrew Craft and wf.
Kochendoerffer, Geo. Philip, b. April 8, 1746; bap. May 8, 1746; spon., Geo. Philip Ruhl and Anna Margaret Roth.

JOH. MICHAEL KOEHL and wf., Mary Catharine.
Koehl, Joh. George, b. Oct. 18, 1760; bap. Oct. 26, 1760; spon., George Koehl and wf., Elizabeth.
Koehl, Anna Catharine (twin), b. July 21, 1762; bap. July 25, 1762; spon., Henry Kettner and wf.
Koehl, Justina (twin), b. July 21, 1762; bap. July 25, 1762; spon., Henry Shepler and wf., Justina Catharine.
Koehl, Joh. Peter, b. Mch. 12, 1764; bap. Apr. 1, 1764; spon., Peter Albert and Eve Kettner, both single.

ANDREW KRAFFT.
Krafft, Joh. Jacob, b. May 17, 1730; bap. Oct. 27, 1730; spon., Joh. Jacob Kitzmiller and wf., Anna Mary.
Krafft, John, b. Sept. 30, 1731; bap. Nov. 14, 1731; spon., Joh. Jacob Kitzmiller and wf., Anna Mary.
Krafft, Anna Mary, b. Apr. 16, 1733; bap. Sept. 16, 1733; spon., Joh. Jacob Kitzmiller and wf., Anna Mary.
Krafft, Anna Margaret, b. Dec. 27, 1734; bap. Dec. 28, 1734; spon., Anna Mary Kitzmiller, represented by Anna Margaret Fay.
Krafft, Mary Catharine, b. Mch. 15, 1736; bap. July 25, 1736; spon., Mary Elizabeth Beyer.
Krafft, Mary Elizabeth, b. Apr. 17, 1737; bap. July 17, 1737; spon., Henry Beyer and wf.
Krafft, Justina Catharine, b. Mch. 4, 1739; bap. Apr. 22, 1739; spon., Justina Catharine Kayser.
Krafft, Andrew, b. Feby. 1, 1741; bap. Apr. 12, 1741; spon., Andrew Kochendoerffer and wf.
Krafft, Mary Magdalene, b. Sept. 7, 1742; bap. Oct. 18, 1742; spon., Michael Krafft and wf., Mary Magdalene.
Krafft, Mary Susanna, b. Apr. 9, 1744; bap. Apr. 29, 1744; spon., Samuel Philbert and wf., Susanna.

HENRY KUEHLER.
Kuehler, Mary Catharine, b. July 19, 1741; bap. Aug. 2, 1741; spon., John Meyer and wf.

JOHN LANG.
Lang, John, b. Aug. 21, 1737; bap. Feby. 5, 1738; spon., John Schaffer and wf., Susanna.
Lang, Anna Margaret, b. Feby. 21, 1740; bap. Mch. 30, 1740; spon., Ludwig Wagner and wf.
Lang, Jacob, b. Jan. 12, 1742; bap. Jan. 24, 1742; spon., Jacob Scharff and wf.
Lang, Joh. George Thomas, b. July 1, 1746; bap. Sept. 6, 1746; spon., Joh. Thomas Kern and wf., Margaret.

MARTIN LANG and wf., Agnes.
Lang, John, b. Apr. 9, 1756; bap. Apr. 18, 1756; spon., John Zopff and wf., Margaret.
Lang, Samuel, b. Aug. 26, 1761; bap. Sept. 1, 1761; spon., John Hoff and wf.

CASPAR LERCH.
Lerch, Anna Elizabeth, b. June 16, 1741; bap. Aug. 11, 1741; spon., Anna Elizabeth Ermentraut.

JACOB LINGEL and wf., Catharine.
Lingel, Joseph, b. Mch. 14, 1787; bap. May 2, 1787; spon., Caspar Lingel.

MATTHIAS LINGEL and wf., Euphrosina.
Lingel, Joel, b. May 28, 1814; bap. ——. —, ——; spon., Michael Schaeffer.

JOHN LINGEL and wf., Susanna.
Lingel, David, b. Feby. 11, 1811; bap. ——. ——, ——; spon., Michael Schaeffer.
Lingel, Salome, b. Apr. 23, 1812; bap.

——. —, ——; spon., Stephen Lingel and wf., Susanna.
Lingel, Henry, b. July 9, 1813; bap. ——. —, ——; spon., Adam Lingel and wf., Elizabeth.
Lingel, John, b. Oct. 20, 1814; bap. ——.
—, ——; spon., David Lingel.
Lingel, Daniel, b. Jan. 1, 1816; bap. ——.
—, ——; spon., Jacob Lingel and wf., Catharine.
Lingel, Isaac, b. May 29, 1817; bap. ——.
—, ——; spon., —— ——.

PAUL LUENGEL.

Luengel, John, b. June 5, 1741; bap. July 5, 1741; spon., John Artzt and wf.
Luengel, Joh. Nicholas, b. Feb. 1, 1743; bap. March 20, 1743; spon., Joh. Nicholas Holder and wf.
Luengel, Joh. Martin, b. July 30, 1761; bap. Aug. 2, 1761; spon., Martin Laey and wf.

JOHN LEONHARD and Mary Magdalene, a free negress. (Not in index.)
Leonhard, Jacob, b. June 14, 1783; bap. Oct. 20, 1783; spon., Jacob Weininger and wf.

JOHN LUTZ and wf. Sarah.

Lutz, Levi, b. Dec. 29, 1836; bap. March 24, 1838; spon., John Schaeffer and wf., Susanna.

MARTIN LINGLE and wf. Elizabeth. (Not in index.)
Lingel, Jacob, b. July 19, 1786; bap. Aug. 3, 1786; spon., Jacob Lingel and wf. Barbara.
Lingel, Mary Salome, b. June 7, 1798; bap. Aug. 5, 1798; spon., Abelona Wagner.

JOHN METH (Meeth in index).
Meeth, Joanna Mary, b. Dec. 13, 1745; bap. Dec. 25, 1745; spon., Philip Meth or Weeth.

CONRAD MESSERSCHMIDT.

Messerschmidt, Joh. Conrad, b. Sept. 13, 1741; bap. Sept. 12, 1741; spon., Joh. Conrad Kerschner.

JOHN MEYER.

Meyer, Tobias, b. Sept. 22, 1740; bap. Nov. 8, 1740; spon., Tobias Bechtel and wf.
Meyer, John, b. Aug. 3, 1742; bap. Sept. 7, 1742; spon., John Meeth.

BENJAMIN MILLER and wf. Eve.
Miller, Salome, b. July 12, 1787; bap. Aug. 13, 1787; spon., Simon Boltz and wf. Christina.

JOHN MILLER and wf. Justina.
Miller, Mary Elizabeth, b. Oct. 25, 1784; bap. Dec. 25, 1784; spon., Matthias Miller and wf. Mary Elizabeth.
Miller, Joh. Jacob, b. March 11, 1774; bap. March 27, 1774; spon., —— (a separate record).
Miller, Matthew, b. Sept. 12, 1780; bap. Oct. — 1780; spon., Matthew Staudt and wf. Margaret.

JOHN MILLER, the tanner, and wf. Mary Salome.
Miller, John, b. Sept. 18, 1790; bap. Oct. 20, 1790; spon., Matthew Miller and wf. Mary.
Miller, Samuel, b. July 4, 1792; bap. July 26, 1792; spon., Conrad Gilbert and wf., Anna Elizabeth.

GEORGE MILLER, the mason, and wf. Elizabeth.
Miller, Michael, b. Sept. 28, 1790; bap. Oct. 2, 1790; spon., Simon and Catharine Miller, both single.
Miller, Elizabeth, b. Nov. 2, 1792; bap. Nov. 22, 1792; spon., Matthew Miller and wf. Mary.

ULRICH MICHAEL.

Michael, Margaret, b. Jan. 8, 1741; bap. Aug. 2, 1741; spon., Elizabeth Haass.

JACOB MUELLER.

Mueller, John Jacob, b. Sept. 24, 1728; bap. Sept. 26, 1728 (bap. in Europe); spon., Frederic William Beckle, Christopher Haist, Joseph Rohr and Joh. David Bauer.
Mueller, John, b. Nov. 9, 1733; bap. Nov. 16, 1733; spon., Joh. Henry Fegner and Mary Elizabeth Barbara Schneider. This one was born in Pennsylvania and bap. by Philip Boehm, Ref. minister on (at) White Marsh.
Mueller, Mary Elizabeth Barbara, b. Sept. 9, 1736; bap. Sept. 28, 1736; spon., Joh. Henry Fegner and Mary Elizabeth Barbara Schneider; bap. by Bartholomew Rugner, Ref. pastor at Germantown at the time.
Mueller, Matthias, b. Oct. 18, 1743; bap. Nov. 6, 1743, by Joh. Casper Stoever; spon., Matthias Schmidt and wf.
Mueller, Elizabeth Barbara, b. June 7, 1755; bap. —— —— ——; spon., Elizabeth Cara.

THOMAS MUELLER.

Mueller, Joh. Michael, b. July 3, 1746; bap. July 6, 1746; spon., Michael Kaeyser and wf.

Mueller, Margaret, b. Dec. 17, 1748; bap. Jan. 11, 1749; spon., Nicholas Lang, John Lang, Anna Mary Lang, Anna Margaret Hoegele.

JOHN MUELLER and wf. Justina Catharine.

Mueller, Cath. Elizabeth, b. April 16, 1768; bap. — — —; spon., Elizabeth Barbara Mueller.

Mueller, Justina, b. March 24, 1760; bap. — — —; spon., John Hess and wf. Catharine Elizabeth.

NOTES AND QUERIES.

Historical, Biographical and Genealogical.

XXXIX.

POLK.

I am the daughter of Allen W. Newsom and Annie M. White; granddaughter of John White and Amanda Adams, his wife; great-granddaughter of Isaac Adams and Nancy Polk, his wife and great-great-granddaughter of Ephraim Polk and Rhoda Morris, his wife. Can you give me the Revolutionary record of Ephraim Polk. W. N.

Carthage, Ind.

[The services of Ephraim Polk may be found in Penna. Archives, second series, vol. xiii, page 673.]

Thirty Thousand Names,

Of Immigrants into Pennsylvania, originally compiled by I. Daniel Rupp, has recently been reprinted by Messrs. Leary, Stuart & Co., No. 9 S. Ninth street, Philadelphia. The great demand for this volume, so useful in genealogical research by our Pennsylvania-German friends, has induced these enterprising booksellers to issue the volume, which they have done in good shape. The former edition has become so scarce that this one will be timely. It is a great repository for genealogists.

History of the Keagy Family,

Is the title of an interesting family genealogy, by Franklin Keagy, of Chambersburg, issued from the press of the Harrisburg Publishing Company. On the title page the author gives this testimony: "Let the twenty-three years of toil in collecting the data for the genealogical record attest the love I bear for the Keagy relationship." Well said, and the six hundred and fifty pages of this volume prove how intense this love for genealogical research worked wonders. The author has done his work conscientiously, as we can fully testify, for here and there are the records of those concerning whom we learned years and years ago, and he has proved a faithful chronicler. The Keagy "freundschaft" owe him a debt of gratitude which they never can repay. Mr. Keagy certainly is deserving of all praise, and the book is a valuable contribution to Pennsylvania-German family history. This volume shows how far-reaching the connections of any one family may extend, for we find allied to the Pennsylvania Keagys, Hon. Thomas F. Bayard, of Delaware, and many others, North as well as South, who have honored their family and country. Among this representative family were those who in the Civil War served in both the Union and Confederate armies, as well as ministers, physicians, lawyers, artists and college professors, a bright array of men of mark in their special walks in life. The book is illustrated with a large number of excellent halftoned engravings of persons and places. Unfortunately we miss two of the representative men—Dr. John M. Keagy, who taught a classical academy at Harrisburg, and Isaac Keagy, a famous printer, on the old "Democratic Union" (not the "Telegraph") nearly fifty years ago. There is one fault we find with the author—there should be a fuller index, especially of surnames. The typographical execution of the volume is excellent, and the Harrisburg Publishing Comany know how to do superb printing.

JOHN FRANKLIN MEGINNESS,

The Historian of the West Branch Valley.

[The Editor of "Notes and Queries," on the afternoon of November 11, 1899, had a two hours delightful visit from his friend of many years, John F. Meginness, of Williamsport, the accomplished historian of the West Branch Valley. Entertaining in his talk, the impression he left was one of pleasure. Little thought the writer that seven hours later, the Death-Angel would have stamped his seal on heart and brain. Reaching his home, perchance somewhat excited, he suddenly fell over dead. The shock at this sudden termination of a brilliant earthly career cannot be described. It was only a few weeks prior (October 25, 1899,) that he bade his friends to the celebration of the fiftieth anniversary of his wedding. Living beyond three score and ten, his apparent good health gave promise of a few more years of historic labor and usefulness. Verily it is well, that while the day is here that one works with his might lest no other dawn on him. Mr. Meginness was an indefatigable delver. He made his researches conscientiously—and truth was his sole aim in historic lore. He accomplished much—he preserved for the years to come great treasure-houses of history, biography and genealogy. If there is any one in the entire West Branch Valley who dare step in his shoes let him come forth. Mr. Meginness was a perfect encyclopedia of West Branch history—and this was only gathered through almost fifty eyars of quiet, faithful delving. Shall we look upon his like again? No, not in this decade nor in the next. Founded upon the data he gathered, the writers for the years to come must depend upon the unrequited labors of that man of toil, of erudition, and research. One by one the scribes of the historic past are going out from the homes of the living. Within the past two years Pennsylvania has lost many gifted in this field of literature, Frederick D. Stone, William S. Baker, John Blair Linn, Dallas Albert, and others—a bright array of the literati of our Commonwealth—while within the month the galaxy of stars has been dimmed by the death of Isaac Craig, Dr. John G. Brinton, Dr. W. J. Hoffman and John F. Meginness. Others may—nay, will—rise up and take their places, but these shall thrive on the legacies left them by the reapers who have gathered up their sheaves. Few of the people of to-day properly appreciate the excellent services of these men of letters, yet the work of their brain will live long after the sensational literature of the present shall be remanded to a deserved oblivion. This much by way of prelude.]

John Franklin Meginness was born July 16, 1827, in Colerain township, Lancaster county, Penn'a, and died November 11, 1899, at Williamsport, Penn'a. He was the eldest son of Benjamin Meginness and his wife, Sarah Johnston. He was brought up on a farm and educated in the public schools of his day. His parents removed to the West in 1843, but John F. returned to Pennsylvania on the eve of the war with Mexico. His military enthusiasm becoming aroused, in company with some young friends he enlisted "for the war" on the 9th of April, 1847. He participated in the campaign in the Valley of Mexico, and served until the ratification of the treaty of peace. He then returned to Pennsylvania, taught two terms of school in Lycoming county, and marrying, October 25, 1849, he settled down at Jersey Shore. In 1852 he became editor of the Jersey Shore "Republican," continuing until 1854, when he assisted in the founding of "The News Letter" in that town. This partnership lasted one year. Conceiving the idea of preparing a history of the West Branch Valley of the Susquehanna, this work was completed, and published in 1856. From 1857 to 1861, Mr. Meginness was engaged in active newspaper work in Illinois. Disposing of his newspaper office in October of the latter year, he removed to Pennsylvania, and located at Williamsport.

During the War for the Union, Mr. Meginness was a clerk in the quartermaster's department—from 1862 to 1865. At the close of the war he received an appointment as clerk in the Treasury Department where he remained until June 1, 1869. After his retirement, he became the managing editor of the daily "Lycoming Gazette," which was subsequently consolidated with the daily evening "Bulletin," under the title of "Gazette and Bulletin," one of the most influential newspapers of the West Branch. He maintained his connection with this paper until November, 1889, when, owing to impaired health, he was obliged to resign.

Soon after retiring from newspaper work, Mr. Meginness resumed his historic labors, in connection with that of newspaper correspondent, over the signature of "John of Lancaster." The following is an imperfect list of his publications:

Otzinachson: A History of the West Branch Valley of the Susquehanna. Phila., 1857, imp. 8 vo., p. 518.

History, Advantages, Resources and Industries of the City of Williamsport. Map and Illus. Williamsport, 1886, imp. 8 vo., p. 87.

Journal of Samuel Maclay, while Assisting in the Survey of the West Branch of the Susquehanna, the Sinnemahoning and Allegheny Rivers in 1790. Williamsport, 1887, imp. 8 vo., p. 63.

The Historical Journal: A Monthly Record of Local History and Biography. Vol. 1. Williamsport, 1888, imp. 8 vo., p. 396, ii.

Otzinachson: A History of the West Branch Valley of the Susquehanna. Revised Edition, vol. 1. Williamsport, 1889, imp. 8 vo., p. 702. v.

Biographical Annals of Deceased Residents of the West Branch Valley of the Susquehanna. Williamsport, 1889, imp. 8 vo., p. 272.

Biography of Frances Slocum, the Lost Sister of Wyoming. Williamsport, 1891, mp. 8 vo., p. 238, iv, 8.

Origin and History of the Mageniss Family. Williamsport, 1891, 8 vo., p. 245, iii.

History of Lycoming County, Pennsylvania. Chicago, 1892, 4to, p. xv, 1268.

Genealogy and History of the Hepburn Family. Williamsport, 1894, 8 vo., p. 181, iv.

History of the Great Island and William Dunn, Its Owner. Illustrated. Williamsport, 1894, 8 vo., p. 128.

Lycoming County and Its First Centennial. Williamsport, 1895, 8 vo., p. 82.

The Centennial Aniversary of Lycoming County, Pa. Williamsport, 1896, imp. 8vo., p. 32.

"Iron" John Thomas. Address at the Reunion of the Thomas Family. Williamsport, Aug. 20, 1890, imp., 8 vo., p. 17.

The Scotch-Irish of the Upper Susquehanna Valley. Harrisburg, 1896, 8 vo., p. 11.

Gen. Arthur St. Clair, His History and Descendants. Harrisburg, 1897, imp. 8vo., p. 32.

Annals of Montoursville, Pa., from the Earliest Times to the Present. Montoursville, 1898, imp., 8 vo., p. 122.

A Bibliography of the West Branch Valley. Williamsport, 1898, imp. 8 vo., p. 32.

Life and Times of Robert Robb, Esq., of Muncy Township. Muncy Luminary, 1899, imp., 8 vo., p. 53.

The following volumes of history were edited in part by Mr. Meginness:

History of Butler County, Penn'a. Chicago, 1895, 4to [299 to 383.]

History of the City of Cincinnati, Ohio, 2 vols. Chicago, 1896, 4to.

History of Tioga County, Penn'a. Harrisburg, 1897, 4to [1 to 437.]

Biographical Encyclopedia of the Juniata Valley, 2 vols. Harrisburg, 1897, 4to.

Biographical and Genealogical History of Delaware, 2 vols. Harrisburg, 1898, 4to.

In conclusion, we are all aware that every workman must have tools. Mr. Meginness gathered, during his lifetime, an exceedingly valuable library of local history, and we know that it was one of his fondest wishes that this should be kept intact. We hope this may be done, and that the liberal citizens of Williamsport will see that it is not scattered to the four winds of heaven. They ought to secure it for their city, as they could pay no greater tribute to his worth and services. It will form the nucleus of a public library which will increase in value as the years roll on.

The Morus Multicaulis Craze.
1836—1841.

Paper prepared by Rudolph F. Kelker, Esq., and read by William A. Kelker before the Historical Society of Dauphin county, Nov. 9, 1899, with additional newspaper data of the period.

Some sixty odd years ago, about 1836 to '38, a considerable interest was excited among our citizens on the subject of silk culture. A party from New England came to Harrisburg and leased from Mr. Aaron Bombaugh a lot of ground on the north side of "Hammond's Lane" (now Herr street) containing five acres, extending from Front street towards Third street. The ground was ploughed and soil prepared as the farmer of the present prepares his ground for raising potatoes. This ground was planted in furrows perhaps three feet apart with the small pieces of the thin limbs or shoots of the morus multicaulis, or white mulberry tree, each piece containing two or three buds. The crop was carefully cultivated and when the autumn arrived, the entire lot was covered with young trees, varying in height from three to six feet. The owner or owners had in the meantime erected a large shed, and on a certain set day, according to previous advertisement, the public were invited to purchase. Long counters were erected in the shed, marked with feet and inches, and the young trees were measured by laying them on the counters and sold to the purchasers at so much per foot. Some residents of the town and farmers in the surrounding counties, as were disposed to try the experiment, either of raising trees to feed silk worms, or to raise mulberry trees for sale, flocked to the premises, and the whole crop was purchased and carried off, every purchaser expecting to reap a rich profit. The strangers departed with the money and were heard of no more.

Next season, an enterprising citizen, hoping to recover from great financial losses (previously incurred) rented eight acres of land lying between the Pennsylvania canal and the Susquehanna river, now intersected by Dock and other streets and alleys in the vicinity, then owned by Judges Valentine Hummel and William Dock, and planted the entire plot with the "morus multicaulis." When the plants had reached the height of a few feet, it was said that he was offered eighteen cents a plant (and there were many thousands of them) but refused the offer, believing that he would realize a much better price in the following autumn. Unfortunately the bubble burst by that time and a total loss ensued. The owners of the land at a great expense a few years afterwards had to have the forest or jungle of trees grubbed up and burned. They had reached the height of ten or twelve feet and had covered the lot with an impenetrable growth.

Some persons undertook to raise trees and begin silk culture, believing that it could be made a profitable industry. Among these was a Mr. Shannon, who erected a large building on Front street, a short distance south of what is now called Reily street. Here he fed many thousands of silk worms daily with the mulberry leaves. He had shelves arranged in tiers along the sides of the interior of the building upon which he fed the worms. It involved constant attention and great labor, for the papers upon which they were placed had to be cleansed at least twice a day and fresh leaves provided. The writer cannot learn what success attended Mr. Shannon's well meant enterprise.

It was soon discovered by the people that the great obstacles to success were our climate and the price of labor. The spirit of speculation was, however, not confined to the citizens of Harrisburg by any means, but spread throughout the country, as will appear by the following advertisements and notices of the morus multicaulis copied from the "Pennsylvania Telegraph" published at Harrisburg, which gives a much better account of the so-called "craze" than the compiler of this paper can render.

[From Pennsylvania Telegraph of 11th May, 1836, taken from Lexington, Ky., Intelligencer.]
CULTURE OF SILK.
The following remarks on the subject of the culture of silk are from a letter of

a gentleman of Lexington, now in Virginia, to his friend.

Valley of Virginia, 5th March, 1836.

Dear Sir:—With some limitation, it is confessedly an axiom truth, that he who, by proper directed efforts, becomes the instrument of causing two blades of grass to spring in place of one, or, in any way multiplying the available means of sustenance—food or raiment, is regarded as one of the greatest temporal benefactors of his race. Believing in common with a comparatively small number (I am sorry to say) of the American people, that an extended field is now certainly open in nearly all latitudes of this widely extended country, for individual enterprise and emolument in the silk culture, I have taken the liberty, for the want of a better subject, to address you briefly within the limits of a single letter, a few conclusions which have been arrived at on this subject by extended trial, in the experience of gentlemen both in the Eastern and Middle States. I write you with the more willingness on this subject, because I recollect to have heard your favorable expressions respecting this branch of national independence and profit—and believing, further, that there are few in my adopted State who have the means more at disposal to take lead by introducing immediately the morus alba and morus multicaulis, or true Chinese mulberry tree, and who would become the organ with more willingness of widely disseminating knowledge to our fellow citizens in the west on this interesting branch of pastoral economy. My principal design shall then be to give you an abstract drawn up by a gentleman of experience, resident in the city of Albany, New York, embracing the expenditures and proceeds for seven successive years, commencing with 200 cuttings, chiefly intended to show that the business may be commenced without capital, successfully, as follows:

First Year.

Rent for one acre for nursery..	$5 00
Two hundred cuttings, say	2 00
Trouble of collecting, setting, etc., ...	2 00
Feeding 500 worms	2 00
	$11 00

Cr. 50,000 eggs sold at 12½ per 1,000	6.25
Net expense first year	$4 75

Second Year.

Rent for nursery	$5 00
Propagating by cuttings or layers 1,000 trees	6 00
Feeding 15,000 worms	10 00
Reeling 6 ℔s silk	4 50
	$25 50
Cr. 6 ℔s silk sold at $5 per ℔..	30 00
Net gain second year	$4 50

Third Year Statement.

Rent	$5 00
Setting 7,000 trees	21 00
Feeding and care 5,000 worms..	25 00
Reeling 20 ℔s silk	15 00
	$66 00
Twenty ℔s silk sold at $5 per ℔	100 00
Net gain third year	$34 00

Statement for Fourth Year.

Rent of nursery	5 00
Rent of field 20 acres at $2....	40 00
Preparing ground and transplanting 1,200 trees	12 00
Attendance of worms and reeling 50 ℔s silk	100 00
	$157 00
Cr. 50 ℔s silk at $5 per ℔	250 00
Net gain fourth year	$93 00

Fifth Year.

Rent nursery and field	$42 00
Transplanting 7,000 trees	35 00
Feeding and care 1,000,000 worms	250 00
Reeling 416 ℔s silk	312 00
	$639 50
416 ℔s silk at $5 per ℔	2,080 00
Net proceeds fifth year	$1,441 50

Sixth Year.

Rent	$42 50
Transplanting 4,700 trees......	235 00
Feeding and care of 2,500,000 worms	300 00
Reeling 1,041 ℔s of silk	205 50

Interest of cocoonery supposed to have been built last year,	210 00
	$1,308.00
1,041 ℔s silk at $5 per ℔	5,205 00
Net gain 6th year	$3,897 00

Seventh Year.

Allowing for rent and interest this year as before, feeding and care of 15,536,000 worms and reeling 6,886 ℔s silk	4,000 00
6,886 ℔s silk, sold at $5 per ℔,	34,430 00
Net proceeds seventh year after liberal allowances	$30,430.00

[Note—Error in sixth year.—W. A. K.]

We are assured that there is nothing visionary in this calculation, and there is no item in which it has not been far outdone in practice—nothing in it but what any practical grower of silk knows can be realized. Comment on the above is unnecessary; every one at a single view may see and decide for him or herself, that even in this notable age and generation for thrift and speculation, that no branch of business or investment can possibly yield such an astounding dividend, after the first few years of preparation. In a national point of view, its importance can only be measured by reference to the item of silk in the treasurer's report, which causes an annual drain from the United States of from six to ten million of dollars. The morus genus will thrive well in the poor lands of Virginia, and I am very happy to say, that M. C. R., esq., my brother, has obtained through a correspondence with Judge Spencer, of Albany, the seed of morus alba, the growing shoots from which I saw in his nursery yesterday.

P. S.—For want of room elsewhere I wish to say here, that the morus multicaulis may be obtained at Prince's Garden, New York; St. Clair's, Baltimore, or Philadelphia, or at Newton, near Boston.

[10th March, 1837.]
Black Horse, Chester County, Pa.
Italian mulberry trees for sale from 6 inches to four feet high, $20 to $60 per 1,000. Chinese mulberry trees can be had in the fall of 1837 at the above mentioned place.
Owen Williams.

[23rd March, 1837.]
Harrisburg, Pa.
* * * * White Italian and Chinese mulberries for sale by
Philip Wolfersberger.

[18th April 1838.]
CHINESE MULBERRY (Morus Multicaulis).
The subscriber (of Lewisberry, York county, Pa.) has for sale 1,000 Chinese mulberry (morus multicaulis- and 1,500 cuttings of the same, which he will dispose of on reasonable terms. He will attend at Harrisburg with a lot of them for a few days previous to the adjourning of the Legislature, to sell and put up for any person who may purchase and will have a supply kept for sale by Mr. Philip Wolfersberger, Market Square, Harrisburg, and contemplates being at Lebanon and Reading immediately after the Legislature adjourns; perhaps he may stop at several of the smaller towns along the pike between Harrisburg and Reading.
Hervey Hammond.

SILK CONVENTION.
[Monday, 25th February, 1839.]
Harrisburg, Pa.
The silk convention that met here on Friday last was composed of from eighty to one hundred delegates, from fifteen or twenty counties of the State. It presented a respectable appearance, and being attended by several gentlemen of other States, among whom was Mr. Olmstead, from Hartford, and Mr. Smith, from Baltimore, who have had several years experience in the business, much information was dissemated and a new impulse given to the enterprise. These gentlemen and others exhibited specimens of sewing and manufactured silk, cocoons, reeling and spinning machinery, etc., which attracted much attention. A State society was formed, consisting of upwards of one hundred members, of which the Hon. Calvin Blythe was chosen president. The convention adopted a report and other

proceedings and adjourned on Saturday evening. Morus multicaulis and the worm is a principal topic now.

[19th June, 1839.]
LANCASTER COUNTY SILK.
(From the Pennsylvania Telegraph taken from the "Lancaster Union.")

We were shown a few days since a number of very beautiful pocket handkerchiefs made of Lancaster county silk reeled and spun by Messrs. R. and H. Carson, merchants of this city. We feel quite confident we never saw a better article of the kind. They were woven in Philadelphia and nearly twice as heavy as imported ones of the same size, retaining all the softness which characterizes the fabric. We were also shown a quantity of sewing silk, but not having much confidence in our knowledge of such matters we submitted to the inspection of one every way qualified to judge of its merits, some skeins presented to us by the manufacturers, and it was pronounced to be for evenness of thread, beauty of colour, and strength not to be surpassed. The Messrs. Carson have an extensive cocoonery and feed a great number of worms. One leaf of the multicaulis grown by them this summer measures 15¾ inches across. We hope they may succeed fully in an enterprise so beneficial to the community."

[19th June, 1839. Copied from the Petersburg, Va., "Constellation" by the Penna. Telegraph.]
MORUS MULTICAULIS.

We believe we write the words "Morus Multicaulis" editorially for the first time in our life, and we do so now to notice what appears to be generally the fact, that the plantings of this spring have to a great extent failed to come up throughout the Union. At the North the culturists have suffered with unprecedented severity in this respect, and in Virginia there is general complaint of the decay and blight of the cuttings. It is our ill-luck to speak experimentally on this subject. As a matter of amusement, rather than with the expectation of gain, we planted about 1,700 buds (obtained from three several dealers) in a soil well adapted to the purpose, one eighth of which only have come up, and promise to do well. Of the buds planted 400 were of Northern growth, 300 raised in Virginia, and 1,000 in North Carolina, and it is not a little remarkable that the Northern buds which appeared to be in the best order—putting out—in fact, a less number came up than those of Virginia and North Carolina growth. In Carolina the mulberry speculators appear to be very unfortunate indeed. The Raleigh Register of the first instant says: "In this city and the vicinity, the business has been extensively engaged in, and in no instance within our knowledge, not more than the half of the plantings have come up. In many cases the failure of the buddings to vegetate is much more discouraging, and this seems to be the general complaint throughout the country, wherever the culture of the multicaulis has been engaged in North and South." The Newbern "Speculator" mentions "that out of 1,500 roots and cuttings planted by one individual in that place only about one dozen came up." The consequence of so universal a failure, will in our humble opinion, inevitably be a brisk demand, and high price next season; it being no longer, as it has heretofore been, a question with us that the culture of the mulberry and the rearing of silk worms is soon to become one of the leading pursuits of the American husbandman. Extensive cocooneries are already erected in several parts of the State, one or more is in progress in the neighborhood of Richmond, and we understand that a project is on foot for the erection of one in this town or immediate vicinity. We shall be pleased to hear from each of our neighbors engaged in the cultivation of the mulberry, the state of their crops, and any other information relative to them which is likely to be of present interest or future utility to the public.

[17th Oct. 1839. Telegraph and Intelligencer, Harrisburg, Penna.]
AMERICAN SILK AGENCY, 95 Walnut street, Philadelphia.

The subscriber having opened a permanent commission agency for the purchase and sale of all articles connected

with the culture and manufacture of silk in the United States offers for sale the different varieties of mulberry trees suitable for raising the silk worms, viz.: Morus Multicaulis, &c., &c. Those wishing to engage trees or eggs, for the coming season, will do well to apply early.
S. C. CLEVELAND, Agent.
April, 1839.

[30th December, 1841, Pennsylvania Telegraph.]
DOMESTIC SILK.

They are making rapid advances in the silk business in the State of Georgia. We see it stated, at a session of one of their courts, the presiding judge appeared on the bench with silk stockings, silk handkerchief, &c., made by his own family, or some of his friends, of the production of their own cocooneries. The next day another of the judges, A. E. Earnest, Esq., appeared in a full suit of silk (including coat, vest, pantaloons, stockings, pocket handkerchief and stock) produced and manufactured wholly and entirely in his own family. Judge Earnest is of the opinion that domestic silk will, before many years, be found the most economical article for negro clothing, as well as ladies' and gentlemen's dresses.

NOTES AND QUERIES,

Historical, Biographical, and Genealogical.

XL.

Genealogical Notes.

BROWN.

Thomas Brown (2d), who laid out the town of Brownsville, Pa., was the son of Thomas Brown (1st) and his wife, Ann Brashear. The former Thomas Brown served as a soldier on the frontiers of Westmoreland county during the Revolution. He married Ruth Brashear, dau. of John and Ruth Brashear. Their son, Thomas (3d), [1769-1806] m. Ann Mercer, and their son, Thomas Mercer Brown, [1806-1886] m. Selina Maria Williams [1810-1878] dau. of William Williams [1782-1865] and his wife Martha Morris [1782-1825]. Thomas Mercer Brown's son, Justus Morris Brown, is at present a colonel in the United State army.

MERCER.
Edward Mercer m. Ann Gamble. A son Aaron Mercer m. Elizabeth Carr, whose daughter Ann m. Thomas Brown (3d) as above.

WILLIAMS.
John Williams [d. 1786] and wife, Ann Edwards, had a son Isaac Williams [1760-1844] who served as a soldier on the frontiers of Westmoreland county. He m. Elizabeth Metlen, and they were the parents of William Williams, above named.

MORRIS.
Morris Morris [1702-1767] was the son of Cadwalader Morris, an early settler in Pennsylvania. He m. in 1736, Gwenthleen Thomas, dau. of William Thomas [1678-1757] and his wife Ann Griffiths [1680-1752]. Morris Morris' son Benjamin Morris [1748-1833] m. in 1770, Mary Mason, daughter of Jonathan Mason [1716-1793] and his wife Mary Crocket. The former were the parents of Martha Morris above named.

AN OFFICAL MAP OF PENNSYLVANIA.

Paper Read Before the Dauphin County Historical Society by Benjamin Matthias Nead.

There does not seem to be very much that is attractive in this title, but, like many other subjects of investigation, when one gets properly into the work, it becomes more or less interesting. The little specimen map, which I take pleasure in presenting to the society, is, so to speak, the text of what I have to say to-night.

The making of maps was considerable of a mystery in early days. Prior to the beginning of the eighteenth century there was scarcely any map gotten up by any government of the world which was anything near being accurate. Some of the early maps made Asia and America very near neighbors; a number, in point of view, brought the antipodes pretty close together. The trouble was that astronomical observation in map-making was not understood, and there was exceeding great difficulty in determining the true longitude of places. DeLisle's map of the world, dated 1700, was the first comparatively accurate map based upon astronomical observations.

Christopher Columbus was a great map maker, and it seemed to run in his family, for his brother, Bartholomew, introduced the first map into England in the year 1489.

There is much of interest attached to the early mapography of Pennsylvania from the time of Peter Lindstroem down to the period of which we are now writing, but the scope of this paper will not admit of any very extended reference to these early map makers.

Of course, the map of Thomas Holmes, the first surveyor of the Province of Pennsylvania, was, from the time of its recognition in 1685 for a considerable period of time, the official map of the Province. Acrelius and Campanius, of our Swedish forebears, contributed not a little to the work. Then, during the period of the Indian wars, maps became of great importance to the Province, and we find that Lewis Evans, about 1754 or 1755, published a pretty good map of Pennsylvania, with a printed account of the country, both of which are said to be preserved in the Philadelphia Library. His information was obtained at public expense, and his map was used during the Braddock campaign, in connection with another map made by Mr. Patten, which was valuable on account of the fact that its distances were accurately marked.

In 1775 John Reed seems to have engaged in the map making business, for on the twenty-eighth of June in that year he was paid by the provincial council "twenty-five dollars for his map."

Of course, we are familiar with Reading Howell's map, which was projected under authority granted by the Supreme Executive Council of the State in 1790.

The general State map, to which the specimen map presented here to-night refers, was conceived as being a matter of no little importance to the State, and so, by a resolution of the Legislature, passed on the thirteenth of March, 1815, it was directed that, in order to make the necessary preparations toward forming a new and correct map of this State, the Secretary of the Commonwealth be authorized to procure from the county officers of the State copies of all the necessary plots or maps and courses and distances of roads, rivers and creeks, together with their names, which may be in their possession, to collect information of the situation and extent of the mountains and valleys, of the towns and villages, mills, furnaces, forges, glass works, factories, churches, academies, and whatsoever else may deserve notice.

This resolution was followed by the passage of an act of Assembly on the nineteenth of March, 1816, directing "the formation of a map of Pennsylvania, and specifying the manner in which it was to be gotten up, and the terms under which the contractor was to perform the work." John Melish, of Philadelphia, was awarded the contract, and the specimen map which appears here to-night was one which he sent to the members of the State Legislature of 1822, as indicative of the progress of his work.

The plan of this map was a most comprehensive one, and contemplated quite intricate work, which was to represent: 1. A statistical table, showing the length, breadth and area of each county; the population for 1800, 1810 and 1820; the number of townships and post offices in each county; the county towns and their population and distances from Harrisburg and Washington, and some of the other principal places. 2. Statistical and geological remarks, exhibiting a view of the length, breadth and area of the State, with an account of the geological formation, rivers, etc.

The elaborate nature of the map may be judged of from the fact that it was to be colored to exhibit five distinct views, namely:

1. By counties.
2. By townships.
3. By the Indian purchases.
4. By the roads and canals.
5. By the geological features.

The Indian purchases were represented by the following colors:

Yellow—the purchase made by Penn from the Swedes and Dutch shortly after his arrival. Green—the first purchase made from the Indians in 1682. Pink—purchases made in 1683, with undefined northern boundaries. Yellow—A large purchase made in 1781, including all the former, and rendering the several deeds indisputable. Green—A purchase made in 1732, extending to the Blue Mountain. Purple—The first purchase beyond the Susquehanna, made in 1736. Green—The first purchase made beyond the Blue Mountain, made in 1749.

Pink—This very large purchase, extending across the State from the northeast corner to the southwest, was made in 1768, and was the last under the provincial government. Blue—the remaining part of the State (except the triangle on Lake Erie) was purchased in 1784. The triangle colored sienna was purchased from the United States in 1792.

The southeast corner and two small stripes extending from the Delaware below Easton to Reading and Pottsgrove, colored sienna and marked A.A.A., are of the primitive formation. The two stripes, colored pink and marked B.B., are transition. The stripe, colored dark blue and marked C., is of the secondary old red sandstone formation. The space west of the Allegheny Mountain, colored light blue and marked D., is of the secondary formation.

These lines were obtained from William Maclure, Esq., the celebrated geologist. They were not given as entirely correct, but as presenting a general view of the leading geological features of the State.

On the fourteenth of March, 1822, the Secretary and Surveyor General reported to the Legislature with reference to the several specimens of the map, and declaring that, in their view, the whole work embracing the plan, the drawing, the engraving and the coloring, were evinsive of the great exertions of the contractor to comply with his engagement, that the map was worthy of the expense incurred.

The report, together with the specimens and the letter of the publisher, were referred to a joint committee of both branches of the Legislature, and that committee, on the twenty-third of March, made report as follows:

The map, even in its present state, is an example of graphic skill, which at once produces a bold, interesting general effect, and displays the author's tasteful care in the arrangement of the names, and in other minute matters of discretion.

The engraving is executed in a very strong, clear, and neatly finished manner, peculiarly suited to maps of this class, and equal, if not superior, to the style of any other map of the same class ever heretofore published.

The geography of the neighboring States, which Mr. Melish, the publisher, has of choice embraced in the map, the committee regard as a judicious addition, which must greatly enhance the value beyond what it would have been according to the original plan.

Besides the information already embodied in the map, it will contain, when finished, a considerable quantity of interesting matter procured by Mr. Melish, and that of a kind which brings the geography of the State, with a most satisfactory completeness, down to the present period.

The latest surveys of roads have been furnished by the Secretary of the Commonwealth, and corrections of, and additions to the natural and civil geography of the several counties, have been afforded by members of Assembly, and other gentlemen well acquainted with particular parts of the State; all which will appear in the map when completed. Besides, there have been portions of the map printed on bank note paper, and forwarded to different county officers, in order to ascertain what townships have been recently divided or otherwise changed; and some additional information will, no doubt, be obtained in that way.

The general correctness of the map cannot be doubted, and can not need to be sustained by an official report. Finally, the committee regard the work as highly creditable to the State, as well as to the gentlemen engaged in the execution of it.

The project was successfully carried through to completion. It was substantially completed on the twenty-sixth of August, 1821, and, after the report of the legislative committee, was formally and officially declared so. The map, when mounted, was six feet six inches by four feet seven inches, measuring nearly thirty square feet. It was the property of the Commonwealth, and cost the sum of $29,276.75. They were sold for the use of the State, by the publisher, at the price, fully mounted and varnished, of twelve dollars; with township lines colored, thirteen dollars.

How many copies of this map do we now know of?

BURIAL RECORDS

From Mennonite Graveyard, Hanover Pa.

[About two miles east of Hanover, in York county, Pa., is situated one of the first Dunkard-Mennonite graveyards west of the Susquehanna river. The location is on the estate of an original settler named Danner, progenitor of the York county family of that name. His estate was very large, comprising, it is said, over a thousand acres of land. The present meeting house is the second or third structure. Notwithstanding most of the descendants of the early settlers no longer cling to the faith of their fathers they nevertheless continue to inter their dead in the ancestral graveyard which has now grown into a well kept cemetery of several acres. In my researches I confined myself to the older class of interments and nearly all herewith given were in German inscription and exceedingly difficult to decipher. Several of the names herewith given are those of emigrants who founded well-known families. The oldest inscription decipherable dates back to 1759; but these were not the earliest burials. A great number of the first graves have simply limestone markers.]

Baer, Christian, b. 1733; d. 1799.
Baer, Elizabeth, wf. b. 1736; d. 1798.
Baer, Barbara, b. 1772; d. 1804.
Baer, Jacob, b. 1791; d. 1865.
Baer, Daniel, b. 1763; d. 1834.
Baer, Maria, wf. b. 1771; d. 1846.
Baer, Barbara, b. 1797; d. 1887.
Binder, Elizabeth Magdalena, wf. of Peter, b. 1715; d. 1760; had five sons and five daughters.
Bernhart, Ulrich, b. 1748; d. 1819.
Bernhart, Catharine, wf. b. 1756; d. 1838.
Brillhart, Magdalena, a born Danner, b. 1739; d. 1815.
Brillhart, Samuel, b. 1757; d. 1813.
Brezler, George, b. 1774; d. 1837.
Bowersox, John, b. 1770; d. 1858.
Bowersox, Anna Margaret, wf. b. 1775; d. 1865.
Bowersox, Susan, wf. of George, b. 1806; d. 1841.
Bechtel, Samuel, b. 1764; d. 1842.
Bechtel, Barbara, wf. b. 1767; d. 1848.
Danner—presumably the emigrant, stone crumbling.
Danner, Susan, b. 1734; d. 1828.
Danner, Henry, b. 1742; d. 1814.
Danner, Elizabeth, wf. b. 1744; d. 1828.
Danner, David, b. 1778; d. 1842.
Eichelberger, Adam, b. 1730; d. 1787.
Eichelberger, Magdalena, b. 1743; d. 1821.
Eichelberger, Susan, b. 1778; d. 1804.
Eichelberger, John Adam, b. 1721; d. 1818.
Eichelberger, Samuel, b. 1769; d. 1828.
Harnish, Jacob, b. 1794; d. 1876.
Hofe, Daniel, b. 1750; d. 1819.
Hoff, David, b. 1768; d. 1832.
Hershey, Christian, b. 1731; d. 1825.
Mummert, William, b. 1756; d. 1822.
Meyer, Martin, b. 1756; d. 1840.
Meyer, Ann Maria, wf. b. 1764; d. 1832.
Meyer, John, b. 1796; d. 1876.
Meyer, Susan, wf. b. 1799; d. 1890.
Rudesill, Andreas, b. 1756; d. 1778.
Thron, George, b. 1709; d. 1778.
Thron, Johann, b. 1736; d. 1789.
Thron, Magdalena, wf. b. 1739; d. 1811.
Thron, Samuel, b. 1766; d. 1816.
Thron, Maria, wf. b. 1768; d. 1861.
Thron, John, b. 1791; d. 1859.
Thomman, Abraham, b. 1767; d. 1832.
Thomman, Elizabeth, wf. born Hinkel, b. 1783; d. 1850.
Thomman, Maria Elizabeth, dau. of John Jacob, b. 1772; d. 1856.

"Barbara E. Wildson, wife of Andrew Rudisill, died July 28, 1859, aged 111 years, 9 months and 22 days. She sweetly sleeps."

A. STAPLETON.
Carlisle, Pa.

BAPTISMAL AND OTHER RECORD

Of "the Little Tulpehocken Church."

III.

Mueller, Susan Catharine, b. Jan. 5, 1762; bap. Jan. 10, 1762; spon., Matthew Mueller and wf.

Mueller, Mary Magdalene, b. Aug. 25, 1763; bap. —— —, ——; spon., Baltzer Umbenhauer and wf. Mary Abalonia (Apollonia).

Mueller, Christian, b. Jan. 28, 1765; bap. Feb. 10, 1765; spon., Jacob Wagner and wf. Abalonia (Apollonia).

Mueller, John, b. July 29, 1771; bap. Aug. 5, 1771; spon., Jacob Mueller and wf. Apelonia (Apollonia).

JOHN JACOB MUELLER — Possibly same as above.

Mueller, John, b. Nov. 8, 1751; bap. Nov. 20, 1751; spon., John Mueller and Mary Zetenbacher.

Mueller, Anna Mary, b. Feb. 23, 1753; bap. March 10, 1753; spon., Michael Kettner and wf.

Mueller, Cath. Margaret, b. —— ——, 1756; bap. Jan. 23, 1756; spon., John Mueller and Cath. Margaret Bacher.

MATTHEW MUELLER.

Mueller, Mary Barbara, b. Jan. 24, 1762; bap. Jan. 31, 1762; spon., Christopher Muench and wf.

Mueller, Mary Magdalene, b. —— ——, 1764 (?); bap. —— ——, 1764; spon., Jacob Wagner and Mary Apollonia.

Mueller, John, b. —— ——, 1767; bap. —— —, 1767; spon., John Mueller and wf.

Mueller, Cath. Charlotte, b. May 21, 1769; bap. June 4, 1769; spon., the grandfather and grandmother.

Mueller, Mary Elizabeth, b. May 22, 1771; bap. —— ——, 1771; spon., Caspar Heckel and wf.

Mueller, Anna Mary, b. Sept. 21, 1772; bapt. Oct. 23, 1772; spon., Anna Mary, d. of Jacob Mueller, single.

Mueller, Susanna Cath., b. March 31, 1774; bap. May 17, 1774; spon., Christopher Winder (Winter) and wf.

CHRISTOPHER MUENCH.

Muench, Mary Margaret, b. Nov. 8, 1762; bap. Nov. 21, 1762; spon., Matthew Weber and wf. Mary Margaret.

PETER MUENCH.

Muench, Joh. Michael, b. Jan. 2, 1738; bap. Jan. 24, 1738; spon., Joh. Michael Becker and wf.

Muench, Joh. Conrad, b. Nov. 28, 1740; bap. Jan. 21, 1741; spon., Conrad Scharff and wf.

JACOB PERSCHINGER.

Perschinger, Joh. Christian. b. Jan. 8, 1742; bap. July 11, 1742; spon., Frederic Wollenweber and wf.

JOH. GEORGE PETRY.

Petry, Anna Elizabeth, b. May 17, 1735; bap. July 23, 1735; spon., Joh. Michael Krauel and wf.

Petry, Joh. Michael, b. July 4, 1736; bap. Aug. 23, 1736; spon., Joh. Michael Krauel.

Petry, Joh. George, b. April 5, 1741; bap. Aug. 2, 1741; spon., Joh. George Ermentraut.

PHILIP PETRY.

Petry, Joh. George, b. —— ——, ——; bap. Nov. 6, 1743; spon., Joh. George Bechtel and Anna Margaret Duterle.

Petry, Anna Catharine, b. April 27, 1745; bap. May 12, 1745; spon., Henry Adolph and wf.

Petry, Cath. Elizabeth, b. Aug. 10, 1746; bap. Aug. 31, 1746; spon., Joh. Nicholas Bechtel and Catharine Krauel in the stead of Miss Elizabeth Bechtel, a minor.

Petry, Joh. Jacob, b. Jan. 21, 1748; bap. Feb. 7, 1748; spon., Joh. Jacob Heck and Mary Elizabeth Gassler.

MARTIN PFATTEICHER.

Pfatteicher, Mary Cath., b. June 25, 1742; bap. July 11, 1742; spon., Conrad Ernst and wf.

SAMUEL PHILBERT.

Philbert, Mary Catharine, b. Oct. 25, 1739; bap. Dec. 30, 1739; spon., Andrew Krafft and wf.

Philbert, Anna Elizabeth, b. Dec. 6, 1741; bap. Dec. 7, 1741; spon., Anna Elizabeth Krafft.

Philbert, Joh. Philip, b. Dec. 7, 1743; bap. Dec. 27, 1743; spon., Philip Meeth.

Philbert, Joh. Peter, b. Aug. 22, 1746; bap. Aug. 31, 1746; spon., Peter Muench and wf.

CASPER PHILIPPS.
Philipps, Joh. Henry, b. Oct. 10, 1746; bap. Oct. 26, 1746; spon., Joh. Henry Adolph and wf.
Philipps, Philip Jacob, b. May 11, 1749; bap. Sept. 3, 1749; spon., Philips Jacob Brodt.

JOHN PHILIPS and wf. Mary.
Philips, a son, b. April 14, 1816; bap. ——
—, ——; spon., Leonard Zerbe and wf. Susan.

MICHAEL PLATTNER.
Plattner, Joh. Conrad, b. Jan. 24, 1738; bap. Feb. 8, 1738; spon., Joh. Conrad Scharpff and wf.
Plattner, Eva, b. Oct. 1, 1739; bap. Nov. 30, 1739; spon., Michael Busch and wf. Eva.
Plattner, Joh. Michael, b. July 2, 1741; bap. Aug. 2, 1741; spon., Joh. Michael Busch and wf.

PETER RADEBACH.
Radebach, Joh. George, b. Aug. 8, 1763; bap. Aug. 21, 1763; spon., George Radebach and wf.
Radebach, N. Peter, b. Aug. 3, 1765; bap. Oct. 15, 1765; spon., Joh. George Hag and wf. Abalona (Apollonia).
Radebach, Samuel, b. May 28, 1767; bap. July 5, 1767; spon., Henry Radebach and wf. Ann Elizabeth.

JOHN RATHEBACH and wf. Mary.
Rathebach, Joh., b. Feb. 6, 1833; bap. July 7, 1833; spon., John Rathebach and wf. Sarah.

JOHN GEORGE RADEBACH (Reidenbach in index.)
Radebach, Catharine, b. March 24, 1760; bap. —— ——, ——; spon., George Gaertner and wf.
Radebach, Joh. Jacob, b. June 9, 1763; bap. June 13, 1763; spon., Nicholas Weigand and wf. Mary Elizabeth.
Radebach, Mary Elizabeth, b. Aug. 30, 1764; bap. —— ——, ——; spon., Christian Gruber and Susanna Beyer.
Radebach, John Adam, b. July 9, 1783; bap. Aug. 3, 1783; spon., Conrad Gilbert and wf. Anna Elizabeth.

JOSEPH RENNO and wf. Elizabeth.
Renno, John, b. Dec. 7, 1816; bap. ——

—, ——; spon., John Minnig and wf. Catharine.

GEORGE WILLIAM RIEGEL.
Riegel, Mary Catharine, b. Dec. 6, 1736; bap. Jan. 2, 1737; spon., John Riegel and Cath. Elizabeth Schirman.
Riegel, Anna Elizabeth, b. April 1, 1738; bap. April 30, 1738; spon., Christian Ewig and wf.
Riegel, John, b. Sept. 25, 1741; bap. Dec. 27, 1741; spon., Joh. Danl. Riegel and Magdalene Plattner.
Riegel, Joh. William, b. Nov. 17, 1743; bap. Dec. 27, 1743; spon., Margaret Busch.
Riegel, Joh. Jacob, b. eleven weeks ago; bap. Oct. 29, 1749; spon., Jacob Mueller and wf.

JOHN RIEGEL.
Riegel, Simon, b. Nov. 5, 1738; bap. Nov. 10, 1738; spon., Simon Schirmann.

DANIEL RIEGEL.
Riegel, John, b. Feb. 2, 1746; bap. Feb. 18, 1746; spon., George Michael Wildfang and Sophia Mary Vertheim.

NICHOLAS RIEHL.
Riehl, Andrew, b. Sept. 26, 1733; bap. Dec. 24, 1733; spon., Andrew Beyer and wf.
Riehl, Simon, b. Oct. 16, 1736; bap. Nov. 7, 1736; spon., Simon Schrirman and wf.
Riehl, Joh. Jacob, b. Nov. 30, 1738; bap. Dec. 13, 1738; spon., Joh. Jacob Wilhelm and wf.
Riehl, Joh. Conrad, b. Oct. 29, 1741; bap. Nov. 8, 1741; spon., Joh. Conrad Ernst and wf.

JOHN RISSER and wf. Eva Catharine.
Risser, Mary, b. April 5, 1802; bap. June 6, 1802; spon., George Scharff and wf. Susanna.

ELIAS ROEGER and wf. Catharine.
Roeger, Simon, b. March 7, 1774; bap. March 27, 1774; spon., —— ——

JOHN ADAM ROHN and wf. Mary Barbara.
Rohn, John, Dec. 6, 1786; bap. March 14, 1787 (by Rev. Schulz); spon., Michael Rohn (single).

JACOB ROST.
Rost, Elizabeth Catharine, b. May 31, 1741; bap. July 5, 1741; spon., Daniel

Riegel and Elizabeth Cath. Pfaffenberger.

LUDWIG SEAMAN.

Seaman, Ludwig, b. Sept. 11, 1764; bap. Sept. 23, 1764; spon., Ludwig Fischer and wf.

PAUL SAP and wf. Margaret.

Sap, Salome, b. Jan. 13, 1773; bap. Feb. 28, 1773; spon., Peter Gerhardt and wf. Salome.

JOHN GEORGE SCHADE.

Schade, Catharine Barbara, b. Feb. 2, 1746; bap. March 16, 1746; spon., George Maeyer and Catharine Gotteskind.

CONRAD SCHARFF.

Scharff, Elizabeth Barbara, b. —— ——; bap. June 25, 1755; spon., Elizabeth Barbara ——.

Scharff, Mary Catharine, b. —— —, ——; bap. June 25, 1755; spon., Mary Catharine ——.

Scharff, Joh. George, b. —— —— —; bap. June 29, 1755; spon., Mrs. John George Bechler.

Scharff, Joh. George, b. Feb. 3, 1758; bap. —— ——; spon., George Bechler.

Scharff, John, b. March 30, 1761; bap. April 12, 1761., spon., John Wenrich and wf. Christina.

ADAM SCHAUER.

Schauer, Cath. Elizabeth, b. Dec. 23, 1744; bap. Dec. 25, 1744; spon., Michael Schauer and wf.

MICHAEL SCHAUER.

Schauer, Anna Mary, b. Nov. 19, 1730; bap. December 13, 1730; spon., Henry Zeller and wf.

FREDERIC SCHAEFER and wf. Catharine.

Schaefer, Catharine, b. Feb. 14, 1784; bap. March 19, 1784; spon., Catharine wf. of David Miller.

JOHN SCHAEFFER and wf. Sybilla.

Schaeffer, Joel, b. —— — 1814; bap. —— ——; spon., Jonas Hechman.

JOHN SCHAEFFER and wf. Mary Magdalene.

Schaeffer, Isaac, b. Sept. 19, 1816; bap. —— ——; spon., parents.

JACOB SCHAEFFER and wf. Catharine.

Schaeffer, Mary, b. June 8, 1819; bap. —— ——; spon., Thomas Wenrich and wf. Catharine.

Schaeffer, a son, b. Aug. 7, 1820; bap. —— ——; spon., John Bechtel and wf. Barbara.

MARTIN SCHELL and wf. Margaret Elizabeth.

Schell, Hermanus, b. Nov. 15, 1740; bap. Dec. 28, 1740; spon., Hermanus Wallborn and wf.

Schell, Martin, b. Sept. 30, 1749; bap. Oct. 15, 1749; spon., Martin Battorf and wf.

PETER SCHELL and wf. Anna Mary.

Schell, Simon, b. Feb. 17, 1772; bap. April —, 1772; spon., Simon Borrao and wf.

Schell, Christian, b. —— — 1776; bap. —— — 1776; spon., Christian Schell and wf.

Schell, John b. April 13, 1778; bap. April 16, 1778; spon., Joseph Maunts and wf.

Schell, Mary Catharine, b. March 15, 1789; bap. April 15, 1789; spon., Henry Knob and wf. Mary Catharine.

JOHN SCHELL and wf., Magdalene.

Schell, Henry, b. June 3, 1814; bap. ——. —, ——; spon., Matthew Miller and wf., Elizabeth.

GEORGE SCHIRMANN.

Schirmann, Simon, b. Jan. 22, 1743; bap. Jan. 23, 1743; spon., Simon Schirmann and wf.

Schirmann, Anna Mar., b. Oct. 3, 1744; bap. Oct. 14, 1744; spon., Philip Adam Schirmann and Adelheit Pfaffenberger.

Schirmann, Joh. Simon, b. Oct. 19, 1746; bap. Oct. 26, 1746; spon., John Riegel and wf.

MATTHIAS SCHMIDT.

Schmidt, Mary Elizabeth, b. Oct. 15, 1738; bap. Nov. 10, 1738; spon., Bernhardt Motz and wf., Mary Elizabeth.

Schmidt, Joh. Jacob, b. Oct. 3, 1741; bap. Oct. 11, 1741; spon., Joh. Jacob Mueller and wf.

ADAM SCHMITT.

Schmitt, John, b. May 27, 1754; bap. Feby. 8, 1755; spon., Matthias Schmitt, Jr., and wf.

Schmitt, Elizabeth Catharine, b. May 27, 1756; bap. ——. —, ——; spon., Michael Schauer and wf.

Schmitt, Christina, b. two weeks before Easter, 1761; bap. Mch. 20 (Good Friday), 1761; spon., Christina Von Kenne, d. of Michael Schauer.

Schmitt, Susanna, b. Nov. 12, 1761; bap.

Nov. 21, 1761; spon., Jacob Schmitt and wf., Susanna.
Schmitt, Anna Elizabeth, b. Feby. 16, 1758; bap. ——. —, ——; spon., Adam Schauer and wf.
Schmitt, Mary Magdalene, b. Aug. 29, 1764; bap. Sept. 16, 1764; spon., ——
JOH. JACOB SCHMITT and wf., Susanna Catharine.
Schmitt, Joh. Adam, b. Sept. 7, 1765; bap. Sept. 29, 1765; spon., Joh. Adam Schmitt and wf., Mary.
Schmitt, Jacob, b. Aug. 27, 1764; bap. Sept. 4, 1764; spon., Jacob Wagner and wf., Apollonia (Abalona).
Schmitt, Anna Catharine, b. Sept. 11, 1767; bap. Sept. 27, 1767; spon., Jacob Ernst and wf.
Schmitt, Joh. b. Dec. 9, 1769; bap. ——. —, ——; spon., Adam Batteicher and wf.

JACOB SCHMIED, JR.
Schmied, Joh. Peter, b. Apr. 9, 1774; bap. May 17, 1774; spon., Peter Radenbach and wf.

JACOB SCHMIDT, Jr., and wf., Elizabeth.
Schmidt, Elizabeth, b. Apr. 30, 1789; bap. May 16, 1789; spon., Joh. Jac. Schmidt and wf., Susanna Cath. (grandparents).
Schmidt, Matthew, b. July 11, 1791; bap. Aug. 7, 1791; spon., Matthew Wagner and Elizabeth Keller (both single).
Schmidt, Catharine, b. Feby. 2, 1793; bap. Mch. 17, 1793; spon., Mrs. Apollonia Wagner, widow.
Schmidt, Peter, b. Apr. 26, 1795; bap. June 14, 1795; spon., Peter Schmidt.

JOHN SCHNEIDER.
Schneider, John, b. Apr. 23, 1742; bap. June 8, 1742; spon., John Ruesser.

JACOB SCHNEYTER.
Schneyter, Justina, b. Dec. 6, 1772; bap. Dec. 14, 1772; spon., John Mueller and wf., Justina.

MICHAEL SCHNEIDER.
Schneider, Mary Elizabeth, b. Feby 21, 1765; bap. Mch. 10, 1765; spon., Mary Elizabeth Christe, single.
Schneider, Joh. Adam, b. Mch 25, 1766; bap. Mch. 30, 1766; spon., Adam Schneyter, the grandfather.
Schneider, Mary Catharine, b. Jan. 3, 1768; bap. Feby. 7, 1768; spon., Martin Troester and wf.

Schneider, John, b. Feby. 17, 1773; bap. Feby. 24, 1773; spon., John Schoch and wf.
Schneider, Andrew, b. Feby. 2, 1775; bap. Feby. 19, 1775; spon., John Mueller and wf., Justina.

JACOB SCHOPP.
Schopp, Mary Catharine, b. May 4, 1744; bap. June 24, 1744; spon., Simon Schirman and wf.
Schopp, Anna Mary, b. May 30, 1746; bap. June 26, 1746; spon., John Schopp and Anna Mary Hubeler (both single).
Schopp, Joh. Jacob, b. Dec. 14, 1749; bap. Jan. 21, 1750; spon., Jacob Miller and wf.

JACOB SOMER.
Somer, Mary Barbara, b. Dec. 7, 1751; bap. Dec. 15, 1751; spon., Mary Barb. Foller and Valentine Eckert.
HENRY SCHOPP and wf., Justina.
Schopp, Joh. George, b. Feby. 15, 1759; bap. Feby. 18, 1759; spon., George Koehl and wf.
Schopp, William, b. Nov. 10, 1761; bap. Nov. 29, 1761; spon., Shepler and wf.

JOH. ADAM SCHROFF.
Schroff, John Nicholas, b. Aug. 10, 1736; bap. Sept. 12, 1736; spon., Joh. Nicholas Riehl and wf.
Schroff, Mary Eva Rosina, b. Dec. —, 1737; bap. Jan. 8, 1738; spon., Joh. Henry Gruber and wf., Mary Eva Rosina.
Schroff, Mary Catharine, b. Jan. 13, 1741; bap. Aug. 10, 1740; spon., Conrad Ernst and wf., Anna Susanna.
Schroff, Christopher, b. Nov. 24, 1742; bap. Dec. 22, 1742; spon., Christopher Besterle and Mrs. Mary Eva Rosina Gruber.

NOTES AND QUERIES.

Historical, Biographical, and Genealogical.

XLI.

Bedford County Genealogical Notes

[The readers of Notes and Queries are indebted to William Filler Lutz for the following abstract of Bedford county wills.]

ADAMS.
Elijah Adams, d. in January, 1798, leaving a wife, Hannah, and children:
i. Robert.
ii. Elijah.
iii. Ephriam.
iv. Obediah.
v. Mordecai.
vi. Jane, m. John Blair.
vii. Ruth, m. Alexander McGregor.
viii. Hannah, m. James Adams.
ix. Susanna.
x. Dinah.
Grandson, Joshua Smith.
The executors were wife Hannah and Alex. McGregor.

CHAPMAN.
Henry Chapman, d. August, 1796, leaving a wife Mary, and children:
i. John.
ii. Henry.
iii. Elizabeth.
iv. Mary.
v. Nathaniel.
Executor, wife Mary.

CESSNA.
John Cessna, Sr., d. in 1802, leaving a wife Elizabeth, and children:
i. Charles.
ii. Evan.
iii. James.
iv. Henry.
v. Sarah-Rose.
Executors, John Cessna, Jonathan Cessna and Henry Williams.

DEVENY.
Aaron Deveny, of York county, made his will August 9, 1775, which was probated Nov. 3, 1777, at Bedford. He left a wife Margaret, and children:
i. John.
ii. Jenkins.
iii. Hannah.
iv. Aaron.
v. Mary.
vi. Jean.
vii. Andrew.
viii. William.
Executors, Abraham Robinson and Andrew Deveny.

ELDER.
George Elder, d. in March, 1800, leaving a wife, not named, and children:
i. William.
ii. Robert.
iii. John.
iv. James.
v. Isabel.
vi. Margaret.
Executors, Thomas Coulter, Esq., and sons John and James.

HAMILL.
Robert Hamill, d. in April, 1799, leaving a wife Lenore, and children:
i. Sarah.
ii. Margaret.
iii. Robert.
iv. Hugh.
v. Martha.
vi. Samuel.
vii. John.
Executors, sons John and Robert.

KENDELL.
John Kendell, d. in November, 1805, leaving a wife Martha, and children:
i. Mary.
ii. Ruth.
iii. William.
iv. Isabella.
v. James.
vi. Francis.
Grandson John, son of Francis.
Executors, sons Francis and James and William Alexander, Sr.

MEANS.
Robert Means, d. in May, 1798, leaving a wife Rachel, and children:
i. Samuel.
ii. John.
iii. Mary.
iv. Ann.
v. Rachel.
vi. Jane.
vii. Elizabeth.
Executor, wife Rachel.

NIXON.
George Nixon, d. in January, 1806, leaving a wife, not named, and children:
i. Mary, m. —— Young.
ii. William.

iii. Sarah, m. —— Guthrie.
iv. Margaret, m. —— Bradshaw.
v. George.
vi. Barbara, m. —— Hughes.
vii. Thomas.
viii. Rebecca, m. —— Ferguson.
Grandson John Nixon.
Executors, Thomas Ferguson and John Piper, Jr.

PLACING.
Conrad Placing, d. in April, 1803, leaving a wife Catrina, and children:
i. Eleanor, m. James Daugherty.
ii. Catrina, m. John Steel.
iii. Elizabeth, m. Francis Oastonday.
iv. Eve.
v. Christiana, m. Peter Park.
vi. Mary, m. John Swisher.
vii. Susannah.
viii. Michael.
ix. Jacob.
x. Conrad.
xi. Philip.
xii. George.
xii. Nicholas.
Executors, wife and John Will.

RICHEY.
Francis Richey, d. in 1805, leaving a wife Catharine, and children:
i. Abraham.
ii. Samuel.
iii. Henry.
iv. Michael.
v. John.
vi. Christiana.
vii. Jacob.
viii. Philip.
ix. Isaac.
x. Abraham.
Grand-daughter Mary Stiffler.
Executor, not named.

SLOAN.
William Sloan, d. in June, 1804, leaving a wife Frances, and children:
i. Mary.
ii. Sarah.
iii. Martha, m.
iv. Ann, m.
v. Susannah, m.
vi. Jean, m.
vii. John.

viii. Thomas.
ix. William.
Executors, wife and son John, and son-in-law, James Neilson.

SOME ADAMS COUNTY RECORDS

Inscriptions From Sunny Side Cemetery, York Springs.

Col. William F. Bonner, b. Apr. 10, 1797; d. Aug. 29, 1886. "He donated the land for this cemetery, 26 acres, in the year 1878."
John Thompson, "patentee of these grounds," d. 1793.
Isabella Thompson, d. Oct. 11, 1778, aged 54y.
Robert Bonner, b. 1720; d. 1770.
Eleanor Bonner, b. 1725; d. 1805.
Robert Bonner, b. 1745; d. 1825.
Thomas Bonner, b. 1750; d. 1830.
Major John Bonner, d. Mar. 13, 1835, aged 80.
Jane Bonner, wf. of John, d. Feb. 13, 1845, in 88th year.
James Thompson Bonner, son of Charles and Hannah, d. Mar. 24, 1833, aged 4m. 16ds.
Hannah Jane Bonner, dau. of Charles and Hannah, d. Jan. 24, 1831, aged 3y. 14d.
Hannah Bonner, wf. of Charles F. Bonner, and dau. of Nicholas and Jane Wierman, d. Jan. 16, 1854, aged 29y. 14d.
Major Thompson T. Bonner, "a Representative in the Pennsylvania Legislature," d. Nov. 22, 1827, aged 34y. 7d.
E. Eurydice Bonner, b. Apr. 10, 1791; d. May 29, 1855.
Robert Bonner ("Redbeard Bonheur"), b. Apr. 28, 1788; d. May 28, 1863.
Elizabeth Bonner, b. Oct. 4, 1781; d. Sept. 25, 1875.
Ephraim Funk, d. Aug. 24, 1822, aged 5y. 7m. 20d.
Dorothy Kenege, wf. of John, d. July 2, 1833, aged 86.
Daniel Funk, b. Mar. 12, 1751; d. July 7, 1826, aged 75y. 3m. 25d.
Elizabeth Funk, d. Dec. 25, 1829, aged 76y. 5m. 8d.
Jacob Funk, b. Aug. 4, 1780, d. Aug. 13, 1839.
Elizabeth Funk, wf. of Jacob, d. Jan. 27, 1861, aged 74y. 5m.

Susanna Peters, wf. of William, b. Mar. 22, 1814; d. July 3, 1849.
Moses Funk, b. Dec. 29, 1783; d. July 8, 1850.
Rachel Funk, wf. of Moses, d. Dec. 6, 1816, aged 25y. 3m. 6d. Also, her infant child, died same day, aged 13d.
Elizabeth Shrader, d. Mar. 18, 1827, aged 60y. 11m. 13d.
James H. Neely, d. Apr. 6, 1862, aged 51y. 3m. 21d.
Mary L. Neely, wf. of James, d. Jan. 24, 1886, aged 75y. 8m. 5d. .
Phebe T. W. Bowers, wf. of Frederick, d. 1873, aged 76y. 24d.
Isaac Shelley, b. Feb. 25, 1784; d. July 25, 1839.
Molly Shelley, d.. Oct. 15, 1826, aged 35y. 3d.
Templeton Brandon, d. June 19, 1850, in 77th year.
Mary S. Brandon, wf. of Templeton, d. June 10, 1847, in 64th year.
Thomas Brandon, d. Aug. 7, 1848, in 65th year.
James Brandon, d. May 3, 1838, in 26th year.
Thomas Long Brandon, d. Dec. 10, 1829, aged 21y. 9m.
Mary Morrison, wf. of John Morrison, of Marsh Creek, aged 80.
William Moorhead, b. Sept. 19, 1790; d. Sept. 10, 1868.
Esther Kinyon Moorhead, wf. of William, b. July 7, 1797; d. Dec. 14, 1876.
[Nearly all the foregoing were removed from Funk's graveyard.]

Inscriptions in Lutheran Church Graveyard at York Springs.

Davalt Kesselring, d. Oct. 7, 1858, aged 90y.
Catharine Kesselring, d. Sept. 3, 1854, aged 47y. 3d.
Susanna Asper, wf. of Phillip, d. March 27, 1860, aged 77y. 1m. 12d.
Mary M. Dottaror, wf. of Henry, d. Feb. 4, 1864, aged about 55y.
Samuel Gardner, b. Aug. 6, 1798; d. Sept. 2, 1868.
Sarah Gardner, b. Aug. 21, 1804; d. Oct. 29, 1869.
Joseba Gardner, b. Jan. 14, 1780; d. Sept. 2, 1878.
Jacob Gardner, Sr., b. March 10, 1777; d. Jan. 10, 1861.
Conrad Moul, d. Oct. 18, 1863, aged 68y.
George Gardner, d. June 7, 1854, aged 56y. 9m. 29d.
Julianna Bittinger, wf. of Henry, b. Nov. 5, 1809; d. March 28, 1837.
Mary Sheffer, wf. of Henry and mother of Dr. Daniel Sheffer, b. Dec. 15, 1759; d. Dec. 15, 1836.
Margaret Spealman, wf. of John, d. Nov. 3, 1841; aged 46y. 2m. 7d.
Jane L. Gardner, wf. of Samuel, d. July 13, 1849, aged 58y, 3m, 9d.
John S. Bridges, "formerly a resident of Baltimore," d. Aug. 8, 1838, aged 47y. 5m. 6d., a native of Norwich, England.
William Gardner, d. Nov. 7, 1857, aged 57y. 1m. 19d.
Christian Picking, d. Dec. 2, 1842, aged 59y. 4m. 21d.
Mary Picking, wf. of G. Picking, d. May 1, 1874, aged 87y. 6m. 4d.
Naomi Sheffer, wf. of Dr. Daniel Sheffer and only child of the late John Wierman, Esq., b. April 8, 1784; d. April 8, 1872.
Dr. Daniel Sheffer, b. May 24, 1783; d. Feb. 16, 1880. "He was a member of the 25th Congress."
Margaret Fickes, wf. of Daniel, d. March 18, 1860, aged 78y, 9m, 26d.
Daniel Fickes, d. Sept. 6, 1859, aged 77y. 7m, 16d.
Jacob Shaeffer, b. Aug. 10, 1796; d. Oct. 17, 1879.
Mary Sheaffer, wf. of Jacob, d. Oct. 9, 1863, aged 48y. 6m. 7d.
Benjamin Gardner, d. Nov. 30, 1875, aged 78y. 2m, 26d. "He was a soldier of the War of 1812; fought at the battles of Lundy's Lane and Fort Erie."
Hephzibah Gardner, wf. of Benjamin, d. July 26, 1858, aged 54y. 5m. 1d.
Pteer Becker, d. Nov. 13, 1839, in 65th year.
Jacob Thorne, b. Nov. 13, 1803; d. Sept. 29, 1840.
Catharine Becker, wf. of Peter, d. March 30, 1853, aged 73y, 8m. 10d.
George Naylor, d. April 24, 1858, aged 59y.
Jacob Tanger, d. July 30, 1848, aged 52y. 5m. 12d.
Catharine Carbaugh, d. April, 1863, aged about 66y.

Samuel Keplinger, d. March, 1858, aged about 80y.
Andrew Hartman, d. May 30, 1876, aged 82y. 8m. 20d.
Elizabeth Hartman, wf. of Andrew, d. April 7, 1888, aged 84y. 6m. 26d. ALBERT COOK MYERS. Philadelphia.

BAPTISMAL AND OTHER RECORDS

Of "The Little Tulpehocken Church."

IV.

ALBRECHT STRAUSS.
Strauss, Mary Barbara, b. Nov. 16, 1735; bap. Jan. 11, 1736; spon., George Graff, Jr., and Mary Barbara Zerwe.
Strauss, John Jacob (twin), b. May 5, 1737; bap. May 19, 1737; spon., John Jacob Zerwe and wf.
Strauss, Mary Elizabeth (twin), b. May 5, 1737; bap May 19, 1737; spon., Henry Beyer and wf.
Strauss, Anna Elizabeth, b. Mch. 25, 1739; bap. Apr. 22, 1739; spon., Martin Zerwe and wf.
Strauss, Joh. Caspar, b. Aug. 1, 1741; bap. Sept. 13, 1741; spon., Joh. Caspar Stoever—Baptizator.
Strauss, Mary Eve Rosina, b. Nov. 6, 1742; bap. Nov. 28, 1742; spon., Henry Gruber and wf.
Strauss, Mary Catharine, b. Mch. 6, 1745; bap. Mch. 17, 1745; spon., Andrew Krafft and wf.
Strauss, Joh. Philip, b. Jan. 4, 1748; bap. Feby. 7, 1748; spon., John. Philip Meeth and wf.

JOH. PHILIP STRAUSS.
Strauss, Anna Magdalena, b. Dec. 21, 1744; bap. Dec. 26, 1744; spon., John Eckert and Anna Magdalena Riemer.
Strauss, Bina Elizabeth, b. Sept. 15, 1746; bap. Sept. 25, 1746; spon., Phinehas (Pinnis) Kuerschner and wf.

JOHN STROH-SCHNEIDER and wf., Margaret.
Stroh-Schneider, Mary Catharine, b. May 13, 1761; bap. May 31, 1761; spon., Henry Radebach and wf., Apollonia.

PETER SCHOENFELDER.
Schoenfelder, John, b. July 23, 1756; bap. Aug. 17, 1756; spon., John Ruhl and wf.

FRANTZ SCHULER.
Schuler, Anna Margaret, b. July 1, 1741; bap. Aug. 2, 1741; spon., Jacob Weickert and wf.

LEWIS THOMAS.
Thomas, Anna Magdalene, b. Jan. 5, 1744; bap. Apr. 1, 1744; spon., Jost Hedderich and wf.

JOHN THORTHEUER.
Thortheuer, Joh. Jacob, b. Aug. 22, 1741; bap. Nov. 8, 1741; spon., Joh. Jacob Cantor and wf.
Thortheuer, Mary Margaret, b. Dec. 15, 1742; bap. Jan. 23, 1743; spon., Thomas Berger and Anna Margaret Roth.

JOH. MARTIN TROESTER.
Troester, Joh. Martin, b. Mch. 2, 1743; bap. Mch. 17, 1743; spon., Ulrich Spies and wf.
Troester, Joh. Michael, b. Nov. 18, 1746; bap. Dec. 21, 1746; spon., Joh. Michael Axer and wf.

CHRISTOPHER UHRICH.
Uhrich, Mary Catharine, b. Jan. 29, 1739; bap. Feby. 24, 1739; spon., George Valentine Unruh and wf.

VALENTINE UNRUH.
Unruh, Mary Catharine, b. Jan. 28, 1743; bap. Feby. 20, 1743; spon., Jacob Wilhelm and wf.

JOH. JACOB VOLLMAR, Snr.
Vollmar, Eva Mary, b. Nov. 1, 1741; bap. Nov. 8, 1741; spon., George Briegel and Anna Mary Zorn.

JACOB VOLLMAR, Jr.
Vollmar, Anna Mary Apollonia, b. Dec. 1, 1742; bap. Dec. 22, 1742; spon., Jacob Vollmar, Snr., and wf., Apollonia.
Vollmar, Joh. Michael, b. Sept. 20, 1744; bap. Oct. 14, 1744; spon., Joh. Michael Vollmar and Barbara Kaerchner.

LEWIS WAGNER.
Wagner, Mary Elizabeth, b. Feby. 17, 1741; bap. Apr. 12, 1741; spon., Mary Elizabeth Fischer and Mary Eva Rosina Gruber.
Wagner, Mary Eva Rosina, b. Aug. 19, 1743; bap. Sept. 11, 1743; spon., Mary Elizabeth Fischer and Mary Eva Rosina Gruber.
Wagner, Lewis Adam, b. Apr. 18, 1746; bap. May 11, 1746; spon., Henry Gruber and Hieronimus Fischer.

MATTHIAS WAGNER.

Wagner, Mary Magdalene, b. Aug. 7, 1741; bap. Sept. 12, 1741; spon., Aug. Kuenig and wf.

Wagner, Joh. George, b. Sept. 6, 1743; bap. Oct. 9, 1743; spon., George Wagner and Adelheit Pfaffenberger.

Wagner, Joh. Matthias, b. Dec. 11, 1745; bap. Dec. 25, 1745; spon., Joh. Matthias Schmidt and Catharine Wagner.

JACOB WAGNER.

Wagner, Joh. Jacob, b. Nov. 22, 1762; bap. Dec. 12, 1762; spon., Joh. Jacob Schmidt and wf., Susanna.

Wagner, John, b. Oct. 23, 1764; bap. Dec. 9, 1764; spon., John Miller and Justina Miller.

JOHN GEORGE WEBER.

Weber, John Adam, b. Feby, 14, 1746; bap. Feby. 17, 1746; spon., none given.

MATTHIAS WENDERICH.

Wenderich, John Balthaser, b. May 18, 1726; bap. May 22, 1726; spon., Balthaser Wenderich and wf., Mary Magdalene.

Wenderich, John, b. July 8, 1727; bap. July 22, 1727; spon., John Lauer.

Wenderich, Matthias, b. May 1, 1729; bap. Sept. 16, 1729; spon., Thomas Matern.

Wenderich, Esther, b. July 25, 1731; bap. July 29, 1731; spon., Francis Wennerich.

Wenderich, John Thomas, b. Sept. 8, 1734; bap. Oct. 17, 1734; spon., Thomas Matern.

Wenderich, Conrad, b. Feby. 1, 1737; bap. Apr. 12, 1737; spon., Conrad Scharff.

Wenderich, Mary Magdalene, b. Mch. 8, 1740; bap. May 21, 1740; spon., Mary Magdalene Schauer.

JOHN WENRICH.

Wenrich, John, b. Nov. 14, 1784; bap. Mch. 20, 1785; spon., John Scharff.

Wenrich, David, b. Sept. 13, 1787; bap. Nov. 4, 1787; spon., John Wenrich and wf., Christina—grandparents.

PAUL WENRICH.

Wenrich, Mary, b. Apr. 17, 1830; bap. ——. —, ——; spon., Catharine Leiss (single).

Wenrich, Rebecca, b. Apr. 16, 1832; bap. ——. —, ——; spon., Adam Seitz and wf., Eve.

Wenrich, James Daniel, b. Feby. 26, 1834; bap. ——. —. ——; spon., Daniel Wenrich and wf., Margaret.

Wenrich, Amanda, b. Oct. 16, 1835; bap. Dec. 6, 1835; spon., John Wenrich and wf., Mary.

Wenrich, Sarah, b. Oct. 30, 1837; bap. ——. —, 1837; spon., Joseph Ernst and wf., Elizabeth.

Wenrich, Melinda, b. Jan. 6, 1840; bap. Feby. 9, 1840; spon., John Groff and wf., Mary.

Wenrich, Emanuel, b. Apr. 3, 1842; bap. May 8, 1842; spon., John Meyer and wf., Elizabeth.

Wenrich, Adam Paul, b. Aug. 11, 1843; spon., William Staut and wf., Mary.

Wenrich, Elonore (twin), b. Nov. 25, 1846; bap. Dec. .27, 1846; spon., Benjamin Troutman and wf., Hannah.

Wenrich, Henrietta (twin), b. Nov. 25, 1846; bap. Dec. 27, 1846; spon., Isaac Leetz and wf., Henrietta.

JOHN WERTZ and wf., Catharine.

Wertz, Benjamin, b. Aug. 30, 1787; bap. Nov. 4, 1787; spon., Samuel Umbenhauer and wf., "Cordia."

JACOB WILHELM.

Wilhelm, Philip Jacob, b. Jan. 10, 1738; bap. Feb. 2, 1739; spon., Jacob Schopff and wf.

Wilhelm, Joh. Adam, b. Oct. 31, 1742; bap. Nov. 28, 1742; spon., Bernhard Motz and wf.

LAZARUS WINGERT.

Wingert, John, b. Dec. 26, 1740; bap. April 12, 1741; spon., John Carl and wf.

PHILIP WITMAYER.

Witmayer, Anna Mary, b. Oct. 10, 1781; bap. Oct. 14, 1781; spon., Caspar Hinckel and wf. Mary Eve.

Witmayer, Catharine Elizabeth, b. June 14, 1784; bap. July 18, 1784; spon., Philip Guengster, Sr., and wf. Cath. Barbara.

—— ZECHMAN.

Zechman, Jonathan, b. Oct. 1, 1791; bap. —— —, ——.

JOHN JACOB ZERWE.

Zerwe, Christina, b. Dec. 25, 1736; bap. Jan. 2, 1737; spon., George Peter Zerwe and wf.

Zerwe, Joh. Michael, b. April 20, 1738; bap. April 30, 1738; spon., Joh. Michael Busch and wf.

Zerwe, Joh. Valentine, b. June 24, 1741; bap. July 6, 1741; spon., Engelhardt Flory.

JOHN ZERWE.

Zerwe, Mary Catharine, b. April 8, 1745; bap. April 14, 1745; spon., Jacob Zerwe and wf.

Zerwe, John. b. March 23, 1748; bap. April 3, 1748; spon., John Eberd and Catharine Heck.

BENJAMIN ZERWE.

Zerwe, Benjamin, b. May 17, 1763; bap. May 21, 1763; spon., Conrad Krichbaum and wf. Anna Mary.

Zerwe, Hermanus, b. March 20, 1765; bap. March 31, 1765; spon., Caspar Henckel and wf. Mary Eve.

LEONARD ZERWE.

Zerwe, Christina, b. Jan. 7, 1781; bap. Dec. 24, 1781; spon., Thomas Lingel and wf.

GEORGE ZERWE.

Zerwe, Susanna Catharine, b. Dec. 10, 1781; bap. Dec. 29, 1781; spon., Adam Leiss and Susanna Unruh, both single.

LEONARD ZERBEN (Zerwe) and wf. Susanna.

Zerben (Zerwe), Margaret, b. March 30, 1805; bap. ———, ———; spon., John Scharff and wf. "Euphrosina."

Zerben (Zerwe), Elizabeth, b. Oct. 4, 1814; bap. ——— ———, ———; spon., Elizabeth Zerben.

Zerben (Zerwe), John, b. April 9, 1817; bap. ——— ———, ———; spon., John Zerben.

CHRISTIAN ZWEYSICH.

Zweysich, Joh. Conrad, b. March 2, 1747; bap. April 12, 1747; spon., Conrad Lang and wf.

Here follow a few not indicated in the index:

——— LIEB.

Lieb, Caspar, b. Sept. 12, 1780; bap. Oct. 8, 1780; spon., Matthew Staudt and wf. Margaret.

CHRISTIAN FREMDLING.

Fremdling, Anna Mary, b. Oct. 28, 1776; bap. ——— ———, ———; spon., Adam Schmitt and wf.

JOHN SALTER and wf. Anna Mary.

Salter, Elizabeth, b. Dec. 22, 1789; bap. Jan. 20, 1790; spon., Anthony Heilman and wf. Sybilla.

GEORGE ROHN and wf. Catharine.

Rohn, John, b. March 18, 1792; bap. June 10, 1792; spon., John Rohn and wf. Justina, grandparents.

JACOB LENGEL and wf.

Lengel, John, b. June 3, 1829; bap. Aug. 16, 1829; spon., John Conrad and wf.

CATHARINE RITSCHART.

A daughter, b. Dec. 9, 1815; bap. April 20, 1816; spon., John Schaeffer and wf. Magdalene.

JOEL HAAG and wf. Susanna.

Haag, Rebecca, b. June 7, 1845; bap. Aug. 24, 1845; spon., Levina Zerbe.

Burials.

Only two deaths and burials in this congregation at the Northkill are found in the record, viz:

1749, July 17, Adam Fischborn's wf. was buried.

1749 July 29, Michael Busch was buried on his own land.

Marriages.

As there are less than thirty in the list and as quite a number of them are not found in Stoever's Record, we give it entire. It will also appear from an examination of this list that when Stoever names Tulpehocken, he generally means this church in Tulpehocken township and not Stouchsburg:

Jan. 7, 1735, Joh. George Petry and Anna Sabina Roth.

April 29, 1735, John Matthias Wagner and Elizabeth Stup.

Jan. 12, 1736, George William Riegel and Anna Mary Plattner.

Jan. 9, 1738, John Riegel and Catharine Elizabeth Schirman.

Feb. 8, 1738, John Kittner and Barbara Heinrich.

Nov. 10, 1738, Lazarus Wagner and Catharine Lauck (not Pauck).

June 12 1739, Andrew Kochendoerfer and Justina Catharine Kaeyser.

Aug. 27, 1739, John Wendel Braun and Mary Elizabeth Knopff.

Dec. 31, 1739, Peter Knopff and Sophia Catharine Gaendling.

May 27, 1740, George Michael Kittner and Mary Catharine Friedrich.

July 28, 1740, Joh. George Arnold and Hannah Knopff.

April 12, 1741, Jacob Zorn and Anna Mary Gottes Kind.

Oct. 11, 1741, Engelhardt Flory and Elizabeth Zerwe.
Dec. 7, 1741, Nicholas Jungblut and Catharine Kappler.
Jan. 25, 1742, Jacob Vollmar, Jr., and Justina Kaercher.
Jan. 26, 1742, Christian Gruber and Anna Kunigunda Stup.
Oct. 31, 1742, Lewis Knopff anl Margaret Froehlich.
Jan. 23, 1743, Philip Petry and Susanna Juliana Emmert.
May 22, 1743, John Ermentraut and Anna Elizabeth Hedderich.
Aug. 30, 1743, Henry Frey and Catharine Schauer.
Jan. 24, 1744, Philip Meeth and Anna Mary Eberdt.
Feb. 28, 1744, Joh. Philip Strauss and Anna Mary Reimer.
Dec. 22, 1746, Valentine Van Huss and Mary Barbara Zerwe.
Dec. 22, 1746, John George Meyer and Caharine Zerwe.
Feb. 16, 1747 John Van Huss and Hannah Cheeck.
Feb. 7, 1748, Matthias Kaempffer and Mary Magdalene Reimer.
Sept. 3, 1749, Adam Fischborn, widower, and Anna Elizabeth Keppeler, widow, in church.
Nov. 12, 1749, Anna Cath. Heck, d. of Jost Heck, in church.
Jan. 17, 1750, George Adam Busch and Dorothea Kattermann.

In the latter part of the book containing this record we also find the following:

"Memorandum, Tulpehacken township, Oct. 26, 1774. When, after there had been great confusion among the members of this congregation in reference to a pastor, extending over several years, as is shown by this book, there was an unexpected change through the withdrawal of Rev. Schultze in April last. Since May 17, the congregation is served a second time by Rev. Stoever, at its earnest solicitation, and if God grant him health and strength he is to continue to serve it. A renewed effort is to be made by the newly elected deacons, John Wenderich and Nicholas Lengel, at least to bring about the desired order in the matter of income and expenditures especially. This arrangement is to be carried out in the following manner:
1774.   Receipts.   £. s. d.
Oct. 26. Paid over by the former
          deacons as per bill
          No. 1, ... 1 4 4
          Expenditures. £. s. d.
There is also the following "List and Register of the Communicants, and more particularly of those who attended the Holy Supper and took part in the preparatory service since 1761."

"March 21 and 22, 1761, the following persons at Northkill handed in their names (angemeldet) as applicants for admission to the Holy Supper, namely:

Conrad Ernst,   Henry Reitebach,
Joh. Adam Schnei-   Matthias Schmitt,
   der,   Mary   Catharine
A. Mary Bechtel,   Glueck,
John Schneider,   William Hedderich,
George Gaensel,   Joh. George Meyerle,
Jacob Miller,
Mrs. Cath. Char-   Jost Hederich,
   lotte Miller,   Melchoir Doebler,
Simon Lieb,   John Miller,
Justina Miller,   Michael Koehl,
Mar. Cath. Koehl,   Martin Pfatteicher,
A. Barbara Pfat-   Frederic Taxis,
   teicher,   Joh. Hertmens,
A. Margr. Aundt,   Philippina Henning,
Justina Vollmar,   Joh. Nicholas Bechtel,
Lewis Fischer,
Mary Cath Fischer."

NOTES AND QUERIES.

Historical, Biographical, and Genealogical.

XLII.

MONTGOMERY.

James Montgomery was a lawyer living in Lancaster city, and died about 1847. I have seen him many a time when a boy.
J. A. B.

HOGE—JENKINS.

Jacob Jenkins, of Hampshire county, Virginia, by his wife Elizabeth, had the following children:

i. Jonathan, m. Ann Hoge.
ii. Mary, m. in 1778, John Hoge, son of William Hoge, of Frederick county, Va.
iii. Evan, m. in 1779, Elizabeth Connard, dau. of James and Jane Connard, of Hampshire county, Va.
iv. Michael, m. in 1787 Rachel Pugh, dau. of Thomas and Ann Pugh, of Frederick county, Va.
v. Anna, m. in 1782, —— Gettis.
vi. Ruth, m. in 1786, Israel Hoge.
vii. Elizabeth, m. in 1792, John Lewis.
viii. Jacob.
Information is desired as to the ancestry of this family of Hoge.
Piqua, O. N. M.
[These Hoges belong to the Virginia branch of that family—although remotely connected with the Pennsylvania Hoges. Mr. R. A. Brock, of Richmond, Va., can furnish data.]

The Ancestry of John L. Dawson.

[The following record of the ancestry of John Littleton Dawson, the eminent lawyer and statesman of Western Pennsylvania, comes to us from an occasional correspondent.]

I. Nicholas Dawson, son of George Dawson, of Montgomery county, Md., settled in Western Pennsylvania prior to the war of the Revolution, in which he took an active part in the defense of the frontiers. He died in Fayette county, Pa., about 1800. He m. Violet Littleton, daughter of John and Violet Littleton. They had two sons:
2. i. George, b. March 17, 1783; m. Mary Kennedy.
3. ii. John, b. July 13, 1788; m. Ann Bailey.

II. George Dawson (Nicholas, George) b. March 17, 1783; d. June 19, 1871,at Brownsville, Pa. He m. Mary Kennedy. They had issue:
i. Sarah.
4. ii. John-Littleton, b. Feb. 13, 1813; m. Mary Clarke.
iii. Mary-Kennedy; d. unm.
iv. Louisa; m. Gen. George W. Cass.
v. Elizabeth; m. Alfred Howell.
vi. Catharine-Harrison; m. A. Evans Willson.
vii. George-Nicholas.
viii. Ellen; m. George W.Cass (second wife).
ix. Samuel-Kennedy; m. Jeannette Weston.
x. George-Fielding; m. Mary Patterson.

III. John Dawson (Nicholas, George), b. July 13, 1788; d. at Uniontown, Pa. He was a lawyer of distinction, and presided for some years as associate judge of the Court of Common Pleas for Fayette county. He m. Ann Bailey, b. Sept. 8, 1799; d. May 6, 1859. They had issue:
i. Ellis-Bailey.
ii. Ellen-Moore; m. Addison Ruby.
iii. Emily-Violet; m. Dr. William Sturgeon.
iv. Maria; m. Henry Baldwin.
v. Henry-Clay.
vi. Ruth-Elizabeth; m. A. K. Johnson.
vii. Louisa-Cass; m. John M. Berry.
viii. John-Nicholas.
ix. Richard-W.

IV.—John Littleton Dawson (George, Nicholas, George), b. Feb. 7, 1813, at Uniontown, Pa.; d. Sept. 18, 1870, near Geneva, a. He m. Oct. 20, 1836, Mary Clarke, dau. of Robert Clarke and his wife Sarah Whaley. They had issue:
i. Sarah-Kennedy, b. Sept. 1838; m. Charles E. Speer.
ii. Louisa-Cass, b. Oct. 4, 1839; m. Henry Whitely Patterson.
iii. Mary-Clarke, b. June 13, 1842; m. Chauncey Forward Black.
iv. George-Littleton, b. March 29, 1846; l. Oct. 17, 1860.

BAPTISMAL AND OTHER RECORDS

Of "The Little Tulpehocken Church."

V.

Communicants.

May 9th, 1761, the following handed in their names and communed on the next day, May 10, Whit. S.:
Michael Kuntz, Mrs. Cath. Weininger,
Mary Magdalene Kuntz, Sarah Radebach,
A. Mary Radebach, Jacob Frederick Lang,
A. Catharine Lieb,

Matthew Mueller,
Susan Cath. Mueller,
Mary Margrt. Kettner,
Mary Eve Kettner,
Kilian Jack,
Lawrence Spindler,
Nicholas Lingel,
John Lingel,
John Wenrich,
Christina Wenrich,
Gottlieb Loeffle,
Susan Mary Loeffle,
Susanna Ernst,
A. Cath. Mueller,
David Mueller,
Jacob Schmitt,
Joh. George Radebach,
Juliana Radebach,
Jacob Ernst,
A. Cath. Ernst,
Mary Cath. Buechler,
Eva Strohschneider,
Elizabeth Schneider,
Geo. Michl. Kettner,
Catharine Kettner,
Cath. Fahringer,

Andrew Vogel,
A. Mary Vollmar,
Cath. Elizbeth Zimmerman,
Mary Magdalene Schell,
Mary Eliz. Bogenreif (crossed out).
Michael Fries,
Margaret Fries,
Martin Lang,
Agnes Lang,
Mary Magdalene Bogenreif,
Conrad Scharff,
Jacob Boeckle,
A. Mary Boeckle,
Theobald Fahringer,
Catharine Fahringer,
Catharine Schmidt,
A. Elizabeth Arnold,
A. Elizabeth Bechtel,
Nicholas Holder,
A. Mary Holder,
Nicholas Bechtel,
Margaret Bechtel,
Elizabeth Barbara Neff.

Catechumens confirmed:
Joh. George Gaensle, 21 yrs.,
Theobald Fahringer, 15 yrs.,
Joh. Jacob Loewegut, 16, schlecht,
Joh. Nicholas Hoern, 16, ziemlich,
Andrew Emrich, 17, artlich,
Gottlieb Glasbrenner, 13½, so,
Michael Zerbe, 18, schlecht,
Valentine Zerbe, 17, einfachtig,
Phil. Leopold Lang, 14½,
Elizabeth Kettner, 17, bloed,
Mary Cath. Kettner, 15, artig,
Catharine Boekle, 16, schlecht,
Veronica Fries, 14, gut,
Esther Regina Scharff, 12½,
Catharine Emert, 16, schlecht,
Catharine Jack, 17.

Sept. 13, 1761, 13th S. aft. Trinity the following appeared:
Martin Lang,
Joh. Miller,
Hermanus Schell,
Matthias Miller,
Justina Miller,
Michael Koehl,
Mary Cath. Koehl,
John Mauntz,
Anna Mary Bechtel,
Anna Barbara Jack,
Anna Mary Bechtel,
Joh. Strohschneider,
Mary Margr. Schneider,
George Michael Kettner,
Catharine Kettner,
Jacob Fischer,
Cath. Fischer,
Mary Eve Kettner,
Catharine Kettner,
Anna Mary Kettner,
Mary Elizabeth Zerbe,
Joh. Adam Schneider,
Jacob Mueller,
Cath. Charlotte Mueller,
Matthew Schmitt,
Cath. Margrt. Schmitt,
Henry Gebbert,
Anna Cath. Gebbert,

Susan Cath. Miller,
Joh. Michael Schneider,
Mary Schmidt,
Eva Margaret Bechtel,
Mary Margrt. Kettner,
Elizabeth Kettner,
Catharine Boeckele,
Susan Cath. Ernst,
Michael Sauser,
Mrs. Anna Sauser,
Anna Mary Badebach,
Mary Cath. Bicker,
Joh. Jacob Ernst,
Anna Cath. Ernst,
Margaret Elizb. Bogenreif,
A. Mary Bockele,
Christopher Muench,
Barbara Muench,
Mary Schwenck,
William Spatz,
George Fries,
Joh. George Meyerle,
John Kraft,
Catharine Lengel,
Nicholas Gaucker,
Caspar Hinckel,
Nicholas Holder,
Eva Holder.

Communicants who received the Holy Supper April 4 (Palmarum), 1762, at the Northkill:
Martin Lang,
Agnes Lang,
Catharine Lauck,
Catharine Volmar,
Joh. Adam Schneider,
Anna Elizabeth Schneider,
Joh. George Maeyerle,
Jacob Fuchs,
A. Catharine Mueller,
Catharine Weininger,
Jacob Mueller,
Michael Fries,
Henry Gebbert,
Henry Frey,
Dietrich Sohl,
Jacob Fredr. Lang,
John Fues,
Simon Lieb,
George Kress,
Henry Sohl,
Caspar Hinckel,
David Mueller,
Jacob Sauser,
Conrad Kriegbaum,
Michael Mueller,
John Fues,
Tobias Fues,

Conrad Scharff, Cath. Charlotte Mueller.
John Mueller,
William Spatz,
Mary Cath. Goecker, Justina Mueller,
Mary Margaret Scharff, Elizabeth Fues, Esther Regina Spies,
Mary Barbara Wilhelm, Veronica Fries, A. Catharine Lieb,
Mary Catharine Lingel, Mary Catharine Jack,
A. Catharine Gebbert, A. Mary Bechtel, John Schwartz Haupt,
Catarine Frey,
Margaret Fries, George Christ,
Mary Eva Hinckel, Jacob Stauch,
Ann Elizabeth Arnold.

Communed on Whit Sunday, May 30th, 1762:
Mathias Smith, Catharine Schmidt,
Joh. Wenrich, A. Cath. Ernst,
Michael Kunz, Catharine Fischer,
Michael Koehl, Susan Radebach,
Nicholas Bechtel, Justina Volmar,
Martin Ernst, Mary Zerbe,
Kilian Jack, A. Elizabeth Zerbe,
George Radebach, Margaret Mauntz,
Henry Radebach, Mary Magdalene Kuntz,
Samuel Bayer,
John Lingle, Barbara Hess,
Nichholas Lingel, M. Elizabeth Roesch,
John Mauntz, Sus. Cath. Miller,
Lewis Fischer, Jhilippina Heninger,
Michael Schneider, Catharine Fischer,
Jacob Lowegut, A. Barbara Muench,
Jacob Ernst, A. Mary Holter,
Matthias Miller, A. Barbara Jack,
Bernhard Zimmerman, A. Elizabeth Bechtel, Margaret Bechtel,
George Fries, Justina Cath.Hepler,
Jacob Pfatteicher, Cath. Margaret Schell,
Christian Roesch,
Jacob Weiniger, Apollonia Wagner.
Lawrence Spingler,

Communicants who handed in their names October 30th and partook of the Holy Supper, October 31st, 1762, at the Northkill:
Joh. George Mayerle, A. Mar. Kriegbaum,
Henry Gebbert, A. Barb. Jack,
John Fuess, Mar. Cath. Bayer,
Michael Kuntz, M. Magalene Kuntz,
Joh. Adam Schaner, Philipina Henning,
Michael Fries, A. Eva Arzt,

Nicholas Holder, Catharine Fischer,
Kilian Jack, Cath. Kettner,
Lawrence Spintler, M. Elizabeth Zerbe,
George Kress, M. Cath. Lengel,
Caspar Hinckel, M. Eva Hinckel,
Benjamin Zerbe, A. M. Holder,
Samuel Bayer, Elizabeth Fues,
Theobold Fahringer, A. Elizbth. Schneider,
Simon Lieb,
John Fues, Cath. Jack,
Mar. Cath. Gicker, Cath. Lieb
Susan Radebach, Veronica Fues,
Mary Elizabeth Becker, Margr. Charlotte Oxerath,
Barbara Wilhelm, M. Barb. Hoff,
Mar. Cath. Lauck, Margr. Kettner,
A. Elizabeth Zerbe, Elizabeth Kettner,
Catharine Gebbert, Elizb. Regina Scharff
Margaret Fries, Magalene Vetter.
Justina Volmar,

Communicants, April 3d, 1763—Easter:
Jacob Mueller, Kilian Jack,
Mathias Schmitt, Adam Schneider,
John Miller, Jacob Schmidt,
Michael Koehl, Joh. Geo. Fries,
John Schneider, Michael Schneider,
A. Gebbert, Nicholas Bechtel,
W. Spatz, Jacob Ernst,
Fredr. Sentzel, Christopher Muench,
Joh. Geo. Maeyerle, David Mueller,
Michael Kuntz, Andrew Krafft,
Joh. Fuess, Tobias Fues.
Charlotte Mueller, A. Mary Schneider,
Cathar. Schneider, A. Mary Jack,
Justina Mueller, E. M. Bechtel,
Barbara Muench, Elizab. Fues,
Margr. Elizab. Bay, A. Mary Bechtel,
Catharine Mueller, Catharine Kettner,
Susanna Schmidt, Eva Kettner,
Catharine Ernst, Veronica Fries,
A. Mary Radebach, Anna Radebach,
Philipina Henning, Elizabeth Kettner,
A. Margr. Staudt, Margaret Kettner,
A. Magdl. Kuntz, Cath. Gebbert.

The following persons handed in their names for communion, May 21st, 1763, and attended the same on the 23d, viz. Whit Sunday:
Geo. Michael Kettner, Mar. Cath. Fischer,
A. Mary Heberling,
Martin Lang, Susanna Radebach,
Michael Fries, Mary Margrt Strohschneider,
Nicholas Holder,

Caspar Hinckel,
Michael Sauser,
George Kress,
Lewis Fischer,
Philip Wagner,
Joh. Strohschneider,
Nicholas Lingel,
Henry Radebach,
Jacob Mountz,
Matthias Sommer,
Matthew Miller,
George Radebach,
Mar. Cath. Lingel,
Agnes Lang,
Barbara Wilhelm,
Susan Cath. Miller,
Anna Cunigunda Sauser,
M. Eve Hinckel,
Justina Volmar,
Elizabeth Wagner,
Margrt. Fries,
Cath. Kettner,
M. Cath. Gicker,
Cath. Gebbert,
A. Elizabeth Schneider,
Mary Blaser.

This completed the list of communicants during the time of service of one pastor. They are all in the same hand. Now there is a space of 11 years in which no record is made. E.

Tulpehocken Township, June 11, 1774. Memorandum of the communicants who were present (i. e. took part in the communion) administered by Rev. Stoever when Rev. Schultz had ceased to serve:
Conrad Scharff,
George Scharff,
Jacob Schmied,
Matthias Schmied,
Martin Battorf,
John Mueller,
John Wendrich,
Joh. Adam Schneider,
Matthew Mueller,
J. Jacob Beyerle,
Adam Schmied,
Mar. Margrt Scharff,
Mary Catharine Scharff,
Susanna Schmied,
Catharine Schmied,
Catharine Mueller,
Anna Cunigunda Gruber,
Susanna Schmied,
Justina Miller,
Catharine Mueller,
Anna Mary Mueller,
Justina Wendrich,
Susanna Catharine Mueller,
Mary Margaret Beyerle,
Anna Mary Schmied,
Anna Elizabeth Schmied.

Communicants on Advent Sunday, November 27, 1774:
Adam Schmied,
Jacob Schmied,
John Badeicher,
Adam Badeicher,
Martin Badeicher,
John Schwartzhaupt,
John Wendrich,
Conrad Scharff,
Joh. George Scharff,
Anna Mary Schmied,
Susanna Schmeid,
Sybilla Badeicher,
Catharine Schmied,
Catharine Mueller,
Mrs. Wendrich,
Mary Margaret Scharff,
Mary Barbara Sommer,
Samuel Baeyer,
Matthias Sommer,
George Schaeffer,
Jacob Beyerle,
Catharine Mueller,
Mary Margaret Beyerle,
Mary Catharine Scharff.

These are plainly in Stoever's own handwriting.

NOTES AND QUERIES.

Historical, Biographical and Genealogical.

XLIII.

HOTTENSTEIN.

I. Jacob Hottenstein was born February 15, 1697, in Eslingen, fi Germany. He came to America with his family after 1740, settling in Maxatawny township, Berks county, Pa. He died March 23, 1753. Jacob Hottenstein m. Dorothea Reber, in Germany. Their children were:

i. Jacob Jr., m. and settled in Richmond township, Berks county. He left issue:
1. Catharine; m. Abraham Biehl.
2. Maria; m. Abraham Deyster.
3. Blondine; m. Caspar Merkel.
4. Susanna; m. Samuel Ely.

ii. William; resided in Cumru township, m. and left besides four daughters, issue:
1. Samuel.
2. William, Jr.
3. Henry.
4. Solomon.
5. David.

iii. David; resided on the homestead farm. His children were:
1. Jacob.
2. David (M. D)
3. Daniel.
4. Catharine; m. Jacob Grim.
5. Dorothea.

iv. Henry; studied medicine, and died at Lancaster.

[From the foregoing data, our Ohio correspondent can make further research.]

YOUNG.

William Young is mentioned in the list of taxables of the township of Lurgan, Franklin county, then a part of Cumberland, in year 1753. From the records of Cumberland county, letters of administration were granted March 6, 1753, to John Davis and Elizabeth Young on the estate of William Young, deceased. In the release of John Young and wife Elizabeth, of Southampton township, Franklin county, Penn'a., to William Young, of the township, county and State aforesaid "of the right, title and interest of a certain tract of land lying and being situate in the township aforesaid, containing 136 acres, which is the same tract that was agreed for by my late father, William Young, with Richard Peters, Esq., and conveyed by the said Richard Peters since my father's death to the present William Young, parties or eldest son to the said William Young, deceased, bearing date June 6, 1761." The above release is dated August 10, 1804. From the release and deeds are found names of six children of William Young, Sr—William, John, Elizabeth (intermarried with John McConnell), Margaret (intermarried with Andrew Hemphill) unknown (married Daniel Slaymaker) and an unknown daughter. From time to time it is shown in the Franklin county deeds that William and John Young bought in the shares of their sisters. The plantation was stuated in Lurgan township, Franklin county. John Young was a private in Col. William Irvine's regiment (Sixth Penn'a battalion) in the Revolutionary War. He was in the third company commanded by Capt. Abraham Smith, and mustered into service in January, 1776. Andrew Hemphill served as a private in the First battalion, Cumberland county militia, in 1777. John McConnell was captain in the Cumberland county battalion in 1776.

Queries—1. Who were the parents of William Young, Sr.?
2. Who was the wife of William Young, Sr.? H. E. K.
Detroit, Mich.

TOMBSTONE INSCRIPTIONS

Warrington Friends Meeting House York County, Penna.

[Near the village of Wellsville, York county, is located the historic old building, called the "Warrington Meeting House." The stone structure is surrounded by a beautiful grove or native trees, and is one of the landmarks in the early settlement of the county. A history of this historic spot cannot be given in this connection, but it is hoped Mr. Myers, who so kindly furnished "Notes and Queries" with the transcript from the stones in the graveyard close by, will give us a sketch in the near future.]

John McCelellan, d. Aug. 30, 1871; aged 75y. 7m. 1d.
Eleanor McClellan, wf. of John, d. Feb. 13, 1882; aged 70y. 4m. 2d.
Rebecca McClellan, b. Sept. 13, 1799; d. Dec. 10, 1870.
James McClellan, d. May, 1862; aged about 23y.
Lydia Walker, wf. of John [and dau. of John and Margaret Marsh] d. 12mo. 19, 1864; aged 85y. 1m. 29d.
John Walker, d. 4mo. 2, 1854; aged 78y. 7m. 22d.
Sarah Hutton, wf. of Benjamin, d. Feb. 10, 1859; aged 70y. 30d.
Benjamin Hutton, d. April 24, 1864; aged 74y. 11m. 1d.
Martha Denison, d. Oct. 16, 1856.
Elizabeth Wall, wf. of Jacob, d. 11mo. 1, 1878; aged 83y 4m. 13d.
David Burkholder, d. Feb. 19, 1858; aged 63y. 8m. 23d.
Sarah Ann E. Moore, d. Feb. 3, 1850; aged 65y.
William Wall, d. June 1, 1839; aged 78y. 5m. 5d.
Mary Wall, wf. of William, d. Jan. 30, 1845.
Hannah Underwood, d. 1mo. 24, 1831; aged near 70y.
Jacob Comfort, d. Oct. 30, 1836; aged 61y. 3m. 1d.
Elizabeth Comfort, wf. of Jacob, d. March 16, 1863; aged 83y. 7m. 9d.
Elizabeth Comfort, b. July 1, 1778; d. March 11, 1854.
Jane Denison, d. May 10, 1840.
Anna Mary Comfort, b. Oct. 25, 1765; d. Dec. 25, 1832.
Samuel John, d. July 9, 1872; in 73d year.
Ann Alcock, d. 8mo. 20, 1802; aged 62y.
Mary Alcock, d. 9mo. 22, 1802; aged 38y.

Robert Gray, d. 6mo. 30, 1796; aged 64y.
Samuel Keller, d. July 23, 1869; aged 77y.
Isaac Gray, b. Feb. 15, 1792; d. Sept. 19, 1860.
Eliza Cadwallader, wf. of David, d. June 22, 1876; aged 71y. 9m. 22d.
William Cadwallader, d. April 1868, in 87th year.
Sarah Cadwallader, wf. of William, d. 11mo. 11, 1839; aged 52y. 7m. 13d.
B. C., d. 1802.
J. C., d. 1801.
R. W., d. 1781.
A. W., d. 1817.
Jacob McMillan, d. 1mo. 1, 1833; aged 55y. 5m.
Ruth McMillan, wf. of Jacob, d. 3mo. 1, 1829, aged 59y. 1m. 9d.
Joseph McMillan, d. 1826.
R. M., d. 1833. (?)
Thomas McMillan, d. 1831.
J. M. [John McMillan] d. 10mo. 17, 1791.
J. M. [Jane McMillan, wf. of John. Her grave was dug 10mo. 14, 1782], d. 1782.
J. M.
S. M. [Sarah McMillan, dau. of John and Jane, b. 3 mo. 3, 1760.], d. 1789.
Db. M., Sr. [Deborah McMillan, wf. of William and dau. of Henry and Lydia (Fell) Holland.], d. 9 mo. 4, 1797.
J. M., d. 11mo., 1791.
Db. M. [Deborah McMillan, dau. of William and Deborah. Her grave was dug 12mo. 10, 1782.], d. 12 mo., 1782.
S. M. [Samuel McMillan, son of William and Deborah, b. 2mo. 26, 1770], d. 4mo. 10, 1777.
T. M. [Thomas McMillan, who came to Pennsylvania in 1738 from Ballynacree, County Antrim, Province of Ulster, Ireland, with wife Deborah and children], d. 9mo., 1753.
D. M. [Deborah McMillan, wf. of Thomas and dau. of Joshua and Elizabeth Marsh], d. 9mo. 22, 1764.
Db. M. [Deborah McMullan, dau. of William and Deborah, b. 9mo. 13, 1764], d. 11mo. 24, 1766.
Ruth Walker, d. 1772; aged 72y.
Benjamin Walker, d. Dec. 31, 1801; aged 77y.

Jarman Walker, d. 8mo. 31, 1782.
Phebe Walker, d. 1mo. 31, 1782.
D. Mc., 95y.
Charles Underwood, d. Oct. 6, 1869, in 81st year.
Margaret Underwood, wf. of Charles, d. April 8, 1895, in 84th year.
Rebecca McMillan, wf of George [and dau. of Benjamin and Susanna (Dunn) Cutler], d. 11mo. 24, 1766.
George McMillan [son of George and Ann (Hinshaw) McMillan], d. 5mo. 24, 1846; aged 83y.
Jane McMillan, second wf. of George [and dau. of Jacob and ——— (McClellan) Laird], d. Sept. 1, 1862; aged 70y. 1m. 10d.
George McMillan [son of Thomas and Deborah (Marsh) McMillan, b. 4mo. 2, 1732], d. 7mo. 11, 1795.
J. Cook [Jesse Cook, son of Jesse and Mary (Wierman) Cook], d. 1799.
W. Cook [William Cook, son of Jesse and Mary (Wierman) Cook], d. 1793.
J. Packer, d. 1788.
Mary Cook [wf. of Henry and dau. of William and Mary Way, b. 7mo. 16, 1767], d. 3 mo. 16, 1836.
Henry Cook [son of Jesse and Mary (Wierman) Cook, b. 2 mo. 29, 1768], d. 4mo. 13, 1835.
Mary Cook [dau. of Henry and Mary (Way) Cook], d. 1 mo. 13, 1832, in 33d year.
Sidney Cook [nee Evans] wf. of Isaac, d. March 12, 1821; aged 51y. 9m. 21d.
Ann Jones, d. 1830.
Jehu Jones, d. 1831.
A. Cook [Ann Cook, dau. of Peter and Sarah (Gilpin) Cook, b. 10 mo. 20, 1741. Her grave was dug 2mo. 12, 1784], d. 1784.
Pet. C. [Peter Cook, son of Peter and Elinor (Norman) Cook, b. 10mo. 4, 1700, at Northwich, Cheshire, England; came with parents to Pennsylvania in 1713], d. 4mo. 28, 1779.
S. Cook [Sarah Cook, wf. of Peter, and dau. of Joseph and Hannah (Glover) Gilpin, b. 4mo. 2, 1706], d. 6 mo. 7, 1783.
Hannah C. [Hannah Cook, wf. of Samuel and dau. of William and Deborah (Roberts) Fisher, b. 3mo. 30, 1741], d. 5mo. 9, 1768.

Notes and Queries.

S. Cook [Sarah Cook, dau. of Jesse and Mary (Wierman) Cook], d. 1800.
Jesse Cook [son of Peter and Sarah (Gilpin) Cook, b. 9mo. 15, 1744], d. 8mo. 18, 1818.
Mary Cook [wf. of Jesse and dau. of Henry and Priscilla (Pope) Wierman, b. 10mo. 19, 1746], d. 12mo. 1, 1824.
Mary Reed, wf of Zachariah [and dau. of Jesse and Mary (Wierman) Cook], d. Dec. 19, 1849; aged 75y.
Lydia G. Walker, b. June 11, 1796; d. June 22, 1869.
Dr. Joseph J. Hayward, d. Sept. 19, 1853; aged 76y. 6m. 19d.
Sally Hayward, wf. of Dr. Joseph Hayward, d. Jan. 19, 1873; aged 72y. 10m.
Israel Cook [son of Samuel and and Ruth (Mode) Cook, b. 8mo. 27, 1774], d. 3mo. 14, 1780..
Samuel Cook [son of Peter and Sarah (Gilpin) Cook, b. 10mo. 15, 1738], d. 8mo. 10, 1800.
Ruth Cook[wf. of Samuel and dau. of Alexander and Rebecca (Allen) Mode, b. 10 mo. 21, 1747], d. 4 mo. 5, 1789.
W. N. [William Nevitt, b. 1719, in Ireland; came from Moat, Leinster Province, Ireland, to Warrington, York county, Pa., in 1751], d. 8mo. 15, 1800.
H. N. [Hannah Nevitt, wf. of William, and dau. of Peter and Sarah (Gilpin) Cook], b. 4mo. 27, 1736; d. in spring of 1806.
Joseph Griffith [son of William and Joanna (Craig) Griffith], d. 7mo. 5, 1854, aged 85y. 9mo.
Rebecca Griffith [wf. of Joseph and dau. of Samuel and Ruth (Mode) Cook].
Catharine Bentz, wf. of Michael, d. June 1, 1827, aged 52y.
Mordecai Pugh, d. 1802.
James Griffith [son of Abraham and Margaret (Cadwallader) Griffith], d. Feb. 18, 1892, aged 83y. 9mo. 13d.
Mary Griffith, wf. of James, d. Jan 30, 1886, aged 73y. 5m. 12d.
Deborah Griffith [dau. of William and Joanna (Craig) Griffith, b. 9 mo. 21, 1772]; d. 2mo. 20, 1845.
J. Mc. [Joanna McMillan, dau. of William and Mary Craig, d. 4mo. 27, 1794. She married first William Griffith and second John McMillan.]
Elizabeth Griffith [nee Ong, 1st wf. of Abraham Griffith], d. Dec. 9, 1805, aged about 55y.
Abraham Griffith [son of William and first wife, Esther (Davis) Griffith], d. June 21, 1841, aged 95y. 8mo. 20d.
Margaret Griffith [second wf. of Abraham, and dau. of James and Mary (Davis) Cadwallader], d. Nov. 7, 1859, aged 86y. 11mo. 29d.
Margaret Ross, d. Feb. 14, 1870, aged 74y.
Margaret Ross, wf. of James, b. Feb. 9, 1793; d. Nov. 2, 1881.
James Ross, b. Apr. 24, 1791; d. Nov. 7, 1867.
John Ross, d. Aug. 19, 1802.
John Ross, d. 1799.
Susan Keller, wf. of Samuel, b. July 19, 1797; d. Apr. 16, 1851.
Elizabeth Kuhn, d. Apr. 15, 1871, aged 82y.
Hannah Cook, wf. of John [and dau. of Abel and Ann (Vale) Walker], d. Mar. 3, 1863, aged 77y. 10mo. 21d.
John Cook [son of Jesse and Mary (Wierman) Cook], d. July 23, 1864, aged 82y. 3mo. 24d.
Solomon Underwood, b. Jan. 27, 1783; d. Oct. 16, 1846, aged 63y. 8mo. 20d.
Ann Underwood, wf. of Solomon; d. Sept. 5, 1861, aged 71y. 6mo. 27d.
John Edmundson, d. Feb. 3, 1784.
Louisa Cookson, d. 1830.
E. C.
H. C.
Sarah Vale, dau. of William and Ann, b. 5mo. 12, 1789; d. 5mo. 4, 1862.
Peter Vale, d. 8mo. 14, 1834, aged 44y. 27d.
Mary Walker, wf. of Asahel, b. Dec. 5, 1787; d. Apr. 18, 1827.
Asahel Walker, b. Sept. 6, 1786; d. Oct. 14, 1877.
M. Walker, d. 1852.
P. W., d. 1837.
Alice Vale, d. 3mo. 1818, aged 28y.
Ann G. Vale, d. 3mo. 1822, aged 24y.
Elisha Vale, d. 5mo. 27, 1855, in 67th year.
R. V. [Robert Vale], d. 8mo. 17, 1799, aged 83y.
Ann Vale, wf. of William, d. 4mo. 5, 1816, aged about 61y.

William Vale, d. 4mo. 5, 1838, aged about 84y.
Ann Hussey, wf. of Jediah, d. 12mo. 6, 1819, aged 33y. 7mo. 6d.
Jediah Hussey, d. 9mo. 10, 1828, aged 51y. 6mo. 13d.
H. Wierman, d. Aug. 5, 1802.
Elihu Underwood, d. 10mo. 26, 1803, aged 57y.
Lydia B. Underwood, wf. of Amos, d. July 30, 1860, aged 77y. 9mo. 19d.
Amos Underwood, b. 1786; d. Feb. 4, 1868.
John Nisbet, d. 1801.
Mary Nisbet, d. 1767.
William Ross, d. 1777.
Jane Ross, d. 1801.
Alexander Ross, d. Mar. 15, 1816, aged 59y. 9mo. 15d.
Margaret Ross, wf. of Alexander, d. July 23, 1829, aged 63y. 7mo. 7d.
Jane Ross, d. Dec. 3, 1818, aged 31y. 6mo. 15d.
James Ross, d. May 14, 1820, aged 26y. 2mo. 14d.
Margaret Ross, wf, of William, d. May 23, 1827, aged 32y. 3mo. 28d.
William Ross, d. July 20, 1863, aged 74y. 2mo. 25d.
Elizabeth Ross, wf. of William, d. May 22, 1872, aged 80y. 5mo. 24d.
Mary M. Harman, wf. of F. Harman, and "mother of fourteen children," d. Jan. 6, 1826, aged 70y.
Abraham Harman, b. Feb. 18, 1787; d. Jan. 4, 1869.
Samuel Cook [son of Jesse and Mary (Wierman) Cook, d. 7mo. 2, 1857, in 85th year.]
Jane Cook [wf. of Samuel Cook, and dau. of James and Mary (Maulsby) Hicks, b. 2mo. 15, 1771; d. 1mo. 28, 1849. Her first husband was —— Warner.]
Robert Erwin, d. 1808.
S. E., d. 1818.
D. F., d. 1mo. 11, 1826.
S. V., d. 1833.
Garret Van Arsdelen, d. 1800.
R. Bradley, d. 1789.
William Squibb, Jr., d. Dec. 20, 1831, aged 46y. 11mo. 6d.
William Squibb, d. Jan. 5, 1826, aged 72y. 1mo. 29d.
Jane Squibb, d. 1800.
John Squibb, d. 1800.

Rebecca Gratz, d. Apr. 30, 1834, in 30th year.
Ann Ramsey, wf. of William, b. Sept. 18, 1805, aged 32y. 7mo. 19d.
John Bell, oldest son of Ebenezer and Rebecca Bell, d. Feb. 27, 1864, aged 77y. 1mo. 14d.
Ann Bell, wf. of John, d. Jan. 17, 1867, aged 71y. 8mo. 4d.
Ebenezer Bell, d. Aug. 31, 1834.
J. B., d. 1793.
J. B., d. 1792.
J. B., d. 1802.
R. M., d. 1822.
James Glass, d. 1802, aged 28y.
Daniel Glass, d. 1802, aged 13y.
Margaret Glass, d. 1804, aged 22y.
P. L., d. 1822.
Peter Cleaver, d. 12mo. 8, 1795, aged 64y. 1mo. 19d.
Miriam Cleaver, d. 5mo. 29, 1798, aged 71y.
Uriah Cleaver, d. 1818.
John Cleaver, d. 5mo. 3, 1823, in 63d year.
Susan Cleaver, d. 7mo. 11, 1823, in 60th year.
D. Cookson, d. 8mo. 17, 1831.
Sarah John, wf. of Samuel, d. Mar. 17, 1837, aged about 37y.
Eli Cookson, son of Daniel, d. 8mo. 5, 1869, aged about 66y.
John Marsh, d. 3mo. 10, 1804, aged 80y.
M. M.
J. M.
John Everitt, b. 2mo. 3, 1771; d. 2mo. 25, 1855.
Robert Vale, d. Aug. 19, 1823, aged 37y. 1mo. 12d.
Benjamin Underwood, d. 1803.
D. Vale, d. 7mo. 26, 1804, aged 40(?)y.
Mary Squibb, wf. of George, d. June 25, 1866, aged 67y. 2mo.; George Squibb, d. June 18, 1866; aged 71y. 1mo. 5d. "The murdered family."
Elijah Underwood, d. 1804.
Rebecca Everitt, d. 4mo. 14, 1858, in 81st year.
William Nelson, d. Dec. 3, 1849, aged 68y.
E. N., d. 1823.
Sarah Nelson, wf. of William, d. Aug. 18, 1880, aged 81y. 5mo.
Abraham Wells, d. Apr. 8, 1851, aged 77y.
Hannah Wells, wf. of Abraham, d. June 19, 1847, aged 68y.

Willing Griest, d. 1833, aged 60y. 10mo. 5d.
Ann Griest [wf. of Willing, and dau. of George and Ann (Hinshaw) McMillan, b. 8mo. 21, 1766], d. 2mo. 23, 1850.
Mary Griest, wf. of Solomon, d. 11mo. 23, 1879, aged 80y. 21d.
Samuel McElwee, d. May 15, 1872, aged 79y. 3d.
Joanna McElwee, d. Sept. 24, 1875, aged 75y. 7mo. 2d.
William Ramsey, d. June 8, 1884, aged 85y. 4mo. 18d.

ALBERT COOK MYERS.
Philadelphia.

NOTES AND QUERIES,

Historical, Biographical, and Genealogical.

XLIV.

DEATHS OF PROMINENT PERSONS.
Sebastian Graff, d. July 2, 1791.
Colonel Thomas Proctor, son of Francis Proctor, d. Dec. 12, 1792.
Mrs. Isabella Mercer, wife of Gen. Hugh Mercer, d. Sept. 17, 1791.
Col. Christopher Stuart, d. May 27, 1791, aged 51 years, buried in Norriton graveyard.
Elizabeth Stuart, widow of Col. Christopher Stuart, and daughter of William and Mary Bull, d. April 4, 1838, aged 85 years.

CURRY.
From the burial records of Norriton graveyard we have the following relating to the family of Curry, inquiry concerning whom has been made:
Agnes Curry, d. Jan. 14, 1803, aged 86y.
Ann Curry, dau. of Archibald and Sarah, d. Jan. 3, 1810, aged 19y.
Archibald Curry, d. May 9, 1824, aged 64y.
James Curry, Sr., d. April 8, 1788, aged 84y.
James Curry, d. 1838, aged 83y.
Mary Curry, d. April 9, 1804, aged 97y.
Robert Curry, d. Nov. 9, 1794, aged 60y.
Sarah Curry, wife of Archibald, d. April 6, 1838, aged 76y., 1m., 4d.

KECK.
According to family tradition, my great-grandfather, John George Keck was a soldier of the Revolution, and was at the battle of Brandywine. His father, Henry Keck, emigrated from Basle, Switzerland, prior to 1750, and settled on Big Lehigh Spring, Northampton county, Pa. John George Keck married Catharine Schaub and at the close of the war removed to Westmoreland county. What were his revolutionary services.
Utica, Ia. J. A. K.
[Henry Keck was a private soldier, enlisted February 26, 1777, in Capt. Yost Dreisbach's company, in Baron de Ottendorff's Corps, attached to the Pennsylvania Line. George Keck was a ranger on the frontiers of Northampton county, Pa. Henry and George Keck are on the assessment lists of Salisbury township, that county up to the close of the Revolution, when they disappear, and in 1786 are located in Hempfield township, Westmoreland county.]

The Latest History of Indiana.

In the controversy between Virginia and Pennsylvania in regard to the boundary lines between the two colonies, Governor Penn claimed for his western boundary a line beginning at 39 degrees north latitude at the distance of five degrees of longitude from the Delaware, thence at the same distance from that river in every point, to north latitude 42 degrees. Lord Dunmore, Governor of Virginia, denied this claim, and insisted that the western boundary of Pennsylvania should be a meridian line run south from the end of five degrees of longitude from the Delaware, on line 42 degrees. By an examination of the map. and laying off the distance with compasses, it appears that both sides were granting far more than was claimed by either. A line conforming to the Delaware and drawn at the distance of five degrees from that river would at one point fall as far east as Latrobe and would leave Pittsburg, which was the main bone of contention, nearly a dozen miles over the border in Virginia; while Dunmore's line would have left it several miles within the limits of Pennsylvannia, so ignorant evidently were both parties to the dispute, of the geography of the country.

On the 31st of August, 1779, joint commissioners for Virginia and Pennsylvania agreed upon the following boundaries: "To extend Mason and Dixon's line due west five degrees of longitude, to be computed from the river Delaware, for the southern boundary of Pennsylvania; and that a meridian, drawn from the western extremity thereof to the northern limit of said State, be the western boundary of Pennsylvania forever."—Veech's The Monongahela of Old, p. 254.

Five degrees of longitude computed from the point where the forty-second parallel crosses the Delaware, westward, and a meridian let fall from the end of that line, is exactly all that Dunmore claimed. Virginia might well be satisfied, and Pennsylvania much more than satisfied, with the adjustment. But five degrees measured westward along the forty-second parallel from the Delaware, would bring one to a point a little southwest of the city of Erie, on the north, and the meridian would fall at the south just a little west of the point where the Monongahela river crosses the State line. Between this meridian and the present western boundary of the State there is a strip of land about twenty-five miles in width. When was the adjustment made by the commissioners in 1779, modified, and this trip of territory added to the State?

In my old Morse's American Geography 1796, that part of what is now West Virginia, bounded on the south by the Little Kenawha, on the east by the Laurel Hill and the Monongahela river, on the north by the southern boundary line of Pennsylvania and by that line extended to the Ohio, and on the west by the Ohio to the mouth of the Little Kenawha, is called "Indiana," and was granted to William Trent and 22 others by a number of tribes of Indians "as compensation for the losses they had sustained by the depredations of the latter, in the year 1763." In 1782 the validity of the claim of Trent, Croghan, &c., was brought into Congress, but no decision could be reached there. It was then decided that Colonel Morgan, who was agent for the proprietors as well as one of the proprietors himself, should present the matter to the Supreme Court. Before taking this step, however, it was resolved to present a memorial to the Virginia Legislature. This memorial was presented accordingly in November, 1790, and there the business "rested," so far as Morse's Geography is concerned. What was the later history of "Indiana?"

Ingram, Pa. T. J. CHAPMAN.

Westmoreland County Families.

[Information is desired relating to the following—especially names of parents, dates of birth, marriage and address of members of families.—S. P. B.]

ALEXANDER.

John Alexander, b. 1811, m. in 1832, Mary Phipps. Where was he born and full names of parents?

ATTLEMAN.

The Christian name of the wife of Andrew A. Sloan, of Venango county, Pa., who was an Attleman.

BURRIETT—DILLEY.

The full names of the parents of George Dilley, of Wilkes-Barre, Pa., who was b. June 12, 1812, and whose mother was a Burriett.

DUNCAN.

Name of wife of James Duncan, whose son was John Duncan, of Westmoreland county.

DEVOR.

Rebecca Devor, b. about 1797; d. September 30, 1871, at New Florence, Pa. She married about 1833, Eli Phipps. Names of her parents in full.

DUNHAM.

Nancy Dunham, of Richland county, O., m. John Clapper Charlton, and after his death married David Matthews and removed to California. Dates of birth and marriage and names of parents of Nancy Dunham wanted.

HALSTEAD.

Mary Halstead lived in Quincy, Ill.; m. William Jeptha Lamley, of Black Oak, Mo., and died in July, 1874, in Colorado. What else is known of her, and of her parentage? ?

KIESTER.

Sarah Kiester was the first wife of Jacob Phipps, son of Nathan and Edith

(Updegraff) Phipps, of Clarion county, Pa. What additional information can be given as to the Kiester and this particular Phipps families?

MISNER.

John Wesley Misner married Mary Lavina Charlton, of Ray county, Mo. Full data of these persons are desired.

SLOAN.

John Sloan, b. about 1786, m. three times; first, about 1811, Ellen Stevenson, and resided in Venango county, Pa. About 1818 he m. secondly Sarah Phipps, widow of Allen McDowell, and later removed to Logan county, O. In 1841 he m. thirdly, Rebecca Dickson. John Sloan d. in January, 1867, at Zanesville, O. Information relating to all the foregoing is desired.

URIE.

Was the maiden name of Catharine Harvey, who m. June 5, 1792, John Phipps, of West Fairfield township, Westmoreland county, Pa., Catharine Urie? If not, what was the relationship between the Urie and Phipps families?

VAUGHN.

William Vaughn, son of John Vaughn, and his wife Lydia Perry, was born about 1813, in Logan county, O. He m. in 1838 Delilah Sloan, of Zanesville, O.

WIER.

What was the Christian name of the wife of Jared Hunter, of Venango county, who was a Wier.

WADE.

Thomas Wade, b. about 1812, was the son of Garland Wade. He m. Delilah Sloan, widow of William Vaughn. What is known concerning these persons?

RENNIE.

William Rennie m. Mary Elizabeth Lamley, of Terry's Grove, Mo. Is supposed to have removed to California. Information requested.

Minneola, L. I., New York.

NORTHUMBERLAND COUNTY

List of Prothonotaries for One Hundred and Twenty-Seven Years.

Northumberland county was organized by act of March 21, 1772, and on the 24th of March following, Governor John Penn appointed "William Plunket, Turbutt Francis, Samuel Hunter, James Potter, William Maclay, Caleb Graydon, Benjamin Alison, Robert Moodie, John Lowdon, Thomas Lemon, Ellis Hughes and Benjamin Weiser, justices of the court of general quarter sessions of the peace and jail delivery." The first court, a private sessions of the peace, was held April 9, 1772, at Fort Augusta, there being no court house. Dr. Wiliam Plunket was chosen president, and he presided at these courts for several years. William Maclay was commissioned to act as prothonotary by the Governor under the Provincial regime; these appointments were made by the Supreme Executive Council under the Constitution of 1776, and by the Governor under the Constitution of 1790, until the Constitution of 1837-38 was adopted, when the office became elective. William Maclay served five years.

Under the various changes in the law since that time, with the dates of their commissions, and the terms which they served by election, the following have been the Prothonotaries of Northumberland county up to the present time:

William Maclay, March 24, 1772, clerk of the peace and quarter sessions of the peace, May 19, 1772; recommissioned March 22, 1777.
David Harris, September 11, 1777.
Matthew Smith, February 4, 1780.
Lawrence Keene. September 25, 1783.
Jasper Ewing, July 28, 1789, August 17, 1791, and January 3, 1800.
Daniel Levy, September 23, 1800.
Hugh Bellas, January 3, 1809.
George W. Brown, February 2, 1818.
Andrew Albright. April 24, 1819.
Martin Weaver, February 9, 1821.
Samuel J. Packer, January 27, 1824.
Martin Weaver, April 9, 1829.
Edward Y. Bright. January 25, 1830, and January 21, 1833.
Daniel Brantigam, January 29, 1836, and January 4, 1839.
Samuel D. Jordan, February 5, 1839—elected in the autumn of that year—1839-45.
John Farnsworth, 1845-51.
James Beard, 1851-57.
Daniel Beckley, 1857-63.
John J. Reimensnyder, 1863-69.
William D. Haupt, 1869-72.

Lloyd T. Rohrback, 1872-79.
Wesley Auten, 1879-85.
H. F. Mann, 1885-91.
S. P. Fausold, 1891-94.
Charles L. Kremer, 1894-99, re-elected.

Since the organization of the county one hundred and twenty-seven years ago, the office of Prothonotary has been filled by only twenty-five different men.

J. F. M.

Campbellstown Evangelical Lutheran Church.

[In Notes and Queries for 1898 will be found the baptismal and other records of the Evangelical Lutheran Church at Campbellstown. Subsequently the Rev. Mr. Early found additional memoranda, which are herewith given. The items were taken from an old, not very carefully arranged book, resembling an old-time copy book, containing about a quire of paper. Some of the accounts were scribbled on the lid and on the last page of the book. It was kept in the altar in front of the pulpit. As the church itself was demolished and whatever records were left in the altar may possibly have been destroyed. It may serve a very useful purpose to publish them at this time.]

	£.	s.	d.
1805. Henry Goetz made settlement and paid Kerber	3	6	9½
1805, July 4. Rec'd of Oehrly & Schantz	2	6	9
1806, May 26. Wm. Early (does not say rec'd or pd. but apparently rec'd from W. E.)	4	4	0
1811, June 3. Oehrle	5	10½	
" July 21, Oehrly	5	10	
" Aug. 18, Oehrly, Comm.	2	2	0
" Sept. 15, Oehrly	4	6	
" Oct. 13, Oehrly	9	1½	
" Dec. 8, Oehrly	10	9	
1812, March, Oehrly	7	4	

Then followed a third column of figures and accounts, with the name Oehrle written a few times and the rest without any names.

Feby. 28, 1813, William Oehrle made settlement:

£. s. d.

During his term of office he received 13 5 1½

Paid out 1 6 3

Paid in full to John Karmene's successor, most probably. There were also settlements of the Lutheran congregation for 1800, 1801 and 1802, but as frequently only amounts, without the names were given, and as the purpose at the time was genealogical research, the figures and amounts were not copied. But there was one very interesting and important slip, simply a part of a sheet, inserted in the book, which is herewith given in English. It was evidently considered of great importance by the congregation, shown by the fact that a special copy in German was made and fastened in this account book of the congregation. It is:

"Extract from the will of Anna M. Palm, deceased."

"I give and bequeath to the Ev. Lutheran congregation at Campbellstown, Twenty dollars, which are to be paid over to the Elders of said congregation one year after my death. They are to invest it with approved (sufficient) security and pay the interest annually to the pastor of the said congregation as part of his salary—one who believes the Augsburg Confession."

"In accordance with this provision the above named sum, viz. $20.00, was paid over by the Executors of the will of the said Anna M. Palm, Wm. Oehrle and George Schneider, to Jacob Oehrle, who was the Elder at the time, and who regularly paid the interest of the money to the Lutheran pastor until the year 1837" (The year of his death).

Although not directly connected with the Campbellstown church, the following is of sufficient importance historically to be ocnneted with it. It is in part a copy of the patent deed, complete as far as it goes, i. e., except the legal phraseology about appurtenances, rights, hereditaments, heirs, assigns, &c., for which there was no time of the "Betimes" farm, south of Palmyra, to which frequent reference has been made.

On the outside there is written:

Patent, John Early.
Betimes 233 $.
Lancaster County.
M. Epple.

The seal has:

"Thomas and John Penn, Proprietors," with "Mercy" and "Justice" beneath.

"Thomas Penn and John Penn, Esqrs. True and absolute Proprietaries & Governors in chief of the Province of Pennsylvania & counties of New Castle, Kent and Sussex, upon Delaware.

"To all whom these presents shall come, Greeting:

"Whereas, in pursuance of a warrant dated the ninth day of October, 1751, granted to Leonard Teninger (Deninger) there hath been surveyed to John Early, to whom the said Teninger conveyed by deed dated the 7th day of December, 1751, a certain tract of land called 'Betimes,' situate in Derry township, in the county of Lancaster, beginning at a marked Wh. Oak on a line of John Balm's land, thence by the same land south fifty-eight degrees, west 170 perches to a post, thence by George Henry's land, McCullem's land, S. E. 259 perches to a marked Bl. Oak, thence by a line of marked trees N. E. 146 perches to a marked Wh. Oak, thence by Conrad Rice's land N. W. 259 perches to place of beginning, containing 233 A. & allow. of six acres pr. A. for roads by the said warrant and survey remaining in the Surveyor General's office and from thence certifyed into our Secretaries office appears."

"Paid thirty-five pounds and thirteen shillings patent.

Adam Tininger alias Deininger.
Adam Gordon, 174.
Advice 3——,"

Recorded in the Rolls office in and for the Province of Pennsylvania—Patent B. A. A., vol. 13, p. 382. Witness our hands and seal of office the 13th day of February, 1773.

Will. Farr, Recorder.

From this it will be seen that the name "Betimes" is not of fanciful derivation, but is good old English, assigned to it by the Proprietaries themselves.

J. W. EARLY.

OBITUARY.

Samuel McIlhenny.

Word reached the city about 2.45 Saturday afternoon, December 30th, 1899, of the death at his home at Linglestown, at 2.30, of Mr. Samuel McIlhenny, the well-known Republican county leader. He had been in declining health for some months, but was able to be about until recently. Friday morning his illness took a dangerous turn and his sons, Deputy Sheriff George McIlhenny and Deputy Recorder William McIlhenny, of this city, were hastily summoned to his bedside. Next morning they sent information to friends here that there had been a slight improvement in their father's condition, notwithstanding that he had passed a very bad night, sufferini much pain in his stomach. But the improvement was only temporary. The news of "Uncle Sam's" death was received in this city with general expression of regret. His was a stalwart, rugged, honest, fearless, generous and whole-souled make-up, and he numbered his friends by the thousands.

Mr. McIlhenny was a son of Samuel and Mary (Carson) McIlhenny, and was born June 4th, 1823, in West Hanover township. He was educated in the public schools of Lower Paxtang township, and was brought up a farmer. At the age of 17 he apprenticed himself to William J. Kaul to learn the trade of tanner, which he followed many years. In 1849 he commenced business for himself at Linglestown, and took an active part in the political affairs of the country. Mr. McIlhenny was elected county auditor in 1869, serving three years, and 1873 was elected one of the County Commissioners, and re-elected, filling that responsible station six years. During his term of office various needed reforms were made in the administration of the public affairs of the county, and much credit is due Mr. McIlhenny for his efforts in this direction. He has filled the various township offices, and in 1879 was appointed one of the inspectors of the Dauphin county prison. Mr. McIlhenny married, January 9th, 1847, Catharine, daughter of Louisa and Sarah Maria (Albert) Cu'p. Their children were: Sarah R., John H., Mary Ann, Kate Ann, Lydia J., Elizabeth E., who married Jacob Balthaser; Samuel C., Susan S., George W., Emma E., William A., Anna Maria and Minnie C.

All of the children but Samuel and Mary, who died in early childhood, survive their father.

NOTES AND QUERIES.

Historical, Biographical, and Genealogical.

XLV.

POWELL.

Rev. Joseph Powell, of Bedford county, d. in November, 1804, leaving a wife, Rachel and children:
i. Mary.
ii. Eleanor.
iii. Ann.
iv. Rebecca.
v. Rachel.
vi. Joseph (eldest son).
vi. Samuel.
viii. John.

The executors were wife, Rachel, and son, Joseph.

[See sketch of Rev. Joseph Powell, a member of the Pennsylvania Constitutional Convention of July 15, 1776, in The Pennsylvania Magazine of History for 1880.]

Stewart of Cumberland Valley.

I. Archibald Stewart, m. Margaret ———. They came from Newry in Ireland, on board ship Happy Return, James Boggs, master, July, 1752, and settled in the Cumberland Valley, near Carlisle in 1753. Their children, all grown up, were:
2. i. William.
ii. John (see Cumberland county wills).
iii. Archibald.

II. William Stewart (Archibald), d. July 29, 1784. He m. Elizabeth Wilson; d. August 12, 1822. He served in the Cumberland county militia. Their children were:
3. i. John, b. June 8, 1770; m. firstly, Elizabeth Walker; m. secondly, Rebecca Johnston.
ii. Wilson, d. May 20, 1814, s. p.
iii. Sarah, m. Abraham Dean.
iv. Mary, m. Noble Crawford.
v. Margaret, m. George Brown.
vi. Gracy, m. Henry Lukins.
vii. Elizabeth, m. Isaac Cook.
viii. Jean, m. Andrew Thompson (tailor).
ix. Rachel, m. John Thompson.
x. Rebecca, m. Andrew Thompson (farmer).

III. John Stewart (William, Archibald), b. June 8, 1778, in the Cumberland Valley; d. April 13, 1831. He. m. first Elizabeth Walker, dau. of David Walker. They had issue:
i. Anna, m. Abraham Lukens and left issue.
ii. Eliza, d. inf.
iii. David, b. April 14, 1806; d. Sept. 20, 1836; m. Elizabeth McAlister.
iv. William, d. March 5, 1834; s. p.
vi. Eliza (second), m. Dr. Cyrus McCurdy, s. Horace McCurdy, of Bloomington, Ill.
vii. Mary, m. Dr. John Irvin.

Wagoning in Ye Olden Time.

The reason that the great Pennsylvania Railroad has been so successful as one of the principal lines of this country is that it is the most direct and shortest communication between the cities of the East and great West. The same cause resulted in that most of the wagoning in former years prior to the construction of canals and railroads, was, through Pennsylvania from the East to the West. It was also the most direct route by Harrisburg and the Cumberland Valley crossing the Allegheny mountains at easier grades.

Before the making of good roads the principal means of transportation through the State, especially the western part, was done on pack horses. When roads were properly constructed wagons superceded them.

Wagoning was done for a number of years on what were then called mud roads, turnpikes not having been made. These roads in the spring were almost impassable, twelve barrels of flour or about one ton of merchandise constituting a full load for five or six horses to draw. The first turnpike made in the State was from Philadelphia to Lancaster, and from Lancaster they were made at different points by different companies until the entire road to Pittsburgh was of stone. A prominent man once astonished an audience in Philadelphia by saying that he expected to live to see the day when the road from Philadelphia to Pittsburgh would be paved with stone.

The pike from Middletown to Harrisburg was only made in 1818, and from the Susquehanna to Carlisle about the same year; and so they were added along the whole distance, made by separate incorporated companies, keeping the road in repair and some times receiving dividends from the toll taken at the gates, which were placed at about six or eight miles apart. Turnpike roads were a great relief to wagoners and horses. The amount handled by wagoners increased from one to three tons.

These roads were well supplied with taverns every few miles, which were generally well kept, as teamsters would only patronize those which kept full and good tables. Merchandise was hauled from New York, Philadelphia and Baltimore to Pittsburgh and Wheeling through the State. In Philadelphia the wagons were all backed against the curb stone on Market street, above Eighth street, as the market houses prevented them going lower down, the horses being fed and kept at the tongues of the wagons, which extended for squares up the street, receiving and discharging their loads into the warehouses. The price of freight was governed by the number of wagons and the amount awaiting transportation. Sometimes freights were very high and at other times prices were low. The stipulations were the safe delivery of the load at its destination in a certain number of days.

Some of the wagons were owned by a company, but mostly by individuals, who employed drivers. During the winter season some farmers would put their wagons on the road to employ their horses. The teamsters as a class had their habits and rules as other classes of men. They were much exposed to all varieties of weather and led a rough, hard life; yet they enjoyed it, many continuing on the road as long as they lived. When on the road they would endeavor to reach certain stations even if night overtook them. All the taverns were well supplied with places for the wagons and strong poles were kept to hang the harness around the wagons, the horses being stabled at the trough which was placed on the tongue. The rule was for the landlord to supply the straw for bedding. The driver was given a segar and one drink morning and evening gratis, charging for the meals eaten, the grain and hay. The drivers carried their bedding, which was placed on the floor of the bar-room, where they slept after their work was done, and, supper over, the time was spent in games or conversation, as there were always several wagons at the same tavern. A. B.

The Butler Wills at Carlisle.

Thomas Butler, of West Pennsboro' township, Cumberland county, Pa.; will dated 20th September, 1787. (Will Book E, pp. 234); wife, Eleanor; sons, Richard, William, Pierce, Edward and Capt. Thomas Butler; daughter, Eleanor. Some of the bequests and devises are: "To my loving son Richard Butler and spouse, one half Johanes;" to my loving son, William Butler, and spouse, one-half Johanes;" "to my loving and worthy son. Capt. Thomas Butler, all my real estate in West Pennsborough township, county of Cumberland, and State of Pennsylvania, excepting what shall be hereafter excepted;" Pierce Butler, 175 pounds (loving son), &c. Proved 23d July, 1791. Executors, his wife, Eleanor, and sons Thomas and Edward.

Richard Butler, of Carlisle, Pa.; will dated "at Fort McIntosh, September 29th, 1785." (Will Book E, pp. 251). Wife, Mary; children, William and Mary, the rearing and education of whom is intrusted to his wife, Mary. Estate: "House and lot in Carlisle;" furniture, plate, &c;" tract of land warranted in name of John Beard, situate on Plumb Creek, Westmoreland county, adjoining land of the late Col. George Croghan; tract in Allegheny; lots in Pittsburgh adjoining lots of William Butler;" one thousand acres of land being a donation of the State of Pennsylvania, and six hundred acres of land a donation of the United States in Congress—these donations are for my services as colonel in the army of the United States." and other property, including "horses, cows and farming utensils, at and near Carlisle." Executors named in will: His wife, Mary, brother William, his "respected friend Thomas Smith, Esq., attorney-at-law, Carlisle, and my friend John Montgomery, Esquire."

Richard Butler's will appears to have been written hurriedly and on the eve of some dangerous expedition, for he says: "Being in perfect health and senses, think it my duty (as I am going far from my family and into some degree of danger more than generally attend at my happy and peaceful home) to make such an arrangement of my worldly affairs, as I wish and desire may take place in case of my death, which I hope, for the sake of my family, the Great and Almighty God will avert."

Martha Butler, of Carlisle, Pa.; will dated January 5th, 1848; devises all her estate, real and personal, to "my sister, Rosanna McCarter." Proved 6th August, 1849. (Will Book M, pp. 20.)

Rev. William Butler, of Carlisle, Pa.; will dated 9th March, 1848. (Will Book M, pp. 163, &c.) Children: Mary Ann Beck, William Henry Butler, Samuel Butler, Margaret Elizabeth and Anna Wesley Butler. Executors named: Nathan Hautch, of Carlisle. This decedent had considerable property. Had a "lot of land in Williamsport, Pa."

Some Family Graveyards.

Tombstone inscriptions in the graveyard on the farm of Christian Lyter, in Lower Paxtang township, Dauphin county:
Sarah, dau. of Christian and Barbara Lyter, d. August 26, 1854, aged 29y. 4m. 7d.
Barbara, wife of Conrad Peck, b. Dec. 1, 1791; d. August 31, 1851.
Maria Leyder, wife of Joseph Leyder, d. March 16, 1838, aged 76y. 8m. 12d.
Joseph Leyder, d. November 15, 1854, aged 86y. 8m. 8d.
John Heisay, d. April 25, 1847, aged 56y. 6m. 16d.
Matthias Sheets, b. Feb. 6, 1789; d. April 7, 1873.
Susannah Baker, wife of Matthias Sheets, b. June 23, 1795; d. Nov. 7, 1852.
Anna Leime, wife of Jacob Leime, d. Feb. 27, 1799, aged 57y.
Isabella, dau. of C. and B. Lyter, d. 1834, aged 3y 9m.
[There are eight or ten graves more of Lyter (Leyder) family without stone, comprising some of the oldest members.]

Tombstone inscriptions in graveyard on the farm of Adam Shope, Jr., in Lower Paxtang township, Dauphin county:
Adam Shope, Sen., b. Dec. 24, 1776; d. Feb. 7, 1866.
Esther Shope, wife of Adam Shope, b. Sept. 20, 1777; d. Oct. 7, 1843.
[There are in addition six large graves, unmarked.]

D. A. FISHER.

NOTES AND QUERIES.

Historical, Biographical and Genealogical.

XLVI.

BERRYHILL.

The following Berryhill data is furnished in reply to a correspondent in Virginia:

Ann Berryhill m. June 24, 1774, Samuel Bell; they had a son named Berryhill Bell.

Samuel Berryhill, of Harrisburg, cabinet maker d. in 1801, leaving a wife, Martha, and children:
i. John.
ii. Samuel.
iii. Hugh.

Andrew Berryhill, of Paxtang, township, then Lancaster county, d. in 1784, leaving a wife Eleanor.

Alexander Berryhill, of Paxtang township, d. in 1788, leaving a wife, Matilda, and children:
i. Amelia.
ii. Andrew.
iii. Clarissa.
iv. Matilda.
v. Cassandra.
vi. Caroline.
vii. Alexander.

McCURDY NOTES.
Archibald McCurdy, of Carlisle, d. in January, 1753, leaving a wife, Elizabeth, and children:
i. John.
ii. (Posthumous child.)
He mentions his mother, Jane McCurdy; sister Margaret; sister Catharine; brother Robert. [He was Captain Robert McCurdy, of the Revolution.]
Arthur McCurdy emigrated from County Antrim prior to the Revolution and settled in Pennsylvania. He left issue, among other:
i. John; settled in Virginia.
ii. James; settled in Franklin, then Cumberland county, Pa., and had issue among others:
1. James, b. 1770; d. 1822; m. Mary Brown and had:
a. Anna; m. John Alexander.
b. Margaret; m. James Rankin.
c. James; m. Eliz. Klippinger.
d. Jane; m. John Carey.
e. Stephen-O.
f. Robert.
g. Hugh.
John McCurdy settled in the Cumberland Valley prior to 1764; thence to York county, and subsequently to Virginia, in Weston county. He m. Mary Foy, and had issue twelve children:
i. Elisha, a minister, b. Oct. 15, 1763, at Carlisle, Pa.; d. July 22, 1845; m. first, in 1796, Sarah Briceland, b. 1771, d. Oct. 26, 1818; dau. of Thomas Briceland. He m. secondly, Mrs. Sarah Brown Colwell.

The Gnadenhutten Massacre.

Our friend, Mr. W. H. Hunter, of the Steubenville (O.) Gazette, in concluding a valuable paper on the Williamson expedition of 1782, gives us the following, which we commend to the careful consideration of the readers of "Notes and Queries.:"

"Referring again to the disposition of the people at the present day to cast reproach of murder upon the men who killed the Moravian Indians at Gnadenhutten, it is well to keep in mind that the British were wholly responsible for this massacre. In fact it was planned by the British at Detroit. The hostile Indians, who were the allies of the British had captured the missionaries having the Moravian Indians in charge, and, with the Christian Indians, had taken them to Sandusky on a trumped-up charge. The winter following was a very severe one and provisions ran short. About one hundred of the Christian Indians were permitted to return to the Tuscarawas Valley to gather corn left growing when they were taken away. At the same time warriors were sent out to murder the whites in the valley, to incense the Americans against the Indians, knowing that they would organize and make cause against the Christian Indians in the Tuscarawas Valley. These red warriors crossed the river at Steubenville and committed all sorts of awful depredations against the settlers, among them the murder of Mrs. Wallace and her babe. The plan laid by the British at Detroit carried out, and Colonel Williamson with his men marched to the Tuscarawas, and finding the Indians there and in possession of Mrs. Wallace's bloody garments, naturally supposed that the Christian Indians had murdered her, just as the British at Detroit had planned they would. There has been much written against Colonel Williamson and the "murder" of the Christian Indians; but those who reproach his memory do not appreciate the conditions then existing. The pioneer to whom we owe everything is entitled to every doubt. He knew the treacherous nature of the Indian as well as of the British, and it was natural and especially during the border warfare of the Revolution, to suspect every Indian and trust none of them, Christian or otherwise; the British were Christians, and they were not trusted, and why should a savage under the flag of Britain be trusted simply because he professed Christianity? The pioneer who made this valley a home of peace for those who came after him, is worthy an enduring monument on every hill and in every valley, instead of clouding his memory with the charge of murder. When we celebrate the wonderful achievement of the pioneer fathers we should rejoice in their bravery, in their fortitude, in their endurance and steadfastness of purpose. They were wonderful men the like of which this country will never see more. The sentimentality that has been wasted on the Moravian Indians and the reproach cast upon Colonel Williamson and his pioneer soldiers, as brave men as ever aimed the long rifle at the savage and made that aim count in one less British ally, has its parallel in the pioneer struggles in Pennsylvania, where the Indians would commit depredations on the hardy settlers, and then seek safety among the Quakers, who seemed to think it all right for the Indians to kill and destroy, but when the 'Paxtang Boys,' as they were known, undertook to retaliate, they were charged with murder, and to this day the Quaker writers have cast a cloud over the memory of these brave men, that seems impossible to efface; but we are pleased to note that our good friend, Dr. Egle, has undertaken the defense of the 'Paxtang Boys,' having gathered data for a history of the affair and will have it in book form for the present year. He has also gathered much matter on the Gnadenhutten massacre, and it is likely that he will publish something on that incident in defense of the American pioneer, who had to fight every step he took in his efforts to make a home for himself and for those who came after him. The descendants of the American pioneer have a right to be proud of their ancestry, for theirs is the royal blood of America."

Death of a Nonogenarian.

On Saturday, the 13th of January, 1900, in the beautiful village cemetery at Churchville (Oberlin P. O.), Dauphin county, was laid to rest the late Mrs. Sarah Metz, after services in the Lutheran Church. Sarah Metz was born April 9, 1809, in Lower Swatara township, Dauphin county, and died January 10, 1900, aged 90 years, 9 months and 1 day. She was the daughter of Daniel Fisher (b. Dec. 24, 1765; d. Nov. 14, 1836) and Catharine Parthemore (b. Jan. 6, 1773; d. Oct. 1, 1836). Her father's ancestor was Philip Fisher, who emigrated from Germany more than a century and a half ago, eventually settling in Lower Swatara township, this county, where he purchased a farm near "Fidler's Elbow," on the Swatara creek. When Philip Fisher came to America he brought with him the seeds of a pear tree which grew on his parents' land in Germany, and from these seeds, which he planted on his farm, grew a number of pear trees which for a century and more produced a lucious and excellent pear, which can be recalled with pleasure by the old citizens of the Swataras; Derry and Londonderry townships.

Susan Fisher married, first, in September, 1835, John Peifer, who died in January, 1837, leaving surviving one son, a resident of Swatara township, who attended the funeral, and it is not often a mother lives long enough to have a son arrive at the age of sixty-four years to be at that parent's funeral. Mrs. Peifer married, secondly, on Jan. 15, 1840, George Metz (b. June 14, 1814; d. Nov. 7, 1878). He was a native of Lykens Valley, where his ancestor was an early settler. She resided and died on one of the beautiful farms northwest of Rutherford Station, in the Lebanon Valley, which her husband had purchased more than half a century ago.

The writer has a recollection of her from his earliest youth, from the fact whenever a death occurred in the Parthemore "freundschaft" old "Aunty Metz," as she was familiarly known, was always present. She carried out that distinctive characteristic among the Pennsylvania Germans to keep up the relationship, which she could show no better than being at the funeral, no matter if the death were a babe, child or grown person; whether cousin, cousin's child, or grandchild.

Early in life Mrs. Metz became a communicant in her father's denomination, Lutheran, to which she strictly adhered until death, being a member of Shoop's Church, in Lower Paxtang township. She is survived, beside the son of the first marriage by the following (surname Metz):

i. Sarah-Ann; m. Solomon Felty, who died quite recently near Ling'estown, where she resides, and they had eight children.

ii. Daniel; residing on the farm where his mother died.

ii. Catharine-Ann; m. Jacob J. Bishop,

residing at Oberlin, and they had seven children.

iv. Mary-E.; m. Abraham W. Whitmer, residing in Lower Swatara, and they had two children.

The funeral sermon was preached by Rev. Solomon Dasher, and the pall-bearers six of her grandsons. The writer has never attended a funeral where he noticed as many aged persons and large number of grand and great-grand-children. What "Aunty Metz" did in her lifetime was fully carried out at her burial by the Parthemore relationship, who were present to pay their last tribute to the old friend and relative, who lived more than nine decades. E. W. S. P.

WILLIAM DARBY

The Eminent American Geographer.

William Darby, son of Patrick Darby and Mary Rice, was born August 14, 1775, on the Dixon farm in Hanover, Lancaster, now Dauphin county, Penna. From an autobiographical letter which came into our possession a few years since, we shall cull such facts as go to make up an interesting biographical sketch of the statistician and geographer. As he says:

"My father was a second husband, and my eldest, but maternal brother only was born in April, 1770. My father began and ended by being poor, and his children had to find education where and as best they could. What little I possess, was truly picked up along the Lanes, Highways and Commons of human life.

"Before leaving Swatara I had learned to read a little, though only about two months turned of six years of age. Plunged into the West, amid savage war and almost unbroken woods, the dangers and imperative wants of life would seem to preclude all thought of improving the mind. Happily for me, my desire of knowledge, even so situated, grew with my growth, and mental hunger was sharpened by food. Every book I could procure I read, and was aided by a tolerable good memory. Books were, however, rare, and when found mostly confined to school books. Before I was twelve years of age I had read the Jewish Scriptures five times, and many parts ten times over. Up to that age Sewell's 'History of the Quakers' was the only work on any branch of general history I obtained. Without making much more intellectual advances, I was, from the poverty of my parents, compelled to labor more as my bodily strength increased.

"I completed my eighteenth year; then by permission of my parents I commenced teaching—don't laugh at the attempt—since, if I was ignorant, I can say without boast, that I had outstript most of my neighbor boys, of course could teach them. Tho' in many respects very irksome business, teaching was of invaluable benefit to me. I had the mornings, evenings and spare days to myself, and as far as other means offered, this leisure was used to effect.

"At Wheeling, in 1793-4, on the then outer border of civilized life, I procured the reading of several very valuable works, among which were Rollin's Ancient History, Ward's Mathematics and Johnson's Lives of English Poets. From Wheeling, in my twenty-first year, I removed to Fayette county, Pennsylvania, and there obtained the perusal of The Universal History from Judge Nathaniel Breading. This immense work occupied my every leisure moments whilst I remained in the vicinity of Red Stone, now Brownsville. In my twenty-second year I removed to Westmoreland county, Pennsylvania, and there became acquainted with a man of the name of Benjamin Gilbert, belonging to the Society of Friends, like your cousin Lindley Murray. With Mr. Gilbert's books an entirely new species of reading was opened to my mind. From this man I procured the reading of Montesquieu's Spirit of Laws, Locke's Essay on the Human Understanding, Reed on the Mind, Blair's Lectures on Elocution, Elements on Criticism, by Henry Home Lord Kaimes, and perhaps the deepest metaphysical work ever written, Edwards on Free Will.

"The latter course of reading produced on my mind a change and course of thinking, which, if I had remained in Pennsylvania, would, it is probable, have led me into the clerical profession, but the death of my father, in 1799, and some other circumstances of greatly less importance, induced me to travel, and I went to Natchez, where, very contrary to my expectations, I married, like your brother, a widow with a family of children, and quite handsome property. What led me into this connexion was a similarity of tastes. Like myself, Mrs. Boardman had been her own teacher, and had acquired a fine stock of information. As a wife she was everything I or any man could wish for, but her family involved us in litigation. I was compelled to quit the pursuits, which habit had endeared to me, to attend to affairs which were, to say the least, to me very repugnant. Out of this troublesome state we would have finally extracted ourselves, it is most likely, but in the spring of 1804 a large and well-filled cotton gin belonging to the estate was consumed by fire, and again, by a strange unity of misfortune, two months afterward, another house also full of cotton and belonging to the estate was lost by similar accident. This double loss involved me in debt, to which I was compelled to yield. I have said these accidents happened by "a strange unity of misfortune," but I recall the words. Had I not lost this property, and been thrown once more on my own resources, I would no doubt have vegetated, a Mississippi cotton planter. I speak this in full respect to cotton planters, and only because the business demanded what I did not possess."

"And, in brief, availing myself of what mathematical knowledge I possessed, I entered on the surveying business, in the service of the United States. In that employment I continued until the middle of 1809, when I conceived the plan of "A Map and Statistical Account of Louisiana," and which I subsequently executed and published. Well for me when I commenced this task that its difficulties were not to be foreseen, for though not much disposed to yield to slight obstacles, yet in that case I must have shrank, had the whole issue been before my mind. But I went on and soon found that all the surveys made under the Government produced documents falling far short of what was requisite to the completion of my plan. I then relinquished the office of Deputy Surveyor, and commenced the extensive exploration to which you allude in your letter.

"All these operations brought the middle of 1814, when, with my projection and manuscripts, I was ready to set out from Louisiana to the cities of New York and Philadelphia in search of a publisher. I had actually departed from my home, at Opelousas, and was on my way to New Orleans, when the news met me that Washington had been taken and burned by the British. This so dispirited my friends that I was advised to postpone my attempt, and did so. In the meantime I made an extensive tour in Florida and Southern Alabama.

"On my return to Baton Rouge, I learned two distressing articles of intelligence almost at the same moment. One was the death of my wife, October 23d, 1814, and the other the great probability that Louisana would be invaded. Before I could proceed to Opelousas and make arrangements for the care of my little daughter and only child, and again return to New Orleans, Louisiana was invaded. I hastened to the camp of our army, below New Orleans, volunteered my services as engineer, and in that capacity made that campaign which humbled the British army and eventually gave the crown to our general. As general or monarch, I never made of him but two requests. As general I demanded and received the office of engineer, and when candidate for the sceptre I asked for and received the following:

"'William Darby, Esqr.: Be it remembered, that during the late war, and whilst the enemy was before New Orleans, William Darby, Esqr., acted as one of my topographical staff, performed his duty much to the satisfaction of the commanding general, and at the close of the war I gave him a written testimonial that his services had obtained for him my full approbation.

'ANDREW JACKSON.'

"The campaign over and without a family or much else to impede my motions, I returned to Pennsylvania in the summer of 1815. Poor in purse, but rich in the accumulated experience gained from near sixteen years of almost incessant motion. —experience which I had reaped with the briars in my fingers; and now in my fortieth year commenced my life as author. The first edition of my Louisiana was published in 1816 and the second in 1818. In 1819 I wrote for Kirk & Mercain of New York, "The Emigrant's Guide." In 1821 I was employed to prepare for publication "Brooks' Gazetteer," which I found in many things relating to America so very defective as to induce me to advise a substitute. My advice was taken, and early in 1823 came out the first and early in 1827 the second edition of "Darby's Geographical Dictionary." In 1833 issued the first and in 1833 the second edition of "Darby and Dwight's United States Gazetteer." Mr. Dwight's name is united with mine in the later work, he furnished all beyond New Jersey and New York inclusive and I the residue. In the second edition Mr. Dwight had no concern. Since 1820 and from the letters M I C H I have supplied nearly all the geographical articles for "Brewster's Encyclopedia."

"In 1829 I commenced supplying tales for 'Atkinson's Casket,' and have written all that species of writing which has appeared under the signature of Mark Bancroft. Recently I have made a regular engagement with Mr. Atkinson for a long series of border tales and I may note here as peculiarly remarkable in our joint case, that the incident of the capture and recapture of your mother-in-law and Boone's daughter has been long since fixed in my eye as a chosen subject, and this added to the extraordinary fact of my having connected in the same tale the families of both your parents gives true interest to the series of circumstances.

"In a life so full of changes and in most part of it but scantily supplied with means of procuring books or securing leisure, most persons would suppose any chance of general reading was out of the question; but I must say I have gone far to render such a conclusion doubtful, at least to anything approaching the usual extent given in such cases. My reading has been desultory, I confess, and far indeed from that of many, but it has been beyond what is commonly attempted by persons of straitened means, and not professionally engaged. You see, I am laying my heart naked to you, and hope no charge of mere vanity will be made when I go a step farther in the dissection, and do so to demonstrate that a tolerable educaton is within the reach of every free white in the United States.

"I was in my thirty-second year when I undertook to study the French language, and long years past, full one-half if not more of all my reading is in that language. The learned languages I never have studied, but in their modern dress, in English and French, have read every one of the most eminent classics. In the 'National Intelligencer' of November 13, 1833, as an editorial preface to my notes on Switzerland, over the signature of Tacitus, it is observed:

"To those who have been long readers of the 'National Intelligencer' we need not say that the gentleman who, under this signature, occasionally enriches our columns with his communications in a person of great intelligence. We can add that he is probably better versed in history 'than any other individual in the Union.' Under any other circumstance I should not dare enclosing such extracts, but take them as given.

* * * * * * * *

"In February, 1816, the year after my return from Louisiana, I intermarried with Elizabeth Tanner, a sister of the well-known engravers of that name in Philadelphia. My daughter, left in Louisiana with her half sisters, died in 1821. By my second wife I have but one surviving child, a young woman in her seventeenth year, so my entire family consists of my wife, child and myself. We live in a fine healthy country, twenty miles north of Washington city, and on a rented farm in a country place, I may repeat, possessing most of the essential advantages without the enormous expense of a city. We keep our own cows, and make their feed from the fields. Our source of living is, however, my pen, which is kept commonly busy. In summer I give courses of lectures, and the rank of intelligence of the people around us may be estimated to advantage by the fact that last summer I had a class of about fifty on general geography.

"My father and mother had eight children, four sons and four daughters; my eldest sister, Arabella, called for your grandmother and one of your aunts, died on the Swatara, and was buried at the Derry meeting house. Two more children died in Washington county, Pennsylvania. One brother, Robert, called for Robert Dixon, died also in the same county, as did my father in 1799. My brother Thomas was drowned in the Ohio river, and your acquaintance, Patrick H., you know died in Kentucky, at Brandenbury, Meade county. My mother died in Tennessee, and her eldest son, and my half brother, in Louisiana. My dear sister Nancy, called for your Aunt Campbell, when I last heard from her, was living in Stewart county, Tennessee, near Dover. Her husband's name in Hugh Barr. They have several sons.

The foregoing autobiography was written in 1834. Beside the works alluded to Mr. Darby was the author of "Plan of Pittsburg and Adjacent Country," published in 1817; "Tour From New York to Detroit," 1819; "Geography and History of Florida," with a map, 1821; "View of the United States," 1828; "Lectures on the Discovery of America." 1829, and "Mnemonica, a Register of Events to 1829." The latter years of Mr. Darby's life were spent in Washington, and connected with one or another of the departments. He was a remarkable man—his life was an active and busy one—his literary labors herculean. He died in that city, October 9, 1854 Of his family, a married daughter, Mrs. Raikes, resides in Ohio.

NOTES AND QUERIES.

Historical, Biographical and Genealogical.

XLVII.

DUNCAN McARTHUR.

I wish to write a sketch of Duncan McArthur, a brigadier general of the War of 1812 and once Governor of Ohio. In his life as given in McDonald's sketches, it is stated that his father, John McArthur, married Margaret Campbell on the Isle of Bute in 1768; that they came to Duchess county, New York, in 1769, and moved thence to Washington county, Pa., the year not given, but supposed to be about 1780. The date of McArthur's birth is given as 1772; that he was enrolled in Major Hall's company of Pennsylvania militia in Harmer's command, in 1790; that he was commissioned an ensign in Pennsylvania militia by Governor Mifflin in 1792, in Captain Enoch's company of scouts, and was in a battle with the Indians at Captina Creek, in Ohio, near present site of Steubenville.

We are supposed to have all of your records in the Newberry Library in this city, and I have tried without success to verify these statements of McDonald by reference to them, yet as McDonald was McArthur's brother-in-law, and was associated with him in pioneer adventures and in the War of 1812, his information should be correct. But I would like to verify these facts if they are facts.

What I would particularly like to know is from what particular part of Pennsylvania General McArthur (my grandfather) entered the militia, for Washington county then embraced all the western part of the State? There is another element of confusion. There are a set of McArthurs who claim to be descendants of John McArthur, the father of Duncan. But they claim that their ancestors were half-brothers, and that John McArthur lived in Vermont and married a Lyon. Our records show that Duncan had only one full sister and the McArthurs referred to have no records. I see by some Duchess county (N. Y.) records that there were McArthurs and McDonalds from Duchess county in the War of Independence, and indeed, the records show that they were there as early as 1750, as a lot of Scotch came over son after the battle of Culloden in 1746.

[In reply to Gen. Anderson. John McArthur took up 400 acres of land in Washington county, December 19, 1775. In 1781 we find his name on the tax list of Bethlehem township that county. Washington county never embraced the whole of western Pennsylvania—but Westmoreland county did. John McArthur served as a soldier on the frontiers of Washington county prior to 1783. For other facts in regard to the McArthurs and McDonalds the records o fWestmoreland and Washington counties should be referred to.]

Application by a Soldier of the Revolution.

[The following application for a pension is valuable not only for the personal narrative, but furnishing data concerning one of the best regiments of the Pennsylvania Line in the War of the Revolution.]

Application of John McConnell, of Franklin township, Westmoreland county, filed November 23, 1825, sets forth: That he was 70 years old; that he enlisted as a private in a company commanded by Capt. Eli Myers in the Eighth Pennsylvania regiment, then commanded by Col. Eneas McCoy, in the month of June, 1776, for the term of three years; that he first did duty at Kittanning, Westmoreland county, and in the succeeding fall was marched to New Jersey; that he was in the battle of Bound-brook; that the regiment was continued with the main army for about one year and a half, after which time it was marched back to the western country to defend it against the Indians; that the regiment was marched by way of Pittsburgh to Beaver Creek; that he assited to build Fort McIntosh; that he was in the campaign carried on under the command of General McIntosh against the Indians on the Tuscarawas, and afterwards in the campaign against the Muncy Indians which was commanded by Col. Brodhead; that he faithfully served three years, the term for which he enlisted, and was honrably discharged at Pittsburgh by Col. Bayard.

JOHN McCONNELL.

[John McConnell died in Franklin township, Westmoreland county, Pa., May 25, 1832, leaving to survive him a widow, Nancy McConnell.]

Craig of the Irish Settlement.

James Craig, of the Irish settlement, Northampton county, Pa., had at least three sons.

I. William Craig, b. ——, 1741; d. March 19, 1818; m. Elizabeth Brown, dau. of Samuel and Jane (Boyd) Brown and had issue:
  i. Jane, b. Dec. 31,, 1781; m. —— Flora and d. Nov. 14, 1873.
  ii. Ann, b. March 1, 1784; d. Nov. 6, 1863.
  iii. James, b. June 15, 1787.
  iv. Elizabeth, b. Sept. 21, 1789; m. —— Johnston; lived in Jerseytown, Pa., in 1881.
  v. William, b. Feb. 25, 1793; m. Feb. 10, 1829, Harriet Bradford.
  vi. Sarah, b. June 8, 1797; m. her cousin, Joseph Craig.
  viii. Samuel, b. Feb. 7, 1802; m. Dec. 4, 1845, Sarah Heacock.
  viii. Margaret, b. Sept. 17, 1804; m. —— McKee.

II. Thomas Craig, no record. Could this be Captain or Col. Thomas Craig?

III. Robert Craig, b. 1746; d. Aug. 4, 1806, and lies buried at Warrior Run Church; m. Esther Brown, dau. of Samuel and Jane (Boyd) Brown and had issue:
  i. James.
  ii. Jane; m. Oct. 24, 1815, John Brown, and was living in North Sewickly township, Beaver county, Pa.
  iii. Mary, b. 1777; d. Oct. 16, 1813, unm.
  iv. Samuel, b. June 15, 1779; d. Dec. 19, 1834, in Clark county, Ohio; m. Jane Miller.
  v. William, d. 1838, unm.
  vi. John, b. Dec. 23, 1784; lived and d. at Lima, Ind.; m. April 29, 1819, Jane Derr.
  vii. Elizabeth, b. 1787; d. Aug. 1860.
  viii. Margaret, b. 1790; d. Jan. 13, 1829; buried at Mill Creek Churchyard, Beaver county, Pa.; m. 1816, James Richart; descendants live at Carbondale, Ill.
  ix. Bobert, b. Jan. 21, 1793; m Oct. 14, 1819, Mary Graham.
  x. Joseph, b. July, 1800; d. Dec. 9, 1845; m. a cousin, Sarah Craig, dau. of his father's brother William.

[Notes to "Craig Family."]

William Allen deeded to James Craig, June 13, 1743, two hundred and fifty acres of his five thousand acre tract.— (Clyde.)

The burying ground and church lots of the Presbyterian congregation of Allen township were transferred to them by James Craig by deeds dated March 11, 1770, and March 11, 1772, respectively. These lots were occupied for burial and church purposes many years previous, but the titles were not perfected until that time.—(Fatzinger.)

James Craig, by deeds dated April 16, 1774, conveyed his landed property to his sons, viz: To Robert 104 acres and 68 perches, and to William and Thomas 162 acres and 46 perches. The wife of James Craig evidently died previous to the above mentioned date. The tract deeded to William and Thomas Craig contained a grist mill formerly called "Craig's Mill," erected about the year 1750. This mill was taken down about 1805 and a new one erected a short distance above the site of the old one. Thomas Craig evidently conveyed his portion of this tract to William Craig, as by deed dated April 1, 1794, William Craig and Elizabeth his wife conveyed a tract of land then containing 268 acres and 140 perches to Henry Epple, which includes the 162 acres and 46 perches above mentioned.—(Fatzinger.) SAMUEL CRAIG.
Wapakoneta, O.

THE SULLIVAN EXPEDITION

To Destroy the Indian Towns, in 1977.

[For some fifteen years the following account and diary of Gen. John Sullivan's expedition to destroy the Indian towns in New York, which were a constant menace to the northern frontiers of Pennsylvania, came into the possession of the Editor of "Notes and Queries." Of historic value, it is herewith given in order for its permanent preservation. At the present writing no information can be given as to its authorship. The details, however, are substantiated by other documents extant and in print.]

On the first of May, 1779, the 2d and 4th N. Y. regiments left their camp near the Hudson, and passing through Warwarsing arrived upon the Delaware the 9th. They crossed the Delaware and passed down the west side to Easton, at which place their stores were collected. From thence they marched towards Wyoming, where they arrived the 17th of June. The delay was occasioned by the great labour required to open a road through woods and over an almost impassable swamp, extending many miles. General Sullivan arrived with the main army on the 23d. On the 31st of July the army left Wyoming for the Indian settlements. The stores and artillery were conveyed up the Susquehanna in 150 boats. The boats formed a beautiful appearance as they moved in order from their moorings, and as they passed the fort received a grand salute, which was returned by the loud cheers of the boatmen. The whole scene formed a military display surpassing any which had ever been exhibited at Wyoming and was well calculated to form a powerful impression upon the minds of those lurking parties of savages which still continued to roam upon the mountains, from which all their movements were visible for many miles.

On the 11th they arrived at Tioga, and encamped in the forks of the river. On the 12th a detachment was sent forward to Chemung, 12 miles distant, where they were attacked by a body of Indians and lost 7 men killed and wounded. The next day, having burned the town, they returned to Tioga. About a mile and a quarter above the junction of the Tioga and Susquehanna these rivers approach each other within a stone's throw. Here a fort was built called Fort Sullivan, while the army lay on what might be called an island below.

In this situation Gen. Sullivan awaited the arrival of Gen. James Clinton. This officer, with the 1st and 3d N. Y. regiments passed up the Mohawk to Canajoharie, where he arrived early in the spring. An expedition was sent out from here by Gen. Clinton against the Onondaga Indians. This detachment consisted of six companies of New York troops, one of Pennsylvania, one of Massachusetts, and one of Rifles, amounting in the whole to 504 rank and file. Col. Van Schaick, of the 1st regiment of New York line, had the command, was accompanied by Lt. Col. Willet and Maj. Cochrane, of the 3d regiment. They rendezvoused at Fort Schuyler and from thence began their march. The whole settlement of the Onondagas, consisting of about 50 houses, and a large quantity of grain were destroyed. They took 37 prisoners and killed between 20 and 30 warriors.

About 100 muskets were taken. On their return they met a small party of Indians, who fired on them, but were soon driven back by the corps of riflemen under Lieut. Evans. They returned to Fort Schuyler in 5½ days from the time of march from thence. The whole distance going and returning was 180 miles.

General Clinton commenced opening a road from Canajoharie to the head of Otsego Lake, distant about 20 miles, and one of the principal sources of the eastern branch of the Susquehannah. This was effected with great labour; his boats were carried across on wagons. It was midsummer before Gen. Clinton found himself with his army and baggage at the head of the lake. This is a beautiful little lake about 9 miles long and in width from one to three miles. Its elevation is 1,193 feet and it is almost surrounded by high land. The water is deep and clear, which is said to be the meaning of its Indian name. The outlet of this lake is narrow. General Clinton, having passed his boats through, caused a dam to be thrown across. The lake was raised several feet. A party was sent forward to clear the river of driftwood. When ready to move the dam was broken up and the boats glided swiftly down the current. The few scattered inhabitants along the river fled, not being able to account for the rapid rise of the river. At Tioga the water flowed back up the Western Branch. On the 22d of August this division arrived at Tioga and joined the main army. The whole force now under Gen. Sullivan consisted of Generals Hands', Clinton's, Maxwell's and Poor's brigades of infantry, Proctor's artillery and a corps of Riflemen, in all between 4,000 and 5,000 men.

On the 26th this army, formidable indeed, if the numbers of the enemy be considered, moved from Tioga up the river of that name in excellent order. Their progress was necessarily slow, and every precaution was taken to guard against surprise. Large flanking parties were kept out on each side and a corps of light troops was thrown forward. On the 28th they destroyed the settlements and grain at Chemung, twelve miles distant from Tioga, and on the morning of the 29th about 10 o'clock fell in with the enemy near Newtown and a short distance from the mouth of Butler's creek (since called Baldwin's creek). They were under the Butlers and Brant, and were in numbers about 600 Indians and 200 Tories. After some reconnoitering and skirmishing the enemy retreated behind their breastworks and made a spirited resistance. They were soon driven from their position by the artillery. In the meantime Generals Clinton's and Poor's brigades filed off to the right, and Gen. Hand's light troops to the left, to gain the enemy's rear, where the land was high. Had this been effected the enemy could not have escaped, but the movement is said to have been discovered by Brant, who ordered an immediate retreat. Nine Indians were left dead on the field; their wounded they carried off. The Americans lost in killed three. Thirty-four were wounded, among whom was Major Titcomb, Captain Clayes and Lieutenant McColley, the latter of whom died of his wounds. Two persons were taken who gave information as to the force of the enemy. This was the only stand made by the Indians. When it was first announced that an army was marching to their country the Indians laughed at their supposed folly, believing it impossible for a regular army to traverse the wilderness such a distance and to drive them from their fastnesses.

The following is an extract from the manuscript journal of an officer who accompanied the expedition:

"1779, Aug. 29. This night encamped on the field of action.

30th. Remained on the ground. Large detachments sent off this morning to destroy the corn, beans, &c., about this place, which was not half destroyed. This evening sent out our wounded, heavy artillery and wagons in boats down the river to Tioga. These boats brought forward such stores as could not be loaded on pack horses. This day put on half allowance.

"31st. Decamped at 8 o'clock. Marched over mountainous grounds until we arrived at the Forks of Newtown; there entered on low bottom; crossed the Cayuga branch and encamped on a pine plain. Much good land about Newtown. Here we left the Tioga branch to our left.

"Sept. 1st. Decamped early in the morning. After marching about three miles, entered a swamp 8 or 9 miles across; roads very bad and no pasture here. The army made a forced march and arrived that night at dark at Catherine's town. The cattle and most part of the pack horses, together with our brigade (Clinton's) lay that night in the swamp without pack or baggage. From this town the enemy seemed to have made a very perceptible retreat.

"2d. About three o'clock came up with the army at the town and encamped.

"3d. Destroyed it, together with the beans, corn, &c. Decamped at 8 o'clock in the morning. After marching three miles fell in on the east side of Seneca lake. This lake runs north and south about 36 miles in length and between 2 and 3 across. At 2 o'clock passed Apple-Tree Town, situated on the banks of the lake. This day marched eleven miles over high, though level ground, timbered chiefly with white oak, and encamped in the woods.

"4th. Marched twelve miles from last encampment; passed several narrow defiles and encamped in the woods beside the lake. This day and yesterday passed several corn fields and scattering houses, which we destroyed as we passed along. The Cayuga lake runs the same direction as this lake, and is about 10 or 12 miles distant. Land tolerably good.

"5th. Decamped in the morning, and about 12 o'clock arrived at Kandaia, a fine town lying about half a mile from the lake. Here we found a great plenty of old apple trees. It evidently appears to be an old inhabited town; their houses are large and elegant; some beautifully painted; their tombs likewise, especially their chief warriors, are beautifully painted boxes which they build over the grave of planks hewn out of timber.

"6th. Decamped at noon and marched about three miles, when we encamped on the edge of the lake. Land timbered with white and black oak, and very good, descending with an easy descent to the lake.

"7th. This day passed the north end or outlet of the lake, which is very narrow, and marched through a narrow defile about one mile in length. The lake on our left and a morass through which no one could pass on our right. Arrived, at Sundown, at the northwest corner of the lake, where we destroyed a town and some corn, and proceeded on to Kanadesago, the capital of the Senecas, where we arrived at 8 o'clock at night. This town lies on a level spot of ground about one and a half miles north of the lake, and consisted of about 60 houses, and great plenty of apple and peach trees. The enemy in their retreat from this place left a white child about 4 years of age, and some horses, cows, &c.

"8th. This day we employed in destroying the corn, beans, &c., at this place, of which there was a great quantity. The riflemen were detached this morning to destroy Kashanguash (Cashong), about 8 miles south. This morning a captain and 50 men detached to the garrison at Tioga with all the sick and lame and such others as could not proceed with us to Genesee.

"9th. Marched nine miles.

"10th. Decamped early in the morning, and about 2 o'clock fell in with a small lake on our left, at the outlet of which lies the town of Canandaigua (Chosentown) consisting of upwards of 20 houses, which we set fire to and decamped. This town from the appearance of the buildings, seems to have been inhabited by white people. Some houses have very neat chimneys, which the Indians have not, but build a fire in the centre around which they gather.

"11th. Decamped earlier than usual to reach the next settlement Honeyoye, where we arrived in season and encamped. The country from Kanandesgo, excepting this day, is exceedingly level and soil very good. This day crossed several mountains between which lie fine, rich valleys. This town lies at the head of a small lake, in a fine rich valley, consisting of 13 or 14 good houses and neatly built. Here we likewise found a great quantity of corn, beans, &c.

"12th. Decamped this morning at 11 o'clock; detained by a heavy rain. Marched over a rough country, passed another small lake, called Konyougheough, and arrived within two miles of Adjontown, and encamped in the woods. The sick, lame and some stores were left with a detachment under the command of Capt. Cummings, who took a post in one of the block houses.

"13th. Decamped this morning at 5 o'clock; marched to the town, where we were employed destroying the corn until noon. From this place Lieutenant Boyd, of the rifle corps, was detached with 15 or 20 men to reconnoitre the next town. On his return found his retreat cut off, and surrounded by 500 or 600 savages, defended himself until his men were all cut off, but himself and one more, when he surrendered—whom we afterwards found in the Genesee Castle, tortured in a most cruel manner. He was the first prisoner taken by the enemy, altho' they had used all their arts to obtain one, in order to learn the number and destination of the army. One of the party under Lieut. Boyd was Hanyerry, an Oneida Indian, who had distinguished himself in the Oriskany battle; he was a man of great courage, and an excellent marksman, and did great execution. His conduct had not passed unnoticed by the hostile Indians, and now when in their power he was literally hewn to pieces by them. Lieut. Boyd was taken before Col. Butler, and being examined, was, according to Butler's statement sent forward with a guard to Niagara.

When passing through Genesee village, an old Indian rushed out and tomahawked him. The same day, 13th, encamped that night at Gachsegwarohare, where we found the enemy paraded before the town and seemed determined to fight us. Clinton's brigade filed off to the right to gain the enemy's rear, which could not be effected; but they retreated in a very perceptible manner.

"14th. This morning the whole army paraded at gunfiring, which was half past 3 in the morning. Lay on our arms until sunrise expecting an attack from the enemy. At 6 o'clock detached large parties to destroy the corn about this place. At 10 the army passed a branch of the Genesee river and entered on the Genesee flats. These flats extended along the borders of the Genesee river about 20 miles in length and 4 in breadth, with a rich soil producing grass 10 feet high. Scarcely a tree was to be seen over the whole extent. The river in a high freshet overflows most of this extensive plain, as appears from several large trunks of trees scattered over the same. After fording the river, raised a considerable, timbered chiefly with white oak, entered another flat on which stands the capital of the Genesee, consisting of upwards of 120 houses, and vast quantities of corn, beans, pumpkins, potatoes, &c. Encamped this evening around the town.

"15th. This morning the whole army paraded at 6 o'clock to destroy the corn, &c., about this place, which could be done in no other way but by gathering the corn in the houses and setting fire to them. Here we likewise found a great quantity of corn gathered in the houses by the savages. At 3 o'clock P. M. we completed the destruction of this place; recrossed the Genesee river, and encamped on the flats, about a half mile north of Gachesegwarohare. This morning a woman taken prisoner at Wyoming last year, came in to us at the Genesee Castle.

"16th. This morning after destroying the corn &c., on the southeast corner of the flats, recrossed the branch of the Genesee river on logs. This river is about 12 paces wide, with very high banks, and the current hardly perceptible. At 10 o'clock passed the last mentioned town, lying on the banks of this branch and encamped this night at Adjonton.

"17th. Decamped very early in the morning, and arrived in good season at Honeyoye, where we encamped this night. Found our store, &c., as we left them.

"18th. Decamped and left Honeyoye with great difficulty; the horses left at this place having strayed so far from the village and could not be found, consequently many packs would have been left on the ground, had not the officers entitled to ride dismounted, of whom General Sullivan was one. This day met 3 Oneida Indians with dispatches for General Sullivan. They informed us the city of New York was left in ashes and evacuated. Arrived at Canandaigua some time before night, passed the outlet of the lake and encamped about a mile from the outlet. This town lies about one-fourth of a mile from a small lake, I suppose of the same name.

"19th. Decamped early, proceeded on our way to Canadesago, where we encamped a little before sunset.

"20th. Remained encamped until 2 o'clock, when we decamped, passed the outlet of Seneca Lake and encamped about a mile from the outlet. This morning detached Col. Butler (Col. William Butler) with the rifle corps and 500 men to the Cayuga Lake to destroy the settlements there. Col. Gansevoort detached at the same time with one hundred men to Fort Schuyler.

"21st. Decamped in the morning, passed Kandaia and encamped about two miles above. This morning detached Lieut. Col. Dearborn with 200 men to destroy the settlements along the south side of Cayuga Lake.

"22d. Decamped early, passed several defiles and encamped within seven miles of Catherine's Town.

"23d. Decamped early and marched about four miles southeast of Catharine's town at the edge of the swamp and encamped.

"Passed the swamp so much dreaded from its badness without any difficulty, and arrived at the Forks of Newtown, where Captain Reid with a detachment of 200 men had thrown up a breastwork to guard some stores and cattle brought forward from Tioga for the army in case of necessity. Saluted by 13 rounds of cannon from the breastwork on our arrival, which number we returned from our artillery.

"25th. This morning the small arms of the whole army were discharged at 5 o'clock, the whole were drawn up in one line, with a field piece on the right of each brigade to fire a feu-de-joy—first, 13 rounds of cannon; second, a running fire of musketry from right to left, which was repeated twice. Five oxen were killed on this occasion, one delivered to each brigade and one to the artillery and staff. This was done in consequence of Spain declaring war against Great Britain.

"26th. Remained encamped. Col. Dearborn's detachment arrived.

"27th. Encamped.

"28th. Col. Butler with his detachment arrived, having destroyed a vast quantity of corn, beans, apple trees, &c., on the east side of the Cayuga Lake, and burnt three towns, among which was the capital of the Cayuga tribe. This morning, Cols. Cortland and Dayton dispatched with three large detachments to destroy corn; the former taking his route up the Tioga branch, to which place he was detached the day before, and destroyed large fields of corn, and the latter taking his route downward and destroyed so much as the army had left in going up.

"29th. Decamped at 8 o'clock, passed the Cayuga branch (Newtown creek) and encamped at old Chemung, three miles below New Chemung. This day forded the Tioga branch.

"30th. Decamped this morning at 7 o'clock; arrived at Fort Sullivan about 1 o'clock. Saluted from the fort by 13 cannon, which we returned from our artillery, after which we passed the fort, and encamped on our old grounds in the forks of the river."